INTRODUCTION *to* SOCIOLOGY

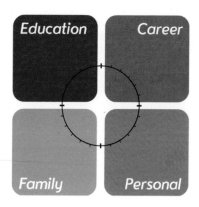

CUSTOM EDITION

Taken from:
Sociology, Ninth Edition
by John J. Macionis

Taken from:

Sociology, Ninth Edition
by John J. Macionis
Copyright © 2003, 2001, 1999, 1997, 1995, 1993, 1991, 1989, 1987 by Pearson Education, Inc.
Published by Prentice Hall, Inc.
Upper Saddle River, New Jersey 07458

This special edition published in cooperation with Pearson Custom Publishing.

Printed in the United States of America

10 9 8 7 6 5 4 3 2 1

ISBN 0-536-81402-3

BA 999250

JC

Please visit our web site at *www.pearsoncustom.com*

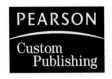

PEARSON CUSTOM PUBLISHING
75 Arlington Street, Suite 300, Boston, MA 02116
A Pearson Education Company

BRIEF CONTENTS

TABLE OF CONTENTS

cyber.scope PART I
WELCOME TO THE INFORMATION
REVOLUTION!   54

PART II
THE FOUNDATIONS OF SOCIETY

PART V
SOCIAL CHANGE

BOXES

APPLYING SOCIOLOGY

DIVERSITY: RACE, CLASS, AND GENDER

CRITICAL THINKING

GLOBAL SOCIOLOGY

CONTROVERSY & DEBATE

FEATURE ESSAYS
NEW INFORMATION TECHNOLOGY AND SOCIETY

 cyber.scope

MAPS

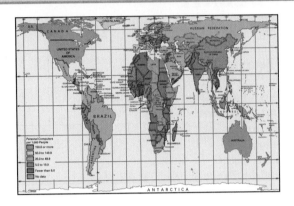

NATIONAL MAPS: SEEING OURSELVES

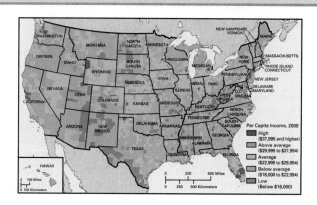

PREFACE

The final manuscript of this book was just about complete when the tragic events of September 11, 2001, took place. Rarely does the news of one day so change everyone's lives. There is little doubt that terrorism will leave its mark on life in the United States and elsewhere for years to come as our concern for security prompts us to reexamine so many dimensions of our everyday lives.

More generally, these events force us to confront the question of what kind of world we live in and what kind of world we want for ourselves and for our children. It is here that readers of this book will discover the importance of the discipline of sociology.

The daily e-mail I receive from students in the United States and around the world stands as testimony to the power of sociology to help people understand their world and, often, to transform people. Indeed, the material in this text was recently used in a presentation to the U.S. Supreme Court (*Falvo v. Owasso Ind. School District*, 2001). All instructors know well the deep satisfaction that comes from making a difference in the lives of our students. There is no greater reward for our work, and, in my case, no better reason for striving for ever-better revisions of *Sociology*, which, along with the briefer *Society: The Basics*, stands out as the discipline's most popular text.

I hope you will find *Sociology* to be authoritative, comprehensive, stimulating, and—as so many students testify—plain fun to read. In addition to the book, every new copy of *Sociology, Ninth Edition*, comes with a second learning tool, a CD-ROM that provides a number of short video selections that illustrate major concepts, ideas, and theories. Included on the CD-ROM is a series of "author's tip" videos—one for each chapter—that focuses on key chapter themes. Finally, the third part of the learning package that is available free with each new book is access to a full-featured Web site at http://www.prenhall.com/macionis From the main page, simply click on the cover of the text and select a chapter; you will find chapter summaries, learning objectives, suggested essay questions and paper topics, and multiple-choice and true-false questions prepared by the author of the text. As the student completes these tests, the server immediately grades them and points out exactly where the student needs more study. Also at this Web site, faculty will find a full complement of teaching resources, including Power Point slides for download and the Prentice Hall syllabus manager system that allows an instructor to post a course syllabus to the Internet without having to learn hypertext markup language (HTML).

Textbook, CD-ROM, and Web site: A three-part, multimedia package that is the foundation for sound learning in this new information age. We invite you to examine all three!

ORGANIZATION OF THIS TEXT

Part I of the textbook and the CD-ROM introduces the foundations of sociology. Underlying the discipline is the *sociological perspective*—the focus of Chapter 1, which explains how this invigorating point of view brings the world to life in a new and instructive way. Chapter 2 spotlights *sociological investigation*, or the "doing of sociology." This chapter explains the scientific, interpretive, and critical orientations of the discipline, and illustrates major research strategies with actual, well-known sociological work.

Part II surveys the foundations of social life. Chapter 3 focuses on the central concept of *culture*, emphasizing the cultural diversity that makes up our society and our world. The focus of Chapter 4 is the concept of *society*, presenting four time-honored models for understanding the structure and dynamics of social organization. This unique chapter provides introductory students with the background to understand the ideas of important thinkers—including Karl Marx, Max Weber, and Emile Durkheim, as well as Gerhard Lenski—that appear in subsequent chapters. Chapter 5 turns to *socialization*, exploring how we gain our humanity as we learn to participate in society. Chapter 6 provides a micro-level look at the patterns of *social interaction* that make up our everyday lives. Chapter 7 offers full-chapter coverage of *groups and organizations*, explaining the importance of group life and investigating how and why large organizations have come to dominate our way of life. Chapter 8 explains how the operation of society generates both *deviance and conformity*, and also surveys the operation of the criminal justice system. Chapter 9 explains the social foundations of *human sexuality*. This chapter surveys sexual patterns in the United States and also explores variations in sexual practices through history and around the world today.

Part III offers unparalleled discussion of social inequality, beginning with three chapters on *social stratification*. Chapter 10 introduces major concepts and presents theoretical explanations of social inequality. This chapter richly illustrates historical changes in stratification and how patterns of inequality vary in today's world. Chapter 11 surveys *social inequality in the United States*, confronting common perceptions of inequality and assessing how well they square with research findings. Chapter 12 extends the analysis with a look at *global stratification*, revealing the disparities in wealth and power that separate rich and poor nations. Both Chapters 11 and 12 pay special attention to how global developments affect stratification in the United States just as they explore our society's role in global inequality. Chapter 13, *gender stratification*, explains how gender is a central element in social stratification in the United States as it is worldwide. *Race and ethnicity*, additional important dimensions of social inequality that often intersect differences based on class and gender, are detailed in Chapter 14. *Aging and the elderly*, a topic of increasing concern to "graying" societies such as our own, is addressed in Chapter 15.

Part IV includes a full chapter on each social institution. Leading off is Chapter 16, *the economy and work*, because most sociologists recognize the economy as having the greatest impact on all other institutions. This chapter traces the rise and fall of industrial production in the United States, the emergence of a global economy, and explains what such transformations mean for the U.S. labor force. Chapter 17, *politics and government*, analyzes the distribution of power in U.S. society as well as surveying political systems around the world. In addition, this chapter includes discussion of the U.S. military, the threat of war, and an expanded discussion of terrorism as a new form of war in the twenty-first century. Chapter 18, *family*, explains the central importance of families to social organization, and underscores the diversity of family life both here and in other societies. Chapter 19, *religion*, addresses the timeless human search for ultimate purpose and meaning, introduces major world religions, and explains how religious beliefs are linked to other dimensions of social life. Chapter 20, *education*, analyzes the expansion of schooling in industrial and postindustrial societies. Here again, schooling in the United States comes to life through contrasts with educational patterns in other countries. Chapter 21, *health and medicine*, reveals health to be a social issue just as much as it is a matter of biological processes. This chapter traces the historical emergence of scientific medicine, analyzes current medical issues and alternative approaches, and compares U.S. patterns to those found in other countries.

Part V examines important dimensions of global social change. Chapter 22 highlights the powerful impact of *population growth* and *urbanization* in the United States and throughout the world with special attention to the *natural environment*. Chapter 23 explores forms of *collective behavior* and explains how people seek or resist social change by joining *social movements*. Chapter 24 concludes the text with an overview of *social*

change that contrasts *traditional, modern, and postmodern societies*. This chapter rounds out the text by explaining how and why world societies change and critically analyzing the benefits and liabilities of traditional, modern, and postmodern ways of life.

CONTINUITY: ESTABLISHED FEATURES OF *SOCIOLOGY*

Everyone knows that introductory sociology texts have some things in common; but differences run deep. The extraordinary success of *Sociology* and *Society: The Basics*, which are far and away the most widely adopted texts by sociologists across North America, results from a combination of the following distinctive features.

The best writing style. Most important, this text offers a writing style widely praised by students and faculty alike as elegant and inviting. *Sociology* is an enjoyable text that encourages students to read—even beyond their assignments. No one says it better than the students themselves, whose recent e-mail includes testimonials such as these:

> Thanks for writing such a brilliant book. It has sparked my sociological imagination. This was the first textbook that I have ever read completely and enjoyed. From the moment that I picked the book up I started reading nonstop.

> I have read four chapters ahead; it's like a good novel I can't put down! I just wanted to say thank you.

> Your book is extremely well written and very interesting. I find myself reading it for pleasure, something I have never done with college texts. It is going to be the only collegiate textbook that I ever keep simply to read on my own. I am also thinking of picking up sociology as my minor due to the fact that I have enjoyed the class as well as the text so much. Your writing has my highest praise and utmost appreciation.

> I am taking a Sociology 101 class using *Sociology*, a book that I have told my professor is the best textbook that I have ever seen, bar none. I've told her as well that I will be more than happy to take more sociology classes as long as there is a Macionis text to go with them.

> I am fascinated by the contents of this textbook. In contrast to texts in my other classes, I actually

enjoy reading *Sociology*. Thank you for such a thought-provoking, well-written textbook.

I absolutely love your sociology text! It is a wonderful book. This is by far the best textbook I have ever used. The CD-ROM has been very helpful and informative. I had no idea that I would love sociology so much!

A global perspective. *Sociology* has taken a leading role in expanding the horizons of our discipline beyond the United States. *Sociology* was the first text to mainstream global content, introduce global maps, and offer coverage of global topics such as stratification and the environment. No wonder this text has been adapted and translated in many languages for use all over the world. Each chapter explores global social diversity as well as explaining why social trends in the United States—from musical tastes to the pace of airport security to the growing disparity of income—are influenced by what happens elsewhere.

A focus on national diversity. *Sociology* invites students from all social backgrounds to discover a fresh and exciting way to see the world and to understand themselves. Readers will find in this text the diversity of U.S. society—people of African, Asian, Middle Eastern, European, and Latino ancestry as well as women and men of various class positions, in all parts of the country, and at all points in the life course. An independent survey of all introductory books gave this text top marks for mainstreaming race and ethnicity (Stone, 1996).

Emphasis on critical thinking. Critical-thinking skills include the ability to challenge common assumptions by formulating questions, identify and weigh appropriate evidence, and reach reasoned conclusions. This text not only teaches but encourages students to discover on their own.

The broadest coverage so instructors can choose. No other text matches *Sociology*'s twenty-four chapter coverage of the field. We offer such breadth—at no greater cost—knowing that few instructors will assign every chapter, but with the goal of supporting instructors as they choose exactly what they wish to teach.

Engaging and instructive chapter openings. One of the most popular features of *Sociology* is the engaging vignettes that begin each chapter. These openings—for instance, using the tragic sinking of the *Titanic* to illustrate the life and death consequences of social inequality, or the story of Linda Brown to explore racial inequality in the United States, or Utah's recent prosecution of Tom Green for polygamy to describe our ideas about

the family—spark the interest of readers as they introduce important themes. This revision retains eleven of the best chapter-opening vignettes found in earlier editions and offers thirteen new ones as well.

Inclusive focus on women and men. Beyond devoting two full chapters to the important concepts of sex and gender, *Sociology* mainstreams gender into *every* chapter, showing how the topic at hand affects women and men differently and explaining how gender operates as a basic dimension of social organization.

Theoretically clear and balanced. *Sociology, Ninth Edition*, makes theory easy. Chapter 1 introduces the discipline's major theoretical approaches, which are used in all the chapters that follow. The text highlights not only the social-conflict, structural-functional, and symbolic-interaction paradigms, but incorporates feminist theory, social-exchange analysis, ethnomethodology, cultural ecology, and sociobiology.

Chapter 4—unique to this text—provides students with an easy-to-understand introduction to important social theorists *before* they encounter their work in later chapters. The ideas of Max Weber, Karl Marx, and Emile Durkheim, as well as Gerhard Lenski's historical overview of human societies, appear in distinct sections that instructors may assign together or refer to separately at different points in the course.

Recent research and the latest data. *Sociology, Ninth Edition*, blends classic sociological statements with the latest research as reported in the leading publications in the field. Some 250 new studies inform this revision, and about half of the 1500 pieces of research cited throughout the book were published since 1995. From chapter to chapter, the text's statistical data are the most recent available and include the results of Census 2000.

Learning aids. This text has many features to help students learn. In each chapter, **key concepts** are identified by boldfaced type, and following each appears *a precise, italicized definition*. A list of key concepts with their definitions appears at the end of each chapter, and a complete **Glossary** is found at the end of the book. Each chapter also contains a numbered **Summary** and four **Critical-Thinking Questions** that help students review material and assess their understanding. Following these are a number of **Applications and Exercises**, which provide students with activities to do on or near the campus. Each chapter also includes an annotated list of worthwhile **Sites to See** on the Internet.

Outstanding images: photography and fine art. This book offers the finest and most extensive program of photography and artwork available in any sociology textbook. The ninth edition of *Sociology* displays about 100 examples of fine art as well as more than 250 color photographs—more than in any other text. Each of these images is carefully selected by the author and appears with an insightful caption. Moreover, both photographs and artwork present people of various social backgrounds and historical periods. For example, alongside art by well-known Europeans such as Vincent Van Gogh and U.S. artists including George Tooker, this edition has paintings by celebrated African American artists Jacob Lawrence and Henry Ossawa Tanner, outstanding Latino artist Diego Rivera, and the engaging Australian painter and feminist Sally Swain.

Thought-provoking theme boxes. Although boxed material is common to introductory texts, *Sociology, Ninth Edition*, provides a wealth of uncommonly good boxes. Each chapter typically contains four boxes, which fall into five types that amplify central themes of the text. **Global Sociology** boxes provoke readers to think about their own way of life by examining the fascinating social diversity that characterizes our world. **Diversity: Race, Class, and Gender** boxes focus on multicultural issues and amplify the voices of women and people of color. **Applying Sociology** boxes show the value of the sociological perspective to understanding the world around us. **Critical Thinking** boxes teach students to ask sociological questions about their surroundings and help them evaluate important controversial issues. Each Critical Thinking box is followed by three "What do you think?" questions. **Controversy & Debate** boxes complete each chapter by presenting several points of view on an issue of contemporary importance. The three "Continue the debate" questions that conclude each box are sure to stimulate spirited class discussion.

Sociology, Ninth Edition, contains ninety-four boxes in all. Fourteen of them are new to this edition and many more are revised and updated. A complete list of the boxes in this text can be found following the table of contents.

An unparalleled program of sixty-seven global and national maps. This is the text that pioneered the use of global and national maps. Windows on the World global maps—thirty-two in all and including eleven new ones—are truly sociological maps offering a comparative look at the number of children typically born to women, income disparity, favored languages and religions, the extent of prostitution, permitted marriage forms, the practice of female genital mutilation, the degree of political freedom, the incidence of HIV infection, and a host of other issues. The global maps use the non-Eurocentric projection devised by cartographer Arno Peters that accurately portrays the relative size of all the continents. A complete listing of the Window on the World global maps follows the table of contents.

Seeing Ourselves national maps—thirty-five in all with four new and many updated for this edition—help to illuminate the social diversity of the United States. Most of these maps offer a close-up look at all 3,014 U.S. counties, highlighting suicide rates, per capita income, labor force participation, college attendance, the prevalence of interracial marriage, most widespread religious affiliation, teen pregnancy rates, and, as measures of popular culture, where people play golf or where households prefer wine or drink beer. Each national map includes an explanatory caption that poses several questions to stimulate students' thinking about social forces. A complete list of the Seeing Ourselves national maps follows the table of contents.

INNOVATION: CHANGES IN THE NINTH EDITION

Each new edition of *Sociology* has broken new ground, one reason that the popularity of this text and its brief version keeps rising. A revision raises high expectations, but, after several years of planning and hard work, we are pleased to offer what we believe is the best revision yet. Here is a brief overview of the innovations that define *Sociology, Ninth Edition*.

Keeping up with the field. As surprising as it may seem, some textbooks fail to reflect new work in the field, making few references to sociology journals and taking little notice of new books. In preparing this revision, I have reviewed new publications—including *American Journal of Sociology, American Sociological Review, Rural Sociology, Social Forces, Sociological Focus, Sociological Forum, Society, The Public Interest, Social Problems, Population Bulletin, Teaching Sociology, Contemporary Sociology*, and *Social Science Quarterly*—as well as popular press publications that keep us abreast of current trends and events.

Improved high-tech! For this edition, the CD-ROM includes a video library, presenting short clips that illustrate important concepts and ideas. This video material, drawn from the video library of ABC News, takes learning to a whole new level.

Students buying new copies of *Sociology, Ninth Edition*, will have open access to an updated Web site at http://www.prenhall.com/macionis Begin by clicking on the cover of this book and follow the easy-to-use menus. At the site, students will find a full range of study materials including computer-graded practice tests. Faculty will find a resource bank including Power Point slides for download and software that allows instructors to put a course syllabus on the Internet without having to know anything about HTML. In addition, all users of this book are invited to make use of videos, biographies, and dozens of links found at the author's personal Web site at http://www.TheSociologyPage.com or http://www.macionis.com

Linking technology to the text. At four or five points in each chapter, the text directs students to visit carefully selected Web sites. These sites provide biographical material about sociologists, useful data, or information about an organization that deals with the topic at hand.

More coverage of rural issues. Although most of the population of the United States lives in urban places, most of our country's counties are rural. Therefore, this revision pays special attention not only to urban social patterns but also to rural issues. Examples of this rural focus include a comparative analysis of rural and urban poverty and homelessness in Chapter 11; discussion of women in coal mining in Chapter 13; a discussion of the aging of U.S. farmers in Chapter 15; a new diversity box in Chapter 17 on the rural-urban divide in U.S. politics; and a discussion of the "rural rebound" in Chapter 22, as well as more photographs and artwork that reflect rural life. In addition, we have recently added *Rural Sociology* to the list of journals that provide new research reported in this text.

New maps! The only way to improve our colorful maps is be sure they are as up to date as possible. This edition features sixty-seven global and national maps, fifteen of them new to this edition.

New chapter-opening vignettes. This revision keeps the best of the popular chapter-opening vignettes and adds thirteen new ones; overall, more than half of the openings are new to this edition.

Many new boxes. A total of ninety-four boxes supports five themes of the text: Global Sociology, Diversity: Race, Class, and Gender, Critical Thinking, Applying Sociology, and, focusing on social policy, Controversy & Debate. Many boxes are revised and updated; fourteen boxes are new to this edition.

The latest statistical data. Instructors count on this text for including the very latest statistical data. The ninth edition comes through again, making use of data from the Internet as well as conventional bound publications of various government agencies and private organizations. The author and Carol A. Singer, a professional government documents librarian at Bowling Green State University (Ohio), have worked together to ensure that the newest statistics are used throughout the text—in many cases for 2000 and even for 2001. These data include reported results of Census 2000. In addition, readers will find 250 new research citations as well as references to many familiar current events to peak their interest.

New topics. The ninth edition of *Sociology* is thoroughly updated with new and expanded discussions in every chapter. Here is a listing, by chapter, of some of the new material:

• **Chapter 1 The Sociological Perspective**: A new chapter opening explores how and why U.S. children are deeply involved in sports; in addition, a new global map highlights the number of children born to women around the world.

• **Chapter 2 Sociological Investigation**: New material includes new end-of-chapter learning ideas and several new Web sites noted throughout the chapter.

• **Chapter 3 Culture**: A new chapter opening describes the visit of members of the Andean Q'ero society to New York City; find an update on the "culture of victimization" thesis, a new journal entry on visiting Disney World, new links to the author's videos on travel and cultural relativism, and a new Global Sociology box comparing the dominant cultures of the United States and Canada.

• **Chapter 4 Society**: There is an update on classic theorists' view of the Information Revolution as well as links to online biographies of sociology's founders.

• **Chapter 5 Socialization**: Find an update on how the violent content in television programming and video games affects young children; a Web link provides a complete chapter on the sociology of the mass media; a new Diversity: Race, Class, and Gender box examines how race and ethnicity affect the personal development of high-school students.

• **Chapter 6 Social Interaction in Everyday Life**: A new national map shows where people are and are not likely to be avid golfers; find updates on reality construction and the sociology of humor (including a few new jokes).

• **Chapter 7 Groups and Organizations**: A new global snapshot highlights arts-related organizations in selected countries; there is an update on McDonaldization as well as new data on the share of incumbents who held their congressional seats in the 2000 elections, discussion of using social networks to find jobs by gender, race, and ethnicity, an update on gender and management positions in the United States, and new material on the controversy surrounding computers, large organizations, and personal privacy.

• **Chapter 8 Deviance**: A new national map shows the risk of violent crime for all U.S. counties; there are updates on U.S. crime rates and a fresh look at the rising debate over capital punishment.

• **Chapter 9 Sexuality**: A new chapter opening illustrates the problems of acceptance faced by transgender individuals; there are updates on U.S. attitudes about sexual practices and a new global map shows the use of contraception around the world.

• **Chapter 10 Social Stratification**: Find an update on the unequal distribution of wealth in the United States; a new global snapshot shows that income inequality is greater in the United States than in high-income European nations.

• **Chapter 11 Social Class in the United States**: A new chapter opening looks at a case of high-flying executive pay; a new national map shows average income for all counties across the United States; we've added a new discussion of rural homelessness and updated statistics on income, wealth, and poverty.

• **Chapter 12 Global Stratification**: A new chapter opening notes natural disasters that are all too common in low-income nations; find new data showing which countries now fall into high-, middle-, and low-income categories as well as a new figure that charts the world's increasing income inequality.

• **Chapter 13 Gender Stratification**: The chapter includes two new global maps illustrating women's power and the practice of female genital mutilation in global perspective; there are updates on the share of women in various job categories, including new data on the number of women in top corporate positions; new statistics show the latest gaps in earnings between women and men and between various racial and ethnic categories; new Web links take readers to recent government reports concerning gender.

• **Chapter 14 Race and Ethnicity**: A new journal entry points out racial and ethnic stratification in everyday life; find Census 2000 data for various racial and ethnic categories as well as updates on income and other measures of social standing by race and ethnicity; there is more on the social construction of ethnicity as well as race, and the intersection of these variables with class and gender.

• **Chapter 15 Aging and the Elderly**: A new chapter opening looks at the role of middle-aged people caring for aging parents; new data show the advancing average age of U.S. farmers and give updates on income for all categories of elderly people in the United States; a number of new Web sites provide access to recent data and analysis of issues related to aging.

• **Chapter 16 The Economy and Work**: A new chapter opener illustrates the power of technology to change the character of work; a new global map shows the share of the labor force in service sector jobs for world nations; the chapter offers new data (which may surprise you) on the relative importance of the three economic sectors in high-, middle-, and low-income nations; new data on the U.S. labor force highlight the increasing share of minorities.

• **Chapter 17 Politics and Government**: Updates the 2000 elections, including a new national map showing the county-by-county results of the presidential race; a new Diversity: Race, Class, and Gender box explains the rural-urban divide in U.S. politics; there is extensive coverage of terrorism and the events of September 11, 2001, including an analysis of terrorism as a new form of "asymmetrical" war.

• **Chapter 18 Family**: A new opening profiles the "plural marriage" of Tom Green and his conviction for bigamy; updates are provided on all family trends including singlehood, divorce, single parenting, and cohabitation as well as family data from Census 2000.

• **Chapter 19 Religion**: Did you know that the number of Muslims in the United States exceeds the number of Episcopalians, Presbyterians, or Jews? Find the most recent data, as well as an update on the ordination of women; there is also a new section on the search for spirituality in postdenominational U.S. society.

• **Chapter 20 Education**: A new chapter opening highlights the far better performance on proficiency tests by children living in high-income communities compared to those from low-income areas; find updates on educational statistics as well as a new discussion of the U.S. teacher shortage.

• **Chapter 21 Health and Medicine**: This chapter offers an update on the share of minority physicians in the United States as well as a new statistical profile of the health of the U.S. population; there is expanded discussion of health care policy in Canada.

• **Chapter 22 Population, Urbanization, and Environment**: Find a new chapter opening as well as a new section describing the "rural rebound" trend; a new Diversity: Race, Class, and Gender box uses Census 2000 to highlight the minority majority in half the nation's largest 100 cities; there are updates on all U.S. demographic data and more on "critical demography."

• **Chapter 23 Collective Behavior and Social Movements**: A new chapter opening describes the massive demonstration at the 1999 meeting of the World Trade Organization in Seattle; there is also a new discussion of moral panics, including the widespread fear in the wake of the events of September 11, 2001.

- **Chapter 24 Social Change: Traditional, Modern, and Postmodern Societies**: A new chapter opening highlights the lives of two families who resided in the same New York City apartment a century apart; a new table provides a snapshot of change in the United States across the twentieth century; a new journal entry describes the appearance of mass society and an updated figure shows support for science in selected nations around the world.

A WORD ABOUT LANGUAGE

This text's commitment to representing the social diversity of the United States and the world carries with it the responsibility to use language thoughtfully. In most cases, we prefer the terms *African American* and *person of color* to the word *black*. We use the terms *Hispanic* and *Latino* to refer to people of Spanish descent. Most tables and figures refer to "Hispanics" because this is the term the Census Bureau uses when collecting statistical data about our population.

Students should realize, however, that many individuals do not describe themselves using these terms. Although the term "Hispanic" is commonly used in the eastern part of the United States, and "Latino" and the feminine form "Latina" are widely heard in the West, across the United States people of Spanish descent identify with a particular ancestral nation, whether it be Argentina, Mexico, some other Latin American country, or Spain or Portugal in Europe.

The same holds for Asian Americans. Although this term is a useful shorthand in sociological analysis, most people of Asian descent think of themselves in terms of a specific country of origin (say, Japan, the Philippines, Taiwan, or Vietnam).

In this text, the term "Native American" refers to all the inhabitants of the Americas (including the Hawaiian Islands) whose ancestors lived here prior to the arrival of Europeans. Here again, however, most people in this broad category identify with their historical society (for example, Cherokee, Hopi, or Zuni). The term "American Indian" designates only those Native Americans who live in the continental United States, not including Native peoples living in Alaska or Hawaii.

Learning to think globally also leads us to use language carefully. This text avoids the word "American"—which literally designates two continents—to refer to just the United States. For example, referring to this country, the term "U.S. economy" is more correct than the "American economy." This convention may seem a small point, but it implies the significant recognition that we in this country represent only one society (albeit a very important one) in the Americas.

SUPPLEMENTS

Sociology, Ninth Edition, is the heart of an unprecedented multimedia learning package that includes a wide range of proven instructional aids as well as several new ones. As the author of the text, I maintain a keen interest in all the supplements to ensure their quality and integration with the text. The supplements for this revision have been thoroughly updated, improved, and expanded. Also, many of them are now available for easy download at http://www.prenhall.com/sociology_central

FOR THE INSTRUCTOR

Annotated Instructor's Edition. The AIE is a complete student text annotated by the author on every page. Annotations—which have been thoroughly revised for this edition—have won praise from instructors for enriching class presentations. Margin notes include summaries of research findings, statistics from the United States or other nations, insightful quotations, information highlighting patterns of social diversity in the United States, and high-quality survey data from the National Opinion Research Center's (NORC) *General Social Survey* and *World Values Survey* data from the Inter-university Consortium for Political and Social Research (CPSR).

Data File. This is the "instructor's manual" that is of interest even to those who have never used one before. The *Data File* provides far more than detailed chapter outlines and discussion questions; it contains statistical profiles of the United States and other nations, summaries of important developments, and significant research and supplemental lecture material for every chapter of the text. The *Data File* is available in Windows format as well as the traditional print version.

Test Item File. A revised test item file prepared by John Macionis is available in both printed and computerized forms. The file contains 2400 items—100 per chapter—in multiple-choice, true/false, and essay formats. Questions are identified as simple "recall" items or more complex inferential issues, and answers to all questions are page referenced to the text. Prentice Hall Custom Test is a test generator designed to allow the creation of personalized exams. It is available in Windows and Macintosh formats. Prentice Hall also provides a test preparation service to users of this text that is as easy as a call to our toll-free 800 number. Please contact your Prentice Hall representative for this number.

Film/Video Guide: Prentice Hall Introductory Sociology, Sixth Edition. Keyed to the chapters of this text, this guide describes more than 300 films and videos appropriate for classroom viewing. It also provides summaries, discussion questions, and rental sources for each film and video.

ABCNEWS **ABC News/Prentice Hall Video Library for Sociology.** Few will dispute that video is the most dynamic supplement you can use to enhance a classroom presentation. However, the quality of the video material and how well it relates to your course still make all the difference. Prentice Hall and ABC News are working together to bring to you the best and most comprehensive video ancillaries available in the college market.

Through its wide variety of award-winning programs—*Nightline, This Week, World News Tonight,* and *20/20*—ABC offers a resource for feature and documentary-style videos related to the chapters in *Sociology, Ninth Edition.* The programs have high production quality, present substantial content, and are hosted by well-versed, well-known anchors.

The authors and editors of Prentice Hall have carefully selected videos on topics that complement *Sociology, Ninth Edition,* and have included notes on how to use them in the classroom. An excellent instructor's guide carefully and completely integrates the videos into your lecture. The guide has a synopsis of each video that shows its relation to the chapter and discussion questions to help students focus on how concepts and theories apply to real-life situations.

Volume I: Social Stratification (0-13-466228-8)
Volume II: Marriage/Families (0-13-209537-8)
Volume III: Race/Ethnic Relations (0-13-458506-2)
Volume IV: Criminology (0-13-375163-5)
Volume V: Social Problems (0-13-437823-7)
Volume VI: Intro to Sociology I (0-13-095066-1)
Volume VII: Intro to Sociology II (0-13-095060-2)
Volume VIII: Intro to Sociology III (0-13-095773-9)
Volume IX: Social Problems (0-13-095774-7)
Volume X: Marriage/Families II (0-13-095775-5)
Volume XI: Race and Ethnic Relations II (0-13-021134-6)
Volume XII: Institutions (0-13-021133-8)
Volume XIII: Introductory Sociology IV (0-13-018507-8)
Volume XIV: Introductory Sociology V (0-13-018509-4)

Prentice Hall Introductory Sociology PowerPoint™ Transparencies. Created by Roger J. Eich of Hawkeye Community College, this PowerPoint slide set combines graphics and text in a colorful format to help you convey sociological principles in a new and exciting way. Created in PowerPoint, an easy-to-use, widely available software program, this set contains over 300 slides keyed to each chapter in the text. For easy download, they are available on our instructor resource site at http://www.prenhall.com/sociology_central

Prentice Hall Color Transparencies: Sociology Series VII. Full-color illustrations, charts, and other visual materials from the text as well as outside sources have been selected to make up this useful in-class tool.

Instructor's Guide to Prentice Hall Color Transparencies: Sociology Series VII. This guide offers suggestions for effectively using each transparency in the classroom.

MEDIA SUPPLEMENTS

Interactive CD-ROM. Using video as a window to the world outside of the classroom, this innovative CD-ROM offers students videos and animations arranged according to theme (Global Perspective, Social Diversity, or Critical Thinking) within each chapter. Students can view relevant ABC News clips and author video tips, interact with the global and national maps, and review sociological concepts through video. The CD-ROM is available free with all new copies of *Sociology, Ninth Edition.*

Census 2000 Update CD-ROM. Capturing the rich picture of our nation drawn by Census 2000, this CD-ROM brings related Census data into your classroom in a multimedia format. It is free when packaged with *Sociology, Ninth Edition.*

Companion Website™. In tandem with the text, students and professors can now take full advantage of the Internet to enrich their study of sociology. The Macionis *Companion Website™* continues to lead the way in providing students with avenues for delving deeper into the topics covered in the text. Features of the Web site include chapter objectives, study questions, and faculty resources, as well as links to interesting material and information from other sites on the Web that will reinforce and enhance the content of each chapter. Use of the site is free to both students and faculty. Please visit the site at http://www.prenhall.com/macionis and click on the cover of *Sociology, Ninth Edition.*

ContentSelect. Developed by Prentice Hall and EBSCO, the world leader in online journal subscription management, ContentSelect is a customized research database for students of sociology. A collection of over 125 sources—peer-reviewed journals as well as popular magazines, but *all* with relevance to sociology—provide students with a reputable starting point for their research. If you would like to integrate this resource into your course, a free student access code can be packaged with *Sociology, Ninth Edition.* Please contact your Prentice Hall representative for more information or visit the ContentSelect Web site at www.prenhall.com/contentselect

Distance Learning Solutions. Prentice Hall is committed to providing our leading content to the growing number of courses being delivered over the Internet by developing relationships with the leading vendors—Blackboard™, Web CT™, and CourseCompass, Prentice Hall's own easy-to-use course management system powered by Blackboard™. Please visit our technology solutions site at http://www.prenhall.com/demo

Sociology on the Internet: A Critical Thinking Guide, 2001. This guide focuses on developing the critical thinking skills necessary to evaluate and use online sources. The guide also provides a brief introduction to navigating the Internet, along with complete references related specifically to the discipline of sociology. This supplementary book is free to students when packaged with *Sociology, Ninth Edition.* Please contact your Prentice Hall representative for more information.

FOR THE STUDENT

Study Guide. This complete guide helps students to review and reflect on the material presented in *Sociology, Ninth Edition.* Each of the twenty-four chapters in the Study Guide provides an overview of the corresponding chapter in the student text, summarizes its major topics and concepts, offers applied exercises, and features end-of-chapter tests with solutions.

Practice Tests. This collection of study questions offers students a learning opportunity that is free when packaged with *Sociology, Ninth Edition.*

The New York Times Supplement, Themes of the Times, for Introductory Sociology. *The New York Times* and Prentice Hall are sponsoring *Themes of the Times*, a program designed to enhance student access to current information relevant to the classroom. Through this program, the core subject matter provided in this text is supplemented by a collection of timely articles from one of the world's most distinguished newspapers, *The New York Times.* These articles demonstrate the vital, ongoing connection between what is learned in the classroom and what is happening in the world around us.

To enjoy the wealth of information of *The New York Times* daily, a reduced subscription rate is available. For information, call toll-free 1-800-631-1222.

Prentice Hall and *The New York Times* are proud to co-sponsor *Themes of the Times.* We hope it will make the reading of both textbooks and newspapers a more dynamic and involving process.

10 Ways to Fight Hate Brochure. Produced by the Southern Poverty Law Center, the leading hate-crime and crime-watch organization in the United States, it walks students through ten steps that they can take on their own campus or in their own neighborhood to fight hate everyday.

Critical Thinking Audiocassette Tape. In keeping with the text's critical thinking approach, a sixty-minute audio tape is available to help students think and read critically.

IN APPRECIATION

The conventional practice of designating a single author obscures the efforts of dozens of women and men that have resulted in *Sociology, Ninth Edition.* I would like to express my thanks to the Prentice Hall editorial team, including Yolanda de Rooy, division president, Laura Pearson, editorial director, Nancy Roberts, publisher, Chris DeJohn, senior acquisitions editor in sociology, and Christina Scalia, editorial assistant, for their steady enthusiasm and for pursuing both innovation and excellence. Day-to-day work on the book is shared by the author and the production team. Susanna Lesan, developmental editor-in-chief at Prentice Hall, has played a vital role in the development of all my texts for more than fifteen years, coordinating and supervising the editorial process. Barbara Reilly, production editor at Prentice Hall, is an essential member of the team. Barbara deserves much of the credit for the attractive page layout of the book; indeed, if anyone "sweats the details" more than the author, it is Barbara! Amy Marsh Macionis, the text's "in house" editor, checks virtually everything, untangling awkward phrases, and eliminating errors and inconsistencies in all the statistical data. Amy is a most talented editor who is relentless in her pursuit of quality; my debt to her is great, indeed.

I also have a large debt to the members of the Prentice Hall sales staff, the men and women who have given this text such remarkable support over the years. Thanks, especially, to Beth Mejia who directs our marketing campaign.

Thanks, too, to Laura Gardner for providing the interior design of the book, which was coordinated by art director Nancy Wells. Developmental and copy editing of the manuscript was provided by Harriett Prentiss, Carol Peschke, and Amy Marsh Macionis. Barbara Salz did the research for our photographs and fine art.

It goes without saying that every colleague knows more about some topics covered in this book than the author does. For that reason, I am grateful to the hundreds of faculty and students who have written to me to offer comments and suggestions. More formally, I am grateful to the following people who have reviewed some or all of this manuscript:

Sampson Lee Blair, Arizona State University
Lovberta Cross, Southwestern Tennessee Community College
Isaac W. Eberstein, Florida State University
Mike Hart, Broward County Community College
Steve Light, SUNY Plattsburgh
Dale Lund, University of Utah
Tim Tuinstra, Kalamazoo Valley Community College
Rich Yinger, Palm Beach Community College

I also wish to thank the following colleagues for sharing their wisdom in ways that have improved this book: Doug Adams (The Ohio State University), Richard Alford (East Central University), Sally Archer (The College of New Jersey), Kip Armstrong (Bloomsburg University), Rose Arnault (Fort Hays State University), Patricia S. Astry (SUNY College at Fredonia), Judith Barker (Ithaca College), Scott Beck (Eastern Tennessee State University), Paul J. Becker (Morehead State University), Lois Benjamin (Hampton University), Philip Berg (University of Wisconsin, La Crosse), Jane Bock (University of Wisconsin—Green Bay), Charlotte Brauchle (Southwest Texas Junior College), Bill Brindle (Monroe Community College), John R. Brouillette (Colorado State University), Cathryn Brubaker (Georgia Perimeter College), Brent Bruton (Iowa State University), Richard Bucher (Baltimore City Community College), Karen A. Callaghan (Barry University), Karen Campbell (Vanderbilt University), Harold Conway (Blinn College), Gerry Cox (Fort Hays State University), Robert Daniels (Mount Vernon Nazarene College), James A. Davis (Harvard University), Sumati Devadutt (Monroe Community College), Keith Doubt (Northeast Missouri State University), Denny Dubbs (Harrisburg Area Community College), Lois Easterom (Onondaga Community College), Travis Eaton (Northeast Louisiana State University), Helen Rose Fuchs Ebaugh (University of Houston), John Ehle (Northern Virginia Community College), Roger Eich (Hawkeye Community College), Heather Fitz Gibbon (The College of Wooster), Kevin Fitzpatrick (University of Alabama-Birmingham), Jerry Flattum (University of Minnesota), Dona C. Fletcher (Sinclair Community College), Abby Foster (University of Colorado at Colorado Springs), Charles Frazier (University of Florida), Karen Lynch Frederick (St. Anselm College), Mary Theresa Bonhage Freund (Alma College), Patricia Gagné (University of Kentucky, Louisville), Pam Gaiter (Collin County Community College), Timothy J. Gallagher (Kent State University), Jarvis Gamble (Owen's Technical College), Steven Goldberg (City College, City University of New York), Charlotte Gotwald (York College of Pennsylvania), Norma B. Gray (Bishop State Community College), Rhoda Greenstone (DeVry Institute), Jeffrey Hahn (Mount Union College), Harry Hale (Northeast Louisiana State University), Dean Haledjian (Northern Virginia Community College), Dick Haltin (Jefferson Community College), Roma Stouall Hanks (University of South Alabama), Marvin Hannah (Milwaukee Area Technical College), Charles Harper (Creighton University), Christine L. Himes (Syracuse University), Gary Hodge (Collin County Community College), Elizabeth A. Hoisington (Heartland Community College), Sara Horsfall (Stephen F. Austin State University), Peter Hruschka (Ohio Northern University), Glenna Huls (Camden County College), Jeanne Humble (Lexington Community College), Cynthia Imanaka (Seattle Central Community College), G. David Johnson (University of South Alabama), Patricia Johnson (Houston Community College), Ed Kain (Southwestern University), Paul Kamolnick (Eastern Tennessee State University), Irwin Kantor (Middlesex County College), Thomas Korllos (Kent State University), Rita Krasnow (Virginia Western Community College), Donald Kraybill (Elizabethtown College),

Michael Lacy (Colorado State University), Michael Levine (Kenyon College), George Lowe (Texas Tech University), Don Luidens (Hope College), Larry Lyon (Baylor University), Li-Chen Ma (Lamar University), N. Jane McCandless (State University of West Georgia), Karen E. B. McCue (University of New Mexico, Albuquerque), Meredith McGuire (Trinity College), Setma Maddox (Texas Wesleyan University), Errol Magidson (Richard J. Daley College), Marguerite Martin (Gonzaga University), Allan Mazur (Syracuse University), Jack Melhorn (Emporia State University), Ken Miller (Drake University), Michael Miller (University of Texas at San Antonio), Richard Miller (Navarro College), Daniel J. Monti (Boston University), Joe Morolla (Virginia Commonwealth University), Craig Nauman (Madison Area Technical College), David Naylor (Charleston Southern University), Toby Parcel (The Ohio State University), Anne Peterson (Columbus State Community College), Marvin Pippert (Roanoke College), Lauren Pivnik (Monroe Community College), Nevel Razak (Fort Hays State College), Jim Rebstock (Broward Community College); George Reim (Cheltenham High School), Virginia Reynolds (Indiana University of Pennsylvania), Laurel Richardson (The Ohio State University), Keith Roberts (Hanover College), Ellen Rosengarten (Sinclair Community College), Howard Schneiderman (Lafayette College), Ray Scupin (Lindenwood University), Steve Severin (Kellogg Community College), Robert Shelly (Ohio University), Harry Sherer (Irvine Valley College), Walt Shirley (Sinclair Community College), Anson Shupe (Indiana University-Purdue University at Fort Wayne), Ree Simpkins (Missouri Southern State University), Glen Sims (Glendale Community College), Blasco Sobrinho (University of Cincinnati), Nancy Sonleitner (University of Oklahoma), Dee Southard (Central Washington University), Steven Spitzer (Suffolk University), Leslie Stanley-Stevens (Tarleton University), Larry Stern (Collin County Community College), Randy Ston (Oakland Community College), Verta Taylor (The Ohio State University), Vickie H. Taylor (Danville Community College), Jan Thomas (Kenyon College), Mark J. Thomas (Madison Area Technical College), Len Tompos (Lorain County Community College), Christopher Vanderpool (Michigan State University), Phyllis Watts (Tiffin University); Murray Webster (University of North Carolina, Charlotte), Debbie White (Collin County Community College), Rhys H. Williams (Southern Illinois University—Carbondale), Marilyn Wilmeth (Iowa University), Stuart Wright (Lamar University), William Yoels (University of Alabama, Birmingham), Dan Yutze (Taylor University), Wayne Zapatek (Tarrant County Community College), and Frank Zulke (Harold Washington College).

Finally, I would like to dedicate this edition of the book to all the men and women who became heroes in the wake of events of September 11, 2001, in ways big and small, including those known to many and those known to just a few. In the face of terror, they rose up, reached out to others even at the cost of their own lives, and displayed the very best that lies within us.

Jan J. Macionis

ABOUT THE AUTHOR

John J. Macionis (pronounced ma-SHOW-nis) was born and raised in Philadelphia, Pennsylvania. He received his bachelor's degree from Cornell University and his doctorate in sociology from the University of Pennsylvania. His publications are wide-ranging, focusing on community life in the United States, interpersonal intimacy in families, effective teaching, humor, new information technology, and the importance of global education. He and Nijole V. Benokraitis have edited the companion volume to this text, *Seeing Ourselves: Classic, Contemporary, and Cross-Cultural Readings in Sociology*. Macionis has also authored *Society: The Basics*, the leading brief text in the field, and he collaborates on international editions of the texts: *Sociology: Canadian Edition* (with Linda M. Gerber, from Prentice Hall Canada), *Society: The Basics, Canadian Edition* (with Cecelia Benoit and Mikael Jansson, also from Prentice Hall Canada), and *Sociology: A Global Introduction* (with Ken Plummer, published by Prentice Hall Europe). *Sociology* is also available in various international and foreign language editions. In addition, Macionis and Vincent Parrillo have written the urban studies text, *Cities and Urban Life* (Prentice Hall). Macionis's most recent new text is *Social Problems* (Prentice Hall), which is the first text to take a social-constructionist approach to the study of social problems and public policy. The latest on all the Macionis textbooks, as well as news, information, and dozens of Internet links of interest to students and faculty in sociology, can be found at the author's personal Web site, http://www.macionis.com or http://www.TheSociologyPage.com Additional information, as well as online study guides for the texts, is available at the Prentice Hall site, http://www.prenhall.com/macionis

John Macionis is Professor and Prentice Hall Distinguished Scholar of Sociology at Kenyon College in Gambier, Ohio. During a career of almost twenty-five years at Kenyon, he has chaired the Anthropology-Sociology Department, directed the college's multidisciplinary program in humane studies, and presided over the campus senate and also the college's faculty.

In 1998, the North Central Sociological Association named Macionis recipient of the Award for Distinguished Contribution to Teaching, citing his work with textbooks and his pioneering use of new technology in sociology.

Professor Macionis has been active in academic programs in other countries, having traveled to some fifty nations. In the fall of 1994, he directed the global education course for the University of Pittsburgh's Semester at Sea program, teaching 400 students on a floating campus that visited twelve countries as it circled the globe.

Macionis writes, "I am an ambitious traveler, eager to learn and, through the texts, to share much of what I discover with students, many of whom know so little about the rest of the world. For me, traveling and writing are all dimensions of teaching. First and foremost, I am a teacher—a passion for teaching animates everything I do." At Kenyon, Macionis offers a wide range of upper-level courses, but his favorite course is Introduction to Sociology, which he schedules every semester. He enjoys extensive contact with students and each term invites his students to enjoy a home-cooked meal.

The Macionis family— John, Amy, and children McLean and Whitney—live on a farm in rural Ohio. Their home serves as a popular bed and breakfast where they enjoy visiting with old friends and making new ones. In his free time, John enjoys bicycling through the Ohio countryside, swimming, sailing, and playing oldies rock and roll on his guitar. He is currently learning to play the Scottish bagpipes.

Professor Macionis welcomes (and responds to) comments and suggestions about this book from faculty and students. Write to the Sociology Department, Palme House, Kenyon College, Gambier, Ohio 43022, or direct e-mail to MACIONIS@KENYON.EDU

CHAPTER

1

John Sloan (1871–1951)
Traveling Carnival, Santa Fe, 1924

Oil on canvas, 76.5 × 91.6 cm.
Smithsonian American Art Museum, Washington, D.C./Art Resource, N.Y.

THE SOCIOLOGICAL PERSPECTIVE

Whitney Linnea is a happy, well-adjusted ten-year-old living in a small Midwestern town in the United States. Like most of her friends, she loves sports. It is a warm fall day, and Whitney is headed from school to soccer practice. She climbs into her mother's van and settles back with a snack for the five-mile trip to the playing fields. Her mother will drive back again in an hour to pick her up. On Saturday, there are soccer games: The away games can be a two-hour drive each way.

Soccer is not the only sport Whitney enjoys. As the weather turns colder, soccer fades and swimming takes

over, with the season lasting until the end of March. Daily practices are held at the pool of the nearby college—a twenty-minute drive each way—with meets around the state on Saturdays.

In spring, Whitney splits her afternoons between soccer and Little League baseball. On Saturdays in April and May, she is likely to hurry from a morning soccer game to a noon baseball game that may be thirty miles away. With all the driving to and from Whitney's practices and sporting events, Whitney's mother and father put more than 5,000 miles on their car (adapted from Ferguson, 1999).

Some 40 million young people in the United States—about three out of four—participate in one or more organized sports from soccer to swimming to squash. If you asked them why they do it, probably most would say they play sports just to have fun. But there is more to the story than children doing what they enjoy. Consider that the United States has a fascination with competitive sports that is far greater than what we find in much of the world. In other words, if we view Whitney's behavior in context, we see that the choices we make every day have much to do with the larger society around us. Here and elsewhere, how people decide to spend their time does not result from the process philosophers call "free will." More correctly—and this is the essential wisdom that we gain from a study of sociology—our social world guides our actions and life choices in much the same way that the seasons influence our selection of clothing and activities.

THE SOCIOLOGICAL PERSPECTIVE

Sociology is *the systematic study of human society*. At the heart of sociology is a distinctive point of view called "the sociological perspective."

SEEING THE GENERAL IN THE PARTICULAR

Peter Berger (1963) described the sociological perspective as *seeing the general in the particular*. By this he meant that sociologists identify general patterns in the behavior of particular people. Although every individual is unique, a society guides people to act in certain ways, such as enjoying competitive sports. In addition, within any one country society acts differently on various *categories* of people (say, women as opposed to men, the rich as opposed to the poor, and children as opposed to adults). We begin to think sociologically by realizing how the general categories into which we fall shape our particular life experiences.

1

We can easily grasp the power of society over the individual by imagining how different our lives would be had we been born in place of any of these children from, respectively, Bolivia, Sri Lanka, Ethiopia, Botswana, the People's Republic of China, and El Salvador.

This text explores the power of society to shape our thoughts, feelings, and actions. People with high incomes, for example, are likely to enjoy expensive sports (such as downhill skiing), whereas people with low incomes prefer less expensive sports (such as baseball and basketball). More generally, people who come from more privileged social backgrounds tend to be confident and optimistic about their lives. This is not surprising when we realize that they have had more opportunities and the training and skills to take advantage of them.

Seeing the world sociologically also makes us aware of the importance of gender. As Chapter 13 ("Gender Stratification") describes, every society attaches meaning to being female or male and gives women and men different kinds of work and family responsibilities. Here, again, society influences us throughout the course of our lives by suggesting that certain sports, college courses, and career goals correspond to our sex.

SEEING THE STRANGE IN THE FAMILIAR

At first, using the sociological perspective amounts to *seeing the strange in the familiar*. This does not mean that sociologists focus on the bizarre elements of society. Rather, looking sociologically means giving up the familiar idea that human behavior is simply a matter of what people *decide* to do in favor of the initially strange notion that society shapes our lives.

For individualistic North Americans, learning to see how society affects us may take a bit of practice. Say someone asked you why you "chose" to enroll at your particular college. In response, you might offer one of the following reasons:

"I wanted to stay close to home."

"I got a basketball scholarship."

"With a journalism degree from this university, I can get a good job."

"My girlfriend goes to school here."

"I didn't get into the school I *really* wanted to attend."

Such responses may well be true. But do they tell the whole story?

Thinking sociologically about going to college, we might first realize that, around the world, about five people in one hundred gets a college degree. Even in the United States a century ago, going to college was not an option for most people. Today a look around the classroom shows that social forces still have much to do with college attendance. Typically, U.S. college students are young, generally between eighteen and twenty-four. Why? Because in our society, attending college is linked to this period of life. But more than age is involved because fewer than half of all young men and women actually end up on campus.

Another factor is cost. Because higher education is so expensive, students tend to come from families with above-average incomes. As Chapter 20 ("Education") explains, if you are lucky enough to belong to a family earning more than $75,000, you are three times as likely to go to college as someone whose family earns less than

 For a closer look at college attendance by family income, go to http://www.prenhall.com/weblinks

$20,000 each year. This is one reason that a greater share of white people (63 percent) than African Americans (59 percent) "choose" to go to college.

INDIVIDUALITY IN SOCIAL CONTEXT

To see the power of society to shape individual choices, consider the number of children women have. In the United States, as shown in Global Map 1–1 on page 4, the average woman has slightly fewer than two children during her lifetime. In India, however, the average is about three; in South Africa, about four; in Cambodia, about five; in Saudi Arabia, about six; and in Niger, about seven.

Why these striking differences? As later chapters explain, women in poor countries have less schooling and fewer economic opportunities, are more likely to remain in the home, and are less likely to use contraception. Clearly, society has much to do with the decisions women and men make about childbearing.

Another illustration of the power of society to shape even our most private choices comes from the study of suicide. What could be a more personal choice than taking one's own life? But Emile Durkheim (1858–1917), one of sociology's pioneers, showed that

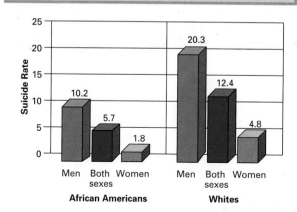

FIGURE 1–1 Rate of Death by Suicide, by Race and Sex, for the United States

Rates indicate the number of deaths by suicide for every 100,000 people in each category for 1998.

Source: U.S. National Center for Health Statistics (2000).

social forces are at work even in the apparently isolated act of self-destruction.

Examining official records in his native France, Durkheim found that some categories of people were more likely than others to take their own lives. He found that men, Protestants, wealthy people, and the unmarried had significantly higher suicide rates than did women, Catholics and Jews, the poor, and married people. Durkheim explained the differences in terms of *social integration*: Categories of people with strong social ties had low suicide rates, whereas more individualistic people had high suicide rates.

In the male-dominated society Durkheim studied, men certainly had more freedom than women. But despite its advantages, freedom also contributes to social isolation and thus a higher suicide rate. Likewise, more individualistic Protestants were more prone to suicide than more traditional Catholics and Jews, whose rituals foster stronger social ties. The wealthy have much more freedom than the poor, but, once again, at the cost of a higher suicide rate. Finally, can you see why single people are at greater risk than married people?

A century later, Durkheim's analysis still holds true (Thorlindsson & Bjarnason, 1998). Figure 1–1 shows suicide rates for four categories of the U.S. population. In 1998, there were 12.4 recorded suicides for every

GLOBAL MAP 1–1 Women's Childbearing in Global Perspective

Is childbearing simply a matter of personal choice? A look around the world shows that it is not. In general, women living in poor countries have many more children than women in rich nations. Can you point to some of the reasons for this global disparity? In simple terms, such differences mean that if you had been born into another society (whether you are female or male), your life might have been quite different from what it is now.

Source: Data from Mackay (2000).

100,000 white people, more than twice the rate for African Americans (5.7). For both races, suicide was more common among men than among women; white men (20.3) were more than four times as likely as white women (4.8) to take their own lives. Among African Americans, the rate for men (10.2) was nearly six times higher than for women (1.8). Following Durkheim's logic, the higher suicide rate among white people and men reflects their greater wealth and freedom; the lower rate among women and people of color follows

The Global Village: A Social Snapshot of Our World

The Earth is home to 6.2 billion people who live in the cities and villages of 192 nations. To grasp the social shape of the world, imagine for a moment that the planet's population is reduced to a single settlement of 1,000 people. In this "global village," more than half (610) of the inhabitants are Asian, including 210 citizens of the People's Republic of China. Next, in terms of numbers, we would find 130 Africans, 120 Europeans, 85 people from Latin America and the Caribbean, 5 from Australia and the South Pacific, and just 50 North Americans, including 45 people from the United States.

A study of the settlement's ways of life would reveal some startling facts:

The village is a rich place, with a seemingly endless array of goods and services for sale. Yet most of the inhabitants only dream about such treasures because 80 percent of the village's total income is earned by just 200 people.

For the majority, the greatest problem is getting enough food. Every year, village workers produce more than enough to feed everyone; even so, half the village's people, including most of the children, do not get enough to eat, and many fall asleep hungry. The worst-off 200 residents (who, together, have less money than the richest person in the village) lack both clean drinking water and safe shelter. Weak and unable to work, some of them fall victim to life-threatening diseases every day.

Villagers boast of their community's many schools, including a fine university. About 50 inhabitants have completed a college degree, but almost half of the village's people can neither read nor write.

We in the United States, on average, would be among the richest people in this global village. Although we tend to credit ourselves for living well, the sociological perspective reminds us that our achievements are largely products of the privileged position our nation holds in the worldwide social system.

Source: Calculations by the author based on data from United Nations and Population Reference Bureau publications.

from their limited social choices. Just as in Durkheim's day, then, we can see general patterns in the personal actions of particular individuals.

THE IMPORTANCE OF GLOBAL PERSPECTIVE

December 10, Fez, Morocco. This exotic medieval city—a web of narrow streets and alleyways—is alive with the laughter of playing children, the silence of veiled women, and the steady gaze of men leading donkeys laden with goods. Fez has changed little over the centuries. Here, in northwest Africa, we are just a few hundred miles from the more familiar rhythms of Europe. Yet this place seems a thousand years away. Never have we had such an adventure! Never have we thought so much about home!

As new information technology draws even the farthest reaches of the Earth closer to each other, many academic disciplines take a **global perspective,** *the study of the larger world and our society's place in it.* What is the importance of a global perspective for sociology?

First, global awareness is a logical extension of the sociological perspective. Sociology shows us that our place in society profoundly affects our life experiences. It stands to reason, then, that the position of our society in the larger world system affects everyone in the United States. The box describes a "global village" to show the social shape of the world and the place of the United States within it.

Global Map 1–2 provides a visual guide to the relative economic development of the world's countries. **High-income countries**[1] are *nations with very*

---

[1]The text favors this terminology over the traditional but outdated "First World," "Second World," and "Third World." See Chapter 12 ("Global Stratification") for a full discussion.

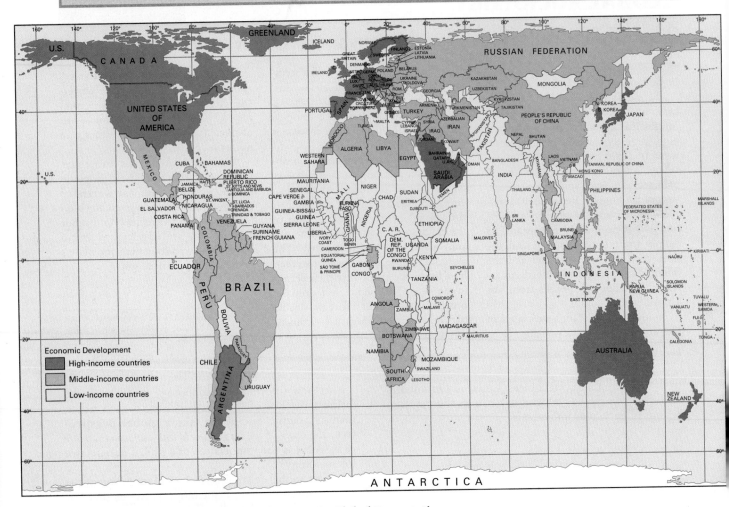

GLOBAL MAP 1–2 Economic Development in Global Perspective

In high-income countries—including the United States, Canada, Argentina, the nations of Western Europe, Israel, Saudi Arabia, Australia, and Japan—a highly productive economy provides people, on average, with material plenty. Middle-income countries—including most of Latin America and the nations of Eastern Europe—are less economically productive, with a standard of living about average for the world as a whole but far below that of the United States. These nations also have a significant share of poor people who barely scrape by with meager housing and diet. In the low-income countries of the world, poverty is severe and extensive. Although small numbers of elites live very well in the poorest nations, most people struggle to survive on a small fraction of the income common in the United States.

Note: Data for this map are provided by the United Nations. High-income countries have a per capita gross domestic product (GDP) of at least $10,000. Many are far richer than this, however; the figure for the United States exceeds $31,000. Middle-income countries have a per capita GDP ranging from $2,500 to $10,000. Low-income countries have a per capita GDP below $2,500. Figures used here reflect the new United Nations "purchasing power parities" system. Rather than directly converting income figures into U.S. dollars, this calculation estimates the local purchasing power of each domestic currency.

Sources: Prepared by the author using data from United Nations Development Programme (2001). Map projection from *Peters Atlas of the World* (1990).

productive economic systems in which most people have relatively high incomes. High-income countries include the United States and Canada, Argentina, the nations of Western Europe, Israel, Saudi Arabia, Japan, and Australia. Taken together, these forty nations produce most of the world's goods and services and control most of the wealth. On average, individuals in these countries live well, not because they are smarter than anyone else, but because they had the good fortune to be born in an affluent region of the world.

The world's **middle-income countries** are *nations with moderately productive economic systems in which people's incomes are about the global average.* Individuals living in any of these roughly ninety nations—most of the countries of Eastern Europe, some of southern Africa, and almost all of Latin America—are as likely to live in rural villages as in cities; to walk or ride tractors, scooters, bicycles, or animals as to drive automobiles; and, on average, to receive just a few years of schooling. Most middle-income countries also have marked social inequality, so that some people are extremely rich (members of the business elite in nations across North Africa, for example), but many more lack safe housing and adequate nutrition.

Finally, about half of the world's people live in the sixty **low-income countries**, *nations with less productive economic systems in which most people are poor.* As Global Map 1–2 shows, most of the poorest countries in the world are in Africa and Asia. Here, again, a few people are very rich, but the majority struggle to get by with poor housing, unsafe water, too little food, limited sanitation, and, perhaps most seriously of all, little chance to improve their lives.

Chapter 12 ("Global Stratification") details the causes and consequences of global wealth and poverty. But every chapter of this text highlights life in the world beyond our own borders for four reasons:

1. **Where we live makes a great difference in shaping our lives.** As we saw in Global Map 1–1, women's lives are strikingly different in rich and poor countries. To understand ourselves and appreciate the plight of others, we must grasp the social landscape of the world—one good reason to pay attention to the thirty global maps found throughout this text.

2. **Societies throughout the world are increasingly interconnected.** Historically, the United States has taken only passing note of the countries beyond its own borders. In recent decades, however, the United States and the rest of the world have become linked as never before. Electronic

One important reason to gain a global understanding is that, living in a high-income nation, we scarcely can appreciate the suffering that goes on in much of the world. This boy is growing up in the African nation of Ghana, where he carries water for cooking and drinking from a public faucet and sewerage flows freely over unpaved streets. In poor nations like this, children have only a fifty-fifty chance to grow to adulthood.

technology now transmits sounds, pictures, and written documents around the globe in seconds.

One consequence of new technology, as later chapters explain, is that people all over the world now share many tastes in music, clothing, and food. With their economic clout, high-income countries such as the United States influence other nations, whose people eagerly gobble up our hamburgers, dance to pop music, and, more and more, speak the English language.

We are spreading our way of life around the world, but the larger world also has an impact on us. Almost 1 million documented immigrants enter the United States each year, and we have been quick to adopt many of their fashions and foods, which greatly enhances the racial and cultural diversity of this country.

Commerce across national boundaries has also created a global economy. Large corporations make and market goods worldwide, and global financial markets linked by satellite communication operate around the clock. Stock traders in New York follow the financial markets in Tokyo and Hong Kong even as wheat farmers in Iowa watch the price of grain in the former Soviet republic of Georgia. With eight out of ten new U.S. jobs involving international trade, global understanding has never been more important.

3. **Many problems that we face in the United States are far more serious elsewhere.** Poverty is a serious problem in the United States, but as Chapter 12 ("Global Stratification") explains, poverty in Latin America, Africa, and Asia is both more common and more serious. Similarly, although women have lower social standing than men in the United States, gender inequality is much greater in poor countries of the world.

4. **Thinking globally is a good way to learn more about ourselves.** We cannot walk the streets of a distant city without becoming keenly aware of what it means to live in the United States. Making global comparisons also leads to unexpected lessons. For instance, in Chapter 12 we visit a squatter settlement in Madras, India. There, despite a lack of basic material goods, people thrive in the love and support of family members. Why, then, is poverty in the United States associated with isolation and anger? Are material comforts—so crucial to our definition of a "rich" life—the best way to gauge human well-being?

In sum, in an increasingly interconnected world, we can understand ourselves only to the extent that we comprehend others (Macionis, 1993).

APPLYING THE SOCIOLOGICAL PERSPECTIVE

It is easy to apply the sociological perspective when we encounter people who differ from us—whether around the world or in our own hometowns—because they remind us that society shapes individual lives. But two other kinds of situations also help us to see the world with a sociological perspective: being socially marginal and living through a social crisis.

SOCIOLOGY AND SOCIAL MARGINALITY

From time to time, everyone feels like an "outsider." For some categories of people, however, being an *outsider*—not part of the dominant group—is an everyday experience. The greater people's social marginality, the better able they are to use the sociological perspective.

For example, no African American grows up in the United States without understanding the importance of race. But white people, as the dominant majority, think less often about race and believe it affects only people of color, not themselves. Women, gay people, people with disabilities, and the very old are also, to some degree, "outsiders." People at the margins of social life are aware of social patterns that others rarely think about. To become better at using the sociological perspective, therefore, we must step back from our familiar routines and look at our lives with new awareness and curiosity.

SOCIOLOGY AND SOCIAL CRISIS

Periods of change or crisis make everyone feel a little off balance and prompt us to use the sociological perspective. U.S. sociologist C. Wright Mills (1959) illustrated this idea with the Great Depression of the 1930s. As the unemployment rate soared to 25 percent, people out of work could not help but see general social forces at work in their particular lives. Rather than saying, "Something is wrong with me; I can't find a job," they took a sociological approach and realized, "The economy has collapsed; there are no jobs to be found!"

Just as social change fosters sociological thinking, sociological thinking can bring about social change. The more we learn how "the system" operates, the more we may want to change it in some way. Becoming aware of the power of gender, for example, many women and men have actively tried to reduce traditional gender role differences.

In short, an introduction to sociology is an invitation to learn a new way of looking at familiar patterns of social life. But is this invitation worth accepting? What are the benefits of applying the sociological perspective?

BENEFITS OF THE SOCIOLOGICAL PERSPECTIVE

Applying the sociological perspective to our daily lives benefits us in four ways:

1. **The sociological perspective helps us assess the truth of "common sense."** We all take many things for granted, but that does not make

The Sociological Imagination:
Turning Personal Problems into Public Issues

The power of the sociological perspective lies not just in changing individual lives but in transforming society. As C. Wright Mills saw it, society, not people's personal failings, is the cause of poverty and other social problems. The sociological imagination brings people together to bring about change by transforming personal *problems* into public *issues*.

In the following excerpt* Mills explains the need for a sociological imagination:

When a society becomes industrialized, a peasant becomes a

*In this excerpt, Mills uses "man" and male pronouns to apply to all people. Note that even an outspoken critic of society such as Mills reflected the conventional writing practices of his time as far as gender was concerned.

worker; a feudal lord is liquidated or becomes a businessman. When classes rise or fall, a man is employed or unemployed; when the rate of investment goes up or down, a man takes new heart or goes broke. When wars happen, an insurance salesman becomes a rocket launcher; a store clerk, a radar man; a wife lives alone; a child grows up without a father. Neither the life of an individual nor the history of a society can be understood without understanding both.

Yet men do not usually define the troubles they endure in terms of historical change. . . . The well-being they enjoy, they do not usually impute to the big ups and downs of the society in which they live. Seldom aware of the intricate

connection between the patterns of their own lives and the course of world history, ordinary men do not usually know what this connection means for the kind of men they are becoming and for the kinds of history-making in which they might take part. They do not possess the quality of mind essential to grasp the interplay of men and society, of biography and history, of self and world. . . .

What they need . . . is a quality of mind that will help them to [see] . . . what is going on in the world and . . . what may be happening within themselves. It is this quality . . . that . . . may be called the sociological imagination.

Source: Mills (1959:3–5).

them true. One good example, noted earlier, is the notion that we are free individuals who are personally responsible for our own lives. If we think people decide their own fate, we may be quick to praise particularly successful people as superior and consider others with more modest achievements personally deficient. A sociological approach, by contrast, encourages us to ask whether commonly held beliefs are actually true and, to the extent that they are not, why they are so widely held.

2. **The sociological perspective helps us assess both opportunities and constraints in our lives.** Sociological thinking leads us to see that, in the game of life, we have a say in how to play our cards, but it is society that deals us the hand. The more we understand the game,

the better players we will be. Sociology helps us size up our world so we can pursue our goals more effectively.

3. **The sociological perspective empowers us to be active participants in our society.** The more we understand about how society works, the more active citizens we become. For some, this may mean supporting society as it is; others may attempt nothing less than changing the entire world in some way. Evaluating any aspect of social life—whatever your goal—requires identifying social forces and assessing their consequences.

In the box, C. Wright Mills describes the power of using the sociological perspective.

4. **The sociological perspective helps us live in a diverse world.** North Americans represent just

5 percent of the world's people, and, as the remaining chapters of this book explain, much of the other 95 percent live very differently than we do. Still, like people everywhere, we tend to define our own way of life as "right," "natural," and "better." The sociological perspective encourages us to think critically about the relative strengths and weaknesses of all ways of life, including our own.

SOCIOLOGY, POLICY, AND CAREERS

The benefits of sociology go well beyond personal growth. Sociologists have helped shape public policy and law in countless ways, involving school desegregation, school busing, pornography, and social welfare. For example, the work that Lenore Weitzman (1985) did on the financial hardships facing women after divorce "had a real impact on public policy and resulted in the passage of fourteen new laws in California" (1996:538).

A background in sociology is also good preparation for the working world. The American Sociological Association reports that sociologists are hired for hundreds of jobs in fields such as advertising, banking, criminal justice, education, government, health care, public relations, and research (Billson & Huber, 1993).

Most men and women who continue beyond a bachelor's degree to earn advanced training in sociology go on to careers in teaching and research. But an increasing number of professional sociologists work in all sorts of applied fields. For example, clinical sociologists work with troubled clients much as clinical psychologists do. A basic difference is that whereas psychologists focus on the individual, sociologists locate difficulties in a person's web of social relationships. Another type of applied sociology is evaluation research. In today's cost-conscious climate, administrators must evaluate the effectiveness of almost every kind of program and policy. Sociologists, especially those with advanced research skills, are in high demand for this kind of work (Deutscher, 1999).

 In a short video, the author offers a personal response to the question, "why would someone want to be a sociologist?" See the Video Gallery at http://www.TheSociologyPage.com

THE ORIGINS OF SOCIOLOGY

Like the "choices" made by individuals, major historical events rarely just happen on their own. The birth of sociology resulted from powerful social forces.

SOCIAL CHANGE AND SOCIOLOGY

Striking transformations during the eighteenth and nineteenth centuries greatly changed European society. Three changes were especially important in the development of sociology: the rise of a factory-based industrial economy, the explosive growth of cities, and new ideas about democracy and political rights.

A New Industrial Economy

During the European Middle Ages, most people tilled fields near their homes or engaged in small-scale *manufacturing* (a word derived from Latin words meaning "to make by hand"). But by the end of the eighteenth century, inventors used new sources of energy—the power of moving water and then steam—to operate large machines in mills and factories. Instead of laboring at home or in tightly knit groups, workers became part of a large and anonymous labor force, toiling for strangers who owned the factories. This change in the system of production separated families and weakened the traditions that had governed community life for centuries.

The Growth of Cities

Across Europe, factories drew people in need of work. Along with this pull came the push of the *enclosure movement*. Landowners fenced off more and more ground, turning farms into grazing land for sheep, the source of wool for the thriving textile mills. Without land, countless tenant farmers left the countryside in search of work in the new factories.

As cities grew to unprecedented size, the new urban dwellers contended with mounting social problems, including pollution, crime, and homelessness. Living on streets crowded with strangers, they adapted to the new, impersonal social environment.

Political Change

During the Middle Ages, people viewed society as an expression of God's will: Royalty claimed to rule by "divine right," and each person up and down the social ladder played a part in the holy plan. This theological view of society is captured in lines from the old Anglican hymn "All Things Bright and Beautiful":

> The rich man in his castle,
> The poor man at his gate,
> God made them high and lowly
> And ordered their estate.

The birth of sociology was prompted by rapid social change. The discipline developed in those regions of Europe where the Industrial Revolution most disrupted traditional ways of life, drawing people from isolated villages to rapidly growing industrial cities.

But economic development and the rapid growth of cities soon brought new political ideas. By about 1600, tradition was under spirited attack. In the writings of Thomas Hobbes (1588–1679), John Locke (1632–1704), and Adam Smith (1723–1790), we see a shift in focus from people's moral obligations to God and their rulers to the idea that people should pursue their own self-interest. In the new political climate, philosophers spoke of *individual liberty* and *individual rights*. Echoing Locke, our own Declaration of Independence asserts that every person has "certain unalienable rights," including "life, liberty, and the pursuit of happiness."

The French Revolution, which began in 1789, symbolized this dramatic break with political and social tradition. French social analyst Alexis de Tocqueville (1805–1859) declared that the changes in society brought about by the French Revolution amounted to "nothing short of the regeneration of the whole human race" (1955:13; orig. 1856).

A New Awareness of Society

Huge factories, exploding cities, a new spirit of individualism—these changes combined to make people aware of their surroundings. As the social ground trembled under people's feet, the new discipline of sociology was born in England, France, and Germany—precisely where the changes were greatest.

SCIENCE AND SOCIOLOGY

The nature of society fascinated the brilliant thinkers of the ancient world, including the Chinese philosopher K'ung Fu-tzu, or Confucius (551–479 B.C.E.), and the Greek philosophers Plato (c. 427–347 B.C.E.) and Aristotle (384–322 B.C.E.).[2] Later, the Roman emperor Marcus Aurelius (121–180), the medieval thinkers St. Thomas Aquinas (c. 1225–1274) and Christine de Pisan (c. 1363–1431), and the great English playwright William Shakespeare (1564–1616) took up the question.

Yet these thinkers were more interested in envisioning the ideal society than in analyzing society as it really was. In creating their new discipline, sociology's pioneers certainly cared how society could be improved, but their major goal was to understand how society actually operates. It was the French social thinker Auguste Comte (1798–1857) who coined the term *sociology* in 1838 to describe this new way of

---

[2]Throughout this text, the abbreviation B.C.E. designates "before the common era." We use this terminology in place of the traditional B.C. ("before Christ") in recognition of the religious plurality of our society. Similarly, in place of the traditional A.D. (*anno Domini*, or "in the year of our Lord"), we use the abbreviation C.E. ("common era").

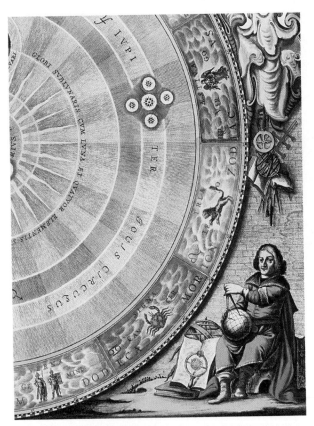

Here we see Copernicus, the sixteenth-century astronomer, taking careful measurements of the world. Just as Copernicus challenged the common sense of his day, sociologists such as Auguste Comte later argued that society is neither fixed by God's will nor set by human nature. On the contrary, Comte claimed, society is a system we can study scientifically, and based on what we learn, we can act intentionally to improve our lives.

Thomas Hobbes (1588–1679), for example, thought that society reflected not the perfection of God so much as the failings of a selfish human nature.

What Comte called the *scientific stage* of history began with the work of early scientists such as the Polish astronomer Copernicus (1473–1543), the Italian astronomer and physicist Galileo (1564–1642), and the English physicist and mathematician Isaac Newton (1642–1727). Comte's contribution came in applying the scientific approach, which was first used to study the physical world, to the study of society.[3]

Comte thus favored **positivism,** defined as *a way of understanding based on science*. As a positivist, Comte believed that society conforms to invariable laws, much as the physical world operates according to gravity and other laws of nature.

At the beginning of the twentieth century, sociology emerged as an academic discipline in the United States, strongly influenced by Comte's ideas. Today, most sociologists still consider science a crucial part of

 For a biographical sketch of Comte, go to the Gallery of Sociologists at http://www. TheSociologyPage.com

sociology. But as Chapter 2 ("Sociological Investigation") explains, we now realize that human behavior is far more complex than the movement of planets or even the actions of other living things. Because humans are creatures of imagination and spontaneity, our behavior can never be fully explained by any rigid "laws of society." In addition, early sociologists such as Karl Marx (1818–1883), whose ideas are discussed in Chapter 4 ("Society"), were deeply troubled by the striking inequality of the new industrial society. They wanted the new discipline of sociology not just to understand society but to bring about change toward social justice.

GENDER AND RACE: MARGINAL VOICES

Auguste Comte and Karl Marx stand among the giants of sociology. In recent years, though, we have come to see the important contributions that others—pushed to the margins of society because of gender or race—have made.

thinking. Therefore, sociology is among the youngest academic disciplines—far newer than history, physics, or economics, for example.

Comte (1975; orig. 1851–54) saw sociology as the product of a three-stage historical development. During the earliest, the *theological stage*, which spanned the time from the beginning of human history to the end of the European Middle Ages about 1350 C.E., people took a religious view of society, seeing it as an expression of God's will.

With the Renaissance, the theological approach gave way to what Comte called the *metaphysical stage*. During this period, people understood society as a natural rather than a supernatural phenomenon.

---

[3]Illustrating Comte's stages, the ancient Greeks and Romans viewed the planets as gods; Renaissance metaphysical thinkers saw them as astral influences (giving rise to astrology); by the time of Galileo, scientists understood planets as natural objects behaving in orderly ways.

We can use the sociological perspective to look at sociology itself. All of the most widely recognized pioneers of the discipline were men. This is because, in the nineteenth century, it was all but unheard of for women to be college professors, and few women took a central role in public life. But women, such as Harriet Martineau in England and Jane Addams in the United States, made contributions to sociology that we now recognize as important and lasting.

Harriet Martineau (1802–1876), born to a wealthy English family, first made her mark in 1853 by translating the writings of Auguste Comte from French into English. Subsequently, she became a noted scholar in her own right, revealing the evils of slavery and arguing for laws to protect factory workers and advance the standing of women.

In the United States, Jane Addams (1860–1935) was a sociological pioneer. Trained as a social worker, Addams spoke out on behalf of immigrants, who were entering the nation at the rate of 1 million per year. In 1889, Addams founded Hull House, a settlement house in Chicago that provided assistance to immigrant families. She also gathered sociologists and politicians to discuss the urban problems of the day. For her work on behalf of immigrants, Addams received the Nobel Peace Prize in 1931.

An important contribution to understanding race in the United States was made by yet another sociological pioneer, William Edward Burghardt Du Bois (1868–1963). Born to a poor Massachusetts family, Du Bois enrolled in Fisk University in Nashville, Tennessee, and then Harvard University, where he earned the first doctorate awarded by that university to a person of color. Like Martineau and Addams, Du Bois believed sociologists should try to solve social problems. He therefore studied the black community (1899), spoke out against racial inequality, and served as a founding member of the National Association for the Advancement of Colored People (NAACP).

Widespread belief in the inferiority of women and African Americans kept Martineau, Addams, and Du Bois at the margins of sociology. Looking back with a

sociological eye, we can see how the forces of society were at work shaping even the history of sociology itself.

SOCIOLOGICAL THEORY

Weaving observations into understanding brings us to another aspect of sociology: theory. A **theory** is *a statement of how and why specific facts are related.* More to the point, the job of sociological theory is to explain social behavior in the real world. Recall Emile Durkheim's theory that categories of people with low social integration (men, Protestants, the wealthy, and the unmarried) are especially prone to suicide. As Durkheim pondered the issue of suicide, he considered a number of possible theories. But which one was correct?

To evaluate a theory, as the next chapter explains, sociologists gather evidence using various methods of scientific research. Facts allow sociologists to confirm some theories while rejecting or modifying others. Thus, Durkheim collected data that revealed patterns showing that certain categories of people are more likely to commit suicide. These patterns allowed Durkheim to settle on a theory that best squared with all available evidence. National Map 1–1 displays the suicide rate for each of the fifty states and gives you a chance to do some theorizing of your own.

In building theory, sociologists face two basic questions: What issues should we study? How should we connect the facts? How they answer these questions depends on their theoretical "road map," or paradigm (Kuhn, 1970). A **theoretical paradigm** is *a*

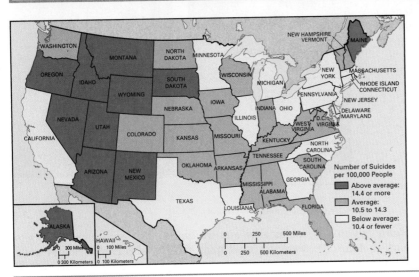

NATIONAL MAP 1–1
Suicide Rates across the United States

This map shows which states have high, average, and low suicide rates. Look for patterns. By and large, high suicide rates occur where people live far apart from one another. More densely populated states have low suicide rates. Do these data support or contradict Durkheim's theory of suicide? Why?

Source: U.S. National Center for Health Statistics (2000).

basic image of society that guides thinking and research. Sociology has three major approaches: the structural-functional paradigm, the social-conflict paradigm, and the symbolic-interaction paradigm.

THE STRUCTURAL-FUNCTIONAL PARADIGM

The **structural-functional paradigm** is *a framework for building theory that sees society as a complex system whose parts work together to promote solidarity and stability.* As its name suggests, this paradigm points to **social structure**, meaning *any relatively stable pattern of social behavior.* Social structure gives our lives shape, whether it be in families, the workplace, or the classroom. Second, this paradigm looks for a structure's **social functions**, or *consequences for the operation of society as a whole.* All social structure—from a simple handshake to complex religious rituals—functions to keep society going, at least in its present form.

The structural-functional paradigm owes much to Auguste Comte, who pointed to the importance of social integration during a time of rapid change. Emile Durkheim, who helped establish sociology in French universities, also based his work on this approach. A third structural-functional pioneer was the English sociologist Herbert Spencer (1820–1903). Spencer compared society to the human body. Just as the structural

parts of the human body—the skeleton, muscles, and various internal organs—function interdependently to help the entire organism survive, social structures work together to preserve society. The structural-functional paradigm, then, organizes sociological observations by identifying various structures of society and investigating their functions.

As sociology developed in the United States, many of the ideas of Comte, Spencer, and Durkheim were carried forward by Talcott Parsons (1902–1979), the major U.S. proponent of the structural-functional paradigm. Parsons treated society as a system, and sought to identify the basic tasks that any and all societies must perform to survive and the ways they accomplish these tasks.

The Gallery of Sociologists includes a biography of Herbert Spencer. Go to http://www. TheSociologyPage.com

Contemporary U.S. sociologist Robert K. Merton critically expanded our understanding of the concept of social function. Merton (1968) explains, first, that people rarely perceive all the functions of social structure. He describes as **manifest functions** *the recognized and intended consequences of any social pattern.* By contrast, **latent functions** are *consequences that are largely unrecognized and unintended.* To illustrate, the obvious function of the U.S. system of higher

The approach of the structural-functional paradigm is conveyed by the painting St. Regis Indian Reservation *by Amy Jones (1937). Here we see society composed of major rounds of life, each serving a particular purpose that contributes to the operation of the entire system.*

Amy Jones, *St. Regis Indian Reservation,* 1937. Photo courtesy Janet Marqusee Fine Arts Ltd.

education is to provide young people with the information and skills they need to perform jobs. Perhaps almost as important, although less often acknowledged, is college's function as a "marriage broker," bringing together people of similar social backgrounds. Another latent function of higher education is keeping millions of young people out of the labor market where, presumably, many of them would not find jobs.

Second, Merton explains, social patterns affect various members of a society differently (Stern, 1998). For example, conventional families may provide a good setting for rearing children, but they also confer privileges on men while limiting the opportunities of women.

Merton makes a third important point: Social structure is not always useful. **Social dysfunctions** are *the undesirable consequences of any social pattern for the operation of society.* People usually disagree about what is useful or harmful. What is functional for one category of people (say, factory owners or landlords) may well be dysfunctional for another category of people (factory workers or tenants).

Critical evaluation. The chief characteristic of the structural-functional paradigm is its vision of society as stable and orderly. The main goal of sociologists who use this approach, then, is to figure out "what makes society tick."

In the mid-1900s, most sociologists favored the structural-functional paradigm. In recent decades, however, its influence has declined. By focusing on social stability and unity, critics point out, structural-functionalism tends to ignore inequalities of social

class, race, and gender, which can generate considerable tension and conflict. In general, focusing on stability at the expense of conflict makes this paradigm somewhat conservative. As a critical response to this approach, sociologists developed another theoretical orientation: the social-conflict paradigm.

THE SOCIAL-CONFLICT PARADIGM

The **social-conflict paradigm** is *a framework for building theory that sees society as an arena of inequality that generates conflict and change.* Unlike the structural-functional emphasis on solidarity, this approach highlights inequality. Sociologists guided by this paradigm investigate how factors such as social class, race, ethnicity, gender, and age are linked to the unequal distribution of money, power, education, and social prestige. A conflict analysis rejects the idea that social structure promotes the operation of society as a whole, pointing out instead how social patterns benefit some people while depriving others. The box highlights a key contribution regarding race made by W. E. B. Du Bois.

Sociologists using the social-conflict paradigm look at ongoing conflict between dominant and disadvantaged categories of people—the rich in relation to the poor, white people in relation to people of color, and men in relation to women. Typically, people on top strive to protect their privileges, while the disadvantaged try to gain more for themselves.

A conflict analysis of our educational system shows how schooling reproduces class inequality in every new generation. For example, secondary schools

An Early Pioneer: Du Bois on Race

One of sociology's pioneers in the United States, William Edward Burghardt Du Bois, did not consider sociology a dry, academic discipline. On the contrary, he wanted to apply sociology to solving the pressing problems of his time, especially racial inequality.

Du Bois spoke out against racial separation and served as a founding member of the National Association for the Advancement of Colored People (NAACP). He helped his colleagues in sociology—and people everywhere—to see the deep racial divisions in the United States. White people can simply be "Americans," Du Bois pointed out; African Americans, however, have a "double consciousness," reflecting their status as citizens who are never able to escape identification based on the color of their skin.

In his sociological classic *The Philadelphia Negro: A Social Study* (1899), Du Bois studied Philadelphia's African American community, identifying both the strengths and weaknesses of people wrestling with overwhelming social problems. He challenged the widespread belief in black

inferiority, attributing the problems of African Americans to white prejudice. His criticism extended also to successful people of color for being so eager to win white acceptance that they gave up all ties with the black community, which needed their help.

Du Bois described race as the major problem facing the United States in the twentieth century. Early in his career, he was optimistic about overcoming racial divisions. By the end of his life, however, he had grown bitter, believing that little had changed. At the age of ninety-three, Du Bois left the United States for Ghana, where he died two years later. Do you think, following Du Bois, that race is still a major problem in the twenty-first century?

Sources: Based, in part, on Baltzell (1967) and Du Bois (1967; orig. 1899).

---

assign students to either college preparatory or vocational training programs. From a structural-functional point of view, such "tracking" benefits everyone by providing schooling that fits students' abilities. But conflict analysis counters that tracking often has less to do with talent than with social background, so that well-to-do students are placed in higher tracks while poor children end up in the lower tracks.

In this way, young people from privileged families receive the best schooling and later pursue high-income careers. The children of poor families, on the other hand, are not prepared for college and, like their parents before them, typically enter low-paying jobs. In both cases, the social standing of one generation is passed on to another, with schools justifying the practice in terms of individual merit (Bowles & Gintis, 1976; Oakes, 1982, 1985).

Social conflict in the United States extends well beyond schools. Later chapters of this book explain

how inequality based on class, gender, and race is rooted in the organization of society itself.

Many sociologists use the social-conflict paradigm not just to understand society but to bring about societal change that would reduce inequality. This was the goal of W. E. B. Du Bois and also Karl Marx, whose writing was especially important in the development of the social-conflict paradigm. Marx had little patience with those who sought only to analyze society. In a well-known declaration (inscribed on his monument in London's Highgate Cemetery), Marx asserted, "The philosophers have only interpreted the world, in various ways; the point, however, is to change it."

Critical evaluation. The social-conflict paradigm has gained a large following in recent decades. Yet, like other approaches, it has had its share of criticism. Because the paradigm focuses on inequality, it largely ignores how shared values and mutual interdependence unify members of a society. In addition, say critics, to the extent that this paradigm pursues political goals, it cannot claim scientific objectivity. As Chapter 2 ("Sociological Investigation") explains, however, conflict theorists counter that *all* theoretical approaches have political consequences, albeit different ones.

A final criticism of both the structural-functional and social-conflict paradigms is that they paint society in broad strokes in terms of "family," "social class," "race," and so on. A third theoretical paradigm depicts society less in terms of broad social structures and more as everyday experiences.

THE SYMBOLIC-INTERACTION PARADIGM

The structural-functional and social-conflict paradigms share a **macro-level orientation,** meaning *a concern with broad patterns that shape society as a whole.* Macro-level sociology takes in the big picture, rather like observing a city from high above in a helicopter and seeing how highways help people move from place to place or how housing differs from rich to poor neighborhoods. Sociology also has a **micro-level orientation,** *a close-up focus on social interaction in specific situations.* Exploring urban life in this way occurs at street level, perhaps observing how children interact on a school playground or how pedestrians respond to homeless people. The **symbolic-interaction paradigm,** then, is *a framework for building theory that sees society as the product of the everyday interactions of individuals.*

How does "society" result from the ongoing experiences of tens of millions of people? One answer, explained in Chapter 6 ("Social Interaction in Everyday Life"), is that society is nothing more than the shared reality that people construct as they interact with one another. That is, human beings are creatures who live in a world of symbols, attaching *meaning* to virtually everything. "Reality," therefore, is simply how we define our surroundings, our obligations toward others, even our own identities.

Of course, this process of definition is subjective and varies from person to person. For example, one person may define a homeless man as "just a bum looking for a handout" and ignore him, but another might see the man as a "fellow human being in need" and offer help. In the same way, one person may feel a sense of security passing by a police officer walking the beat, while another may be seized by nervous anxiety. Sociologists who take a symbolic-interaction approach, therefore, view society as a complex, ever-changing mosaic of subjective meanings.

The painting Furnishings, *by Paul Marcus, presents the essential wisdom of social-conflict theory: Society operates in a way that conveys wealth, power, and privilege to some at the expense of others. Looking at the painting, what are most of the people doing? What do you make of the head hanging on the wall? The classi cal scene between the drapes? What categories of people does the artist suggest are disadvantaged?*
© Paul Marcus, *Furnishings,* oil painting on canvas, 64 in. × 48 in. Studio SPM, Inc.

The symbolic-interaction paradigm has roots in the thinking of Max Weber (1864–1920), a German sociologist who emphasized the need to understand a setting from the point of view of the people in it. Weber's approach is discussed in Chapter 4 ("Society").

Since Weber's time, sociologists have taken micro-level sociology in a number of directions. Chapter 5 ("Socialization") discusses the ideas of George Herbert Mead (1863–1931), who explored how we build our personalities from social experience. Chapter 6 ("Social Interaction in Everyday Life") presents the work of Erving Goffman (1922–1982), whose *dramaturgical analysis* describes how we resemble actors on a stage as

To understand how the symbolic-interaction paradigm views society, consider Emil Bisttram's painting Domingo Chorus. *Society is never at rest; it is an ongoing process by which interacting individuals define and redefine reality.*

Emil Bisttram, American (1895–1976). *Domingo Chorus*, 1936, gouache and pencil on paper, 57.8 × 43.5 cm. Private Collection/Christie's Images/The Bridgeman Art Library.

we play out our various roles. Other contemporary sociologists, including George Homans and Peter Blau, have developed *social-exchange analysis*. In their view, social interaction is guided by what each person stands to gain and lose from others (Molm, 1997; Mulford et al., 1998). In the ritual of courtship, for example, people seek mates who offer at least as much—in terms of physical attractiveness, intelligence, and wealth—as they themselves have to offer.

Critical evaluation. The social-interaction paradigm corrects some of the bias found in macro-level approaches to society. Without denying the existence of macro-level social structures such as "the family" and

"social class," the symbolic-interaction paradigm reminds us that society basically amounts to *people interacting*. That is, micro-level sociology tries to convey how individuals actually experience society. The other side of the coin is that, by focusing on day-to-day interactions, the symbolic-interaction paradigm ignores larger social structures, the effects of culture, and factors such as class, gender, and race.

Table 1–1 summarizes the main characteristics of the structural-functional paradigm, the social-conflict paradigm, and the symbolic-interaction paradigm. Each paradigm is helpful in answering particular kinds of questions. However, the fullest understanding of society comes from using the sociological perspective with all three, as we show with the following analysis of sports in the United States.

APPLYING THE PARADIGMS: THE SOCIOLOGY OF SPORT

In the opening to this chapter, we noted how people in the United States love sports. Not only do most young people engage in organized sports, but—for old and young alike—television is filled with sporting events, and a large share of daily news reports sports scores. In the United States, outstanding players such as Mark McGwire (baseball), Shaquille O'Neal (basketball), and Venus Williams (tennis) are among our most famous celebrities. Overall, sports in the United States are a multibillion-dollar industry. What sociological insights can the three theoretical paradigms give us about this familiar part of everyday life?

The Functions of Sports

A structural-functional approach directs attention to the ways in which sports help society operate. Their manifest functions include providing recreation, physical conditioning, and a relatively harmless way to "let off steam." Sports have important latent functions as well, from fostering social relationships to generating tens of thousands of jobs. Perhaps most important, sports encourage competition and the pursuit of success, both of which are central to our way of life.

Sports also have dysfunctional consequences. For example, colleges and universities intent on fielding winning teams sometimes recruit students for their athletic ability rather than their academic aptitude. Not only does this practice pull down the academic standards of a school, but it shortchanges athletes who devote little time to academic work (Upthegrove, Roscigno, & Charles, 1999).

TABLE 1–1 The Three Major Theoretical Paradigms: A Summary

Theoretical Paradigm	Orientation	Image of Society	Core Questions
Structural-functional	Macro-level	A system of interrelated parts that is relatively stable because of widespread agreement on what is morally desirable; each part has a particular function in society as a whole.	How is society integrated? What are the major parts of society? How are these parts interrelated? What are the consequences of each part for the overall operation of society?
Social-conflict	Macro-level	A system based on social inequality; each part of society benefits some categories of people more than others; social inequality leads to conflict, which, in turn, leads to social change.	How is society divided? What are the major patterns of social inequality? How do some categories of people try to protect their privileges? How do other categories of people challenge the status quo?
Symbolic-interaction	Micro-level	An ongoing process of social interaction in specific settings based on symbolic communication; individual perceptions of reality are variable and changing.	How is society experienced? How do human beings interact to create, maintain, and change social patterns? How do individuals try to shape the reality that others perceive? How does individual behavior change from one situation to another?

Sports and Conflict

A social-conflict analysis begins by pointing out that sports are closely linked to social inequality. Some sports—including tennis, swimming, golf, and skiing—are expensive, so participation is largely limited to the well-to-do. Football, baseball, and basketball, however, are accessible to people of all income levels. In short, the games people play are not simply a matter of choice but also reflect social standing.

Throughout history, sports have been oriented mainly toward males. For example, the first modern Olympic Games, held in 1896, barred women from competition; in the United States, even Little League teams in most parts of the country did not let girls play until recently. Such exclusion has been defended by incorrect notions that girls and women lack the strength and stamina to play sports or that they lose their femininity when they do. Thus, our society encourages men to be athletes while expecting women to be attentive observers and cheerleaders. Today, more women play professional sports than ever before, yet they continue to take a back seat to men, particularly in sports with the most earnings and social prestige.

Although our society long excluded people of color from big league sports, the opportunity to earn high incomes in professional sports has expanded in recent decades. Major League Baseball first admitted African American players when Jackie Robinson broke the color line and joined the Brooklyn Dodgers in 1947. More than fifty years later, in 2000, after professional baseball retired the legendary Robinson's number 42 on *all* teams, African Americans (12 percent of the U.S. population) accounted for 13 percent of Major League Baseball players, 67 percent of National Football League (NFL) players, and 78 percent of National Basketball Association (NBA) players (Center for the Study of Sport in Society, 2001).

One reason for the increasing proportion of people of African descent in professional sports is that athletic performance—in terms of batting average or number of points scored per game—can be precisely measured and is not influenced by racial prejudice. It is also true that some people of color make a particular effort to excel in athletics, where they perceive greater opportunity than in other careers (Steele, 1990; Hoberman, 1997, 1998; Edwards, 2000; Harrison, 2000). In recent years, in fact, African American athletes have earned higher salaries, on average, than white players.

But racial discrimination still taints professional sports in the United States. For one thing, race is linked to the *positions* athletes play on the field, in a pattern called "stacking." Figure 1–2 shows the result

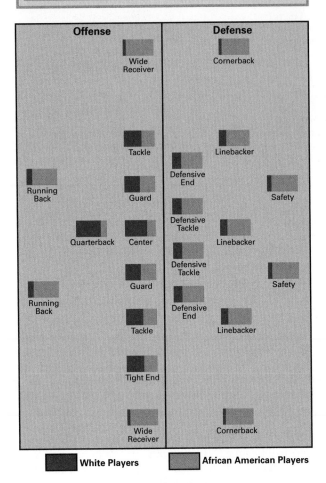

DIVERSITY SNAPSHOT

Offense

Wide Receiver

Tackle

Running Back

Guard

Quarterback   Center

Guard

Running Back

Tackle

Tight End

Wide Receiver

Defense

Cornerback

Linebacker

Defensive End

Safety

Defensive Tackle

Linebacker

Defensive Tackle

Safety

Defensive End

Linebacker

Cornerback

■ White Players   ▪ African American Players

FIGURE 1–2 Race and Sport: "Stacking" in Professional Football

Source: Center for the Study of Sport in Society (2001).

of a study of race in football. Notice that white players dominate in offense and also play the central positions on both sides of the line. More broadly, African Americans figure prominently in only five

 For a look at racial "stacking" in professional baseball, go to http://www.prenhall.com/ weblinks

sports: baseball, basketball, football, boxing, and track. Across all of professional sports, the vast majority of managers, head coaches, and owners of sports teams are white (Gnida, 1995; Smith & Leonard, 1997).

We might ask who benefits the most from professional sports. Although individual players get astronomical salaries, and millions of fans enjoy following their teams, sports are big business, generating property for a small number of people (predominantly white men). In sum, sports in the United States are bound up with inequalities based on gender, race, and economic power.

Sports as Interaction

At a micro-level, a sporting event is a complex drama of face-to-face interaction. In part, play is guided by the players' assigned positions and the rules of the game. But players are also spontaneous and unpredictable. Informed by the symbolic-interaction paradigm, then, we see sports less as a system than as an ongoing process.

From this point of view, too, we expect each player to understand the game a little differently. Some thrive in a setting of stiff competition, whereas, for others, love of the game may be greater than the need to win. (The ancient Romans coined the word *amateur*, literally, "lover," to designate someone who engages in some activity for the sheer love of it.)

Beyond different attitudes toward competition, team members also shape their particular realities according to the various prejudices, jealousies, and ambitions they bring to the game. Then, too, the behavior of any single player may change over time. A rookie in professional baseball, for example, may feel self-conscious during the first few games in the big leagues. In time, however, most players fit in comfortably with the team. Coming to feel at home on the field was slow and painful for Jackie Robinson (the first African American to play in the major leagues, beginning in 1947), who knew that many white players, and millions of white fans, resented his presence. In time, however, his outstanding ability and his confident and cooperative manner won him the respect of the entire nation.

The three theoretical paradigms—structural-functional, social-conflict, and symbolic-interaction—provide different insights, but none is more correct than the others. Applied to any issue, each paradigm generates its own interpretations; to appreciate fully the power of the sociological perspective, you should become familiar with all three. Together, they stimulate debates and controversies. In the final box, we review many of the ideas presented in this chapter by asking how sociological generalizations differ from common stereotypes.

Is Sociology Nothing More Than Stereotypes?

"Protestants are the ones who kill themselves!"

"People in the United States? They're rich, they love to marry, and they love to divorce!"

"Everybody knows that you have to be black to play professional basketball!"

Everyone, including sociologists, loves to generalize. But beginning students of sociology may wonder how generalizations differ from stereotypes. For example, are the preceding statements sound generalizations or stereotypes?

These three statements are **stereotypes,** *exaggerated descriptions applied to every person in some category.* First, rather than describing averages, each statement paints every individual in a category with the same brush; second, each ignores facts and distorts reality (even though many stereotypes do contain an element of truth); third, a stereotype sounds more like a "put-down" than a fair-minded assertion.

Good sociology, by contrast, involves making generalizations, but with three important conditions. *First, sociologists do*

not indiscriminately apply any generalization to all individuals; second, sociologists are careful that a generalization squares with available facts; third, sociologists offer generalizations fair-mindedly, with an interest in getting at the truth.

Earlier in this chapter, we noted that the suicide rate among Protestants is higher than among Catholics or Jews. However, the statement "Protestants are the ones who kill themselves" is not a reasonable generalization because most Protestants do no such thing. Moreover, it would be just as wrong-headed to assume that a particular friend, because he is a Protestant male, is on the verge of self-destruction. (Imagine refusing to lend money to a roommate who happens to be a Baptist, explaining, "Well, given your risk of suicide, I might never get paid back!")

Second, sociologists shape their generalizations to available facts. A more factual version of the second statement at the beginning of this box is that, on average and by world standards, the U.S. population has a very high standard of living. It is also true that our marriage rate is one of the highest in the world. And, although few

people take pleasure in divorcing, so is our divorce rate.

Third, sociologists strive to be fair-minded; that is, they are motivated by a passion for truth. The third statement, about African Americans and basketball, is not good sociology for two reasons. First, it is simply not true, and, second, it seems motivated by bias rather than truth-seeking.

Good sociology stands apart from harmful stereotyping. But a sociology course is an excellent setting for talking over common stereotypes. The classroom encourages discussion and offers the factual information you need to decide whether a particular assertion is accurate or just a stereotype.

Continue the debate . . .

1. *Do people in the United States have stereotypes of sociologists? What are they? Are they valid?*

2. *Do you think taking a sociology course dispels people's stereotypes? Why or why not?*

3. *Can you cite a stereotype of your own that sociology challenges?*

SUMMARY

1. The sociological perspective shows "the general in the particular," or the power of society to shape our individual lives.

2. Because our culture emphasizes individual choice, seeing the power of society in our lives may seem, at first, like "seeing the strange in the familiar."

3. Differences in the number of children born to women around the world, as well as Emile

Durkheim's research on suicide rates among some categories of people, show that society affects even our most personal choices and actions.

4. Global awareness is an important part of the sociological perspective because, first, people live very differently in various nations; second, societies around the world are becoming increasingly interconnected; third, many social problems are most

serious beyond the borders of the United States; and, fourth, global awareness helps us better understand ourselves.

5. Socially marginal people are more likely than others to see the power of society. For everyone, periods of social crisis foster sociological thinking.

6. The benefits of using the sociological perspective include, first, helping us assess common beliefs; second, helping us appreciate the opportunities and limits in our lives; third, encouraging more active participation in society; and, fourth, increasing our awareness of social diversity in the world around us.

7. Sociology arose in response to vast changes in Europe during the eighteenth and nineteenth centuries. Three changes—the rise of an industrial economy, the explosive growth of cities, and the emergence of new political ideas—focused people's attention on how society operates.

8. Auguste Comte gave sociology its name in 1838. Earlier social thinkers focused on what society ought to be, but Comte's new discipline used scientific methods to understand society as it is.

9. A theory weaves observations into insight and understanding. Sociologists use various theoretical paradigms to construct theories.

10. The structural-functional paradigm focuses on how patterns of behavior contribute to the operation of society. This approach highlights stability and integration while minimizing inequality and conflict.

11. While emphasizing inequality, conflict, and change, the social-conflict paradigm downplays a society's integration and stability.

12. In contrast to these broad, macro-level approaches, the symbolic-interaction paradigm is a micro-level framework that focuses on face-to-face interaction in specific settings.

13. Because each paradigm highlights different dimensions of any social issue, the richest sociological understanding is derived from applying all three.

14. Sociological thinking involves generalizations. But unlike a stereotype, a sociological statement (1) is not applied indiscriminately to everyone in some category, (2) is supported by facts, and (3) is put forward in the fair-minded pursuit of truth.

KEY CONCEPTS

sociology (p. 1)   the systematic study of human society

global perspective (p. 5)   the study of the larger world and our society's place in it

high-income countries (p. 5)   nations with very productive economic systems in which most people have relatively high incomes

middle-income countries (p. 7)   nations with moderately productive economic systems in which people's incomes are about the global average

low-income countries (p. 7)   nations with less productive economic systems in which most people are poor

positivism (p. 12)   a way of understanding based on science

theory (p. 13)   a statement of how and why specific facts are related

theoretical paradigm (p. 13)   a basic image of society that guides thinking and research

structural-functional paradigm (p. 14)   a framework for building theory that sees society as a complex system whose parts work together to promote solidarity and stability

social structure (p. 14)   any relatively stable pattern of social behavior

social functions (p. 14)   the consequences of any social pattern for the operation of society as a whole

manifest functions (p. 14)   the recognized and intended consequences of any social pattern

latent functions (p. 14)   the unrecognized and unintended consequences of any social pattern

social dysfunctions (p. 15)   the undesirable consequences of any social pattern for the operation of society

social-conflict paradigm (p. 15)   a framework for building theory that sees society as an arena of inequality that generates conflict and change

macro-level orientation (p. 17)   a concern with broad patterns that shape society as a whole

micro-level orientation (p. 17)   a close-up focus on social interaction in specific situations

symbolic-interaction paradigm (p. 17)   a framework for building theory that sees society as the product of the everyday interactions of individuals

stereotypes (p. 21)   exaggerated descriptions applied to every person in some category

CRITICAL-THINKING QUESTIONS

1. How would you contrast psychology and sociology in terms of perspective?

2. In what ways does using the sociological perspective make us seem less in control of our lives? How does it give us greater power over our surroundings?

3. What factors help explain why sociology developed where and when it did?

4. Guided by the discipline's three major theoretical paradigms, what questions might you ask about (a) television, (b) war, and (c) colleges and universities?

APPLICATIONS AND EXERCISES

1. Packaged in the back of this new textbook is an interactive CD-ROM that offers a variety of study and review materials intended to help you better understand the material covered in this chapter. For this chapter, the CD-ROM contains an author's tip video, Real Life Sociology videos, interactive map animations, audio journal entries from the author, Web links, and much more. It also offers an interactive version of the timeline that is inside the front cover of this textbook.

2. Spend several hours exploring your local area until you can draw a sociological map of the community. The map might indicate the categories of people and types of buildings found in various places (for example, "big single-family homes," "run-down business area," "new office buildings," "student apartments," and so on). What patterns do you see?

3. Look ahead to Figure 18–3, which shows the U.S. divorce rate over the last century. Try to identify societal factors that pushed the divorce rate down after 1930, up again after 1940, down in the 1950s, and up again after 1960.

4. During a class, carefully observe the behavior of the instructor and other students. What patterns do you see in who speaks? What about how people use space? What categories of people are taking the class in the first place?

SITES TO SEE

http://www.prenhall.com/macionis

The author and publisher of this book invite you to visit the interactive *Companion Website*™ that accompanies this text. Begin by clicking on the cover of your book. You will find a chapter-by-chapter study guide, practice tests, and a significant portion of the text for online review, as well as many suggested Web links.

http://www.macionis.com
(or http://www.TheSociologyPage.com)

You can find dozens of additional links to Internet sites, as well as information—including short videos—about the discipline of sociology, at the author's home page. Bookmark this page as your doorway to the discipline.

http://www.nationalgeographic.com
http://www.nationalatlas.gov

These two sites provide a number of maps showing patterns and trends of interest to sociologists.

http://quickfacts.census.gov/qfd
http://www.countrywatch.com

The first of these sites provides statistical data and other information about the United States, your own state, and your own county. The second offers a range of data about all 192 nations in the world.

INVESTIGATE WITH CONTENTSELECT

Investigate issues discussed in this chapter using the ContentSelect database of scholarly journals and popular publications. To access ContentSelect through this book's *Companion Website*™, visit http://www.prenhall.com/macionis Click on the cover of your book. Select this or any chapter and click "Begin." Once in the chapter, click the ContentSelect icon at the bottom left of your screen. You will be prompted to enter your ContentSelect access code and then asked to create your personal User ID and Password. For all repeat visits, simply enter your personal User ID and Password. Enter keywords such as "sociology," "Auguste Comte," and "sports," and the search engine will help you become an effective researcher.

CHAPTER

2

Edvard Munch (1863–1944)
Rue Lafayette

SOCIOLOGICAL INVESTIGATION

While on a visit to the city of Atlanta during the winter holiday season, sociologist Lois Benjamin (1991) called on the mother of an old friend from college. Benjamin was eager for news of her friend, Sheba, a woman who she knew had shared her own dream of earning a graduate degree, landing a teaching job, and writing books. Benjamin had fulfilled her lifelong dream, but as she soon found out, the news was not good for Sheba, who had fallen disastrously short of her goal.

There had been early signs of trouble, Benjamin recalled. After college, Sheba began graduate work at a university in Canada. But in her letters to Benjamin, Sheba became more and more critical of the world and seemed to be cutting herself off from others. The problem, as Sheba saw it, was racism. As an African American woman, she felt she was the target of racial hostility. Before long, she flunked out of school, blaming her white professors for her failure. Then she left North America, finally earning a PhD from an English university and settling in Nigeria. Since then, Benjamin had not heard a word from her long-time friend.

Benjamin was happy to learn that Sheba had returned to Atlanta. But her delight dissolved into shock when she saw Sheba and

realized that her friend, suffering a mental breakdown, was barely responsive to anyone.

For months after, Sheba's emotional collapse troubled Benjamin. She knew that many factors combine to cause such personal tragedy. But having experienced the sting of racism herself, Benjamin believed it had played a major role in Sheba's story. Partly as a tribute to her old friend, Benjamin set out to explore the effects of racial prejudice on the lives of bright and well-educated people of color in the United States.

Benjamin realized she was challenging the conventional wisdom that race poses less of a barrier today than in previous generations, especially to talented African Americans (Wilson, 1978). But her own experiences—and, she believed, Sheba's—seemed to contradict such thinking.

To test her ideas, Benjamin spent the next two years of her life asking 100 successful African Americans across the country how race affected their lives. In the words of these "Talented One Hundred"[1] men and women, she found evidence that, even among privileged African Americans, racism remains a heavy burden.

---

[1] Benjamin derived her concept from the term "Talented Tenth" used by W. E. B. Du Bois (1899) to describe African American leaders in his day.

Later in this chapter, we will take a closer look at Lois Benjamin's research. For the moment, notice how the sociological perspective helped her spot broad social patterns operating in the lives of individuals. Just as important, Benjamin's work demonstrates the *doing* of sociology, the process of *sociological investigation*.

Many people think that scientists work only in laboratories, carefully taking measurements using complex equipment. But as this chapter explains, whereas some sociologists conduct scientific research in laboratories, most work on neighborhood streets, in homes and workplaces, in schools and hospitals, in bars and prisons—in short, wherever people can be found.

This chapter examines the methods sociologists use to conduct research. Along the way, we shall see that research involves not just procedures for gathering information but controversies about values: Should researchers strive to be objective? Or should they point to the need for change? Certainly, Lois Benjamin did not undertake her study simply to show that racism exists; she wanted to bring racism out in the open as a way to challenge it. We shall tackle questions of values after addressing the basics of sociological investigation.

THE BASICS OF SOCIOLOGICAL INVESTIGATION

Sociological investigation starts with two simple requirements. The first was the focus of Chapter 1: *Use the sociological perspective.* This point of view reveals curious patterns of behavior all around us that call for further study. It was Lois Benjamin's sociological imagination that prompted her to wonder how race affects the lives of talented African Americans.

The first requirement of sociological investigation leads directly to the second: *Be curious and ask questions.* Benjamin sought to learn more about how race affects people with significant personal achievements. She asked questions: Who are the leaders of this nation's black community? What effect does being part of a racial minority have on their self-identity? On the way white people perceive them and their work?

Seeing the world sociologically and asking questions are fundamental to sociological investigation. Yet they are only the beginning. They spark our curiosity, but then we face the task of finding answers to our questions. To understand the kinds of insights sociology offers, we need to realize that there are various kinds of "truth."

SCIENCE AS ONE FORM OF TRUTH

When we say we "know" something, we can mean many things. Most members of U.S. society, for instance, claim to believe in the existence of God. Few would claim to have direct contact with God, but they say they believe all the same. We call this kind of knowing "belief" or "faith."

A second kind of truth rests on the pronouncement of some recognized expert. For example, parents with questions about raising their children may read books by an "expert" or consult a child psychologist.

A third type of truth is based on simple agreement among ordinary people. We come to "know" that, say, sexual intercourse among young children is wrong because just about everyone says it is.

People's "truths" differ the world over, and we often encounter "facts" at odds with our own. Imagine being a Peace Corps volunteer who has just arrived in a small, traditional village in Latin America. Your job is to help local people increase their crop yield. On your first day in the fields, you observe a curious practice: After planting the seeds, the farmers lay dead fish on top of the soil. In response to your question, they reply that the fish are a gift to the god of the harvest. A village elder adds sternly that the harvest was poor one year when no fish were offered.

From that society's point of view, using fish as gifts to the harvest god makes sense. The people believe in it, their experts endorse it, and everyone seems to agree that the system works. But with scientific training in agriculture, you shake your head and wonder. The scientific truth in this situation is something entirely different: The decomposing fish fertilize the ground, producing a better crop.

Science represents a fourth way of knowing. **Science** is *a logical system that bases knowledge on direct, systematic observation.* **Scientific sociology**, then, is *the study of society based on systematic observation of social behavior.* Standing apart from faith, the wisdom of experts, and general agreement, scientific knowledge rests on **empirical evidence,** that is, *information we can verify with our senses.*

Our Peace Corps example does not mean that people in traditional villages ignore what their senses tell them, or that members of technologically advanced societies reject nonscientific ways of knowing. A medical researcher using science to develop a new drug for treating cancer, for example, may still practice her religion as a matter of faith; she may turn to experts when making financial decisions; and she may derive political opinions from family and friends. In short, we all hold various kinds of truths at the same time.

Myths as well as scientific facts are an important dimension of human existence. In his painting, The Creation of the Earth, *Mexican painter Diego Rivera (1886–1957) offers a mythic account of human origins. A myth (from the Greek, meaning "story" or "word") may or may not be factual in the literal sense. Yet, it conveys some basic truth about the meaning and purpose of life. Indeed, it is science, rather than art, that has no power to address such questions of meaning.*

Diego Rivera, Mexican (1886–1957). *The Creation of the Earth* page from *Popol Vuh*, watercolor on paper. Museo Casa Diego Rivera (INBA), Guanajuato, Mexico. Index/The Bridgeman Art Library. © 2003 Banco de Mexico Diego Rivera and Frida Kahlo Museums Trust.

COMMON SENSE VERSUS SCIENTIFIC EVIDENCE

Scientific evidence sometimes challenges our common sense. Here are six statements that many North Americans assume are true:

1. **Poor people are far more likely than rich people to break the law.** Watching a television show such as *Cops*, one might well conclude that police arrest only people from "bad" neighborhoods. Chapter 8 ("Deviance") explains that poor people do stand out in the official arrest statistics. But research also shows that police and prosecutors are more likely to respond leniently to wrong-doing by well-to-do people. Furthermore, some laws are written in a way that criminalizes poor people more and affluent people less.

2. **The United States is a middle-class society in which most people are roughly equal.** Data presented in Chapter 11 ("Social Class in the United States") show that the richest 5 percent of our people control more than half the nation's total wealth. If people are equal, then some are much "more equal" than others.

3. **Most poor people don't want to work.** Research described in Chapter 11 indicates that this statement is true of some but not most poor people. In fact, about half of poor people in the United States are children and elderly people whom no one would expect to work.

4. **Differences in the behavior of females and males reflect "human nature."** Much of what we call "human nature" is constructed by the society in which we are raised, as Chapter 3 ("Culture") explains. Furthermore, as Chapter 13 ("Gender Stratification") argues, some societies define "feminine" and "masculine" very differently from the way we do.

5. **People change as they grow old, losing many interests as they focus on their health.** Chapter 15 ("Aging and the Elderly") reports that aging changes our personalities very little. Problems of health increase in old age, but, by and large, elderly people keep their distinctive personalities.

6. **Most people marry because they are in love.** To members of U.S. society, few statements are so self-evident. Surprisingly, however, in many societies marriage has little to do with love. Chapter 18 ("Family") explains why.

These examples confirm the old saying that "It's not what we don't know that gets us into trouble as much as things we *do* know that just aren't so." We have

 For another example of sociology challenging common sense, go to http://www.prenhall.com/weblinks

all been brought up believing conventional truths, being bombarded

Common sense suggests that, in a world of possibilities, people fall in love with that "special someone." Sociological research reveals that the vast majority of people select partners who are very similar in social background to themselves.

by expert advice, and being pressured to accept the opinions of people around us. As adults, we need to evaluate critically what we see, read, and hear. Sociology can help us to do just that.

SCIENCE: BASIC ELEMENTS AND LIMITATIONS

In Chapter 1, we explained how early sociologists such as Auguste Comte and Emile Durkheim applied science to the study of society just as natural scientists investigate the physical world. The scientific approach to knowing, called *positivism*, assumes that an objective reality exists "out there." The job of the scientist is to discover this reality by gathering empirical evidence, facts we can verify with our senses.

In this chapter, we begin by introducing the major elements of scientific sociology. Then we shall discuss some limitations of scientific (or positivist) sociology and present alternative approaches.

CONCEPTS, VARIABLES, AND MEASUREMENT

A basic element of science is the **concept,** *a mental construct that represents some part of the world in a simplified form.* "Society" is a concept, as are the structural parts of societies, such as "the family" and "the economy." Sociologists also use concepts to describe individuals, as when we speak of someone's "race" or "social class."

A **variable** is *a concept whose value changes from case to case.* The familiar variable "price," for example, changes from item to item in a supermarket. Similarly, we use the concept "social class" to identify people as upper class, middle class, working class, or lower class.

The use of variables depends on **measurement,** *a procedure for determining the value of a variable in a specific case.* Some variables are easy to measure, as when the checkout clerk adds up the cost of our groceries. But measuring sociological variables can be far more difficult. For example, how would you measure a person's social class? You might look at clothing, listen to patterns of speech, or note a home address. Or, trying to be more precise, you might ask about income, occupation, and education.

Because almost any variable can be measured in more than one way, sociologists often have to make a judgment about which factors to consider. For example, having a very high income might qualify a person as "upper class." But what if the income comes from selling automobiles, an occupation most people think of as "middle class"? Would having only an eighth-grade education make the person "lower class"? In this case, sociologists sensibly (but arbitrarily) combine these three measures—income, occupation, and education—to assign social class, as described in Chapter 10 ("Social Stratification") and Chapter 11 ("Social Class in the United States").

Sociologists face another interesting problem in measuring variables: dealing with vast numbers of people. For instance, how do you describe income for millions of U.S. families? Reporting streams of numbers carries little meaning and tells us nothing about the people as a whole. Therefore, sociologists use *statistical measures* to describe people. The box explains how.

Defining Concepts

Measurement is always somewhat arbitrary because the value of any variable partly depends on how it is

Three Useful (and Simple) Statistical Measures

We all talk about "averages," whether it is the average price of a gallon of gasoline or the average salary for new college graduates. Sociologists, too, are interested in averages, and they use three different statistical measures to describe what is typical.

Assume that we want to describe the salaries paid to seven members of a sociology department at a local college:

$35,000 $41,700 $35,000 $35,000
$43,000 $42,000 $78,295

The simplest statistical measure is the *mode*, the value that occurs most often in a series of numbers. In this example, the mode is $35,000 because that value occurs three times and each of the others occurs only once. If all the values occurred only once, there would be no mode; if two values occurred three times (or twice), there would be two modes. Although it is easy to identify, sociologists rarely use the mode because it is a very crude measure of the "average."

A more common statistical measure, the *mean*, is the arithmetic average of a series of numbers, calculated by adding all the values together and dividing by the number of cases. The sum of the seven incomes is $309,995; dividing by seven yields a mean income of $44,285. But notice that the mean is higher than the income of six of the seven sociologists. Because the mean is pulled up or down by an especially high or low value (in this case, the $78,295 paid to one sociologist, who also serves as a dean), it has the drawback of giving a distorted picture of any distribution that contains extreme scores.

The *median* is the middle case: the value that occurs midway in a series of numbers arranged from lowest to highest. Here the median income for the seven people is $41,700 because three incomes are higher and three are lower. (With an even number of cases, the median is halfway between the two middle cases.) Because a median is unaffected by an extreme score, it gives a better picture of what is "average" than the mean does.

Calculate simple statistics on your own. An example is found at http://www.prenhall.com/weblinks

---

defined. In addition, deciding what abstract concepts such as "love," "family," or "intelligence" mean in real life can lead to lengthy debates before any attempt is made to measure them as variables.

Good research, therefore, includes **operationalizing a variable,** which means *specifying exactly what one is to measure before assigning a value to a variable.* Before measuring the concept of social class, for example, we would have to decide exactly what we were going to measure (say, income level, years of schooling, occupational prestige). Sometimes sociologists measure several of these things; in such cases, they need to specify exactly how they plan to combine these variables into one overall score. When reading about research, always notice the way researchers operationalize each variable. How they define terms can greatly affect the results.

When deciding how to operationalize variables, sociologists may take into account the opinions of the people they study. Since 1977, for example, researchers

at the U.S. Census Bureau defined race and ethnicity as white, black, Hispanic, Asian or Pacific Islander, and American Indian or Alaskan Native. One problem with this list is that someone can be both Hispanic and white or black; similarly, people of Arab ancestry might not identify with any of these choices. Just as important, an increasing number of people in the United States are *multiracial* (Cose, 1997; O'Hare, 1998). As a result of such problems, the census in the year 2000 allowed people to describe their race and ethnicity by selecting more than one category.

Reliability and Validity

For a measurement to be useful, it must be reliable and valid. **Reliability** refers to *consistency in measurement.* In other words, the procedure must yield the same result if repeated time after time. But consistency is no guarantee of **validity,** which means *precision in measuring exactly what one intends to measure.* In other words, valid yields consistent results (making it reliable), it can still miss the real, intended target (and lack validity). Later on, in Chapter 19 ("Religion"), we suggest that measuring religiosity should take account of not only church attendance but also a person's beliefs and the degree to which a person lives by religious convictions. In sum, careful measurement is vital to sociological research and often a challenge.

Relationships between Variables

Once measurements are made, investigators can pursue the real payoff: seeing how variables are related. The scientific ideal is **cause and effect,** *a relationship in which change in one variable causes change in another.* Cause-and-effect relationships occur around us every day, as when studying for an exam results in a high grade. *The variable that causes the change* (in this case, studying) is called the **independent variable.** *The variable that changes* (the exam grade) is called the **dependent variable.** In other words, the value of one variable depends on the value of another. Why is linking variables in terms of cause and effect important? Because this kind of relationship allows us to *predict* how one pattern of behavior will produce another.

But just because two variables change together does not mean that they are linked by a cause-and-effect relationship. For instance, the marriage rate in the United States falls to its lowest point in January, exactly the same month that our national death rate peaks. This hardly means that people die because they fail to marry (or that they don't marry because they die). In fact, it is the dreary weather in much of the nation during January (and maybe also the post-holiday blahs) that causes both a low marriage rate and a high death rate. The converse holds as well: The warmer and sunnier summer months have the highest marriage rates and the lowest death rates. Thus researchers must look below the surface to untangle cause-and-effect relationships.

To take a second case, sociologists have long recognized that juvenile delinquency is more common among young people who live in crowded housing. Say we operationalize the variable "juvenile delinquency" as the number of times (if any) a person under age eighteen has been arrested, and we define "crowded housing" to mean a home's amount of square feet of living space per person. We would find the variables related; that is, delinquency rates are high in densely populated neighborhoods. But should we conclude that crowding in the home (in this case, the independent variable) is what causes delinquency (the dependent variable)?

Young people who live in the crowded inner city are more likely than those who live in the spacious suburbs to have trouble with the police. But does this mean that crowding causes delinquency? Researchers know that crowding and arrest rates do vary together, but they have demonstrated that the connection is spurious: Both factors rise in relation to a third factor—declining income.

measurement means more than hitting the same spot on a target again and again; it means hitting the bull's-eye.

Valid measurement is more difficult than it may at first seem. Say you want to study how religious people are. A reasonable strategy might be to ask how often respondents attend religious services. But is going to a church or temple really the same thing as being religious? It may be that religious people attend services more frequently, but people also join in religious rituals out of habit or because someone else wants them to. Moreover, some devout believers avoid organized religion altogether. Thus, even when a measurement

Not necessarily. **Correlation** is *a relationship by which two (or more) variables change together*. We know that density and delinquency are correlated because they change together, as shown in part (a) of Figure 2–1. This relationship *may* mean that crowding causes misconduct, but it could also mean that some third factor is at work causing change in *both* of the variables under observation. To identify a third variable, think what kind of people live in crowded housing: people with little money and few choices—the poor. Poor children are also more likely to end up with police records. Therefore, crowded housing and juvenile delinquency are found together because *both* are caused by a third factor—poverty—as shown in part (b) of Figure 2–1. In short, the apparent connection between crowding and delinquency is "explained away" by a third variable—low income—that causes them both to change. So our original connection turns out to be a **spurious correlation,** *an apparent, although false, relationship between two (or more) variables caused by some other variable.*

Unmasking a correlation as spurious takes a bit of detective work, assisted by a technique called **control,** *holding constant all variables except one in order to see clearly the effect of that variable.* In this example, we suspect that income level may be causing a spurious link between housing density and delinquency. To check, we control for income (that is, we hold income constant by looking at only young people of one income level) and see whether a correlation between density and delinquency remains. If the correlation between density and delinquency is still there despite the control (that is, if young people living in more crowded housing show higher rates of delinquency than young people in less crowded housing, all with the same family income), we have more reason to think that crowding does, in fact, cause delinquency. But if the relationship disappears when we control for income, as shown in part (c) of the figure, we then know we have a spurious correlation. In fact, research shows that the correlation between crowding and delinquency just about disappears if income is controlled (Fischer, 1984). So we have now sorted out the relationships between the three variables, as illustrated in part (d) of the figure. Housing density and juvenile delinquency have a spurious correlation; evidence shows that both variables rise or fall according to people's income.

To sum up, correlation means only that two or more variables change together. Cause and effect rests on three conditions: (1) demonstrated correlation, (2) an independent (or causal) variable that precedes the dependent variable in time, and (3) no evidence that a

FIGURE 2–1 Correlation and Cause: An Example

(a)

| Density of living conditions | ←— *Correlation* —→ | Delinquency rate |

If two variables vary together, they are said to be correlated. In this example, density of living conditions and juvenile delinquency increase and decrease together.

(b)

| Density of living conditions | ←— *Correlation* —→ | Delinquency rate |

Cause ← Income level → *Cause*

Here we consider the effect of a third variable: income level. Low income level may cause *both* high-density living conditions *and* a high delinquency rate. In other words, as income level decreases, both density of living conditions and the delinquency rate increase.

(c)

| Density of living conditions | *Correlation disappears* | Delinquency rate |

Income level controlled

If we control income level—that is, examine only cases with the same income level—do those with higher-density living conditions still have a higher delinquency rate? The answer is *no*. There is no longer a correlation between these two variables.

(d)

| Density of living conditions | *Spurious correlation* | Delinquency rate |

Cause ← Income level → *Cause*

This finding leads us to conclude that income level is a cause of both density of living conditions and delinquency rate. The original two variables (density of living conditions and delinquency rate) are thus correlated, but neither one causes the other. Their correlation is therefore *spurious*.

THE IDEAL OF OBJECTIVITY

Assume that ten people who work for a magazine in Fort Lauderdale, Florida, are collaborating on a story about that city's best restaurants. With the magazine picking up the tab, they head out on the town for a week of fine dining. Later, they get together to compare notes. Do you think one restaurant will be everyone's clear favorite? That hardly seems likely.

In scientific terms, each of the ten probably operationalizes the concept "best restaurant" differently. For one, it might be a place that serves delicious steaks at reasonable prices; for another, the choice might turn on a menu keyed to nutrition and health; for still another, stunning decor and attentive service might be the deciding factors. Like so many other things in life, the best restaurant turns out to be mostly a matter of individual taste.

Personal values are fine when it comes to restaurants, but they pose a challenge to scientific research. Remember, science assumes an objective reality. Scientists need to study this reality without changing it in any way. Therefore, science demands that researchers strive for **objectivity,** *a state of personal neutrality in conducting research*. Objectivity means that researchers carefully hold to scientific procedures while reining in their own attitudes and beliefs in order not to bias the results.

Scientific objectivity is an ideal rather than a reality, of course, because no one can be completely neutral about anything. Even the subject a researcher chooses to study reflects a personal interest of one sort or another, as Lois Benjamin's research on race attests. But the scientific ideal is to keep a professional sense of detachment from how the results turn out. Holding to this ideal, we do our best to see that conscious or unconscious biases do not distort research. As an extra precaution, many researchers inform their readers about their personal leanings so that their conclusions are taken in the proper context.

Max Weber: Value-Free Research

The influential German sociologist Max Weber expected that people would select their research topics according to their personal beliefs and interests. After all, why else would one person study world hunger, another investigate the effects of racism, and still another examine how children fare in one-parent families? Knowing that people select topics that are *value-relevant*, Weber cautioned researchers to be *value-free* in their investigations. Only by being dispassionate (as we expect any professional to be) can researchers study the world *as it*

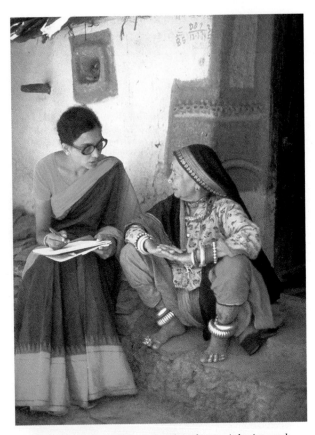

One principle of scientific research is that sociologists and other investigators should strive to be objective in their work, so that their personal values and beliefs do not distort their findings. But such an aloof attitude may discourage the relationship needed in order for people to open up and share information. Thus, as sociologists study human relationships, they have to be especially mindful of their own—when it comes to their subjects.

third variable could be causing a spurious correlation between the two.

Natural scientists usually have an easier time than social scientists identifying cause-and-effect relationships because they can control many variables in a laboratory. Carrying out research in a workplace or on the streets, however, is a more difficult task, and sociologists often must be satisfied with demonstrating only correlation. Moreover, human behavior is highly complex, involving dozens of causal variables at any one time, so establishing all the cause-and-effect relationships in any situation is extremely difficult.

A basic lesson of social research is that being observed affects how people behave. Researchers can never be certain precisely how this will occur; while some people resent public attention, others become highly animated when they think they have an audience.

is rather than tell how they think *it should be*. For Weber, this detachment is a crucial element of science that sets it apart from politics. In other words, politicians are committed to particular outcomes; scientists try to maintain an open-minded readiness to accept the results of their investigations, whatever they may be.

Weber's argument still carries much weight in sociology, although most sociologists concede that we can never be completely value-free or even aware of all our biases (Demerath, 1996). Moreover, sociologists are not "average" people: Most are white people who are highly educated and more politically liberal than the population as a whole (Wilson, 1979). Sociologists need to remember that they, too, are influenced by their own social backgrounds.

One way to limit distortion caused by personal values is **replication,** *repetition of research by other investigators.* If other researchers repeat a study using the same procedures and obtain the same results, we gain confidence that the results are accurate. The need for replication in scientific investigation probably explains why the search for knowledge is called *re*-search in the first place.

In any case, keep in mind that the logic of science does not guarantee objective, absolute truth. What science offers is an approach to knowledge that is *self-correcting* so that, in the long run, researchers stand the best chance of overcoming their biases. Thus, objectivity and truth lie not in any particular research but in the scientific process itself.

SOME LIMITATIONS OF SCIENTIFIC SOCIOLOGY

Science is one important way of knowing. Yet, applied to social life, science has several important limitations:

1. **Human behavior is too complex for sociologists to predict precisely any individual's actions.** Astronomers calculate the movement of objects in the heavens with remarkable precision, but comets and planets are unthinking objects. Humans, by contrast, have minds of their own, so no two people react to any event in exactly the same way. Sociologists, therefore, must be satisfied with showing that *categories* of people typically act in one way or another. This is not a failing of sociology. It simply reflects the reality of what we do: study creative, spontaneous people.

2. **Because humans respond to their surroundings, the mere presence of a researcher may affect the behavior being studied.** An astronomer's gaze has no effect whatever on a distant comet. But most people react to being observed. Some become anxious, angry, or defensive; others try to "help" by doing what they think the researcher expects of them.

3. **Social patterns change; what is true in one time or place may not hold true in another.** The laws of physics apply tomorrow as well as

today; they hold true all around the world. But human behavior is so variable that there are no unchanging sociological laws.

4. **Because sociologists are part of the social world they study, being value-free when conducting social research is difficult.** Barring a laboratory mishap, chemists are rarely personally affected by what goes on in test tubes. But sociologists live in their "test tube": the society they study. Therefore, social scientists face a greater challenge in controlling, or even recognizing, personal values that may distort their work.

A SECOND FRAMEWORK: INTERPRETIVE SOCIOLOGY

All sociologists agree that studying social behavior scientifically presents some real challenges. But some sociologists go further, suggesting that science as it is used to study the natural world misses a vital part of the social world: *meaning*.

Human beings do not simply act; we engage in *meaningful* action. Max Weber, who pioneered this framework, argued that the proper focus of sociology, therefore, is *interpretation*, or understanding the meanings involved in everyday life. **Interpretive sociology** is *the study of society that focuses on the meanings people attach to their social world.*

Interpretive sociology differs from scientific, or positivist, sociology in three ways. First, scientific sociology focuses on action, what people do; interpretive sociology, by contrast, focuses on the meaning people attach to behavior. Second, whereas scientific sociology sees an objective reality "out there," interpretive sociology sees reality constructed by people themselves in the course of their everyday lives. Third, whereas scientific sociology tends to favor *quantitative* data—that is, numerical measurements of social behavior—interpretive sociology favors *qualitative* data, researchers' perceptions of how people understand their surroundings.

In sum, the scientific approach is well suited to research in a laboratory, where investigators stand back and take careful measurements. The interpretive approach is better suited to research in a natural setting where investigators interact with people, learning how they make sense of their everyday lives.

Weber believed that the key to interpretive sociology lay in *Verstehen*, the German word for "understanding." It is the interpretive sociologist's job not just to observe *what* people do but to share in their world of meaning and come to appreciate *why* they act

as they do. Subjective thoughts and feelings—which science tends to dismiss as "bias"—now become the focus of the researcher's attention (Berger & Kellner, 1981; Neuman, 1997).

A THIRD FRAMEWORK: CRITICAL SOCIOLOGY

There is a third methodological approach in sociology. Like the interpretive approach, critical sociology developed in reaction to scientific research. This time, however, the issue was the scientific goal of objectivity.

Scientific sociology holds that reality is "out there," and the researcher's task is to study and document this reality. But Karl Marx, who founded the critical approach, rejected the idea that society exists as a natural system with a fixed order. To assume this, he claimed, amounts to saying that society cannot be changed. From this point of view, scientific sociology ends up supporting the status quo.

Critical sociology, by contrast, is *the study of society that focuses on the need for social change.* Rather than asking the scientific question "How does society work?" critical sociologists ask moral and political questions, especially "Should society exist in its present form?" Their answer, typically, is that it should not. The point, said Marx (1972:109; orig. 1845), is not merely to study the world as it is but to *change* it. In making value judgments about how society should be improved, critical sociology rejects Weber's goal that researchers be value-free.

Sociologists using the critical approach seek to change not only society but also the character of research itself. They consider their research subjects equals and encourage their participation in deciding what to study and how to do the work. Often, researchers and subjects use their findings to provide a voice for less powerful people and advance the political goal of a more equal society (Nielsen, 1990; Stanley, 1990; Reinharz, 1992; Wolf, 1996; Hess, 1999).

Scientific sociologists object to taking sides in this way, charging that critical sociology (whether feminist, Marxist, or some other critical approach), because of its political nature, lacks objectivity and is unable to correct for its own biases. Critical sociologists respond that *all* research is political or biased in that either it calls for change or it does not. Sociologists thus have no choice about their work being political, but they can choose *which* positions to support.

Critical sociology is an activist approach tying knowledge to action, seeking not just to understand the world but also to improve it. Generally speaking, scientific

TABLE 2–1 Three Methodological Approaches in Sociology

	Scientific	Interpretive	Critical
What Is Reality?	Society is an orderly system; reality is "out there."	Society is ongoing interaction; reality is socially constructed meanings.	Society is patterns of inequality; reality is that some dominate others.
How Do We Conduct Research?	Gather empirical data, ideally, quantitative; researcher tries to be an objective observer.	Develop a qualitative account of the subjective sense people make of their world; researcher is a participant.	Research is a strategy to bring about desired change; researcher is an activist.
Corresponding Theoretical Paradigm	Structural-functional paradigm	Symbolic-interaction paradigm	Social-conflict paradigm

sociology tends to appeal to researchers with more conservative political views; critical sociology appeals to those whose politics range from liberal to radical-left.

What about the link between methodological approaches and theory? There is no precise connection; a sociologist who favors the critical approach, for example, may well use scientific methods to collect data. But each of the three methodological approaches does stand closer to one of the theoretical paradigms presented in Chapter 1 ("The Sociological Perspective"). The scientific approach corresponds to the structural-functional paradigm, the interpretive approach to the symbolic-interaction paradigm, and the critical approach to the social-conflict paradigm. Table 2–1 summarizes the differences between the three methodological approaches. Many sociologists favor one approach over another; however, it is important to become familiar with all three (Gamson, 1999).

GENDER AND RESEARCH

In recent years, sociologists have become aware that research is affected by **gender,** *the personal traits and social positions that members of a society attach to being female and male.* Margrit Eichler (1988) identifies five ways in which gender can shape research:

1. **Androcentricity.** *Androcentricity* (*andro* is the Greek word for "male"; *centricity* means "being centered on") refers to approaching an issue from a male perspective. Sometimes researchers act as if only men's activities are important, ignoring what women do. For years researchers studying occupations focused on the paid work of men and overlooked the housework and child care traditionally performed by women. Clearly, research

that seeks to understand human behavior cannot ignore half of humanity.

Gynocentricity—seeing the world from a female perspective—is equally limiting to sociological investigation. However, in our male-dominated society, this problem arises less often.

2. **Overgeneralizing.** This problem occurs when researchers use data drawn from people of only one sex to support conclusions about "humanity" or "society." Gathering information about a community from a handful of male public officials and then drawing conclusions about the entire community illustrates the problem of overgeneralizing. In another case, studying child-rearing practices by collecting data only from women would allow researchers to draw conclusions about "motherhood" but not about the more general issue of "parenthood."

3. **Gender blindness.** Failing to consider the variable of gender at all is called "gender blindness." As is evident throughout this book, the lives of men and women differ in countless ways. A study of growing old in the United States would be flawed by gender blindness if it overlooked the fact that most elderly men live with spouses whereas elderly women typically live alone.

4. **Double standards.** Researchers must be careful not to distort what they study by judging men and women differently. For example, a family researcher who labels a couple "man and wife" may define the man as the "head of household" and treat him accordingly while assuming that the woman simply engages in family "support work."

5. **Interference.** Gender distorts a study if a subject reacts to the sex of the researcher and

thereby interferes with the research operation. While studying a small community in Sicily, for instance, Maureen Giovannini (1992) found many men responding to her as a woman rather than as a researcher. Gender dynamics prevented her from performing certain activities such as private conversations with men, which were considered inappropriate for a single woman. Local residents also denied Giovannini access to places they considered off-limits to women.

There is nothing wrong with focusing research on one sex or the other. But all sociologists, as well as people who read their work, should be mindful of the importance of gender in any investigation.

RESEARCH ETHICS

Like all other researchers, sociologists are aware that research can harm as well as help subjects or communities. For this reason, the American Sociological Association (ASA)—the major professional association of sociologists in North America—has established formal guidelines for conducting research (1997).

Sociologists must strive to be both technically competent and fair-minded in their work. Sociologists must disclose all research findings, without omitting significant data. They are ethically bound to make their results available to other sociologists, especially those who want to replicate a study.

Sociologists must also ensure the safety of subjects taking part in a research project. Should research develop in a manner that threatens the well-being of participants, investigators must stop their work immediately. Researchers must also protect the privacy of anyone involved in a research project. This last promise can be difficult to keep because researchers sometimes come under pressure (even from the police or courts) to disclose information. Therefore, researchers must think carefully about their responsibility to protect subjects, and they should discuss this issue with participants. In fact, ethical research requires the *informed consent* of participants, which means that subjects understand the responsibilities and risks that the research involves and agree—before the work begins—to take part.

Another important guideline concerns funding. Sociologists must include in their published results the sources of all financial support. They must also avoid

 Read the American Sociological Association's code of ethics at http://www.asanet.org

conflicts of interest that may compromise the integrity of their work. For example, researchers must never accept funding from an organization that seeks to influence the research results for its own purposes.

Finally, there are global dimensions to research ethics. Before beginning research in other countries, investigators must become familiar enough with that society to understand what people *there* are likely to perceive as a violation of privacy or a source of personal danger. In a multicultural society such as the United States, the same rule applies to studying people whose cultural background differs from one's own. The box offers some tips about how outsiders can effectively and sensitively study Hispanic communities.

THE METHODS OF SOCIOLOGICAL RESEARCH

A **research method** is *a systematic plan for conducting research.* The remainder of this chapter introduces four commonly used methods of sociological investigation. None is inherently better or worse than any other. Rather, in the same way that a carpenter selects a particular tool for a specific task, researchers choose a method according to who they want to study and what they want to learn.

TESTING A HYPOTHESIS: THE EXPERIMENT

The logic of science is most clearly expressed in the **experiment,** *a research method for investigating cause and effect under highly controlled conditions.* Experimental research is *explanatory,* meaning that it asks not just what happens but why. Typically, researchers devise an experiment to test a **hypothesis,** *an unverified statement of a relationship between variables.*

The ideal experiment consists of four steps. First, the experimenter specifies the variable that changes (the dependent variable, or "the effect") and the variable that one assumes is causing the change in the dependent variable (the independent variable, or "the cause"). Second, the investigator measures the dependent variable. Third, the investigator exposes the dependent variable to the independent variable (the "treatment"). Fourth, the researcher again measures the dependent variable to see whether the predicted change took place. If the expected change did occur, the experiment supports the hypothesis; if not, the hypothesis must be modified.

DIVERSITY: RACE, CLASS, AND GENDER

Studying the Lives of Hispanics

In a society as racially, ethnically, and religiously diverse as the United States, sociologists are always studying people who differ from themselves. Learning—in advance—some of the distinctive traits of any category of people can ease the research process and ensure that no hard feelings are left when the work is finished.

Gerardo Marín and Barbara VanOss Marín have identified five areas of concern in conducting research with Hispanics:

1. **Terminology.** The Maríns point out that the term "Hispanic" is a label of convenience used by the Census Bureau. Few people of Spanish descent think of themselves as "Hispanic" or "Latino"; most identify with a particular country (generally, with a Latin American nation such as Mexico or Argentina, or with Spain).

2. **Cultural values.** By and large, the United States is a nation of individualistic, competitive people. Many Hispanics, by contrast, have a more collective orientation. Therefore, an outsider may judge the behavior of a Hispanic subject as conformist or overly trusting when, in fact, the person is simply trying to be courteous. Researchers should also realize that Hispanic respondents might agree with a particular statement out of politeness rather than conviction.

3. **Family dynamics.** Generally speaking, Hispanic cultures have strong family loyalties. Asking subjects to reveal information about another family member may make them uncomfortable or even angry. The Maríns add that, in the home, a researcher's request to speak privately with a Hispanic woman may provoke suspicion or outright disapproval from her husband or father.

4. **Time and efficiency.** Spanish cultures, the Maríns explain, tend to be

more concerned with the quality of relationships than with simply getting a job done. A non-Hispanic researcher who tries to hurry an interview with a Hispanic family, perhaps wishing not to delay the family's dinner, may be considered rude for not proceeding at a more sociable and relaxed pace.

5. **Personal space.** Finally, as the Maríns point out, people of Spanish descent typically maintain closer physical contact than many non-Hispanics. Consequently, researchers who seat themselves across the room from their subjects may appear "standoffish." Conversely, researchers may inaccurately label Hispanics "pushy" when they move closer than the non-Hispanic researcher finds comfortable.

Of course, Hispanics differ among themselves, just like people in every other category, and these generalizations apply to some more than to others. But the challenge of being culturally aware is especially great in the United States, where hundreds of categories of people make up our multicultural society.

Source: Marín & Marín (1991).

But a change in the dependent variable could be due to something other than the supposed cause. To be certain that they identify the correct cause, researchers carefully control other factors that might intrude into the experiment and affect the outcome. Such control is most easily accomplished in a laboratory, a setting specially constructed for research purposes. Another strategy for neutralizing outside influences is dividing subjects into

an *experimental group* and a *control group*. Early in the study, the researcher measures the dependent variable for subjects in both groups but later exposes only the experimental group to the independent variable or treatment. (The control group typically gets a *placebo*, a treatment that seems to be the same but really has no effect on the experiment.) Then the investigator measures the subjects in both groups again. Any factor occurring during the

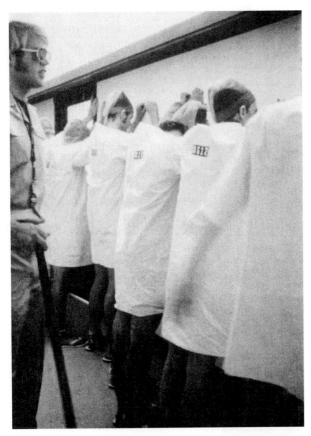

Philip Zimbardo's research helps to explain why violence is a common element in our society's prisons. At the same time, his work demonstrates the dangers that sociological investigation poses for subjects and the need for investigators to observe ethical standards that protect the welfare of people who participate in research.

its Hawthorne factory near Chicago (Roethlisberger & Dickson, 1939). One experiment tested the hypothesis that increasing the available lighting would raise worker output. First, researchers measured worker productivity (the dependent variable). Then they increased the lighting (the independent variable) and measured output a second time. Productivity increased, supporting the hypothesis. But when the research team later turned the lighting back down, productivity increased again. What was going on? In time, the researchers realized that the employees were working harder (even if they could not see as well) simply because people were paying attention to them. From this research, social scientists coined the term **Hawthorne effect** to refer to *a change in a subject's behavior caused simply by the awareness of being studied.*

An Illustration: The Stanford County Prison

Prisons can be violent settings, but is this simply a result of the "bad" people who end up there? Or, as Philip Zimbardo suspected, does the prison itself somehow generate violent behavior? This question led Zimbardo to devise a fascinating experiment, which he called the "Stanford County Prison" (Zimbardo, 1972; Haney, Banks, & Zimbardo, 1973).

Zimbardo contended that, once inside a prison, even emotionally healthy people are prone to violence. Thus, Zimbardo treated the *prison setting* as the independent variable capable of causing *violence*, the dependent variable.

To test this hypothesis, Zimbardo's research team first constructed a realistic-looking "prison" in the basement of the psychology building on the campus of Stanford University. Then they placed an ad in a Palo Alto newspaper, offering to pay young men to help with a two-week research project. To each of the seventy who responded they administered a series of physical and psychological tests and then selected the healthiest twenty-four.

The next step was to assign randomly half the men to be "prisoners" and half to be "guards." The plan called for the guards and prisoners to spend the next two weeks in the mock prison. The prisoners began their part of the experiment soon afterward when the Palo Alto police "arrested" them at their homes. After searching and handcuffing the men, the police drove them to the local police station, where they were fingerprinted. Then police transported their captives to the Stanford prison, where the guards locked them up. Zimbardo started his video camera rolling and watched to see what would happen next.

course of the research that influences people in the experimental group (say, a news event) would do the same to those in the control group, thus "washing out" the factor. By comparing the before and after measurements of the two groups, a researcher can assess how much of the change is due to the independent variable.

The Hawthorne Effect

Another concern of experimenters is that subjects may change their behavior simply because they are getting special attention, as one classic experiment revealed. In the late 1930s, the Western Electric Company hired researchers to investigate worker productivity in

The experiment turned into more than anyone had bargained for. Both guards and prisoners soon became embittered and hostile toward one another. Guards humiliated the prisoners by assigning them tasks such as cleaning out toilets with their bare hands. The prisoners resisted and insulted the guards. Within four days, the researchers removed five prisoners who displayed "extreme emotional depression, crying, rage and acute anxiety" (Haney, Banks, & Zimbardo, 1973:81). Before the end of the first week, the situation had become so bad that the researchers canceled the experiment. Zimbardo explains,

> The ugliest, most base, pathological side of human nature surfaced. We were horrified because we saw some boys (guards) treat others as if they were despicable animals, taking pleasure in cruelty, while other boys (prisoners) became servile, dehumanized robots who thought only of escape, of their own individual survival and of their mounting hatred for the guards. (Zimbardo, 1972:4)

The events that unfolded at the "Stanford County Prison" supported Zimbardo's hypothesis that prison violence is rooted in the social character of jails themselves, not in the personalities of guards and prisoners. This finding raises questions about our society's prisons, suggesting the need for basic reform. But also note how this experiment reveals the potential of research to threaten the physical and mental well-being of subjects. Such dangers are not always as obvious as they were in this case. Therefore, researchers must consider carefully the potential harm to subjects at all stages of their work and end any study, as Zimbardo did, if subjects may suffer harm of any kind.

ASKING QUESTIONS: SURVEY RESEARCH

A **survey** is *a research method in which subjects respond to a series of statements or questions in a questionnaire or an interview.* The most widely used of all research methods, surveys are particularly well suited to studying attitudes—such as beliefs about politics, religion, or race—because there is no way to observe directly what people think. Sometimes surveys provide clues about cause and effect, but typically they yield *descriptive* findings, painting a picture of people's views on some issue.

Population and Sample

A survey targets a **population,** *the people who are the focus of research.* In her study of racism described at the

beginning of this chapter, Lois Benjamin's population was talented African Americans. At the broadest level, political pollsters predict election returns using surveys that treat every adult in the country as the population.

Obviously, contacting millions of people would overwhelm even the most well-funded and patient researcher. Fortunately, there is an easier way that yields accurate results: Researchers collect data from a **sample,** *a part of a population that represents the whole.* Everyone uses the logic of sampling all the time. If you look around the classroom and notice five or six heads nodding off, you might conclude that the class finds the day's lecture dull. In reaching this conclusion, you are making a judgment about *all* the people (the "population") from observing *some* of the people (the "sample"). But how can we know if a sample actually represents the entire population?

A good way to do this is *random sampling*, in which researchers draw a sample from the population by chance so that every element in the population has an equal opportunity to be selected. The mathematical laws of probability dictate that a random sample is quite likely to represent the population.

Beginning researchers sometimes make the mistake of assuming that "randomly" walking up to people on a street produces a sample that is representative of the entire city. Unfortunately, such a strategy does not give every person an equal chance to be included in the sample. For one

 For a discussion of the use of polls in political campaigns, go to http://www.faculty. vassar.edu/lowry/polls.html

thing, any street, whether in a rich neighborhood or a college town, contains more of some kinds of people than others. For another, any researcher is apt to find some people more approachable than others, again introducing a bias.

Although good sampling is no simple task, it can save a great deal of time and money. We are spared the tedious work of contacting everyone in a population, yet we can obtain essentially the same results.

Using Questionnaires

Selecting subjects is only the first step in carrying out a survey. Also needed is a plan for asking questions and recording answers. Most surveys do this with a questionnaire.

A **questionnaire** is *a series of written questions a researcher presents to subjects.* One type of questionnaire provides not only the questions but a series of fixed responses (similar to a multiple-choice examination).

Survey Questions: A Word or Two Makes All the Difference

Do people approve of their president? Pollsters find that approval ratings rise or fall depending on a few small words. During the Clinton years, surveys showed that a majority of adults held a favorable opinion of Mr. Clinton as president. But when researchers asked people what they thought of Mr. Clinton *as a person*, his approval ratings typically tumbled 20 percent.

This difference shows that how researchers word questions affects people's responses. In 1998, *Newsweek* magazine hired a team of researchers to measure public attitudes toward abortion. The results of this national survey showed once again just how important a few words can be in shaping public response. One question put it this way: "Do you personally believe that abortion is wrong?" In this case, 57 percent of respondents said "yes," and 36 percent said "no" (the rest either were not sure or did not answer). Looking at these results, one might well conclude that a majority of people are antiabortion. Another question was worded this way: "Whatever your own personal view of abortion, do you favor or oppose a woman in this country having the choice to have an abortion with the advice of her doctor?" Now 69 percent favored available abortion, and just 24 percent opposed it—clear support for the abortion-rights side of the debate.

Are people of two minds on the abortion question? Probably most people listen carefully to the wording of the questions. Although a slight majority *personally* consider abortion wrong, a larger majority believe that women—with medical advice—should be able to have an abortion if they decide to.

One final example: Look at the wording in these questions. The first is "Do you think that the police force is doing a good job?" The second is "Do you agree that the police force is doing a good job?" Which one is more likely to show stronger support for the police? Why?

Source: Data from Witt (1999).

This *closed-ended format* makes it easy to analyze the results, but by narrowing the range of responses, it can also distort the findings. For example, Frederick Lorenz and Brent Bruton (1996) found that how many hours per week students say they study for a college course depends on the options offered to them. When the researchers presented students with options ranging from one hour or less to nine hours or more, 75 percent said that they studied four hours or less per week. But when a comparable group was given choices ranging from four hours or less to twelve hours or longer (a higher figure that suggests that students should study more) they suddenly became more studious, with only 34 percent reporting that they studied four hours or less each week.

A second type of questionnaire, using an *open-ended format*, allows subjects to respond freely, expressing various shades of opinion. The drawback of this approach is that the researcher has to make sense out of what can be a bewildering array of answers.

The researcher must also decide how to present questions to subjects. Most often, researchers use a *self-administered survey*, mailing or e-mailing questionnaires to respondents and asking them to complete the form and send it back. Because no researcher is present when subjects read the questionnaire, it must be both inviting and clearly written. *Pretesting* a self-administered questionnaire with a small number of people before sending it to the entire sample can avoid the costly problem of finding out—too late—that instructions or questions were confusing.

Using the mail or e-mail allows a researcher to contact a large number of people over a wide geographic area at minimal expense. But many people treat such questionnaires as junk mail, so that typically no more than half of the questionnaires are completed and returned (in 2000, the public returned just two-thirds of U.S. Census Bureau forms as requested). Researchers must send follow-up mailings (or, as the Census Bureau does, visit people's homes) to coax reluctant subjects to respond.

Finally, keep in mind that many people are not capable of completing a questionnaire on their own. Young children obviously cannot, nor can many hospital patients, and a surprising number of adults simply lack the necessary reading and writing skills.

Conducting Interviews

An **interview** is *a series of questions a researcher administers in person to respondents*. In a closed-format design, researchers read a question or statement and then ask the subject to select a response from several alternatives. Generally, interviews are open-ended so that subjects can respond as they choose and researchers can probe with follow-up questions. However, the researcher must guard against influencing a subject, which is as easy as raising an eyebrow when a person begins to answer.

Although subjects are more likely to complete a survey if contacted personally by the researcher, interviews have some disadvantages: Tracking people down is costly and time-consuming, especially if subjects do not live in the same area. Telephone interviews allow far greater "reach," but the impersonality of cold calls by telephone (and reaching answering machines) can lower the response rate.

In both questionnaires and interviews, how a question is worded greatly affects how people answer. For example, when asked whether they object to homosexuals serving in the military, most adults in the United States say "yes." Yet, when asked whether the government should exempt homosexuals from military service, most say "no" (NORC, 1991). Emotionally loaded language can also sway subjects. For instance, using the term "welfare mothers" rather than "women who receive public assistance" adds an emotional element to a question that encourages people to answer negatively. The box takes a closer look at the importance of wording in conducting public opinion polls.

Finally, researchers may confuse respondents by asking a double question, such as "Do you think that the government should reduce the deficit by cutting spending and raising taxes?" The problem here is that a subject could agree with one part of the question but reject the other, so that forcing a subject to say "yes" or "no" distorts the opinion the researcher is trying to measure.

An Illustration:
Studying the African American Elite

We opened this chapter by recounting how Lois Benjamin came to investigate the effects of racism on talented African American men and women. Benjamin suspected that personal achievement did not prevent hostility based on color. She based this view on her own experiences as the only black professor in the history of the University of Tampa. But was she the exception or the rule? To answer this question, Benjamin

These African American women and men are members of the Congressional Black Caucus; they are movers and shakers on the national scene. But, according to Lois Benjamin, who conducted interviews with 100 highly successful African Americans, "making it" does not eliminate the sting of racial prejudice. On the contrary, she found, even the highest achievers still have to contend with barriers based on skin color.

set out to discover whether—and how—racism had plagued others like her.

Opting to conduct a survey, Benjamin chose to interview subjects rather than distribute a questionnaire because, first, she wanted to enter into a conversation with her subjects, to ask follow-up questions, and to pursue topics that she could not anticipate. A second reason Benjamin favored interviews over questionnaires is that racism is a sensitive topic. A supportive investigator can make it easier for subjects to respond to painful questions (Bergen, 1993).

Choosing to conduct interviews made it necessary to limit the number of people in the study. Benjamin settled for 100 men and women. Even this small number kept Benjamin busy for more than two years scheduling, traveling, and meeting with respondents.

TABLE 2–2 The Talented One Hundred: Lois Benjamin's African American Elite

Sex	Age	Childhood Racial Setting	Childhood Region	Highest Educational Degree	Occupational Sector	Income	Political Orientation
Male 63%	35 or younger 6%	Mostly black 71%	West 6%	Doctorate 32%	College or university 35%	More than $50,000 64%	Radical left 13%
Female 37%	36 to 54 68%	Mostly white 15%	North or Central 32%	Medical or law 17%	Private, profit 17%	$35,000 to $50,000 18%	Liberal 38%
	55 or older 26%	Racially mixed 14%	South 38%	Master's 27%	Private, nonprofit 9%	$20,000 to $34,999 12%	Moderate 28%
			Northeast 12%	Bachelor's 13%	Government 22%		Conservative 5%
			Other 12%	Less 11%	Self-employed 14%	Less than $20,000 6%	Depends on issue 14%
					Retired 3%		Unknown 2%
100%	100%	100%	100%	100%	100%	100%	100%

Source: Adapted from Lois Benjamin, *The Black Elite: Facing the Color Line in the Twilight of the Twentieth Century* (Chicago: Nelson-Hall, 1991), p. 276.

She spent two more years transcribing the tapes of her interviews, sorting out what the hours and hours of talk told her about racism, and writing up her results.

In selecting a sample, Benjamin first considered using all the people listed in *Who's Who in Black America*. But she rejected this idea in favor of starting out with people she knew and asking them to suggest others. This strategy is called *snowball sampling* because the number of subjects included grows rapidly over time.

Snowball sampling is appealing because it is an easy way to do research: We begin with familiar people who provide introductions to their friends and colleagues. The drawback is that snowball sampling rarely produces a sample that is representative of the larger population. Benjamin's sample probably contained many like-minded individuals, and it was certainly biased toward people willing to talk openly about race. She understood these problems and tried to make her sample as varied as she could in terms of sex, age, and region of the country. Table 2–2 presents a statistical profile of Benjamin's respondents; the box provides some tips on how to read tables.

Benjamin based all her interviews on a series of questions, with an open-ended format so that her subjects could say whatever they wanted. As usually happens, the interviews took place in a wide range of settings. She met subjects in offices (hers or theirs), in hotel rooms, and in cars. In each case, Benjamin tape-recorded the conversation, which lasted from two-and-one-half to three hours, so she would not be distracted by taking notes.

As research ethics demand, Benjamin offered full anonymity to participants. Even so, many—including notables such as Vernon E. Jordan, Jr. (former president of the National Urban League) and Yvonne Walker-Taylor (first woman president of Wilberforce University)—were accustomed to being in the public eye and permitted Benjamin to use their names.

What surprised Benjamin most about her research was how eagerly many informants responded to her request for an interview. These normally busy men and women appeared to go out of their way to contribute to her project. Furthermore, once the interviews were underway, many became very emotional. Benjamin reports that, at some point in the conversation, about forty of her subjects cried. For them, apparently, the research provided an opportunity to release feelings and share experiences never revealed before. How did Benjamin respond to such sentiments? She reports that she laughed and cried along with her respondents.

Benjamin's research is less scientific and more interpretive sociology (she wanted to find out what race

Reading Tables: An Important Skill

A table provides a lot of information in a small amount of space, so learning to read tables can increase your reading efficiency. When you spot a table, look first at the title to see what information it contains. The title tells you that Table 2–2 presents a profile of the 100 subjects participating in Lois Benjamin's research. Across the top of the table, you will see eight variables that define these men and women. Reading down each column, note the categories within each variable; the percentages in each column add up to 100.

Starting at the top left, we see that Benjamin's sample was mostly men (63 percent men versus 37 percent women). In terms of age, most of the respondents (68 percent) were in the middle stage of life, and most grew up in a predominantly black community in the South, North, or Central regions of the United States.

These people are, indeed, a professional elite. Notice that half have earned either a doctorate (32 percent) or a medical or law degree (17 percent). Given their extensive education (and Benjamin's own position as a professor),

we should not be surprised that the largest share (35 percent) work in academic institutions. In terms of income, these are well-off individuals, with most (64 percent) earning more than $50,000 annually (a salary that only 25 percent of all U.S. workers made at the time).

Finally, we see that these 100 people are generally left-of-center in their political orientation. In part, this reflects their extensive schooling (which encourages progressive thinking) and the tendency of academics to fall on the liberal side of the political spectrum.

---

meant to her subjects) and critical sociology (she undertook the study partly to document that racial prejudice still exists). Indeed, many subjects reported fearing that race might someday undermine their success, and others spoke of a race-based "glass ceiling" preventing them from reaching the highest positions in our society. Summarizing her findings, Benjamin concluded that despite the improving social standing of African Americans, black people in the United States still feel the sting of racial hostility.

IN THE FIELD: PARTICIPANT OBSERVATION

Lois Benjamin's research demonstrates that sociological investigation takes place not only in laboratories but in the field, that is, where people carry on their everyday lives. The most widely used strategy for field study is **participant observation,** *a research method in which investigators systematically observe people while joining in their routine activities.*

Participant observation allows researchers an inside look at social life in settings ranging from nightclubs to religious seminaries. Cultural anthropologists commonly use participant observation (which they call *fieldwork*) to

study communities in other societies. They call their descriptions of unfamiliar cultures *ethnographies.* Sociologists prefer to call their accounts of people in particular settings *case studies.*

At the outset of a field study, most investigators do not have a specific hypothesis in mind. In fact, they may not yet realize what the important questions will turn out to be. Thus, most field research is *exploratory* and *descriptive.*

As its name suggests, participant observation has two sides. On one hand, getting an "insider's" look depends on becoming a participant in the setting: spending time with others, trying to act, think, and even feel the way they do. Compared with experiments and survey research, then, participant observation has fewer rules. But it is precisely this flexibility that allows investigators to explore the unfamiliar and adapt to the unexpected.

Unlike other research methods, participant observation requires that the researcher become immersed in the setting, not for a week or two but for months or even years. At the same time, however, the researcher must maintain some distance as an observer, mentally stepping back to record field notes and eventually to interpret them. Because the investigator must both "play the participant" to win acceptance and gain access to

Anthropologists and photographers Angela Fisher and Carol Beckwith have documented fascinating rituals around the world. As part of their fieldwork, they lived for months with the Himba in Namibia, in order to gain their acceptance and trust. During this time, a village man was killed by a lion. Later, his wives fell under the control of a lion spirit, apparently sent by the husband to bring these women to him in the afterlife. In the ritual shown above, photographed by Fisher and Beckwith, the women seek to rid themselves of the curse.

people's lives and "play the observer" to maintain the distance needed for thoughtful analysis, there is an inherent tension in this method. Carrying out the twin roles of insider participant and outsider observer often comes down to a series of careful compromises.

Most sociologists carry out participant observation alone, so they—and readers—must remember that the results depend on the work of a single individual. Participant observation usually falls within interpretive sociology, yielding mostly qualitative data—impressions and understandings—although researchers sometimes collect some quantitative (numerical) data. From a scientific point of view, participant observation is a "soft" method that relies heavily on personal judgment and lacks scientific rigor. Yet, its personal approach is also a strength: Whereas a highly visible team of sociologists attempting to administer, say, formal surveys would disrupt many social settings, a sensitive participant-observer can often gain considerable insight into people's natural behavior.

An Illustration: *Street Corner Society*

In the late 1930s, a young graduate student at Harvard University named William Foote Whyte (1914–2000)

was fascinated by the lively street life of a nearby, run-down section of Boston. His curiosity ultimately led him to carry out four years of participant observation in this neighborhood, which he called "Cornerville," in the process producing a sociological classic.

At the time, Cornerville was home to first- and second-generation Italian immigrants. Many were poor, and popular wisdom in Boston considered Cornerville a place to avoid: a poor, chaotic slum inhabited by racketeers. Unwilling to accept easy stereotypes, Whyte set out to discover for himself exactly what kind of life went on inside this community. His celebrated book, *Street Corner Society* (1981; orig. 1943), describes Cornerville as a highly organized community with a distinctive code of values, complex social patterns, and particular social conflicts.

In beginning his investigation, Whyte considered a range of research methods. He could have taken questionnaires to one of Cornerville's community centers and asked local people to fill them out. Or he could have invited members of the community to come to his Harvard office for interviews. But it is easy to see that such formal strategies would have prompted little cooperation from the local people and yielded few insights. Therefore, Whyte decided to ease into Cornerville life and patiently build an understanding of this rather mysterious place.

Soon enough, Whyte discovered the challenges of getting started in field research. After all, an upper-middle-class graduate student from Harvard did not exactly fit into Cornerville life. He soon found out, for example, that even a friendly overture, made by an outsider, could seem pushy and rude. Early on, Whyte dropped in at a local bar, hoping to buy a woman a drink and encourage her to talk about Cornerville. But looking around the room, he could find no woman alone. Presently, he thought he might have an opportunity when a man sat down with two women. He gamely asked, "Pardon me. Would you mind if I joined you?" Instantly, he realized his mistake:

> There was a moment of silence while the man stared at me. Then he offered to throw me down the stairs. I assured him that this would not be necessary, and demonstrated as much by walking right out of there without any assistance. (1981:289)

As this incident suggests, gaining entry to a community is the crucial (and sometimes hazardous) first step in field research. "Breaking in" requires patience, ingenuity, and a little luck. Whyte's big break came in the form of a young man named "Doc," whom he met in a local social service agency. Listening to Whyte's account of his bungled efforts to make friends in Cornerville, Doc was sympathetic and decided to take Whyte under his wing and introduce him to others in the community. With Doc's help, Whyte soon became a neighborhood regular.

Whyte's friendship with Doc illustrates the importance of a *key informant* in field research. Such people not only introduce a researcher to a community but often remain a source of information and help. Using a key informant also has its risks. Because any person has a particular circle of friends, a key informant's guidance is certain to "spin" the study in one way or another. Moreover, in the eyes of others, the reputation of the key informant—for better or worse—usually rubs off on the investigator. In sum, a key informant is helpful at the outset, but a participant-observer soon must seek a broad range of contacts.

Having entered the Cornerville world, Whyte began his work in earnest. But he soon realized that a field researcher needs to know when to speak up and when simply to look, listen, and learn. One evening, he joined a group discussing neighborhood gambling. Wanting to get the facts straight, Whyte asked innocently, "I suppose the cops were all paid off?" In a heartbeat,

The gambler's jaw dropped. He glared at me. Then he denied vehemently that any policeman had been paid off and immediately switched the conversation to another subject. For the rest of that evening I felt very uncomfortable.

The next day, Doc offered some sound advice:

> "Go easy on that 'who,' 'what,' 'why,' 'when,' 'where' stuff, Bill. You ask those questions and people will clam up on you. If people accept you, you can just hang around, and you'll learn the answers in the long run without even having to ask the questions." (1981:303)

In the months and years that followed, Whyte became familiar with life in Cornerville and even married a local woman, with whom he spent the rest of his life. In the process, he learned that this neighborhood was hardly the stereotypical slum. On the contrary, most immigrants worked hard, many were successful, and some even boasted of sending children to college. In short, Whyte's book is fascinating reading about the deeds, dreams, and disappointments of one ethnic community, and it contains a richness of detail that can come only from long-term participant observation.

Whyte's work shows that participant observation is a method rife with tensions and contrasts. Its flexibility allows a researcher to respond to the unexpected, but it also makes replication difficult. Participation means getting close to people, but observation depends on keeping some distance. Because no elaborate equipment or laboratory is needed, little expense is involved. But this method is costly in terms of time: Most studies take a year or more, which probably explains why participant observation is used less often than the other methods described in this chapter. Yet the depth of understanding gained through interpretive research of this kind greatly enriches our knowledge of many types of human communities.

USING AVAILABLE DATA: SECONDARY AND HISTORICAL ANALYSIS

Not all research requires investigators to collect their own data. Sometimes, sociologists conduct **secondary analysis,** *a research method in which a researcher uses data collected by others.*

The most widely used statistics in social science are gathered by government agencies (for easy access to many data links, visit http://www.TheSociologyPage.com).

The Census Bureau continuously updates information on the U.S. population. Comparable data on Canada are available from Statistics Canada, a branch of that nation's government. For international data, consult various publications of the United Nations and the World Bank. In short, a wide range of data about the whole world is as close as your library or the Internet.

Using available data—whether government statistics or the findings of individual researchers—saves time and money. Therefore, this approach has special appeal to sociologists with low budgets. Even more important, government data generally are better than what most researchers could obtain on their own.

Still, secondary analysis has inherent problems. For one thing, available data may not exist in precisely the form needed. Furthermore, there are always questions about the meaning and accuracy of work done by others. For example, in his classic study of suicide, Emile Durkheim acknowledged that there was no way to know whether a death classified as a suicide was really an accident or vice versa. In addition, various agencies use different procedures and categories in collecting data, making comparisons difficult. In the end, then, using secondhand data is a little like shopping for a used car: Bargains are plentiful, but you have to shop carefully to avoid ending up with a "lemon."

To illustrate, let's assume that reading about Lois Benjamin's account of African American elites sparks our interest in this country's well-off minorities. How many such people are there? Where do they live? National Map 2–1 graphically displays Census Bureau data that address these questions. These statistics are the best available and at no cost. Yet to use them means accepting the Census Bureau's racial and ethnic categories (until 2000, for example, people could check only one racial category). It also means accepting people's self-reported income on government questionnaires as accurate. Furthermore, if you were to use this map for your own purposes, you would also have to accept the given definitions of "well-off" and "above average" even though they may not exactly fit your purpose.

An Illustration: A Tale of Two Cities

To people trapped in the present, secondary analysis offers a key to unlocking secrets of the past. The award-winning study *Puritan Boston and Quaker Philadelphia*, by E. Digby Baltzell (1979b), exemplifies a researcher's power to analyze the past using historical sources.

A chance visit to Bowdoin College in Maine prompted Baltzell to begin his investigation. Entering the college library, he gazed at portraits of the celebrated author Nathaniel Hawthorne, the eminent poet Henry Wadsworth Longfellow, and Franklin Pierce, the fourteenth U.S. president. He was startled to learn that all three of these great men were members of a single class at Bowdoin, graduating in 1825. How could it be, Baltzell mused, that this small college had graduated more famous people in a single year than his own, much bigger University of Pennsylvania had graduated in its entire history? To answer this question, Baltzell was soon poring over historical documents to see whether New England had indeed produced more famous individuals than his native Pennsylvania.

For data, Baltzell turned to the *Dictionary of American Biography*, twenty volumes profiling more than 13,000 outstanding men and women in fields such as politics, law, and the arts. The *Dictionary* told Baltzell *who* was great; but he also wanted some way to measure *how* great people were. He decided to base his ranking on the *Dictionary*'s statement that, the more impressive the person's achievements, the longer the biography. So counting the number of lines in a biography yielded a reasonable measure of "greatness."

By the time Baltzell had identified the seventy-five individuals with the longest biographies, he saw a striking pattern. Massachusetts had the most by far, with twenty-one of the seventy-five top achievers. The New England states combined claimed thirty-one of the entries. By contrast, Pennsylvania could boast of only two, and the entire Middle Atlantic region had just twelve. Looking more closely, Baltzell discovered that most of New England's great achievers had grown up in and around the city of Boston. Again, in stark contrast, almost no one of comparable standing came from his own Philadelphia, a city with many more people than Boston.

What could explain this remarkable pattern? Baltzell drew inspiration from the German sociologist Max Weber (1958; orig. 1904–5), who argued that a region's record of achievement was largely a result of its predominant religious beliefs (see Chapter 4, "Society"). In the religious differences that set Boston apart from Philadelphia, Baltzell found the answer to his puzzle. Boston was a Puritan settlement, founded by people who were determined in their pursuit of excellence and public achievement. Philadelphia, by contrast, was settled by Quakers, who were equally determined to shun public notice.

Both the Puritans and the Quakers were fleeing religious persecution in England, but the two religious

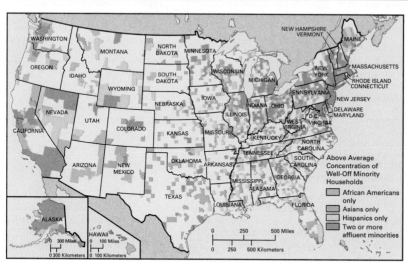

NATIONAL MAP 2–1
Well-Off Minorities across the United States

Based on 1990 census data, this map identifies the counties of the United States with an above-average share of well-off minority households—people earning at least $50,000 annually. (For the entire country in 2000, about one-third of African American and Hispanic families and more than half of Asian families fell into this category.) Where in the United States do well-off members of each minority category live? Do members of one category tend to live where members of another category predominate? Can you explain this pattern?

Adapted from *American Demographics* magazine, December 1992, pp. 34–35. Reprinted with permission. © 1992, *American Demographics* magazine, Ithaca, New York. Data from the 1990 decennial census.

beliefs produced very different cultural patterns. Convinced of humanity's innate sinfulness, Boston Puritans built a rigid society in which family, church, and school regulated people's behavior. They celebrated hard work as a means of glorifying God and viewed public success as a reassuring sign of God's blessing. In other words, Puritanism fostered a disciplined life in which people both sought and respected achievement.

Philadelphia's Quakers, on the other hand, built their way of life on the belief that all human beings are basically good. They saw little need for strong social institutions to "save" individuals from sinfulness. They believed in equality, so that even people who became rich considered themselves no better than anyone else. Thus, rich and poor alike lived modestly and discouraged one another from standing out by seeking fame or even public office.

In Baltzell's sociological imagination, Boston and Philadelphia took the form of two social "test tubes": Puritanism was poured into one, Quakerism into the other. Centuries later, we can see that different "chemical reactions" occurred in each case. The two belief systems apparently led to different attitudes toward personal achievement, which, in turn, shaped the history of each region. Moreover, we can see the results of these cultural differences even today. Boston's Kennedy family (despite being Catholic) still exemplifies the Puritan pursuit of recognition and leadership, but there has never been a family with such public stature in the entire history of Philadelphia.

Baltzell's study uses scientific logic, but it also illustrates the interpretive approach. His research reminds us that sociological investigation often involves various methodological approaches and a lively sociological imagination.

Table 2–3 on page 48 summarizes the four major methods of sociological investigation. We now turn to our final consideration: the link between research results and sociological theory.

THE INTERPLAY OF THEORY AND METHOD

No matter how they gather data, sociologists must turn facts into meaning by building theory. They do this in two ways: inductive logical thought and deductive logical thought.

Inductive logical thought is *reasoning that transforms specific observations into general theory*. In this mode, a researcher's thinking runs from the specific to

TABLE 2–3 Four Research Methods: A Summary

Method	Application	Advantages	Limitations
Experiment	For explanatory research that specifies relationships between variables; generates quantitative data	Provides the greatest opportunity to specify cause-and-effect relationships; replication of research is relatively easy	Laboratory settings have an artificial quality; unless the research environment is carefully controlled, results may be biased
Survey	For gathering information about issues that cannot be directly observed, such as attitudes and values; useful for descriptive and explanatory research; generates quantitative or qualitative data	Sampling, using questionnaires, allows surveys of large populations; interviews provide in-depth responses	Questionnaires must be carefully prepared and may yield a low return rate; interviews are expensive and time-consuming
Participant observation	For exploratory and descriptive study of people in a "natural" setting; generates qualitative data	Allows study of "natural" behavior; usually inexpensive	Time-consuming; replication of research is difficult; researcher must balance roles of participant and observer
Secondary analysis	For exploratory, descriptive, or explanatory research whenever suitable data are available	Saves time and expense of data collection; makes historical research possible	Researcher has no control over possible biases in data; data may only partially fit current research needs

the general and goes something like this: "I have some interesting data here; I wonder what they mean?" E. Digby Baltzell's research illustrates the inductive logical model. His data showed that one region of the country (the Boston area) had produced many more high achievers than another (the Philadelphia region). He worked upward, from ground-level observations to the more general theory that religious values were a key factor that shaped people's attitudes toward achievement.

A second type of logical thought moves downward: **Deductive logical thought** is *reasoning that transforms general theory into specific hypotheses suitable for testing.* The researcher's thinking runs from the general to the specific: "I have this hunch about human behavior; let's collect some data and put it to the test." Working deductively, the researcher first states the theory in the form of a hypothesis and then selects a method by which to test it. To the extent that the data support the hypothesis, we conclude that the theory is correct; data that refute the hypothesis tell us that the theory should be revised or perhaps rejected entirely.

Philip Zimbardo's Stanford County Prison experiment illustrates deductive logic. Zimbardo began with the general idea that prisons change human behavior. He then developed a specific, testable hypothesis:

Placed in a prison setting, even emotionally well-balanced young men will behave violently. The violence that erupted soon after his experiment began supported Zimbardo's hypothesis. Had his experiment produced friendly behavior between prisoners and guards, his original theory clearly would have needed reformulation.

Just as researchers often use several methods over the course of one study, they typically make use of *both* kinds of logical thought. Figure 2–2 illustrates both types of reasoning: inductively building theory from observations and deductively making observations to test a theory.

Finally, turning facts into meaning usually involves organizing and presenting statistical data. Precisely how sociologists arrange their numbers affects the conclusions they reach. In short, preparing one's results amounts to spinning reality in one way or another.

Often, we conclude that an argument must be true simply because there are statistics to back it up. However, we must look at statistics with a cautious eye. After all, researchers choose what data to present, they interpret their statistics, and they may use tables and graphs to steer readers toward particular conclusions. The final box, on pages 50–51, takes a closer look at this important issue.

PUTTING IT ALL TOGETHER: TEN STEPS IN SOCIOLOGICAL INVESTIGATION

We can draw the material in this chapter together by outlining ten steps in the process of carrying out sociological investigation. Each step is represented by an important question:

1. **What is your topic?** Being curious and using the sociological perspective can generate ideas for social research any time and any place. The issue you choose for study is likely to have some personal significance.

2. **What have others already learned?** You are probably not the first person with an interest in some issue. Visit the library to see what theories and methods other researchers have applied to your topic. In reviewing the existing research, note problems that have come up.

3. **What, exactly, are your questions?** Are you seeking to explore an unfamiliar social setting? To describe some category of people? To investigate cause and effect between variables? If your study is exploratory or descriptive, identify *who* you want to study, *where* the research will take place, and *what* kinds of issues you want to explore. If it is explanatory, you also must formulate the hypothesis to be tested and operationalize each variable.

4. **What will you need to carry out research?** How much time and money are available to you? Are special equipment or skills necessary? Can you do the work yourself? You should answer all these questions as you plan the research project.

5. **Are there ethical concerns?** Not all research raises serious ethical questions, but you must be sensitive to the possibility. Can the research cause harm or threaten anyone's privacy? How might you design the study to minimize the chances for injury? Will you promise anonymity to the subjects? If so, how will you ensure that anonymity is maintained?

6. **What method will you use?** Consider all major research strategies, as well as combinations of approaches. Keep in mind that the appropriate method depends on the kinds of questions you are asking and the resources available to you.

7. **How will you record the data?** The research method you choose is the system for data collection. Record all information accurately and in a way that will make sense later (it may be some time before you write up the results of your work). Be alert for any bias that may creep into the research.

8. **What do the data tell you?** Study the data in terms of your initial questions and decide how to interpret the data you have collected. If your study involves a specific hypothesis, you must decide whether to confirm, reject, or modify the hypothesis. Keep in mind that there may be several ways to look at your data, depending on which theoretical paradigm you apply, and you should consider all interpretations.

9. **What are your conclusions?** Prepare a final report stating your conclusions. How does your work advance sociological theory? Improve research methods? Does your study have policy implications? What would the general public find interesting in your work? Finally, evaluate your own work, noting problems that arose and questions left unanswered.

10. **How can you share what you've learned?** Consider sending your research paper to a campus newspaper or magazine or making a presentation to a class, campus gathering, or perhaps a meeting of professional sociologists. The point is to share what you have learned with others and to let them respond to your work.

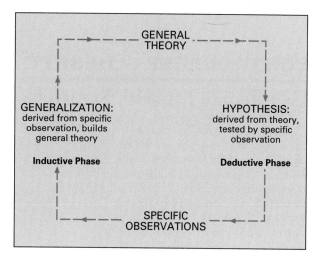

FIGURE 2–2 Deductive and Inductive Logical Thought

CONTROVERSY & DEBATE

Can People Lie with Statistics?

Is research—especially research involving numbers—always as "factual" as we think? Not according to the great English politician Benjamin Disraeli, who remarked, "There are three kinds of lies: lies, damned lies, and statistics!" In a world that bombards us with numbers—often described as "scientific facts" or "official figures"—it is worth pausing to consider that statistical evidence is not necessarily the same as truth. For one thing, any researcher can make mistakes. For another, because data do not speak for themselves, someone has to interpret what they mean. Sometimes, people dress up their data the way politicians deliver campaign speeches: with an eye more to winning you over than getting at the truth.

The best way not to fall prey to statistical manipulation is to understand how people can mislead with statistics:

1. **People select their data.** Many times, the data presented are not wrong, but they are not the whole story. Let's say someone who thinks that television is ruining our way of life presents statistics indicating that

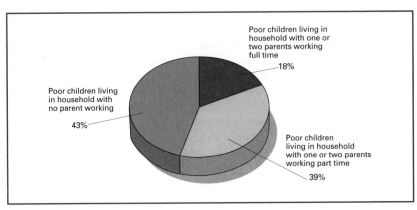

we watch more TV today than a generation ago. Moreover, during the same period, SAT scores have fallen. Both sets of data may be correct, but the suggestion that television is lowering test scores remains unproven. Moreover, a person more favorable to television might counter with the additional "fact" that the U.S. population spends much more money buying books today than it did a generation ago, suggesting that television creates new intellectual interests. In sum,

people can find statistics that seem to support just about any argument.

2. **People interpret their data.** Another way people manipulate statistics is to package them with a ready-made interpretation, as if numbers can mean only one thing. One publication, for example, presented the results of a study of U.S. children living in poverty (National Center for Children in Poverty, cited in *Population Today*, 1995). As the figure shows, the researchers

SUMMARY

1. Two basic requirements for sociological investigation are (1) using the sociological perspective and (2) being curious and asking questions about the world around us.

2. Scientific sociology studies society by systematically observing social behavior. This methodological approach requires carefully operationalizing concepts and ensuring that measurement is both reliable (consistent) and valid (precise).

3. A goal of science is to discover how variables are related. Correlation means that two or more variables change

value together. A cause-and-effect relationship means that change in one variable causes the change in another variable. When a cause-and-effect relationship exists, a researcher who knows the value of an independent variable can predict the value of some dependent variable.

4. Although investigators select topics according to their personal interests, the scientific ideal of objectivity demands that they try to suspend personal values and biases as they conduct research.

5. Interpretive sociology is a methodological approach that focuses on the meaning that people attach to

reported that 43 percent of these children lived in a household with no working parent, 39 percent lived in a household with one or two parents employed part time, and 18 percent lived in a household with one or two parents working full time. The researchers labeled this figure "Majority of Children in Poverty Live with Parents Who Work." Do you think this interpretation is accurate or misleading?

3. **People use graphs to spin the truth.** Especially in newspapers and other popular media, we find statistics in the form of charts and graphs. Graphs help explain data, showing, for example, an upward or downward trend. But they also give people the opportunity to "spin" data in various ways. What trend we think we see depends, in part, on the time frame used in a graph. Looking at just the last few years, for instance, we would see the U.S. crime rate going downward. But looking at the last few decades, we would see an opposite trend: The crime rate pushes sharply upward.

The scale used to draw a graph is also important because it lets a researcher "inflate" or "deflate" a trend. Both of the following graphs present identical data for College Board SAT scores between 1967 and 2000. But the left-hand graph stretches the scale to show a dip in the middle; the right-hand graph compresses the scale, making the dip disappear. So, understanding what statistics mean—or don't mean—depends on being a careful reader!

Continue the debate . . .

1. *Why do you think people are so quick to accept statistics as true?*

2. *From a scientific point of view, is spinning the truth acceptable? What about from a critical approach, trying to advance social change?*

3. *Can you find a news story on some social issue that you think presents biased data or conclusions? What are the biases?*

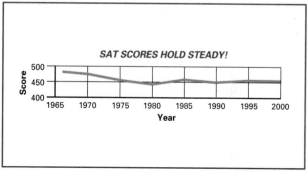

their behavior. Reality is not "out there" but is constructed by people in their everyday interactions.

6. Critical sociology is a methodological approach that uses research as a means of social change. Critical sociology rejects the scientific principle of objectivity, claiming that all research has a political character.

7. The logic of science is most clearly expressed in the experiment, which is performed under controlled conditions and tries to specify cause-and-effect relationships between two (or more) variables.

8. Surveys measure people's attitudes or behavior using questionnaires or interviews.

9. Participant observation is a method in which a researcher directly observes a social setting while participating in it for an extended period of time.

10. Secondary analysis is making use of existing data. This method is easier and often more efficient than collecting data firsthand and allows the study of historical issues.

11. Theory and research are linked in two ways. Deductive logical thought starts with general theories and generates specific hypotheses suitable for testing. Inductive logical thought starts with specific observations and builds general theories.

KEY CONCEPTS

science (p. 26) a logical system that bases knowledge on direct, systematic observation

scientific sociology (p. 26) the study of society based on systematic observation of social behavior

empirical evidence (p. 26) information we can verify with our senses

concept (p. 28) a mental construct that represents some part of the world in a simplified form

variable (p. 28) a concept whose value changes from case to case

measurement (p. 28) a procedure for determining the value of a variable in a specific case

operationalizing a variable (p. 29) specifying exactly what one is to measure before assigning a value to a variable

reliability (p. 29) consistency in measurement

validity (p. 29) precision in measuring exactly what one intends to measure

cause and effect (p. 30) a relationship in which change in one variable (the independent variable) causes change in another (the dependent variable)

independent variable (p. 30) a variable that causes change in another (dependent) variable

dependent variable (p. 30) a variable that is changed by another (independent) variable

correlation (p. 31) a relationship by which two (or more) variables change together

spurious correlation (p. 31) an apparent, although false, relationship between two (or more) variables caused by some other variable

control (p. 31) holding constant all variables except one in order to see clearly the effect of that variable

objectivity (p. 32) a state of personal neutrality in conducting research

replication (p. 33) repetition of research by other investigators

interpretive sociology (p. 34) the study of society that focuses on the meanings people attach to their social world

critical sociology (p. 34) the study of society that focuses on the need for social change

gender (p. 35) the personal traits and social positions that members of a society attach to being female and male

research method (p. 36) a systematic plan for conducting research

experiment (p. 36) a research method for investigating cause and effect under highly controlled conditions

hypothesis (p. 36) an unverified statement of a relationship between variables

Hawthorne effect (p. 38) a change in a subject's behavior caused simply by the awareness of being studied

survey (p. 39) a research method in which subjects respond to a series of statements or questions in a questionnaire or an interview

population (p. 39) the people who are the focus of research

sample (p. 39) a part of a population that represents the whole

questionnaire (p. 39) a series of written questions a researcher presents to subjects

interview (p. 41) a series of questions a researcher administers in person to respondents

participant observation (p. 43) a research method in which investigators systematically observe people while joining in their routine activities

secondary analysis (p. 45) a research method in which a researcher uses data collected by others

inductive logical thought (p. 47) reasoning that transforms specific observations into general theory

deductive logical thought (p. 48) reasoning that transforms general theory into specific hypotheses suitable for testing

CRITICAL-THINKING QUESTIONS

1. What does it mean to say that there are various kinds of truth? What are the advantages and limitations of science as a way of knowing?

2. How does interpretive sociology differ from scientific sociology? What about critical sociology? Which approach best describes the work of each of these sociology founders: Emile Durkheim, Max Weber, and Karl Marx?

3. Why do some sociologists argue that objectivity is essential to sound research? Why do other sociologists disagree?

4. What are some differences between "hard" research (such as scientific experiments) and "soft" research (such as participant observation)?

APPLICATIONS AND EXERCISES

1. Imagine that you are observing your instructor in an effort to assess his or her skills as a teacher. Operationalize the concept "good teaching." What specific traits might you identify as relevant evidence? Do you think students are always good judges of strong teaching?

2. Drop by to see at least three sociology instructors (or other social science instructors) during their office hours. Ask each the extent to which sociology is an objective science. Do they agree about the character of their discipline? Why or why not?

3. Conduct a practice interview with a roommate or friend on the general topic of "How do I expect that completing a college education will affect the rest of my life?" Before the actual interview, prepare a list of specific questions or issues you think are relevant. Afterward, give some thought to why carrying out an effective interview is much harder than it initially may seem.

4. You can do sociological research while watching television. In recent years, some critics have claimed that African Americans are not very visible on prime-time television. Select a sample of prime-time shows and systematically keep track of the race of major characters. Notice that you will have to decide what "prime-time" means, what a "major" character is, how to gauge someone's "race," and other issues before you begin. Sketch out a research plan.

5. Packaged in the back of this new textbook is an interactive CD-ROM that offers a variety of study and review materials intended to help you better understand the material covered in this chapter. For this chapter, the CD-ROM contains an author's tip video, Real Life Sociology videos, other relevant audio and video, interactive map animations, audio journal entries from the author, Web links, and much more.

 SITES TO SEE

http://www.prenhall.com/macionis
Visit the interactive *Companion Website*™ that accompanies this text. Begin by clicking on the cover of your book. You will find a chapter-by-chapter study guide, practice tests, and a significant portion of the text for on-line review, as well as many suggested Web links.

http://www.macionis.com
(or http://www.TheSociologyPage.com)

You can find more than fifty Web links to sociological journals and other sources of data and information by visiting the Links Library at the author's personal Web site.

http://www.ropercenter.uconn.edu

To learn more about public opinion research, visit the Roper Center's Web site.

http://quickfacts.census.gov/qfd/

Data for any county in the United States are available from this Census Bureau Web site. Visit this site and prepare a profile of your local area.

http://ssda.anu.edu.au/

Learn more about Australia by visiting this Web site that provides social science data for that country.

 INVESTIGATE WITH CONTENTSELECT

Follow the instructions found on page 23 of this textbook to enter this chapter of the book's *Companion Website*™. Once in the chapter, click on the Content-Select icon at the bottom left of your screen and enter your personal User ID and Password. Enter keywords such as "science" and "objectivity," and the search engine will help you become an effective researcher.

cyber.scope

WELCOME TO THE INFORMATION REVOLUTION!

Now that we have begun a new century (and a new millennium), we are witnessing astounding changes brought on by a new kind of technology. For the last two centuries, the Industrial Revolution has shaped our society, dictating the kind of work people do and how we think about the world. But now another transformation is underway—dubbed the Information Revolution—that is already redefining our world in novel ways.

At the end of each of the five parts of this text, we present a special section called "cyber.scope." These features highlight how computers and new information technology affect the issues raised in the preceding chapters. In this first cyber.scope, we extend our discussion of the sociological perspective (Chapter 1) and sociological research (Chapter 2) to explain what the Information Revolution is all about.

The Age of Machines: Industrial Society

The time line found inside the front cover of this book places the onset of the modern era about 250 years ago, the dawn of the Industrial Revolution. At that time—first in England and soon afterward in the United States—new sources of energy led imaginative people to create new products in new ways. First rivers and then steam generated by coal furnaces provided the power to operate large machines. Soon afterward, the Industrial Revolution was changing all aspects of social life, drawing people away from home to

work in the new factories and demanding that they learn the skills needed to operate machinery. As time went on, the increasing size and number of factories encouraged migration from the countryside to rapidly growing cities, where most people experienced a faster-paced, more impersonal way of life and, in time, came to enjoy a higher material standard of living. As we have noted, these changes sparked people's interest in studying society and played a key role in the birth of sociology.

The Age of Computers: Information Society

The final decades of the twentieth century witnessed the unfolding of another technological transformation—the Information Revolution—which promises to change our world once again. The technology that will define the twenty-first century is

based on *information:* the computer and related technology including the Internet, facsimile machines, modems and cellular telephones, as well as fiber optics and satellite communications. The fact that we already have shorthand names for such devices—the "Net," "fax," "cell phone," and "dish"—suggests how quickly they have become a part of our lives.

The age of the computer began in 1946 when U.S. engineers in a Philadelphia laboratory switched on a room-sized machine stuffed with wires and vacuum tubes. Despite its giant size, this "mother of all computers" could do no more than today's ten-dollar hand-held calculator. No wonder Thomas Watson, head of IBM, thought his company would end up selling "maybe five computers." Thirty years later, Ken Olson, founder of Digital Equipment Corporation, was just as skeptical, stating, "There is no reason anyone would want a computer in the home" (quoted in Lunsford, 1996).

For better or worse, these two men were quite wrong. In the final decades of the twentieth century, increasingly sophisticated computers quickly became a basic element of our lives. We now find microprocessors at work in the vast majority of U.S. households and businesses, and in cars and trucks as well. Surveys show that in

Familiarity with computers is far more common among younger members of our society than older generations. Today's young people, who will live out their lives during the twenty-first century, will find computers a natural and indispensable part of day-to-day living.

2001, almost 55 percent of U.S. households had at least one personal computer, and almost 45 percent of U.S. households

 For the latest government reports on computer use and Internet availability, visit http://www.census.gov/population/www/socdemo/computer.html

were connected to the Internet (U.S. Census Bureau, 2001). As computers become more numerous—as well as more powerful, smaller, and more portable—they will rewrite the rules of social life in the twenty-first century just as monstrous machines defined the industrial era now coming to a close.

What's different about new information technology? Most basically, the change involves the kind of work people do. Yesterday's industrial technology empowered people to create more and more *things*; information technology leads us to work with *ideas*, creating and manipulating symbols. The industrial age was represented by the factory's assembly line, with workers toiling to make steel or assemble cars. But the typical worker in the information age peers at a computer screen, entering data, writing, calculating, composing, drawing, or designing.

A second key change brought about by the Information Revolution is the declining importance of distance and physical space. Just as industrial technology demands that people work in centralized factories (where the machinery and energy sources are located), information

The earliest computers, including the 1946 ENIAC (Electronic Numerical Integrator and Computer) were monstrous contraptions that filled an entire room. (In fact, in 1949, Popular Mechanics *magazine confidently predicted that computers in the future would weigh no more than 1.5 tons!) It wasn't until the development of small, personal computers in the 1980s that the Information Revolution began to change the everyday lives of most people in the United States.*

technology allows people to work almost anywhere that they can carry a computer or flip on a cell phone. Note, too, that when we use this technology to communicate with others, we often have no idea where they are. The term "cyberspace" suggests that our emerging world is less and less bounded by physical dimensions. Of course, just as we gauged the output of industrial engines with a reference to the "horse-power" they made obsolete, so we now cling to older, physical images in describing new cyber-realities: We talk about the information superhighway,[1] read electronic bulletin boards, and enter online chat rooms. Yet these places are a "virtual reality," meaning that they are computer simulations that we see

and interact with, yet they have no physical existence. In fact, they exist only in the flow of electrons that illuminates our computer, electrons that can circle the world at the speed of light.

As later chapters of the text explain, this new technology is changing nearly every dimension of our lives: reshaping culture and how we learn about the world, connecting us to people in new ways, generating new kinds of crime as well as new ways of pursuing criminals, and even altering patterns of social inequality. There is little doubt that as we move through the new century we will see more changes that will spark people's sociological interest in the surrounding world.

New Information Technology: Thoughts on Theory

Chapter 1 ("The Sociological Perspective") discusses sociology's three major theoretical paradigms. What insights do these paradigms give us into new information technology?

A structural-functional analysis would point up the fact that because society is a system of countless interdependent elements, a new form of technology is likely to affect nearly all aspects of our lives. Since

---

[1]The rapidly increasing number of people logging on to the Internet has overwhelmed existing telephone lines and sometimes results in long delays in transmitting and receiving information. Until high-speed connections are more common, the information "superhighway" may remain more of a "dirt road."

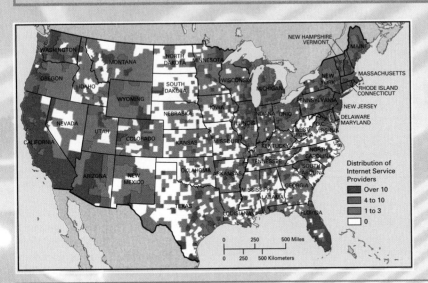

**NATIONAL MAP Cyber I-1
Available Internet Service
across the United States**

The counties that have the most Internet
service providers are those with high
population densities and thus large
markets. These same counties also have a
large number of affluent people who can
afford to log on. Thus, although high
technology is transforming the United
States, the pace of change is faster in
urban than rural areas.

Source: *Time*, March 22, 1999. Copyright © 1999,
Time, Inc. Reprinted by permission.

the invention of television in 1939,
more than 2 billion TV sets have
been built (and, in high-income nations such as the United States, we
add televisions faster than we add
people). Television has altered what
we know, how we learn, patterns of
recreation, and even the ways family
members interact. The computer
will almost certainly change our
lives even more. Its manifest (that is,
intended and expected) effects will
range from decentralizing the workplace to encouraging entire cities to
spread outward because talking to
or working with others no longer
requires being physically with them.
The latent (that is, unintended) effects are certainly harder to foresee,
but they may well include new kinds
of human communities as people
pay less attention to their physical
neighbors and spend more time
communicating online with like-
minded others.

A social-conflict analysis of the
rise of new information technology

offers contrasting insights, especially regarding social inequality.
Here, we might note that the
spread of new information technology has been rapid among affluent
people but far less among the poor,
a pattern illustrated in National
Map Cyber I-1. There is already
evidence that the information age
will be marked by two distinct
classes: educated people with sophisticated symbolic skills (who are
likely to prosper) and people without symbolic skills (who are likely
to remain in low-income jobs). Statistical comparisons show that,
among workers in the same job,
those able to use a computer earn
15 percent more than those who
cannot (Ratan, 1995).

Finally, the symbolic-interaction
paradigm asks questions at the
micro-level of analysis. For example,
how does communication via electronic mail differ from face-to-face
interaction? Obviously, lacking
facial expression or tone of voice,

electronic communication cannot
convey emotion very well. For this
reason, as shown in Figure Cyber
I–1, people have creatively turned
the characters found on their keyboards into symbols, generating a
new cyber-language.

New Information Technology: What about Research?

How is new information technology
changing sociological research, the
focus of Chapter 2? A generation of
sociologists has been trained to use
computers to select random sam-
ples, to perform complex statistical
analysis, and prepare written reports efficiently. Obviously, electronic mail enables researchers to
"travel" almost anywhere almost instantly and with minimal cost. In
the coming years, more and more
surveys will take place online. Electronic surveys raise some interesting
questions: Will this technology improve survey response rates or be
discarded as electronic junk mail?

Will cyber-surveys end up protecting respondents' anonymity or threatening their privacy?

What seems sure is that new information technology will greatly enhance communication between researchers throughout the world. The Internet—highlighted in the next cyber.scope, on pages 244–45—now links some 400 million people in almost all of the world's 192 nations. It gives sociologists a powerful tool for building networks, sharing information, and joining together to conduct research. Just as important, faculty and students now have ready access to a rapidly increasing amount of statistical information. For example, the U.S. Census Bureau (see their Web site at http://www.census.gov) publishes reports of all kinds online and will respond to questions from individuals doing research of their own.

Visit Us Online!

Please visit the Web site that accompanies this text. Travel to the author's home page at http://www.TheSociologyPage.com (or http://www.macionis.com) to review our family of textbooks, read sociological news, view videos, enter the Gallery of Sociologists, and find a library of links to a wide range of interesting organizations. The author and publisher have also prepared an interactive Web site that serves as a study guide to help you throughout this course. Visit http://www.prenhall.com/macionis and click on the cover of this book. There, you will find a chapter-by-chapter study guide, self-scoring practice tests, and many links to other instructive Web sites. These sites, along with the CD-ROM that is included with your new textbook, are our invitation to you to join the Information Revolution. Welcome, and enjoy!

FIGURE Cyber I-1 Cyber-Symbols: An Emerging Language

It all started with the "smiley" figure that shows one is happy or telling a joke. Now a new language of gestures is emerging as creative people use computer keystrokes to create emoticons, symbols that convey thoughts and emotions. Here is a sampling of the new cyber-language. (Rotate this page 90° to the right to appreciate the emoticon faces.)

: -)	I'm smiling at you.
: `-)	I'm so happy (laughing so hard) that I'm starting to cry.
: - O	Wow!
: - x	My lips are sealed!
: -||	I'm angry with you!
: - P	I'm sticking my tongue out at you!
: - (	I feel sad.
: - |	Things look grim.
% -}	I think I've had too much to drink.
-:(	Somebody cut my hair into a mohawk!
+O:-)	I've just been elected Pope!
@}——>———	Here's a rose for you!

Computers are as popular in Japan as they are in the United States. The Japanese have their own emoticons:

(^_^)	I'm smiling at you.
(*^o^*)	This is exciting!
(^o^)	I am happy.
\(^o^)/	Banzai! This is wonderful!

How far will this new keyboard language go? If you're creative enough, anything is possible. Here's a routine that has been making the rounds on the Internet. It's called "Mr. Asciihead learns the Macarena"! To see Mr. Asciihead in action, go to the link at http://www.TheSociologyPage.com

```
 o      o      o      o      o     <o    <o>     o>      o
.l.    \l.    \l/    //     X      \      l      <l     <l>
/\     >\     /<     >\     /<     >\     /<     >\      /<
```

Sources: Pollak (1996) and Krantz (1997). "Mr. Asciihead" is the creation of Leow Yee Ling.

CHAPTER

3

Diego Rivera (1866–1957)
La Piñata, 1953

CULTURE

Don Domingo is a priest and member of the Q'ero, a small society that lives 15,000 feet up in the peaks of the Andes, South America's highest mountain range. The Q'ero are among the most socially isolated people on Earth, rarely making contact with the world beyond their home. But in 2000, the world came to the Q'ero. A messenger from the United Nations arrived to invite Don Domingo and several other Q'ero people to attend the Millennium World Peace Summit in New York City. Don Domingo considered the invitation but made one request: He asked whether the UN officials would provide horses for the group to travel the three days needed to reach the nearest paved road. When the messenger agreed, Don Domingo smiled at the thought of visiting the United States.

A few weeks later, Don Domingo and five of his fellow priests were in Peru's ancient capital city, Cuzco, boarding a DC-10 airliner. Because the Quechua language has no word for "airplane," they spoke of the plane using their word for "big bird." As the plane roared down the runway, the men anxiously gazed out the window. Then, shortly after takeoff, they smiled and nodded as the flight attendant handed them cans of Coke, although they had no idea what to do with them.

Hours later, the plane

touched down at Newark Airport, a few miles west of New York. In their brightly colored clothing, the visitors followed their UN hosts to a waiting van. Only minutes later, the van was stuck in the late afternoon traffic that clogs the New Jersey Turnpike. "A horse moves faster than this," Don Domingo commented to the others. Alongside the highway was a small rocky hill, which prompted the question, "What is the name of this mountain?" The interpreter shook her head and responded that, as far as she knew, the hill had no name. This disturbed the Q'ero priests, who view all mountains as gods. As the traffic began to move, the van headed into the Lincoln Tunnel. The five priests became even more uneasy. "Uccu Pacha," Don Domingo said quietly to the others, "We are entering the underworld."

United Nations officials pronounced the conference a success, having brought together people from hundreds of societies—large and small—to discuss ways to promote peace and protect the Earth's natural environment. The Q'ero priests, too, were pleased with their travels. Back in the Andes, Don Domingo and the others have spent many hours trying to convey to the Q'ero people something of life in New York, including the mysterious trip to the underworld that people make in cars that barely move (based on Van Biema, 2000).

Human beings around the globe create diverse ways of life. Such differences begin with outward appearance: Contrast the women shown here from Brazil, Kenya, New Guinea, and Morocco, and the men from Taiwan (Republic of China), India, Peru, and New Guinea. Less obvious, but of even greater importance, are internal differences, since culture also shapes our goals in life, our sense of justice, and even our innermost personal feelings.

The world is home to more than 6 billion human beings, who have developed thousands of different ways of life. As the Q'ero visitors discovered, the differences can delight, puzzle, and disturb us. Indeed, we might imagine the reaction of a small group of New Yorkers if they were parachuted into a tiny Q'ero village at the top of the Andes.

For additional photos of the Q'ero, visit http://www1.suu.edu/faculty/Gordon/Images/photos/PhotoAlbum/Qero.html

Some differences in how people live are not important. Whereas many New Yorkers wear conservative business suits, the Q'ero prefer clothing that is brightly colored. Other cultural differences, however, can be quite profound. A survey of the world's people would show that some people have many children, whereas others have few; some honor the elderly, while others push them aside; some are peaceful, and others are warlike; and people have thousands of different religious beliefs and ideas about what is polite or rude, beautiful or ugly, pleasant or repulsive. This amazing capacity for difference is a matter of human culture.

WHAT IS CULTURE?

Culture is *the values, beliefs, behavior, and material objects that, together, form a people's way of life*. Culture includes what we think, how we act, and what we own. Culture is both a bridge to our past and a guide to the future (Soyinka, 1991).

To understand all that culture entails, we must distinguish between thoughts and things. **Nonmaterial culture** is *the intangible world of ideas created by members of a society*, ideas that range from altruism to zen. **Material culture,** on the other hand, is *the tangible things created by members of a society*, everything from armaments to zippers.

Not only does culture shape what we do, it also helps form our personalities—what we commonly, but wrongly, describe as "human nature." The warlike Yąnomamö of the Brazilian rain forest think aggression is natural, whereas, halfway around the world, the Semai of Malaysia live in peace and cooperation. The cultures of the United States and Japan both stress achievement and hard work, but members of our society value individualism more than the Japanese, who are more traditional and group-oriented.

Given the extent of cultural differences in the world and people's tendency to view their own way of life as better or more "natural" than others, it is no wonder that travelers—such as the Q'eros described in

Behavior people in one society consider routine can be chilling to members of another culture. In the Russian city of St. Petersburg, this young mother and her six-week-old son brave the 17°F temperatures for a dip in a nearby lake. To Russians, this is something of a national pastime. To some members of our society, however, this practice may seem cruel or even dangerous.

the opening to this chapter—often feel uneasy when they enter a different culture. This uneasiness is known as **culture shock,** *personal disorientation when experiencing an unfamiliar way of life*. The box on page

The author offers a short video discussing the challenges and benefits of travel at http://www.TheSociologyPage.com

62 presents another experience of culture shock: the story of a researcher making his first visit to the home of the Yąnomamö people living in the Amazon region of South America.

December 1, Istanbul, Turkey. Harbors everywhere, it seems, have two things in common: ships and cats. Istanbul, the tenth port on our voyage, is awash with felines, prowling about in search of an easy meal. People certainly change from place to place—but not cats.

Confronting the Yąnomamö: The Experience of Culture Shock

A small aluminum motorboat chugged steadily along the muddy Orinoco River, deep within South America's vast tropical rain forest. Anthropologist Napoleon Chagnon was nearing the end of a three-day journey to the home territory of the Yąnomamö, one of the most technologically simple societies on Earth.

Some 12,000 Yąnomamö live in villages scattered along the border of Venezuela and Brazil. Their way of life could hardly be more different from our own. The Yąnomamö wear little clothing and live without electricity, automobiles, or other familiar conveniences. Their traditional weapon, used for hunting and warfare, is the bow and arrow. Most Yąnomamö have had little contact with the outside world, so Chagnon would be as strange to them as they would be to him.

By 2:00 in the afternoon, Chagnon had almost reached his destination. The hot sun and humid air were almost unbearable. He was soaked with perspiration, and his face and hands swelled from the bites of gnats swarming around him. But he scarcely noticed, so excited was he that in just a few moments he would be face to face with people unlike any he had ever known.

Chagnon's heart pounded as the boat slid onto the riverbank. Chagnon and his guide climbed from the boat and headed toward the sounds of a nearby village, pushing through the dense undergrowth. Chagnon describes what happened next:

> I looked up and gasped when I saw a dozen burly, naked, sweaty, hideous men staring at us down the shafts of their drawn arrows! Immense wads of green tobacco were stuck between their lower teeth and lips making them look even more hideous, and strands of

dark green slime dripped or hung from their nostrils—strands so long that they clung to their [chests] or drizzled down their chins.

> My next discovery was that there were a dozen or so vicious, underfed dogs snapping at my legs, circling me as if I were to be their next meal. I just stood there holding my notebook, helpless and pathetic. Then the stench of the decaying vegetation and filth hit me and I almost got sick. I was horrified. What kind of welcome was this for the person who came here to live with you and learn your way of life, to become friends with you? (1992:11–12)

Fortunately for Chagnon, the Yąnomamö villagers recognized his guide and lowered their weapons. Though reassured that he would survive the afternoon, Chagnon was still shaken by his inability to make any sense of the people surrounding him. And this was to be his home for a year and a half! He wondered why he had forsaken physics to study human culture in the first place.

Source: Chagnon (1992).

No way of life is "natural" to humanity, even though most people around the world view their own behavior that way. What comes naturally to members of our species is creating culture. Every other form of life—from ants and crocodiles to robins and zebras—behaves in uniform, species-specific ways. To a traveler, the enormous diversity of human life stands out in contrast to the behavior of, say, cats, which is the same everywhere. This uniformity follows from the fact that most living creatures are guided by *instinct*, biological programming over which an animal has no control. A few animals—notably chimpanzees and related primates—have the capacity for limited culture, as researchers have noted by observing them use tools and teach simple skills to their offspring. But the creative power of humans far exceeds that of any other form of life. In short, *only humans rely on culture rather than instinct to ensure the survival of their kind* (Harris, 1987).

with numerous new medical or psychological conditions ranging from the "Cinderella complex" to the "Casanova complex" and even "soap opera syndrome." And U.S. courts are clogged by lawsuits blaming someone for misfortunes that we used to accept as part of life.

What's going on here? Is U.S. culture changing? Historically, our cultural ideal was rugged individualism, the idea that people are responsible for whatever triumph or tragedy befalls them. But this value has been eroded in a number of ways. First, everyone is more aware (partly through the work of sociologists) of how society shapes our lives. Therefore, categories of people other than those who have suffered real historical disadvantages (such as Native Americans, African Americans, and women) now say they are victims. The latest victims include white men who claim that "everybody gets special treatment but us."

Second, especially since they began advertising their services in 1977, many lawyers have encouraged a sense of injustice among clients they hope to represent in court. The number of million-dollar lawsuit awards has risen more than twenty-five–fold in the last twenty-five years.

Finally, a proliferation of "rights groups" promotes what Amitai Etzioni calls "rights inflation." Beyond the traditional constitutional liberties are many newly claimed rights: those of hunters (as well as animals), the rights of smokers (and nonsmokers), the right of women to control their bodies (and the rights of the unborn), and the right to own a gun (and the right to be safe from violence). Expanding claims for unmet rights create victims (and victimizers) on all sides.

Does this shift toward victimization signal a fundamental realignment in our individualistic culture? Perhaps, but the new popularity of being a victim also

springs from some established cultural forces. For example, the claim to victimization depends on a longstanding belief that everyone has the right to life, liberty, and the pursuit of happiness. What is new, however, is that the explosion of "rights" now does more than alert us to clear cases of injustice: It lessens our responsibility for our own lives.

What do you think?

1. *Do you think our cultural emphasis on individualism is weaker today than in the past? Why?*

2. *Do you think the United States has experienced "rights inflation"? Why or why not?*

3. *Does using the sociological perspective encourage us to view people as victims? Why or why not?*

Sources: Based on Etzioni (1991), Taylor (1991), Hollander (1995), and Roche (1999).

Values: Sometimes in Conflict

Looking over Williams's list, we see that some values are inconsistent and even opposed to one another (Lynd, 1967; Bellah et al., 1985; Ray, 1997). For example, people in the United States believe in equality of opportunity, yet they may also discriminate against others because of their sex or race.

Conflict between values reflects the cultural diversity of U.S. society and also cultural change by which new trends develop alongside older traditions. Recently, for example, what some observers call a "culture of victimization" has arisen to challenge our society's longstanding belief in individual responsibility (Best, 1997; Furedi, 1998). The box takes a closer look.

Value conflict causes strain and often leads to awkward balancing acts in our beliefs. Sometimes we

decide one value is more important than another by, for example, supporting equal opportunity while opposing the acceptance of homosexual people in the U.S. military. In such cases, we simply learn to live with the contradictions.

NORMS

Most people in the United States are eager to gossip about "who's hot" and "who's not." Members of Peru's Q'ero society, however, condemn such behavior as rude and divisive. Both patterns illustrate the operation of **norms**, *rules and expectations by which a society guides the behavior of its members.* Some norms are *proscriptive:* They state what we should *not* do, as, for example, when health officials warn us to avoid casual sex. *Prescriptive* norms, on the other hand, state what

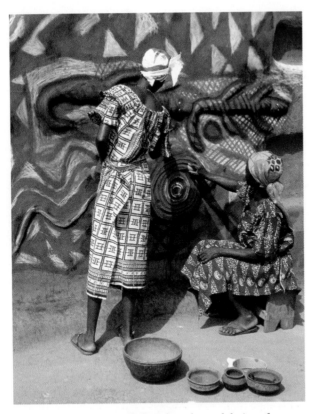

Standards of beauty—including the color and design of everyday surroundings—vary significantly from one culture to another. These two Nankani women put the finishing touches on their lavishly decorated homes. Members of North American and European societies, by contrast, make far less use of bright colors and intricate detail so that their housing appears much more subdued.

we *should* do, as when U.S. schools teach "safe-sex" practices.

Most important norms in a culture apply everywhere and at all times. For example, parents expect obedience from young children regardless of the setting. Other norms depend on the situation. In the United States, we expect the audience to applaud after a musical performance, we may applaud (although it is not expected) at the end of a classroom lecture, but we do not applaud when a priest or rabbi finishes a sermon.

Mores and Folkways

William Graham Sumner (1959; orig. 1906), an early U.S. sociologist, recognized that some norms are more important to our lives than others. Sumner coined the term **mores** (pronounced "more-ays") to refer to *norms that are widely observed and have great moral significance*. Mores, or *taboos*, include our society's prohibition against adults engaging in sexual relations with children.

People pay less attention to **folkways**, *norms for routine, casual interaction*. Examples include ideas about appropriate greetings and proper dress. In short, mores distinguish between right and wrong, whereas folkways draw a line between right and rude. A man who does not wear a tie to a formal dinner party may raise eyebrows for violating folkways. However, if he were to arrive at the party wearing *only* a tie, he would violate cultural mores and invite more serious sanctions.

Social Control

Mores and folkways are the basic rules of everyday life. Although we sometimes bristle when others pressure us to conform, we all can see that norms make our dealings with others more orderly and predictable. Observing or breaking the rules of social life prompts a response from others, in the form of reward or punishment. *Sanctions*—whether an approving smile or a raised eyebrow—operate as a system of **social control**, *various means by which members of a society encourage conformity to norms*.

As we learn cultural norms, we acquire the capacity to evaluate our own behavior. Doing wrong (say, downloading a term paper from the Internet) can cause both *shame* (the painful sense that others disapprove of our actions) and *guilt* (a negative judgment we make of ourselves). Only cultural creatures can experience shame and guilt. This is probably what Mark Twain had in mind when he remarked that people "are the only animals that blush—or need to."

"IDEAL" AND "REAL" CULTURE

Values and norms do not describe actual behavior so much as they suggest how we *should* behave. We must remember that *ideal* culture always differs from *real* culture—what actually occurs in everyday life. To illustrate, most women and men agree on the importance of sexual fidelity in marriage. Even so, in one study, about 25 percent of married men and 10 percent of married women reported being sexually unfaithful to their spouses at some point in their marriage (Laumann et al., 1994). But a culture's moral prodding is important all the same, calling to mind the old saying "Do as I say, not as I do."

MATERIAL CULTURE AND TECHNOLOGY

In addition to intangible elements such as values and norms, every culture includes a wide range of tangible (from the Latin word meaning "touchable") human creations, which sociologists call *artifacts*. The Chinese eat with chopsticks rather than knives and forks, the Japanese put mats rather than rugs on the floor, many men and women in India prefer flowing robes to the close-fitting clothing common in the United States. The material culture of a people may seem as strange to outsiders as their language, values, and norms.

A society's artifacts partly reflect underlying cultural values. The warlike Yạnomamö carefully craft their weapons and prize the poison tips on their arrows. By contrast, our society's emphasis on individualism and independence goes a long way toward explaining our high regard for the automobile: We own some 208 million motor vehicles—one for every licensed driver—and, on average, U.S. cars are the biggest in the world. Figure 3–1 shows that, even compared with other high-income nations, the United States stands out as a car-loving nation.

In addition to reflecting values, material culture also reflects a society's **technology**, *knowledge that people use to make a way of life in their surroundings*. The more complex a society's technology, the more its members are able (for better or worse) to shape the world for themselves.

Because we attach great importance to science and praise sophisticated technology, people in our society tend to judge cultures with simpler technology as less advanced. Some facts support such an assessment. For example, life expectancy for children born in the United States now exceeds seventy-six years; the life span of the Yạnomamö is only about forty years.

However, we must be careful not to make self-serving judgments about other cultures. Although many Yạnomamö are eager to acquire modern technology (such as steel tools and shotguns), they are generally well fed by world standards, and most are very satisfied with their lives (Chagnon, 1992). Also, although our powerful and complex technology has produced work-reducing devices and seemingly miraculous medical treatments, it has also contributed to unhealthy levels of stress, degraded the natural environment, and created weapons capable of destroying in a blinding flash everything that humankind has achieved.

Finally, technology is not equally distributed within our population. Although many of us cannot imagine life without personal computers, televisions,

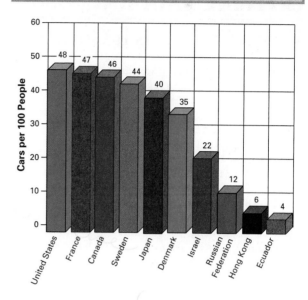

GLOBAL SNAPSHOT

FIGURE 3–1 Car Ownership in Global Perspective
Source: The World Bank (2001).

and CD players, many members of U.S. society cannot afford these luxuries. Others, including the Amish, reject them on principle. These "Plain People," who live in small farming communities across Pennsylvania, Ohio, and Indiana, shun most modern conveniences on religious grounds. With their traditional black garb and horse-drawn buggies, the Amish may seem like a curious relic of the past. Yet their communities flourish, grounded in strong families that give everyone a sense of identity and purpose. Some researchers have studied the Amish only to conclude that these communities are "islands of sanity in a culture gripped by commercialism and technology run wild" (Hostetler, 1980:4; Kraybill, 1994:28).

NEW INFORMATION TECHNOLOGY AND CULTURE

Many high-income nations, including the United States, have entered a postindustrial phase in which an increasing share of economic activity is based on computers and

Virtual Culture: Is It Good for Us?

January 16, Orlando, Florida. Disney World is a delight to the kids but a little disturbing to sociologists. It is ready-made culture: Streets, stores, and events re-create a nineteenth-century small town, populated with Disney characters. Here, life is carefully controlled to ensure a good time, with the ultimate purpose of relieving us of whatever cash we have left.

The Information Revolution is generating symbols—words, sounds, and images—faster than ever before and spreading these symbols across the nation and around the world. What does this new information technology mean for our way of life?

In centuries past, culture was a way of life transmitted from generation to generation. It was a heritage—a society's collective memory—that was authentically our own because it belonged to our ancestors (Schwartz, 1996). But in the emerging cyber-society, more and more cultural symbols are new, intentionally *created* by a small cultural elite of composers, writers, filmmakers, and others who work in the expanding information economy.

To illustrate, consider the changing character of cultural heroes, people who serve as role models and represent cultural ideals. A century ago, our heroes were real men and women who made a difference in the life of this nation: George Washington, Abigail Adams, Betsy Ross, Davy Crockett, Daniel Boone, Abraham Lincoln, and Harriet Tubman. Of course, when a society makes a hero of someone (almost always well after the person has died), they "clean up" the person's biography, highlighting the successes and overlooking the shortcomings. Even so, these people were authentic parts of our history.

Today's youngsters, by contrast, are fed a steady diet of *virtual culture*, images that spring from the minds of contemporary culture makers and reach them via a screen: on television, in the movies, or through computer networks. Today's "heroes" are Crocodile Dundee, Rug Rats, Pokémon, Batman, Barbie, Barney, a continuous flow of Disney characters, and the ever-smiling Ronald McDonald. Some of these cultural icons embody values that shape our way of life. But they have no historical reality, and almost all have been created for a single purpose: to make money.

What do you think?

1. *As the Information Revolution proceeds, do you think virtual culture will become increasingly important? Why or why not?*

2. *Does virtual culture erode or enhance our cultural traditions? Is that good or bad?*

3. *What image of this country do U.S. movies and television shows give to people abroad?*

Source: Thanks to Roland Johnson (1996) for the basic idea for this box.

new information technology. Whereas industrial production is centered on factories and machinery generating material goods, postindustrial production is based on computers and other electronic devices that create, process, store, and apply information.

In an information economy, workers need symbolic skills in place of the mechanical skills of the industrial age. Symbolic skills include the ability to speak, write, compute, design, and create images in art, advertising, and entertainment. New information technology also enables us to *generate culture* on an unprecedented scale. The box takes a closer look.

CULTURAL DIVERSITY: MANY WAYS OF LIFE IN ONE WORLD

In the United States, we are aware of our cultural diversity when we hear the distinctive accents of people from various geographic regions of the country, including New England, the Midwest, and the deep South. Ours is also a nation of religious pluralism, a land of class differences, and a home to individualists who try to be like no one else. Over the centuries, heavy immigration has made the United States the most *multicultural* of all high-income countries. By

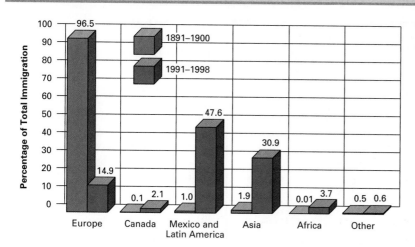

FIGURE 3–2
Recorded Immigration to the United States, by Region of Birth, 1891–1900 and 1991–1998

Sources: U.S. Department of Commerce (1930) and U.S. Immigration and Naturalization Service (1999).

contrast, historic isolation has made Japan the most *monocultural* of all high-income nations.

Between 1820 (when the U.S. government began keeping track of immigration) and 2000, more than 65 million people have come to these shores. Moreover, our cultural mix continues to increase as each year almost 1 million more people arrive. A century ago, as shown in Figure 3–2, almost all immigrants hailed from Europe; today, most newcomers are from Latin America and Asia. To understand the reality of life in the United States, we must move beyond broad cultural patterns and shared values to consider cultural diversity.

HIGH CULTURE AND POPULAR CULTURE

Cultural diversity can involve social class. In fact, in everyday talk, we usually use the word "culture" to mean art forms such as classical literature, music, dance, and painting. We describe people who regularly go to the opera or the theater as "cultured" because we think they appreciate the "finer things in life."

We speak less generously of ordinary people, assuming that everyday culture is somehow less worthy. We are tempted to judge the music of Beethoven as "more cultured" than the blues, couscous as better than cornbread, and polo as more polished than Ping-Pong.

Such judgments imply that many cultural patterns are readily accessible to only some members of a society (Hall & Neitz, 1993). Sociologists use the term **high culture**[1] to refer to *cultural patterns that distinguish a society's elite*; **popular culture** designates *cultural patterns that are widespread among a society's population*. At the same time, because common sense seems to suggest that high culture is superior to popular culture, sociologists prefer the term "culture" to refer to *all* elements of a society's way of life, including patterns of rich and poor alike.

Moreover, we should resist distinctions between high culture and popular culture for two reasons. First, neither elites nor ordinary people share all the same tastes and interests; people in both categories differ in numerous ways. Second, do we praise high culture because it is inherently better than popular culture or simply because its supporters have more money, power, and prestige? For example, there is no difference between a violin and a fiddle; however, we name the instrument one way when it is used to produce music typically enjoyed by a person of higher position and the other way when the musician plays works appreciated by people with lower social standing.

---

[1]The term "high culture" is derived from the term "highbrow." A century ago, people influenced by phrenology—the bogus nineteenth-century notion that personality was affected by the shape of the human skull—praised the tastes of those they called "highbrows" while dismissing the appetites of "lowbrows."

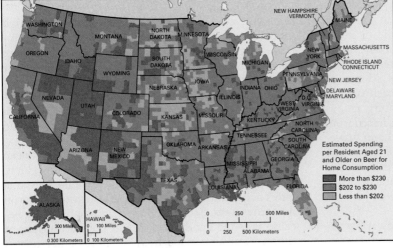

NATIONAL MAP 3–1
What'll Ya Have?
Popular Beverages across the United States

What people consume is one mark of their status as a "highbrow" or "lowbrow." Drinking wine at home is an indicator of highbrow standing. Well-to-do people not only enjoy a glass of wine with dinner but drink water from bottles rather than the tap, prefer Grey Poupon to Gulden's mustard, and favor Häagen-Dazs over the local Tastee-Freeze. Drinking beer, on the other hand, marks a person as a "lowbrow." Such a person has a low to moderate income, consumes a good deal of snack foods, and frequents fast-food restaurants. Looking at the maps, where have the "highbrows" and the "lowbrows" created centers of "high culture" and "popular culture"?

Source: *American Demographics* magazine, March 1998, p. 19. Reprinted with permission. © 1998, *American Demographics* magazine, Ithaca, New York.

National Map 3–1 looks at preferred alcoholic beverages to show the distribution of high and popular culture across the United States.

SUBCULTURE

The term **subculture** refers to *cultural patterns that set apart some segment of a society's population.* Young people who enjoy rap music, Polish Americans, frequent-flyer executives, New England Yankees, Colorado cowboys, the southern California beach crowd, jazz musicians, computer "nerds," campus poets, and wilderness campers—all display subcultural patterns.

It is easy, but often inaccurate, to place people in some subcultural category because almost everyone participates in many subcultures without necessarily having much commitment to any of them. In some cases, however, ethnicity and religion set people apart from one another, sometimes with tragic results.

Whether visual expression in lines and color is revered as "art" or dismissed as "graffiti" or even condemned as "vandalism" depends on the social standing of the creator. How would you characterize images such as this one, common in cities across North America? Is this art? Why or why not?

Consider the former nation of Yugoslavia in southeastern Europe. The recent Balkan war is only the latest chapter in a long history of hatred based on cultural differences. Before its breakup, this *one* small country used *two* alphabets, professed *three* religions, spoke *four* languages, was home to *five* major nationalities, was divided into *six* political republics, and absorbed the cultural influences of *seven* surrounding countries. Clearly, subcultures are a source not only of pleasing variety but also of tension and outright violence (cf. Sekulic, Massey, & Hodson, 1994).

Historically, we have viewed the United States as a melting pot where many nationalities blend into a single "American" culture. But given our cultural diversity, how accurate is the "melting pot" image? For one thing, subcultures involve not just *difference* but *hierarchy*. Too often, what we view as "dominant" or "mainstream" culture is a set of patterns favored by powerful segments of the population, and we view the lives of disadvantaged people as "subculture." Some sociologists, therefore, prefer to level the playing field of society by emphasizing multiculturalism.

MULTICULTURALISM

Multiculturalism is *an educational program recognizing the cultural diversity of the United States and promoting*
the equality of all cultural traditions. Multiculturalism is a sharp turn away from the past, when our society downplayed cultural diversity and defined itself primarily in terms of its European (and especially English) immigrants. Today, a spirited debate asks whether we should continue to stress these historical traditions or highlight our cultural diversity (Orwin, 1996; Rabkin, 1996).

E pluribus unum, the familiar Latin phrase that appears on all U.S. coins, means "out of many, one." This motto symbolizes not only our national political union but also the idea that immigrants from around the world have come together to form a new way of life.

From the outset, however, the many cultures did not melt together so much as harden into a hierarchy. At the top were the English, who formed a majority early in U.S. history and established English as the nation's dominant language. Further down, people of other backgrounds were advised to model themselves after "their betters." In practice, then, "melting" was really a process of Anglicization (adoption of English ways). As multiculturalists see it, early in our history, this society set up the English way of life as an ideal to which all should aspire and by which all should be judged.

Ever since, historians have reported events from the point of view of the English and other people of European ancestry, paying little attention to the perspectives and accomplishments of Native Americans

Any society is actually made up of countless different cultural patterns, some of which may seem strange, indeed, to most people. What cultural values are evident in the pierced noses and tattoos of these two men? Are these values completely at odds with our individualistic way of life?

and people of African and Asian descent. Multiculturalists call this view **Eurocentrism,** *the dominance of European (especially English) cultural patterns.* Molefi Kete Asante, an advocate of multiculturalism, argues that, like "the fifteenth-century Europeans who could not cease believing that the Earth was the center of the universe, many today find it difficult to cease viewing European culture as the center of the social universe" (1988:7).

One contested issue involves language. Some people believe English should be the official language of the United States. By 2001, legislatures in twenty-six states had enacted such laws. But some 45 million men and women—nearly one in six—speak a language other than English at home. Spanish is the second most commonly spoken language, but several hundred other tongues are also heard across the country, including Italian, German, French, Filipino, Japanese, Korean, Vietnamese, and a host of Native American languages. National Map 3–2 shows where in the United States large numbers of people speak a language other than English at home.

Proponents also paint multiculturalism as a way of coming to terms with our country's increasing social diversity. With the Asian and Hispanic populations of this country increasing rapidly, some analysts predict that today's children will live to see people of African, Asian, and Hispanic ancestry become a *majority* of this country's population.

Proponents also claim that multiculturalism is a good way to strengthen the academic achievement of African American children. To offset Eurocentrism, some multicultural educators are calling for **Afrocentrism,** *the dominance of African cultural patterns,* which they see as a corrective for centuries of minimizing or ignoring the cultural achievements of African societies and African Americans.

Although multiculturalism has found favor in recent years, it has provoked criticism as well. Opponents say it encourages divisiveness rather than unity, urging people to identify with their own category rather than with the nation as a whole. Instead of recognizing any common standards of truth, say critics, multiculturalism maintains that we should evaluate ideas according to the race (and sex) of those who present them. Our common humanity thus dissolves into an "African experience," an "Asian experience," and so on.

The bottom line, say critics, is that multiculturalism does not help minorities, as its supporters claim. Some multicultural policies (from African American studies to all-black dorms) seem to endorse the same racial segregation that our nation has struggled so long to end. Furthermore, in the early grades an Afrocentric curriculum may deny children a wide range of important knowledge and skills by teaching only certain topics from a single point of view. The historian Arthur Schlesinger, Jr. (1991:21), puts the matter bluntly: "If a Kleagle of the Ku Klux Klan wanted to use the schools to handicap black Americans, he could hardly come up with anything more effective than the 'Afrocentric' curriculum."

Is there any common ground in this debate? Almost everyone agrees that we need greater appreciation of our cultural diversity. But precisely where the balance is to be struck—between the *pluribus* and the *unum*—is likely to remain an issue for some time to come.

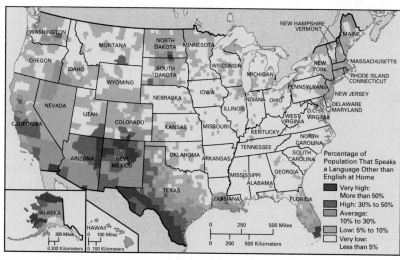

NATIONAL MAP 3–2
Language Diversity
across the United States

Of nearly 255 million people over the age of five in the United States, the 2000 census reports that 45 million (18 percent) typically speak a language other than English at home. Of these people, 60 percent speak Spanish, 15 percent use an Asian language, and the remaining 25 percent communicate with some other tongue (the Census Bureau lists 25 languages, each of which is favored by more than 100,000 people in the United States). The map shows that non–English speakers are concentrated in certain regions of the country. Which ones? What do you think accounts for this pattern?

COUNTERCULTURE

Cultural diversity also includes outright rejection of conventional ideas or behavior. **Counterculture** consists of *cultural patterns that strongly oppose those widely accepted within a society.*

In many societies, counterculture is linked to youth (Spates, 1976, 1983; Spates & Perkins, 1982). The youth-oriented counterculture of the 1960s, for example, rejected mainstream culture as overly competitive, self-centered, and materialistic. Instead, hippies and other counterculturalists favored a cooperative lifestyle in which "being" took precedence over "doing," and the capacity for personal growth—or "expanded consciousness"—was prized over material possessions such as homes and cars. Such differences led some people to "drop out" of the larger society.

Countercultures are still flourishing. In the 1990s, militaristic bands of men and women, deeply suspicious of the federal government, advocated dropping out of the political system. Countercultural extremism of this kind led to the bombing of the Oklahoma City federal building in 1995, killing 168 people.

CULTURAL CHANGE

Perhaps the most basic human truth of this world is "All things shall pass." Even the dinosaurs, which thrived on this planet for 160 million years (see the time line), remain today only as fossils. Will humanity survive for millions of years to come? All we can say with certainty is that, given our reliance on culture, for as long as we survive, the human record will show continuous change.

Table 3–1 compares student attitudes in 1968 (the height of the 1960s counterculture) and 2000. Some attitudes have changed only slightly. Today, as they did a generation ago, most men and women look forward to raising a family. But today's students are much more interested in making money than in developing a philosophy of life.

Change in one dimension of a culture usually sparks changes in others. For example, women's increased participation in the labor force parallels changing family patterns, including first marriages at a later age and a rising divorce rate. Such connections illustrate the principle of **cultural integration,** *the close relationships among various elements of a cultural system.*

TABLE 3–1 Attitudes among Students Entering U.S. Colleges. 1968 and 2000				
Life Objectives ("Essential" or "Very Important")		1968*	2000	Change
Develop a philosophy of life	Men	79%	43%	–36%
	Women	87	42	–45
Keep up with political affairs	Men	52	32	–20
	Women	52	25	–27
Help others in difficulty	Men	50	53	+ 3
	Women	71	69	– 2
Raise a family	Men	64	73	+ 9
	Women	72	73	+ 1
Be successful in my own business	Men	55	45	–10
	Women	32	35	+ 3
Be very well off financially	Men	51	76	+25
	Women	27	71	+44

*To allow comparisons, data from the early 1970s rather than 1968 are used for some items.

Sources: Richard G. Braungart and Margaret M. Braungart, "From Yippies to Yuppies: Twenty Years of Freshmen Attitudes," *Public Opinion*, vol. 11, no. 3 (September–October 1988): 53–56; Linda J. Sax, Alexander W. Astin, William S. Korn, and Kathryn M. Mahoney, *The American Freshman: National Norms for Fall 2000* (Los Angeles: UCLA Higher Education Research Institute, 2000).

Cultural Lag

Some elements of culture change faster than others. William Ogburn (1964) observed that technology moves quickly, generating new elements of material culture (such as test-tube babies) faster than nonmaterial culture (such as ideas about parenthood) can keep up with them. Ogburn called this inconsistency **cultural lag**, *the fact that some cultural elements change more quickly than others, which may disrupt a cultural system.* How are we to apply traditional notions about motherhood and fatherhood when one woman can give birth to a child using another woman's egg, which has been fertilized in a laboratory with the sperm of a total stranger?

Causes of Cultural Change

Cultural changes are set in motion in three ways. The first is *invention*, the process of creating new cultural elements. Invention has given us the telephone (1876), the airplane (1903), and the computer (the late 1940s), each of which has had a tremendous impact on our way of life. The process of invention goes on constantly, as indicated by the thousands of applications submitted annually to the U.S. Patent Office. The time line inside the front cover of this text shows other inventions that have changed our way of life.

Discovery, a second cause of cultural change, involves recognizing and better understanding something already in existence—from a distant star, to the foods of another culture, to women's athletic prowess. Many discoveries result from painstaking scientific research, but others are a stroke of luck, as in 1898, when Marie Curie left a rock on a piece of photographic paper, noticed that emissions from the rock exposed the paper, and thus discovered radium.

The third cause of cultural change is *diffusion*, the spread of cultural traits from one society to another. Because new information technology sends information around the globe in seconds, cultural diffusion has never been greater than it is today.

Certainly our own society has contributed many significant cultural elements to the world, ranging from jazz music to computers. Of course, diffusion works the other way, too, so that much of what we assume to be "American" actually comes from elsewhere. Clocks, newspapers, money, most clothing and furniture, and even the English language are derived from other cultures (Linton, 1937a).

ETHNOCENTRISM AND CULTURAL RELATIVISM

December 10, a small village in rural Morocco. Watching many of our shipmates browsing through a tiny ceramic factory, we feel confident in saying that North Americans are among the world's greatest shoppers. We delight in admiring hand-woven carpets in China or India, inspecting finely crafted metals in Turkey, or collecting the beautifully colored porcelain tiles we find here in Morocco. And, of course, all these items are wonderful bargains. But one major reason for the low prices is unsettling: Many products from the world's low- and middle-income countries are produced by children—some as young as five or six—who work long days for extremely low wages.

We think of childhood as a time of innocence and freedom from adult burdens such as regular work. In poor countries throughout the world, however, families depend on income earned by children. So what people in one society think of as right and natural, people elsewhere find puzzling and even immoral. Perhaps the Chinese philosopher Confucius had it right when he noted that "All people are the same; it's only their habits that are different."

Just about every imaginable idea or behavior is commonplace somewhere in the world, and this cultural variation causes travelers equal measures of excitement and distress. The Australians flip light switches down to turn them on, whereas North Americans flip them up; the Japanese name intersections rather than streets, a practice that regularly confuses North Americans, who do the opposite; Egyptians stand very close to others in conversation, which irritates North Americans, used to maintaining several feet of "personal space." In rural Morocco, most bathrooms lack toilet paper, causing considerable consternation among Westerners unaccustomed to using the left hand for bathroom hygiene.

Given that a particular culture is the basis for everyone's reality, it is no wonder that people everywhere exhibit **ethnocentrism,** *the practice of judging another culture by the standards of one's own culture.* Some ethnocentrism is necessary for people to be emotionally attached to their way of life. But ethnocentrism also generates misunderstanding and sometimes conflict.

Even our language is culturally biased. Centuries ago, people in Europe and North America called China the "Far East." But this term, unknown to the Chinese, is an ethnocentric expression for a region that is far east *of us.* The Chinese name for their country translates as "Central Kingdom," suggesting that they, like us, see their own society as the center of the world. The map on page 80 shows ethnocentrism at work in a "down under" view of the Western Hemisphere.

The logical alternative to ethnocentrism is **cultural relativism,** *the practice of evaluating a culture by its own standards.* Cultural relativism is a difficult attitude to adopt: It requires understanding unfamiliar values and norms and suspending cultural standards we have known all our lives. At the same time, as people of the world come into increasing contact with one another, the importance of understanding other cultures becomes ever greater.

Businesses in the United States are learning that success in the global economy depends on cultural awareness. For example, General Motors learned the hard way that its Nova wasn't selling well

Most people in the affluent United States take for granted that childhood should be a carefree time of life devoted to learning and play. In low-income societies of the world, however, poor families depend on the income earned by children, some of whom perform long days of heavy physical labor. We may not want to accept all cultural practices as "natural" just because they exist. But what universal standards can be used to judge social patterns as either right or wrong?

in Spanish-speaking nations because the name in Spanish means "No Go." Coors's phrase "Turn It Loose" startled customers by proclaiming that the beer would cause diarrhea. Braniff Airlines turned "Fly in Leather" into clumsy Spanish reading "Fly Naked." Eastern Airlines transformed its slogan "We Earn Our Wings Daily"

 In two brief videos, the author considers issues of cultural relativism: http://www. TheSociologyPage.com

The View from "Down Under"

North America should be "up" and South America "down," or so we think. But, because we live on a globe, such notions are conventions rather than absolutes. The reason that this map of the Western Hemisphere looks wrong to us is not that it is geographically inaccurate; it simply violates our ethnocentric assumption that the United States should be "above" the rest of the Americas.

into "We Fly Every Day to Heaven." Frank Purdue fell victim to poor marketing when his pitch "It Takes a Tough Man to Make a Tender Chicken" ended up as "A Sexually Excited Man Will Make a Chicken Affectionate" in Spanish (Helin, 1992).

But cultural relativism introduces problems of its own. If almost any kind of behavior is normative *somewhere* in the world, does that mean everything is equally right? Does the fact that poor Moroccan families benefit from having their children work long hours justify child labor?

Because we all are members of a single species, surely there must be some universal standards of proper conduct. But what are they? And, in trying to develop them, how can we avoid imposing our own standards of fair play on others? There are no simple answers. But when confronting an unfamiliar cultural practice, resist making judgments before grasping what members of that culture think of the issue. Remember, also, to think about your own way of life as others might see it. After all, what we gain most from studying others is better insight into ourselves.

A GLOBAL CULTURE?

Today, more than ever before, we can observe many of the same cultural practices the world over. Walking the streets of Seoul (South Korea), Kuala Lumpur (Malaysia), Madras (India), Cairo (Egypt), and Casablanca (Morocco), we find jeans, hear familiar pop music, and see advertising for many of the same products we use at home. Recall from Global Map 3–1 that English is rapidly emerging as the preferred second language of most of the world. Are we witnessing the birth of a single global culture?

It is true that societies around the world have more contact with one another than ever before, involving the flow of goods, information, and people:

1. **The global economy: the flow of goods.** There has never been more international trade. The global economy has spread many of the same consumer goods (from cars and TV shows to music and fashions) throughout the world.

2. **Global communication: the flow of information.** Satellite-based communication enables people to experience the sights and sounds of events taking place thousands of miles away, often as they happen.

3. **Global migration: the flow of people.** Knowing about the rest of the world motivates people to move where they imagine life will be better. Moreover, today's transportation technology, especially air travel, makes relocating easier than ever before. As a result, in most countries, significant numbers of people were born elsewhere (including some 30 million people who are now in the United States, 11 percent of the population).

These global links make the cultures of the world more similar. But there are three important limitations to the global culture thesis. First, the global flow of goods, information, and people is uneven. Generally speaking, urban areas (centers of commerce, communication, and people) have stronger ties to one another, and rural villages remain isolated. Furthermore, the greater economic and military power of North America and Western Europe means that these regions influence the rest of the world more than happens the other way around.

Second, the global culture thesis assumes that people everywhere are able to afford various new goods and services. As Chapter 12 ("Global Stratification") explains, desperate poverty in much of the world deprives people of even the basic necessities of a safe and secure life.

Third, although many cultural practices are found throughout the world, people everywhere do not attach the same meanings to them. Do teenagers in Tokyo understand hip hop the way their counterparts in New York or Los Angeles do? Similarly, we enjoy foods from around the world while knowing little about the lives of the people who created them. In short, people everywhere look at the world through their own cultural lenses (Featherstone, 1990; Hall & Neitz, 1993).

THEORETICAL ANALYSIS OF CULTURE

Culture helps us make sense of ourselves and the surrounding world. And sociologists have the special task of comprehending culture. They use several theoretical approaches.

STRUCTURAL-FUNCTIONAL ANALYSIS

The structural-functional paradigm depicts culture as a complex strategy for meeting human needs. Borrowing from the philosophical doctrine of *idealism*, this approach considers values as the core of a culture (Parsons, 1966; Williams, 1970). In other words, cultural values give meaning to life and bind people together. Countless other aspects of culture function in various ways to support a way of life.

Thinking functionally helps us understand an unfamiliar way of life. Take, for example, the Amish farmer plowing hundreds of acres of an Ohio farm with a team of horses. His farming methods may violate our cultural value of efficiency, but from the Amish point of view, hard work functions to develop the discipline necessary for a highly religious way of life. Long days of working together make the Amish self-sufficient while unifying families and communities.

Of course, Amish practices have dysfunctions as well. The hard work and strict religious discipline are too demanding for some, who end up leaving the community. Then, too, religious devotion sometimes prevents compromise, resulting in lasting divisions within the Amish world (Hostetler, 1980; Kraybill, 1989; Kraybill & Olshan, 1994).

If cultures are strategies for meeting human needs, we would expect to find many common patterns around the world. **Cultural universals** are *traits that are part of*

Following the structural-functional paradigm, what do you make of the Amish practice of "barn raising," by which everyone in a community joins together to raise a family's new barn in a day? Why is such a ritual almost unknown in rural areas outside of Amish communities?

every known culture. Comparing hundreds of cultures, George Murdock (1945) identified dozens of cultural universals. One common element is the family, which functions everywhere to control sexual reproduction and oversee the care of children. Funeral rites, too, are found everywhere, because all human communities cope with the reality of death. Jokes are another cultural universal, serving as a safe means of releasing social tensions.

Critical evaluation. The strength of the structural-functional paradigm is showing how culture operates to meet human needs. Yet, by emphasizing a society's dominant cultural patterns, this approach largely ignores cultural diversity. Moreover, because this approach emphasizes cultural stability, it downplays the importance of change. In short, cultural systems are not as stable or as free of conflict as structural functionalism leads us to believe.

SOCIAL-CONFLICT ANALYSIS

The social-conflict paradigm stresses the link between culture and inequality. From this point of view, any cultural trait benefits some members of society at the expense of others.

We might well begin a conflict analysis by asking why certain values dominate a society in the first place. Many conflict theorists, especially Marxists, argue that culture is shaped by a society's system of economic production. "It is not the consciousness of men that determines their being," Marx asserted, "it is their social being that determines their consciousness" (Marx & Engels, 1978:4; orig. 1859). Social-conflict theory, then, is rooted in the philosophical doctrine of *materialism*, which holds that a society's system of material production (such as our own industrial-capitalist economy) has a powerful effect on the rest of a culture. This materialist approach contrasts with the idealist leanings of structural functionalism.

Social-conflict analysis ties our competitive values to our society's capitalist economy, which serves the interests of our nation's wealthy elite. The culture of capitalism further teaches us to think that rich and powerful people have more energy and talent than others and therefore deserve their wealth and privileges. Viewing capitalism as somehow "natural" also discourages efforts to reduce economic disparity.

Eventually, however, the strains of inequality erupt into movements for social change. Two recent examples in the United States are the civil rights movement and the women's movement. Both seek greater equality, and both encounter opposition from defenders of the status quo.

Critical evaluation. The social-conflict paradigm proposes that cultural systems do not address human needs

Using an evolutionary perspective, sociobiologists point to a double standard by which men treat women as sexual objects more than women treat men that way. While this may be so, many sociologists counter that behavior—such as that shown in Ruth Orkin's photograph, American Girl in Italy*—is more correctly understood as resulting from a culture of male domination.*
Copyright 1952, 1980 Ruth Orkin/Getty Images, Inc.

equally, allowing some people to dominate others. This inequity, in turn, generates pressure toward change.

Yet, by stressing the divisiveness of culture, this paradigm understates the ways in which cultural patterns integrate members of society. Therefore, we should consider both social-conflict and structural-functional insights for a fuller understanding of culture.

SOCIOBIOLOGY

We know culture is a human creation, but does human biology influence how culture unfolds? A third theoretical paradigm, standing with one leg in biology and one in sociology, is **sociobiology,** *a theoretical paradigm that explores ways in which human biology affects how we create culture.*

Sociobiology rests on the theory of evolution proposed by Charles Darwin (1859) in his book *On the Origin of Species.* Darwin asserted that living organisms change over long periods of time as a result of *natural selection,* a matter of four simple principles. First, all living things live to reproduce themselves. Second, the blueprint for reproduction is in the genes, the basic units of life that carry traits of one generation into the next. Third, random variation in genes allows a species to "try out" new life patterns in a particular environment. This variation allows some organisms to survive better than others

and pass on their advantageous genes to their offspring. Finally, over thousands of generations, the genetic patterns that promote reproduction survive and become dominant. In this way, as biologists say, a species *adapts* to its environment, and dominant traits emerge as the "nature" of the organism.

Sociobiologists claim that the large number of cultural universals reflects the fact that all humans are members of a single biological species. It is our common biology that underlies, for example, the apparently universal "double standard" of sexual behavior. As sex researcher Alfred Kinsey put it, "Among all people everywhere in the world, the male is more likely than the female to desire sex with a variety of partners" (quoted in Barash, 1981:49). But why?

We all know that children result from joining a woman's egg with a man's sperm. But the biological importance of a single sperm and of a single egg are quite different. For healthy men, sperm are a renewable resource produced by the testes throughout most of the life course. A man releases hundreds of millions of sperm in a single ejaculation—technically, enough to fertilize every woman in North America (Barash, 1981:47). A newborn female's ovaries, however, contain her entire lifetime allotment of follicles, or immature eggs. A woman generally releases a single egg cell from her ovaries each month. So, whereas a man is biologically capable of fathering thousands of offspring, a woman is able to bear only a small number of children.

The United States and Canada: Are They Culturally Different?

To many people in the United States, this country *is* "America." But, to the north lies another large, high-income nation: Canada. How does the culture of Canada compare with U.S. culture?

One important point to make at the start is that both nations are *multicultural*. Just as immigration has brought people to the United States from all over the world, it has done the same in Canada. Also as in the United States, most early immigrants came from Europe, and most recent immigrants have come from Asia and Latin America. Vancouver, for example, on the western Canadian coast, has a large Chinese community on the same order as the Spanish community in Los Angeles.

Canada and the United States differ in one important respect. Historically, Canada has had *two* dominant cultures: French (about 25 percent of the population) and British (roughly 40 percent). People of French ancestry are a large majority of the province of Quebec (where French is the official language) and a large minority of New Brunswick (which is officially bilingual).

Otherwise, do Canada and the United States share the same dominant values? Seymour Martin Lipset (1985) finds that the two nations differ to some degree. The United States declared independence from Great Britain in 1776; Canada formally separated from Great Britain only in 1982. Thus, Lipset continues, the dominant culture of Canada lies somewhere between the cultures of the United States and Great Britain.

For example, the culture of the United States is more individualistic, whereas Canada's is more collective. In the United States, individualism is seen in the historical importance of the cowboy—a self-sufficient person—and even outlaws such as Jessie James and Billy the Kid are looked on as heroes because they bucked authority. In Canada, by contrast, it is the Mountie—Canada's well-known police officer—who is looked on with great respect.

Politically, people in the United States tend to think individuals ought to do things for themselves. In Canada, however, there is a strong sense that government should look after the interests of everyone, much as there is in Great Britain. This is one reason, for example, that Canada has a much broader social welfare system (including universal health care) than the United States (the only high-income nation without such a program). Likewise, about half of all U.S. households own one or more guns, and the idea that individuals are entitled to own a gun is strong—although controversial—in this country. In Canada, few households have a gun, and government greatly restricts gun ownership, as in Great Britain.

Sources: Lipset (1985) and Macionis & Gerber (2001).

Given this biological difference, men reproduce their genes most efficiently by being promiscuous, readily engaging in sex. However, this scheme opposes the reproductive interests of women. Each of a woman's pregnancies demands that she carry the child for nine months, give birth, and provide care for some time afterward. Therefore, efficient reproduction on the part of the woman depends on carefully selecting a mate whose qualities (beginning with the likelihood that he will simply stay around) will contribute to their child's survival and, later, successful reproduction (Remoff, 1984).

The "double standard" certainly involves more than biology and is tangled up with the historical domination of women by men (Barry, 1983). But sociobiology suggests that this cultural pattern, like many others, has an underlying bio-logic. Simply put, the double standard exists around the world because women and men everywhere tend toward distinctive reproductive strategies.

Critical evaluation. Sociobiology has generated intriguing theories about the biological roots of some cultural patterns. But the approach remains controversial for several reasons.

First, some critics fear that sociobiology may revive biological arguments from a century ago that touted the superiority of one race or sex. But defenders counter that sociobiology rejects the past pseudo-science of racial superiority. In fact, sociobiology unites all of humanity because all people share a single evolutionary history. Sociobiology does assert that men and women differ biologically in some ways that culture cannot overcome. But, far from claiming that males are somehow more important than females, sociobiology emphasizes that both sexes are vital to human reproduction.

Second, say the critics, sociobiologists have little evidence to support their theories. Research to date suggests that biological forces do not determine human behavior in any rigid sense. Rather, humans *learn* behavior within a cultural system. The contribution of sociobiology, then, lies in explaining why some cultural patterns are learned more readily than others (Barash, 1981).

CULTURE AND HUMAN FREEDOM

Underlying the discussion in this chapter is an important question: To what extent are cultural creatures free? Does culture bind us to each other and to the past? Or does culture enhance our capacity for individual thought and independent choices?

CULTURE AS CONSTRAINT

Humans cannot live without culture. But the capacity for culture does have some drawbacks. We may be the only animals who name ourselves, but living in a symbolic world means that we are also the only creatures who experience alienation. Moreover, culture is largely a matter of habit, limiting our choices and driving us to repeat troubling patterns, such as racial prejudice, in each new generation. In addition, in this age of new information technology, we may wonder at the extent to which business-dominated media manipulate our culture in pursuit of profits.

Finally, our society's emphasis on competitive achievement urges us toward excellence, yet this pattern also isolates us from one another. Material things comfort us in some ways but divert us from the security and satisfaction that come from close relationships and spiritual strength.

CULTURE AS FREEDOM

For better or worse, human beings are cultural creatures, just as ants and bees are prisoners of their biology. But there is a crucial difference. Biological instincts create a ready-made world; culture, by contrast, forces us to choose as we make and remake a world for ourselves. No better evidence of this freedom exists than the cultural diversity of our own society and the even greater human diversity around the world.

Learning more about this cultural diversity is one goal shared by sociologists. The final box offers some contrasts between the cultures of the United States and Canada. But, wherever we may live, the better we understand the workings of the surrounding culture, the better prepared we are to use the freedom it offers us.

SUMMARY

1. Culture is a way of life shared by members of a society. Several species have limited capacity for culture, but only human beings rely on culture for survival.

2. As the human brain evolved, the first elements of culture appeared some 3 million years ago; culture replaced biological instincts as our species' primary strategy for survival.

3. Culture relies on symbols. Language is the symbolic system by which one generation transmits culture to the next.

4. Values are culturally defined standards of what ought to be; beliefs are statements that people who share a culture hold to be true.

5. Cultural norms, which guide human behavior, are of two kinds: Mores have great moral significance, whereas folkways are everyday matters of politeness.

6. High culture consists of patterns that distinguish a society's elite; popular culture consists of widespread social patterns.

7. The United States stands among the most culturally diverse societies in the world. Subculture consists of distinctive cultural patterns supported by some part of a population, and counterculture of patterns strongly at odds with a conventional way of life. Multiculturalism is an educational effort to enhance awareness and appreciation of cultural diversity.

8. Invention, discovery, and diffusion all generate cultural change. Cultural lag results as some parts of a cultural system change faster than others.

9. Ethnocentrism involves judging others by the standards of one's own culture. By contrast, cultural relativism means evaluating another culture according to its own standards.

10. Global cultural patterns result from the worldwide flow of goods, information, and people.

11. Structural-functional analysis views culture as a generally stable system built on core values. Cultural patterns function to maintain the overall system.

12. The social-conflict paradigm envisions culture as a dynamic arena of inequality and conflict. Cultural patterns benefit some categories of people more than others.

13. Sociobiology studies how evolution shapes the human creation of culture.

14. Culture can constrain social possibilities, yet as cultural creatures, we have the capacity to shape and reshape our world to meet our needs and pursue our dreams.

KEY CONCEPTS

culture (p. 61) the values, beliefs, behavior, and material objects that, together, form a people's way of life

nonmaterial culture (p. 61) the intangible world of ideas created by members of a society

material culture (p. 61) the tangible things created by members of a society

culture shock (p. 61) personal disorientation when experiencing an unfamiliar way of life

symbols (p. 63) anything that carries a particular meaning recognized by people who share culture

language (p. 65) a system of symbols that allows people to communicate with one another

cultural transmission (p. 65) the process by which one generation passes culture to the next

Sapir-Whorf thesis (p. 65) the thesis that people perceive the world through the cultural lens of language

values (p. 67) culturally defined standards by which people assess desirability, goodness, and beauty and that serve as broad guidelines for social living

beliefs (p. 67) specific statements that people hold to be true

norms (p. 69) rules and expectations by which a society guides the behavior of its members

mores (p. 70) norms that are widely observed and have great moral significance

folkways (p. 70) norms for routine, casual interaction

social control (p. 70) various means by which members of a society encourage conformity to norms

technology (p. 71) knowledge that people use to make a way of life in their surroundings

high culture (p. 73) cultural patterns that distinguish a society's elite

popular culture (p. 73) cultural patterns that are widespread among a society's population

subculture (p. 74) cultural patterns that set apart some segment of a society's population

multiculturalism (p. 75) an educational program recognizing the cultural diversity of the United States and promoting the equality of all cultural traditions

Eurocentrism (p. 76) the dominance of European (especially English) cultural patterns

Afrocentrism (p. 76) the dominance of African cultural patterns

counterculture (p. 77) cultural patterns that strongly oppose those widely accepted within a society

cultural integration (p. 77) the close relationships among various elements of a cultural system

cultural lag (p. 78) the fact that some cultural elements change more quickly than others, which may disrupt a cultural system

ethnocentrism (p. 79) the practice of judging another culture by the standards of one's own culture

cultural relativism (p. 79) the practice of evaluating a culture by its own standards

cultural universals (p. 81) traits that are part of every known culture

sociobiology (p. 83) a theoretical paradigm that explores ways in which human biology affects how we create culture

CRITICAL-THINKING QUESTIONS

1. In the United States, hot dogs, hamburgers, French fries, and ice cream have long been considered national favorites. What cultural patterns help explain the love for these kinds of foods?

2. What cultural lessons do games such as King of the Mountain, Tag, or Keep-Away teach our children? What about a schoolroom spelling bee? What cultural values are expressed by children's stories such as *The Little Engine That Could* and board games such as "Chutes and Ladders," "Monopoly," and "Risk"?

3. To what extent, in your opinion, is a global culture emerging? Do you regard the prospect of a global culture as positive or negative? Why?

4. Have you ever identified with one or more subcultures? If so, which? How are they distinctive?

APPLICATIONS AND EXERCISES

1. Try to find someone on campus who has lived in another country. Ask for a chance to discuss how the culture of that society differs from the way of life here. Does the other person see U.S. culture differently from most of us?

2. Make a list of words with the prefix *self* (*self-service*, *self-image*, *self-esteem*, *self-destructive*, and so on); there are hundreds of them. What does this high number suggest about our way of life?

3. An easy way to study popular culture is to pick up a number of superhero comic books. Examine them to see why some people are defined as heroes and others as villains. Does gender figure in this process? (cf. Hall & Lucal, 1999)

4. Watch a Disney film such as *The Little Mermaid, Aladdin, Pocahontas,* or *Mulan.* All of these films share cultural themes, which explains their popularity. According to these films, how should young people behave toward their parents? What makes these films especially "American"?

5. Packaged in the back of this new textbook is an interactive CD-ROM that offers a variety of study and review materials intended to help you better understand the material covered in this chapter. For this chapter, the CD-ROM contains an author's video, Real Life Sociology videos, other relevant audio and video, interactive map animations, audio journal entries from the author, Web links, and much more.

SITES TO SEE

http://www.prenhall.com/macionis

Visit the interactive *Companion Website*™ that accompanies this text. Begin by clicking on the cover of your book. You will find a chapter-by-chapter study guide, practice tests, and a significant portion of the text for on-line review, as well as many suggested Web links.

http://www.macionis.com
(or http://www.TheSociologyPage.com)

Visit the author's Web page to view short videos on the lessons and challenges of traveling in an unfamiliar setting.

http://www.nationalgeographic.com

Visit the Web site for the National Geographic Society.

This site offers information on world cultures, including search engines and a library of maps.

http://www.gorilla.org

The Gorilla Foundation operates a Web site where you can follow the progress researchers are making in teaching a 450-pound gorilla named Koko to use sign language.

http://www.aaanet.org

Anthropologists study cultures all over the world. This is the Web site for the American Anthropological Association, where you can find out more about this discipline, which is closely related to sociology.

INVESTIGATE WITH CONTENTSELECT

Follow the instructions found on page 23 of this textbook to enter this chapter of the book's *Companion Website*™. Once in the chapter, click on the ContentSelect icon at the bottom left of your screen and enter your personal User ID and Password. Enter keywords such as "Amish," "multiculturalism," and "immigration," and the search engine will help you become an effective researcher.

Tosa (attributed to)
People along the River

Detail from screen representing the River Festival. 17th century. Painting on paper. Photo: Arnaudet. Musée des Arts Asiatiques–Guimet, Paris, France. Réunion des Musées Nationaux/Art Resource, N.Y.

SOCIETY

Sididi Ag Inaka has never logged on to the Internet, sent a fax, or even spoken on a cell phone. In today's high-technology world, these facts may seem strange enough. But neither Inaka nor anyone else in his family has ever seen a television or read a newspaper.

Who are these people? They are Tuareg nomads who wander the vastness of the Sahara in western Africa, north of the city of Timbuktu in the nation we know as Mali. Known as the "blue men of the desert" for the flowing blue robes worn by both men and women, the Tuareg herd camels, goats, and sheep and live in camps where the sand blows and the daytime temperature often reaches 120 degrees. Life is hard, but most try to

hold onto traditional ways. With a look of determination, Inaka says, "My father was a nomad, his father was a nomad, I am a nomad, my children will be nomads."

The Tuaregs are among the poorest people of the world, living a simple and difficult existence. When the rains fail to come, they and their animals are at risk for their lives. Inaka and his people are a society set apart, isolated from the rest of humanity and nearly untouched by modern ideas and advanced technology. To many, no doubt, they seem a curious throwback to the past. But Inaka does not complain: "This is the life of my ancestors. This is the life that we know" (Buckley, 1996; Matloff, 1997; Lovgren, 1998).

Many kinds of human societies have existed in the past, and we still find remarkable diversity today, as the story of the Tuareg shows. But what is a society? How and why have societies changed over the course of human history?

Society is *people who interact in a defined territory and share culture.* In this chapter, we shall examine this deceptively simple term from four different angles. We begin with **Gerhard Lenski,** who described the changing character of human societies over the last 10,000 years. He explained the importance of *technology* and its revolutionary consequences for social life. Then we turn to three of sociology's founders. **Karl Marx,** like Lenski, understood human history as a long and complex process. For Marx, however, the story of society centered on *social conflict* that arises from how people produce material goods. **Max Weber** took another approach, showing that the power of *ideas* also shapes society. Weber contrasted the traditional thinking of simple societies with the rational thought that dominates our modern way of life. Finally, **Emile Durkheim** helped us see the different

ways in which traditional and modern societies hang together.

All four visions of society answer important questions: What makes people like the Tuareg of the Sahara so different from the society familiar to us? How and why do all societies change? What forces divide a society? What forces hold it together? Finally, after looking at the trends over time, we conclude this chapter by asking whether societies are getting better or worse.

GERHARD LENSKI: SOCIETY AND TECHNOLOGY

Members of our society, who take telephones and television as well as schools and hospitals for granted, must wonder at the nomads of the Sahara, who live the same simple life their ancestors did centuries ago. The work of Gerhard Lenski (Lenski, Nolan, & Lenski, 1995; Nolan & Lenski, 1999) helps us understand the great differences among societies that have flourished and declined throughout human history.

In technologically simple societies, successful hunting wins men great praise. However, the gathering of vegetation by women is a more dependable and easily available source of nutrition.

Lenski uses the term **sociocultural evolution** to refer to *the changes that occur as a society acquires new technology.* Societies with simple technology, such as the Tuareg, have little control over nature, so they can support only a small number of people. Technologically complex societies, though not necessarily better, support large numbers of people who live highly specialized lives.

In addition, the more technological information a society has, the faster it changes. Technologically simple societies change very slowly; Sididi Ag Inaka says he "lives the life of his ancestors." Modern, high-technology societies, on the other hand, change so quickly that dramatic transformations can occur during a single lifetime. Imagine asking someone who lived just a few generations ago for his or her opinion of beepers, phone sex, artificial hearts, test-tube babies, genetic engineering, e-mail, smart bombs, space shuttles, the threat of nuclear holocaust, transsexualism, computer hackers, and "tell all" talk shows.

In short, new technology sends ripples of change through a society's entire way of life. When our ancestors first discovered how to harness the power of the wind using a sail, they set the stage for building sailing ships, which took them to new lands, stimulated trade, and increased their military might. As a more recent example, consider how our lives are being changed by the spread of computer technology.

Drawing on Lenski's work, we will describe five types of societies according to their technology: hunting and gathering societies, horticultural and pastoral societies, agrarian societies, industrial societies, and postindustrial societies.

HUNTING AND GATHERING SOCIETIES

The simplest of all kinds of societies live by **hunting and gathering,** *the use of simple tools to hunt animals and gather vegetation.* From the emergence of our species 3 million years ago until just 12,000 years ago, *all* humans were hunters and gatherers. Even in 1800, there were many hunting and gathering societies in the world. Today, however, just a few remain, including the Aka and Pygmies of central Africa, the Bushmen of southwestern Africa, the Aborigines of Australia, the Kaska Indians of northwest Canada, and the Batek and Semai of Malaysia (Endicott, 1992; Hewlett, 1992).

With little control over their environment, hunters and gatherers spend most of their time searching for game and collecting edible plants. Only in lush areas where food is plentiful do hunters and gatherers have leisure time. Moreover, it takes a lot of land to support even a few people, so hunting and gathering societies are small bands with a few dozen members. They must also be nomadic, moving on as they deplete vegetation in an area or follow migratory animals. Although they return periodically to favored sites, they rarely form permanent settlements.

Hunting and gathering societies are built on kinship. The family obtains and distributes food, protects its members, and teaches the children. Everyone's life is much the same and is focused on getting the next meal. There is some specialization related to age and gender. The very young and the very old contribute what they can, and healthy adults secure most of the food. Women gather vegetation—the most reliable food source—and men take on the less certain task of hunting. Although men and women perform different tasks, most hunters and gatherers probably saw the sexes as having about the same social importance (Leacock, 1978).

Hunting and gathering societies have few formal leaders. Most recognize a *shaman,* or spiritual leader, who enjoys high prestige but receives no greater material rewards and must work to find food like everyone else. In short, hunting and gathering societies are egalitarian.

Hunters and gatherers use simple weapons—the spear, bow and arrow, and stone knife—but rarely to

Pastoralism historically has flourished in regions of the world where arid soil does not support crops. Pastoral people still thrive in northern Africa, living today much as they did a thousand years ago.

wage war. Their real enemy is the forces of nature: Storms and droughts can destroy their food supply, and there is little they can do in the event of accident or illness. Such vulnerability encourages cooperation and sharing, raising everyone's odds of survival. Nonetheless, many die in childhood, and no more than half reach age twenty (Lenski, Nolan, & Lenski, 1995:104).

During the twentieth century, technologically complex societies slowly closed in on the few remaining hunters and gatherers, reducing their food supply. Lenski claims that hunting and gathering societies are now disappearing from the Earth. Fortunately, study of this way of life has produced valuable information about human history and our fundamental ties to the natural world.

HORTICULTURAL AND PASTORAL SOCIETIES

Ten to twelve thousand years ago, a new technology began to change the lives of human beings (see the time line inside the front cover). People discovered **horticulture,** *the use of hand tools to raise crops.* Using a hoe to work the soil and a digging stick to punch holes in the ground to plant seeds may seem simple and obvious, but horticulture allowed people to give up gathering in favor of "growing their own." Humans first planted gardens in the fertile regions of the Middle East and then in Latin America and Asia. Within 5,000 years, cultural diffusion spread knowledge of horticulture throughout most of the world.

Not all societies abandoned hunting and gathering in favor of horticulture. Hunters and gatherers living amid plentiful vegetation and game probably took little note of the new technology (Fisher, 1979). Then, too, people inhabiting arid regions (such as the Sahara in western Africa or the Middle East) or mountainous areas found horticulture of little value. Such people (including the Tuareg) turned to **pastoralism,** *the domestication of animals.* Today, societies that mix horticulture and pastoralism thrive in South America, Africa, and Asia.

Domesticating plants and animals greatly increased food production, so societies could support not dozens but hundreds of people. Pastoralists remained nomadic, leading their herds to fresh grazing lands. Horticulturalists, by contrast, formed settlements, moving only when they depleted the soil. Joined by trade, these settlements formed societies with populations climbing into the thousands.

Once a society is capable of producing a *material surplus*—more resources than needed to support day-to-day living—not everyone has to secure food. Some make crafts, engage in trade, cut hair, apply tattoos, or

Of Egypt's 130 pyramids, the Great Pyramids at Giza are the largest. Each of the three major structures stands more than forty stories high and is composed of 3 million massive stone blocks. Some 4,500 years ago, tens of thousands of people labored to construct these pyramids so that one man, the pharaoh, might have a godlike monument for his tomb. Clearly social inequality in this agrarian society was striking.

serve as priests. Compared with hunting and gathering societies, then, horticultural and pastoral societies are more specialized and complex.

Hunters and gatherers believe many spirits inhabit the world. Horticulturalists practice ancestor worship and conceive of God as Creator. Pastoral societies carry this belief further, seeing God directly involved in the well-being of the entire world. This view of God ("The Lord is my shepherd," Psalm 23) is widespread among members of our own society because Christianity, Islam, and Judaism all began as Middle Eastern pastoral religions.

Expanding productive technology creates social inequality. As some families produce more food than others, they assume positions of power and privilege. Forging alliances—including marriage—with other elite families allows social advantages to endure over generations. Along with social hierarchy, simple government, backed by military force, emerges to shore up the dominance of elites. However, without the ability to communicate or to travel over large distances, a ruler can control only a small number of people, so there is little empire building.

Domestication of plants and animals made simpler societies more productive. But advancing technology is never entirely beneficial. Lenski points out that, compared with hunters and gatherers, horticulturalists and pastoralists have more social inequality and, in many cases, engage in slavery, protracted warfare, and even cannibalism.

AGRARIAN SOCIETIES

About 5,000 years ago, another technological revolution was underway in the Middle East and eventually transformed most of the world. This was the discovery of **agriculture,** *large-scale cultivation using plows harnessed to animals or more powerful energy sources.* So great was the social significance of the animal-drawn plow and other technological innovations of the period—including irrigation, the wheel, writing, numbers, and various metals—that this era qualifies as "the dawn of civilization" (Lenski, Nolan, & Lenski, 1995:177).

Using animal-drawn plows, farmers could cultivate fields vastly larger than the garden-sized plots worked by horticulturalists. Plows have the additional advantage of turning and aerating the soil to increase fertility. As a result, farmers work the same land for generations, which, in turn, encourages permanent settlements. Large food surpluses, transported on animal-powered wagons, allow agrarian societies to expand their land area and population greatly. About 100 C.E., for example, the agrarian Roman Empire boasted a population of 70 million spread over 2 million square miles (Stavrianos, 1983; Nolan & Lenski, 1999).

As before, increasing production meant more specialization. Tasks once performed by everyone, such as clearing land and securing food, became distinct occupations. Specialization also made the early barter

DIVERSITY: RACE, CLASS, AND GENDER

Technology and the Changing Status of Women

In the earliest human societies, women produced more food than men did. Hunters and gatherers valued meat highly, but men's hunting was not a dependable source of nourishment. The vegetation gathered by women was the primary means of ensuring survival. Similarly, it was women who took charge of the tools and seeds used in horticulture. For their part, men engaged in trade and tended herds of animals. Only at harvest time did men and women work side by side.

Then, about 5,000 years ago, humans discovered how to mold metals. This technology spread by cultural diffusion, primarily along male-dominated trade networks. Therefore, it was men who developed the metal plow and, because they already managed animals, thought to hitch the implement to a cow.

The metal plow marked the beginning of agriculture, and for the first time men took over the dominant role in food production. Elise Boulding explains how this technological breakthrough undermined the social standing of women:

The shift of the status of the woman farmer may have happened quite rapidly, once there were two male specializations relating to

agriculture: plowing and the care of cattle. This situation left women with all the subsidiary tasks, including weeding and carrying water to the fields. The new fields were larger, so women had to work just as many hours as they did before, but now they worked at more secondary tasks. . . . This would contribute further to the erosion of the status of women.

Sources: Based on Boulding (1976) and Fisher (1979).

---

system obsolete, and money became the standard of exchange. Because money made trade easier, cities grew, and their populations soared into the millions.

Agrarian societies exhibit dramatic social inequality. In many cases, including the United States early in its history, peasants or slaves represent a significant share of the population. Freed from manual work, elites can then engage in the study of philosophy, art, and literature. This explains the historical link between "high culture" and social privilege noted in Chapter 3.

Among hunters and gatherers and also among horticulturists, women are the primary providers of food. Agriculture, however, propels men into a position of social dominance (Boulding, 1976; Fisher, 1979). The box looks more closely at the declining position of women at this point in the course of sociocultural evolution.

In many societies, religion reinforces the power of agricultural elites by defining work as a moral obligation. Many of the wonders of the ancient world, such as the Great Wall of China and the Great Pyramids of Egypt, were possible only because emperors and pharaohs wielded absolute power, commanding their people to a lifetime of labor without wages.

In agrarian societies, then, elites acquire unparalleled power. To maintain control of large empires, leaders need the services of a wide range of administrators. Therefore, along with the growing economy, the political system emerges as a distinct sphere of life.

 To see several wonders of the ancient world, all made primarily with muscle power, click on http://unmuseum.mus.pa.us/wonders.htm

Of the societies described so far, agrarian societies have the greatest specialization and the most social inequality. Agrarian technology also gives people a greater range of life choices, which is why agrarian societies differ more from one another than horticultural and pastoral societies do.

INDUSTRIAL SOCIETIES

Industrialism, as found in the United States, Canada, and other rich nations of the world, is *the production of goods using advanced sources of energy to drive large machinery.* Until the industrial era, the major source of energy was the muscles of humans and other animals. But

**FIGURE 4–1 The Increasing Number
of Technological Innovations**

This figure illustrates the dramatic change in the number of technological innovations in Western Europe after the beginning of the Industrial Revolution in the mid-eighteenth century. Technological innovation occurs at an accelerating rate because each innovation combines with existing cultural elements to produce many additional innovations.

Source: Lenski, Nolan, & Lenski (1995).

in about 1750, mills and factories began to use water and then steam boilers to power ever-larger machinery.

With industrial technology, societies began to change faster, as shown in Figure 4–1. Industrial societies transformed themselves more in one century than they had during the past thousand years. As explained in Chapter 1 ("The Sociological Perspective"), this stunning change prompted the birth of sociology itself. During the nineteenth century, railroads and steamships revolutionized transportation, and steel-framed skyscrapers dwarfed the cathedrals that symbolized an earlier age.

In the twentieth century, automobiles further changed Western societies, and electricity powered modern conveniences such as lighting, refrigerators, elevators, and washing machines. Electronic communication,

including the telephone, radio, and television, soon followed, making the world seem smaller and smaller. During the last generation, computers have dramatically increased our ability to process information.

Work also has changed. In agrarian societies, most men and women work in the home or in the nearby fields. Industrialization draws people away from home to factories situated near energy sources (such as coal fields) and filled with large machinery. Industrial workers are far more productive, of course, but lost in the process are close working relationships, strong kinship ties, and many of the traditional values, beliefs, and customs that guide agrarian life.

Occupational specialization has become more pronounced than ever. In fact, industrial people begin to size up one another in terms of their jobs rather than according to their kinship ties (as nonindustrial people do). Rapid change and movement from place to place also generate anonymity, cultural diversity, and numerous subcultures and countercultures, as described in Chapter 3.

Industrial technology recasts the family, too, lessening its traditional significance as the center of social life. No longer does the family serve as the primary setting for economic production, learning, and religious worship. And, as Chapter 18 ("Family") explains, technological change also underlies the trend away from traditional families to greater numbers of single people, divorced people, single-parent families, and stepfamilies.

Lenski explains that early in the industrialization process, only a small segment of the population enjoys the benefits of advancing technology. In time, however, wealth spreads and more people live longer and more comfortably. Although poverty remains a serious problem in industrial societies, compared with a century before the standard of living has risen fivefold and social inequality has declined. Some social leveling, described in Chapter 10 ("Social Stratification"), occurs because industrial societies need an educated and skilled labor force. Whereas most people in nonindustrial societies are illiterate, industrial societies provide state-funded schooling and confer numerous political rights on almost everyone. In fact, industrialization intensifies demands for a political voice, as seen most recently in South Korea, Taiwan, the People's Republic of China, the nations of Eastern Europe, and the former Soviet Union.

POSTINDUSTRIAL SOCIETIES

Many industrial societies, including the United States, have entered yet another phase of technological development, and we can extend Lenski's analysis to take

Type of Society	Settlement Pattern	Social Organization	Examples
Hunting and Gathering Societies	Nomadic	Family centered; specialization limited to age and sex; little social inequality	Pygmies of central Africa Bushmen of southwestern Africa Aborigines of Australia Semai of Malaysia Kaska Indians of Canada
Horticultural and Pastoral Societies	Horticulturalists form small permanent settlements; pastoralists are nomadic	Family centered; religious system begins to develop; moderate specialization; increased social inequality	Middle Eastern societies about 5000 B.C.E. Various societies today in New Guinea and other Pacific islands Yąnomamö today in South America
Agrarian Societies	Cities become common, but they generally contain only a small proportion of the population	Family loses significance as distinct religious, political, and economic systems emerge; extensive specialization; increased social inequality	Egypt during construction of the Great Pyramids Medieval Europe Numerous predominantly agrarian societies of the world today
Industrial Societies	Cities contain most of the population	Distinct religious, political, economic, educational, and family systems; highly specialized; marked social inequality persists, diminishing somewhat over time	Most societies today in Europe and North America, Australia, and Japan generate most of the world's industrial production
Postindustrial Societies	Population remains concentrated in cities	Similar to industrial societies, with information processing and other service work gradually replacing industrial production	Industrial societies noted above are now entering postindustrial stage

splendid affluence and wretched squalor. A handful of aristocrats and industrialists lived in luxury in mansions staffed by dozens of servants. But most people labored long hours for low wages and lived in slums or even slept in the streets, where many eventually died from disease brought on by poor nutrition.

Marx wrestled with a basic contradiction: In a society so rich, how could so many be so poor? Just as important, Marx asked, how can this situation be changed? Many people think Karl Marx set out to tear societies apart. But he was motivated by compassion and sought to help a badly divided society forge a new and just social order.

The key to Marx's thinking is the idea of **social conflict,** *struggle between segments of society over valued resources.* Of course, social conflict can take many forms: Individuals may quarrel, some colleges have longstanding sports rivalries, and nations sometimes go to war. For Marx, however, the most significant form of social conflict was class conflict arising from the way a society produces material goods.

SOCIETY AND PRODUCTION

Living in the nineteenth century, Marx observed the early stage of industrial capitalism in Europe. He noted that this economic system turned a small part of the population into **capitalists,** *people who own and operate factories and other businesses in pursuit of profits.* A capitalist seeks profit by selling a product for more than it costs to produce. Capitalism transforms most of the population into industrial workers, whom Marx called the **proletarians,** *people who sell their productive labor for wages.* To Marx, conflict between capitalists and workers is inevitable in a system of capitalist production. To keep profits high, capitalists keep wages low. Workers, naturally, want higher wages. Because profits and wages come from the same pool of funds,

Norbert Goeneutte's painting Pauper's Meal on a Winter's Day in Paris *suggests the numbing poverty common to migrants drawn to cities as the Industrial Revolution was getting underway. Karl Marx saw in such suffering a fundamental contradiction of modern society: Industrial technology promises material plenty for all, but capitalism concentrates wealth in the hands of a few.*

conflict is the result. As Marx saw it, this conflict could end only with the end of capitalism itself.

All societies are composed of **social institutions,** defined as *the major spheres of social life, or societal subsystems, organized to meet human needs.* In his analysis of society, Marx argued that one institution—the economy—dominates all the others and defines the character of a society. Drawing on the philosophical doctrine of *materialism,* which says that how humans produce material goods shapes their experiences, Marx believed that the political system, family, religion, and education operate largely to support a society's economy. Just as Lenski argued that technology molds a society, Marx argued that the economy is a society's "real foundation" (1959:43; orig. 1859).

Marx viewed the economic system as society's *infrastructure* (*infra* is Latin for "below"). Other social institutions, including the family, the political system, and religion, are built on this foundation, forming society's *superstructure.* These institutions apply economic principles to other areas of life, as illustrated in Figure 4–2. In practical terms, social institutions maintain capitalists' dominant position by protecting their wealth and lawfully transmitting property from one generation to the next through the family.

Generally speaking, members of industrial-capitalist societies do not view their legal or family systems as hotbeds of social conflict. On the contrary, individuals come to see their right to private property as "natural." People in the United States find it easy to think that affluent people have earned their wealth and that those who are poor or out of work lack skills or motivation. Marx rejected this reasoning, arguing that grand wealth clashing with grinding poverty is merely one set of human possibilities—the one generated by capitalism (Cuff & Payne, 1979).

Therefore, Marx rejected capitalist beliefs as **false consciousness,** *explanations of social problems as the shortcomings of individuals rather than the flaws of society.* Marx was saying, in effect, that industrial capitalism itself is responsible for many social problems. False consciousness, he continued, harms people by hiding the real cause of their problems.

CONFLICT AND HISTORY

Marx believed that most societies evolve gradually over time. But sometimes they erupt in rapid, revolutionary change. Marx observed (as did Lenski) that change is caused partly by technological advance. But most change, he maintained, results from social conflict.

To put Lenski's analysis in Marxist terms, early hunters and gatherers formed primitive communist societies. *Communism* is a system by which people share roughly equally in the production of food and other material goods. Although resources were meager, they were shared by all rather than privately owned. In addition, everyone did much the same work, so there was little chance for social conflict.

Horticulture introduced social inequality, Marx noted. Among horticultural, pastoral, and early agrarian societies—which Marx lumped together as the "ancient world"—warfare was frequent, and the victors made their captives slaves. A small elite (the "masters") and their slaves were locked into an irreconcilable pattern of social conflict (Zeitlin, 1981).

Agriculture brought still more wealth to members of the elite, fueling further social conflict. Agrarian serfs, occupying the lowest reaches of European feudalism from about the twelfth to the eighteenth century, were only slightly better off than slaves. In Marx's view, both the church and the state defended the feudal system as God's will. Thus, to Marx, feudalism amounted to little more than "exploitation, veiled by religious and political illusions" (Marx & Engels, 1972:337; orig. 1848).

Gradually, new productive forces eroded the feudal order. As trade increased steadily, the merchants and skilled craftsworkers in cities formed a class, the *bourgeoisie* (a French word meaning "of the town"). Expanding trade made the bourgeoisie richer and richer. After about 1800, the bourgeoisie also controlled factories, becoming true capitalists with power that soon rivaled that of the ancient, landed nobility. For their part, the nobility looked down their noses at this upstart "commercial" class, but, in time, it was the capitalists who gained control of European societies. To Marx's way of thinking, then, new technology was only part of the Industrial Revolution. It was also a class revolution by which capitalists overthrew the old, agrarian elite.

Industrialization also led to the growth of the proletariat. English landowners converted fields once tilled by serfs into grazing land for sheep to produce wool for the textile mills. Forced from the land, serfs migrated to cities to work in factories. Marx envisioned these workers one day joining together to form a unified class and thereby setting the stage for a historic confrontation. This time, he hoped, the class revolution would lift the exploited workers over the oppressing capitalists.

CAPITALISM AND CLASS CONFLICT

"The history of all hitherto existing society is the history of class struggles." With these words, Marx and his collaborator, Friedrich Engels, began their best-known statement, the *Manifesto of the Communist Party* (1972:335; orig. 1848). Industrial capitalism, like earlier types of society, contains two major social classes—the ruling class and the oppressed—reflecting the two basic positions in the productive system. Like masters and slaves in the ancient world and nobles and serfs in feudal systems, capitalists and proletarians are engaged in class conflict now. Today, as in the past, one class controls the other as productive property. Marx used the term **class conflict** (and sometimes *class struggle*) to refer to *conflict between entire classes over the distribution of a society's wealth and power.*

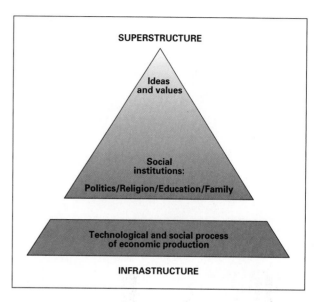

FIGURE 4–2 Karl Marx's Model of Society

This diagram illustrates Marx's materialist view that economic production underlies and shapes the entire society. Economic production involves both technology (industry, in the case of capitalism) and social relationships (for capitalism, the relationship between the capitalists, who control economic production, and the workers, who are a source of labor). On this infrastructure, or foundation, rests society's superstructure, which includes its major social institutions as well as core cultural values and ideas. Marx maintained that every part of a society supports the economic system.

Class conflict is nothing new. What distinguishes the conflict in capitalist society, Marx pointed out, is how out in the open it is. Agrarian nobles and serfs, for all their differences, were bound together by long-standing traditions and mutual obligations. Industrial capitalism dissolved those ties so that pride and honor were replaced by "naked self-interest." With no personal ties to their oppressors, Marx saw no reason for the proletarians to put up with their situation.

Although industrial capitalism brought class conflict out in the open, Marx realized that revolution would not quickly follow. First, workers must *become aware* of their oppression and see capitalism as its true cause. Second, they must *organize and act* to address their problems. This means workers must replace false consciousness with **class consciousness,** *workers' recognition of themselves as a class unified in opposition to*

CAPITALISM AND ALIENATION

Marx also condemned capitalism for producing **alienation,** *the experience of isolation and misery resulting from powerlessness.* Dominated by capitalists, workers are nothing more than a commodity—a source of labor—hired and fired at will. Dehumanized by their jobs (especially monotonous, repetitive factory work), workers find little satisfaction and feel unable to improve their situation. Here we see another contradiction of capitalist society: As people develop technology to gain power over the world, the capitalist economy gains more control over people.

Marx cited four ways in which capitalism alienates workers:

1. **Alienation from the act of working.** Ideally, people work to meet immediate needs and to develop their personal potential. Capitalism, however, denies workers a say in what they make or how they produce it. Furthermore, much work is tedious, a constant repetition of routine tasks. The fact that we replace workers with machines whenever possible would not have surprised Marx. As far as he was concerned, capitalism had turned human beings into machines long ago.

2. **Alienation from the products of work.** The product of work belongs not to workers but to capitalists, who sell it for profit. Therefore, Marx reasoned, the more workers invest of themselves in their work, the more they lose.

3. **Alienation from other workers.** Through work, Marx claimed, people build bonds of community. However, industrial capitalism makes work competitive rather than cooperative. As the box illustrates, factory work provides little opportunity for human companionship.

4. **Alienation from human potential.** Industrial capitalism alienates workers from their human potential. Marx argued that a worker "does not fulfill himself in his work but denies himself, has a feeling of misery rather than well-being, does not freely develop his physical and mental energies, but is physically exhausted and mentally debased. The worker, therefore, feels himself to be at home only during his leisure time, whereas at work he feels homeless" (1964a:124–25; orig. 1844). In short, industrial capitalism distorts activity that should express the best qualities in human beings into a dull and dehumanizing experience.

Karl Marx, shown here at work on the Manifesto of the Communist Party *with his friend, benefactor, and collaborator Friedrich Engels, was surely the pioneering sociologist who had the greatest influence on the world as a whole. Through the second half of the last century, 1 billion people—nearly one-fifth of humanity—lived in societies organized on Marxist principles.*

capitalists and, *ultimately, to capitalism itself.* Because the inhumanity of early capitalism was plain for him to see, Marx concluded that industrial workers would soon rise up to destroy capitalism.

And what of the capitalists? The capitalists' vast wealth made them strong. But Marx saw a weakness in the capitalist armor. Motivated by a desire for personal gain, capitalists fear competition with other capitalists. Therefore, Marx thought that capitalists would be slow to band together even though they, too, share common interests. Furthermore, he reasoned, because capitalists keep employees' wages low to maximize profits, the workers' resolve grows ever stronger. In the long run, Marx believed, capitalists contribute to their own undoing.

Alienation and Industrial Capitalism

These excerpts from the book *Working* by Studs Terkel illustrate how dull, repetitive jobs can alienate a worker.

Phil Stallings is a twenty-seven-year-old auto worker in a Ford assembly plant in Chicago:

I start the automobile, the first welds. From there it goes to another line, where the floor's put on, the roof, the trunk, the hood, the doors. Then it's put on a frame. There is hundreds of lines. . . . I stand in one spot, about two- or three-feet area, all night. The only time a person stops is when the line stops. We do about thirty-two jobs per car, per unit. Forty-eight units an hour, eight hours a day. Thirty-two times forty-eight times eight. Figure it out. That's how many times I push that button.

The noise, oh it's tremendous. You open your mouth and you're liable to get a mouthful of sparks. [Shows his arms.] That's a burn, these are burns. You don't compete against the noise. You go to yell and at the same time you're straining to maneuver the gun to where you have to weld.

You got some guys that are uptight, and they're not sociable. It's too rough. You pretty much stay to yourself. You get involved with yourself. You dream, you think of things you've done. I drift back continuously to when I was a kid and what me and my brothers did. The things you love most are what you drift back into.

It don't stop. It just goes and goes and goes. I bet there's men who have lived and died out there, never seen the end of the line. And they never will—because it's endless. It's like a serpent. It's just all body, no tail. It can do things to you.

Twenty-four-year-old Sharon Atkins is a college graduate working as a telephone receptionist for a large midwestern business:

I don't have much contact with people. You can't see them. You don't know if they're laughing, if they're being satirical or being kind. So your conversations become very abrupt. I notice that in talking to people. My conversation would be very short and clipped, in short sentences, the way I talk to people all day on the telephone. . . .

You try to fill up your time with trying to think about other things: what you're going to do on the weekend or about your family. You have to use your imagination. If you don't have a very good one and you bore easily, you're in trouble. Just to fill in time, I write real bad poetry or letters to myself and to other people and never mail them. The letters are fantasies, sort of rambling, how I feel, how depressed I am. . . .

I never answer the phone at home.

Source: Terkel (1974).

Marx viewed alienation, in its various forms, as a barrier to social change. But he hoped that industrial workers would overcome their alienation by uniting into a true social class, aware of the cause of their problems and ready to transform society.

REVOLUTION

The only way out of the trap of capitalism, argued Marx, is to remake society. He envisioned a more humane productive system, one in which people would be equals. He called this system *socialism*. Although Marx understood the obstacles to a socialist revolution, he was nevertheless disappointed that he did not live to see workers in England rise up. Convinced of the immorality of capitalism, he was sure that, in time, the working majority would realize that they hold the key to a better future. This change would certainly be revolutionary, and perhaps even violent. In the end, Marx believed, a socialist society could meet the needs of all.

Chapter 10 ("Social Stratification") explains more about changes in industrial-capitalist societies since Marx's time and why the revolution he wanted never took place. In addition, as Chapter 17 ("Politics and Government") explains, Marx failed to see that the revolution he imagined would take the form of repressive

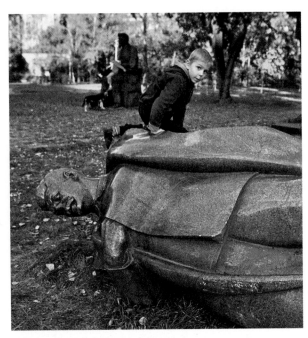

For years, the conventional wisdom in the United States was that, once established, socialism stifled its opposition, rendering government immune to overthrow. But that notion collapsed along with the socialist regimes of Eastern Europe and the Soviet Union. The political transformation of this world region during the 1990s was symbolized, in city after city, by the removal of statues of Joseph Stalin and Vladimir Lenin, earlier Soviet leaders.

regimes—such as Stalin's government in the Soviet Union—that would take the lives of tens of millions of people (Hamilton, 2001). But, in his own time, Marx looked toward the future with hope (Marx & Engels, 1972:362; orig. 1848): "The proletarians have nothing to lose but their chains. They have a world to win."

MAX WEBER:
THE RATIONALIZATION OF SOCIETY

With knowledge of law, economics, religion, and history, Max Weber (1864–1920) produced what many regard as the greatest individual contribution to sociology. This scholar, born to a prosperous family in Germany, generated ideas so wide ranging that, in this discussion, we can touch on only his vision

 For biographical information about Max Weber, visit http://www.TheSociologyPage.com and click on his name in the Gallery of Sociologists.

of how modern society differs from earlier types of social organization.

In line with the philosophical approach called *idealism,* Weber emphasized how human ideas shape society. He understood the power of technology, and he shared many of Marx's ideas about social conflict. But he countered Marx's materialist analysis by arguing that societies differ mainly in terms of how their members think about the world. For Weber, then, ideas—especially beliefs and values—are the key to understanding society. Weber saw modern society as the product not just of new technology and capitalism but also of a new way of thinking. This emphasis on ideas, in contrast with Marx's focus on production has led scholars to describe Weber's work as "a debate with the ghost of Karl Marx" (Cuff & Payne, 1979:73–74).

Weber compared social patterns in different times and places. To make the comparisons, he relied on the **ideal type,** *an abstract statement of the essential characteristics of any social phenomenon.* He explored religion by contrasting the "ideal Protestant" with the "ideal Jew," "ideal Hindu," and "ideal Buddhist," knowing that these models precisely described no actual individuals. Note that Weber's use of the word *ideal* does not mean that something is "good" or "the best." We can analyze criminals as well as priests in ideal terms. We have already used ideal types in comparing hunting and gathering societies with industrial societies and capitalism with socialism.

TWO WORLDVIEWS:
TRADITION AND RATIONALITY

Rather than categorizing societies by their technology or productive systems, Max Weber focused on ways people view the world. In simple terms, Weber said, members of preindustrial societies are *traditional,* whereas people in industrial-capitalist societies are *rational.*

By **tradition,** Weber meant *sentiments and beliefs passed from generation to generation.* In other words, traditional people are guided by the past. They consider particular actions right and proper solely because they have been accepted for so long.

But, argued Weber, people in modern societies favor **rationality,** *deliberate, matter-of-fact calculation of the most efficient means to accomplish a particular task.* Sentiment has no place in a rational worldview, which treats tradition simply as one kind of information. Typically, modern people choose to think and act on the basis of present and future consequences, evaluating jobs, schooling, and even relationships in terms of what they put into them and what they expect to receive in return.

Weber viewed both the Industrial Revolution and capitalism as evidence of a surge of rationality. He used the phrase **rationalization of society** to mean *the historical change from tradition to rationality as the dominant mode of human thought.* He went on to say that modern society has been "disenchanted" as scientific thinking and technology have swept away sentimental ties to the past.

The willingness to adopt the latest technology, then, is one strong indicator of how rationalized a society is. To illustrate the global pattern of rationalization, Global Map 4–1 on page 104 shows where in the world personal computers are found. In general, the high-income countries of North America and Europe use personal computers the most, whereas in low-income nations they are rare.

Using Weber's comparative perspective and the data found in the map, we can say that various societies value technological advance differently. What one society might consider a breakthrough another might deem unimportant and a third might strongly oppose as a threat to tradition. The Tuareg nomads, described at the beginning of this chapter, shrug off the notion of using telephones: Why would anyone want such a thing in the desert? In the United States, the Amish refuse to have telephones in their homes for religious reasons.

In Weber's view, then, the extent of technological innovation in a society depends on how people understand their world. Many people throughout history have had the opportunity to adopt new technology; however, only in the rational cultural climate of Western Europe did people exploit scientific discoveries to spark the Industrial Revolution (1958; orig. 1904–5).

IS CAPITALISM RATIONAL?

Is industrial capitalism a rational economic system? Here, again, Weber and Marx came down on opposite sides. Weber considered industrial capitalism the essence of rationality because capitalists pursue profit in whatever ways they can. Marx believed capitalism was irrational because it failed to meet the basic needs of most of the people (Gerth & Mills, 1946:49).

WEBER'S GREAT THESIS: PROTESTANTISM AND CAPITALISM

To look more closely at Weber's analysis we must consider how industrial capitalism emerged in the first place. Weber contended that industrial capitalism is

A key element of U.S. culture has long been a "work ethic," with its roots in the Calvinist thinking that fascinated Max Weber. This Currier and Ives lithograph from 1875 makes a statement that people should shun the stock market, race track, lotteries, and even labor strikes as ways to improve their lives in favor of climbing the "Ladder of Fortune" based on personal virtue and individual effort.

the legacy of Calvinism, a Christian religious movement that arose from the Protestant Reformation. Calvinists, Weber explained, approached life in a highly disciplined and rational way. Moreover, central to the religious doctrine of John Calvin (1509–1564) was *predestination,* the idea that an all-knowing and all-powerful God has predestined some people for salvation and others for damnation. With everyone's fate set before birth, Calvinists believed that people could do nothing to change their destiny. Worse, they did not even know what their destiny was. Therefore, Calvinists swung between hopeful visions of spiritual salvation and anxious fears of eternal damnation.

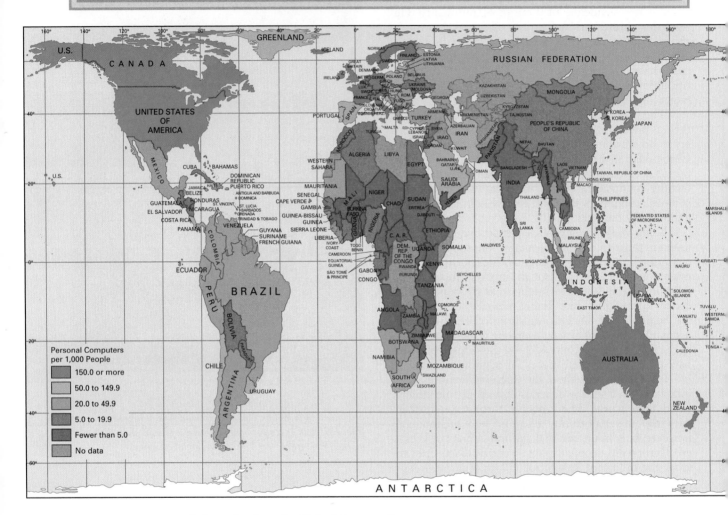

GLOBAL MAP 4–1 High Technology in Global Perspective

Countries with traditional cultures either cannot afford, ignore, or sometimes even resist technological innovation; nations with highly rationalized ways of life quickly embrace such changes. Personal computers, central to today's high technology, are numerous in high-income countries such as the United States. In low-income nations, by contrast, they are unknown to most people.

Source: *World Bank Atlas* by The World Bank. Copyright © 2001 by World Bank. Reproduced with permission of World Bank in textbook format via Copyright Clearance Center.

Not knowing one's fate was intolerable, and Calvinists gradually came to a resolution of sorts. Why shouldn't those chosen for glory in the next world, they reasoned, see signs of divine favor in *this* world? Such a conclusion prompted Calvinists to interpret worldly prosperity as a sign of God's grace. Eager to acquire this reassurance, Calvinists threw themselves into a quest for success, applying rationality, discipline, and hard work to their tasks. Their pursuit of wealth was not for its own sake because self-indulgent spending was clearly sinful. But neither were Calvinists moved to share their wealth with the poor because poverty was a sign of God's rejection. Their duty was to carry forward what they held to be a personal *calling* from God: reinvesting their profits for still greater success. Calvinists thus built the foundation of capitalism. With religious conviction, they used wealth to create more wealth, saved their money, and eagerly adopted new technology that helped their efforts.

The pursuit of wealth distinguished Calvinism from other world religions. For example, Catholicism, the traditional religion in most of Europe, gave rise to a passive, "otherworldly" view: Good deeds performed humbly on earth would bring rewards in heaven. For Catholics, material wealth had none of the spiritual significance that motivated Calvinists. And so it was, Weber concluded, that industrial capitalism developed primarily in areas of Europe where Calvinism was strong.

Weber's study of Calvinism provides striking evidence of the power of ideas to shape society (compared with Marx's contention that ideas merely reflect the process of economic production). But Weber was not one to accept simple explanations; he knew that industrial capitalism has many causes. In fact, one purpose of Weber's research was to counter Marx's narrow, strictly economic explanation of modern society.

Although later generations of Calvinists were less religious, their success-seeking and personal discipline remained, and a *religious* ethic became simply a *work* ethic. In other words, industrial capitalism can be seen as "disenchanted" religion, with wealth now valued for its own sake. It is revealing that the practice of "accounting," which to early Calvinists meant keeping a daily record of moral deeds, before long was simply a matter of keeping track of money.

RATIONAL SOCIAL ORGANIZATION

According to Weber, then, rationality gave rise to the Industrial Revolution and capitalism and thereby defined modern society. Weber went on to identify seven characteristics of rational social organization:

1. **Distinctive social institutions.** Among hunters and gatherers, the family is the center of all activity. Gradually, however, other social institutions, including religious, political, and economic systems, become separate from family life. In modern societies, new institutions—education and health care—also appear. The separation of social institutions is a rational way to meet human needs efficiently.

2. **Large-scale organizations.** Modern rationality is evident in the spread of large-scale organizations. As early as the horticultural era, political officials oversaw religious observances, public works, and warfare. In medieval Europe, the Catholic church grew into a huge organization with thousands of officials. In our modern, rational society, the federal government employs millions, and most people work for one large organization or another.

3. **Specialized tasks.** Unlike members of traditional societies, individuals in modern societies perform a wide range of specialized jobs. Flipping through the classified section of any city's telephone directory shows just how many different occupations there are today.

4. **Personal discipline.** Modern society puts a premium on self-discipline. For early Calvinists, discipline was rooted in religious belief. Although now distanced from its religious origins, discipline is still encouraged by cultural values such as achievement, success, and efficiency.

5. **Awareness of time.** In traditional societies, people measure time according to the rhythm of the sun and seasons. Modern people, by contrast, schedule events precisely by the hour and even the minute. Interestingly, clocks began appearing in European cities some 500 years ago, about the time commerce began to expand. Soon, people began to think (to borrow Benjamin Franklin's phrase) that "time is money."

6. **Technical competence.** Members of traditional societies size up one another on the basis of *who* they are—how they are joined to others in the web of kinship. Modern rationality prompts us to judge people according to *what* they are—that is, with an eye toward their skills and abilities.

7. **Impersonality.** Finally, in a rational society technical competence takes priority over close relationships, making the world impersonal. People interact as specialists concerned with particular tasks rather than as individuals broadly concerned with one another. Because feelings are difficult to control, modern people tend to devalue emotion.

Max Weber agreed with Karl Marx that modern society is alienating to the individual, but the two thinkers identified different causes of this estrangement. For Marx, economic inequality is the culprit; for Weber, the issue is pervasive and dehumanizing bureaucracy. George Tooker's painting Landscape with Figures *echoes Weber's sentiments.*

George Tooker, *Landscape with Figures*, 1963, egg tempera on gesso panel, 26 x 30 in. Private collection.

Rationality and Bureaucracy

The medieval church grew large, Weber explained, but it remained basically traditional and resisted change. Truly rational organizations that are both efficient and open to change appeared only in the last few centuries. The kind of organization Weber called *bureaucracy* arose along with capitalism as an expression of the rationality that shapes modern society. Indeed, Weber explained, bureaucracy and capitalism have much in common:

> Today, it is primarily the capitalist market economy which demands that the official business of public administration be discharged precisely, unambiguously, continuously, and with as much speed as possible. Normally, the very large capitalist enterprises are themselves unequaled models of strict bureaucratic organization. (1978:974; orig. 1921)

As Chapter 7 ("Groups and Organizations") explains, we find aspects of bureaucracy in today's businesses, government agencies, labor unions, and universities. Weber considered bureaucracy highly rational because its elements—offices, duties, and policies—help achieve specific goals as efficiently as possible. Therefore, Weber concluded, the defining elements of modern society—capitalism, bureaucracy, and science—are all expressions of the same underlying factor: rationality.

Rationality and Alienation

Max Weber joined with Karl Marx in recognizing the efficiency of industrial capitalism. Weber also agreed that modern society generates widespread alienation, although he offered different reasons. Whereas Marx thought alienation was caused by economic inequality, Weber blamed the stifling effect of bureaucracy's countless rules and regulations. Bureaucracies treat people as a series of cases rather than as unique individuals, Weber warned. In addition, working for large organizations entails highly specialized and often tedious routines. In the end, Weber envisioned modern society as a vast and growing system of rules seeking to regulate everything and threatening to crush the human spirit.

Like Marx, Weber found it ironic that modern society, meant to serve people, turns on its creators and enslaves them. Just as Marx described the human toll of industrial capitalism, Weber portrayed the modern individual as "only a small cog in a ceaselessly moving mechanism that prescribes to him an endlessly fixed routine" (1978:988; orig. 1921). Although Weber could see the advantages of modern society, he was

Durkheim's observation that people with weak social bonds are prone to self-destructive behavior stands as stark evidence of the power of society to shape individual lives. When rock-and-roll singers become famous, they are wrenched out of familiar life patterns and existing relationships, sometimes with deadly results. The history of rock and roll contains many tragic stories of this kind, including (from left) Janis Joplin's and Jimi Hendrix's deaths by drug overdose (both 1970) and Jim Morrison's (1971) and Kurt Cobain's (1994) suicides.

deeply pessimistic about the future. He feared that, in the end, the rationalization of society would reduce human beings to robots.

EMILE DURKHEIM: SOCIETY AND FUNCTION

"To love society is to love something beyond us and something in ourselves." These are the words of

 Durkheim is included in the Gallery of Sociologists at http://www.TheSociologyPage.com

Emile Durkheim (1858–1917), another of sociology's founders. In this curious statement (1974:55; orig. 1924) we find one more influential vision of human society.

STRUCTURE: SOCIETY BEYOND OURSELVES

Emile Durkheim's great insight was recognizing that society exists beyond ourselves. Society is more than the individuals who compose it; society has a life of its own that stretches beyond our personal experience. Society is here long before we are born, it shapes us while we live, and it will remain long after we are gone. Patterns of human behavior—cultural norms, values, and beliefs—exist as established structures and thus are *social facts* that have an objective reality beyond the lives of individuals.

Because society looms larger than any one of us, it has the *power* to guide our thoughts and actions. This is why studying individuals alone (as many psychologists

or biologists do) can never capture the essence of the human experience. Society is more than the sum of its parts; it exists as a complex organism rooted in our collective life. A classroom of third graders taking a math test, a family gathered around a table sharing a meal, people quietly waiting their turn in a doctor's office—all are examples of the countless situations that have a familiar organization apart from any particular individual who has ever participated in them.

Once created by people, then, society takes on a life of its own and demands a measure of obedience from its creators. We experience the reality of society in the order of our lives or as we face temptation and feel the tug of morality.

FUNCTION: SOCIETY AS SYSTEM

Having established that society has structure, Durkheim turned to the concept of *function*. The significance of any social fact, he explained, is more than what individuals see in our immediate lives; social facts help society as a whole to operate.

To illustrate, consider crime. Of course, individuals experience pain and loss as a result of crime. But, taking a broader view, Durkheim saw that crime is vital to the ongoing life of society itself. As Chapter 8 ("Deviance") explains, only by defining acts as criminal do people construct and defend morality, which gives purpose and meaning to our collective life. For this reason, Durkheim rejected the common view of crime as "pathological." On the contrary, he concluded, crime is

Historically, members of human societies engaged in many of the same activities: searching out food and securing shelter. Modern societies, explained Durkheim, display a rapidly expanding division of labor. Increasing specialization is evident in the streets of countries in the process of industrialization: On a Bombay street, a man earns a small fee for cleaning ears.

"normal" for the most basic reason: A society could not exist without it (1964a, orig. 1893; 1964b, orig. 1895).

PERSONALITY: SOCIETY IN OURSELVES

Durkheim contended that society is not only "beyond ourselves" but also "in ourselves." In other words, each of us builds a personality by internalizing social facts. How we act, think, and feel—our essential humanity—is drawn from the society that nurtures us. Moreover, society regulates our behavior through moral discipline. Durkheim held that human beings are naturally insatiable and in constant danger of being overpowered by their own desires. That is, "the more one has, the more one wants, since satisfactions received only stimulate instead of filling needs" (1966:248; orig. 1897). Having given us life, then, society must also rein us in.

Nowhere is the need for societal regulation better illustrated than in Durkheim's study of suicide (1966; orig. 1897), described in Chapter 1 ("The Sociological Perspective"). Why is it that rock stars—from Janis Joplin to Jim Morrison and Jimi Hendrix to Kurt Cobain—seem so prone to self-destruction? Durkheim had the answer long before anyone made electric music: A century ago, just as today, the *least* regulated categories of people suffer the *highest* rates of suicide.

The enormous freedom of the young, rich, and famous exacts a high price in terms of the risk of suicide.

MODERNITY AND ANOMIE

Compared with traditional societies, modern societies impose fewer restrictions on everyone. Durkheim acknowledged the advantages of modern-day freedom, but he warned of increased **anomie,** *a condition in which society provides little moral guidance to individuals.* The pattern by which many celebrities are "destroyed by fame" well illustrates the destructive effects of anomie. Sudden fame tears people from their families and familiar routines, it disrupts established values and norms, and it breaks down society's support and regulation of an individual, sometimes with fatal results. Therefore, Durkheim explains, an individual's desires must be balanced by the claims and guidance of society—a balance that is sometimes difficult in the modern world.

EVOLVING SOCIETIES: THE DIVISION OF LABOR

Like Marx and Weber, Durkheim saw firsthand the rapid social transformation of Europe during the nineteenth century. But Durkheim made his own sense of this change.

In preindustrial societies, explained Durkheim, tradition operates as the social cement that binds people together. In fact, what he called the *collective conscience* is so strong that the community moves quickly to punish anyone who dares to challenge conventional ways of life. Durkheim used the term **mechanical solidarity** to refer to *social bonds based on common sentiments and shared moral value that are strong among members of preindustrial societies.* In practice, mechanical solidarity springs from *likeness.* Durkheim called these bonds "mechanical" because people feel an automatic sense of belonging together.

With industrialization, Durkheim continued, mechanical solidarity becomes weaker and weaker, and people cease to be bound by tradition. But this does not mean that society dissolves. Modern life generates a new type of solidarity. Durkheim called this new social integration **organic solidarity,** *social bonds based on specialization and interdependence that are strong among members of industrial societies.* Where solidarity was once rooted in likeness, it is now based on *differences* among people who find that their specialized work—as plumbers, consultants, midwives, or sociology instructors—make them rely on one another for many of their daily needs.

The Information Revolution:
What Would Durkheim (and Others) Have Thought?

New technology is rapidly reshaping our society. Were they alive today, the founding sociologists discussed in this chapter would be eager observers of the current scene. Let's imagine for a moment the questions Emile Durkheim, Max Weber, and Karl Marx might ask about the effects of computer technology on society.

Emile Durkheim, who emphasized the increasing division of labor in modern society, probably would wonder whether new information technology is pushing specialization even further. There is good reason to think that it is. Because electronic communication (say, a Web site) gives anyone a vast market (already, 400 million people access the Internet), people can specialize far more than if they were confined to a limited geographic area. For example, whereas most small-town lawyers have a general practice, an information-age attorney (living anywhere) could become a specialist in, say, prenuptial agreements or electronic copyright law. Indeed, as we move into the electronic age, the number of highly specialized

microbusinesses in all fields—some of which become very large—is increasing rapidly.

Durkheim might also point out that the Internet threatens to increase anomie. In part, this is because computer use tends to isolate people, weakening personal relationships. Also, as the Internet offers a flood of information, it provides little in the way of moral guidance about what is true or worth knowing.

Max Weber believed that modern societies are distinctive because their members share a rational worldview, and nothing illustrates this better than bureaucracy. But will bureaucracy continue to dominate the social scene in the new century? Here is one reason to think it may not: Although it may make sense for organizations to regulate workers performing the kinds of routine tasks that were common in the industrial era, much work in the postindustrial era involves imagination. Consider such "new age" work as designing homes, composing music, and writing software. The creativity involved cannot

be regulated in the same way as, say, building automobiles on an assembly line. Perhaps this is why many high-technology companies have done away with dress codes and time clocks.

Finally, what might Karl Marx make of the Information Revolution? Because Marx considered the earlier Industrial Revolution a *class* revolution that allowed the owners of industry to dominate society, he would probably wonder whether a new symbolic elite is gaining power over us. For example, some analysts point out that film and television writers, producers, and performers now enjoy vast wealth, international prestige, and enormous power (Lichter, Rothman, & Lichter, 1990). Similarly, just as people without industrial skills stayed at the bottom of the class system in past decades, so people without symbolic skills are likely to become the "underclass" in the new century.

Durkheim, Weber, and Marx gave us an understanding of industrial societies. As we continue into the postindustrial age, there is plenty of room for new generations of sociologists to carry on.

For Durkheim, then, the key to change in a society is an expanding **division of labor,** or *specialization of economic activity.* Max Weber said that modern societies specialize in order to become more efficient, and Durkheim filled out the picture by showing that members of modern societies count on tens of thousands of others—most of them strangers—for the goods and services needed every day. That is, as members of modern societies, we depend more and more on people we trust less and less. Why do we look to people we hardly know and whose

beliefs may well differ from our own? Durkheim's answer is, "Because we can't live without them."

So modernity rests far less on *moral consensus* and far more on *functional interdependence.* Herein lies what we might call "Durkheim's dilemma": The technological power and greater personal freedom of modern society come at the cost of declining morality and the rising risk of anomie.

Like Marx and Weber, Durkheim worried about the direction society was taking. But of the three,

Durkheim was the most optimistic. He praised our greater freedom and privacy while hoping we could create laws to regulate our behavior.

Finally, can we apply Durkheim's views to the Information Revolution? The box on page 109 suggests that he and the other theorists we have considered in this chapter would have had much to say about new computer technology.

CRITICAL EVALUATION: FOUR VISIONS OF SOCIETY

This chapter opened with several important questions about society. We conclude by summarizing how each of the four visions of society answers these questions.

What Holds Societies Together?

How is something as complex as society possible? Lenski believes that members of a society are united by a shared culture, although cultural patterns vary according to a society's level of technological development. He also points out that as technology becomes more complex, inequality divides a society more and more, although industrialization reduces inequality somewhat.

Marx saw not unity but social division based on class position. From his point of view, elites may force an uneasy peace, but true social unity will come about only if production becomes a cooperative endeavor. To Weber, members of a society share a worldview. Just as tradition joined people together in the past, modern societies have created rational, large-scale organizations that connect people's lives. Finally, Durkheim made solidarity the focus of his work. He contrasted the mechanical solidarity of preindustrial societies, which is based on shared morality, with modern society's organic solidarity, which is based on specialization.

How Have Societies Changed?

According to the Lenski model of sociocultural evolution, societies differ primarily in terms of changing technology. Modern society stands out in this regard with its enormous productive power. Marx also stressed historical differences in productive systems yet pointed to the persistence of social conflict (except perhaps among hunters and gatherers). For Marx, modern society is distinctive only because it brings that conflict out in the open. Weber considered the question of change from the perspective of how people look at the world. Members of preindustrial societies have a traditional outlook, whereas modern people take a rational worldview. Finally, for Durkheim, traditional societies are characterized by mechanical solidarity based on moral likeness. In industrial societies, mechanical solidarity gives way to organic solidarity based on productive specialization.

Why Do Societies Change?

As Lenski sees it, social change is first and foremost a matter of technological innovation that, over time, transforms an entire society. Marx's materialist approach highlights the struggle between classes as the "engine of history," pushing societies toward revolution and reorganization. Weber pointed out how ideas contribute to social change. He demonstrated how a particular world view—Calvinism—advanced the Industrial Revolution, which, in turn, reshaped just about all of society. Finally, Durkheim pointed to an expanding division of labor as the key dimension of social change.

The fact that these four approaches are so different does not mean that any one of them is right or wrong in an absolute sense. Society is exceedingly complex, and we benefit from using all four visions, as shown in the final box.

SUMMARY

Gerhard Lenski

1. Sociocultural evolution explores the effects of technological advances on societies.

2. The earliest hunting and gathering societies were composed of a small number of family-centered nomads. Such societies have all but vanished from today's world.

3. Horticulture began some 12,000 years ago as people created hand tools for cultivation. Pastoral societies domesticate animals and trade extensively.

4. Agriculture, about 5,000 years old, is large-scale cultivation using animal-drawn plows. This technology allows societies to expand into vast empires, with greater productivity, more specialization, and increasing inequality.

Greek god of love). Second, we also have an aggressive drive he called the death instinct, or *thanatos* (from the Greek word meaning "death"). These opposing forces operate at an unconscious level and generate deep inner tension.

Freud's Model of Personality

Freud joined basic needs with the influence of society to devise a model of personality with three parts: id, ego, and superego. The **id** (the Latin word for "it") represents *the human being's basic drives*, which are unconscious and demand immediate satisfaction. Rooted in biology, the id is present at birth, making a newborn a bundle of demands for attention, touching, and food. But society opposes the self-centered id, which is why one of the first words a child learns is "no."

To avoid frustration, a child must learn to approach the world realistically. This is done through the **ego** (Latin for "I"), which is *a person's conscious efforts to balance innate pleasure-seeking drives with the demands of society.* The ego develops as we become aware of ourselves but also realize that we cannot have everything we want.

Finally, the human personality develops the **superego** (Latin meaning "above" or "beyond" the ego), which is *the cultural values and norms internalized by an individual.* The superego operates as our conscience, telling us *why* we cannot have everything we want. The superego begins to form as a child becomes aware of parental control and matures as the child comes to understand that everyone's behavior must take into account cultural norms.

Personality Development

To the id-centered child, the world is a bewildering array of physical sensations that bring either pleasure or pain. As the superego develops, however, the child learns the moral concepts of right and wrong. In other words, initially children can feel good only in a physical way, but after three or four years, they feel good or bad according to how they judge their behavior against cultural norms.

The id and superego remain in conflict, but in a well-adjusted person, the ego manages these two opposing forces. When conflicts are not resolved during childhood, they may surface as personality disorders later on.

Culture, in the form of superego, *represses* selfish demands, forcing people to look beyond themselves. Often, the competing demands of self and society

result in a compromise that Freud called *sublimation.* Sublimation redirects selfish drives into socially acceptable behavior. Sexual urges, for example, may lead to marriage, just as aggression gives rise to competitive sports.

Critical evaluation. Freud's work was controversial in his own time. More recently, critics charge that Freud's work presents humans in male terms and devalues women (Donovan & Littenberg, 1982). But Freud influenced everyone who later studied the human personality. Of special importance to sociology is his notion that we internalize social norms and that childhood experiences have a lasting impact on our personalities.

JEAN PIAGET: COGNITIVE DEVELOPMENT

Swiss psychologist Jean Piaget (1896–1980) studied human *cognition*—how people think. As Piaget

 For a closer look at Piaget and his work, go to http://www.piaget.org

watched his own three children, he wondered not just *what* they knew but *how* they made sense of the world. Piaget went on to identify four stages of cognitive development.

The Sensorimotor Stage

Stage one is the **sensorimotor stage,** *the level of human development at which individuals experience the world only through their senses.* For about the first two years of life, the infant knows the world only through the five senses: touching, tasting, smelling, looking, and listening. "Knowing" to young children amounts to direct, sensory experience.

The Preoperational Stage

About age two, children enter the **preoperational stage,** *the level of human development at which individuals first use language and other symbols.* Now children begin to think about the world mentally and with imagination. But "pre-op" children between about two and six still attach meaning only to specific experiences and objects. They can identify a favorite toy but cannot explain what *kinds* of toys they like.

Lacking abstract concepts, a child also cannot judge size, weight, or volume. In one of his best-known experiments, Piaget placed two identical glasses containing equal amounts of water on a table. He asked

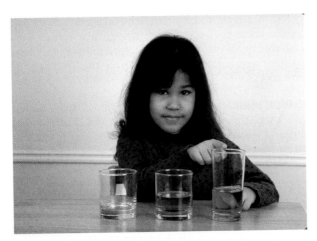

In a well-known experiment, Jean Piaget demonstrated that children over the age of seven had entered the concrete operational stage of development because they could recognize that the quantity of liquid remained the same when poured from a wide beaker into a tall one.

several children ages five and six whether the amount in both glasses was the same. They nodded that it was. The children then watched Piaget take one of the glasses and pour its contents into a taller, narrower glass, raising the level of the water. He asked again whether the glasses held the same amount. The children insisted that the taller glass held more water. By about age seven, children are able to think abstractly and realize that the amount of water stays the same.

The Concrete Operational Stage

Next comes the **concrete operational stage,** *the level of human development at which individuals first perceive causal connections in their surroundings.* Between ages seven and eleven, children focus on how and why things happen. In addition, children in this stage attach more than one symbol to a particular event or object. For example, if you say to a child of five, "Today is Wednesday," she might respond, "No, it's my birthday!" indicating that she can use just one symbol at a time. But a ten-year-old at the concrete operational stage would be able to respond, "Yes, and this Wednesday is my birthday!"

The Formal Operational Stage

The last stage in Piaget's model is the **formal operational stage,** *the level of human development at which individuals think abstractly and critically.* At about age twelve, young people begin to reason abstractly rather than thinking only of concrete situations. For example, if you were to ask a child of seven, "What would you like to be when you grow up?" you might receive a concrete response such as "a teacher." But most teenagers can think more abstractly and might reply, "I would like a job that helps others." This capacity for abstract thought also lets young people understand metaphors. Hearing the expression "A penny for your thoughts" might lead a child to ask for a coin, but the adolescent will recognize a gentle invitation to intimacy.

Critical evaluation. Whereas Freud saw human beings torn by opposing forces of biology and culture, Piaget saw the mind as active and creative. He saw an ability to engage the world unfolding in stages as the result of both biological maturation and social experience.

But do people in all societies pass through all four of Piaget's stages? Living in a traditional society that changes slowly limits the capacity for abstract and critical thought. Even in our own society, perhaps 30 percent of people never reach the formal operational stage (Kohlberg & Gilligan, 1971).

LAWRENCE KOHLBERG: MORAL DEVELOPMENT

Lawrence Kohlberg (1981) built on Piaget's work in studying *moral reasoning*, the ways in which individuals judge situations as right or wrong. Here, again, development occurs in stages.

Young children who experience the world in terms of pain and pleasure (Piaget's sensorimotor stage) are at the *preconventional* level of moral development. At this early stage, "rightness" amounts to "what feels good to me."

The *conventional* level, Kohlberg's second stage, appears by the teen years (corresponding to Piaget's final, formal operational stage). At this point, young people lose some of their selfishness as they learn to define right and wrong in terms of what pleases parents and what is consistent with broader cultural norms. Individuals at this stage also try to assess intention in reaching moral judgments instead of simply observing what others do.

In Kohlberg's final stage of moral development, the *postconventional* level, individuals move beyond their society's norms to consider abstract ethical principles. Now they think about liberty, freedom, or justice, perhaps arguing that what is legal still may not be right.

The Importance of Gender in Research

Carol Gilligan, an educational psychologist at Harvard University, has shown how gender guides social behavior. Her early work exposed the gender bias in studies by Kohlberg and others who had used only male subjects. But as her research progressed, Gilligan (1990) made a major discovery: Boys and girls use different strategies in making moral decisions. Thus, by ignoring gender, we end up with an incomplete view of human behavior.

More recently, Gilligan has looked at the effect of gender on self-esteem. Her research team interviewed more than 2,000 girls, ages six to eighteen, over a five-year period. She found a clear pattern: Young girls start out eager and confident, but their self-esteem slips away as they pass through adolescence.

Why? Gilligan claims that the answer lies in the way our culture defines females. In our society, the ideal woman is calm, controlled, and eager to please. Also, as girls move from the elementary grades to secondary school, they encounter fewer women teachers and find that most authority figures are men. As a result, by their late teens, girls must struggle to regain the personal strength they had a decade before.

Ironically, when Gilligan and her colleagues returned to a private school—one site of their research—to present their findings, they found further evidence of their theory. Most younger girls who had been interviewed were eager to have their names appear in the forthcoming book, but the older girls were hesitant: Many were fearful that they would be talked about.

What do you think?

1. *How does Gilligan's research show the importance of gender in understanding society?*

2. *How does her work show that socialization may not be a direct and linear progression?*

3. *Do you think boys are subject to some of the same pressures and difficulties as girls? How?*

Sources: Gilligan (1990) and Winkler (1990).

Critical evaluation. Like the work of Piaget, Kohlberg's model presents moral development in distinct stages. But, here again, whether this model applies to people in all societies remains unclear. Many people in the United States apparently never reach the postconventional level of moral reasoning, although exactly why is still an open question.

Another problem with Kohlberg's research is that his subjects were all boys. Kohlberg commits the research error, described in Chapter 2 ("Sociological Investigation"), of generalizing the results of male subjects to all people. This problem led a colleague, Carol Gilligan, to investigate how gender affects moral reasoning.

CAROL GILLIGAN: THE GENDER FACTOR

Carol Gilligan, whose approach is highlighted in the box, compared the moral development of girls and boys and concluded that the two sexes use different standards of rightness.

Gilligan (1982, 1990) claims that males have a *justice perspective*, relying on formal rules to define right and wrong. Girls have a *care and responsibility perspective*, judging a situation with an eye toward personal relationships. For example, as boys see it, stealing is wrong because it breaks the law. Girls are more likely to wonder why someone would steal and to be sympathetic toward a person who steals to, say, feed a hungry child.

Kohlberg considers rule-based male reasoning superior to the person-based female approach. But Gilligan notes that impersonal rules dominate men's lives in the workplace, whereas personal relationships are more relevant to women's lives as mothers and caregivers. Why, then, Gilligan asks, should we set up male standards as the norms by which to judge everyone?

Critical evaluation. Gilligan's work sharpens our understanding of human development and gender issues in research. But what accounts for the differences she documents between females and males? Is it nature or nurture? In Gilligan's view, cultural conditioning is at work. Therefore, as more women organize their lives

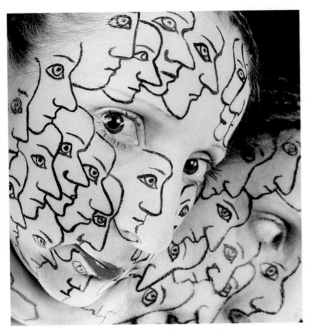

George Herbert Mead wrote: "No hard-and-fast line can be drawn between our own selves and the selves of others." The painting Manyness *by Rimma Gerlovina and Valeriy Gerlovin conveys this important truth. Although we tend to think of ourselves as unique individuals, each person's characteristics develop in an ongoing process of interaction with others.*

Rimma Gerlovina & Valeriy Gerlovin, *Manyness*, 1990. © the artists, New City, N.Y.

around the workplace, the moral reasoning of women and men will become more similar.

GEORGE HERBERT MEAD: THE SOCIAL SELF

George Herbert Mead (1863–1931) developed a theory of *social behaviorism* to explain how social experience creates individual personality (1962; orig. 1934). His approach calls to

A short biography of George Herbert Mead is included in the Gallery of Sociologists at http:// www.TheSociologyPage.com

mind the behaviorism of psychologist John B. Watson, described earlier. Both saw the power of environment to shape behavior. But whereas Watson focused on outward behavior, Mead studied inward *thinking*, humanity's defining trait.

The Self

Mead's central concept is the **self**, *the part of an individual's personality composed of self-awareness and self-image.*

Mead's genius was in seeing the self as the product of social experience.

First, said Mead, *the self develops only with social experience.* The self is not part of the body, and it does not exist at birth. Mead rejected the position that personality is guided by biological drives (as Freud asserted) or biological maturation (as Piaget claimed). For Mead, self develops only as the individual interacts with others. In the absence of interaction, as we see from cases of isolated children, the body grows, but no self emerges.

Second, Mead explained, *social experience is the exchange of symbols.* Only people use words, a wave of the hand, or a smile to create meaning. We can train a dog by rewarding correct behavior, but the dog attaches no meaning to its actions. Human beings, by contrast, find meaning in action by imagining people's underlying intentions. In short, a dog responds to *what you do*; a human responds to *what you have in mind* as you do it. Thus, you can train a dog to go to the hallway and bring back an umbrella. But without understanding intention, if the dog cannot find the umbrella, it is incapable of the *human* response: to look for a raincoat instead.

Third, Mead continues, *understanding intention requires imagining the situation from the other's point of view.* Using symbols, we imagine ourselves "in another person's shoes" and see ourselves as that person does. We can therefore anticipate how others will respond to us even before we act. A simple toss of a ball requires stepping outside ourselves to imagine how another will catch our throw. Social interaction, then, involves seeing ourselves as others see us—a process Mead called *taking the role of the other*.

The Looking-Glass Self

In effect, others represent a mirror (which people used to call a "looking glass") in which we can see ourselves. What we think of ourselves, then, depends on what we think others think of us. For example, if we think others see us as clever, we will think of ourselves in the same way. But if we feel they think of us as clumsy, then that is how we will see ourselves. Charles Horton Cooley (1864–1929) used the phrase **looking-glass self** to mean *a self-image based on how we think others see us* (1964; orig. 1902).

The I and the Me

Mead's fourth point is that *by taking the role of the other, we become self-aware.* The self, then, has two parts. As subject, the self is active and spontaneous. Mead called

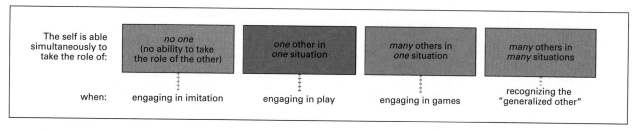

The self is able simultaneously to take the role of:	*no one* (no ability to take the role of the other)	*one* other in *one* situation	*many* others in *one* situation	*many* others in *many* situations
when:	engaging in imitation	engaging in play	engaging in games	recognizing the "generalized other"

FIGURE 5–1 Building on Social Experience

George Herbert Mead described the development of the self as a process of gaining social experience. That is, the self develops as we expand our capacity to take the role of the other.

the active side of the self the *I* (the subjective form of the personal pronoun). But the self is also an object, as we imagine ourselves as others see us. Mead called the objective side of the self the *me* (the objective form of the personal pronoun). All social experience has both components: We initiate an action (the I-phase of self) and then we continue the action (or not) based on how others respond to us (the me-phase of self).

Development of the Self

The key to developing the self, then, is learning to take the role of the other. With limited social experience, infants can do this only through *imitation*. That is, they mimic behavior without understanding underlying intentions, and so they have no self.

As children learn to use language and other symbols, the self emerges through *play*, which involves taking the roles of *significant others*, especially parents. Playing "mommy and daddy" (often putting themselves literally "in the shoes" of a parent) helps young children imagine the world from a parent's point of view.

Gradually, children learn to take the roles of several others at once. They can move from simple play (say, playing catch) involving one other to complex *games* (such as baseball) involving many others. By about age seven, most children have the social experience needed to engage in team sports.

Figure 5–1 charts the progression from imitation to play to games. But a final stage in the development of self remains. A game involves taking the role of others in just one situation, but social life demands that we see ourselves in terms of cultural norms as *anyone* else might. Mead used the term **generalized other** to refer to *the widespread cultural norms and values we use as a reference in evaluating ourselves.*

As life goes on, the self continues to change along with our social experiences. But no matter how much

events and circumstances affect us, we always remain creative beings. Thus, Mead concluded, we play a key role in our own socialization.

Critical evaluation. Mead's work explores the character of social experience itself. In symbolic interaction, he found the root of both self and society.

Some critics say Mead's view is completely social, allowing no biological element at all. In this, Mead stands apart from Freud (who identified general drives within the organism) and Piaget (whose stages of development are tied to biological maturity).

Be careful not to confuse Mead's concepts of the I and the me with Freud's id and superego. For Freud, the id originates in our biology, whereas Mead rejected any biological element of self (although he never specified the origin of the I). Moreover, whereas the id and superego are locked in continual combat, the I and the me work together cooperatively (Meltzer, 1978).

ERIK H. ERIKSON: EIGHT STAGES OF DEVELOPMENT

All the thinkers discussed so far point to childhood as the crucial time when personality takes shape. Erik H. Erikson (1902–1994) took a broader view of socialization. He believed that we face challenges throughout the life course (1963; orig. 1950).

Stage 1—Infancy: the challenge of trust (versus mistrust). Between birth and about eighteen months, infants face the first of life's challenges: to establish a sense of trust that their world is a safe place. Family members play a key role in how the child meets this challenge.

Stage 2—Toddlerhood: the challenge of autonomy (versus doubt and shame). The

Sociological research indicates that affluent parents tend to encourage creativity in their children while poor parents tend to foster conformity. While this general difference may be valid, parents at all class levels can and do provide loving support and guidance by simply involving themselves in their children's lives. Henry Ossawa Tanner's painting The Banjo Lesson *stands as a lasting testament to this process.*

Henry Ossawa Tanner, *The Banjo Lesson*, 1893. Oil on canvas. Hampton University Museum, Hampton, Virginia.

next challenge, up to age three, is to learn skills to cope with the world in a confident way. Failing to gain self-control leads children to doubt their abilities.

Stage 3—Preschool: the challenge of initiative (versus guilt). Four- and five-year-olds must learn to engage their surroundings—including people outside the family—or experience guilt at failing to meet the expectations of parents and others.

Stage 4—Preadolescence: the challenge of industriousness (versus inferiority). Between ages six and thirteen, children enter school, make friends, and strike out on their own more and more. They feel proud of their accomplishments, or fear that they do not measure up.

Stage 5—Adolescence: the challenge of gaining identity (versus confusion). During the teen years, young people struggle to establish their own identity. In part, teenagers identify with others, but they also want to be unique. Almost all teens experience some confusion as they struggle to establish an identity.

Stage 6—Young adulthood: the challenge of intimacy (versus isolation). The challenge for young adults is to form and maintain intimate relationships. Falling in love (as well as making close friends) involves balancing the need to bond with the need to have a separate identity.

Stage 7—Middle adulthood: the challenge of making a difference (versus self-absorption). The challenge of middle age is contributing to the lives of others in the family, at work, and in the larger world. Failing at this, people become stagnant, caught up in their own limited concerns (think of Scrooge in Dickens's classic *A Christmas Carol*).

Stage 8—Old age: the challenge of integrity (versus despair). Near the end of our lives, Erikson explains, people hope to look back on what they have accomplished with a sense of integrity and satisfaction. For those who have been self-absorbed, old age brings only a sense of despair over missed opportunities.

Critical evaluation. Erikson's theory views personality formation as a lifelong process. Furthermore, success at one stage (say, an infant gaining trust) prepares us for meeting the next challenge.

One problem with this model is that not everyone confronts these challenges in the exact order presented by Erikson. Nor is it clear that failure to meet the challenge of one stage of life means that a person is doomed to fail later on. A broader question, raised earlier in our discussion of Piaget's ideas, is whether people in other cultures and in other times in history would define a successful life in the same terms as Erikson.

In sum, Erikson's model helps us make sense of socialization and points out how the family, the school, and other settings shape us. We turn now to take a close look at these agents of socialization.

AGENTS OF SOCIALIZATION

Every social experience we have affects us in at least a small way. However, several familiar settings have special importance in the socialization process.

THE FAMILY

The family has the greatest impact on socialization. Infants are totally dependent on others, and the responsibility typically falls on parents and other family members. At least until children begin school, the family also has the job of teaching children skills, values, and beliefs. Even teenagers continue to place their greatest trust in their parents, according to a recent survey shown in Figure 5–2. Overall, research suggests, nothing is more likely to produce a happy, well-adjusted child than being in a loving family (Gibbs, 2001).

Not all family learning results from intentional teaching by parents. Children also learn from the kind of environment that adults create. Whether children learn to see themselves as strong or weak, smart or stupid, loved or simply tolerated, and, as Erik Erikson suggests, whether they see the world as trustworthy or dangerous, depends largely on their surroundings.

The family also gives children a social position in terms of race, religion, ethnicity, and class. In time, all these elements become part of a child's self-concept.

Research shows that the class position of parents affects how they raise their children (Ellison, Bartkowski, & Segal, 1996). Class position shapes not just how much money parents have to spend but also what they expect of their children. Surveys show that when asked to pick from a list of traits that are most desirable in a child, lower-class people in the United States favor obedience and conformity. Well-to-do people, by contrast, choose good judgment and creativity (NORC, 2001).

Why the difference? Melvin Kohn (1977) explains that people of lower social standing usually have limited education and perform routine jobs under close supervision. Expecting that their children will hold similar positions, they encourage obedience and may even use physical punishment such as spanking to get it. Well-off parents, with more schooling, usually have jobs that demand imagination and provide more personal freedom. Therefore, these parents try to inspire the same qualities in their children. In short, parents act in ways that encourage their children to follow in their footsteps.

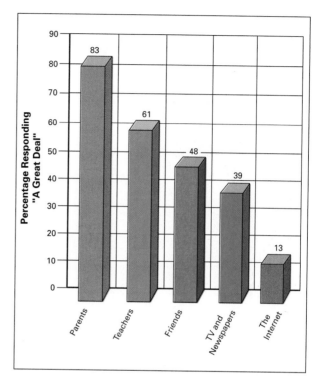

FIGURE 5–2 Whom Do You Trust?

Survey Question: "How much do you trust the information you get from . . . ?"

Sample of 409 U.S. teens, ages 13 to 17, 341 (83%) responding using the Internet. Survey taken April 1999 by Yankelovich Partners, Inc.

Source: Data from Okrent (1999).

THE SCHOOL

Schooling enlarges children's social worlds to include people with backgrounds different from their own. In the process, they learn the importance that society attaches to race and gender. Studies confirm that children tend to cluster in play groups made up of one race and gender (Lever, 1978; Finkelstein & Haskins, 1983).

Schools teach children a wide range of knowledge and skills. But schools informally convey other lessons, which might be called the *hidden curriculum*. Activities such as spelling bees and sports foster the value of competition and showcase success. Children also receive countless informal lessons that their society's way of life is morally good.

School is also most children's first experience with bureaucracy. The school day runs on impersonal rules and a strict time schedule. Not surprisingly, these are

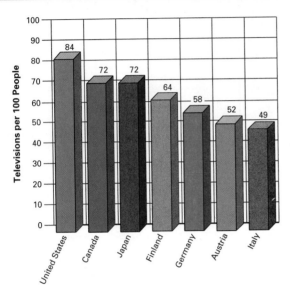

**FIGURE 5–3 Television Ownership
in Global Perspective**

Source: The World Bank (2001).

the hallmarks of the many organizations that will employ them later in life.

Finally, schools socialize children into gender roles. Raphaela Best (1983) notes that at school, boys engage in more physical activities and spend more time outdoors, whereas girls often volunteer to help teachers with various housekeeping chores. Gender differences continue in college as women tend toward majoring in the arts or humanities and men lean toward economics, the physical sciences, and computing.

PEER GROUPS

By the time they enter school, children have discovered the **peer group,** *a social group whose members have interests, social position, and age in common.* Unlike the family and school, the peer group lets children escape the direct supervision of adults. Among their peers, children learn how to form relationships on their own. Peer groups also offer the chance to discuss interests that adults may not share (such as clothing and popular music) or tolerate (such as drugs and sex).

Not surprisingly, then, parents express concern about who their children's friends are. In a rapidly changing society, peer groups have great influence, and the attitudes of young and old may differ because of a "generation gap." The importance of peer groups typically peaks during adolescence, when young people begin to break away from their families and think of themselves as adults.

Even during adolescence, however, parental influence on children remains strong. Peers may affect short-term interests such as music or films, but parents retain greater sway over long-term goals such as going to college (Davies & Kandel, 1981).

Finally, any neighborhood or school is a social mosaic of many peer groups. As Chapter 7 ("Groups and Organizations") explains, individuals tend to view their own group in positive terms and discredit others. Moreover, people are influenced by peer groups they would like to join, a process sociologists call **anticipatory socialization,** *learning that helps a person achieve a desired position.* In school, for example, young people may mimic the styles and slang of the group they hope to join. Or a young lawyer who hopes to become a partner in her law firm may conform to the attitudes and behavior of the firm's partners in order to be accepted.

THE MASS MEDIA

September 29, the Pacific Ocean, nearing Japan. We have been out of sight of land for two weeks now, which makes this ship our entire social world. But more than land, many of the students miss television! A few students have brought videotapes of old "Beverly Hills 90210" shows, which are a hot item.

The **mass media** are *impersonal communications aimed at a vast audience.* The term "media" comes from the Latin word meaning "middle," suggesting that media connect people. *Mass* media arise as communication technology (first newspapers and then radio and television) spreads information on a mass scale.

In the United States today, the mass media have an enormous effect on our attitudes and behavior. Television, introduced in 1939, soon became the dominant medium: 98 percent of U.S. households have a TV (just 94 percent have telephones), and 88 percent have more than one. Two out of three households also have cable television. As Figure 5–3 shows, the United States has the highest rate of television ownership in

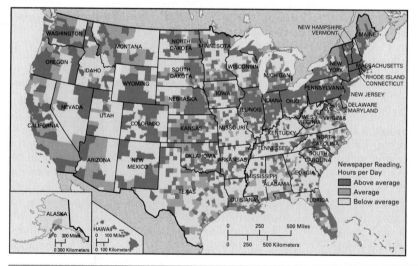

NATIONAL MAP 5–1
Television Viewing and Newspaper Reading across the United States

The map on the left identifies U.S. counties where television watching is above average, average, and below average. The map below provides comparable information for time devoted to reading newspapers. What do you think accounts for the high level of television viewing across much of the South and in rural West Virginia? Does your theory also account for patterns of newspaper reading?

Source: *American Demographics* magazine, August 1993, p. 64; *American Demographics* magazine, November 1998, p. 46. Reprinted with permission. © 1993, 1998 *American Demographics* magazine, Ithaca, New York.

the world. Some categories of people, including those with lower incomes, spend more time watching TV than others do. National Map 5–1 shows where in the United States people are more likely to be television watchers and where they are more likely to spend their leisure time reading newspapers.

Just how "glued to the tube" are we? Survey data show that the average household has at least one set turned on for seven hours each day, and people spend almost half their free time watching television

(Nielsen, 1997; Seplow & Storm, 1997; Cornell, 2000). A study by the Kaiser Family Foundation found that youngsters between age two and age eighteen average five-and-one-half hours per day "consuming media," including almost three hours a day watching television and the rest divided between watching videotapes and playing video games (McPherson, 1999).

Years before children learn to read, television watching is a regular routine. In fact, children grow up

How Should the Media Portray Minorities?

On an old *Saturday Night Live* sketch, director Ron Howard tells comedian Eddie Murphy about a new film, *Night Shift*, in which two mortuary workers decide to open their own sideline business: a prostitution ring. Murphy asks whether there are any black actors in the film; Howard shakes his head "no." Murphy then thunders, "A story about two pimps and there wasn't no brothers in it? I don't know whether to thank you or punch you in the mouth, man!"

Murphy's response points to twin criticisms of the U.S. mass media: Films and television either portray minorities in stereotypical fashion or ignore them altogether (Press, 1993:219). Back in the 1950s, minorities were all but absent from television and films. Even the wildly successful comedy *I Love Lucy* initially was turned down by major television studios because it featured Desi Arnaz—a Cuban—in a starring role. Since then, the media have steadily included more minorities. But despite top-rated programs such as *The Cosby Show* in the 1980s, *visibility* remains an issue: The 1990s came to an end with just a handful of African American stars on prime time television.

But what about *how* the media portray minorities? The few African Americans who managed to break into television in the 1950s played stereotypical low-status characters such as Amos and Andy and Jack Benny's butler, Rochester. Today, more television shows feature African American stars, but most are situation comedies that feature crude humor and bumbling characters.

Certainly, the image of minorities in the mass media is better than it used to be. But how minorities should be portrayed on television is still a matter of debate (MacDonald, 1992). Should television portray minorities *as they are*, which risks perpetuating stereotypes? Should shows present minorities *as they should be*, which risks being unrealistic about our nation's problems? Or should programs just present *individuals*, who may or may not match anyone's expectations?

---

spending as many hours in front of a television as they do in school or interacting with their parents. This is so despite research that suggests that television makes children more passive and less likely to use their imagination (Singer & Singer, 1983; APA, 1993; Fellman, 1995).

Comedian Fred Allen once quipped that we call television a "medium" because it is rarely well done. For a variety of reasons, television (as well as other mass media) provokes plenty of criticism. Some liberal critics argue that television shows mirror our society's patterns of inequality and rarely challenge the status quo. Most programs involve men in positions of power over women. Moreover, although racial and ethnic minorities watch about 40 percent more television than white people, they are largely absent from programming (Gans, 1980; Cantor & Pingree, 1983; Ang, 1985; Parenti, 1986; Brown, 1990). The box provides a closer look at how the U.S. entertainment industry characterizes minorities.

On the other side of the fence, conservative critics charge that the television and film industries are led by a liberal "cultural elite." In recent years, they claim, "politically correct" media have advanced liberal causes—including feminism and gay rights—while excluding a conservative perspective (Lichter, Rothman, & Rothman, 1986; Woodward, 1992b; Prindle, 1993; Prindle & Endersby, 1993; Rothman, Powers, & Rothman, 1993).

A final concern involves the mass media and violence. In 1996, the American Medical Association (AMA) declared that violence in the mass media, especially television and films, had reached levels that were hazardous to the well-being of this country's people. More recently, a study found a strong link between the amount of time elementary school children spend watching television and using video games and aggressive behavior (Robinson et al., 2001). The public as a whole seems to share concerns over the violent content of the mass media: Three-fourths of U.S. adults reported having walked out of a movie or turned off a television show because of high levels of violence. A more recent national study found that almost two-thirds of television programs contain violence and that

In recent decades, some analysts suggest that U.S. society is shortening childhood by pushing children to grow up faster and faster. What role do you think the mass media have in this process? What about the rising number of children left to fend for themselves while their parents work? What other factors are affecting the experience of childhood today?

in most violent scenes, characters show no remorse and are not punished (Wilson, 1998).

In 1997, the television industry adopted a rating system for shows. But larger questions remain: Does watching sexual or violent programming harm people as much as critics say? More important, why do the mass media contain so much sex and violence in the first place?

In sum, television and the other mass media enrich our lives with entertaining and educational programming. The media also increase our exposure to diverse cultures and provoke discussion of current issues. At the same time, the power of the media, especially television, to shape how we think remains highly controversial.

Finally, other spheres of life beyond the family, school, peer groups, and the media also play a part in social learning. For most people in the United States, these include religious organizations, the workplace, the military, and social clubs. Considering the variety of sources, we end up with different messages. In the end, therefore, socialization proves to be not a simple matter of learning but a complex process of taking in and evaluating all sorts of conflicting information.

SOCIALIZATION AND THE LIFE COURSE

Although childhood has special importance in the socialization process, learning continues throughout our lives. An overview of the life course reveals that our

society organizes human experience according to age: childhood, adolescence, adulthood, and, finally, old age.

CHILDHOOD

A few years ago, the Nike corporation, maker of sportswear and athletic shoes, came under fire. Their shoes are made in Taiwan and Indonesia, in many cases by young children who work in factories rather than going to school. Some 250 million of the world's children work, at least 120 million of them full time, earning about fifty cents an hour (Human Rights Watch, 2001). Global Map 5–1 shows that child labor is most common in the nations of Africa and Asia.

Criticism of Nike sprang from the fact that most North Americans think of *childhood*—roughly the first twelve years of life—as a carefree time for learning

 A Web site that reports on the state of children serving as soldiers around the world is http://www.hrw.org/campaigns/crp/

and play. But a century ago, children in North America and Europe led much the same life as children in poor countries today: Many worked long hours, often under dangerous conditions, for little pay. In fact, explains historian Philippe Ariès (1965), the whole idea of childhood is fairly new. During the Middle Ages, children of four or five were treated like adults and expected to fend for themselves.

We defend our idea of childhood because youngsters are biologically immature. But a look back in time and around the world shows that the concept of childhood is grounded in culture. In rich countries, not

GLOBAL MAP 5–1 Child Labor in Global Perspective

Industrialization prolongs childhood and discourages children from work and other activities deemed suitable only for adults. Thus, child labor is uncommon in the United States and other high-income countries. In less economically developed nations of the world, however, children are a vital economic asset, and they typically begin working as soon as they are able.

Source: The World Bank (2001) and author estimates; map projection from *Peters Atlas of the World* (1990).

everyone has to work, so childhood can be extended to allow time for young people to learn the skills they will need in a high-technology workplace.

Given this extended childhood, many people worry about children growing up too fast. According to one executive of a children's television channel, today's ten- to twelve-year-olds have many of the same interests and experiences typical of twelve- to fourteen-year-olds a generation ago (Hymowitz, 1998). In part, this "hurried child" syndrome results from changes in the family—including high divorce rates and both parents in the labor force—that leave children with less supervision. Then, too, "adult" programming on television (not to mention films and the Internet) carries grown-up concerns such as sex, drugs, and violence into young people's lives. Perhaps it should be no surprise that, compared with kids fifty years ago, today's children have higher levels of stress and anxiety (Gorman, 2000).

ADOLESCENCE

Just as industrialization created childhood as a distinct stage of life, adolescence emerged as a buffer between childhood and adulthood. We generally link adolescence, or the teenage years, to emotional and social turmoil as parents spar with young people who are trying to develop their own identities. We are tempted to attribute teenage turbulence to the biological changes of puberty, but this turmoil more correctly reflects cultural inconsistency. For example, the mass media glorify sex, and schools hand out condoms, while, at the same time, parents urge restraint. An eighteen-year-old male may face the adult duty of going to war, but he lacks the adult right to drink alcohol. In short, adolescence is a time of social contradictions when people are no longer children but not yet adults.

As is true of all stages of life, adolescence varies according to social background. Most young people from working-class families move directly from high school into the adult world of work and parenting. Wealthier teens, however, have the resources to attend college and perhaps graduate school, thereby stretching adolescence into the late twenties and even the thirties.

ADULTHOOD

Adulthood, which begins between the late teens and early thirties, depending on social background, is a time of accomplishment. Having completed their schooling, people embark on careers and raise families of their own. Personalities are now largely formed, although a marked change in a person's environment—such as unemployment, divorce, or serious illness—may cause significant change in the self.

Early Adulthood

During early adulthood—until about age forty—young adults learn to manage day-to-day affairs for themselves, often juggling conflicting priorities: parents, partner, children, schooling, and work (Levinson et al., 1978). Women, especially, often try to "do it all," because our culture gives them major responsibility for child rearing and housework even if they have demanding jobs outside the home (Hochschild & Machung, 1989).

Middle Adulthood

In middle adulthood—roughly ages forty to sixty—people sense that their life circumstances are pretty well set. They also become more aware of the fragility of health, which the young typically take for granted. Women who have spent many years raising a family find middle adulthood especially trying. Children grow up and need less attention, and husbands become absorbed in their careers, leaving some women with spaces in their lives that are difficult to fill. Many women who divorce also face serious financial problems (Weitzman, 1985, 1996). For all these reasons, an increasing number of women in middle adulthood return to school and seek new careers.

For everyone, growing older means facing physical decline, a prospect our culture makes more painful for women. Because good looks are defined as more important for women, wrinkles, added weight, and graying hair can be traumatic. Of course, men have their own difficulties. Some must admit that they are never going to reach their career goals. Others realize that the price of career success has been neglect of family or personal health (Farrell & Rosenberg, 1981; Wolf, 1990).

OLD AGE

Old age—the later years of adulthood and the final stage of life itself—begins about the mid-sixties. Again, societies attach different meanings to this stage of life. As explained in Chapter 15 ("Aging and the Elderly"), traditional societies often give older people control over most of the land and other wealth. Also, because traditional societies change slowly, older people amass great wisdom during their lifetime, which earns them much respect (Sheehan, 1976; Hareven, 1982).

In industrial societies, however, most younger people work apart from the family, becoming independent of their elders. Rapid change fosters a youth orientation that leads us to define what is old as unimportant or even obsolete. To younger people, the elderly appear unaware of new trends and fashions, and their knowledge and experience may seem of little value.

It is likely that U.S. society's anti-elderly bias will diminish as the share of older people steadily increases. The percentage of the U.S. population over age sixty-five has more than tripled since the beginning of the

The Development of Self among High School Students

Adolescence is a time when people are concerned about identity, asking questions such as "Who am I?" and "What should I strive to become?" Depending on their race and ethnicity, however, young people develop very different answers to these questions.

Grace Kao (2000) investigated the identity and aspirations of students enrolled in Johnstown High School, a large (3,000-student) school in a Chicago suburb. Johnstown High is considered a good school, with above-average test scores. It is also racially and ethnically diverse: 47 percent of the students are white, 43 percent are African American, 7 percent are Hispanic, and 3 percent are of Asian descent.

Kao interviewed sixty-three Johnstown students—female and male—both in small groups with others of their race and ethnicity and also individually. From these interviews, she documented the importance of racial and ethnic stereotypes in the students' developing sense of self. Moreover, Kao found, not only is there wide agreement about these stereotypes, but students in various racial and ethnic categories apply these stereotypes to themselves.

What are these stereotypes? White students are seen as hard working and studious, motivated by a desire for high grades. African American students, by contrast, are viewed as less studious. As some see it, this is because they are less intelligent; as others see it, this is simply because they don't try as hard. Hispanics are seen as destined for manual occupations—as gardeners or laborers—so that doing well in school is less important to them. Finally, Asian American students are seen as hard working and high achievers. Again, some attribute this achievement to "being smart," whereas others see it as a focus on academics rather than, say, sports.

From her interviews, Kao concludes that most students take these stereotypes very personally. That is, they assume these beliefs are true and that they will perform in school the way the stereotype predicts. One reason for this, Kao explains, is that white, black, Hispanic, and Asian students tend to socialize—both in and out of school—with others like themselves, which reinforces existing beliefs.

Another reason is that although students of all racial and ethnic categories say they *want* to do well in school, they measure success *only in relation to their own category*. In other words, to African American students "success" means doing as well as other black students and not flunking out. To Hispanics, "success" means avoiding manual labor and ending up with any job in an office. Whites and Asians, by contrast, define "success" as earning high grades and living up to the high achievement embodied in the stereotype. For all these young people, then, "self" develops through the lens of how U.S. society defines race and ethnicity.

Source: Kao (2000).

---

twentieth century, so that today there are more seniors than there are teenagers. Moreover, because life expectancy is still increasing, most men and women in their mid-sixties (the "young elderly") can look forward to decades more of life. In the twenty-first century, the Census Bureau (1999) predicts that the fastest-growing segment of our population may be those over eighty-five ("the oldest old"), whose numbers could soar nearly fivefold.

Old age differs in an important way from earlier stages in the life course. Growing up typically means entering new roles and assuming new responsibilities. Growing old, by contrast, is the opposite experience: leaving roles that provided both satisfaction and social identity. Retirement can be a period of restful activity, or it can mean the loss of valued routines and sometimes outright boredom. Like any life transition, retirement demands learning new, different patterns while *un*learning familiar habits from the past. A nonworking wife or husband who must now accommodate a partner at home has an equally difficult transition to make.

DYING

Through most of human history, low living standards and simple medical technology meant that death, caused by disease or accident, came at any stage of life. Today, however, more than 85 percent of people in the United States die after the age of fifty-five (U.S. National Center for Health Statistics, 2001).

After observing many dying people, Elisabeth Kübler-Ross (1969) described death as an orderly transition involving five distinct responses. A person's first reaction to the prospect of dying usually is *denial*, because our culture tends to ignore the reality of death. The second phase is *anger*, when a person facing death views it as a gross injustice. Third, anger gives way to *negotiation* as the person imagines avoiding death by striking a bargain with God. The fourth response, *resignation*, is often accompanied by psychological depression. Finally, adjustment to death is completed in the fifth stage, *acceptance*. Rather than being paralyzed by fear and anxiety, the person whose life is ending now sets out to make the most of whatever time remains.

As the share of women and men in old age increases, we can expect our culture to become more comfortable with the idea of death. In recent years, for example, people in the United States and elsewhere discuss death more openly, and the trend is to view dying as preferable to painful or prolonged suffering. Moreover, more married couples now prepare for death with legal and financial planning. This openness may ease somewhat the pain of the surviving spouse, a consideration for women who, more often than not, outlive their husbands.

THE LIFE COURSE: AN OVERVIEW

This survey of the life course leads us to two major conclusions. First, although each stage of life is linked to the biological process of aging, the life course is largely a social construction. For this reason, people in other societies may experience a stage of life very differently, or they may not recognize it at all. Second, in any society, the stages of the life course present characteristic problems and transitions that involve learning something new and, in many cases, unlearning familiar routines.

Societies organize the life course according to age, but other forces such as class, race, ethnicity, and gender also shape people's lives. Therefore, the general patterns we have described apply somewhat differently to various categories of people (cf. Duncan et al., 1998). The box provides an example, showing how race and ethnicity can shape the academic performance of high-school students.

The penal system's requirement that new inmates suffer the indignity of having their heads shaved is more than a matter of hair style; such a degrading ritual is also the first stage in the process by which a total institution attempts to break down an individual's established social identity.

Finally, people's life experiences also vary according to when, in the history of the society, they are born. A **cohort** is *a category of people with a common characteristic, usually their age.* Age cohorts are likely to be influenced by the same economic and cultural trends so that members have similar attitudes and values (Riley, Foner, & Waring, 1988). Women and men born in the 1940s and 1950s, for example, grew up during a time of economic expansion that gave them a sense of optimism. Today's college students, who have grown up in an age of economic uncertainty, are less confident of the future.

RESOCIALIZATION: TOTAL INSTITUTIONS

A final type of socialization, currently experienced by more than 2 million people in the United States, involves being confined—often against their will—in prisons or mental hospitals. This is the special world of the **total institution,** *a setting in which people are isolated from the rest of society and manipulated by an administrative staff.*

Are We Free within Society?

Throughout this chapter, we have stressed one key theme: Society shapes how we think, feel, and act. If this is so, then in what sense are we free? To answer this question, consider the Muppets, puppet stars of television and film. Watching the antics of Kermit the Frog, Miss Piggy, and the rest of the troupe, we almost believe they are real rather than objects animated from backstage. Similarly, as the sociological perspective points out, human beings are like puppets in that we, too, respond to backstage forces. Society gives us a culture and shapes our lives according to class, race, and gender. In the face of such social forces, can we really claim to be free?

Sociologists speak with many voices when addressing this question. One response, with politically liberal overtones, is that individuals are *not* free of society; in fact, as social creatures, we never could be. But if we are constrained to life within society, it is important to make our home as just as possible. That is, we should work to lessen class differences and other barriers to opportunity for minorities, including women.

Another approach, this time with conservative overtones, is that we *are* free because society can never dictate our dreams. Our history as a nation, right from the revolutionary act that led to its founding, is one story after another of individuals pursuing personal goals despite great odds.

We find both attitudes in George Herbert Mead's analysis of socialization. Mead recognized that society makes demands on us and sometimes limits us. But he also saw that human beings are spontaneous and creative, capable of continually acting back—individually and collectively—on society. Thus Mead noted the power of society while still affirming the human capacity to evaluate, criticize, and, ultimately, to choose and change.

In the end, then, we may resemble puppets, but only on the surface. A crucial difference—one that gives us a large measure of freedom—is that we can stop, look up at the "strings" that animate much of our action, and even yank on them defiantly (Berger, 1963:176). If our pull is persistent enough, we can do more than we might think. As Margaret Mead once mused, "Do not make the mistake of thinking that concerned people cannot change the world; it's the only thing that ever has."

Continue the debate . . .

1. *Do you think our society affords more freedom to males than to females? Why or why not?*

2. *What about modern, high-income countries compared with traditional, low-income nations: Are some of the world's people more free than others?*

3. *Does an understanding of sociology increase your freedom? Why?*

According to Erving Goffman (1961), total institutions have three distinctive characteristics. First, staff members supervise all spheres of daily life, including where residents (often called "inmates") eat, sleep, and work. Second, the environment of a total institution is highly standardized, with institutional food, uniforms, and one set of activities for everyone. Third, formal rules and daily schedules dictate when, where, and how inmates perform their daily routines.

Total institutions impose such regimentation for one purpose: **resocialization,** *radically changing an inmate's personality by carefully controlling the environment.* Prisons and mental hospitals physically isolate inmates behind fences, barred windows, and locked doors and control their access to the telephone, mail, and visitors. The institution becomes the inmate's entire world, making it easier for the staff to produce long-term change—or at least short-term compliance—in the inmate.

Resocialization is a two-part process. First, the staff breaks down the new inmate's existing identity, using what Goffman describes as "abasements, degradations, humiliations, and profanations of self" (1961:14). For example, an inmate must give up personal possessions, including clothing and grooming articles used to maintain a distinctive appearance. Instead, the staff provides standard-issue clothes so everyone looks alike. The staff subjects new inmates

To most people in the United States, these expressions convey anger, fear, disgust, happiness, surprise, and sadness. But do people elsewhere in the world define them in the same way? Research suggests that all human beings experience the same basic emotions and display them to others in the same basic ways. But culture plays a part by specifying the situations that trigger one emotion or another.

him whatsoever. He stared through them, round them, over them—eyes lost in space. The beach might have been empty. If by chance a ball was thrown his way, he looked surprised; then let a smile of amusement light his face (Kindly Preedy), looked around dazed to see that there were people on the beach, tossed it back with a smile to himself and not a smile *at* the people. . . .

[He] then gathered together his beach-wrap and bag into a neat sand-resistant pile (Methodical and Sensible Preedy), rose slowly to stretch his huge frame (Big-Cat Preedy), and tossed aside his sandals (Carefree Preedy, after all). (1956; quoted in Goffman, 1959:4–5)

Without uttering a single word, Mr. Preedy offers a great deal of information about himself to anyone observing him. This illustrates the process of **nonverbal communication,** *communication using body movements, gestures, and facial expressions rather than speech.*

People use many parts of the body to generate *body language* through which they convey information to others. Facial expressions are the most significant form of body language. Smiling conveys pleasure, for instance, although we distinguish between the deliberate smile of Kindly Preedy on the beach, a spontaneous smile of joy at seeing a friend, a pained smile of embarrassment, and the full, unrestrained smile of

Hand gestures vary widely from one culture to another. Yet people everywhere define a chuckle, grin, or smirk in response to someone's performance as an indication that one does not take another person seriously. Therefore, the world over, people who cannot restrain their mirth tactfully cover their faces.

self-satisfaction we often associate with the "cat who ate the canary."

Eye contact is another crucial element of nonverbal communication. Generally, we use eye contact to invite social interaction. Someone across the room "catches our eye," sparking a conversation. Avoiding another's eyes, by contrast, discourages communication. Hands, too, speak for us. Common hand gestures in our society can convey, among other things, an insult, a request for a ride, an invitation for someone to join us, or a demand that others stop in their tracks. Gestures also supplement spoken words. Pointing in a menacing way at someone gives greater emphasis to a word of warning, just as shrugging the shoulders adds an air of indifference to the phrase "I don't know," and rapidly waving the arms lends urgency to the single word "Hurry!"

Body Language and Deception

As any actor knows, it is very difficult to pull off a perfect performance. In everyday performances, unintended body language can contradict our planned meaning. A teenage boy offers an explanation for getting home late, for example, but his mother doubts his words because he avoids looking her in the eye. The movie star on a television talk show claims that her recent flop at the box office is "no big deal," but the nervous swing of her leg suggests otherwise. In practical terms, careful observation of nonverbal communication

(most of which is not easily controlled) provides clues to deception, in much the same way that a lie detector records telltale changes in breathing, pulse rate, perspiration, and blood pressure.

Look at the two photographs in the box. Can you tell which smile is honest and which one is meant to deceive? Detecting phony performances is difficult

 For more information about facial expression and honesty, visit the following Web site: http://www.bbc.co.uk/science/humanbody/humanface/expertarticle_ekman.shtml

because no bodily gesture directly indicates that one is lying. Even so, because any performance involves so many expressions, few people can lie without making a slip and raising the suspicions of a careful observer. Therefore, the key to detecting deceit is to scan the whole performance with an eye for inconsistencies. The box provides a closer look at everyday lie detection.

GENDER AND PERSONAL PERFORMANCES

Because women are socialized to be less assertive than men, they tend to be more sensitive to nonverbal communication. Moreover, gender plays an important part in personal performances. Based on the work of Nancy Henley, Mykol Hamilton, and Barrie Thorne (1992), we can extend our discussion of personal performances to spotlight the importance of gender.

APPLYING SOCIOLOGY

Hide Those Lyin' Eyes: Can You Do It?

Poker players and police officers have long realized that a good liar has a real advantage. Deception is a familiar element of everyday interaction, if only because common politeness sometimes demands that we not say what we really think.

Can you tell when another person is trying to deceive you? Paul Ekman suggests paying close attention to four elements of a performance: words, voice, body language, and facial expressions.

1. **Words.** Good liars mentally rehearse their lines, but they cannot always avoid a simple slip of the tongue—something the performer did not mean to say in quite that way. For example, a young man who is deceiving his parents by claiming that his roommate is a male friend rather than a female lover might mistakenly use the word "she" rather than "he" in conversation. The more complicated the deception, the more

likely a performer is to make a revealing mistake.

2. **Voice.** Tone and patterns of speech contain clues to deception because they are hard to control. Especially when trying to hide a powerful emotion, a person cannot easily prevent the voice from trembling or breaking. Similarly, the person may speak more quickly (suggesting anger) or slowly (indicating sadness). Nervous laughter, inappropriate pauses between words, or nonwords, such as "ah" and "ummm," also hint at discomfort.

3. **Body language.** A "leak" from body language may tip off an observer to deception as well. Subtle body movements, for example, give the impression of nervousness, as does sudden swallowing or rapid breathing. These are especially good clues to deception because few people can control them. Sometimes, *not* using the body in the expected way—as when a person's body fails to confirm words that suggest excitement—also reveals deception.

4. **Facial expressions.** Because facial expressions, too, are hard to control, they give away many phony performances. Have you picked the lying face? It's the one on the left. Whereas a real smile usually has a relaxed expression and lots of "laugh lines" around the eyes, a phony smile seems forced and unnatural, with fewer wrinkles around the mouth and eyes.

Sources: Based on Ekman (1985) and Golden (1999b).

Demeanor

Demeanor—general conduct or deportment—is a clue to personal power. Simply put, powerful people enjoy more freedom in how they act; subordinates act more formally and self-consciously. Off-color remarks, swearing, or putting one's feet on the desk may be acceptable for the boss but not for a secretary. Similarly, powerful people can interrupt others whenever they want, whereas subordinates are expected to display deference through silence (Smith-Lovin & Brody,

1989; Henley, Hamilton, & Thorne, 1992; Johnson, 1994).

Because women generally occupy positions of lesser power, demeanor is a gender issue as well. As Chapter 13 ("Gender Stratification") explains, about half of all working women in the United States hold clerical or service jobs that place them under the control of supervisors, who are usually men. Women, then, craft their personal performances more carefully than men and defer to others more often in everyday interaction.

Use of Space

How much space does a personal performance require? Power plays a key role because using more space is a sign of personal importance. Men typically command more space than women, whether pacing back and forth before an audience or casually lounging on a beach. Why? Our culture traditionally has measured femininity by how *little* space a woman occupies (the standard of "daintiness") and masculinity by how *much* territory a man controls (the standard of "turf").

For both sexes, the concept of **personal space** refers to *the surrounding area over which a person makes some claim to privacy*. In the United States, people typically position themselves several feet apart when speaking; throughout the Middle East, by contrast, people stand much closer. But just about everywhere, men routinely intrude into women's personal space. A woman's encroachment into a man's personal space, however, is often seen as a sexual overture. Here, again, women have less power in everyday interaction than men.

Staring, Smiling, and Touching

Eye contact encourages interaction. Women more than men work to sustain eye contact. But men have their own distinctive brand of eye contact: *staring*. As Henley, Hamilton, and Thorne see it, men staring at women are claiming dominance and defining women as sexual objects.

Although often conveying pleasure, *smiling* can also be a sign of appeasement or submission. In a male-dominated world, therefore, women smile more than men.

Finally, mutual *touching* conveys intimacy and caring. Apart from close relationships, however, touching generally is something men do to women (and rarely, in our culture, to other men). A male physician touches the shoulder of his female nurse as they examine a report, a young man touches the back of his woman friend as he guides her across the street, or a male skiing instructor touches young women as he teaches them to ski. In such examples, the touching may evoke little response, but it amounts to a subtle ritual by which men claim dominance over women.

IDEALIZATION

Complex motives underlie human behavior. Even so, Goffman suggests, we construct performances to *idealize* our intentions. That is, we try to convince others (and perhaps ourselves) that what we do reflects ideal cultural standards rather than selfish motives.

Idealization is easily illustrated in the world of physicians and patients. In a hospital, physicians engage in a performance commonly called "making rounds." Entering the room of a patient, the physician often stops at the foot of the bed and silently examines the patient's chart. Afterward, physician and patient converse briefly. In ideal terms, this routine involves a physician making a personal visit to inquire about a patient's condition.

In reality, the picture is not so perfect. A physician may see several dozen patients a day and remember little about many of them, so that reading the chart is a chance to recall the patient's name and medical problems. Revealing the impersonality of such medical care would undermine the cultural ideal of the physician as one who is deeply concerned about the welfare of others.

Physicians, college professors, and other professionals typically idealize their motives for entering their chosen careers. They describe their work as "making a contribution to science," "helping others," "serving the community," and even "answering a calling from God." Rarely do they concede the less honorable, but common, motives of seeking the income, power, prestige, and leisure these occupations provide.

More generally, idealization is part of civility. Smiling and speaking politely to people we do not like are little lies that ease our way through social interactions. Even when we suspect that others are putting on an act, we are unlikely to challenge their performances, for reasons we explain next.

EMBARRASSMENT AND TACT

The visiting speaker mispronounces the college's name; the senator rises from the table to speak, unaware of the napkin that still hangs from her neck; the president becomes ill at a state dinner. As carefully as people craft their performances, slip-ups of all kinds occur. The result is *embarrassment*, or discomfort resulting from a spoiled performance. Goffman describes embarrassment simply as "losing face."

Embarrassment is an ever-present danger because, first, all performances typically contain some deception. And second, most performances involve many elements that, in a thoughtless moment, can shatter the intended impression.

A curious fact is that an audience usually overlooks flaws in a performance, allowing an actor to avoid embarrassment. If we do point out a misstep ("Excuse me, but did you know your fly is open?"), we do it quietly and only to help someone avoid even greater loss of face. In Hans Christian Andersen's classic fable "The Emperor's New Clothes," the child who blurts out that the emperor is parading about naked tells the truth but is scolded for being rude.

Often, members of an audience actually help the performer recover a flawed performance. *Tact* amounts to helping someone "save face." After hearing a supposed expert make an embarrassingly inaccurate remark, for example, people may tactfully ignore the comment as if it were never spoken. Or mild laughter may indicate that they choose to treat what was said as a joke. Or a listener may simply respond, "I'm sure you didn't mean that," noting the statement but not allowing it to destroy the actor's performance. With this in mind, we can understand Abraham Lincoln's comment that "Tact is the ability to describe others the way they see themselves."

Why is tact so common? Because embarrassment provokes discomfort not only for the actor but for everyone. Just as a theater audience feels uneasy when an actor forgets a line, people who observe awkward behavior are reminded of how fragile their own performances are. Socially constructed reality thus works like a dam holding back a sea of chaos. If one person's performance springs a leak, others tactfully help make repairs. After all, everyone lends a hand in building reality, and no one wants it suddenly swept away.

In sum, Goffman's research shows that although behavior is spontaneous in some respects, it is more patterned than we like to think. Almost 400 years ago, Shakespeare captured this idea in memorable lines that still ring true:

All the world's a stage,
And all the men and women merely players:
They have their exits and their entrances;
And one man in his time plays many parts.
(*As You Like It*, II)

INTERACTION IN EVERYDAY LIFE: TWO APPLICATIONS

We have examined the major elements of social interaction. The final sections of this chapter apply these lessons to two important yet very different aspects of everyday life: language and humor.

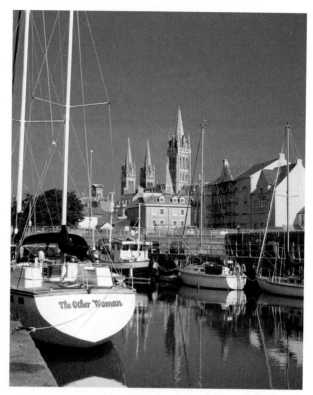

Why do we associate ownership with men and characterize what is owned as feminine? How easily can you imagine renaming this boat with the gender reversed?

LANGUAGE: THE GENDER ISSUE

As Chapter 3 ("Culture") explains, language is the thread that joins members of a society in the symbolic web we call culture. Language conveys not only a surface meaning but also deeper levels of meaning. One such level involves gender. Language defines men and women differently in at least three ways, involving power, value, and attention.[1]

Language and Power

A young man astride his new motorcycle proudly rolls up his friend's driveway and eagerly asks, "Isn't she a beauty?" On the surface, the question has little to do

---

[1]The following sections draw primarily on Henley, Hamilton, & Thorne (1992). Additional material comes from Thorne, Kramarae, & Henley (1983) and Romaine (1999).

Gender and Language: "You Just Don't Understand!"

In the story that opened this chapter, a couple faces a situation that rings all too true to many people: When lost, men grumble to themselves, perhaps blame their partners, but avoid asking others for directions. For their part, women can't seem to understand such behavior.

Deborah Tannen, who has conducted extensive research on the linguistic differences that separate the sexes, explains. Men, she claims, see most daily encounters as competitive situations; getting lost is bad enough without asking for help and thereby letting someone else get "one up" on them. By contrast, because women in the United States hold a generally subordinate position, they are socialized to ask for help. Sometimes, Tannen points out, women ask for assistance even when they don't need it.

A similar gender-linked problem common to couples involves what men call "nagging." Consider the following exchange (Adler, 1990:74):

SYBIL: What's wrong, honey?

HAROLD: Nothing . . .

SYBIL: Something is bothering you; I can tell.

HAROLD: I told you nothing is bothering me. Leave me alone.

SYBIL: But I can see that something is wrong.

HAROLD: OK. Just why do you think something is bothering me?

SYBIL: Well, for one thing, you're bleeding all over your shirt.

HAROLD [NOW IRRITATED]: It doesn't bother me.

SYBIL [LOSING HER TEMPER]: "WELL, IT SURE IS BOTHERING ME!"

HAROLD: "I'll go change my shirt."

The problem couples face in communicating is that what one partner *intends* by a comment is not always what the other *hears* in the words. To Sybil, her opening question is an attempt at cooperative problem solving. She can see that something is wrong with Harold (who has cut himself while doing yard work), and she wants to help him. But Harold interprets her pointing out his problem as belittling, and he tries to close off the discussion. Sybil, confident that Harold needs just to understand that she only wants to be helpful, repeats herself. This reaction sets in motion a vicious circle in which Harold, thinking his wife is nagging because she must believe he cannot take care of himself, responds by digging in his heels. His response, in turn, makes Sybil all the more sure that she needs to do something. And around and around it goes until somebody gets really angry.

In the end, Harold gives in only to the extent that he agrees to change his shirt. But notice that he still refuses to discuss the original problem—his injury. Misunderstanding his wife's motives, Harold just wants Sybil to leave him alone. Likewise, Sybil fails to understand her husband's view of the situation and walks away thinking that he is a stubborn grouch.

Sources: Adler (1990) and Tannen (1990).

with gender. Yet why does he use the pronoun "she" rather than "he" or "it" to refer to his prized possession? The answer is that men often use language to establish control over their surroundings. That is, a man attaches a female pronoun to a motorcycle (or car, boat, or other object) because it reflects the power of *ownership*.

Another power function of language relates to people's names. Traditionally in the United States and in many other parts of the world, a woman takes the family name of her husband when she marries. Although few people in this country consider this an explicit statement of a man's ownership of a woman, many think it reflects male dominance. For this reason, an increasing share of married women (almost 15 percent) have kept their own name or merged the two family names.

Language and Value

The English language usually treats as masculine whatever has greater value, force, or significance. For instance, the adjective "virtuous," meaning "morally worthy" or "excellent," is derived from the Latin word *vir*, meaning "man." By contrast, the disparaging adjective "hysterical" is derived from the Greek word *hyster*, meaning "uterus."

In many familiar ways, language also confers different value on the two sexes. Traditional masculine terms such as "king" and "lord" have retained their positive meaning, whereas comparable terms, such as "queen," "madam," and "dame" have acquired negative connotations in contemporary usage. Language thus both mirrors social attitudes and helps perpetuate them.

Similarly, use of the suffixes "ette" and "ess" to denote femininity usually devalues the words to which they are added. For example, a "major" has higher standing than a "majorette," as does a "host" in relation to a "hostess." And, certainly, men's groups with names such as the *Los Angeles Rams* carry more stature than women's groups with names such as the *Radio City Music Hall Rockettes*.

Language and Attention

Language also shapes reality by directing greater attention to masculine activity. In the English language, the plural pronoun "they" is gender-neutral. But the corresponding singular pronouns "he" and "she" specify gender. According to traditional grammatical practice, many people use "he," along with the possessive "his" and objective "him," to refer to *all* people. Thus, we assume that the bit of wisdom "He who hesitates is lost" refers to women as well as to men. But this practice also reflects the cultural pattern of neglecting the existence of women.

The English language has no gender-neutral, third-person singular personal pronoun. In recent years, however, the plural pronouns "they" and "them" have gained some currency as a singular pronoun ("A person should do as they please"). This usage violates grammatical rules, yet there is no doubt that English is changing to accept such gender-neutral constructions.

Grammar aside, the mix of gender and language is likely to remain a source of miscommunication between women and men. In the box, Harold and Sybil, whose misadventures in trying to find a friend's home opened this chapter, return to illustrate how the two sexes often seem to be speaking different languages.

HUMOR: PLAYING WITH REALITY

Humor is an important part of everyday life. But, although everyone laughs at jokes, few people think about what makes something funny or why humor is a part of every culture in the world. We can apply many of the ideas developed in this chapter to explore the character of humor.[2]

The Foundation of Humor

Humor is a product of reality construction; specifically, it stems from the contrast between two different realities. Generally, one reality is *conventional*, that is, what people expect in a specific situation. The other reality is *unconventional*, an unexpected violation of cultural patterns. Thus, humor arises from contradiction, ambiguity, and double meanings found in differing definitions of the same situation. Note how this principle works in the newspaper headlines in the box on page 156.

There are countless ways to mix realities and thereby generate humor. Contrasting realities emerge from statements that contradict themselves, such as "Nostalgia is not what it used to be." Switching words can create humor, as in Oscar Wilde's line: "Work is the curse of the drinking class." Even reordering syllables does the trick, as in the case of the (probably fictitious) country song, "I'd rather have a bottle in front of me than a frontal lobotomy."

Of course, a joke can be built the other way around, so that the comic leads the audience to *expect* an unconventional answer then delivers a very ordinary one. When a reporter asked the famous desperado Willy Sutton why he robbed banks, for example, he replied dryly, "Because that's where the money is." However a joke is constructed, the greater the opposition or incongruity between the two definitions of reality, the greater the humor.

---

[2]The ideas discussed here are those of the author (1987), except as otherwise noted. The general approach draws on work discussed in this chapter, especially on the ideas of Erving Goffman.

Double Take: Real Headlines That Make People Laugh

Humor is generated by mixing two distinct and opposing realities. Here are several real headlines from newspapers. Read each one and identify the conventional meaning intended by the writer as well as the unconventional interpretation that generates humor.

"Include Your Children
　　When Baking Cookies"

"Drunk Gets Nine Months
　　in Violin Case"

"Survivor of Siamese Twins
　　Joins Parents"

"Iraqi Head Seeks Arms"

"Stud Tires Out"

"Prostitutes Appeal to Pope"

"Panda Mating Fails:
　　Veterinarian Takes Over"

"Soviet Virgin Lands Short
　　of Goal Again"

"Typhoon Rips Through Cemetery:
　　Hundreds Dead"

"Squad Helps Dog Bite Victim"

"Miners Refuse to Work after Death"

"Killer Sentenced to Die
　　for Second Time in Ten Years"

"Something Went Wrong
　　in Jet Crash"

"British Left Waffles
　　on Falkland Islands"

"Stolen Painting Found by Tree"

What do you think?

1. *For each headline, do you see the expected and unexpected meanings?*

2. *Which headlines are funniest? Why?*

3. *Can you think of other everyday examples of humor?*

Source: Thanks to Kay Fletcher.

When telling jokes, the comedian can strengthen this opposition in various ways. One common technique is for the comic to present the first, or conventional, remark in conversation with another actor, then to turn toward the audience to deliver the second, unexpected line. In a Marx Brothers film, Groucho waxes philosophical when he says, "Outside of a dog, a book is a man's best friend." Then, dropping his voice and turning to the camera, he counters, "And *inside* of a dog, it's too dark to read!" Such "changing channels" underscores the incongruity of the two parts. Following the same logic, stand-up comics may "reset" the audience to conventional expectations by interjecting "But, seriously, folks . . ." after one joke and before the next one.

To construct the strongest contrast in meaning, comedians pay careful attention to their performances—the precise words they use and the timing of their delivery. A joke is "well told" if the comic creates the sharpest possible opposition between the realities, just as humor falls flat in a careless performance. Because the key to humor lies in the opposition of realities, we can see why the climax of a joke is called the "*punch* line."

The Dynamics of Humor: "Getting It"

Someone who does not understand both the conventional and unconventional realities in a joke may complain, "I don't get it." To "get" humor, the audience must understand the two realities involved well enough to appreciate their difference. But comics may make getting the joke harder still by leaving out some important piece of information. Therefore, the audience must pay attention to the *stated* elements of the joke and then fill in the missing pieces on their own.

As a simple case, consider the reflection of movie producer Hal Roach upon reaching his one hundredth birthday: "If I had known I would live to be one hundred, I would have taken better care of myself!" Here, getting the joke depends on realizing that Roach must have taken pretty good care of himself because he lived to be one hundred in the first place. Or take one of W. C. Fields's lines: "Some weasel took the cork out of my lunch." "Some lunch!" we think to ourselves to "finish" the joke.

Here is an even more complex joke: What do you get if you cross an insomniac, a dyslexic, and an agnostic? Answer: A person who stays up all night wondering whether there is a dog. To get this one, you must know, first, that insomnia is an inability to sleep; second, that dyslexia causes a person to reverse letters in words; and, third, that an agnostic doubts the existence of God.

Why would an audience be required to make this sort of effort in order to understand a joke? Simply because our enjoyment of a joke is heightened by the pleasure of having completed the puzzle. In addition, getting the joke confers a favored insider status. We can also understand the frustration of *not* getting a joke: fear of being judged stupid coupled with being excluded from a pleasure shared by others. Not surprisingly, outsiders in such a situation sometimes fake getting the joke, or someone may tactfully explain the joke so the other person doesn't feel left out.

But, as the old saying goes, if you have to explain a joke, it won't be very funny. Besides taking the edge off the language and timing on which the punch depends, an explanation removes the mental involvement and greatly reduces the listener's pleasure.

The Topics of Humor

People throughout the world smile and laugh, making humor a universal human trait. But the world's people differ in what they find funny, so humor rarely travels well.

October 1, Kobe, Japan. Can you share a joke with people who live halfway around the world? At dinner, I ask two Japanese college women to tell me a joke. "You know 'crayon'?" Asako asks. I nod. "How do you ask for a crayon in Japanese?" I respond that I have no idea. She laughs out loud as she says what sounds like "crayon crayon." Her companion, Mayumi, laughs, too. My wife and I sit awkwardly, straight-faced. Asako relieves some of our embarrassment by explaining that the Japanese word for "give me" is <u>kureyo</u>, which sounds like <u>crayon</u>. I force a smile.

What is humorous to the Japanese, then, may not seem funny in China, Iraq, or the United States. To some degree, too, the social diversity of our own country means that different types of people find humor in different situations. New Englanders, southerners, and

Because humor involves challenging established conventions, most U.S. comedians—including Margaret Cho—have been social "outsiders," members of racial and ethnic minorities.

westerners have their own brands of humor, as do Latinos and Anglos, fifteen- and forty-year-olds, Wall Street bankers and southwestern rodeo riders.

But, for everyone, humor deals with topics that lend themselves to double meanings or *controversy*. For example, the first jokes many of us learned as children were about culturally taboo bodily functions. The mere mention of "unmentionable acts" or even certain parts of the body can dissolve young faces in laughter.

Are there jokes that break through the culture barrier? Yes, but they must touch upon universal human experiences such as betraying a friend.

I think of a number of jokes, but none seems likely to work. Understanding jokes about the United States is difficult for people who have never been there. Is there something more universal? Inspiration: "Two fellows

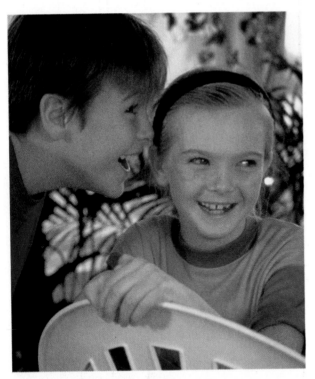

There are two sides to humor. On the one hand, people use humor as a safety valve to express potentially disruptive sentiments with little harm. On the other hand, people also make fun of others, elevating themselves at the expense of someone else.

are walking in the woods and come upon a huge bear. One guy leans over and tightens up the laces on his running shoes. 'Jake,' says the other, 'what are you doing? You can't outrun this bear!' 'I don't have to outrun the bear,' responds Jake, 'I just have to outrun you!' Smiles all around.

Humor and health have always been related. During the Middle Ages, people used the word *humors* (derived from the Latin word *humidus*, meaning "moist") to mean a balance of bodily fluids that regulate a person's well-being. Researchers today document the power of humor to reduce stress and improve health, confirming the old saying "Laughter is the best medicine" (Robinson, 1983; Haig, 1988). But, at the extreme, people who always take conventional reality

lightly risk being defined as deviant or even mentally ill (a common stereotype depicts insane people as laughing uncontrollably, and we have long dubbed mental hospitals "funny farms").

Also, every social group considers certain topics too sensitive for humorous treatment. One can joke about such things, but doing so may bring criticism for telling a "sick" joke (and, therefore, *being* sick). People's religious beliefs, tragic accidents, or appalling crimes are the stuff of "sick" jokes.

The Functions of Humor

Humor is found everywhere because it works as a safety valve that vents potentially disruptive sentiments with little harm. That is, humor provides a way to express an opinion on a sensitive topic without being serious. Having said something controversial, a person can also use humor to diffuse the situation by simply stating, "I didn't mean anything by what I said; it was just a joke!"

Similarly, people use humor to relieve tension in uncomfortable situations. One study of medical examinations found most patients begin to joke with doctors to ease their own nervousness (Baker et al., 1997).

Humor and Conflict

If humor holds the potential to comfort those who laugh, it can also be used to harm others. Men who tell jokes about women, for example, typically are voicing some measure of hostility toward them (Powell & Paton, 1988; Benokraitis & Feagin, 1995). Similarly, jokes at the expense of homosexuals reveal the tensions surrounding sexual orientation in the United States. Humor often is a sign of real conflict in situations in which one or both parties choose not to bring the conflict out into the open (Primeggia & Varacalli, 1990).

"Put-down" jokes make one category of people feel good at the expense of another. After collecting and analyzing jokes from many societies, Christie Davies (1990) concluded that conflict between ethnic groups is one driving force behind humor almost everywhere. The typical ethnic joke makes fun of some disadvantaged category of people, thereby making the jokester and the audience superior. Given the Anglo-Saxon traditions of U.S. society, Poles and other ethnic and racial minorities have long been the butt of jokes, as have Newfoundlanders ("Newfies") in eastern Canada, the Irish in Scotland, Sikhs in India, Turks in Germany, Hausas in Nigeria, Tasmanians in Australia, and Kurds in Iraq.

Disadvantaged people also make fun of the powerful, although usually with some care. Women in the United States joke about men, just as African Americans find humor in white people's ways, and poor people poke fun at the rich. Throughout the world, people target their leaders with humor, and officials in some countries take such jokes seriously enough to suppress them (cf. Speier, 1998).

In sum, the significance of humor is much greater than we may think. Humor is a means of mental escape from a conventional world that is never entirely to our liking (Flaherty, 1984, 1990; Yoels & Clair, 1995). Indeed, this fact explains why so many of our nation's comedians come from among the ranks of historically oppressed peoples, including Jews and African Americans. As long as we maintain a sense of humor, we assert our freedom and are not prisoners of reality. By putting a smile on our faces, we change ourselves and the world just a little.

SUMMARY

1. Social structure provides guidelines for behavior, which helps to make everyday life understandable and predictable.

2. A major component of social structure is status. Within an entire status set, a master status has special significance for a person's identity.

3. Ascribed statuses are involuntary, whereas achieved statuses are earned. In practice, most statuses are both ascribed and achieved.

4. Role is the dynamic expression of a status. Incompatible roles linked to two or more statuses generate role conflict; likewise, incompatible roles linked to a single status cause role strain.

5. "The social construction of reality" refers to the idea that we build the social world through our interactions with others.

6. The Thomas theorem states that situations defined as real become real in their consequences.

7. Ethnomethodology reveals the assumptions and understandings people have of their social world.

8. Dramaturgical analysis views everyday life as theatrical performance, noting that people try to create particular impressions in the minds of others.

9. Social power affects performances, which is one reason men's behavior typically differs from women's.

10. Everyday behavior carries the ever-present danger of embarrassment, or "loss of face." People use tact to prevent others' performances from breaking down.

11. Language is vital to the process of socially constructing reality. In various ways, language defines women and men differently, generally to the advantage of men.

12. Humor stems from the difference between conventional and unconventional definitions of a situation. Because humor is an element of culture, people throughout the world find different situations funny.

KEY CONCEPTS

social interaction (p. 139) the process by which people act and react in relation to others

status (p. 140) a social position that an individual occupies

status set (p. 140) all the statuses a person holds at a given time

ascribed status (p. 140) a social position a person receives at birth or assumes involuntarily later in life

achieved status (p. 141) a social position a person assumes voluntarily that reflects personal ability and effort

master status (p. 141) a status that has special importance for social identity, often shaping a person's entire life

role (p. 141) behavior expected of someone who holds a particular status

role set (p. 142) a number of roles attached to a single status

role conflict (p. 143) conflict between the roles corresponding to two or more statuses

role strain (p. 143) tension between roles connected to a single status

social construction of reality (p. 144) the process by which people creatively shape reality through social interaction

Thomas theorem (p. 145) W. I. Thomas's assertion that situations that are defined as real are real in their consequences

ethnomethodology (p. 146) Harold Garfinkel's term for the study of the way people make sense of their everyday surroundings

dramaturgical analysis (p. 147) Goffman's term for the study of social interaction in terms of theatrical performance

presentation of self (p. 147) Goffman's term for an individual's efforts to create specific impressions in the minds of others

nonverbal communication (p. 149) communication using body movements, gestures, and facial expressions rather than speech

personal space (p. 152) the surrounding area over which a person makes some claim to privacy

CRITICAL-THINKING QUESTIONS

1. Consider ways in which a physical disability can serve as a master status. What assumptions do people commonly make about the mental ability of someone with a physical disability such as cerebral palsy? What assumptions are made about the person's sexuality?

2. The word "conversation" has the same root as the religious term "convert," suggesting that we engage one another with the expectation of change on the part of everyone involved. In what sense, then, does good-faith conversation necessitate open-mindedness on everyone's part?

3. George Jean Nathan once quipped, "I only drink to make other people interesting." What does this mean in terms of reality construction? Can you identify the elements of humor in this statement?

4. Here is a joke about sociologists: "Question—How many sociologists does it take to change a light bulb? Answer—None, because there is nothing wrong with the light bulb; it's *the system* that needs to be changed!" What makes this joke funny? What sort of people are likely to get it? What kind of people probably won't? Why?

APPLICATIONS AND EXERCISES

1. Write down as many of your own statuses as you can. Do you consider any of your statuses a master status? To what extent is each of your statuses ascribed and achieved?

2. During the next twenty-four hours, every time somebody asks, "How are you?" stop and actually give a truthful answer. What happens when you respond to a "polite" question in an unexpected way? (Listen to what people say and also note their body language.) What does this experiment suggest about everyday interactions?

3. This chapter illustrated Erving Goffman's ideas with a description of a physician's office. Investigate the offices of several professors in the same way. What furniture is there, and how is it arranged? What "props" do professors use? How are the offices of physicians and professors different? Which are tidier? Why?

4. Spend an hour or two walking around the businesses of your town (or shops at a local mall). Observe the presence of women and men at each location. Based on your observations, would you conclude that physical space is "gendered"?

5. Packaged in the back of this new textbook is an interactive CD-ROM that offers a variety of study and review materials intended to help you better understand the material covered in this chapter. For this chapter, the CD-ROM contains an author's tip video, Real Life Sociology videos, other relevant audio and video, interactive map animations, audio journal entries from the author, Web links, and much more.

SITES TO SEE

http://www.prenhall.com/macionis

Visit the interactive *Companion Website*™ that accompanies this text. Begin by clicking on the cover of your book. You will find a chapter-by-chapter study guide, practice tests, and a significant portion of the text for on-line review, as well as many suggested Web links.

http://www.census.gov/genealogy/www/

Many interesting patterns of everyday life involve names. This Census Bureau Web site has a search engine for names. Study the frequency of different last names (or investigate first names) in the U.S. population. What patterns can you find? How many others share your own name?

http://www.ai.mit.edu/projects/humanoid-robotics-group/kismet.html

Is it possible to build a machine capable of human interaction? That is the goal of robotics engineers at the Massachusetts Institute of Technology. Their Web site provides

details and photographs. Look over their work and think about issues raised in this chapter. In what ways are machines able—and unable—to mimic human behavior?

http://www.georgetown.edu/faculty/tannend/

Here is the personal home page for Deborah Tannen, whose research is noted in the chapter.

http://www.achievement.org/autodoc/page/par0pro-1

Read more about the life and activism of Rosa Parks, who helped launch the civil rights movement in 1955.

http://www.paulekman.com

Discover more about Paul Ekman's research on human emotions.

http://www.people.brandeis.edu/~teuber/goffmanbio.html

Read more about the life and work of Erving Goffman at this site.

INVESTIGATE WITH CONTENTSELECT

Follow the instructions found on page 23 of this textbook to enter this chapter of the book's *Companion Website*™. Once in the chapter, click on the ContentSelect icon at the bottom left of your screen and enter your personal User ID and Password. Enter keywords such as "ethnomethodology," "Goffman," and "emotions," and the search engine will help you become an effective researcher.

CHAPTER

7

Colin William Moss (b. 1914, English)
Hunger Marchers, 1936

Oil on canvas, 64 × 76.5 cm.
The Bridgeman Art Library.

GROUPS AND ORGANIZATIONS

Back in 1948, people in Pasadena, California, paid little attention to the opening of a new restaurant. Yet one small business—owned by brothers Maurice and Richard McDonald—would not only transform the restaurant industry but also introduce a new organizational model copied by countless businesses of all kinds.

The McDonald brothers' basic concept, which we now call "fast food," was to serve meals quickly and cheaply to large numbers of people. The brothers trained employees to perform highly specialized jobs, so that one person grilled hamburgers while others "dressed" them, made French fries, whipped up milkshakes, and presented the food to the customers in assembly-line fashion.

As the years went by, the McDonald brothers prospered, and they decided to move their single restaurant from Pasadena to San Bernardino. It was there, in 1954, that Ray Kroc, a traveling blender and mixer merchant, paid them a visit.

Kroc was fascinated by the efficiency of the brothers' system and saw the potential for a whole chain of fast-food restaurants. The three launched the plan as partners. Soon, however, Kroc bought out the McDonalds, and he went on to become one of the greatest success stories of all time. Today, about 28,000 McDonald's restaurants have served more than 150 billion hamburgers to people throughout the United States and in 120 other nations around the world.

The success of McDonald's is evidence of more than just the popularity of hamburgers. The larger importance of McDonald's lies in the extent to which the principles that guide this company are coming to dominate social life in the United States and elsewhere (Ritzer, 1993, 1998, 2000).

We begin with an examination of *social groups*, the clusters of people with whom we interact in much of our daily lives. As we shall see, the scope of group life expanded greatly during the course of the twentieth century. Having evolved from a close-knit world of families, local neighborhoods, and small businesses, our society now turns on the operation of huge businesses and other bureaucracies that sociologists describe as *formal organizations*. Understanding how this expanding scale of life came to be—and what it means for us as individuals—are this chapter's main objectives.

SOCIAL GROUPS

Almost everyone seeks a sense of belonging, which is the experience of group life. A **social group** is made up of *two or more people who identify and interact with one another*. Human beings come together in couples, families, circles of friends, churches, clubs, businesses, neighborhoods, and large organizations. Whatever its form, a group is made up of people with shared experiences, loyalties, and interests. In short, while keeping their individuality, members of social groups also think of themselves as a special "we."

Not every collection of individuals can be called a group. People with a status in common, such as women, homeowners, gay men, soldiers, millionaires, and Roman Catholics, are not a group but a *category*. Although they know others who hold the same status, most are strangers to one another.

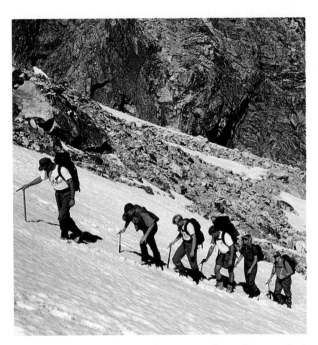

As human beings, we live our lives as members of groups. Such groups may be large or small, temporary or long-lasting. The United States is regarded as a country where people are especially likely to form groups based on kinship, heritage, or some shared interest.

What about students sitting together in a lecture hall or bathers enjoying a hot day at the beach? Some people in such settings may interact, but only with a few others. These temporary, loosely formed collections of people are better termed a *crowd*. In general, crowds are too anonymous and transitory to qualify as groups.

The right circumstances, however, can turn a crowd into a group. People riding in an elevator that stalls between floors generally recognize their common plight and turn to each other for help. Sometimes out of accidents and disasters, people form lasting relationships.

PRIMARY AND SECONDARY GROUPS

Acquaintances commonly greet one another with a smile and a "Hi! How are you?" The response is usually, "Just fine, thanks. How about you?" This answer is often more scripted than truthful. In most cases, providing a detailed account of how you are *really* doing would make most people feel so awkward they would beat a hasty retreat.

Sociologists designate two types of social groups, depending on the degree of genuine personal concern that members show for one another. According to Charles Horton Cooley (1864–1929), a **primary group** is *a small social group whose members share personal and enduring relationships*. Bound by *primary relationships*, people typically spend a great deal of time together, engage in a wide range of activities, and feel that they know one another well. Although not without conflict from time to time, members of primary groups display real concern for each other's welfare. The family is every society's most important primary group.

For a biographical sketch of Charles Horton Cooley, see the Gallery of Sociologists at http://www.TheSociologyPage.com

Cooley called these personal and tightly integrated groups *primary* because they are among the first groups we experience in life. In addition, the family and early play groups hold primary importance in the socialization process, shaping attitudes, behavior, and social identity.

Primary relationships give people a comforting sense of security. In the familiar social circle of family or friends, people feel they can "be themselves" without worrying about the impression they are making.

Members of primary groups help one another in many ways, but they generally think of their ties as ends in themselves rather than as means to some other end. In other words, we prefer to think that kinship and friendship link people who belong together. Moreover, members of a primary group tend to view each other as unique and irreplaceable. Especially in the family, we are bound to others by emotion and loyalty. Brothers and sisters may not always get along, but they always remain siblings.

In contrast to the primary group, the **secondary group** is *a large and impersonal social group whose members pursue a specific goal or activity*. In most respects, secondary groups have precisely the opposite characteristics of primary groups. *Secondary relationships* involve weak emotional ties and little personal knowledge of one another. Most secondary groups are short term, beginning and ending without particular significance. Students in a college sociology course, for instance, who probably will not see many of the others again after the semester ends, exemplify the secondary group.

Secondary groups include many more people than primary groups. For example, dozens or even hundreds of people may work together in the same office, yet most of them pay only passing attention to one another. In some cases, time may transform a group from secondary to primary, as with co-workers who share an office for many years. But, generally, members of a secondary group do not think of themselves as "we."

Whereas members of primary groups display a *personal orientation*, people in secondary groups have a *goal orientation*. Secondary ties need not be hostile or cold, of course. Interaction between students, co-workers, and business associates often is pleasant even if it is impersonal. But whereas primary group members define themselves according to *who* they are in terms of kinship or personal qualities, people in secondary groups look to one another for *what* they are or what they can do for each other. Put simply, people in secondary groups tend to "keep score," mindful of what they give others and what they receive in return. This goal orientation means that secondary group members usually remain formal and polite. In a secondary relationship, therefore, we ask the question "How are you?" without expecting a truthful answer.

Table 7–1 summarizes the characteristics that distinguish primary and secondary groups. Keep in mind that these traits define two types of groups in ideal terms; many real groups contain elements of both. But putting these concepts at opposite ends of a continuum helps us describe and analyze group life.

Many people think that small towns and rural areas have mostly primary relationships and that large cities are characterized by more secondary ties. This generalization holds much truth, but some urban neighborhoods—especially those populated by people of a single ethnic or religious category—are very tightly knit.

GROUP LEADERSHIP

How do groups operate? One important element of group dynamics is leadership. Many small friendship groups have no leader at all, but most large secondary groups have a formal chain of command.

Two Leadership Roles

Groups typically benefit from two kinds of leadership. **Instrumental leadership** is *group leadership that emphasizes the completion of tasks.* Members look to instrumental leaders to get things done. **Expressive leadership,** on the other hand, is *group leadership that focuses on collective well-being.* Expressive leaders take less of an interest in achieving goals than in raising group morale and minimizing tension and conflict between members.

Because they concentrate on performance, instrumental leaders usually have formal, secondary relationships with other group members. Instrumental

TABLE 7–1 Primary Groups and Secondary Groups: A Summary		
	Primary ◄——► Secondary Group Group	
Quality of Relationships	Personal orientation	Goal orientation
Duration of Relationships	Usually long term	Variable; often short term
Breadth of Relationships	Broad; usually involving many activities	Narrow; usually involving few activities
Subjective Perception of Relationships	As ends in themselves	As means to an end
Typical Examples	Families; circles of friends	Co-workers; political organizations

leaders give orders and reward or punish members according to their contribution to the group's efforts. Expressive leaders build more personal, primary ties. They offer sympathy to a member going through a tough time, keep the group united, and lighten a tense moment with humor. Whereas successful instrumental leaders enjoy more *respect* from members, expressive leaders generally receive more personal *affection*.

In the traditional North American family, the two types of leadership are linked to gender. Historically, cultural norms bestowed instrumental leadership on men, who, as fathers and husbands, assumed primary responsibility for earning income and making major family decisions. Expressive leadership traditionally belonged to women: Mothers and wives encouraged supportive and peaceful relationships between family members. One result of this division of labor was that many children had greater respect for their fathers but closer personal ties with their mothers (Parsons & Bales, 1955; Macionis, 1978a).

Greater equality between men and women has blurred this gender-based distinction between instrumental and expressive leadership. In most group settings, women and men now assume both leadership roles.

Three Leadership Styles

Sociologists also characterize leadership in terms of decision-making style. *Authoritarian leadership* focuses

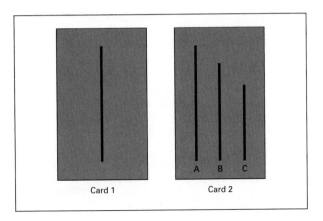

FIGURE 7–1 Cards Used in Asch's Experiment in Group Conformity

Source: Asch (1952).

on instrumental concerns, takes personal charge of decision making, and demands strict compliance from subordinates. Although this leadership style may win little affection from the group, a fast-acting authoritarian leader is appreciated in a crisis.

Democratic leadership is more expressive and makes a point of including everyone in the decision-making process. Although less successful when crises leave little time for discussion, democratic leaders generally draw on the ideas of all members to develop creative solutions to problems.

Laissez-faire leadership (a French phrase roughly meaning "to leave alone") allows the group to function largely on its own. This style typically is the least effective in promoting group goals (White & Lippitt, 1953; Ridgeway, 1983).

GROUP CONFORMITY

Groups influence the behavior of members and promote conformity. "Fitting in" provides a secure feeling of belonging, but, at the extreme, group pressure can be unpleasant and, at times, dangerous. Moreover, even strangers can foster conformity, as experiments by Solomon Asch and Stanley Milgram showed.

Asch's Research

Solomon Asch (1952) conducted a classic experiment that showed the power of groups to generate conformity. Asch recruited students allegedly for a study of visual perception. Before the experiment began, he explained to all but one member in a small group that

their real purpose was to put pressure on the remaining person. Arranging six to eight students around a table, Asch showed them a "standard" line, as drawn on Card 1 in Figure 7–1, and asked them to match it to one of three lines on Card 2.

Anyone with normal vision could easily see that the line marked "A" on Card 2 is the correct choice. Initially, as planned, everyone made the matches correctly. But then Asch's secret accomplices began answering incorrectly, leaving the naive subject (seated at the table in order to answer next to last) bewildered and uncomfortable.

What happened? Asch found that one-third of all subjects conformed to the others by answering incorrectly. Apparently, many of us are willing to compromise our own judgment to avoid being different, even from people we do not know.

Milgram's Research

Stanley Milgram, a former student of Solomon Asch, conducted conformity experiments of his own. In Milgram's controversial study (1963, 1965; Miller, 1986), a researcher explained to male recruits that they would be taking part in a study of how punishment affects learning. One by one, he assigned subjects to the role of "teacher" and placed another individual—actually an accomplice of Milgram—in a connecting room to pose as a "learner."

The teacher watched as the learner was seated in a contraption that looked like an electric chair. The researcher applied electrode paste to one of the learner's wrists, explaining that this would "prevent blisters and burns." The researcher then attached an electrode to the wrist and secured the leather straps, explaining that these would "prevent excessive movement while the learner is being shocked." Although the shocks would be painful, the researcher assured the teacher that they would cause "no permanent tissue damage."

The researcher then led the teacher back to the next room, explaining that the "electric chair" was connected to a "shock generator," a phony but realistic-looking piece of equipment with a label that read "Shock Generator, Type ZLB, Dyson Instrument Company, Waltham, Mass." On the front was a dial that supposedly regulated electric current from 15 volts (labeled "Slight Shock") to 300 volts (marked "Intense Shock") to 450 volts (marked "Danger: Severe Shock").

Seated in front of the "shock generator," the teacher was told to read aloud pairs of words. Then the teacher was to repeat the first word of each pair and wait for the learner to recall the second word. Whenever the learner failed to answer correctly, the teacher was told to apply an electric shock.

The researcher directed the teacher to begin at the lowest level (15 volts) and to increase the shock by 15 volts every time the learner made a mistake. And so the teacher did. At 75, 90, and 105 volts, the teacher heard moans from the learner; at 120 volts, shouts of pain; at 270 volts, screams; at 315 volts, pounding on the wall; after that, deadly silence. None of forty subjects assigned to the role of teacher during the initial research even questioned the procedure before reaching 300 volts, and twenty-six of the subjects—almost two-thirds—went all the way to 450 volts. Even Milgram was surprised at how readily people obeyed authority figures.

Milgram (1964) then modified his research to see whether Solomon Asch had documented such a high degree of group conformity only because the task he used to measure group conformity was trivial. Could groups of ordinary people—not authority figures—also pressure people to administer electrical shocks?

This time, Milgram formed a group of three teachers, two of whom were his accomplices. Each of the three teachers was to suggest a shock level when the learner made an error; the group would then administer the *lowest* of the three suggestions. This arrangement gave the naive subject the power to deliver a lesser shock regardless of what the others proposed.

The accomplices suggested increasing the shock level with each error, putting pressure on the third member to do the same. And, in fact, they succeeded. The subjects applied voltages three to four times higher than subjects who acted alone under control conditions. Thus Milgram's research suggests that people are likely to follow directions from not only "legitimate authority figures" but also from groups of ordinary individuals, even when it means inflicting harm on another person.

Janis's Research

Experts also cave in to group pressure, says Irving L. Janis (1972, 1989). Janis contends that a number of U.S. foreign policy errors, including the failure to foresee the Japanese attack on Pearl Harbor during World War II and the ill-fated Vietnam War, resulted from group conformity among our highest-ranking political leaders.

Common sense tells us that group discussion improves decision making. Janis counters that group members often seek consensus that closes off other points of view. Janis called this process **groupthink**, *the tendency of group members to conform, resulting in a narrow view of some issue.*

A classic example of groupthink led to the disastrous 1961 invasion of the Bay of Pigs in Cuba. Looking back, Arthur Schlesinger, Jr., an advisor to President Kennedy, confessed to feeling guilty for "having kept so quiet during those crucial discussions in the Cabinet Room," adding that the group discouraged anyone from challenging what, in hindsight, Schlesinger considered "nonsense" (quoted in Janis, 1972:30, 40).

REFERENCE GROUPS

How do we assess our own attitudes and behavior? Often we use a **reference group,** *a social group that serves as a point of reference in making evaluations and decisions.*

A young man who imagines his family's response to a woman he is dating is using his family as a reference group. Similarly, a supervisor who tries to gauge her employees' reactions to a new vacation policy is using them as a standard of reference. As these examples suggest, reference groups can be primary or secondary. In either case, our need to conform means that others' attitudes greatly affect us.

We also use groups that we do *not* belong to for reference. Being well prepared for a job interview means showing up dressed the way people in that company dress for work. Conforming to groups we do not belong to as a strategy to win acceptance illustrates the process of *anticipatory socialization*, described in Chapter 5 ("Socialization").

Stouffer's Research

Samuel A. Stouffer (1949) conducted a classic study of reference group dynamics during World War II. Researchers asked soldiers to rate their own or any competent soldier's chances of promotion in their army unit. One might guess that soldiers serving in outfits with a high promotion rate would be optimistic about their own advancement. Yet Stouffer's research pointed to the opposite conclusion: Soldiers in army units with low promotion rates actually were more positive about their chances to move ahead.

The key to understanding Stouffer's results lies in the groups against which soldiers measured themselves. Those having assignments with lower promotion rates looked around them and saw people making no more headway than they were. That is, although

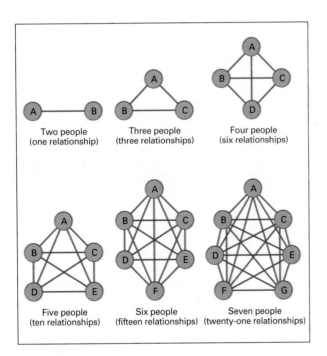

FIGURE 7–2 Group Size and Relationships

Two people
(one relationship)

Three people
(three relationships)

Four people
(six relationships)

Five people
(ten relationships)

Six people
(fifteen relationships)

Seven people
(twenty-one relationships)

they had not been promoted, neither had many others, so they did not feel deprived. On the other hand, soldiers in units with a higher promotion rate could easily think of people who had been promoted sooner or more often than they had. With such people in mind, even soldiers who had been promoted were likely to feel shortchanged.

The lesson is that we do not make judgments about ourselves in isolation, nor do we compare ourselves with just anyone. Regardless of our situation in *absolute* terms, we form a subjective sense of our well-being by looking at ourselves in relation to specific reference groups (Merton, 1968; Mirowsky, 1987).

INGROUPS AND OUTGROUPS

Everyone favors some groups over others, whether because of political outlook, social prestige, or just manner of dress. On the college campus, for example, left-leaning student activists may look down on fraternity members, whom they consider conservative; the Greeks, in turn, may snub the computer "nerds" and "grinds," who work too hard. Nearly every social landscape has a comparable mix of positive and negative evaluations.

Such judgments illustrate another element of group dynamics: the opposition of ingroups and outgroups. An **ingroup** is *a social group commanding a member's esteem and loyalty.* An ingroup exists in relation to an **outgroup,** *a social group toward which one feels competition or opposition.* Ingroups and outgroups are based on the idea that "we" have valued traits that "they" lack.

Tensions among groups sharpen their boundaries and give people a clearer social identity. At the same time, these group dynamics foster stereotypes and distort reality. Specifically, members of ingroups generally hold overly positive views of themselves and unfairly negative views of various outgroups.

Power also plays a part in intergroup relations. A powerful ingroup can define others as a lower-status outgroup. Historically, for example, white people have viewed people of color as an outgroup and subordinated them socially, politically, and economically. Internalizing these attitudes, minorities must struggle to overcome negative self-images. In short, ingroups and outgroups foster loyalty but also generate conflict (Tajfel, 1982; Bobo & Hutchings, 1996).

GROUP SIZE

If you are the first person to arrive at a party, you are in a position to watch some fascinating group dynamics. Until about six people enter the room, everyone usually shares a single conversation. But as more people arrive, the group soon divides into two or more clusters. Size plays an important role in how group members interact.

To understand the effects of group size, consider the mathematical number of relationships between two to seven people. As Figure 7–2 shows, two people form a single relationship, adding a third person results in three relationships, and adding a fourth person yields six. Increasing the number of people one at a time expands the number of relationships much more rapidly because every new person can interact with everyone already there. Thus, by the time seven people join one conversation, twenty-one "channels" connect them. With so many open channels at this point, the group usually divides.

The Dyad

German sociologist Georg Simmel (1858–1918) studied the social dynamics in the smallest groups. Simmel (1950; orig. 1902) used the term **dyad** to designate *a social group with two members.*

Simmel explained that social interaction in a dyad typically is more intense than in larger groups because

 For more about Georg Simmel, see his biography in the Gallery of Sociologists at http://www. TheSociologyPage.com

neither member shares the other's attention with anyone else. In the United States, love affairs, marriages, and the closest friendships are dyadic.

But like a stool with only two legs, dyads are unstable. Both members of a dyad must work to keep the relationship going; if either withdraws, the group collapses. Because the stability of marriages is important to society, the marital dyad is supported with legal, economic, and often religious ties.

The Triad

Simmel also studied the **triad**, *a social group with three members*. A triad contains three relationships, each joining two of the three people. A triad is more stable than a dyad because one member can act as a mediator should the relationship between the other two become strained. Such group dynamics help explain why members of a dyad (say, a married couple) often seek out a third person (a counselor) to air tension between them.

On the other hand, two of the three can pair up to press their views on the third, or two may intensify their relationship, leaving the other feeling left out. For example, when two of the three develop a romantic interest in each other, they will understand the old saying, "Two's company, three's a crowd."

As groups grow beyond three people, they become more stable and capable of withstanding the loss of even several members. At the same time, increases in group size reduce the intense personal interaction possible only in the smallest groups. Larger groups therefore are based less on personal attachment and more on formal rules and regulations. Such formality helps a group persist over time, although the group is not immune to change. After all, their numerous members give large groups more contact with the outside world, opening the door to new attitudes and behavior (Carley, 1991).

SOCIAL DIVERSITY:
RACE, CLASS, AND GENDER

Race, ethnicity, class, and gender also affect group dynamics. Peter Blau (1977; Blau, Blum, & Schwartz, 1982; South & Messner, 1986) points out four ways in which social diversity influences intergroup contact:

The triad, illustrated by Jonathan Green's painting Friends, includes three people. A triad is more stable than a dyad because conflict between any two persons can be mediated by the third member. Even so, should the relationship between any two become more intense in a positive sense, those two are likely to exclude the third.

Jonathan Green, *Friends*, 1992. Oil on masonite, 14 in. × 11 in. © Jonathan Green, Naples, Florida. Collection of Patric McCoy.

1. **Large groups turn inward.** Blau explains that the larger a group, the more likely its members are to have relationships just between themselves. Say a college is trying to enhance social diversity by increasing the number of international students. These students may add a dimension of difference, but as their numbers rise, they become more likely to form their own social group. Thus, efforts to promote social diversity may have the unintended effect of promoting separatism.

2. **Heterogeneous groups turn outward.** The more internally diverse a group is, the more

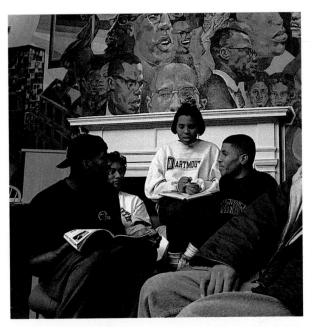

Today's college campuses value social diversity. One of the challenges of this movement is ensuring that all categories of students are fully integrated into campus life. This is not always easy. Following Blau's theory of group dynamics, as the number of minority students increases, these men and women are able to form a group unto themselves, perhaps interacting less with others.

likely its members are to interact with outsiders. Campus groups that recruit people of both sexes and various social backgrounds typically have broader social contact than those with members of one social type.

3. **Social equality promotes contact.** To the extent that all groups have the same social standing, members of all the groups will interact. Thus, whether groups keep to themselves depends on how much the groups form a social hierarchy.

4. **Physical boundaries create social boundaries.** To the extent that a social group is physically segregated from others (by having its own dorm or dining area, for example), its members are less likely to associate with other people.

NETWORKS

A **network** is *a web of weak social ties.* Think of a network as a "fuzzy" group containing people who come into occasional contact but who lack a sense of boundaries and belonging. If we think of a group as a "circle of friends," then we might describe a network as a "social web" expanding outward, often reaching great distances and including large numbers of people.

Some networks are close to being groups, as is the case with college friends who stay in touch after graduation by e-mail and telephone. More commonly, however, a network includes people we *know of*—or who *know of us*—but with whom we interact rarely, if at all. As one woman with a widespread reputation as a community organizer explains, "I get calls at home, someone says, 'Are you Roseann Navarro? Somebody told me to call you. I have this problem'" (quoted in Kaminer, 1984:94).

Network ties often give us the sense that we live in a small world. In another classic experiment, Stanley Milgram (1967; Watts, 1999) gave letters to subjects in Kansas and Nebraska intended for a few specific people in Boston who were unknown to the original subjects. No addresses were supplied, and the subjects in the study were instructed to send the letters to others they knew personally who might know the target people. Milgram found that letters reached the target people with, on average, six subjects helping out. This result led Milgram to conclude that just about everyone is connected to everyone else with "six degrees of separation."

Network ties may be weak, but they can be a powerful resource. For immigrants seeking to become established in a new community, businesspeople seeking to expand their operations, or anyone looking for a job, *whom you know* is often just as important as *what you know* (cf. Luo, 1997; Hagan, 1998; Petersen, Saporta, & Seidel, 2000).

Networks are based on people's colleges, clubs, neighborhoods, political parties, and personal interests. Obviously, some networks contain people with much more wealth, power, and prestige than others, which is what the expression "well connected" means. The networks of more privileged categories of people—including whites in comparison to African Americans and Hispanics—are a more valuable form of "social capital," which is more likely to land people in those categories higher-paying jobs, for example (Kasinitz & Rosenberg, 1996; Green, Tigges, & Diaz, 1999).

Some people also have denser networks than others; that is, they are connected to more people. Typically, the most extensive social networks include people who are young, well educated, and living in large cities (Markovsky et al., 1993; Kadushin, 1995;

The Internet: A Global Network

Its origins are reminiscent of the film popular during the cold war in the 1960s, *Dr. Strangelove.* Three decades ago, government officials and scientists were trying to figure out how to run the country after an atomic attack, which, they assumed, would knock out telephones and television. The brilliant solution was to devise a communication system with no central headquarters, no one in charge, and no main power switch—in short, an electronic web that would link the country in one vast network.

By 1985, a web of high-speed data lines was in place, and the Internet was about to be born. Today, the Internet connects thousands of colleges and universities and tens of thousands of government offices, all of which share in the cost of its operation. Tens of millions of businesses and individuals at home also connect to this "information superhighway" using modems and

subscriptions to commercial Internet service providers.

How many people use the Internet? A rough estimate is that, in 2002, more than 400 million people in 180 (of 192) countries around the world are connected by the largest network in history.

What does the network offer to individuals? Popular search engines such as YAHOO! (type in http://www.yahoo.com) provide site listings for just about any topic you can imagine. Through electronic mail you can start a cyber-romance with a pen pal, write to your textbook author (macionis@kenyon.edu), or even send a message to the president of the United States (president@whitehouse.gov). You can also use the Internet to join discussion groups, take "virtual tours" of museums, locate data from government agencies (a good starting point is http://www.census.gov), explore Web pages of sociological interest (try the author's Web site, at http://

www.TheSociologyPage.com), or review for exams in this course (http://www.prenhall.com/macionis). With no formal rules for its use, the Internet's potential is limited only by our imagination.

Ironically, perhaps, it is precisely this freedom that disturbs some people. Critics claim that "electronic democracy" threatens our political system, parents fear that their children will access sexually explicit sites, and purists bristle as the Internet becomes flooded with advertising.

In its "anything-goes" character, the Internet is like the real world. Not surprisingly, therefore, more and more people now use passwords, fees, and other "gates" to create restricted subnetworks limited to people like themselves. From one vast network, then, is emerging a host of social groups.

Sources: Based on Elmer-DeWitt (1993, 1994b), Hafner (1994), and O'Connor (1997).

O'Brien, Hassinger, & Dershem, 1996; Fernandez & Weinberg, 1997; Podolny & Baron, 1997).

Gender also shapes networks. Although the networks of men and women typically are the same size, women include more relatives (and other women) in their networks, whereas men include more co-workers (and other men). Research suggests that women's ties do not carry quite the same clout as typical "old boy" networks. Even so, as gender equality increases in the United States, the networks of women and men are becoming more alike (Moore, 1991, 1992; Wright, 1995; Mencken & Winfield, 1999; Reskin & McBrier, 2000).

Finally, new information technology has generated a global network of unprecedented size in the form of the Internet. The box takes a closer look at this twenty-first century form of communication, and

Global Map 7–1 on page 172 shows access to the Internet around the world.

FORMAL ORGANIZATIONS

A century ago, most people in the United States lived in small groups of family, friends, and neighbors. Today, our lives revolve increasingly around **formal organizations,** *large secondary groups that are organized to achieve their goals efficiently.*

Formal organizations, such as business corporations and government agencies, differ from families and neighborhoods in an important way: Their greater size makes social relations less personal and fosters a formal, planned atmosphere. In other words, formal organizations operate in a deliberate way, not

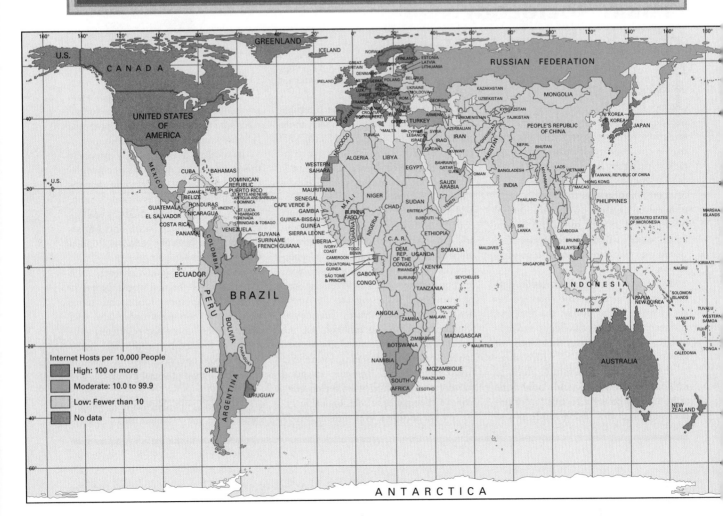

GLOBAL MAP 7–1 Access to the Internet in Global Perspective

This map shows access to the Internet around the world in terms of the number of Internet hosts for every 10,000 people. Most high-income countries and many middle-income nations are rated as having high Internet access. By contrast, about half the world's nations (mostly those with low average incomes) offer little access. What effect does this have on people's access to information? What are the likely consequences of this disparity for the future in terms of global inequality?

Source: The World Bank (2001).

to meet personal needs but to accomplish complex jobs.

When you think about it, organizing some 285 million members of society is an incredible accomplishment, involving countless jobs, from collecting taxes to delivering the mail. To carry out most of these tasks, we rely on large formal organizations. The U.S. government, the nation's largest formal organization, employs more than 5 million people in hundreds of agencies and the armed forces. Large formal organizations develop lives and cultures of their own so that, as members come and go, their operation can stay the same over many years.

TYPES OF FORMAL ORGANIZATIONS

Amitai Etzioni (1975) identified three types of formal organizations, distinguished by the reasons people participate: utilitarian organizations, normative organizations, and coercive organizations.

Utilitarian Organizations

Just about everyone who works for income belongs to a *utilitarian organization*, one that pays people for their efforts. For example, large businesses generate profits for their owners and income for their employees. Joining utilitarian organizations usually is a matter of individual choice, although, obviously, most people must join one or another utilitarian organization to make a living.

Normative Organizations

People join *normative organizations* not for income but to pursue some goal they think is morally worthwhile. Sometimes called *voluntary associations*, these include community service groups (such as the Lions Club, the League of Women Voters, and the Red Cross), as well as political parties and religious organizations. In global perspective, people in the United States tend to join voluntary associations (Curtis, Grabb, & Baer, 1992). Figure 7–3 provides a comparative glance at membership in arts-related organizations for selected countries.

Coercive Organizations

Coercive organizations have an involuntary membership. That is, people are forced to join these organizations as a form of punishment (prisons) or treatment (psychiatric hospitals). Coercive organizations have special physical features, such as locked doors and

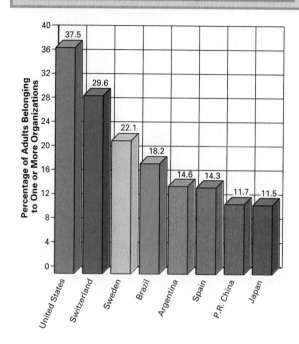

GLOBAL SNAPSHOT

FIGURE 7–3 Membership in Arts-Related Organizations

Source: Inglehart et al. (2000).

barred windows, and are supervised by security personnel. They isolate people as "inmates" or "patients" for a period of time, seeking to change attitudes and behavior radically. Recall from Chapter 5 ("Socialization") the power of *total institutions* to transform a human being's sense of self.

From differing vantage points, any particular organization may fall into all of these categories. A psychiatric hospital, for example, serves as a coercive organization for a patient, a utilitarian organization for a psychiatrist, and a normative organization for a part-time hospital volunteer.

ORIGINS OF BUREAUCRACY

Formal organizations date back thousands of years. Elites who controlled early empires relied on officials to collect taxes, undertake military campaigns, and construct monumental structures, from the Great Wall of China to the pyramids of Egypt.

Although formal organization is vital to modern, high-income nations, it is far from new. Twenty-five centuries ago, the Chinese philosopher and teacher K'ung Fu-Tzu (known to Westerners as Confucius) endorsed the idea that government offices should be filled by the most talented young men. This led to what was probably the world's first system of civil service examinations. Here, would-be bureaucrats compose essays to demonstrate their knowledge of Confucian texts.

These early organizations had two limitations, however. First, they lacked the technology to communicate quickly, to travel over large distances, and to collect and store information. Second, tradition is strong in preindustrial societies, so organizational goals were to preserve cultural systems, not to change them. But during the last few centuries, what Max Weber called a "rational worldview" emerged in parts of the world, a process described in Chapter 4 ("Society"). In Europe and North America, the Industrial Revolution ushered in a new organizational structure concerned with efficiency, which Weber called *bureaucracy.*

CHARACTERISTICS OF BUREAUCRACY

Bureaucracy is *an organizational model rationally designed to perform tasks efficiently.* Bureaucratic officials deliberately enact and revise policy in order to increase efficiency. To appreciate the power and scope of bureaucratic organization in the twenty-first century, consider this: Any one of nearly 300 million phones in the United States can connect you, within seconds, to any other phone—in homes, businesses, automobiles, or even a hiker's backpack on a remote mountain trail in the Adirondacks. Such instant communication was beyond the imagination of people who lived in the ancient world.

Of course, the telephone system depends on technology such as electricity, fiberoptics, and computers. But the system could not exist without the organizational ability to keep track of every telephone call—noting which phone called which other phone, when, and for how long—and then present this information in the form of more than 100 million monthly telephone bills.

What are the specific traits that promote organizational efficiency? Max Weber (1978; orig. 1921) identified six key elements of the ideal bureaucratic organization:

1. **Specialization.** Our ancestors spent most of their time looking for food and shelter. Bureaucracy, by contrast, assigns individuals highly specialized duties.

2. **Hierarchy of offices.** Bureaucracies arrange personnel in a vertical ranking of offices. Each person is supervised by "higher-ups" in the organization while supervising others in lower positions. Usually, with few people at the top and many at the bottom, bureaucratic organizations take the form of a pyramid.

3. **Rules and regulations.** Cultural tradition counts for little in a bureaucracy. Instead, rationally enacted rules and regulations guide a bureaucracy's operation. Ideally, a bureaucracy seeks to operate in a completely predictable way.

4. **Technical competence.** Bureaucratic officials and staff have the technical competence to carry out their duties. Bureaucracies typically recruit new members according to set criteria and regularly monitor their performance. Such impersonal evaluation contrasts sharply with the ancient custom of favoring relatives, whatever their talents, over strangers.

5. **Impersonality.** Bureaucracy puts rules ahead of personal whim so that clients as well as workers are treated uniformly. From this detached approach stems the notion of the "faceless bureaucrat."

6. **Formal, written communication.** According to an old saying, the heart of bureaucracy is not people but paperwork. Rather than casual, face-to-face talk, bureaucracy relies on formal, written memos and reports, which accumulate in vast files and guide the operation of the organization.

Bureaucratic organization promotes efficiency by carefully recruiting personnel and limiting the unpredictable effects of personal taste and opinion. Table 7–2 summarizes the differences between small social groups and large formal organizations.

ORGANIZATIONAL ENVIRONMENT

No organization operates in a vacuum. How any organization performs depends not only on its own goals and policies but also on the **organizational environment,** *factors outside the organization that affect its operation.* These factors include technology, economic and political trends, the available work force, and other organizations.

Modern organizations are shaped by the *technology* of computers, telephone systems, and copiers. Computers give employees access to more information and people than ever before. At the same time, computer technology allows managers to monitor closely the activities of workers (Markoff, 1991).

Economic and political trends affect organizations. All organizations are helped or hindered by periodic economic growth or recession. Most industries also face competition from abroad as well as changes in law—such as new environmental standards—at home.

Population patterns, such as the size and composition of the surrounding populace, also affect organizations. The average age, typical education, and social diversity of a local community determine the available work force and, sometimes, the market for an organization's products or services.

Other organizations also contribute to the organizational environment. To be competitive, a hospital must be responsive to the insurance industry and organizations representing doctors, nurses, and other workers. It must also keep abreast of the equipment and procedures available at nearby facilities, as well as their prices.

TABLE 7–2 Small Groups and Formal Organizations: A Comparison

	Small Groups	Formal Organizations
Activities	Members typically engage in many of the same activities	Members typically engage in distinct, highly specialized activities
Hierarchy	Often informal or nonexistent	Clearly defined, corresponding to offices
Norms	Informal application of general norms	Clearly defined rules and regulations
Membership Criteria	Variable, often based on personal affection or kinship	Technical competence to carry out assigned tasks
Relationships	Variable; typically primary	Typically secondary, with selective primary ties
Communications	Typically casual and face to face	Typically formal and in writing
Focus	Person-oriented	Task-oriented

THE INFORMAL SIDE OF BUREAUCRACY

Weber's ideal bureaucracy deliberately regulates every activity. In actual organizations, however, human beings are creative (and stubborn) enough to resist bureaucratic blueprints. Informality may amount to simply cutting corners in one's job, but it can also provide needed flexibility (Scott, 1981).

Informality comes partly from the personalities of organizational leaders. Studies of U.S. corporations document that the qualities and quirks of individuals—including personal charisma and interpersonal skills—can have a great effect on organizational outcomes (Halberstam, 1986; Baron, Hannan, & Burton, 1999).

Authoritarian, democratic, and laissez-faire types of leadership (described earlier in this chapter) reflect individual personality as much as they do any organizational plan. Also, in the real world of organizations, leaders and their cronies sometimes seek to benefit personally by abusing organizational power. Perhaps even more commonly, leaders take credit for the efforts of their subordinates. For example, many executive assistants have far more authority

George Tooker's painting Government Bureau *is a powerful statement about the human costs of bureaucracy. The artist depicts members of the public in monotonous similitude—reduced from human beings to mere "cases" to be disposed of as quickly as possible. Set apart from others by their positions, officials are "faceless bureaucrats" concerned more with numbers than with providing genuine assistance (notice that the artist places the fingers of the officials on calculators).*

George Tooker, *Government Bureau*, 1956. Egg tempera on gesso panel, 19⅝ x 29⅝ inches. The Metropolitan Museum of Art, George A. Hearn Fund, 1956 (56.78). Photograph © 1984 The Metropolitan Museum of Art.

and responsibility than their official job titles and salaries suggest.

Communication offers another example of informality within large organizations. Memos and other written communications are the formal way to spread information through the organization. Typically, however, individuals create informal networks, or "grapevines," that spread information quickly, if not always accurately. Grapevines, using both word-of-mouth and e-mail, are particularly important to subordinates because higher-ups may try to keep important information from them.

The spread of e-mail has "flattened" organizational hierarchies somewhat, because it allows even the lowest-ranking employee to bypass immediate superiors and communicate directly with the organization's leader or even with all fellow employees at once. Some organizations object to "open-channel" communication and limit employees' use of e-mail. Microsoft Corporation (whose founder, Bill Gates, has an unlisted address yet still receives hundreds of e-mail messages a day) has developed "screens" that allow messages only from approved people to reach a particular computer terminal (Gwynne & Dickerson, 1997).

Using new information technology and age-old human ingenuity, members of organizations try to personalize their procedures and surroundings. Such efforts suggest that we should now take a closer look at some of the problems of bureaucracy.

PROBLEMS OF BUREAUCRACY

We rely on bureaucracy to manage countless dimensions of everyday life, but many people are uneasy about large organizations. Bureaucracy can dehumanize and manipulate us, and some say it poses a threat to political democracy.

Bureaucratic Alienation

Max Weber touted bureaucracy as a model of productivity. Nonetheless, Weber was keenly aware of bureaucracy's ability to *dehumanize* the people it is supposed to serve. The same impersonality that fosters efficiency also keeps officials and clients from responding to each other's unique, personal needs. On the contrary, officials must treat each client impersonally, as a standard "case."

According to Weber, formal organizations create *alienation* by reducing the human being to "a small cog in a ceaselessly moving mechanism" (1978:988; orig. 1921). Although formal organizations are intended to benefit humanity, Weber feared that people could end up serving formal organizations.

Bureaucratic Inefficiency and Ritualism

Inefficiency, the failure of an organization to carry out the work that it exists to perform, is a familiar problem. According to one report, the General Services Administration, the government agency that buys

GLOBAL SOCIOLOGY

The Japanese Model: Will It Work in the United States?

What the company wants is for us to work like the Japanese. Everybody go out and do jumping jacks in the morning and kiss each other when they go home at night. You work as a team, rat on each other, and lose control of your destiny. That's not going to work in this country.

> John Brodie
> President, United Paperworkers
> Local 448
> Chester, Pennsylvania

Competition from Asia and, increasingly, from Europe is forcing U.S. companies to rethink how corporate organizations should operate in a global marketplace. Business leaders are looking at the Japanese manufacturing plants built here in the United States. These "transplant organizations," operated in the United States by Honda, Nissan, and Toyota, have adapted well to a new environment, achieving the same level of efficiency and quality that won these companies praise in Japan. They have

also provided more than 250,000 jobs for U.S. workers.

Yet some voices in this country—from the ranks of workers, union leaders, and managers—speak as bitterly about importing Japanese organizational techniques as they do about importing Japanese cars. Our corporate culture still favors hierarchy, praises individualism, and remembers its long history of labor-management conflict. As a result, workers and managers are wary of traditional Japanese practices, such as worker participation.

Some employees in the United States think worker participation ends up increasing their workload. While still responsible for building cars, for instance, workers also have to worry about quality control, unit costs, and overall efficiency—concerns usually shouldered by management. Moreover, some employees see the broad training favored by the Japanese as endlessly moving from job to job, always having to learn new skills. Many union leaders fear that any alliance of workers and managers undermines union strength.

Some managers, too, look warily on worker participation programs. Sharing the power to set production goals or schedule vacations does not come easily in light of past practices. Finally, U.S. corporations have a short-term outlook on profits, which discourages investing time and money in organizational restructuring.

But the pressure of rising global competition is slowly changing U.S. organizations. The government reports that 70 percent of large businesses have begun at least some reforms of this kind. Productivity and profits usually are higher when workers have a say in decision making. Moreover, most employees in worker participation programs—even those who may not want to sign up for morning jumping jacks—seem happier about their jobs. Workers who have long used only their bodies are now enjoying the opportunity to use their minds as well.

Sources: Hoerr (1989) and Florida & Kenney (1991).

---

4. **Broad-based training.** U.S. workers are highly specialized, and many spend an entire career doing one thing. But a Japanese organization trains workers in all phases of its operation, again with the idea that employees will remain with the company for life.

5. **Collective decision making.** In the United States, key executives make the important decisions. Although Japanese leaders also take responsibility for their organization's performance, they involve workers in "quality circles" to discuss decisions that affect them. A closer working relationship is also encouraged by Japan's lower

salary difference between executives and workers: about 10 percent of the difference that is typical in the United States.

These characteristics give the Japanese a strong sense of organizational loyalty. Because their personal interests are tied to company interests, workers realize their ambitions through the organization. In recent years, Japanese companies have become more like their U.S. counterparts by, for example, laying off some workers. Even so, the Japanese emphasis on *groupism* is the cultural equivalent of our society's emphasis on *individual* achievement.

The recent trend is toward breaking down the rigid structure of conventional bureaucracy. One example of more flexible organizational form is the self-managed work team, whose members have the skills to carry out their tasks creatively and with minimal supervision.

Many U.S. companies have been influenced by Japanese organizations. But transplanting an organizational system from one culture to another is not easy, as the box on page 181 explains.

THE THIRD CHALLENGE: THE CHANGING NATURE OF WORK

Beyond rising global competition, pressure to modify conventional organizations is also coming from changes in the nature of work itself. Chapter 4 ("Society") described the shift from industrial to postindustrial production. Rather than working in factories using heavy machinery to make *things*, more and more people are using computers and other electronic technology to create or process *information*. The postindustrial society, then, is characterized by information-based organizations.

Frederick Taylor developed his concept of scientific management at a time when jobs involved tasks that, though often backbreaking, were routine. Workers shoveled coal, poured liquid iron into molds, welded body panels to automobiles on an assembly line, or shot hot rivets into steel girders to build skyscrapers. In addition, a large proportion of U.S. workers in Taylor's day were immigrants, most of whom had little schooling and many of whom knew little English. The routine nature of industrial jobs coupled with the limited skills of the labor force led Taylor to treat work as a series of fixed tasks set down by management and followed by employees.

Many of today's information age jobs are very different: The work of designers, artists, writers, composers, programmers, business owners, and others now demands creativity and imagination. What does this mean for formal organizations? Here are several ways in which today's organizations differ from those of a century ago:

1. **Creative autonomy.** Organizations know that employees with information age skills are a vital resource. Executives can set production goals but cannot dictate how to accomplish tasks involving imagination and discovery. Thus, highly skilled workers have *creative autonomy*, which means they have little day-to-day supervision as long as they generate good ideas in the long run.

2. **Competitive work teams.** Many organizations give several groups of employees the freedom to work on a problem, offering the greatest rewards to those who come up with the best solution. Competitive work teams, a strategy first used by Japanese organizations, draw out the creative contributions of everyone and, at the same time, reduce the alienation often found in conventional organizations (Yeatts, 1991, 1994; Maddox, 1994).

3. **A flatter organization.** By spreading responsibility for creative problem solving throughout the work force, organizations take on a flatter shape. That is, the pyramid shape of conventional bureaucracy is replaced by an organizational form with fewer levels in the chain of command, as shown in Figure 7–5.

4. **Greater flexibility.** The typical industrial age organization was a rigid structure guided from the

FIGURE 7–5 Two Organizational Models

The conventional model of bureaucratic organizations has a pyramid shape, with a clear chain of command. Directives flow from the top down, and reports of performance flow from the bottom up. Such organizations have extensive rules and regulations, and their workers have highly specialized jobs. More open and flexible organizations have a flatter shape, more like a football. With fewer levels in the hierarchy, responsibility for generating ideas and making decisions is shared throughout the organization. Many workers do their jobs in teams and have a broad knowledge of the entire organization's operation.

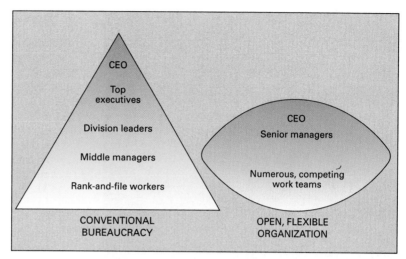

Source: Created by the author.

top. Such organizations may accomplish a good deal of work, but they are not especially creative or able to respond quickly to changes in their larger environment. The ideal model in the information age is a *flexible* organization, one that both generates new ideas and, in a rapidly changing global marketplace, adapts quickly.

As important as these changes are, many of today's jobs do not involve creative work at all. On the contrary, the postindustrial economy has created two very different types of work: highly skilled creative work and low-skill service work. For example, work in the fast-food industry is routine and highly supervised and thus has much more in common with factory work of a century ago than with the work of teams in information organizations. Whereas some organizations have taken on a flexible, flatter form, others continue to use the rigid chain of command, as we now explain.

THE "McDONALDIZATION" OF SOCIETY[1]

As noted in the opening to this chapter, McDonald's has enjoyed enormous success, now operating 28,000 restaurants in the United States and around the world. Japan has more than 2,400 Golden Arches, and the world's largest McDonald's is found in China's capital city of Beijing.

October 9, Macau. Here we are, halfway around the world, in the Portuguese colony of Macau—a little nub jutting from the coast of China. Few people here speak English, and life on the streets seems a world apart from the urban rhythms of New York, Chicago, or Los Angeles. Then I turn the corner and stand face to face with (who else?) Ronald McDonald! After eating who-knows-what for so long, forgive me for giving in to the lure of the Big Mac. But the most amazing thing is that the food—the burger, the fries, and the drink—looks, smells, and tastes exactly the same as it does back home 10,000 miles away!

McDonald's may be found almost everywhere these days but, in the United States, it is more than a restaurant: It is a symbol of our way of life. Not only do people around the world associate McDonald's with the United States, but, here at home, one poll found that 98 percent of schoolchildren could identify Ronald McDonald, making him as well known as Santa Claus.

[1]Much of the material in this section is based on Ritzer (1993, 1998, 2000).

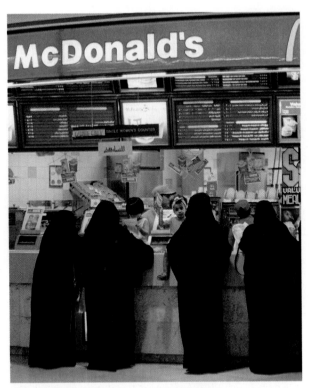

Is McDonaldization becoming a global trend? Yes and no. The spread of McDonald's and other fast-food corporations around the world has been dramatic, and the company now earns most of its revenue from outside the United States. But in some nations, McDonald's has altered its formula to take account of local cultural norms. For example, these women in a shopping mall in Dhahran, Saudi Arabia, are ordering food from a "ladies only" counter, which reflects the traditional gender norms of that nation.

Even more important, the organizational principles that underlie McDonald's are coming to dominate our entire society. Our culture is becoming "McDonaldized," an awkward way of saying that we model many aspects of life on this restaurant chain: Parents buy toys at worldwide chain stores such as Toys 'Я' Us; we drive to Jiffy Lube for a ten-minute oil change; face-to-face communication is sliding more and more toward voice mail, e-mail, and junk mail; more vacations take the form of resort and tour packages; television presents news in the form of ten-second sound bites; college admissions officers size up students they have never met by their GPA and SAT scores; and professors assign ghost-written textbooks[2] and evaluate students with tests mass-produced by publishing companies. The list goes on and on.

McDonaldization: Four Principles

What do all such developments have in common? According to George Ritzer (1993), the McDonaldization of society involves four basic organizational principles:

1. **Efficiency.** Ray Kroc, the marketing genius behind the expansion of McDonald's, set out to serve a hamburger, French fries, and milkshake to a customer in fifty seconds. Today, one of the company's most popular items is the Egg McMuffin, an entire breakfast in a single sandwich. In the restaurant, customers bus their own trays, or they drive away from the pickup window taking the packaging and whatever mess they make with them.

   Efficiency is now central to our way of life. We tend to think that anything done quickly is, for that reason alone, good.

2. **Calculability.** The first McDonald's operating manual set the weight of a regular raw hamburger at 1.6 ounces, its size at 3.875 inches across, and its fat content at 19 percent. A slice of cheese weighs exactly half an ounce. Fries are cut precisely 9/32 of an inch thick.

   Think about how many objects around your home, the workplace, and campus are designed and mass-produced according to a uniform plan. Not just our environment but our life experiences—from traveling the nation's interstates to sitting at home viewing television—are more standardized than ever before.

3. **Uniformity and predictability.** A person can walk into a McDonald's restaurant almost anywhere and receive the same sandwiches, drinks, and desserts prepared in precisely the same way.[3] Predictability is the result of a highly rational system that specifies every course of action and leaves nothing to chance.

4. **Control through automation.** The most unreliable element in the McDonald's system is human beings. People, after all, have good and bad days, sometimes let their minds wander, or simply

---

[2]Several popular sociology texts were not authored by the person or persons whose names appear on the cover. This book is not one of them.

decide to try something a different way. To minimize the unpredictable human element, McDonald's has automated its equipment to cook food at fixed temperatures for set lengths of time. Even the cash register at a McDonald's is little more than pictures of the items, so that the task of ringing up a customer's order is made as simple as possible.

Similarly, automatic teller machines are replacing banks, highly automated bakeries now produce bread with scarcely any human intervention, and chickens and eggs (or is it eggs and chickens?) emerge from automated hatcheries. In supermarkets, laser scanners are phasing out checking groceries by hand. We do most of our shopping in malls, where everything—from temperature and humidity to the kinds of stores and products—is carefully controlled and supervised (Ide & Cordell, 1994).

Can Rationality Be Irrational?

There can be no argument about the popularity or efficiency of McDonald's. But there is another side to the story.

Max Weber observed the expansion of formal organizations with alarm, fearing that they would cage the imagination and crush the human spirit. As Weber saw it, rational systems were efficient but dehumanizing, and McDonaldization bears him out. Each of the four principles just discussed limits human creativity, choice, and freedom. Echoing Weber, Ritzer states that "the ultimate irrationality of McDonaldization is that people could lose control over the system and it would come to control us" (1993:145).

 To learn more about Max Weber, go to http://www. TheSociologyPage.com

---

[3]As McDonald's has "gone global," a few products have been added or modified according to local tastes. For example, in Uruguay, customers enjoy the McHuevo (hamburger with poached egg on top); Norwegians can buy McLaks (grilled salmon sandwiches); the Dutch favor Groenteburger (vegetable burger); in Thailand, McDonald's serves Samurai pork burgers (pork burgers with teriyaki sauce); the Japanese can purchase Chicken Tatsuta Sandwich (chicken seasoned with soy and ginger); Filipinos eat McSpaghetti (spaghetti with tomato sauce and bits of hot dogs); and in India, where Hindus eat no beef, McDonald's sells a vegetarian Maharaja Mac (Sullivan, 1995).

THE FUTURE OF ORGANIZATIONS: OPPOSING TRENDS

Early in the twentieth century, ever-larger organizations arose in the United States, most taking on the bureaucratic form described by Max Weber. In many respects, these organizations resembled armies led by powerful generals who issued orders to their captains and lieutenants. Foot soldiers, working in the factories, did what they were told.

With the emergence of a postindustrial economy after mid-century and with rising competition from abroad, many organizations have evolved toward a flatter, more flexible model that prizes communication and creativity. Such "intelligent organizations" (Pinchot & Pinchot, 1993) have become more productive than ever. Just as important, for highly skilled people whose information age work demands creative autonomy, these organizations create less of the alienation that so worried Max Weber.

But this is only half the story. Although the postindustrial economy has created many highly skilled jobs, it has created even more routine service jobs, as exemplified by McDonald's, where one in eight adults in the United States has worked at some time (Ritzer, 1998). Work of this kind, which Ritzer calls "McJobs," offers few of the benefits that today's highly skilled workers enjoy. On the contrary, the automated routines that define work in the fast-food industry, telemarketing, and similar fields are very much the same as Frederick Taylor described a century ago.

Moreover, the organizational flexibility that gives better-off workers more autonomy carries, for rank-and-file employees, the ever-present threat of "downsizing" (Sennett, 1998). That is, organizations facing global competition are eager to have creative employees, but they are just as eager to cut costs by eliminating as many routine jobs as possible. The net result is that some people are better off than ever while others worry about holding their jobs and struggle to make ends meet—a trend that Chapter 11 ("Social Class in the United States") explores in detail.

In sum, many analysts conclude that U.S. organizations remain the envy of the world for their productive efficiency. Indeed, there are few places on earth where the mail arrives as quickly and dependably as it does in the United States (J. Wilson, 1991). But we should remember that the future is far brighter for some than for others. In addition, as the final box on pages 186–87 explains, organizations pose an increasing threat to our privacy—something to keep in mind as we envision our organizational future.

Computer Technology, Large Organizations, and the Assault on Privacy

Joe finishes dressing and calls a 1-800 number to check the pollen count. As he listens to a recorded message, a Caller ID computer identifies Joe, records the call, and pulls up Joe's profile from a public records database. The computer adds to the profile the fact that Joe suffers from allergies. Several weeks later, tens of thousands of profiles are sold to a drug company, which sends Joe and others a free sample of its new allergy medication.

At a local department store, Nina uses her American Express card to buy an expensive new watch and some sleepwear. The store's computer adds Nina's name to its database of "buyers of expensive jewelry" and "buyers of sexy lingerie." The store trades its database with other companies, and within a month Nina receives four jewelry catalogues and an adult video brochure (Bernstein, 1997).

Are these organizations providing consumers with interesting products, or are they violating people's privacy? The answer is both: The same systems that help organizations operate efficiently also let them invade our lives and manipulate us. So as large organizations have expanded in the United States, privacy has diminished.

Small-town life in the past gave people little privacy, but at least if people knew something about you, you were just as likely to know something about them. Today, unknown people can access information about any of us at any time.

In part, the loss of privacy is a result of more and more complex computer technology. Are you aware that every e-mail you send and every chat room message you post is recorded in one or more computers and can be retrieved by people you don't know? Even visiting a Web site leaves an electronic "footprint" that can be traced by anyone interested in your tastes and shopping habits.

Another part of today's loss of privacy reflects the number and size of formal organizations. As we have explained in this chapter, large organizations tend to treat people impersonally, and they have a huge appetite for information. Mix large organizations with ever-more complex computer technology, and it is no wonder that most people in the United States are concerned about who knows what about them and what people are doing with this information.

For decades, the level of personal privacy in the United States has been declining. Early in the twentieth century, when state agencies began issuing driver's licenses, for example, they generated files for every licensed driver. Today, officials can send this information at the touch of a button to other organizations, including police. Similarly, the Internal Revenue Service, the Social Security Administration, and government agencies that benefit veterans, students, the unemployed, and the poor all collect extensive information.

Business organizations now do much the same thing, although, as these examples show, people may not be aware that their choices and activities end up in a company's database. Most people find credit cards a great convenience—the U.S. population now holds more than 1 billion of them, averaging more than five per adult—but few people stop to think that credit card purchases automatically generate records that can end up almost anywhere.

Then there are the small cameras found in stores, public buildings, parking garages, and college campuses. The number of surveillance cameras that

SUMMARY

1. Social groups are building blocks of society that connect individuals with each other and perform various tasks.

2. Primary groups tend to be small and person-oriented; secondary groups are large and goal-oriented.

3. Instrumental leadership is concerned with realizing a group's goals; expressive leadership focuses on members' morale and well-being.

4. Because group members often seek consensus, groups may pressure members toward conformity.

monitor our movements is rapidly increasing with each passing year. Such cameras may improve public safety in some ways—say, by discouraging muggers—but only at the cost of some of the privacy we have left.

Concern about the erosion of privacy in the United States is also on the rise. Across the United States, who is most concerned about the growing assault on privacy? National Map 7–1 provides some insights.

There is some legal protection. All the states have enacted laws giving citizens rights to examine some records about themselves kept by employers, banks, and credit bureaus. The U.S. Privacy Act of 1974 also limits the exchange of personal information between government agencies and permits citizens to examine and correct most government files. But so many private and public organizations now have information about us—experts estimate that 90 percent of U.S. households are profiled in databases somewhere—that current laws simply do not address the extent of the privacy problem. In the last ten years, the Internet revolution has made the problem of personal privacy more serious than ever, yet there are no national standards that protect public privacy.

Continue the debate . . .

1. *Look over National Map 7–1. Where are people most concerned about losing their privacy? Can you explain this pattern?*

2. *Internet search engines such as Yahoo! (http://www.yahoo.com) have "people search" programs that let you locate almost anyone. Do you think such programs pose a threat to privacy?*

3. *How have concerns about privacy changed in the wake of the September 11th terrorist attacks on the United States?*

SEEING OURSELVES

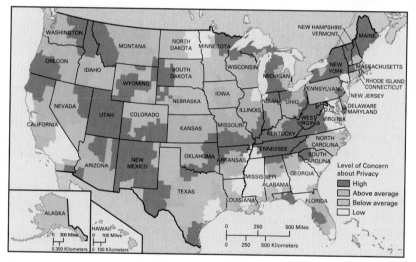

NATIONAL MAP 7–1 Concerns about Privacy across the United States

Source: *Business Geographics* © 1994 GIS World, Inc., 2101 S. Arlington Heights Boulevard, Arlington Heights, Ill., 60005-4185.

Sources: Bernstein (1997), Wright (1998), *Business Week* (2000), and Rosen (2000).

5. Individuals make use of reference groups—both ingroups and outgroups—to form attitudes and make evaluations.

6. Georg Simmel characterized the dyad—a social group with two members—as intense but unstable; a triad, he added, can easily dissolve into a dyad by excluding one member.

7. Peter Blau explored how group size, homogeneity, and social standing and physical segregation of groups all affect members' behavior.

8. Social networks are relational webs that link people with little common identity and limited interaction. The Internet is a vast electronic network linking millions of people worldwide.

9. Formal organizations are large secondary groups that seek to perform complex tasks efficiently. They are classified as utilitarian, normative, or coercive, based on their members' reasons for joining.

10. Bureaucratic organization expands in modern societies to perform tasks efficiently. Bureaucracy is based on specialization, hierarchy, rules and regulations, technical competence, impersonal interaction, and formal, written communications.

11. Technology, political and economic trends, population patterns, and other organizations all combine to form the environment in which a particular business or agency must operate.

12. Ideally, bureaucracy promotes efficiency, but it can also lead to alienation and oligarchy and contribute to the erosion of privacy.

13. Frederick Taylor's principles of scientific management shaped U.S. organizations a century ago. Since then, organizations have evolved toward a more open and flexible form as they have included a larger share of women and other minorities, responded to global competition, especially from Japan, and shifted their focus from industrial production to postindustrial information processing.

14. Reflecting the collective spirit of Japanese culture, formal organizations in Japan are based more on personal ties than their counterparts in the United States.

15. The "McDonaldization" of society involves increasing automation and impersonality.

16. The future of organizations probably will involve opposing trends: toward more creative autonomy for highly skilled information workers and toward supervision and discipline for less skilled service workers.

KEY CONCEPTS

social group (p. 163) two or more people who identify and interact with one another

primary group (p. 164) a small social group whose members share personal and enduring relationships

secondary group (p. 164) a large and impersonal social group whose members pursue a specific goal or activity

instrumental leadership (p. 165) group leadership that emphasizes the completion of tasks

expressive leadership (p. 165) group leadership that focuses on collective well-being

groupthink (p. 167) the tendency of group members to conform, resulting in a narrow view of some issue

reference group (p. 167) a social group that serves as a point of reference in making evaluations and decisions

ingroup (p. 168) a social group commanding a member's esteem and loyalty

outgroup (p. 168) a social group toward which one feels competition or opposition

dyad (p. 168) a social group with two members

triad (p. 169) a social group with three members

network (p. 170) a web of weak social ties

formal organization (p. 171) a large secondary group organized to achieve its goals efficiently

bureaucracy (p. 174) an organizational model rationally designed to perform tasks efficiently

organizational environment (p. 175) factors outside an organization that affect its operation

bureaucratic ritualism (p. 177) a preoccupation with rules and regulations to the point of thwarting an organization's goals

bureaucratic inertia (p. 177) the tendency of bureaucratic organizations to perpetuate themselves

oligarchy (p. 177) the rule of the many by the few

scientific management (p. 178) Frederick Taylor's term for the application of scientific principles to the operation of a business or other large organization

CRITICAL-THINKING QUESTIONS

1. How do primary groups differ from secondary groups? Identify examples of each in your own life.

2. According to Max Weber, what are the six characteristic traits of bureaucracy? In what ways do new, more flexible organizations differ?

3. George Ritzer (1996:1), a critic of "McDonaldization," suggests that fast-food restaurants carry the following label: "Sociologists warn us that habitual use of McDonald's systems are destructive to our physical and psychological well-being as well as to society as a whole." Do you agree? Why or why not?

4. The twentieth century was the first one with the widespread use of initials, such as IRS, IRA, IMF, IBM, CIA, WPA, PLO, NATO, CNN, WB, WWF, and CDC. What does this change suggest about social trends?

APPLICATIONS AND EXERCISES

1. Spend several hours observing customers at a fast-food restaurant. Think about ways in which both employees and customers are trained to behave in certain ways. For example, customer norms include lining up to order and finding their own table. What other norms are at work?

2. Visit a large public building with an elevator. Observe groups of people as they approach the elevator, and enter the elevator with them. Watch their behavior: What happens to conversations as the elevator doors close? Where do people fix their eyes? Can you account for these patterns?

3. Make a list of ingroups and outgroups on your campus. What traits account for groups falling into each category? Ask several people to comment on your list to see whether they agree with your classifications.

4. Using available publications (and some assistance from an instructor), try to draw an organizational pyramid for your college or university showing the key offices and how they supervise and report to each other.

5. Packaged in the back of this new textbook is an interactive CD-ROM that offers a variety of study and review materials intended to help you better understand the material covered in this chapter. For this chapter, the CD-ROM contains an author's tip video, Real Life Sociology videos, other relevant audio and video, interactive map animations, audio journal entries from the author, Web links, and much more.

 ## SITES TO SEE

http://www.prenhall.com/macionis

Visit the interactive *Companion Website*™ that accompanies this text. Begin by clicking on the cover of your book. You will find a chapter-by-chapter study guide, practice tests, and a significant portion of the text for on-line review, as well as many suggested Web links.

http://www.saturnbp.com

Visit the Saturn car company Web site to read about Saturn's flatter organizational structure.

http://www.mte.com/riot_site/webcam.html

This Web site uses a camera placed at New York City's Fifth Avenue at Forty-fifth Street. Do you think Internet technology of this kind threatens people's privacy? Why or why not?

http://groups.yahoo.com/local/news.html

A number of Web sites, including this one, let people build their own social groups for chat or posting photos and other information. Take a look and see what you think about "virtual groups."

 ## INVESTIGATE WITH CONTENTSELECT

Follow the instructions found on page 23 of this textbook to enter this chapter of the book's *Companion Website*™. Once in the chapter, click on the ContentSelect icon at the bottom left of your screen and enter your personal User ID and Password. Enter keywords such as "Max Weber," "bureaucracy," "social network," and "McDonald's," and the search engine will help you become an effective researcher.

CHAPTER

8

Emil Kazaz
Saratoga, 1998

Oil on linen, 60 in. × 72 in.
Collection of Rafael and Marina Akopian. Courtesy of Noah's Ark Fine Art.

DEVIANCE

Ricky McGinn sat in his prison cell in Huntsville, Texas, wiping his mouth and looking at the floor. He had just finished the cheeseburger, French fries, and Dr. Pepper that he thought would be his last meal. Forty-three-year-old McGinn had been convicted of the brutal murder of his twelve-year-old stepdaughter and sentenced to death for his crime. In just several hours, the execution would be carried out.

Then, eighteen minutes before McGinn was to die, Texas governor George W. Bush halted the execution. Defense lawyers claimed that a DNA test would prove McGinn's innocence. The governor agreed to a postponement (Alter, 2000).

In recent years, public opinion about capital punishment has been

changing. The greatest fear is that people convicted of serious crimes and sentenced to death may be innocent. In 2000, Illinois Governor George Ryan ordered a halt to executions in that state in the wake of evidence that thirteen men on death row in Illinois prisons were actually innocent. Since 1973, nationwide, eighty-seven people sentenced to die have been set free based on new evidence.

In the case of Ricky McGinn, however, the reprieve was brief. Officials carried out the DNA tests McGinn's lawyers requested, and the evidence confirmed his guilt. With no further options to appeal, on September 27, 2000, McGinn again ordered a last meal and was put to death by lethal injection.

This chapter explores the problem of violent crime and other criminal offenses, profiles offenders, and looks at the criminal justice system. First, however, we tackle the broader issue of why societies develop standards of right and wrong in the first place. As we shall see, law is simply one part of a complex system of social control: Society teaches us all to conform, at least most of the time, to countless rules. We begin our investigation by defining several basic concepts.

WHAT IS DEVIANCE?

Deviance is *the recognized violation of cultural norms.* Because norms guide almost all human activities, the concept of deviance is quite broad. One category of deviance is **crime,** *the violation of a society's formally enacted criminal law.* Even criminal deviance spans a wide range of behavior, from minor traffic violations to sexual assault to murder.

Most examples of nonconformity that come readily to mind are negative instances of rule breaking, such as stealing from a convenience store, abusing a child, or driving while intoxicated. But we also define especially righteous people—students who speak up too much in class or people who are overly enthusiastic about new computer technology—as deviant, even if we accord them a measure of respect (Huls, 1987). What deviant actions or attitudes—whether negative or positive—have in common is some element of *difference* that causes us to regard another person as an "outsider" (Becker, 1966).

Not all deviance involves action or even choice. The very *existence* of some categories of people can be troublesome to others. To the young, elderly people may seem hopelessly "out of it," and to some whites, the mere presence of people of color may cause discomfort. Able-bodied people often view people with disabilities as an outgroup, just as affluent people may shun the poor for falling short of their standards.

191

SOCIAL CONTROL

All of us are subject to **social control,** *attempts by society to regulate people's thought and behavior.* Often, this process is informal, as when parents praise or scold their children or friends make fun of someone's musical taste. Serious deviance may involve the **criminal justice system,** *a formal response by police, courts, and prison officials to alleged violations of the law.*

In sum, deviance is much more than a matter of individual choice or personal failing. *How* a society defines deviance, *who* is branded as deviant, and *what* people decide to do about deviance all have to do with the way society is organized. Only gradually have people recognized this fact, as we shall now explain.

 Visit the Juvenile Justice and Delinquency Prevention Web site to see their available research reports: http://ojjdp. ncjrs.org/pubs/alpha.html

THE BIOLOGICAL CONTEXT

Chapter 5 ("Socialization") explained that people a century ago understood—or, more correctly, misunderstood—human behavior as an expression of biological instincts. Early interest in criminality thus emphasized biological causes. In 1876, Caesare Lombroso (1835–1909), an Italian physician who worked in prisons, proposed that criminals could be identified by physical traits: low foreheads, prominent jaws and cheekbones, big ears, lots of body hair, and unusually long arms. All in all, Lombroso claimed that criminals resembled our apelike ancestors.

But the physical features that Lombroso pointed to can be found throughout the entire population. We now know that no physical attributes of the kind described by Lombroso set off criminals from noncriminals (Goring, 1972; orig. 1913).

At mid-century, William Sheldon (Sheldon, Hartl, & McDermott, 1949) took a different tack, suggesting that body shape predicted criminality. He crosschecked hundreds of young men for body type and criminal history and concluded that criminality was most common among boys with muscular, athletic builds. Sheldon Glueck and Eleanor Glueck (1950) confirmed Sheldon's conclusion but cautioned that a powerful build does not necessarily cause criminality. Parents, they suggested, tend to be somewhat distant from powerfully built sons, who, in turn, grow up to show less sensitivity toward others. Moreover, in a self-fulfilling prophesy, people who expect muscular boys to act like bullies may provoke such aggressive behavior.

Today, genetics research seeks possible links between biology and crime. Although no conclusive evidence connects criminality to any specific genetic trait, people's overall genetic makeup, in combination with social influences, probably accounts for some tendency toward criminality. In other words, biological factors may have a real but modest effect on whether an individual becomes a criminal (Rowe, 1983; Rowe & Osgood, 1984; Wilson & Herrnstein, 1985; Jencks, 1987; Pallone & Hennessy, 1998).

Critical evaluation. At best, biological theories offer a limited explanation of crime. Researchers point out that violent crime is overwhelmingly male and that parents are more likely to abuse foster children than natural children. But we know too little about the links between genes and human behavior to draw firm conclusions (Daly & Wilson, 1988).

Furthermore, because a biological approach looks at the individual, it offers no insight as to how some kinds of behaviors come to be defined as deviant in the first place. Therefore, although there is much to be learned about how human biology may affect behavior, research currently puts far greater emphasis on social influences (Gibbons & Krohn, 1986; Liska, 1991).

PERSONALITY FACTORS

Like biological theories, psychological explanations of deviance focus on individual abnormality. Some personality traits are hereditary, but most psychologists think that personality is shaped primarily by social experience. Deviance, then, is viewed as the product of "unsuccessful" socialization.

Research by Walter Reckless and Simon Dinitz (1967) illustrates the psychological approach. Reckless and Dinitz began by asking a number of teachers to categorize twelve-year-old male students as either likely or unlikely to get into trouble with the law. They then interviewed both the boys and their mothers to assess each boy's self-concept and how he related to others. Analyzing their results, Reckless and Dinitz found that the "good boys" displayed a stronger conscience (what Freud called superego), could handle frustration, and identified with cultural norms and values. The "bad boys," by contrast, had a weaker conscience, displayed little tolerance for frustration, and felt out of step with conventional culture.

As we might expect, the "good boys" had fewer run-ins with the police than the "bad boys." Because all the boys lived in an area where delinquency was widespread, the investigators attributed staying out of trouble to a personality that reined in deviant impulses. Based on this idea, Reckless and Dinitz called their analysis *containment theory*.

Critical evaluation. Psychologists have shown that personality patterns have some connection to deviance. However, the fact is that most serious crimes are committed by people whose psychological profiles are normal.

Overall, both biological and psychological research view deviance as an individual trait, without exploring how conceptions of right and wrong initially arise, why people define some rule breakers but not others as deviant, or what role power plays in shaping a society's system of social control. To explore these issues, we now turn to a sociological analysis of deviance.

THE SOCIAL FOUNDATIONS OF DEVIANCE

Although we tend to view deviance in terms of the free choice or personal failings of individuals, all behavior— deviance as well as conformity—is shaped by society. Three social foundations of deviance are identified here and explained in later sections of the chapter:

1. **Deviance varies according to cultural norms.**
   No thought or action is inherently deviant; it becomes deviant only in relation to particular norms. Norms vary from place to place, so deviance also varies. Parts of Nevada permit prostitution, a practice outlawed in all other states. Casinos in Atlantic City and Las Vegas and on Mississippi riverboats and numerous Native American reservations beckon high rollers, but everywhere else in the United States gambling is illegal. Furthermore, most cities and towns have at least one unique statute. For example, South Padre Island, Texas, bans wearing ties; Mount Prospect, Illinois, has a law against keeping pigeons or bees; Los Angeles bans gas-powered leaf blowers; Hoover, South Dakota, outlaws fishing with a kerosene lantern; and Beverly Hills regulates the number of tennis balls allowed on the court at one time (Sanders & Horn, 1998; Steele, 2000).
   Around the world, what is considered deviant is even more diverse. Albania outlaws any public display of religious faith, such as "crossing" oneself; Cuba and Vietnam can prosecute their citizens for "consorting with foreigners"; Singapore bans the sale of chewing gum; police in

The kind of deviance people create reflects the moral values they embrace. The Berkeley campus of the University of California has long celebrated its open-minded tolerance of sexual diversity. Thus, in 1992, when Andrew Martinez decided to attend classes wearing virtually nothing, people were reluctant to accuse "The Naked Guy" of immoral conduct. However, in Berkeley's politically correct atmosphere, it was not long before school officials banned Martinez from campus—charging that his nudity constituted a form of sexual harassment.

Iran can arrest a woman for wearing makeup; U.S. citizens risk arrest by traveling to Libya or Iraq.

2. **People become deviant as others define them that way.** Everyone violates cultural norms, sometimes to the extent of breaking the law. For example, most of us sometimes walk around talking to ourselves or "borrow" pens from the workplace. Whether such behavior defines us as mentally ill or criminal depends on how others perceive, define, and respond to our behavior.

3. **Both rule-making and rule-breaking involve social power.** The law, claimed Karl Marx, is the

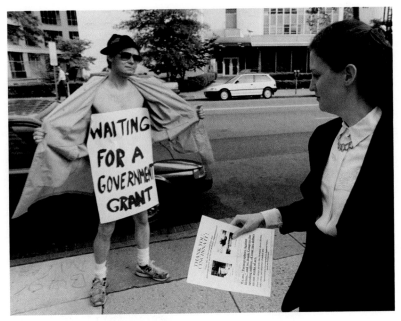

Artists have an important function in any society: to explore alternatives to conventional notions about how to live. For this reason, while we celebrate artists' creativity, we also accord them a mildly deviant identity. In today's more conservative political climate, some government officials have objected to art that seems to challenge traditional morality. For their part, some artists have found expressive ways to show their displeasure with such thinking.

means by which powerful people protect their interests. A homeless person who stands on a street corner denouncing the government risks arrest for disturbing the peace; a mayoral candidate during an election campaign does exactly the same thing and receives police protection. In short, norms and how we apply them reflect social inequality.

THE FUNCTIONS OF DEVIANCE: STRUCTURAL-FUNCTIONAL ANALYSIS

The key insight of the structural-functional paradigm is that deviance is a necessary part of social organization. This point was made a century ago by Emile Durkheim.

EMILE DURKHEIM: THE FUNCTIONS OF DEVIANCE

In his pioneering study of deviance, Emile Durkheim (1964a, orig. 1893; 1964b, orig. 1895) made the surprising statement that there is nothing abnormal about deviance. In fact, it performs four essential functions:

1. **Deviance affirms cultural values and norms.** As moral creatures, people must prefer some

attitudes and behaviors to others. But any conception of virtue rests on an opposing notion of vice: There can be no good without evil and no justice without crime. Deviance, then, is needed to define and sustain morality.

2. **Responding to deviance clarifies moral boundaries.** By defining some people as deviant, society draws a boundary between right and wrong. For example, a college marks the line between academic honesty and cheating by punishing students who plagiarize.

3. **Responding to deviance promotes social unity.** People typically react to serious deviance with collective outrage. In this way, Durkheim explained, they reaffirm the moral ties that bind them. For example, after the terrorist attacks on the World Trade Center and the Pentagon in 2001, feelings of anguish and outrage brought together not just those communities but the entire nation.

4. **Deviance encourages social change.** Deviant people push a society's moral boundaries, suggesting alternatives to the status quo and encouraging change. Today's deviance, declared Durkheim, can become tomorrow's morality (1964b:71). For example, rock and roll—condemned as morally degenerate in the 1950s—became a multibillion-dollar industry just a few years later.

An Illustration: The Puritans of Massachusetts Bay

Kai Erikson's (1966) study of the Puritans of Massachusetts Bay brings Durkheim's theory to life. Erikson shows that even the Puritans, a disciplined and highly religious group, created deviance to clarify their moral boundaries. In fact, Durkheim might well have had the Puritans in mind when he wrote,

> Imagine a society of saints, a perfect cloister of exemplary individuals. Crimes, properly so called, will there be unknown; but faults which appear [insignificant] to the layman will create there the same scandal that the ordinary offense does in ordinary consciousness. . . . For the same reason, the perfect and upright man judges his smallest failings with a severity that the majority reserve for acts more truly in the nature of an offense. (1964b:68–69)

In short, deviance is not a matter of a few "bad apples"; it is a necessary condition of "good" social living.

Deviance may be universal, but the *kind* of deviance people generate depends on the moral issues they seek to clarify. For example, the Puritans experienced a number of "crime waves," including the well-known outbreak of witchcraft in Salem in 1692. With each response, the Puritans sharpened their views on crucial moral issues. They answered questions about the range of proper beliefs by celebrating some of their members and condemning others as deviant.

Perhaps most fascinating of all, Erikson discovered that even though the offenses changed, the proportion of people the Puritans defined as deviant remained steady over time. This stability, concludes Erikson, confirms Durkheim's contention that deviants serve to mark a society's changing moral boundaries. In other words, by constantly defining a small number of people as deviant, the Puritans gave a moral shape to their society.

MERTON'S STRAIN THEORY

Some deviance may be necessary for a society to function, but Robert Merton (1938, 1968) argued that excessive deviance results from particular social arrangements. Specifically, the extent and kind of deviance depend on whether a society provides the *means* (such as schooling and job opportunities) to achieve cultural *goals* (such as financial success).

Conformity, says Merton, lies in pursuing conventional goals through approved means. Thus, our success stories celebrate people who acquire wealth

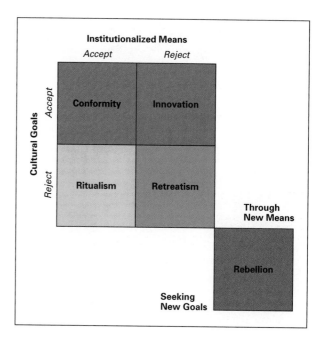

FIGURE 8–1 Merton's Strain Theory of Deviance
Source: Merton (1968).

and prestige through talent and hard work. But not everyone who seeks conventional success has the opportunity to attain it. People raised in poverty may see little chance of becoming successful if they play by the rules. As a result, they may try to make money through crime—say, by dealing cocaine. Merton called this type of deviance *innovation:* using unconventional means (drug sales) to achieve a culturally approved goal (becoming rich). Figure 8–1 shows that innovation involves accepting a cultural goal while rejecting the conventional means of getting there.

According to Merton, the strain between our culture's emphasis on wealth and the limited opportunity to get rich gives rise to theft and the sale of drugs or other street crime, especially among the poor. In some respects, notorious gangster Al Capone was quite conventional: He pursued the fame and fortune at the heart of the "American dream." But, like many minorities who find the doors to "legitimate" success hard to open, Capone blazed his own trail to the top. As one analyst put it,

> The typical criminal of the Capone era was a boy who had . . . seen what was rated as success in the society he had been thrust into—the Cadillac, the big bankroll, the elegant apartment. How could

In Kosovo, as in the United States, young people (especially males) cut off from legitimate opportunity may form deviant subcultures as a strategy to gain the prestige denied them by the larger society.

he acquire that kind of recognizable status? He was almost always a boy of outstanding initiative, imagination, and ability; he was the kind of boy who, under different conditions, would have been a captain of industry or a key political figure of his time. But he hadn't the opportunity of going to Yale and becoming a banker or broker; there was no passage for him to a law degree from Harvard. There was, however, a relatively easy way of acquiring these goods that he was incessantly told were available to him as an American citizen, and without which he had begun to feel he could not properly count himself as an American citizen. He could become a gangster. (Allsop, 1961:236)

Perhaps we should not be surprised that Capone, with little chance of attending Yale or Harvard, landed his first job with a gangster who called himself Mr. Frankie Yale and owned a nightclub named the "Harvard Inn."

The inability to become successful by normative means may also lead to another type of deviance that Merton calls *ritualism* (see Figure 8–1). Low-level bureaucrats, knowing they will achieve only limited financial success, stick closely to the rules in order to feel and appear respectable.

A third response to the inability to succeed is *retreatism*, the rejection of both cultural goals and means. In effect, one "drops out" of mainstream culture. Some alcoholics, drug addicts, and street people are retreatists. The deviance of retreatists lies in their unconventional lifestyle and, perhaps more seriously, in their choosing to live this way.

The fourth response to failure is *rebellion*. Like retreatists, rebels reject both the cultural definition of success and the normative means of achieving it. Rebels—such as radical "survivalists"—go one step further by forming a counterculture and advocating alternatives to the existing social order.

DEVIANT SUBCULTURES

Richard Cloward and Lloyd Ohlin (1966) extended Merton's theory, proposing that crime results not just from limited legitimate (legal) opportunity but also from readily accessible illegitimate (illegal) opportunity. In short, deviance or conformity arises from the *relative opportunity structure* that frames a person's life.

The life of Al Capone shows how an ambitious person denied legitimate opportunity could take advantage of an illegal opportunity: supplying alcohol during Prohibition (1920–1933). In other words, illegal opportunities foster the development of *criminal subcultures* that provide people with the knowledge, skills, and other resources to succeed in unconventional ways. Capone, for example, built a criminal empire. Indeed, gangs may specialize in one or another form of criminality according to available opportunities and resources (Sheley et al., 1995).

But what happens when people cannot identify *any* kind of opportunity, legal or illegal? Then, deviance often surfaces in the form of *conflict subcultures* (armed street gangs), where violence is ignited by frustration and a desire for respect. Alternatively, those who fail to succeed, even using criminal means, may fall into *retreatist subcultures*, dropping out through alcohol or other drug abuse.

Albert Cohen (1971; orig. 1955) suggests that delinquency is most pronounced among lower-class youths because they have the least opportunity to achieve conventional success. Neglected by society, they seek self-respect by creating a delinquent subculture that "defines as meritorious the characteristics they *do* possess, the kinds of conduct of which they *are* capable" (1971:66). Being feared on the street may win few points with society as a whole, but it may satisfy a youth's desire to "be somebody" in the local neighborhood.

Walter Miller (1970; orig. 1958) adds that delinquent subcultures are characterized by (1) *trouble*, arising from frequent conflict with teachers and police; (2) *toughness*, the value placed on physical size and strength, especially among males; (3) *smartness*, the ability to succeed on the streets, to outsmart or "con" others, and to avoid being similarly taken advantage of; (4) *a need for excitement*, the search for thrills, risk, or danger; (5) *a belief in fate*, a sense that people lack control over their own lives; and (6) *a desire for freedom*, often expressed as hostility toward figures of authority.

Finally, Elijah Anderson (1994) explains that most people in poor, urban neighborhoods conform to conventional ("decent") values. Some young men, however, faced with neighborhood crime and violence, hostility from police, and sometimes even neglect from their own parents, adopt a "street code." To show that he can take care of himself and thus survive on the street, a young man displays "nerve," a willingness to stand up to any threat. According to this code, explains Anderson, even a violent death is better than being "dissed" (disrespected) by others. Some manage to escape the dangers, but the risk of ending up in jail—or worse—is very high for these young men pushed to the margins of our society.

Critical evaluation. Durkheim made an important contribution by pointing out the functions of deviance. However, evidence shows that a community does not always come together in reaction to crime; sometimes fear of crime drives people to withdraw from public life (Liska & Warner, 1991; Warr & Ellison, 2000).

Merton's strain theory has been criticized for explaining some kinds of deviance (theft, for example) far better than others (such as crimes of passion or mental illness). Moreover, not everyone seeks success in conventional terms of wealth, as strain theory implies.

The general argument of Cloward and Ohlin, Cohen, Miller, and Anderson—that deviance reflects the opportunity structure of society—has been confirmed by subsequent research (cf. Allan & Steffensmeier, 1989; Uggen, 1999). However, these theories fall short in assuming that everyone shares the same cultural standards for judging right and wrong. Moreover, we must be careful not to define deviance in ways that unfairly target poor people. If we define crime to include stock fraud as well as street theft, then more affluent people will be counted among criminals. Finally, all structural-functional theories imply that everyone who breaks the rules is labeled deviant. However, becoming deviant is actually a highly complex process, as the next section explains.

LABELING DEVIANCE: SYMBOLIC-INTERACTION ANALYSIS

The symbolic-interaction paradigm explains how people define deviance in everyday situations. From this point of view, definitions of deviance and conformity are surprisingly flexible.

LABELING THEORY

The central contribution of symbolic-interaction analysis is **labeling theory**, *the assertion that deviance and conformity result not so much from what people do as from how others respond to those actions.* Labeling theory stresses the relativity of deviance, meaning that people may define the same behavior in any number of ways. Thus, deviance is nothing more than behavior that people define as deviant (Becker, 1966).

Consider these situations: A woman takes an article of clothing from a roommate; a married man at a convention has sex with a prostitute; a mayor gives a big city contract to a major campaign contributor. In each case, "reality" depends on the response of others. Is the first situation a matter of borrowing or theft? The consequences of the second case depend largely on whether the man's behavior becomes known back home. In the third situation, is the official choosing a good contractor or paying off a political debt? The social construction of reality, then, is a highly variable process of detection, definition, and response.

More broadly, because "reality" depends on time and place, it is no surprise that one society's conformity may be another's deviance. The box describes cockfighting. Is this sport an important cultural ritual or a vicious abuse of animals?

Primary and Secondary Deviance

Edwin Lemert (1951, 1972) observed that some episodes of norm violation—say, skipping school or underage drinking—provoke slight reaction from others and have little effect on a person's self-concept. Lemert calls such episodes *primary deviance*.

But what happens if other people notice someone's deviance and make something of it? For example, if people begin to describe a young man as a "boozer" and evict him from their social circle, he may become embittered, drink even more, and seek the company of others who approve of his behavior. In this way, the response to initial deviance sets in motion *secondary deviance*, by which a person repeatedly violates a norm and begins to take on a deviant identity. The development of secondary deviance

Cockfighting: Cultural Ritual or Abuse of Animals?

You won't see it on television, but one of the world's most popular sports—from North America to Europe to Asia—is cockfighting. It is legal in parts of Louisiana, Texas, New Mexico, and Arizona, big business in Mexico, and something of a national pastime in the Philippines. There, the local cock pit is as important as the town square in the U.S. Midwest: Every village has one, and it draws a crowd on weekends and fiesta days.

On the surface, cockfights are about gambling. An afternoon or evening event might include ten fights. A fight begins with the cock owners displaying their birds to one another, calling out for bets as to the stronger bird. Members of the audience weigh in with cash. Keeping track of the bets is the *cristo*,

someone who stands, arms extended, taking money.

With the odds set and the money on the table, actual combat begins. Each rooster is outfitted with a small, sharp blade strapped to the rear of the left leg. The cocks need little encouragement to fight, but the owners do a bit of strutting themselves, swinging their birds in front of each other before dropping them on lines drawn in the pit sand. Upon hitting the ground, the birds fly at one another, merging in a blur of legs and feathers.

Within a few minutes, one bird may collapse from exhaustion; the owner steps in to revive his cock and the process is repeated. Before long, however, a blade finds its mark. The victor, the bird that will live to fight another day, perches on the vanquished, which will not.

In many parts of the world, cockfighting is an important male ritual. Men raise their roosters for about two years, often at great expense, and care for them like sons. In the ritual of the cockfight itself, men test their claims to manhood, establish their standing in the community's pecking order, and pass on to their sons lessons about honor, competition, and masculinity.

Many outside observers are repulsed by the spectacle. But cockfighting is obviously important to insiders. Should one condemn it as brutality or respect it as ceremony?

Sources: Based on *The Economist* (1994), Harris (1994), and the author's research in the Philippines.

---

is one application of the Thomas theorem (discussed in Chapter 6, "Social Interaction in Everyday Life"), which states that "situations defined as real become real in their consequences."

Stigma

Secondary deviance marks the start of what Erving Goffman (1963) calls a *deviant career*. As people develop a stronger commitment to deviant behavior, they typically acquire a **stigma,** *a powerfully negative label that greatly changes a person's self-concept and social identity.*

Stigma operates as a master status (see Chapter 6), overpowering other aspects of social identity so that a person is discredited in the minds of others, becoming socially isolated. Sometimes an entire community formally stigmatizes a person through what Harold Garfinkel (1956) calls a *degradation ceremony*. A criminal prosecution is one example, operating much like a high school graduation in reverse: A person stands

before the community to be labeled in a negative rather than a positive way.

Retrospective and Projective Labeling

Once people stigmatize a person, they may engage in *retrospective labeling,* interpreting someone's past in light of some present deviance (Scheff, 1984). For example, after discovering that a priest has sexually molested a child, others rethink his past, perhaps musing, "He always did want to be around young children." Retrospective labeling distorts a person's biography by being highly selective and helps deepen a deviant identity.

Similarly, people may engage in *projective labeling* of a stigmatized person. That is, they use a deviant identity to predict future action. People might say of the priest, for example, "He's just going to keep at it until he gets caught." Such expectations may increase the likelihood that they will come true.

Labeling and Mental Illness

Is a woman who believes that Jesus rides the bus to work with her every day mentally ill or just expressing her strong religious faith? Is a homeless man who refuses to allow police to take him to a city shelter on a cold night mentally ill or simply trying to live independently?

The psychiatrist Thomas Szasz (1961, 1970, 1994, 1995) charges that people apply the label "insanity" to what is only "difference." Therefore, he concludes, we should abandon the concept of mental illness entirely. Illness is physical, he continues, and afflicts only the body; "mental" illness is a myth. The world is full of people whose "differences" in thought or action may irritate us, but such differences are no grounds for defining someone as mentally ill. Such labeling, Szasz claims, simply enforces conformity to the standards of people powerful enough to impose their will on others.

Most health care professionals reject the notion that mental illness is a fiction. But some hail Szasz's work for pointing out the danger of using medicine to promote conformity. After all, most of us experience periods of extreme stress or other mental instability from time to time. Such episodes, although upsetting, usually are of passing importance. However, if others respond with negative labeling, the long-term result may be further deviance as a self-fulfilling prophecy (Scheff, 1984; Rosenfeld, 1997).

THE MEDICALIZATION OF DEVIANCE

Labeling theory, particularly the ideas of Szasz and Goffman, helps explain an important shift in the way our society understands deviance. Over the last fifty years, the growing influence of psychiatry and medicine in the United States has encouraged the **medicalization of deviance,** *the transformation of moral and legal deviance into a medical condition.*

Medicalization amounts to swapping one set of labels for another. In moral terms, we evaluate people or their behavior as "bad" or "good." However, the scientific objectivity of modern medicine passes no moral judgment, instead using clinical diagnoses such as "sick" or "well."

To illustrate, until the middle of this century, people generally viewed alcoholics as morally weak and easily tempted by the pleasure of drink. Gradually, however, medical specialists redefined alcoholism so that most people now consider alcoholism a disease, making people "sick" rather than "bad." Similarly, overeating, drug addiction, child abuse, sexual promiscuity, and other behaviors that used to be moral matters

The world is full of people who are unusual in one way or another. This Indian man grew the fingernails on one hand for more than thirty years just to do something that no one else had ever done. Should we define such behavior as harmless eccentricity or as evidence of mental illness?

are widely defined today as illnesses for which people need help rather than punishment.

The Difference Labels Make

Whether we define deviance as a moral or medical issue has three consequences. First, it affects *who responds* to deviance. An offense against common morality usually brings about a reaction from members of the community or the police. A medical label, however, places the situation under the control of clinical specialists, including counselors, psychiatrists, and physicians.

A second difference is *how people respond* to deviance. A moral approach defines the deviant as an "offender" subject to punishment. Medically, however, "patients" need treatment (for their own good, of course). Therefore, whereas punishment is designed to fit the crime, treatment programs are tailored to the patient and may

When people step out of line, should we consider their behavior "bad" or "sick"? In 2000, Atlanta Braves pitcher John Rocker made comments about minorities that many considered offensive. Rocker was reprimanded and was also required to undergo psychological testing, suggesting that he has an illness. Do you think these kinds of cases warrant "treatment," or is "punishment" more appropriate? Why?

involve almost any therapy that a specialist thinks will prevent future illness (von Hirsh, 1986). As a result, whereas punishment is closely monitored by the law, treatment provides less assurance of "due process."

Third, and most important, the two labels differ on *the personal competence of the deviant person.* Morally speaking, whether we are right or wrong, at least we take responsibility for our own behavior. Once defined as sick, however, we are seen as lacking the capacity to control (or, if "mentally ill," even understand) our actions. People who are incompetent are, in turn, subject to treatment against their will. For this reason alone, attempts to define deviance in medical terms should be made only with extreme caution.

SUTHERLAND'S DIFFERENTIAL ASSOCIATION THEORY

Learning any behavioral pattern—whether conventional or deviant—is a social process that takes place in groups. Therefore, according to Edwin Sutherland (1940), a person's tendency toward conformity or deviance depends on the amount of contact with others who encourage or reject conventional behavior. This is Sutherland's theory of *differential association.*

We can illustrate Sutherland's theory with a study of drug and alcohol use among young adults in the United States (Akers et al., 1979). Questionnaires completed by juniors and seniors in high school showed a close connection between the extent of alcohol and drug use and the degree to which peer groups encouraged such activity. The researchers concluded that young people accept delinquent patterns to the extent that they receive praise and other rewards for defining deviance—rather than conformity—in positive terms.

HIRSCHI'S CONTROL THEORY

The sociologist Travis Hirschi (1969; Gottfredson & Hirschi, 1995) developed *control theory,* which states that social control depends on imagining the consequences of one's behavior. Hirschi assumes that everyone finds at least some deviance tempting. But imagining the reaction of family and friends deters most people; almost everyone else would stop at the prospect of a ruined career. On the other hand, people who feel they have little to lose from deviance are likely to become rule-breakers.

Specifically, Hirschi continues, there are four types of social control:

1. **Attachment.** Strong social attachments encourage conformity; weak relationships in the family, peer group, and school leave people freer to engage in deviance.

2. **Commitment.** The greater a person's commitment to legitimate opportunity, the greater the advantages of conformity. By contrast, someone with little confidence in future success is more likely to drift toward deviance.

3. **Involvement.** Extensive involvement in legitimate activities—such as holding a job, going to school, and playing sports—inhibits deviance. People who simply "hang out," waiting for something to happen, have time and energy for deviant activity.

4. **Belief.** Strong belief in conventional morality and respect for authority figures control tendencies toward deviance. People with a weak conscience who are left unsupervised are more vulnerable to temptation (Osgood et al., 1996).

Hirschi's analysis draws together a number of earlier ideas about the causes of deviant behavior. Note someone they have arrested before, presumably because previous arrest suggests guilt. Fifth, *are bystanders present?* Smith and Visher claim that the presence of observers prompts police to take stronger control of a situation, if only to move the encounter from the street (the suspect's turf) to the police department (where law officers have the edge). Sixth, *what is the suspect's race?* All else being equal, Smith and Visher contend, police are more likely to arrest people of color than whites, perceiving suspects of African or Hispanic descent as either more dangerous or more likely to be guilty.

COURTS

After arrest, a court determines a suspect's guilt or innocence. In principle, our courts rely on an adversarial process involving attorneys—one representing the defendant and another the state—in the presence of a judge, who monitors legal procedures.

In practice, however, about 90 percent of criminal cases are resolved prior to court appearance through **plea bargaining,** *a legal negotiation in which a prosecutor reduces a charge in exchange for a defendant's guilty plea.* For example, the state may offer a defendant charged with burglary a lesser charge of possessing burglary tools in exchange for a guilty plea.

Plea bargaining is widespread because it spares the state the time and expense of court trials. A trial is unnecessary if there is little disagreement as to the facts of the case. Moreover, because the annual number of cases entering the system has doubled over the last decade, prosecutors could not possibly bring every case to trial. By quickly resolving most of their work, the courts channel their resources into the most important cases.

But plea bargaining pressures defendants (who are presumed innocent) to plead guilty. A person can exercise the right to a trial, but only at the risk of receiving a more severe sentence if found guilty. Furthermore, low-income defendants enter the process with the guidance of a public defender: an attorney, often underpaid, who may devote little time to even a serious case (Novak, 1999). Overall, plea bargaining may be efficient, but it compromises the adversarial process as well as the rights of some defendants.

PUNISHMENT

When a young girl is murdered—as in the case described in the opening to this chapter—some people may wonder why, but almost everyone believes that someone should have to pay for the crime. Indeed,

During the 1990s, the United States built prisons at an unprecedented rate. There are now almost twice as many people in jail—2 million—than there were in 1990. The public's "get tough with criminals" attitude has also led to the spread of "road gangs"—a return of the "chain gangs" common in the early decades of the twentieth century. As some see it, putting criminals to work along busy highways reminds the public of the consequences of law-breaking.

sometimes the desire to punish an offender is so great that justice is lost.

Such cases force us to ask why a society should punish its wrongdoers. Over many years, scholars have pointed to four basic reasons to punish: retribution, deterrence, rehabilitation, and societal protection.

Retribution

The oldest justification for punishment is the public's craving for revenge. Knowing the power of this passion, U.S. Supreme Court justice Oliver Wendell Holmes stated that "the law has no choice but to satisfy [that] craving" (quoted in Carlson, 1976).

The first reason to punish, then, is to satisfy a society's need for **retribution,** *an act of moral vengeance by which society inflicts suffering on an offender comparable to that caused by the offense.* Retribution rests on a view of society as a moral balance. When criminality upsets this balance, punishment exacted in comparable measure

FIGURE 8–4 Nations with the Highest Incarceration Rates, 2000

Source: Walmsley (2000).

restores the moral order, as suggested in the biblical dictum "An eye for an eye."

During the Middle Ages, most people viewed crime as a sin—an offense against God as well as society—that warranted a harsh response. Today, although critics point out that retribution does little to reform the offender, many people consider vengeance reason enough for punishment.

Deterrence

A second justification for punishment is **deterrence,** *the use of punishment to discourage criminality.* Deterrence is based on the eighteenth-century Enlightenment idea that humans are calculating and rational creatures who will not break the law if they think that the pain of punishment will outweigh the pleasure of crime.

Deterrence emerged as reform in response to the harsh punishments based on retribution. Why put someone to death for stealing, reformists reasoned, if theft can be discouraged with a prison sentence? As the concept of deterrence gained widespread acceptance, execution and physical mutilation of criminals in most industrial societies were replaced by milder forms of punishment such as imprisonment.

Punishment can deter in two ways. *Specific deterrence* convinces an individual offender that crime does not pay. Through *general deterrence*, the punishment of one person serves as an example to others.

Rehabilitation

The third justification for punishment is **rehabilitation,** *a program for reforming the offender to prevent subsequent offenses.* Rehabilitation arose along with the social sciences in the nineteenth century. Sociologists of that time (and also since) saw crime and other deviance springing from a social environment marked by poverty or a lack of parental supervision. Logically, then, if offenders learn to be deviant, they can also learn to obey the rules; the key is controlling the environment. *Reformatories* or *houses of correction* provided controlled settings where people could learn proper behavior (recall the description of total institutions in Chapter 5, "Socialization").

Like deterrence, rehabilitation motivates the offender to conform. But rehabilitation emphasizes constructive improvement, whereas deterrence and retribution make the offender suffer. In addition, where retribution demands that the punishment fit the crime, rehabilitation tailors treatment to each offender. Thus, identical crimes would prompt similar acts of retribution but might call for different rehabilitation programs.

Societal Protection

A final justification for punishment is **societal protection,** *a means by which society renders an offender incapable of further offenses temporarily through incarceration or permanently by execution.* Like deterrence, societal protection is a rational approach to punishment intended to protect society from crime.

Currently, 2 million people are incarcerated in the United States, and another 4.5 million are on parole or probation. In response to tougher public attitudes and an increasing number of arrests for drug offenses, the U.S. prison population has tripled since 1980. The size of inmate populations is going up in most high-income countries, yet as Figure 8–4 shows, the

United States incarcerates a larger share of its population than all other countries in the world (Sutton, 2000; Walmsley, 2000).

Critical evaluation. Table 8–2 summarizes the four justifications for punishment. Assessing the actual consequences of punishment, however, is no simple task.

The value of retribution lies in Durkheim's contention that punishing the deviant person increases people's moral awareness. Appropriately, then, punishment traditionally was carried out in public. Although the last public execution in the United States took place in Kentucky in 1937, today's mass media ensure that the population is aware of executions carried out within prison walls (Kittrie, 1971).

Certainly, punishment deters some crime. Yet our society also has a high rate of **criminal recidivism,** *subsequent offenses by people convicted of crimes.* About three-fourths of state prisoners have been jailed before and, once released, about half will be back in prison within a few years (McNulty, 1994; Petersilia, 1997). In light of such patterns, we may well wonder about the extent to which punishment really deters crime. Furthermore, only about one-third of all crimes are known to police, and only about one in five of these crimes results in an arrest. The adage "Crime doesn't pay" rings hollow when we consider that only a small share of offenses are ever punished.

General deterrence is even harder to investigate scientifically because we have no way of knowing how people might act if they were unaware of punishments given to others. In the debate over capital punishment, opponents point to research suggesting that the death penalty has limited value as a general deterrent. Moreover, the United States is the only Western, high-income society that routinely executes offenders. Even more troubling is the fact that some death sentences turn out to be flawed as noted at the beginning of this chapter, and since 1973, eighty-seven people have been released from death row, which amounts to putting the death penalty itself on trial (Sellin, 1980; van den Haag & Conrad, 1983; Archer & Gartner, 1987; Lester, 1987; Bailey & Peterson, 1989; Bailey, 1990; Bohm, 1991; Tanber, 1998; Alter, 2000). National Map 8–2 on page 216 identifies the thirty-eight states that have the death penalty and shows that half the prisoners on death row are in just five of these states.

Prisons provide short-term societal protection by keeping offenders off the streets, but they do little to reshape attitudes or behavior in the long term (Carlson, 1976; Wright, 1994). Perhaps rehabilitation is an unrealistic expectation because, according

TABLE 8–2 Four Justifications for Punishment: A Summary	
Retribution	The oldest justification for punishment. Punishment is atonement for a moral wrong; in principle, punishment should be comparable in severity to the deviance itself.
Deterrence	An early modern approach. Deviance is considered social disruption, which society acts to control. People are viewed as rational and self-interested; deterrence works because the pains of punishment outweigh the pleasures of deviance.
Rehabilitation	A modern strategy linked to the development of social sciences. Deviance is viewed as the product of social problems (such as poverty) or personal problems (such as mental illness). Social conditions are improved; treatment is tailored to the offender's condition.
Societal Protection	A modern approach easier to implement than rehabilitation. If society is unable or unwilling to rehabilitate offenders or reform social conditions, people are protected by incarcerating or executing the offender.

to Sutherland's theory of differential association, locking up criminals together for years probably strengthens criminal attitudes and skills. Incarceration also severs whatever social ties inmates may have to the outside world, which, following Hirschi's control theory, leaves them likely to commit more crimes upon their release.

 Rape in prison is an old problem that is gaining more attention. To read a report on prison rape by the activist organization Human Rights Watch, go to http://www.hrw.org/reports/2001/prison/

Finally, the stigma of being an ex-convict can be a powerful barrier to building a new life. One study of young offenders in Philadelphia found that boys who were sentenced to long prison terms—and thus were likely to acquire a criminal stigma—went on to commit both more crimes and more serious ones when released (Wolfgang, Figlio, & Sellin, 1972).

Ultimately, we should never assume that the criminal justice system can eliminate crime. As the box on page 217 explains, police, courts, and prisons have played a part in the recent downturn in crime rates. But more is involved. As this chapter has described, crime and other deviance result not just from the acts of "bad people" but from the operation of society itself.

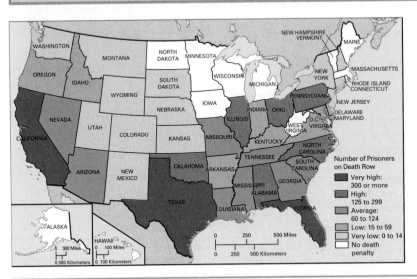

NATIONAL MAP 8–2
Capital Punishment across the United States

The United States and Japan are the only high-income nations in which the government imposes the death penalty. Yet within the United States, the fifty states have broadly divergent capital punishment laws: Half of the 3,527 prisoners on death row are in five states. What regional pattern do you see in the map? Can you account for this pattern?

Source: U.S. Bureau of Justice Statistics (2000).

SUMMARY

1. *Deviance* refers to norm violations ranging from mild breaches of etiquette to serious violence.

2. Biological research, from Caesare Lombroso's nineteenth-century observations of convicts to recent research in human genetics, has not offered much insight into the causes of deviance.

3. Psychological study links deviance to abnormal personality resulting from either biological or environmental causes. Psychological theories help explain some kinds of deviance.

4. Deviance has societal rather than individual roots because it (a) varies according to cultural norms, (b) is socially defined, and (c) reflects patterns of social power.

5. Using the structural-functional paradigm, Durkheim explained that deviance affirms norms and values, clarifies moral boundaries, promotes social unity, and encourages social change.

6. The symbolic-interaction paradigm is the basis of labeling theory, which holds that deviance lies in people's reaction to a person's behavior, not in the behavior itself. Acquiring a stigma of deviance can lead to secondary deviance and a deviant career.

7. Based on Karl Marx's ideas, social-conflict theory holds that laws and other norms reflect the interests of powerful members of society. Although white-collar and corporate crime cause extensive social harm, offenders rarely are branded as criminals.

8. Official statistics indicate that arrest rates peak in late adolescence, then drop steadily with advancing age. Seventy percent of those arrested for property crimes and 83 percent of those arrested for violent crimes are male.

9. People of lower social position commit more street crime than people with greater social privilege. When white-collar and corporate crimes are included among criminal offenses, however, the disparity in overall criminal activity goes down.

10. More whites than African Americans are arrested for street crimes. However, African Americans are arrested more often than whites in proportion to their respective populations. Asian Americans have lower-than-average rates of arrest.

11. Police exercise a great deal of discretion in their work. Arrest is more likely if the offense is serious, bystanders are present, or the accused is African American or Hispanic.

Violent Crime Is Down—But Why?

During the 1980s, crime rates shot upward. Just about everyone lived in fear of violent crime, and in many larger cities, the numbers killed and wounded turned whole neighborhoods into war zones. There seemed to be no solution to the problem.

Then, in the 1990s, something good and unexpected happened: Serious crime rates began to fall until, by 2000, they were at levels not seen in more than a generation. Why? Applying the perspectives and theories presented in this chapter, we can identify several reasons:

1. **A reduction in the youth population.** We have already noted that young people (particularly males) are responsible for much violent crime. Between 1990 and 2000, the share of the population aged fifteen to twenty-four dropped by about 5 percent (in part because abortion was legalized in 1973), presumably making a modest contribution to the decline in serious crime.

2. **Changes in policing.** Much of the drop in crime (and the earlier rise in crime) has taken place in large cities. New York City, where the number of murders fell from 2,245 in 1990 to just 673 in 2000, has adopted a policy of *community policing*, which means that police are concerned not just with making

arrests but with preventing crime before it happens. Officers get to know the areas they patrol and stop young men for jaywalking or other minor infractions to check them for concealed weapons (the word has gotten around that you risk arrest for carrying a gun). Moreover, there are *more* police at work in large cities. For example, Los Angeles added more than 2,000 police during the 1990s, and it, too, has seen its violent crime rate fall.

3. **More prisons.** From 1985 until 2000, the number of inmates in U.S. jails and prisons soared from 750,000 to 2 million. The main reason for this increase is tough laws that demand prison time for many crimes, especially drug offenses. As one analyst put it, "When you lock up an extra million people, it's got to have some effect on the crime rate" (Zimring, cited in Witkin, 1998:31).

4. **A better economy.** The U.S. economy has boomed during the last ten years. With unemployment down, more people are working, which reduces the likelihood that some will turn to crime out of economic desperation. The logic here is simple: More jobs, fewer crimes. However, as the economy weakened after 2000, reductions in crime have also slowed.

5. **The declining drug trade.** Many analysts agree that the most important factor in reducing violent crime rates is the decline of crack cocaine. Crack came on the scene about 1985, and violence spread as young people—especially in the inner cities and increasingly armed with guns—became part of a booming drug trade. With legitimate job opportunities low and rising opportunity to make money illegally, a generation of young people became part of a wave of violence. Widespread crack cocaine use also explains the trend, noted earlier, of the younger age of violent criminals.

By the early 1990s, however, the popularity of crack began to fall as people saw the damage it was causing to entire communities. This realization, coupled with steady improvement in the economy and stiffer sentences for drug offenses, brought the turnaround in violent crime.

Keep in mind that the current picture looks better compared with what it was a decade ago. The crime problem, says one researcher, "looks better, but only because the early 1990s were so bad. So let's not fool ourselves into thinking everything is resolved. It's not."

Sources: Based on Boggess & Bound (1997), Blumstein & Rosenfeld (1998), Fagan, Zimring, & Kim (1998), Witkin (1998), Winship & Berrien (1999), and Donahue & Leavitt (2000).

---

12. In the United States, most prosecutions of criminal cases never go to trial but are resolved through the process of plea bargaining. Though efficient, it is widely believed that this method puts less powerful people at a disadvantage.

13. Justifications of punishment include retribution, deterrence, rehabilitation, and societal protection. Because its consequences are difficult to evaluate scientifically, punishment—like deviance itself—sparks controversy among sociologists and the public as a whole.

KEY CONCEPTS

deviance (p. 191) the recognized violation of cultural norms

crime (p. 191) the violation of a society's formally enacted criminal law

social control (p. 192) attempts by society to regulate people's thought and behavior

criminal justice system (p. 192) a formal response by police, courts, and prison officials to alleged violations of the law

labeling theory (p. 197) the assertion that deviance and conformity result not so much from what people do as from how others respond to those actions

stigma (p. 198) a powerfully negative label that greatly changes a person's self-concept and social identity

medicalization of deviance (p. 199) the transformation of moral and legal deviance into a medical condition

white-collar crime (p. 202) crime committed by people of high social position in the course of their occupations

corporate crime (p. 203) the illegal actions of a corporation or people acting on its behalf

organized crime (p. 203) a business supplying illegal goods or services

hate crime (p. 204) a criminal act against a person or person's property by an offender motivated by racial or other bias

crimes against the person (p. 206) (violent crimes) crimes that direct violence or the threat of violence against others

crimes against property (p. 206) (property crimes) crimes that involve theft of property belonging to others

victimless crimes (p. 207) violations of law in which there are no readily apparent victims

plea bargaining (p. 213) a legal negotiation in which a prosecutor reduces a charge in exchange for a defendant's guilty plea

retribution (p. 213) an act of moral vengeance by which society inflicts suffering on an offender comparable to that caused by the offense

deterrence (p. 214) the use of punishment to discourage criminality

rehabilitation (p. 214) a program for reforming the offender to prevent subsequent offenses

societal protection (p. 214) a means by which society renders an offender incapable of further offenses temporarily through incarceration or permanently by execution

criminal recidivism (p. 215) subsequent offenses by people convicted of crimes

CRITICAL-THINKING QUESTIONS

1. How does a sociological view of deviance differ from the common-sense notion that bad people do bad things?

2. List Durkheim's functions of deviance. From his point of view, can society ever be free from deviance? Why or why not?

3. You probably have heard the old saying, "Sticks and stones can break my bones, but names can never hurt me." Explain how labeling theory challenges this statement.

4. A recent study found that one in three black men between the ages of twenty and twenty-nine is in jail, on probation, or on parole (The Sentencing Project, 2000). What factors noted in this chapter help explain this pattern?

APPLICATIONS AND EXERCISES

1. Research computer crime. What new kinds of crime are emerging in the information age? Is computer technology also generating new ways to track lawbreakers?

2. Rent a wheelchair (check with a local pharmacy or medical supply store) and use it as much as possible for a day or two. Not only will you gain a firsthand understanding of the physical barriers to getting

around, but you will also discover that people respond to you in many different ways.

3. Watch an episode of the real-action police show *COPS*. Based on this program, how would you profile the people who commit crimes?

4. Packaged in the back of this new textbook is an interactive CD-ROM that offers a variety of study and review materials intended to help you better understand the material covered in this chapter. For this chapter, the CD-ROM contains an author's tip video, Real Life Sociology videos, other relevant audio and video, interactive map animations, audio journal entries from the author, Web links, and much more.

 ## SITES TO SEE

http://www.prenhall.com/macionis

Visit the interactive *Companion Website*™ that accompanies this text. Begin by clicking on the cover of your book. You will find a chapter-by-chapter study guide, practice tests, and a significant portion of the text for on-line review, as well as many suggested Web links.

http://www.telalink.net/~police/risk/

Visit this site, run by the Nashville Police Department, that rates your chances of becoming a victim of a serious crime.

http://www.civilrights.org/

The Leadership Conference on Civil Rights maintains this site on hate crimes and other civil rights issues.

http://www.igc.apc.org/spr/

The organization Stop Prisoner Rape hosts this site dealing with the problem of rape in U.S. prisons.

http://www.ncadp.org
http://www.uaa.alaska.edu/just/death/intl.html

These sites provide information on the death penalty. The first presents the views of the National Coalition to Abolish the Death Penalty. The second provides data on the death penalty in global perspective.

http://www.cybercrime.gov

This site, operated by the U.S. Department of Justice, provides a great deal of information on computer crime and intellectual property issues.

http://www.crime.com/info/jailcam_redirect.html

This site provides live video coverage inside the Maricopa County, Arizona, jail.

 ## INVESTIGATE WITH CONTENTSELECT

Follow the instructions found on page 23 of this textbook to enter this chapter of the book's *Companion Website*™. Once in the chapter, click on the ContentSelect icon at the bottom left of your screen and enter your personal User ID and Password. Enter keywords such as "crime," "murder," "prisons," and "cyber-crime," and the search engine will help you become an effective researcher.

CHAPTER

9

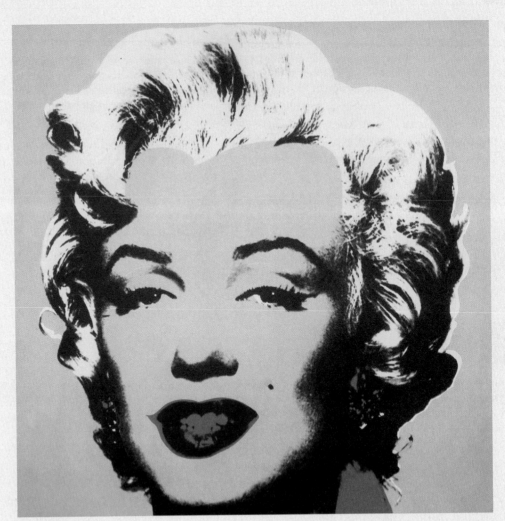

Andy Warhol
Marilyn, 1967
© 2001 Andy Warhol Foundation for the Visual Arts/Artists Rights Society (ARS), New York. Tate Gallery,
London/Art Resource, N.Y.(TM) 2002 Marilyn Monroe LLC under license authorized by GMG Worldwide Inc.
Indianapolis, Indiana 46256 USA/www.MarilynMonroe.com.

SEXUALITY

It was a typical autumn day in Sacramento, California, and students were buzzing as they returned to Center High School for the beginning of classes. Large groups of young people moved together down the hallways as young men and women exchanged stories about summer vacation and caught up with friends. But one story dominated the discussion: the return of teacher David Warfield, who, over the summer, changed his sex from being a man to being a woman and adopted the new name Dana Rivers.

Warfield, who had taught at Center High for almost ten years, was a popular, award-winning journalism teacher who also served as announcer for the school's football games. The previous year, he had informed school officials of his "gender dysphoria," a medical condition whereby he was physically a man but felt himself to be a woman. This condition went back to his childhood, he explained. As much as he had tried to "be a man," he just couldn't do it. Warfield had already begun hormone treatments and planned to undergo a sex-change operation to become a woman within the following year.

School board officials were uneasy about Warfield's plan. They insisted that upon returning to classes in the fall she not share any details about her operation or transformation. However, Rivers discussed her change with a number of students, leading several parents to file complaints. The incident divided the school community between those who supported and those who opposed keeping Rivers as a teacher. Soon after, the school board fired Rivers (Hornblower, 1999).

One thing that is clear about the Dana Rivers case is that in U.S. society, sexuality is an important—and controversial—issue. It is also clear that many young people, and a number of their parents, understand too little about sexuality. This chapter presents some of what researchers have learned about human sexuality. From a sociological point of view, our main concern is how society defines sexuality and how people sexually express themselves.

UNDERSTANDING SEXUALITY

How much of the day goes by without your giving any thought at all to sexuality? If you are like most people, the answer is "not very much." That is because sexuality is not just about "having sex." Sexuality is a theme found throughout society and apparent on campus, in the workplace, and especially in the mass media. In addition, the sex industry—including pornography and prostitution—is a multibillion-dollar business in its own right. As Dana Rivers's story shows us, sexuality is an important part of how we think about ourselves and how others evaluate us. In truth, there are few areas of life in which sexuality does *not* play some part.

But despite its importance, few people understand sexuality. Through much of our history, sex has been a cultural taboo so that, at least in polite conversation, people do not talk about it. As a result, although sex can produce much pleasure, it also causes confusion and sometimes outright fear. Even scientists long considered sex off limits as a research topic. It was not until the mid-twentieth century that researchers turned their attention to this vital dimension of social life. Since then, as this chapter reports, we have learned a great deal about human sexuality.

We claim that beauty is in the eye of the beholder, which suggests the importance of culture in setting standards of attractiveness. All of the people pictured here—from Morocco, South Africa, Nigeria, Myanmar (Burma), Japan, and Ecuador—are beautiful to members of their own society. At the same time, sociobiologists point out that, in every society on Earth, people are attracted to youthfulness. The reason is that, as sociobiologists see it, attractiveness underlies our choices about reproduction, which is most readily accomplished in early adulthood.

SEX: A BIOLOGICAL ISSUE

Sex is *the biological distinction between females and males.* From a biological point of view, sex is the means by which humans reproduce. A female ovum and a male sperm, each containing twenty-three chromosomes (biological codes that guide physical development), combine to form a fertilized embryo. One of these pairs of chromosomes determines the child's sex. To this pair the mother contributes an X chromosome and the father contributes either an X or a Y. An X chromosome from the father combines with the mother's X to produce a female (XX) embryo; a Y from the father produces a male (XY) embryo. Thus, a child's sex is determined biologically at the moment of conception.

Within weeks, the sex of an embryo starts to guide its development. If the embryo is male, testicular tissue starts to produce testosterone, a hormone that triggers the development of male genitals. If no testosterone is present, the embryo develops female genitals. In the United States, about 105 boys are born for every 100 girls, but a higher death rate among males reverses this trend and makes females a slight majority by the time people reach their mid-thirties (U.S. National Center for Health Statistics, 2001).

SEX AND THE BODY

What sets females and males apart are differences in the body. Right from birth, the two sexes have different **primary sex characteristics,** namely, *the genitals, organs used for reproduction.* At puberty, as people reach sexual maturity, additional sex differentiation takes place. At this point, people develop **secondary sex characteristics,** *bodily development apart from the genitals, that distinguishes biologically mature females and males.* To allow for pregnancy, childbirth, and breast feeding, mature females have wider hips, breasts, and soft fatty tissue that provides a reserve supply of nutrition. Mature males typically develop more muscle in the upper body, more extensive body hair, and deeper voices. Of course, these are general differences: Some males are smaller and have less body hair and higher voices than some females.

Hermaphrodites

Sex is not always as clear-cut as we have just described. In rare cases, a hormone imbalance before birth produces a **hermaphrodite** (a word derived from Hermaphroditus, the offspring of the mythological Greek gods Hermes and Aphrodite, who embodied both sexes), *a human being with some combination of female and male genitalia.*

Because our culture is uneasy about sexual ambiguity, some people respond to hermaphrodites with confusion or even disgust. But other cultures lead people to respond quite differently. For example, the Pokot of eastern Africa pay little attention to what they consider a simple biological error, and the Navajo look on hermaphrodites with awe, seeing in them the full potential of both the female and the male (Geertz, 1975).

Transsexuals

Some hermaphrodites undergo genital surgery to appear (and occasionally function as) a sexually normal female or male. Other people deliberately change their sex: **Transsexuals** are *people who feel they are one sex even though biologically they are the other.* This was the case with Dana Rivers. In fact, tens of thousands of people in the United States feel trapped in a body of the wrong sex. Most become *transgendered,* meaning that they begin to disregard conventional ideas about how females and males should look and behave. Many go one step further and become transsexuals by surgically altering their genitals (Tewksbury & Gagné, 1996; Gagné, Tewksbury, & McGaughey, 1997).

Like so many elements of our lives, notions about kissing vary from place to place. The Maori people of New Zealand rub noses to show affection.

SEX: A CULTURAL ISSUE

Sexuality has a biological foundation. But like all dimensions of human behavior, sexuality is also very much a cultural issue. Biology is sufficient to explain the fascinating mating rituals of the animal world, but humans have no similar biological program. That is, humans have a biological "sex drive" in the sense that they find sex pleasurable and want to engage in sexual activity, but our biology does not dictate any specific way of being sexual any more than our desire to eat dictates any particular foods or table manners.

Cultural Variation

Almost any sexual practice shows wide variation from one society to another. In his pioneering study of sexuality in the United States, Alfred Kinsey (1948) found that most couples in the United States reported having intercourse in a single position: face to face, with the woman on the bottom and the man on top. Halfway around the world, in the South Seas, most couples *never* have sex in this way. In fact, when the people of the South Seas learned of this practice from Western missionaries, they poked fun at it as the strange "missionary position."

Even the simple practice of showing affection has extensive cultural variation. Whereas most people in the United States readily kiss in public, the Chinese kiss only in private. The French kiss publicly, often twice (once on each cheek), and Belgians kiss three times (starting on either cheek). The Maoris of New Zealand rub noses, and most people in Nigeria don't kiss at all.

Modesty also is a culturally variable matter. If a woman entering a bath is disturbed, what body parts does she cover? Helen Colton (1983) reports that an Islamic woman covers her face, a Laotian woman covers her breasts, a Samoan woman her navel, a Sumatran woman her knees, and a European woman covers her breasts with one hand and her genital area with the other.

Around the world, some societies tend to restrict sexuality, and others are more permissive. In China, for example, norms closely regulate sexuality so that few people have sexual intercourse before they marry. In the United States, at least in recent decades intercourse before marriage has become the norm, and people may choose to have sex even when there is no strong commitment between them.

THE INCEST TABOO

Are any cultural views of sex the same everywhere? The answer is yes. One cultural universal—an element found in every society the world over—is the **incest taboo,** *a norm forbidding sexual relations or marriage between certain relatives.* In the United States, the law and cultural mores prohibit close relatives (including brothers and sisters, parents and children) from having sex or marrying. But exactly which family members are included in a society's incest taboo varies from one place to another. Some societies (such as the North American Navajo) apply incest taboos to the mother and others on her side of the family. There are also societies (including ancient Peru and Egypt) on record that have approved brother-sister marriages among the nobility (Murdock, 1965; orig. 1949).

Why does the incest taboo exist everywhere? Biology is part of the reason: Reproduction between close relatives of any species risks offspring with mental or physical problems. But this fact does not explain why, of all living species, only humans observe an incest taboo. In other words, controlling sexuality among close relatives seems a necessary element of social organization. First, the incest taboo limits sexual competition in families by restricting sex to spouses (ruling out, for example, sex between parent and child). Second, because family ties define people's

rights and obligations toward each other, reproduction between close relatives would hopelessly confuse kinship; if a mother and son had a daughter, for example, what would the child's relationship be to the other two? Third, by requiring people to marry outside their immediate families, the incest taboo integrates the larger society as people look widely for partners to form new families.

The incest taboo has been an enduring sexual norm in the United States and elsewhere. But in this country, many sexual norms have changed over time. During the twentieth century, as we now explain, our society experienced both a sexual revolution and, later, a sexual counterrevolution.

SEXUAL ATTITUDES IN THE UNITED STATES

What do people in the United States think about sex? Our cultural orientation toward sexuality has always been inconsistent. On one hand, most European immigrants arrived with rigid notions about "correct" sexuality, which ideally meant that sex was only for the purpose of reproduction within marriage. As explained in Chapter 8 ("Deviance"), the Puritan settlers of New England demanded conformity in all attitudes and behavior, and they imposed severe penalties for any misconduct, even if the sexual "misconduct" took place in the privacy of one's home. Efforts to regulate sexuality continued long after: As late as the 1960s, for example, some states legally banned the sale of condoms in stores. Even today, a number of states have laws on the books banning homosexuality and various "unnatural" acts.

But this is just one side of the story of sexuality in the United States. As Chapter 3 ("Culture") explains, our culture is also individualistic, and many believe in giving people freedom to do pretty much as they wish, as long as they cause no direct harm to others. Such thinking—that what people do in the privacy of their own home is *their* business—makes sex a matter of individual freedom and personal choice.

So which is it? Is the United States a restrictive or a permissive society when it comes to sexuality? The answer is that we are both. On one hand, many people in the United States still view sexual conduct as an important indicator of personal morality. On the other, sex is exploited and glorified everywhere in our culture and strongly promoted by the mass media.

Within this general framework, we turn now to changes in sexual attitudes and behavior over the course of the twentieth century. As we shall see, sexual attitudes have changed considerably over time.

THE SEXUAL REVOLUTION

During the twentieth century, people witnessed profound changes in sexual attitudes and practices. The first indications of this change occurred in the 1920s as millions of women and men migrated from farms and small towns to rapidly growing cities. There, living apart from their families and meeting in the workplace, young people enjoyed greater sexual freedom. Indeed, this is one reason the decade became known as the "Roaring Twenties."

In the 1930s and 1940s, the Great Depression and World War II slowed the rate of change. But in the postwar period, after 1945, Alfred Kinsey set the stage for what later came to be known as the *sexual revolution*. Kinsey and his colleagues published their first study of sexuality in the United States in 1948, and it raised eyebrows everywhere. It was not so much what Kinsey said about sexual behavior—although he did present some surprising results—as simply the fact that scientists were studying sex that set off a national conversation. At that time, after all, many people were uneasy talking about sex even privately at home.

Kinsey's two books (1948, 1953) became best-sellers partly because they revealed that people in the United States, on average, were far less conventional in sexual matters than most had thought. Thus, these books fostered a new openness toward sexuality, which helped advance the sexual revolution.

In the late 1960s, the sexual revolution truly came of age. Youth culture dominated public life, and expressions such as "if it feels good, do it" and "sex, drugs, and rock and roll" summed up a new freedom about sexuality. Some people were turned off by the idea of "turning on," of course, but the baby boom generation, born between 1945 and 1960, became the first cohort in U.S. history to grow up with the idea that sex was part of everyone's life, married or not.

Technology also played a part in the sexual revolution. "The pill," introduced in 1960, not only prevented pregnancy but made sex more convenient. Unlike a condom or diaphragm, which has to be used at the time of intercourse, the pill could be taken any time during the day. Now women as well as men could engage in sex without any special preparation.

The sexual revolution had special significance for women because historically women were subject to greater sexual regulation than men. According to the

The sexual revolution was well underway by the late 1960s, when the youth counterculture embraced the idea of "free love." This term is something of an exaggeration, but many people did enter into more casual sexual relationships.

double standard, society allows (and even encourages) men to be sexually active while expecting women to remain chaste before marriage and faithful to their husbands afterward. The survey data shown in Figure 9–1 on page 226 support this conclusion. Among people born in the United States between 1933 and 1942 (that is, people in their sixties today), 56 percent of men but just 16 percent of women report having had two or more sexual partners by the time they were age twenty. Compare this wide gap with the pattern among the baby boomers born between 1953 and 1962 (people now in their forties), who came of age after the sexual revolution. In this category, 62 percent of men and 48 percent of women say they had two or more sexual partners by age twenty (Laumann et al., 1994:198). Thus, the sexual revolution increased

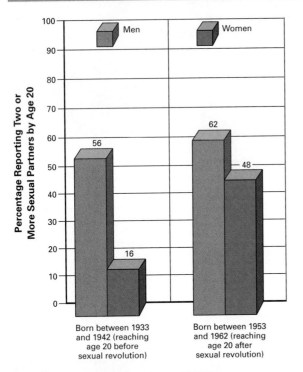

FIGURE 9–1 The Sexual Revolution: Closing the Double Standard

Source: Laumann et al. (1994:198).

sexual activity overall, but it changed behavior among women more than among men.

A general trend, then, is greater openness about sexuality as societies develop economically and as the opportunities for women increase. With these facts in mind, we can understand the global pattern of birth control use shown in Global Map 9–1.

THE SEXUAL COUNTERREVOLUTION

The sexual revolution made sex a topic of everyday discussion and sexual activity more a matter of individual choice. But given that U.S. society has always had two minds about sex, the sexual revolution was also controversial. By 1980, the climate of sexual freedom that had marked the late 1960s and 1970s was

criticized by some as evidence of our country's moral decline. Thus, the *sexual counterrevolution* began.

Politically speaking, the sexual counterrevolution was a conservative call for a return to "family values," replacing sexual freedom with sexual responsibility. In practice, this turnaround meant moving sex back within marriage. Critics objected not just to the idea of "free love" but to trends such as cohabitation (living together) and having children out of wedlock.

Looking back, we can see that the sexual counterrevolution did not greatly change the idea that individuals should decide for themselves when and with whom to have a sexual relationship. What did happen, however, is that more people began choosing to limit their number of sexual partners or to abstain from sex entirely. In many cases, such decisions are made on moral grounds. For others, however, the decision to limit sexual activity reflects a fear of sexually transmitted diseases (STDs). As Chapter 21 ("Health and Medicine") explains, although rates of most infectious diseases fell after 1960, rates of STDs rose sharply. Moreover, the fact that some STDs (such as genital herpes) are incurable and others (AIDS) are deadly has given people good reason to consider carefully their sexual choices.

PREMARITAL SEX

In light of the sexual revolution and the sexual counterrevolution, how much has sexual behavior in the United States really changed? One interesting trend involves premarital sex, that is, the likelihood that young people will have sexual intercourse before marriage.

Consider first what U.S. adults *say* about premarital intercourse. Table 9–1 on page 228 shows that about 35 percent characterize sexual relations before marriage as "always wrong" or "almost always wrong." Another 20 percent consider premarital sex "wrong only sometimes," and about 40 percent say premarital sex is "not wrong at all." Public opinion is more accepting of premarital sex today than a generation ago, but even so, our society remains divided on this issue.

Now first consider what young people *do* regarding premarital intercourse. For women, there has been marked change over time. The Kinsey studies (1948, 1953; see also Laumann et al., 1994) reported that for people born in the early 1900s, about 50 percent of men but just 6 percent of women had premarital sexual intercourse before age nineteen. Studies of baby boomers born after World War II show a slight increase in premarital intercourse among men but a large increase—to about one-third—among women.

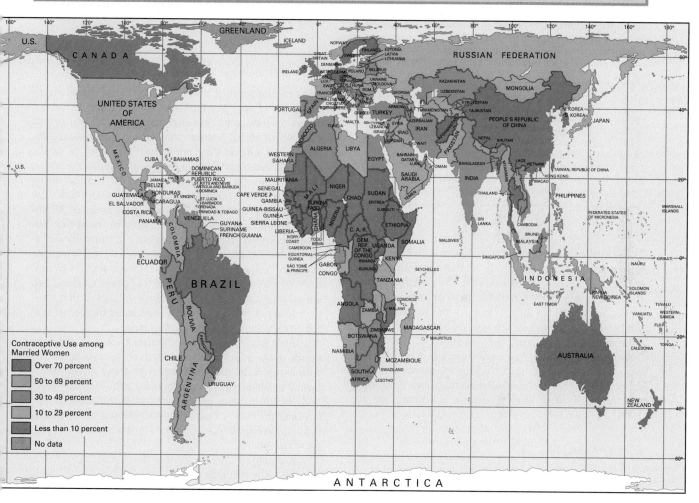

GLOBAL MAP 9–1 Contraceptive Use in Global Perspective

The map shows the percentage of married women using modern contraception methods (such as barrier methods, contraceptive pill, implants, injectables, intra-uterine contraceptive devices [IUD], or sterilization). In general, how do high-income nations differ from low-income nations? Can you explain this difference?

Source: Data from Mackay (2000).

The most recent studies, targeting men and women born in the 1970s, show that 76 percent of men and 66 percent of women had premarital sexual intercourse by their senior year in high school (Laumann et al., 1994:323–24). Thus, although general public attitudes remain divided on premarital sex, the behavior is broadly accepted among young people.

SEX BETWEEN ADULTS

To hear the mass media tell it, people in the United States are very active sexually. But do popular images exaggerate reality? The Laumann study (1994) found that frequency of sexual activity varied widely in the U.S. population. The patterns break down like this:

TABLE 9–1 How We View Premarital and Extramarital Sex

Survey Question: "There's been a lot of discussion about the way morals and attitudes about sex are changing in this country. If a man and a woman have sexual relations before marriage, do you think it is always wrong, almost always wrong, wrong only sometimes, or not wrong at all? What about a married person having sexual relations with someone other than the marriage partner?"

	Premarital Sex	Extramarital Sex
"Always wrong"	26.7%	77.8%
"Almost always wrong"	8.4	10.6
"Wrong only sometimes"	20.5	7.0
"Not wrong at all"	39.9	2.5
"Don't know"/No answer	4.5	2.1

Source: *General Social Surveys, 1972–2000: Cumulative Codebook* (Chicago: National Opinion Research Center, 2001), pp. 17–18.

One-third of adults report having sex with a partner a few times a year or not at all; another one-third have sex once or several times a month; the remaining one-third have sex with a partner two or more times a week. In short, no single stereotype accurately describes sexual activity in the United States.

Moreover, despite the widespread image of "swinging singles," it is married people who have sex with partners the most. In addition, married people report the highest level of satisfaction, both emotional and physical, with their partners (Laumann et al., 1994).

EXTRAMARITAL SEX

What about married people having sex with someone other than their marriage partner? What people commonly call "adultery" (sociologists prefer a more neutral term such as "extramarital sex") is widely condemned. Table 9–1 shows that nearly 90 percent of U.S. adults consider a married person having sex with someone other than the marital partner "always wrong" or "almost always wrong." The norm of sexual fidelity within marriage has been and remains a strong element of U.S. culture.

But in terms of behavior, the cultural ideal often differs from real life. It probably comes as no surprise that extramarital sexual activity is more common than people say it should be. At the same time, extramarital sex is not as frequent as many believe. The Laumann study reports that about 25 percent of married men and 10 percent of married women have had at least

one extramarital sexual experience. Or, the other way around, 75 percent of men and 90 percent of women remain sexually faithful to their partners throughout their married lives (Laumann et al., 1994:214; NORC, 2001:1135).

SEXUAL ORIENTATION

Over recent decades, public opinion about sexual orientation has changed remarkably. **Sexual orientation** is *a person's romantic and emotional attraction to another person*. The norm in all human societies is **heterosexuality** (*hetero* is a Greek word meaning "the other of two"), meaning *sexual attraction to someone of the other sex*. Yet in every society a significant share of people favor **homosexuality** (*homo* is the Greek word for "the same"), *sexual attraction to someone of the same sex*. When thinking about these categories, keep in mind that homosexuality and heterosexuality are not mutually exclusive. That is, people do not necessarily fall into one category or the other but may have both sexual orientations to varying degrees. Figure 9–2 presents these two sexual orientations as a continuum, indicating that most people actually experience at least some degree of sexual attraction to people of both sexes.

The fact that sexual orientation is not clear-cut points to the importance of a third category: **bisexuality,** which refers to *sexual attraction to people of both sexes*. Some bisexual people are equally attracted to males and females; many others are more attracted to one sex over the other. Finally, one additional sexual orientation is **asexuality,** meaning *no sexual attraction to people of either sex*.

It is also important to note that sexual *attraction* is not the same thing as sexual *behavior*. No doubt, many people have experienced attraction to someone of the same sex, but fewer ever experience same sex behavior. This is in large part because of cultural constraints on our actions.

Cultural systems do not accept all sexual orientations equally. In the United States and around the world, heterosexuality is the norm because, biologically speaking, heterosexual relations permit human reproduction. Even so, most societies tolerate homosexuality. In fact, among the ancient Greeks, upper-class men considered homosexuality the highest form of relationship, partly because they looked down on

For a summary of recent research on sexual orientation, go to http://www.davidmyers.org/sexorient/

women as intellectually inferior. As men saw it, heterosexuality was necessary only so they could have children, and "real" men preferred homosexual relations (Kluckhohn, 1948; Ford & Beach, 1951; Greenberg, 1988).

WHAT GIVES US A SEXUAL ORIENTATION?

The question of *how* people come to have a sexual orientation in the first place is vigorously debated. But the arguments cluster into two general positions: first, that sexual orientation is a product of society, and second, that sexual orientation is a product of biology.

Sexual Orientation: A Product of Society

This view argues that people in any society construct a set of meanings that lets them make sense of sexuality. Therefore, understandings of sexuality differ from place to place and over time. For example, Michel Foucault (1990; orig. 1978) points out that there was no distinct category of people called "homosexuals" until a century ago, when scientists and, eventually, the public as a whole began labeling people that way. Through most of history, in other words, some people no doubt had what we would call homosexual experiences. But neither they nor others saw in this behavior the basis for any special identity.

Anthropologists provide further evidence that sexual orientation is socially constructed. Studies show that various kinds of homosexuality exist in different societies. In Siberia, for example, the Chukchee Eskimo have a ritual practice in which one man dresses like a woman and does a woman's work. The Sambia, who dwell in the eastern highlands of New Guinea, have a ritual in which young boys perform oral sex on older men in the belief that ingesting semen will enhance their masculinity. The existence of such diverse patterns around the world points to the fact that sexual orientation and sexual expression have much to do with society itself (Herdt, 1993; Murray & Roscoe, 1998).

Sexual Orientation: A Product of Biology

A growing body of evidence suggests that sexual orientation is innate, that it is rooted in human biology, in much the same way that people are born right-handed or left-handed. Arguing this position, Simon LeVay (1993) links sexual orientation to the structure of the human brain. LeVay studied the brains of both homosexual and heterosexual men and found a small

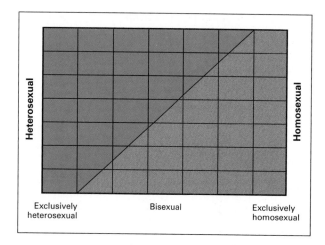

FIGURE 9–2 The Sexual Orientation Continuum
Source: Adapted from Kinsey et al. (1948).

but important difference in the size of the hypothalamus, a part of the brain that regulates hormones. Such an anatomical difference, some claim, plays a part in shaping sexual orientation.

Genetics also may influence sexual orientation. One study of forty-four pairs of brothers, all homosexual, found that thirty-three pairs had a distinctive genetic pattern involving the X chromosome. Moreover, the gay brothers had an unusually high number of gay male relatives, but only on their mother's side, the source of the X chromosome. Such evidence leads some researchers to think there may be a "gay gene" (Hamer & Copeland, 1994).

Critical evaluation. Mounting evidence supports the conclusion that sexual orientation is rooted in biology, although the best guess at present is that it is derived from *both* society and biology (Gladue, Green, & Hellman, 1984; Weinrich, 1987; Troiden, 1988; Isay, 1989; Puterbaugh, 1990; Angier, 1992; Gelman, 1992). Furthermore, we must bear in mind that sexual orientation is not a matter of neat categories. That is, most people who think of themselves as homosexual have had some heterosexual experiences, just as many people who think of themselves as heterosexual have had some homosexual experiences. Thus, the task of explaining sexual orientation is extremely complex.

 The American Psychological Association posts answers to commonly asked questions regarding sexual orientation at http://www.apa.org/pubinfo/answers.html

FIGURE 9–3 Sexual Orientation in the United States: Survey Data

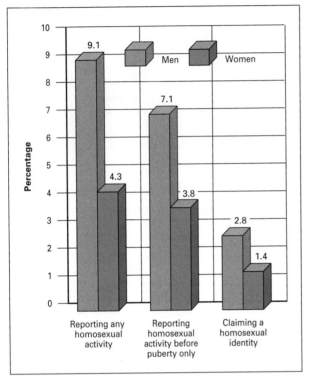

(a) How Many Gay People?

Source: Adapted from Laumann et al. (1994).

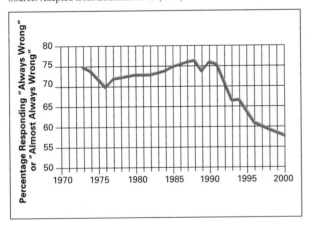

(b) Attitudes toward Homosexual Relations, 1973–2000

Survey Question: "What about sexual relations between two adults of the same sex—do you think it is always wrong, almost always wrong, wrong only sometimes, or not wrong at all?"

Source: NORC (2001).

There is also a political issue here with great importance for gay men and lesbians. To the extent that sexual orientation is based in biology, homosexuality is not a matter of choice any more than, say, skin color. If this is so, shouldn't gay men and lesbians expect the same legal protection from discrimination as African Americans? (Herek, 1991)

HOW MANY GAY PEOPLE?

What share of the U.S. population is gay? This is a difficult question to answer because, as we have explained, sexual orientation not a matter of neat categories. Moreover, people are not always willing to reveal their sexuality to strangers or even to family members. Pioneering sex researcher Alfred Kinsey (1948, 1953) estimated that about 4 percent of males and 2 percent of females have an exclusively same-sex orientation, although he thought that at least one-third of men and one-eighth of women have at least one homosexual experience leading to orgasm.

In light of the Kinsey studies, many social scientists put the gay share of the population at 10 percent. But a more recent national survey of sexuality in the United States indicates that how one operationalizes "homosexuality" makes a big difference in the results (Laumann et al., 1994). As part (a) of Figure 9–3 shows, about 9 percent of U.S. men and about 4 percent of U.S. women between ages eighteen and fifty-nine reported homosexual activity *at some time* in their lives. The second set of numbers shows that a significant share of men (less so women) have a homosexual experience during childhood but not after puberty. And 2.8 percent of men and 1.4 percent of women define themselves as partly or entirely homosexual.

Finally, Kinsey treated sexual orientation as an "either/or" trait: To be more homosexual was, by definition, to be less heterosexual. But same-sex and other-sex attractions can operate independently. At one extreme, then, bisexual people feel strong attraction to people of both sexes; at the other, asexual people experience little sexual attraction to people of either sex.

In the national survey mentioned earlier, less than 1 percent of adults described themselves as bisexual. But bisexual experiences appear to be fairly common (at least for a time) among younger people, especially on college campuses (Laumann et al., 1994; Leland, 1995). Many bisexuals, then, do not think of themselves as either gay or straight, and their behavior reflects elements of both gay and straight living.

THE GAY RIGHTS MOVEMENT

In recent decades, the public attitude toward homosexuality has been moving toward greater acceptance. In 1973, as shown in part (b) of Figure 9–3, about three-fourths of U.S. adults claimed homosexual relations were "always wrong" or "almost always wrong." That percentage changed little during the 1970s and 1980s, but by 2000 it dropped to less than 60 percent (NORC, 2001:243).

In large measure, this change came about through the gay rights movement that arose in the middle of the twentieth century (Chauncey, 1994). At that time, most people did not discuss homosexuality, and it was common for companies (including the federal government and the armed forces) to fire anyone who was thought to be gay. Mental health professionals also took a hard line, describing homosexuals as "sick," and sometimes sending them to mental hospitals where, presumably, they might be cured.

In this climate of intolerance, most lesbians and gay men remained "in the closet," closely guarding the secret of their sexual orientation. But the gay rights movement gained strength during the 1960s. One early milestone occurred in 1973, when the American Psychiatric Association declared that homosexuality was not an illness but simply "a form of sexual behavior."

Gay rights advocates also began using the term **homophobia** to describe *the dread of close personal interaction with people thought to be gay, lesbian, or bisexual* (Weinberg, 1973). The concept of homophobia (literally, "fear of sameness") turns the tables on society: Instead of asking "What's wrong with gay people?" the question becomes "What's wrong with people who can't accept a different sexual orientation?"

SEXUAL CONTROVERSIES

Sexuality lies at the heart of a number of controversies in the United States. Here we take a look at four issues: teen pregnancy, pornography, prostitution, and sexual violence.

TEEN PREGNANCY

Being sexually active—especially having intercourse—demands a high level of responsibility because pregnancy can result. Teenagers may be biologically mature, but many are not socially mature and may not appreciate all the consequences of their actions. Indeed, although the rate of teen pregnancy has been

This gathering took place on June 27, 1999, at New York's Stonewall Inn to celebrate the thirtieth anniversary of the so-called "Stonewall Riot" in 1969, when gay people first fought back against harassment by the police, sparking the gay rights movement.

dropping, surveys indicate that 1 million U.S. teens become pregnant each year, and most did not intend to.

Pregnancy means not only that many young women (and sometimes young fathers-to-be) cannot finish school, but they are at high risk of poverty. As Figure 9–4 on page 232 shows, this country's rate of births among teens is higher than that of other high-income countries.

Did the sexual revolution lead to an increase in teenage pregnancy? Surprisingly, perhaps, the answer is no. The rate in 1950 was actually higher than the rate today, but this is because people

 Find out about a global report from the Alan Guttmacher Institute on teenage sex and pregnancy: http://www.agi-usa. org/pubs/new_world_engl.html

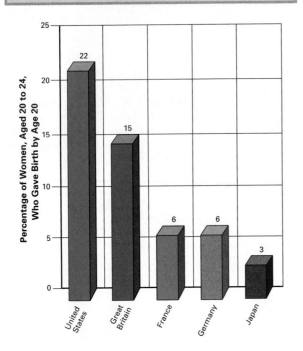

FIGURE 9–4 Births to Teenage Women

Source: The Alan Guttmacher Institute (2000).

married younger at the time. Also, many pregnancies led to quick marriages. As a result, there were many pregnant teenagers, but most were married women. Today, by contrast, most teenagers who become pregnant are not married. In about half of all cases, these women have abortions; in the other half, they keep their babies (Voydanoff & Donnelly, 1990; Holmes, 1996a). National Map 9–1 shows the distribution of births to females between ages fifteen and nineteen in the United States.

Concern about the high rate of teenage pregnancy has led to sex education programs in schools. But such programs are controversial, as the box explains.

PORNOGRAPHY

In general terms, **pornography** is *sexually explicit material that causes sexual arousal*. But what exactly is or is not pornographic has long been a matter of debate. Recognizing that people view the portrayal of sexuality differently, the U.S. Supreme Court gives local communities the power to decide for themselves what violates "community standards" of decency and lacks any redeeming social value.

Definitions aside, pornography is surely popular in the United States: X-rated videos, commercial telephone numbers for sexual conversations, and a host of sexually explicit movies and magazines together constitute roughly a $10-billion-a-year industry. The figure is rising as people find more pornography at more and more sites—now estimated to be in the hundreds of thousands—on the Internet.

Traditionally, people have criticized pornography on *moral* grounds. As national surveys confirm, 60 percent of U.S. adults are concerned that "sexual materials lead to a breakdown of morals" (NORC, 2001:244). Today, however, pornography is also seen as a *power* issue because it depicts women as the sexual playthings of men.

Some critics also see pornography as a cause of violence against women. Although it is difficult to document a scientific cause-and-effect relationship between what people view and how they act, research does support the idea that pornography makes men think of women as objects rather than as people. The public shares a concern about pornography and violence, with almost half of adults holding the opinion that pornography encourages people to commit rape (NORC, 2001:245).

People everywhere object to material they find offensive, but many also value freedom of speech and artistic expression. Nevertheless, opposition to pornography is building from an unlikely coalition of conservatives (who condemn pornography on moral grounds) and progressives (who oppose it for political reasons).

PROSTITUTION

Prostitution is *the selling of sexual services*. Often called "the world's oldest profession," prostitution has always been widespread, and about one in five adult men in the United States reports having paid for sex at some time (NORC, 2001:1135). Even so, to the extent that people think of sex as an expression of interpersonal intimacy, they find the idea of sex for money disturbing. As a result, prostitution is against the law everywhere in the United States, except for parts of Nevada.

Around the world, prostitution is greatest in lower-income countries where patriarchy is strong and traditional cultural norms limit women's ability to earn a living. Global Map 9–2 on page 234 shows where in the world prostitution is most widespread.

CRITICAL THINKING

Sex Education: Solution or Problem?

Most schools today have sex education programs that teach the basics of sexuality. Instructors explain to young people how their bodies grow and change, how reproduction occurs, and how to avoid pregnancy by using birth control or abstaining from sex.

Because half of teenage boys in the United States report having sex by the time they reach sixteen, and half of girls report doing so by seventeen, "sex ed" programs seem to make sense. But critics point out that as the number of sex education programs has expanded, the level of teenage sexual activity has gone *up*. This trend seems to suggest that sex education may not be discouraging sex among youngsters and, maybe, that learning more about sex encourages young people to become sexually active sooner. Critics also say that it is parents who should be instructing their children about sex because, unlike teachers, parents can also teach their beliefs about what is right and wrong.

But supporters of sex education counter that research does not support the conclusion that sex education results in young people being more sexually active. More generally, they argue that it is the larger culture—one that celebrates sexuality—that encourages children to become sexually active. If this is the case, the sensible strategy is to ensure that they understand what they are doing and that they take reasonable precautions to protect themselves from unwanted pregnancy and sexually transmitted diseases.

What do you think?

1. *Schools can teach the facts about sexuality. But do you think they can address the emotional issues that often accompany sex? What about the moral issues involved? Why or why not?*

2. *What about parents? Are they doing their job in instructing children about sex? Ask members of your class how many received instruction in sexual matters from their parents.*

3. *Overall, do you think young people know too little about sexuality? Do you think they know too much? What specific changes would you suggest to address the problem of unwanted pregnancy among teens?*

SEEING OURSELVES

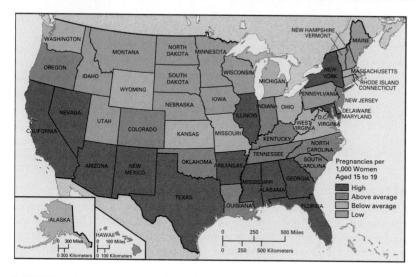

NATIONAL MAP 9-1 Teenage Pregnancy Rates across the United States

The map shows pregnancy rates in the mid-1990s for women aged fifteen to nineteen. In what regions of the country are rates high? Where are they low? What explanation can you offer for these patterns?

Source: The Alan Guttmacher Institute (1999).

Sources: Gibbs (1993), Stodghill (1998), and Voss & Kogan (2001).

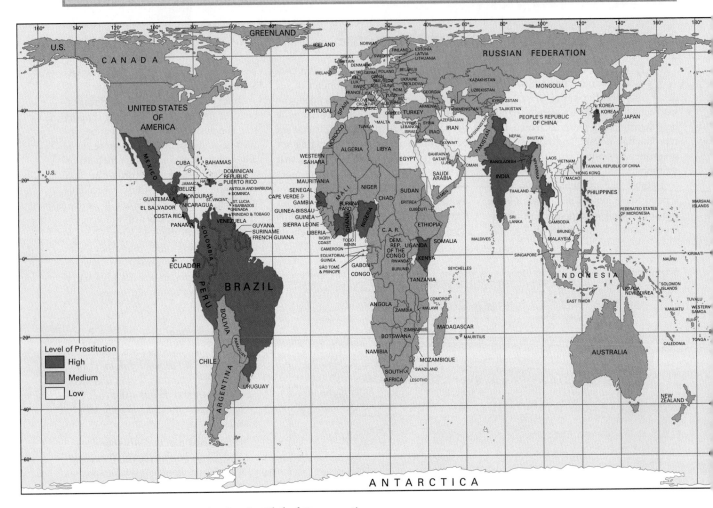

GLOBAL MAP 9–2 Prostitution in Global Perspective

Generally speaking, prostitution is widespread in societies where women have low standing. Officially, at least, the People's Republic of China boasts of gender equality, including the elimination of "vice," such as prostitution, which oppresses women. By contrast, in much of Latin America, where patriarchy is strong, prostitution is common. In many Islamic societies patriarchy is also strong, but religion is a counterbalance, so prostitution is limited. Western, high-income nations have a moderate amount of prostitution.

Sources: *Peters Atlas of the World* (1990) and Mackay (2000).

Types of Prostitution

Most prostitutes (many prefer the morally neutral term "sex workers") are women, but they fall into different categories. *Call girls* are elite prostitutes, typically women who are young, attractive, and well educated and arrange their own appointments with clients by telephone. The classified pages of any large city newspaper contain numerous ads for "escort services," through which women (and a much smaller number of men) offer both companionship and sex for a fee.

Sex workers in a middle category are employed in "massage parlors" or brothels under the control of managers. These people have less choice about their clients, receive less money for their services, and get to keep no more than half of what they make.

At the bottom of the sex-worker hierarchy are *street walkers*, women and men who work the streets of large cities. Female street walkers often are under the control of male pimps who take most of their earnings. Street walkers are at the highest risk of violence from pimps and clients (Gordon & Snyder, 1989; Davidson, 1998).

Most prostitutes offer heterosexual services. Gay prostitutes also trade sex for money. Researchers report that many gay prostitutes have suffered rejection by family and friends because of their sexual orientation (Weisberg, 1985; Boyer, 1989; Kruks, 1991).

A Victimless Crime?

Prostitution is against the law almost everywhere in the United States, but many people consider it a victimless crime (see Chapter 8, "Deviance"). Therefore, instead of enforcing prostitution laws all the time, police stage occasional crackdowns. Our society seems to want to control prostitution while assuming that nothing will eliminate it.

Is selling sex a victimless crime that hurts no one? Certainly, many people who take a "live and let live" attitude about prostitution would say it is. But this view overlooks the fact that prostitution subjects many women to abuse and violence and plays a part in spreading sexually transmitted diseases, including AIDS. In addition, many poor women become trapped in a life of selling sex, generally to the benefit of others, while they put their own lives at risk.

SEXUAL VIOLENCE AND ABUSE

Although sexual activity often occurs within a loving relationship, sex can be twisted by hate and violence. Sexual violence, which ranges from verbal abuse to rape and assault, is widespread in the United States.

Rape

Although some people think rape is a form of sex, it is actually an expression of power, a violent act that uses sex to hurt, humiliate, or control another person. The U.S. Federal Bureau of Investigation reports that about 90,000 women are raped each year. This number reflects only the reported cases, and the actual number of rapes is several times higher (McCormick, 1994; U.S. Federal Bureau of Investigation, 2001).

The official definition of rape, according to the federal government, is "the carnal knowledge of a female forcibly and against her will." Thus, official rape statistics include only victims who are women. But men, too, are raped—in perhaps 10 percent of all cases. Most men who rape men are not homosexual: They are heterosexuals who are motivated by a desire not for sex but to dominate another person (Groth & Birnbaum, 1979; Gibbs, 1991a).

Date Rape

A common myth is that rape involves strangers. In reality, however, most rapes involve people who know one another, and they usually take place in familiar surroundings, especially the home. For this reason, the terms "date rape" and "acquaintance rape" refer to forcible sexual violence against women by men they know.

Many victims of date rape do not report the crime. A new government report on the sexual victimization of college women is available at http://www.ojp.usdoj.gov/bjs/abstract/svcw.htm Some believe that because they know the offender, an attack could not have been rape. But the tide is turning, with more and more women speaking out. The box on page 236 takes a closer look.

THEORETICAL ANALYSIS OF SEXUALITY

We can better understand human sexuality by using sociology's various theoretical paradigms. In the following sections, we apply the three major paradigms in turn.

STRUCTURAL-FUNCTIONAL ANALYSIS

The structural-functional approach highlights the contributions of any social pattern to the overall operation of society. Because sexuality is an important dimension of social life, society regulates sexual behavior.

The Need to Regulate Sexuality

From a biological point of view, sex allows our species to reproduce. But culture and social institutions regulate *with whom* and *when* people reproduce. For example, most societies condemn married people for having sex with someone other than their spouse. To do otherwise—to give the forces of sexual passion free

CRITICAL THINKING

Date Rape: Exposing Dangerous Myths

April Sanders was beside herself with excitement: She had a date with Bob McMahon, a senior she had admired all semester. On Saturday night, she met Bob at 10 o'clock at the south end of the Arts Quad, and they talked easily as they walked across campus to a party. The more Bob talked, the more April liked him.

The music was live and loud as they joined the crowd at a favorite campus hangout, and the beer was flowing freely. They had a few beers and danced. Then they joined some of Bob's friends at a table where everyone was downing shots of hard liquor. Bob handed April a glass. She paused, but then smiled and drank it down. He kept refilling her glass, and soon April's head was spinning. She knew she had drunk too much and just wanted to go home and lie down. Embarrassed, she said she wanted to go back to her dorm room. "No problem," Bob responded, insisting on walking her home.

When they reached her room, April let Bob come in while she looked for some aspirin. They were sitting on her couch talking, when Bob tried to kiss her. At that point, he seemed to change, forcefully pushing April into having sex. "Bob, no!" April pleaded, overcome with fear. But Bob was determined and strong, and she simply could not stop him.

Ten minutes later, the attack was over, and Bob got up and left. April's first reaction was to take a shower. "I felt so filthy," she recalled later. "I washed myself over and over." For hours, she sat crying, trying to make sense of a night that had gone terribly wrong. "Was I raped?" she asked herself, "I told him 'no,' I tried to stop him." But she also worried, "Who will believe me? We were out drinking together. I let him into my room."

In the morning, April Sanders went to the dean's office to report the attack. Later that day, she spoke with two city police officers. The police conducted an investigation, but they were reluctant to act because Bob claimed the sex was consensual, and there was no other evidence such as bruises, a medical ex-amination, or torn clothes to back up April's story.

The case of April Sanders is all too typical. In fact, at least half of all victims of sexual attack make no report to police. One reason is that many women and men do not understand what rape is. In fact, three wrong ideas about rape are so common in the United States that they might be called "rape myths."

Myth #1: Rape involves strangers. A sexual attack brings to mind a strange man lurking in the shadows who suddenly springs on an unsuspecting victim. In four out of five rapes, however, the victim knows the offender. For this reason, it is more realistic to speak of *acquaintance rape* or *date rape*.

Myth #2: Women provoke their attackers. Many people think a woman who has been raped must have done something to make the man think she wanted to have sex. In April Sanders's case, didn't she agree to go drinking? Didn't she let Bob into her room late at night? Such self-doubt often paralyzes

---

rein—would threaten family life and, especially, the raising of children.

Another example, discussed earlier in this chapter, is the incest taboo. The fact that this norm exists everywhere clearly shows that no society permits completely free choice in sexual partners. Reproduction by family members other than married partners would break down the system of kinship and muddle relationships between people.

Historically, the social control of sexuality was strong, mostly because sex commonly led to childbirth. Moreover, offspring, as well as parents, were subject to these controls. We see this in the traditional distinction between "legitimate" reproduction (within marriage) and "illegitimate" reproduction (outside of marriage). But once a society can effectively control births, its norms become more permissive. This occurred in the United States where, over the course of the twentieth century, sex moved beyond its basic reproductive function and became accepted as a form of intimacy and even recreation (Giddens, 1992).

Latent Functions: The Case of Prostitution

It is easy to see that prostitution is harmful because it spreads disease and exploits women. But are there latent functions that help explain why prostitution is widespread despite society's attempts to limit it? Definitely, victims. But going out with a man—or even inviting him into her room—is not consent to have sex with him any more than it would be consent to have him beat her with a club.

Myth #3: Rape is simply sex. If there is no knife held to a woman's throat or if she is not bound and gagged, what's the crime? The answer is that, under the law, forcing a woman to have sex without her consent is a *violent crime*. "Having sex" implies intimacy, caring, and, most important of all, consent, none of which is present in rape. Beyond the brutality of being physically violated, rape by an acquaintance also undermines a victim's sense of trust. Psychological scars are especially serious among the half of rape victims who are under eighteen; one-third of these young victims are attacked by their own fathers or stepfathers (Greenfield, 1996).

The more people believe rape myths, the more women will fall victim to sexual violence. The ancient Babylonians stoned married women who were raped, convinced that they had committed adultery. Ideas about rape have

Is a person who drinks alcohol to excess capable of making a responsible decision about having sex? What role does alcohol play in date rape on the campus?

changed little over thousands of years, which helps explain why, even today, only about one in twenty rapes results in an offender being sent to jail.

Nowhere has the issue of date rape been more widely discussed than on campuses. The collegiate environment promotes easy friendships and encourages trust. At the same time, many young students have much to learn about relationships and about themselves. So although college life encourages communication, it also invites sexual violence.

To counter the problem, many schools now actively address myths about rape and the place of alcohol in campus life. College men and women alike need to understand two simple truths: Sex without a woman's consent is rape, and when a woman says "no," she means just that.

What do you think?

1. *In your opinion, why are myths about rape so widespread?*

2. *What programs or policies exist on your campus to address sexual assault?*

3. *What else needs to be done?*

Sources: Gibbs (1991a, 1991b) and Gilbert (1992).

---

explains Kingsley Davis (1971): Prostitution performs several useful functions. Prostitution is one way to meet the sexual needs of a large number of people who do not have ready access to sex, including soldiers, travelers, and people who are not physically attractive or who have trouble establishing relationships. Moreover, adds Davis, the availability of sex without commitment may even help stabilize some loveless marriages that might otherwise collapse.

Critical evaluation. The structural-functional paradigm helps us appreciate how sexuality plays an important part in the way society is organized. The incest taboo and other cultural norms also suggest that

society has always paid attention to who has sex with whom and, especially, who reproduces with whom.

At the same time, this approach pays little attention to the great diversity of sexual ideas and practices found within every society. Moreover, sexual patterns change over time, just as they differ in remarkable ways around the world. To appreciate the varied and changeable character of sexuality, we turn to the symbolic-interaction paradigm.

SYMBOLIC-INTERACTION ANALYSIS

The symbolic-interaction paradigm highlights how, as people interact, they construct everyday reality. As

Chapter 6 ("Social Interaction in Everyday Life") explains, the process of constructing reality is highly variable, so that one group's or society's views of sexuality may well differ from another's. In the same way, how people understand sexuality can and does change over time.

The Social Construction of Sexuality

Almost all social patterns involving sexuality changed greatly over the course of the twentieth century. One good illustration is the changing importance of virginity. A century ago, our society's norm—for women, at least—was virginity before marriage. This norm was strong because, without effective birth control, virginity was the only assurance a man had that his bride-to-be was not carrying another man's child. Today, however, we have gone a long way toward separating sex from reproduction, and, as a result, the virginity norm has weakened. In the United States, among those born between 1963 and 1974, just 16.3 percent of men and 20.1 percent of women report being virgins at first marriage (Laumann et al., 1994:503).

Another example of our society's construction of sexuality involves young people. A century ago, childhood was a time of innocence in sexual matters. In recent decades, however, our thinking has changed. Although we expect that children will not be sexually active, most people believe children should be educated about sex by the time they are teenagers so that they can make intelligent choices about their sexual behavior.

Global Comparisons

The broader our view, the more variation we see in the meanings people attach to sexuality. One classic study showed that some cultures are far more accepting of childhood sexuality than others. Anthropologist Ruth Benedict (1938), who spent years learning the ways of life of the Melanesian people of southeast New Guinea, reported that adults paid little attention when young children engaged in sexual experimentation with one another. Parents in Melanesia shrugged off such activity because, before puberty, sex cannot lead to reproduction. Is it likely that most parents in the United States would respond the same way?

Sexual practices, too, vary as a part of culture. Male circumcision of infant boys (the practice of removing all or part of the foreskin of the penis) is common in the United States but rare in most other parts of the world. Similarly, female circumcision (the practice of removing the clitoris) is rare in the United States but common in parts of Africa and the Middle East (Crosette, 1995, Huffman, 2000). (For more about female circumcision, see the box in Chapter 13 ["Gender Stratification"] on page 342.)

Critical evaluation. The strength of the symbolic-interaction paradigm lies in revealing the constructed character of familiar social patterns. Understanding that people "construct" sexuality, we can better appreciate the variety of sexual practices found over the course of history and around the world.

One limitation of this approach is that not everything is so variable. Throughout our own history—and around the world—men are more likely to see women in sexual terms than the other way around. If this pattern is widespread, some broader social structure must be at work, as we shall see in the next section.

SOCIAL-CONFLICT ANALYSIS

The social-conflict paradigm highlights dimensions of inequality. Therefore, this approach shows how sexuality both reflects patterns of social inequality and helps create them.

Sexuality: Reflecting Social Inequality

Recall our discussion of prostitution, a practice outlawed almost everywhere in the United States. Even so, enforcement is uneven at best, especially when it comes to who is and is not likely to be arrested. Although two parties are involved, the record shows that police are far more likely to arrest (less powerful) female prostitutes than (more powerful) male clients. Similarly, of all women engaged in prostitution, it is street walkers—women with the least income and those most likely to be minorities—who face the highest risk of arrest (COYOTE, 2000). Also, we might wonder whether so many women would be involved in prostitution at all if they had equal economic opportunities with men.

Sexuality: Creating Social Inequality

Social-conflict theorists, especially feminists, point to sexuality as the root of inequality between women and men. How can this be? Defining women in sexual terms amounts to devaluing them from full human beings into objects of men's interest and attention. Is it any wonder that the word "pornography" comes from the Greek word *porne*, meaning "a man's sexual slave"?

If men define women in sexual terms, it is easy to see why many people consider pornography—almost all of which is consumed by males—a power issue. Because pornography typically depicts women seeking to please men, it supports the idea that men have power over women.

Some more radical critics doubt that this element of power can ever be removed from heterosexual relations (Dworkin, 1987). Whereas most social-conflict theorists do not reject heterosexuality entirely, they do agree that sexuality can and does degrade women. Critics point out that our culture often depicts sexuality in terms of sport (men "scoring" with women) and violence ("slamming," "banging," and "hitting on," for example, are verbs used for both fighting and sex).

Queer Theory

Finally, social-conflict theory has taken aim not only at men dominating women but also at heterosexuals dominating homosexuals. In recent years, just as many lesbians and gay men have come out in search of public acceptance, some sociologists have tried to add a gay voice to their discipline. **Queer theory** is *a growing body of research findings that challenges the heterosexual bias in U. S. society.*

Queer theory begins with the assertion that our society is characterized by **heterosexism,** *a view stigmatizing anyone who is not heterosexual as "queer."* Our heterosexual culture victimizes a wide range of people, including gay men, lesbians, bisexuals, transsexuals, and even asexual people. Furthermore, although most people agree that bias against women (sexism) and people of color (racism) is wrong, heterosexism is widely tolerated and sometimes well within the law. This country's military forces, for example, cannot legally discharge a female soldier for "acting like a woman," because that would be a clear case of gender discrimination. But the military forces can discharge her for homosexuality if she is a sexually active lesbian.

Heterosexism also exists at a more subtle level in our everyday understanding of the world. When we describe something as "sexy," for example, don't we really mean attractive to *heterosexuals?*

Critical evaluation. Applying the social-conflict paradigm shows how sexuality is both a cause and effect of inequality. In particular, this paradigm helps us understand men's power over women and heterosexual people's domination of homosexual people.

The control of women's sexuality is a common theme in human history. During the Middle Ages, Europeans devised the "chastity belt"—a metal device locked about a woman's groin that prevented sexual intercourse (and probably interfered with other bodily functions as well). While such devices are all but unknown today, the social control of sexuality continues. Can you point to examples?

At the same time, this approach overlooks the fact that sexuality is not a power issue for everyone: Many couples enjoy a vital sexual relationship that deepens their commitment to one another. In addition, the social-conflict paradigm pays little attention to strides our society has made toward eliminating injustice. Men, in public at least, are less likely to describe women as sex objects than they were a few decades ago; moreover, our rising public concern about sexual harassment (see Chapter 13, "Gender Stratification") has had some effect in reducing the role of sexuality in the workplace. Likewise, there is ample evidence that the gay rights movement has secured greater opportunities and social acceptance for homosexuals.

We close this chapter with a look at what is perhaps the most divisive sexuality issue of all: **abortion,** *the deliberate termination of a pregnancy.* Many people on both sides of this issue feel strongly about abortion because, as we shall see in the box on pages 240–41, it cuts to the heart of almost everyone's sense of justice.

The Abortion Controversy

A black van pulls up in front of the storefront in a busy section of the city. Two women get out of the front seat and cautiously scan the sidewalk. After a moment, one nods to the other and they open the rear door to let a third woman out of the van. Standing to the right and left of their charge, the two quickly whisk her into the building.

Is this a description of two federal marshals escorting a convict to a police station? It might be. But it is actually an account of two clinic workers escorting a woman who has decided to have an abortion. Why are they so cautious? Anyone who has read the papers in recent years knows about the heated confrontations at abortion clinics across North America. In fact, some opponents have even targeted and killed several doctors who perform abortions. Overall, the 1.3 million abortions performed each year make this probably the most hotly contested issue in the United States today.

Abortion has not always been so controversial. During the colonial era, midwives and other healers performed abortions with little community opposition and with full approval of the law. But controversy arose about 1850, when early medical doctors sought to eliminate the competition they faced from midwives and other traditional health providers, whose income was derived largely from terminating pregnancies. By 1900, medical doctors succeeded in getting every state to pass a law banning abortion.

Such laws did not end abortion, but they greatly reduced the numbers. In addition, these laws drove abortion underground, so that many women—especially those who were poor—had little choice but to seek help from unlicensed "back alley" abortionists, sometimes with tragic results.

By the 1960s, opposition to abortion laws was rising. In 1973, the U.S. Supreme Court rendered a landmark decision (in the cases of *Roe* v. *Wade* and *Doe* v. *Bolton*), striking down all state laws banning abortion. In effect, this action established a woman's legal access to abortion.

In the wake of the Court's decision, the abortion controversy has grown. On one side of the issue are people who describe themselves as "pro-choice," supporting a woman's right to choose abortion. On the other side are those who call themselves "pro-life," opposing abortion as morally wrong; these people would like to see the Supreme Court reverse its 1973 decision.

How strong is the support for each side of the abortion controversy? A recent national survey asked a sample of adults this question: "Should it be possible for a pregnant woman to obtain a legal abortion if the woman wants it for any reason?" In response, 37.9 percent said "yes" (placing them in the pro-choice camp) and 57.1 percent said "no" (the pro-life position); the remaining 5.0 percent offered no opinion (NORC, 2001:234).

However, a closer look shows that particular circumstances make a big difference in how people see this issue. The figure shows that a large majority of U.S. adults favor legal abortion if a pregnancy seriously threatens a woman's health, if she became pregnant as a result of rape, or if a fetus is very likely to have a serious defect. The bottom line,

SUMMARY

1. U.S. culture had long defined sex as a taboo topic, until the Kinsey studies (1948, 1953). They were among the first publications by social scientists on human sexuality.

2. Sex is the biological distinction between females and males, which is determined at conception when a male sperm joins a female ovum.

3. Males and females are distinguished not only by their genitals (primary sex characteristics) but also by

bodily development as they mature (secondary sex characteristics). Hermaphrodites have some combination of both male and female genitalia. Transsexuals are people who feel that they are one sex, although, biologically, they are the other.

4. For most species, sex is rigidly directed by biology, but for human beings sex is a matter of cultural definition as well as personal choice. Patterns of kissing, modesty, and beauty vary around the world, revealing the cultural foundation of sexual practices.

then, looks like this: About 38 percent support access to abortion under *any* circumstances, but about 80 percent support access to abortion under *some* circumstances.

Many pro-life people feel strongly that abortion is nothing more than killing unborn children. To them, people never have the right to end innocent life in this way. But pro-choice people are no less committed to their position. As they see it, the abortion debate is really about the standing of women in society.

Why? For the simple reason that women must have control over their own sexuality. If pregnancy dictates the course of women's lives, women will never be able to compete with men on equal terms, whether it is on campus or in the workplace. Thus, the pro-choice position concludes, women must have access to legal, safe abortion as a necessary condition to full participation in society.

Continue the debate . . .

1. *The more conservative pro-life people see abortion as a moral issue, whereas more liberal pro-choice people see abortion as a power issue. Can you see a parallel to how conservatives and liberals view the issue of pornography?*

2. *Surveys show that men and women have almost the same opinions about abortion. Does this surprise you? Why?*

3. *Why do you think the abortion controversy is often so bitter? Why has our nation been unable to find a middle ground on which all can agree?*

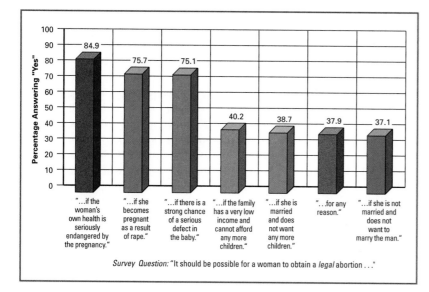

Survey Question: "It should be possible for a woman to obtain a *legal* abortion . . ."

When Should the Law Allow a Woman to Choose Abortion?
Source: NORC (2001).

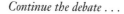

Sources: Based in part on Luker (1984), Tannahill (1992), and various news reports.

5. Historically, our society has held rigid attitudes toward sexuality, although these attitudes have become more permissive over time. Thus, we see that sex is a social, as well as a biological, issue.

6. The sexual revolution, which has roots back to the 1920s but came of age in the 1960s and 1970s, increased openness in matters of sexuality. Research shows that changes in sexuality were greater for women than for men. By 1980, a sexual counterrevolution was taking form, condemning permissiveness and urging a return to more conservative "family values."

7. The share of people in the United States who have premarital sexual intercourse increased during the twentieth century. Research shows that about three-fourths of young men and two-thirds of young women have intercourse by their senior year in high school.

8. The level of sexual activity varies within the population of U.S. adults: One-third report having sex with a partner a few times a year or not at all; another one-third have sex once or several times a month; the remaining one-third have sex with a partner two or more times a week.

9. Although extramarital sex is widely condemned, about 25 percent of married men and 10 percent of married women report being sexually unfaithful to their spouses at some time.

10. Sexual orientation refers to a person's romantic and emotional attraction to another person. Four major orientations are heterosexuality, homosexuality, bisexuality, and asexuality. Sexual orientation is caused by some combination of biological factors, cultural factors, and human choice.

11. The share of the population that is homosexual depends on how researchers define "homosexuality." About 9 percent of adult men and 4 percent of adult women report having some homosexual experience, compared with 2.8 percent of men and 1.4 percent of women who say they have a homosexual identity.

12. The gay rights movement has worked to gain greater acceptance for homosexuals. Largely because of this movement, the share of the U.S. population condemning homosexuality as morally wrong has steadily decreased and stands now at about half.

13. Some 1 million teenagers become pregnant each year in the United States. The rate of teenage pregnancy has dropped since 1950, when many teens married and had children. Today, however, most pregnant teens are not married and, especially when they drop out of school, are at high risk of poverty.

14. With no universal definition of pornography, the law allows local communities to set standards of decency. Many conservatives condemn pornography as immoral; by contrast, many liberals condemn it as demeaning to women.

15. Prostitution, the selling of sexual services, is illegal almost everywhere in the United States. Although many people think of prostitution as a victimless crime, it victimizes women and spreads sexually transmitted diseases.

16. Some 90,000 rapes are reported each year, but the actual number is several times greater. Although many people think of rape as a sexual act, rape is really a violent expression of power. Most rapes involve people who know one another.

17. Structural-functional theory highlights society's need to regulate sexual activity. A universal norm in this regard is the incest taboo, which keeps kin relationships clear.

18. The symbolic-interaction paradigm emphasizes how people attach various meanings to sexuality. Thus, societies differ from one another in terms of sexual attitudes and practices; similarly, sexual patterns change within any one society over time.

19. Social-conflict theory links sexuality to inequality. From this point of view, men dominate women in part by devaluing them as sexual objects.

KEY CONCEPTS

sex (p. 222) the biological distinction between females and males

primary sex characteristics (p. 223) the genitals, organs used for reproduction

secondary sex characteristics (p. 223) bodily development, apart from the genitals, that distinguishes biologically mature females and males

hermaphrodite (p. 223) a human being with some combination of female and male genitalia

transsexuals (p. 223) people who feel they are one sex even though biologically they are the other

incest taboo (p. 224) a norm forbidding sexual relations or marriage between certain relatives

sexual orientation (p. 228) a person's romantic and emotional attraction to another person

heterosexuality (p. 228) a sexual orientation in which a person is sexually attracted to someone of the other sex

homosexuality (p. 228) a sexual orientation in which a person is sexually attracted to someone of the same sex

bisexuality (p. 228) a sexual orientation in which a person is sexually attracted to people of both sexes

asexuality (p. 228) a sexual orientation in which a person is not sexually attracted to people of either sex

homophobia (p. 231) the dread of close personal interaction with people thought to be gay, lesbian, or bisexual

pornography (p. 232) sexually explicit material that causes sexual arousal

prostitution (p. 232) the selling of sexual services

queer theory (p. 239) a growing body of research findings that challenges the heterosexual bias in U. S. society

heterosexism (p. 239) a view stigmatizing anyone who is not heterosexual as "queer"

abortion (p. 239) the deliberate termination of a pregnancy

CRITICAL-THINKING QUESTIONS

1. What do sociologists mean by the term "sexual revolution"? What did the sexual revolution change? Can you suggest some reasons that these changes occurred?

2. What is sexual orientation? Why is this characteristic difficult for researchers to measure?

3. Do you think laws should regulate the portrayal of sex in books, films, or on the Internet? Why or why not?

4. In what ways do societies regulate sexuality? In what ways does sexuality play a part in social inequality?

APPLICATIONS AND EXERCISES

1. The most complete study of sexual patterns in the United States to date is *The Social Organization of Sexuality: Sexual Practices in the United States* by Edward Laumann and others. You can find this book in your campus or community library. Get a copy and browse through some of the chapters most interesting to you. Afterwards, think about the value of doing sociological research on sexuality.

2. Contact your school's student services office and ask for information about the extent of sexual violence on your campus. Do people report such crimes? What policies and procedures does your school have to respond to sexual violence?

3. Do some research on transgendered people such as Dana Rivers, profiled in the opening to this chapter. When you first read her story, would you have supported or opposed firing Rivers? After reading this chapter, do you hold the same opinion? Why?

4. Packaged in the back of this new textbook is an interactive CD-ROM that offers a variety of study and review materials intended to help you better understand the material covered in this chapter. For this chapter, the CD-ROM contains an author's tip video, Real Life Sociology videos, other relevant audio and video, interactive map animations, audio journal entries from the author, Web links, and much more.

 ## SITES TO SEE

http://www.prenhall.com/macionis

Visit the interactive *Companion Website*™ that accompanies this text. Begin by clicking on the cover of your book. You will find a chapter-by-chapter study guide, practice tests, and a significant portion of the text for on-line review, as well as many suggested Web links.

http://www.teenpregnancy.org

Visit the Web site of the National Campaign to Prevent Teen Pregnancy, an organization formed to guide teens toward responsible sexual behavior. You can find data for your state at this site. What are the key parts of this orga-

nization's program? How effective would you imagine it is? Why?

http://www.qrd.org

This Web site, the Queer Resources Directory, looks at a wide range of issues—including family, religion, education, and health—from a queer theory perspective. Visit this site to see in what ways various social institutions can be considered heterosexist. Do you agree? Why?

http://www.gay.com

This is a search engine for all sorts of information on issues involving homosexuality.

 ## INVESTIGATE WITH CONTENTSELECT

Follow the instructions found on page 23 of this textbook to enter this chapter of the book's *Companion Website*™. Once in the chapter, click on the ContentSelect icon at the bottom left of your screen and enter your personal

User ID and Password. Enter keywords such as "sexuality," "incest taboo," "transgender," and "abortion," and the search engine will help you become an effective researcher.

cyber.scope

HOW NEW TECHNOLOGY IS CHANGING OUR WAY OF LIFE

Marshall McLuhan (1969) summed up his pioneering research in the study of communications this way: "Any new technology tends to create a new human environment." In other words, technology not only affects how we work but also shapes and colors our entire way of life. In this second cyber.scope, we pause to reflect on some of the ways the Information Revolution is changing our culture and society.

The Information Revolution and Cultural Values

Chapter 3 ("Culture") noted the importance members of our society attach to material comfort. Throughout our history, many people have defined "success" to mean earning a good income and enjoying the things money will buy, including a home, a car, and fashionable clothing.

But there are signs that as we move through this new century, our values may shift from a single-minded focus on the accumulation of things (the products of industrial

 "Travel" to an Adirondack mountaintop and enjoy the view by visiting http://adirondack.net/adnet/bluemt/bluemt1.html or tour the Tower of London at http://www.toweroflondontour.com

technology) to an appreciation of ideas (the product of information technology). Such new-age ideas include both travel and countless experiences with virtual reality, to concern with well-being, including the self-actualization that has become popular in recent decades (Newman, 1991).

Socialization in the Computer Age

Half a century ago, television rewrote the rules for socialization in the United States, and as Chapter 5 ("Socialization") explained, young people now spend more time watching TV than talking to their parents. Today, screens are not just for television; they are our windows into a cyber-world in which we look to computers to link, entertain, and educate us. But this trend toward cyber-socialization raises several important questions.

First, will the spread of computer-based information erode the regional diversity that has marked this country's history, setting off New England from the Deep South and the Midwest from the West Coast? We know that new information technology is linking our nation and the world, so we might well expect to see a more national culture emerge and, with time, a more global culture as well.

Second, how will this cyber-culture affect our children? Is having computers at the center of their lives good for them? For most children, at least, computer-based images and information play a significant role in teaching them about themselves and the world. Is this trend reducing the importance of parents in children's lives, as television did? Cyber-socialization can certainly entertain and instruct, but can it meet the emotional needs of children? Will it contribute to their moral development? After all, there is nothing more important to a child—and more "low-tech"—than a warm hug.

Almost unlimited access to information can be a mixed blessing, as parents can well understand. How can we prevent children from gaining access to pornography or other objectionable material on the Internet? Or, should we?

Third, who will control cyber-socialization? Just as parents have long expressed concerns about what their children watch on television, they now worry about what kids encounter as they surf the 'Net. To date, the federal courts have taken the position that the Internet should operate with minimal government interference. Do we, as citizens and as parents, have expectations for the content of virtual culture? Should the information industry operate for profit? Should there be standards to ensure some measure of educational content? Who should decide?

The Cyber-Self

A person using the name "VegDiet" enters one of thousands of chat rooms found on the Internet, the vast global network described in Chapter 7 ("Groups and Organizations"). Within a few seconds, VegDiet is actively debating the state of the world with three other people: "MrMaine," "Ferret," and "RedWine."

The growing popularity of computer chat gives us a chance to highlight ways in which online interaction differs from more conventional modes of interaction. After studying online interaction, Dennis Waskul (1997) described the self we transmit via a computer as "disembodied." Using Erving Goffman's dramaturgical approach (see Chapter 6), Waskul notes that computer technology screens out a host of "cues" about people's identities—where they are, what they look like,

how they dress, and their age and sex—and conveys only the identities they choose to present.

Cyberspace thus affords us great freedom to try on identities, with few or no lasting consequences. As one chat room participant explained, "Online is a game. . . . Only here, I play with who I am" (Waskul, 1997:21).

But Wait a Minute: The Neo-Luddites

In the eighteenth century, groups of English weavers who opposed the Industrial Revolution traveled about demolishing new machinery whenever they could gain access to a factory. The Luddites (named after Ned Ludd, their leader) were convinced that the new technology of their day would end up eliminating jobs and generally make life worse (Zachary, 1997).

"On the Internet, nobody knows you're a dog."

Peter Steiner © 1993 from The New Yorker Collection. All rights reserved.

Although the Luddites lost their battle to stem the tide of change, their spirit lives on today in people opposed to the Information Revolution. These neo-Luddites, as they are called, speak with many voices. But they agree that we should not race headlong into a cyber-future without thinking critically about how new technology is likely to make our lives better and worse.

The neo-Luddites remind us, first, that technology is never socially neutral. That is, technology does not simply exist in the world: It *changes* the world, pushing human lives in one direction while closing off other alternatives. By venerating technology as good in and of itself, Theodore Roszak (1986) points out, we give up the power to decide for ourselves how we should live. Is putting computers in the classroom a substitute for good teaching? We might well remember that no computer ever created a painting, penned a poem, or composed a symphony. Perhaps most important, computers have no ability to address ethical questions about right and wrong.

Living in a forward-looking culture, we easily imagine the benefits of new technology. But we need to remember that just as technology can serve us, it also can diminish us and even destroy us. After all, the Luddites were not anti-technology; they simply wanted to be sure that technology responded to human needs—and not the other way around.

CHAPTER

10

Paul Marcus
Upstairs–Downstairs

© Paul Marcus, *Upstairs–Downstairs*,
Studio SPM, Inc.

The rate of change increased in 1990, with Nelson Mandela's release from prison. In 1994, the first national election open to all people of all races elected Mandela president, ending centuries of white minority rule.

Despite this dramatic political change, social stratification in South Africa is still based on race. Even with the right to own property, one-third of black South Africans have no jobs, and the majority remain dirt poor. The worst off are some 7 million *ukuhleleleka*, which means "marginal people" in the Xhosa language. Soweto-by-the-Sea may sound like a summer getaway, but it is home to thousands of ukuhleleleka who live crammed into shacks made of packing cases, corrugated metal, cardboard, and other discarded materials. There is no

electricity for lights or refrigeration. Without plumbing, people use buckets to haul sewerage; women line up to take a turn at a single water tap that serves more than 1,000 people. Any job is hard to come by, and those who do find work are lucky to earn $200 a month.

South Africa's current president, Thabo Mbeki, elected in 1999, leads a nation still twisted by centuries of racial caste. Tourism is up and holds out promise of an economic boom in years to come. But the country can shed its past only by providing all its people with real opportunity.

Sources: Fredrickson (1981), Wren (1991), Hawthorne (1999), and Mabry & Masland (1999).

In a pure meritocracy, social position would depend entirely on a person's ability and effort. Such a system would have ongoing social mobility, blurring social categories as individuals continuously move up or down in the system, depending on their latest performance. In caste societies, "merit" (from the Latin word meaning "worthy of praise") means persisting in low-skill jobs such as farming. Caste systems honor those who do their work dutifully and remain "in their place."

Caste systems waste human potential, of course, but they are very orderly. And herein lies the answer to an important question: Why do industrial and postindustrial societies keep castelike qualities (such as letting wealth pass from generation to generation) rather than becoming complete meritocracies? Simply because a pure meritocracy diminishes the importance of families and other social groupings. Economic performance is not everything, after all. Would we want to evaluate our family members solely on their jobs? Probably not. Therefore, class systems in high-income nations move toward meritocracy to promote productivity and efficiency but retain caste elements to maintain order and social cohesion.

Status Consistency

Status consistency is the *degree of consistency in a person's social standing across various dimensions of social inequality.* A caste system has limited social mobility and high status consistency, so that the typical person has the same relative ranking with regard to wealth, power, and prestige. The greater mobility of class systems, however, produces less status consistency. In the United States, then, a college professor with an advanced degree might enjoy high social prestige but earn only a modest income. Low status consistency means that *classes* are less well defined than *castes*.

ASCRIPTION AND ACHIEVEMENT: THE UNITED KINGDOM

The mix of caste and meritocracy in class systems is well illustrated by the United Kingdom (composed of England, Wales, Scotland, and Northern Ireland), an industrial nation with a long agrarian history.

The Estate System

In the Middle Ages, England had a castelike system of three *estates*. The *first estate* was a hereditary nobility composed of barely 5 percent of the population; they controlled most of the land, the chief form of wealth (Laslett, 1984). Most nobles had no occupation because they deemed engaging in trade or any other work for income beneath them. Well tended by servants, nobles used their leisure time to develop skills in riding and the martial arts and to cultivate a refined taste in art, music, and literature.

To prevent vast landholdings from being divided by heirs, the law of *primogeniture* (from the Latin words meaning "first born") demanded that all landholdings pass to the oldest son or other male relation. Younger sons had to find other means of support. Some entered the clergy—often called the *second estate*—where their spiritual power was upheld by the church's extensive landholdings. Other young men of high birth became military officers or lawyers or took up other professions considered honorable for gentlemen. In an age when no woman could inherit her father's property and few women had the opportunity to earn a living, a noble daughter depended for her security on marrying well.

Below the nobility and the clergy, most men and women formed the *third estate*, or commoners. Most commoners were serfs working land owned by nobles. With little education, most were illiterate.

As the Industrial Revolution expanded England's economy, some commoners living in cities made enough money to challenge the nobility. Greater emphasis on meritocracy, the growing importance of money, and expanded schooling and legal rights eventually blurred social rankings and gave rise to a class system.

Perhaps it is a sign of the times that these days traditional titles are put up for sale by nobles who simply need the money. In 1996, for example, the title "Lord of Wimbledon" was put on the block by the Earl Spencer—Princess Diana's brother—to raise the $300,000 he needed to redo the plumbing in one of his large homes (McKee, 1996).

The United Kingdom Today

Today, the United Kingdom has a class system, though it retains the mark of a long, feudal past. A small cluster of British families own inherited estates, attend expensive schools, and exercise great political influence. A traditional monarch, Queen Elizabeth II, stands as the United Kingdom's head of state, and Parliament's House of Lords is composed of peers, about half of noble birth. However, control of the government has passed to the House of Commons, where the prime minister and other commoners typically attain positions by achievement—winning an election—rather than by birth.

Further down, roughly one-fourth of the British people form the "middle class." Many earn comfortable incomes from professions and business and are likely to have investments in the form of stocks and bonds.

Below the middle class, about half of all Britons think of themselves as "working class," earning modest incomes through manual work. In recent decades, the decline of British industries such as coal mining and steel production has led to high unemployment among working-class families. Some have slipped into poverty, joining the remaining one-fourth of Britons who are socially and economically deprived. Lower-class people—or, more simply, the poor—are heavily concentrated in northern and western regions of the United Kingdom, which are plagued by economic decay.

Today's British class system mixes caste elements and meritocracy, producing a highly stratified society in which people are quite unequal, although some move upward or downward. One legacy of the historical estate system is that social mobility is less

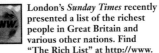 London's *Sunday Times* recently presented a list of the richest people in Great Britain and various other nations. Find "The Rich List" at http://www.sunday-times.co.uk/richlist/

common in the United Kingdom than in the United States (Kerckhoff, Campbell, & Winfield-Laird, 1985). This more rigid system of inequality in the United Kingdom is reflected in the importance attached to accent. Distinctive patterns of speech develop in any society when people are separated from one another over many generations. Whereas people in the United States treat accent as a clue to where one lives (there is little mistaking a Midwestern "twang" or a southern "drawl"), Britons use accent as a mark of social class, distinguishing elites who speak the "King's English" from all others. So different are these two accents that the British seem to be a single people divided by a common language, as the saying goes.

ANOTHER EXAMPLE: JAPAN

Social stratification in Japan also mixes caste and meritocracy. Japan is at once the world's oldest, continuously operating monarchy and a modern society where wealth follows individual achievement.

The traditional caste system, with its concern for people's different social rankings, is still evident in Japan today. Here the women who work at a Japanese inn bow as a sign of respect to a male guest as he departs (in a vintage U.S. automobile that looks to be a 1957 Plymouth).

Feudal Japan

By the fifth century C.E., Japan was an agrarian society with a rigid caste system composed of nobles and commoners and ruled by an imperial family. The emperor ruled by divine right, and his military leader (or *shogun*) oversaw a number of regional warlords.

Below the nobility were the *samurai*, a warrior caste whose name means "to serve." This second rank of Japanese society was made up of soldiers who learned martial skills and who lived by a code of honor based on absolute loyalty to their leaders.

As in Great Britain, most people in Japan at this time in history were commoners who labored to scrape out a bare subsistence. Unlike their European counterparts, however, Japanese commoners were not lowest in rank. At the bottom were the *burakumin*, or "outcasts," shunned by lord and commoner alike. Much like the lowest caste groups in India, these outcasts lived apart from others, performed the most distasteful work, and, like everyone else, could not change their standing.

Japan Today

By the 1860s (the time of the Civil War in the United States), the nobles realized that Japan could not enter the modern, industrial era with its traditional caste system. Besides, as in Britain, some nobles were happy to have their children marry wealthy commoners who

had more money than they did. As Japan opened up to the larger world, the traditional caste system weakened. In 1871, the Japanese legally banned the social category of "outcast," although even today people look down on descendants of this rank. After Japan's defeat in World War II, the nobility lost legal standing, and the emperor remains only as a symbol of Japan's traditions, with little real power.

Social stratification in Japan is a far cry from the rigid caste system of centuries ago. Today, Japanese society consists of "upper," "upper-middle," "lower-middle," and "lower" classes. But no firm boundaries exist, and many people move between classes over time. But because Japanese people revere tradition, family background is never far from the surface in sizing up someone's social standing. Officially, everyone has equal standing before the law, although in practice many people still look at one another through the centuries-old lens of caste (Hiroshi, 1974; Norbeck, 1983).

Finally, traditional ideas about gender continue to shape Japanese society. Legally, the two sexes are equal, but men dominate women in many ways. Japanese parents are more likely to send sons rather than daughters to college, so a significant gender gap exists in education (Brinton, 1988). Consequently, most women who work have lower-level support positions in the corporate world, only rarely assuming leadership roles. Thus, individual

 For information on Japanese society, visit this University of Pittsburgh site: http://www.library.pitt.edu/libraries/jic/jic.html

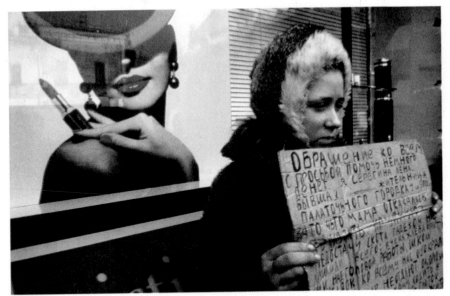

After the collapse of the Soviet Union in 1991, that nation began a transition toward a market economy. Since then, some people have become quite rich, but others have lost their jobs as old, inefficient factories closed. As a result, the problem of poverty has become widespread, affecting perhaps one-third of the Russian people. Scenes like this one—a Moscow woman begging for money—have become all too common.

achievement in Japan's modern class system operates in the shadow of centuries of traditional male privilege.

THE FORMER SOVIET UNION

The former Union of Soviet Socialist Republics (U.S.S.R.), which rivaled the United States as a military superpower during much of the twentieth century, was born out of revolution in 1917. The Russian Revolution ended the feudal estate system ruled by a hereditary nobility and transferred farms, factories, and other productive property from private ownership to state control.

A Classless Society?

The Russian Revolution was guided by the ideas of Karl Marx, who wrote that private ownership of productive property is the basis of social classes (see Chapter 4, "Society"). When the state took control of the economy, Soviet officials boasted that they had engineered the first classless society.

Outside the Soviet Union, however, analysts were skeptical of this claim (Lane, 1984). They pointed out that the jobs people held actually fell into four unequal categories. At the top were high government officials, or *apparatchiks*. Next came the Soviet intelligentsia, including lower government officials, college professors, scientists, physicians, and engineers. Below them were

manual workers and, at the lowest level, the rural peasantry.

These categories enjoyed very different living standards, so the former Soviet Union was not really classless at all. But putting factories, farms, colleges, and hospitals under state control did limit economic inequality (although doing so probably increased differences of power) compared with that of capitalist societies such as the United States.

The Second Russian Revolution

After decades of organizing Soviet society according to the ideas of Karl Marx (and revolutionary leader Vladimir Lenin), the Soviet Union shook with change after Mikhail Gorbachev became president in 1985. Gorbachev introduced a program popularly known as *perestroika*, meaning "restructuring." He saw that although the Soviet system had reduced economic inequality, nearly everyone was poor, and living standards lagged far behind those of higher-income nations in the West. Gorbachev sought to generate economic expansion by reducing inefficient centralized control of the economy.

Gorbachev's economic reforms turned into one of the most dramatic social movements in history. Throughout Eastern Europe, socialist governments toppled, and in 1991 the Soviet Union itself collapsed. People blamed their poverty and their lack of basic freedoms on a repressive ruling class of Communist party officials. In the Soviet Union, for example, just 6 percent of the population formed the Communist party, which ran the whole country.

The Soviet story shows that social inequality involves more than economic resources. Soviet society may not have had the extremes of wealth and poverty found in Great Britain, Japan, and the United States. But an elite class existed all the same, one based on power rather than wealth. Thus, despite the fact that both Mikhail Gorbachev and his successor, Boris Yeltsin, earned far less than a U.S. president, they wielded awesome power.

What about social mobility in the Soviet Union? During the twentieth century there was as much upward social mobility in the Soviet Union as in Great Britain, Japan, and even the United States. Rapidly expanding industry and government drew many poor rural peasants into factories and offices (Dobson, 1977; Lane, 1984; Shipler, 1984). This trend illustrates what sociologists call **structural social mobility,** *a shift in the social position of large numbers of people due more to changes in society itself than to individual efforts.*

November 24, Odessa, Ukraine. The first snow of our voyage flies over the decks as our ship puts in at Odessa, the former Soviet Union's southernmost port on the Black Sea. A short distance from the dock, we gaze up the Potemkin Steps—the steep stairway leading to the city proper where the first shots of the Russian Revolution rang out. It has been six years since our last visit, and much has changed; indeed, the Soviet Union itself has collapsed. Has life improved? For some people, certainly: There are now chic boutiques where well-dressed shoppers buy fine wines, designer clothes, and imported perfumes. Outside, shiny new Volvos, Mercedes, and even a few Cadillacs stand next to the small Ladas from the "old days." But for most, life seems much worse. Flea markets line the curbs as families sell home furnishings. Many are desperate in a town where meat sells for $4 a pound and the average person earns about $30 a month. Even the city has to save money by shutting off street lights at eight o'clock. The spirits of most people seem as dim as Odessa's streets.

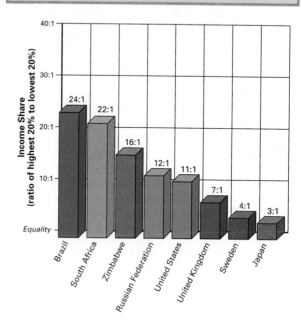

GLOBAL SNAPSHOT

FIGURE 10–1 Economic Inequality in Selected Countries, 1990–2000

These data are the most recent available, representing income share for various years between 1990 and 2000.
Sources: U.S. Census Bureau (2001) and The World Bank (2001).

During the 1990s structural social mobility in the Russian Federation took a downturn. In fact, between 1990 and 1998, the average life span for Russian men dropped by eight years and for women, two years. Many factors are involved in this decline, including Russia's poor health care system, but the Russian people clearly are suffering from a turbulent period of economic change (Róna-Tas, 1994; Specter, 1997b; Bohlen, 1998; Gerber & Hout, 1998).

In the long run, closing inefficient state industries may improve the nation's economic performance. In the short run, however, most citizens face hard times as living standards fall. Moreover, as state-run businesses become privately owned, the gulf between rich and poor grows, a trend reflected in Figure 10–1. Thus, while some praise the recent changes, others do little more than hang on, hoping for a higher living standard.

Medieval Europeans accepted rigid social hierarchy as part of a divine plan for the world. This fifteenth-century painting by the Limbourg brothers shows nobles and high church officials well served by soldiers and servants.

Limbourg Brothers, *Les Tres Riches Heures–January–Purged*, 1400–D. 1416, Flemish. By courtesy of The Board of Trustees of The Victoria & Albert Museum, London/Bridgeman Art Library, London/SuperStock.

IDEOLOGY: THE POWER BEHIND STRATIFICATION

Noting the extent of social inequality around the world, we might wonder how societies persist without sharing resources more equally. Castelike systems in Great Britain and Japan lasted for centuries, placing land and power in the hands of several hundred families. For 2,000 years, people in India have accepted the idea that they should be privileged or poor because of the accident of birth.

A major reason social hierarchies endure, then, is **ideology**, *cultural beliefs that justify social stratification.* A belief—for example, the idea that the rich are smart and the poor are lazy—is ideological to the extent that it defines the wealthy as worthy and suggests that poor people deserve their plight.

Plato and Marx on Ideology

The ancient Greek philosopher Plato (427–347 B.C.E.) defined *justice* as agreement about who should have what. Every culture considers some type of inequality "fair," Plato explained. Karl Marx, too, understood this fact, although he was far more critical of inequality than Plato. Marx took capitalist societies to task for channeling wealth and power to a few and defending the process as "a law of the marketplace." Capitalist law defines the right to own property, Marx continued, and inheritance ensures that money stays within the same families from one generation to the next. In short, Marx concluded, culture and institutions combine to shore up a society's elite, which is why established hierarchies last a long time.

Historical Patterns of Ideology

Ideology changes as a society's economy and technology change. Because agrarian societies depend on the routine labor of their people, they develop caste systems that view performing the duties of one's "station" as a moral responsibility within a natural order. With the rise of industrial capitalism, personal initiative acquires value, and an ideology of meritocracy develops. Wealth and power become prizes won by those who perform the best. Under industrial capitalism, the poor, the object of charity under feudalism, are scorned as personally undeserving. This harsh view is expressed in the work of Herbert Spencer, as explained in the box.

History shows how difficult it is to change social stratification. However, challenges to the status quo always arise. Traditional notions of a "woman's place," for example, are giving way to economic opportunity for women. The continuing progress toward racial equality in South Africa also exemplifies widespread rejection of the ideology of apartheid.

THE FUNCTIONS OF SOCIAL STRATIFICATION

Why are societies stratified at all? One answer, consistent with the structural-functional paradigm, is that social inequality plays a vital part in the operation of

Is Getting Rich "The Survival of the Fittest"?

"The survival of the fittest"—we have all heard these words used to describe society as a competitive jungle. The phrase was coined by one of sociology's pioneers, Herbert Spencer (1820–1903), whose ideas about social inequality are still widespread today.

Spencer, who lived in England, eagerly followed the work of the natural scientist Charles Darwin (1809–1882). Darwin's theory of biological evolution holds that a species changes physically over many generations as it adapts to the natural environment. Spencer, thinking to apply Darwin's theory to the operation of society, proposed that society is a "jungle," with the "fittest" people rising to the top and the weak gradually sinking into miserable poverty.

In the United States, Spencer's distortion of Darwin's theory was popular among the powerful industrialists of that time. John D. Rockefeller (1839–1937), who made a vast fortune building the oil industry, recited Spencer's "social gospel" to young children in Sunday school. As Rockefeller saw it, the growth of giant corporations—and the astounding wealth of their owners—was merely a basic fact of nature. Neither Spencer nor Rockefeller had much sympathy for the poor, seeing poverty as evidence of not measuring up in a competitive world. Spencer opposed social welfare programs for penalizing society's "best" members (through taxes) and rewarding society's "worst" members (through welfare benefits).

Today's sociologists are quick to point out that social standing is not a simple matter of personal effort, as Spencer contended. Nor is it the case that companies or people who generate more money necessarily benefit society. Yet Spencer's view that people get what they deserve in life remains part of our individualistic culture.

What do you think?

1. *What did Herbert Spencer mean when he said society encourages "the survival of the fittest"?*

2. *Why do you think Spencer's ideas are still popular in the United States?*

3. *In what sense do highly paid people benefit society? In what ways do they not?*

---

society. This argument was set forth more than fifty years ago by Kingsley Davis and Wilbert Moore (1945).

THE DAVIS-MOORE THESIS

The **Davis-Moore thesis** states that *social stratification has beneficial consequences for the operation of a society.* How else, ask Davis and Moore, can we explain the fact that some form of social stratification has been found in every known society?

Davis and Moore note that modern societies have hundreds of occupational positions of varying importance. Certain jobs—say, washing windows or answering telephones—are fairly easy and can be performed by almost anyone. Other jobs—such as designing computers or transplanting human organs—are difficult and demand the scarce talents of people with extensive (and expensive) training.

Therefore, Davis and Moore explain, the greater the functional importance of a position, the more

rewards a society attaches to it. This strategy promotes productivity and efficiency because rewarding important work with income, prestige, power, and leisure encourages people to do these jobs and to work better, longer, and harder. Unequal rewards benefit some individuals, then, and a system of unequal rewards (which is what social stratification is) benefits society as a whole.

Davis and Moore concede that any society can be egalitarian, but only to the extent that people are willing to let *anyone* perform *any* job. Equality also demands that someone who carries out a job poorly be rewarded the same as someone who performs well. Such a system clearly offers little incentive for people to try their best and thereby reduces a society's productive efficiency.

The Davis-Moore thesis suggests why some form of stratification exists everywhere; it does not state precisely what rewards a society should give to any occupational position or just how unequal the rewards

Big Bucks: Are the Rich Worth What They Earn?

For an hour of work, a Los Angeles priest earns about $5, a hotel maid in New Orleans about $7, a bus driver in San Francisco about $15, a Phoenix bartender about $20, and a Detroit auto worker roughly $25. By comparison, Barry Bonds earns $40,000 per hour playing baseball for the San Francisco Giants. And what about the $100,000 actor Jim Carrey makes for every hour he spends making a movie? Or the $200,000 Oprah Winfrey collects for each hour she chats with guests before the television cameras? Or the $1 million Tim Allen recently earned for filming each half-hour episode of the sitcom *Home Improvement*?

The Davis-Moore thesis suggests that rewards reflect an occupation's value to society. But are the talents of Michael Jordan, who earned $33 million in just one year playing basketball (more than all the other Chicago Bulls combined) worth more than the efforts of all 100 U.S. senators or 1,000 police officers? In short, do earnings really reflect people's social importance?

In industrial-capitalist societies such as the United States, salaries reflect the market forces of supply and demand. In simple terms, the more you create value in a market system, the more rewards you command. According to this view, movie and television stars, top athletes, writers of popular songs, doctors and other professionals, and many business executives have rare talents that are much in demand; thus, they earn many times more than the typical worker in the United States. Even Elvis Presley's estate—more than twenty-five years after the popular singer's death—still pulls in about $35 million in royalties each year.

But critics of the Davis-Moore thesis question whether the market is really a good evaluator of occupational importance. First, they say, the U.S. economy is dominated by a small proportion

Julia Roberts is among the highest-paid women in the film industry, making millions for starring in each picture. Why does she earn so much more than many lower-paid actors?

of people who manipulate the system for their own benefit. Corporate executives pay themselves multimillion-dollar salaries and bonuses whether their companies do well or not. Lawrence Ellison, CEO of Oracle computer corporation, earned more than $350 million in 2000, even as the price of his company's stock fell dramatically. Moreover, say the critics, many people who make very real contributions to society get little reward in return. The average teacher would have to work more than 10,000 years to earn Ellison's 2000 income.

Equating income with social worth, then, is risky business. Those who defend the market as a measure of occupational worth ask what would be better. But as critics see it, our economic system amounts to a closed game in which only a handful of people have the money to play.

What do you think?

1. *Do you think that highly paid entertainers such as Julia Roberts deserve a thousand times more than an average worker? Why or why not?*

2. *We would all agree that parents perform a vital task as they raise children. Why is parenting unpaid work?*

3. *What about the argument that higher pay would improve the quality and performance of teachers? Do you agree? Why or why not?*

should be. Davis and Moore merely point out that positions a society considers very important must carry enough reward to draw talent away from less important work.

Critical evaluation. Although the Davis-Moore thesis is an important contribution to sociological analysis, it has provoked criticism. Melvin Tumin (1953) wondered, first, how we assess how important any occupation is.

Obviously, we cannot say that important jobs are simply those with high rewards because that amounts to circular reasoning (that is, we assume important jobs have high rewards, but then we define a job's importance by its level of reward so that our thesis is correct by definition). Perhaps the high rewards our society gives to, say, physicians, results partly from deliberate efforts by the medical profession to limit the supply of physicians and thereby increase the demand for their services.

Moreover, do rewards really reflect the contribution someone makes to society? With an income approaching $100 million per year, television personality Oprah Winfrey earns more in two days than George W. Bush makes all year as president. Would anyone argue that hosting a talk show is more important than leading the country? The box takes a critical look at the link between pay and societal importance.

 Do corporate CEOs deserve their high salaries? The AFL-CIO offers a critical view at their site where they track CEO salaries: http://www.aflcio.org/paywatch/index.htm

Second, Tumin claims that the Davis-Moore thesis ignores ways in which social stratification can *prevent* the development of individual talent. Born to privilege, rich children may develop their abilities, something many gifted poor children may never do.

Third, by suggesting that social stratification benefits all of society, the Davis-Moore thesis ignores how social inequality promotes conflict and even outright revolution. This criticism leads us to the social-conflict paradigm, which provides a very different explanation for social hierarchy.

STRATIFICATION AND CONFLICT

Social-conflict analysis argues that rather than benefiting society as a whole, social stratification provides some people with advantages over others. This analysis draws heavily on the ideas of Karl Marx, with contributions from Max Weber.

KARL MARX: CLASS AND CONFLICT

Karl Marx, whose ideas are discussed fully in Chapter 4 ("Society"), explained that most people have one of two basic relationships to the means of production: They can either own productive property or work for others. This productive role is the basis of social class. In medieval Europe, the nobility and church officials owned the productive land; peasants toiled as farmers. Similarly, in industrial class systems, the capitalists (or the bourgeoisie) control factories, which use the labor of workers (the proletariat).

Marx saw great inequality in wealth and power arising from capitalism, which, he argued, made class conflict inevitable. In time, he believed, oppression and misery would drive the working majority to organize and ultimately overthrow capitalism.

Marx lived at a time when a small number of industrialists were amassing huge fortunes. Andrew Carnegie, J. P. Morgan, John D. Rockefeller, and John Jacob Astor (one of the few very rich passengers to perish on the *Titanic*) lived in fabulous mansions adorned with priceless art and staffed by dozens of servants. Their wealth was staggering: Andrew Carnegie, founder of U.S. Steel, reportedly earned some $20 million a year at the beginning of the twentieth century (more than $100 million in today's dollars), at a time when the average worker earned roughly $500 a year (Baltzell, 1964; Pessen, 1990).

But according to Marx, the capitalist elite draws strength not just from the operation of the economy. Through the family, opportunity and wealth are passed down from generation to generation. Moreover, the legal system defends private property and inheritance. Finally, elite children mix at exclusive schools, forging social ties that will benefit them throughout their lives. In short, from Marx's point of view, capitalist society *reproduces the class structure in each new generation.*

Critical evaluation. Marx's analysis of how capitalism creates conflict between classes has greatly influenced sociological thinking. But because it is revolutionary, calling for the overthrow of capitalist society, Marxism is also highly controversial.

One of the strongest criticisms of Marxism is that it denies a central tenet of the Davis-Moore thesis: that motivating people to perform various social roles requires some system of unequal rewards. Marx separated reward from performance, endorsing a roughly equal system based on the principle of "from each according to his ability; to each according to his needs" (1972:388; orig.1848). Critics argue that severing rewards from performance is exactly what caused low productivity in the former Soviet Union and other socialist economies around the world.

Defenders of Marx counter that there is much evidence supporting Marx's view of humanity as inherently social rather than selfish (Clark, 1991; Fiske, 1991). Therefore, we should not assume that individual rewards (much less, money alone) are the only way to motivate people to perform their social roles.

This cartoon, titled "Capital and Labour," appeared in the English press in 1843, when the ideas of Karl Marx were first gaining attention. It links the plight of that country's coal miners to the privileges enjoyed by those who owned coal-fired factories.

CAPITAL AND LABOUR.

A second problem is that the revolutionary developments Marx considered inevitable within capitalist societies have, by and large, failed to happen. The next section explores why the socialist revolution Marx predicted has not occurred, at least not in advanced capitalist societies.

WHY NO MARXIST REVOLUTION?

Despite Marx's prediction, capitalism is still thriving. Why have workers in the United States and other industrial societies not overthrown capitalism? Ralf Dahrendorf (1959) suggests four reasons:

1. **The fragmentation of the capitalist class.** Today, millions of stockholders, rather than single families, own most large companies. Moreover, day-to-day operation of large corporations is now in the hands of a managerial class, whose members may or may not be major stockholders. With stock widely held—by the late 1990s, about 40 percent of U.S. adults were in the market— more and more people have a direct stake in preserving the capitalist system.

2. **A higher standard of living.** As Chapter 16 ("The Economy and Work") explains, a century ago most workers were in factories or on farms performing **blue-collar occupations,**

lower-prestige work that involves mostly manual labor. Today, most workers hold **white-collar occupations,** *higher-prestige work that involves mostly mental activity.* These jobs are in sales, management, and other service fields. Most of today's white-collar workers do not think of themselves as an "industrial proletariat." Just as important, the average U.S. worker's income rose almost tenfold over the course of the twentieth century, even allowing for inflation, and the workweek decreased. As a result, most workers consider themselves better off than their parents and grandparents, a case of structural mobility encouraging people to accept the present system (Edwards, 1979; Gagliani, 1981; Wright & Martin, 1987).

3. **More worker organizations.** Workers today have organizational clout that they lacked a century ago. With the right to organize into labor unions, workers make demands of management backed up by threats of work slowdowns and strikes. In other words, worker-management disputes are settled without threatening the capitalist system.

4. **More extensive legal protections.** During the twentieth century, the government passed laws to make the workplace safer and developed programs such as unemployment insurance,

TABLE 10–1 Two Explanations of Social Stratification: A Summary

Structural-Functional Paradigm	Social-Conflict Paradigm
Social stratification keeps society operating. Linking greater rewards to more important social possessions benefits society as a whole.	Social stratification is the result of social conflict. Differences in social resources serve the interests of some and harm others.
Social stratification matches talents and abilities to appropriate occupational positions.	Social stratification ensures that much talent and ability in society will not be developed at all.
Social stratification is both useful and inevitable.	Social stratification is useful only to some people; it is not inevitable
The values and beliefs that legitimize social inequality are widely shared throughout society.	Values and beliefs tend to be ideological; they reflect the interests of the more powerful members of society.
Because systems of social stratification are useful to society as a whole and are supported by cultural values and beliefs, they are usually stable over time.	Because systems of social stratification reflect the interests of only part of society, they are unlikely to remain stable over time.

Source: Adapted in part from Arthur L. Stinchcombe, "Some Empirical Consequences of the Davis-Moore Theory of Stratification," *American Sociological Review*, Vol. 28, No. 5 (October 1963):808.

disability protection, and Social Security to provide workers with greater financial security.

A Counterpoint

These developments suggest that society has smoothed many of capitalism's rough edges. Yet many claim that Marx's analysis of capitalism is still largely valid (Miliband, 1969; Edwards, 1979; Giddens, 1982; Domhoff, 1983; Stephens, 1986; Boswell & Dixon, 1993; Hout, Brooks, & Manza, 1993). First, wealth remains highly concentrated, with 40 percent of all privately owned property in the hands of just 1 percent of our population (Keister, 2000). Second, many of today's white-collar jobs offer no more income, security, or satisfaction than factory work did a century ago. Third, many benefits enjoyed by today's workers came about through the class conflict Marx described, and workers still struggle to hold on to what they have. Fourth, although workers have gained legal protections, the law still protects the private property of the rich. Therefore, social-conflict theorists conclude, the absence of a socialist revolution in the United States does not negate Marx's analysis of capitalism.

Table 10–1 summarizes the contributions of the two contrasting sociological approaches to understanding social stratification.

MAX WEBER: CLASS, STATUS, AND POWER

Max Weber, whose approach to social analysis is described in Chapter 4 ("Society"), agreed with Karl Marx that social stratification causes social conflict, but he considered Marx's two-class model simplistic. Instead, he thought social stratification involves three distinct dimensions of inequality.

The first dimension is economic inequality—the issue so vital to Marx—which Weber called *class* position. Weber did not think of "classes" as crude categories but as a continuum ranging from high to low. Weber's second dimension of social stratification is *status*, or social prestige, and the third is *power*.

The Socioeconomic Status Hierarchy

Marx viewed social prestige and power as simple reflections of economic position and did not treat them as distinct dimensions of inequality. But Weber noted that status consistency in modern societies often is quite low: A local government official, for instance, might wield great power yet have little wealth or social prestige.

Weber's contribution, then, is portraying social stratification in industrial societies as a multidimensional ranking rather than a hierarchy of clearly defined classes. In line with Weber's thinking, sociologists use the term **socioeconomic status (SES)** to refer to *a composite ranking based on various dimensions of social inequality.*

Because people vary on the three dimensions of class, status, and power, Weber saw society not in terms of distinct classes, as Marx did, but as a broad range of self-interested social categories. For Weber, social conflict is therefore both variable and complex.

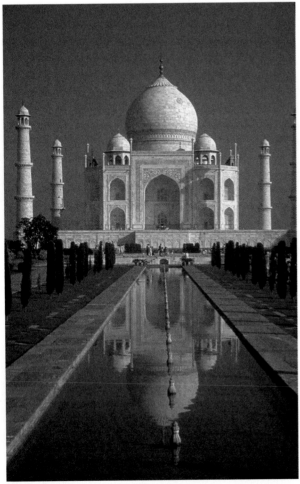

The extent of social inequality in agrarian systems is greater than that found in industrial societies. One indication of the unchallenged power of rulers is the monumental structures built over years with the unpaid labor of common people. Although the Taj Mahal in India is among the world's most beautiful buildings, it is merely a tomb for a single individual.

Inequality in History

Weber noted that each of his three dimensions of social inequality stands out at different points in the evolution of human societies. Agrarian societies emphasize status or social prestige, typically in the form of honor. Members of these societies gain status by conforming to cultural norms that correspond to their rank.

Industrialization and the development of capitalism level traditional rankings based on birth but generate striking financial inequality. Thus, Weber argued, the crucial difference between people in industrial societies is the economic dimension of class.

Over time, industrial and, especially, postindustrial societies witness the growth of a bureaucratic state. Bigger government and the spread of all kinds of other organizations make power more important in the stratification system. Especially in socialist societies, because government regulates many aspects of life, high-ranking officials become the new elite.

Historical analysis points to a final difference between Weber and Marx. Marx thought societies could eliminate social stratification by abolishing private ownership of productive property. Weber doubted that overthrowing capitalism would significantly diminish social stratification. It might lessen economic disparity, he reasoned, but socialism would simultaneously increase inequality by expanding government and concentrating power in the hands of a political elite. Popular uprisings against entrenched bureaucracies in Eastern Europe and the former Soviet Union support Weber's position.

Critical evaluation. Weber's multidimensional view of social stratification has strongly influenced sociologists. But critics (particularly those who favor Marx's ideas) argue that although social class boundaries may have blurred, industrial and postindustrial nations still show striking patterns of social inequality.

Moreover, as we shall see in Chapter 11 ("Social Class in the United States"), income inequality has increased in recent years. In light of this trend, whereas some people favor Weber's multidimensional hierarchy, others think Marx's view of the rich versus the poor is closer to the mark.

STRATIFICATION AND TECHNOLOGY: A GLOBAL PERSPECTIVE

We can weave together a number of observations made in this chapter by considering the relationship between a society's technology and its type of social stratification. This analysis draws on Gerhard Lenski's model of sociocultural evolution, detailed in Chapter 4 ("Society").

HUNTING AND GATHERING SOCIETIES

With simple technology, hunters and gatherers produce only what is necessary for day-to-day living. Some people may produce more than others, but the group's survival depends on all sharing what they have. Thus, no categories of people emerge as better off than others.

HORTICULTURAL, PASTORAL, AND AGRARIAN SOCIETIES

As technological advances create a surplus, social inequality increases. In horticultural and pastoral societies, a small elite controls most of the surplus. Large-scale agriculture is more productive still, and marked inequality—as great as any time in human history—means that various categories of people lead strikingly different lives. Agrarian nobility typically exercises godlike power over the masses.

INDUSTRIAL SOCIETIES

Industrialization turns the tide, lessening inequality. Prompted by the need to develop individual talents, meritocracy takes hold and erodes the power of traditional elites. Industrial productivity also raises the standard of living of the historically poor majority. Furthermore, the specialized work performed in industrial societies demands schooling for all, sharply reducing illiteracy. A literate population, in turn, presses for a greater voice in political decision making, further diminishing social inequality and lessening men's domination of women.

Over time, even wealth becomes somewhat less concentrated (countering the trend predicted by Marx). In the 1920s, the richest 1 percent of the U.S. population owned about 36 percent of all wealth, a figure that fell to 30 percent by the 1980s (Williamson & Lindert, 1980; Beeghley, 1989; *1991 Green Book*). Such trends help explain why Marxist revolutions occurred in *agrarian* societies—such as the former Soviet Union (1917), Cuba (1959), and Nicaragua (1979)—where social inequality is most pronounced, rather than in industrial societies, as Marx predicted. However, wealth inequality turned up again after 1990 (Keister, 2000).

THE KUZNETS CURVE

In human history, technological progress first increases but then moderates the extent of social stratification. Greater inequality is functional for agrarian societies, but industrial societies benefit from a more egalitarian climate. This historical trend, recognized by the Nobel

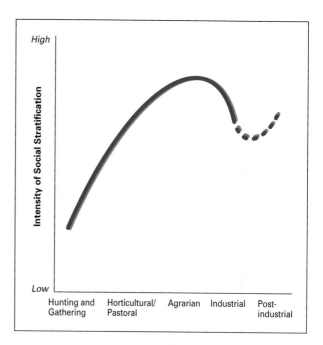

FIGURE 10–2 Social Stratification and Technological Development: The Kuznets Curve

The Kuznets curve shows that greater technological sophistication generally is accompanied by more pronounced social stratification. The trend reverses itself as industrial societies relax rigid castelike distinctions in favor of greater opportunity and equality under the law. Political rights are more widely extended, and there is even some leveling of economic differences. The Kuznets curve may also be usefully applied to the relative social standing of the two sexes. However, the emergence of postindustrial society has brought an upturn in economic inequality, as indicated by the broken line added by the author.

Source: Created by the author, based on Kuznets (1955) and Lenski (1966).

Prize–winning economist Simon Kuznets (1955, 1966), is illustrated by the Kuznets curve, shown in Figure 10–2.

Patterns of social inequality around the world today generally square with the Kuznets curve. Global Map 10–1 on page 264 shows that high-income nations that have passed through the industrial era (including the United States, Canada, and nations of Western Europe) have somewhat less income inequality than nations in which agriculture remains a major part of the economy (as is common in Latin America

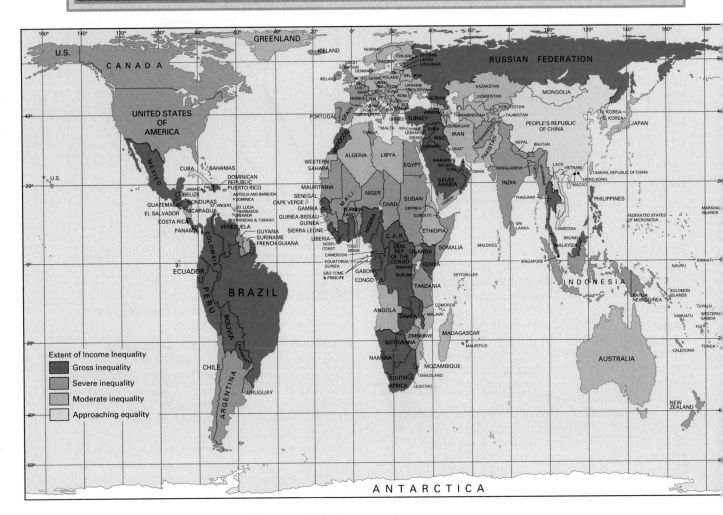

GLOBAL MAP 10–1 Income Disparity in Global Perspective

Societies throughout the world differ in the rigidity and extent of social stratification and in overall standard of living. This map highlights income inequality. Generally speaking, countries that have centralized, socialist economies (including the People's Republic of China and Cuba) display the least income inequality, although their standard of living is low. Postindustrial societies with predominantly capitalist economies, including the United States and most of Western Europe, have higher overall living standards accompanied by severe income disparity. The less economically developed countries of Latin America and Africa (including Mexico, Brazil, and the Democratic Republic of the Congo), as well as the Russian Federation and much of the Arab world, exhibit the most pronounced inequality of income.

Sources: *Peters Atlas of the World* (1990); updates by the author from United Nations Development Programme (1999).

The early industrial era, according to Simon Kuznets, is marked by extreme social inequality that affords aristocratic people a life of leisure while others toil at manual labor for pennies a day. U.S. artist Ford Madox Brown (1821–1893) captures such class distinctions in his painting, Work. Today, more than a century after Brown lived, do you think class differences in the United States have become smaller or greater? Why?

and Africa). Of course, income disparity reflects not just technological development but also political and economic priorities. Of all high–income nations, the United States has the most income inequality.

And what of the future? A glance back at Figure 10–2 shows that we have extended the trend described by Kuznets to the postindustrial era (the broken line) to show increased social inequality. That is, as the Information Revolution moves ahead, we are experiencing some economic polarization (discussed in the next chapter), suggesting that the long-term trend may differ from what Kuznets observed half a century ago (Nielsen & Alderson, 1997).

SOCIAL STRATIFICATION: FACTS AND VALUES

The year was 2081 and everybody was finally equal. They weren't only equal before God and the law. They were equal every which way. Nobody was smarter than anybody else. Nobody was better looking than anybody else. Nobody was stronger or quicker than anybody else. All this equality was due to the 211th, 212th, and 213th Amendments to the Constitution and the unceasing vigilance of agents of the Handicapper General.

With these words, novelist Kurt Vonnegut, Jr. (1961) begins the story of *Harrison Bergeron*, an imaginary account of a future United States in which all social inequality has been abolished. Vonnegut warns that although perhaps appealing in principle, equality can be a dangerous concept in practice. His story describes a nightmare of social engineering whereby every individual talent that makes one person different from another is systematically neutralized by the government.

To eradicate differences that make one person "better" than another, Vonnegut's state requires that physically attractive people wear masks that make them average looking, that intelligent people wear earphones that generate distracting noise, and that the best athletes and dancers be fitted with weights to make them as clumsy as everyone else. In short, although we may imagine that social equality would liberate people to make the most of their talents, Vonnegut concludes that an egalitarian society could exist only by reducing everyone to the lowest common denominator.

Like Vonnegut's story, all of this chapter's explanations of social stratification involve value judgments.

The Bell Curve Debate: Are Rich People Really Smarter?

It is rare when a social science book captures the attention of people across the country. But *The Bell Curve: Intelligence and Class Structure in American Life*, by Richard J. Herrnstein and Charles Murray, did that and more. The book ignited a firestorm of controversy over why social stratification divides our society and, just as important, what should be done about it.

The Bell Curve is a long (800-page) book that addresses many complex issues, but at bottom it puts forth eight propositions:

1. There exists something we can describe as "general intelligence"; people with more of it tend to be more successful in their careers than those with less.

2. At least half the variation in human intelligence is transmitted genetically from one generation to another; the remaining variability results from environmental factors.

3. Over the course of the twentieth century—and especially since the Information Revolution began several decades ago—intelligence has become more necessary in our society's most important jobs.

4. At the same time, the best U.S. colleges and universities have shifted their admission policies away from favoring children of inherited wealth to admitting young people with high grades and the highest scores on standardized tests, such as the Scholastic Assessment Test (SAT), American College Testing Program (ACT), and Graduate Record Examination (GRE).

5. As a result of these changes in the workplace and higher education, our society is coming to be dominated by a "cognitive elite," who are, on average, not only better trained than most people but actually more intelligent.

6. Intelligent people tend to interact with others like themselves—both on the campus and in the workplace—which raises the odds that they will pair up, marry, and have intelligent children, thus extending the "cognitive elite" into another generation.

7. The same process is at work at the other end of the social ladder: Poor people, who have lower intelligence on average, are also socially segregated, tend to marry others with similar social background, and thus pass along their more modest abilities to their children.

Thus, Herrnstein and Murray conclude,

8. Because membership in the affluent elite or the impoverished underclass is at least partly rooted in intelligence received mostly by genetic inheritance, we should not be

---

The Davis-Moore thesis states not only that social stratification is universal but that it is actually necessary to efficient social organization. Class differences in U.S. society, then, reflect both variation in human abilities and the relative importance of different jobs. From this point of view, equality is undesirable because it could be achieved only through oppressive measures to impose uniformity on the population.

Social-conflict analysis, advocated by Karl Marx, reflects egalitarian values. Marx considered inequality dysfunctional to societies, causing both suffering and conflict. As he saw it, social stratification springs from injustice and greed. Therefore, he advocated sharing resources equally. Marx believed that equality would not diminish but enhance human well-being.

The box addresses the connection between intelligence and social class. This issue—also a mix of fact and value—is among the most troublesome in social science. The difficulty lies partly in defining and measuring "intelligence" and partly in the very idea that elites are somehow "better" than others, which challenges our democratic culture.

Chapter 11 ("Social Class in the United States") examines inequality in our own nation, highlighting recent economic polarization. Then, in Chapter 12 ("Global Stratification"), we survey the entire world, asking why some nations have so much more wealth than others. At all levels, as we shall see, the study of social stratification involves a mix of facts and values about the shape of a just society.

surprised that the poor contend with high levels of social problems, such as crime and drug abuse. Furthermore, we should expect that programs to help the poor (including Head Start and Affirmative Action) will have few practical results.

Evaluating the claims made in *The Bell Curve* must begin with a hard look at the concept of intelligence. Critics of the book argue that most of what we call "intelligence" is the result not of genetic inheritance but of socialization. In other words, intelligence tests do not measure cognitive *ability* as much as they measure cognitive *performance*. If this is so, we might well expect rich children to perform better on such tests because they have had the best schooling. In short, whatever innate abilities children have can develop only in a supportive environment.

Most researchers who study intelligence agree that genetics plays a part in children's intelligence, but the consensus is that no more than 25 to 40 percent is inherited—less than what Herrnstein and Murray claim. Therefore, *The Bell Curve* misleads readers into thinking that social stratification is both natural and inevitable. In fact, say critics, this book amounts to a new version of the social Darwinism popular a century ago, which justified the great wealth of industrial tycoons as "the survival of the fittest."

Perhaps the more today's competitive society seems like a jungle, the more people think of stratification as a matter of blood rather than upbringing. But despite any flaws, *The Bell Curve* raises issues we cannot easily ignore. If some people are, indeed, smarter than others, shouldn't we expect that most will end up in higher social positions? Is that fair or not? Wouldn't we want the top people in various fields to be at least a little smarter than the rest of us? Are there also dangers in having a smart elite? Is it true that our society's elites live apart from the problems—including crime, homelessness, and poor schools—that plague most of the population? Finally,

what can our society do to ensure that all people have the opportunity to develop their abilities as fully as possible?

Continue the debate . . .

1. *Do you think there is such a thing as "general intelligence"? Why or why not?*

2. *Do you think that well-off people, on average, are more intelligent than people of low social position? If so, how do we know which factor is causing the other?*

3. *Do you think social scientists should study controversial issues such as differences in human intelligence? Why or why not?*

Sources: Herrnstein & Murray (1994), Jacoby & Glauberman (1995), and Kohn (1996).

SUMMARY

1. Social stratification is the ranking of people in a hierarchy. Stratification (a) is a trait of society, not just a result of individual differences, (b) endures over many generations; (c) is universal yet variable in form; and (d) is supported by cultural beliefs.

2. Caste systems, common in agrarian societies, are based on ascription (birth), permit little social mobility, and shape a person's entire life, including occupation and marriage.

3. Class systems, with an element of meritocracy, are found in industrial and postindustrial societies and allow social mobility based on individual achievement.

4. With public ownership of productive property, socialist societies claim to be classless. Although such societies usually exhibit less economic inequality than their capitalist counterparts, there is much greater inequality in power.

5. Social stratification is difficult to change because it is supported by various social institutions and because cultural values and beliefs—ideology—define certain kinds of inequality as both natural and just.

6. The Davis-Moore thesis states that social stratification is universal because it promotes economic productivity in a society. In class systems, unequal

rewards attract the most able people to the most important jobs.

7. Critics of the Davis-Moore thesis note that (a) it is difficult to assess objectively the functional importance of any job; (b) stratification prevents many people from developing their abilities; and (c) social stratification benefits some at the expense of others, causing social conflict.

8. For Karl Marx, the main architect of social-conflict analysis, conflict in industrial societies places the capitalists (bourgeoisie), who own the means of production and seek to maximize profits, in opposition to the proletariat, who provide labor in exchange for wages.

9. The socialist revolution Marx predicted has not occurred in high-income nations such as the United States. Some sociologists consider this evidence that Marx's analysis was flawed; others point out that our society is marked by pronounced social inequality and class conflict.

10. Max Weber identified three dimensions of social inequality: economic class, social status or prestige, and power. Because people's standing on the three dimensions may differ, stratification takes the form of a multidimensional hierarchy rather than distinct classes.

11. Historically, says Gerhard Lenski, technological advances have made societies more unequal. Some reversal of this trend occurs in industrial societies, as shown by the Kuznets curve. However, the new postindustrial economy in the United States shows some increase in economic inequality.

12. The study of social inequality deals not only with facts but also with politics and values concerning how a society should be organized.

KEY CONCEPTS

social stratification (p. 247) a system by which a society ranks categories of people in a hierarchy

social mobility (p. 248) change in one's position in the social hierarchy

caste system (p. 248) social stratification based on ascription, or birth

class system (p. 250) social stratification based on both birth and individual achievement

meritocracy (p. 250) social stratification based on personal merit

status consistency (p. 251) the degree of consistency in a person's social standing across various dimensions of social inequality

structural social mobility (p. 255) a shift in the social position of large numbers of people due more to changes in society itself than to individual efforts

ideology (p. 256) cultural beliefs that justify social stratification

Davis-Moore thesis (p. 257) the assertion that social stratification is a universal pattern because it benefits the operation of a society

blue-collar occupations (p. 260) lower-prestige work that involves mostly manual labor

white-collar occupations (p. 260) higher-prestige work that involves mostly mental activity

socioeconomic status (SES) (p. 261) a composite ranking based on various dimensions of social inequality

CRITICAL-THINKING QUESTIONS

1. How is social stratification a creation of society rather than simply a reflection of individual differences?

2. How do caste and class systems differ? What do they have in common? In what ways does industrialization introduce a measure of meritocracy to social stratification?

3. According to the Davis-Moore thesis, why should a college president earn more than a professor or a secretary? What would happen if all employees were paid the same?

4. In what respects have Karl Marx's predictions about capitalism failed? In what respects are they correct?

APPLICATIONS AND EXERCISES

1. Is social stratification evident on your college campus? What categories of people are unequal? In what ways are they unequal?

2. Sit down with parents, grandparents, or other relatives and assess how your family's lifestyle has changed over the last three generations. Has social mobility taken place? If so, describe the change. Was it caused by the efforts of individuals or changes in society itself?

3. What are the "seven deadly sins," the human failings recognized by the Catholic church during the Middle Ages? Why are these traits dangerous to an agrarian caste system? Are they a threat to a modern, capitalist class system? Why?

4. Packaged in the back of this new textbook is an interactive CD-ROM that offers a variety of study and review materials intended to help you better understand the material covered in this chapter. For this chapter, the CD-ROM contains an author's tip video, Real Life Sociology videos, other relevant audio and video, interactive map animations, audio journal entries from the author, Web links, and much more.

 SITES TO SEE

http://www.prenhall.com/macionis

Visit the interactive *Companion Website*™ that accompanies this text. Begin by clicking on the cover of your book. You will find a chapter-by-chapter study guide, practice tests, and a significant portion of the text for on-line review, as well as many suggested Web links.

http://www.macionis.com
(or http://www.TheSociologyPage.com)

You can find additional links pertaining to social stratification at the author's home page.

http://www.bea.doc.gov

This Web site is run by the U.S. government's Bureau of Economic Analysis. Here you will find income data by county and many other statistics about social inequality. See what you can learn about stratification in your part of the country.

http://www.cbpp.org

This site, developed by the Center on Budget and Policy Priorities, provides data and analysis of issues involving social inequality.

 INVESTIGATE WITH CONTENTSELECT

Follow the instructions found on page 23 of this textbook to enter this chapter of the book's *Companion Website*™. Once in the chapter, click on the ContentSelect icon at the bottom left of your screen and enter your personal User ID and Password. Enter keywords such as "social class," "meritocracy," "Karl Marx," and "apartheid," and the search engine will help you become an effective researcher.

CHAPTER

11

Beauford Delaney (1901–1979)
Can Fire in the Park, 1946

Oil on canvas, 24 × 30 in. (61.0 × 76.2 cm).
Smithsonian American Art Museum, Washington, D.C./Art Resource, N.Y.

The Color of Money: Being Rich in Black and White

African American families earn 64 cents for every dollar a white family earns, which helps explain why black families are three times as likely to be poor. But there is another side to black America—an affluent side—that has expanded dramatically in recent decades.

The number of affluent families—those with annual incomes over $80,000—is increasing faster among African Americans than among whites. In 2000, 1.2 million African American families (13 percent) were financially privileged, 50 percent more than the number in 1990 and ten times the number in 1970, taking account of inflation. About 12 percent of Latino families also rank as well-off, along with 30 percent of non-Hispanic white families.

The color of money is the same for everyone, but black and white affluence differs in several ways. First, well-off people of African descent are not *as rich* as their white counterparts. Sixty-five percent of affluent non-Hispanic white families (20 percent of all non-Hispanic white families) earn more than $100,000 a year, compared to 60 percent

of affluent African American families (8 percent of all black families).

Second, African Americans are more likely than white people to achieve affluence through multiple incomes. From another angle, 10.5 percent of non-Hispanic white men and 2.5 percent of non-Hispanic white women earn more

Rich people come in all colors. But are they all the same?

than $80,000, compared to just 2.9 percent of black men and 1.0 percent of black women. Rich black families, then, are more likely to contain two, and perhaps more, working people.

Third, affluent African Americans are more likely to derive their income from salaries rather than from investments. Among wealthy white families, more than 80 percent of families have investment income, compared to two-thirds of affluent African American families.

Beyond differences in income, affluent people of color contend with social barriers that do not limit whites. Even African Americans with the money to purchase a home, for example, may find that they are unwelcome as neighbors. This is one reason that a smaller share of well-off African American families (40 percent) live in the suburbs (the richest areas of the country) than affluent white families (61 percent).

Affluent Americans come in all colors. Yet race has a powerful effect on the lives of rich people, just as it does on the lives of us all.

Sources: O'Hare (1989), Weicher (1995), Lach (1999), and U.S. Census Bureau (2001).

Upper-Uppers

The *upper-upper class*, sometimes called "blue bloods" or simply "society," includes less than 1 percent of the U.S. population (Warner & Lunt, 1941; Coleman & Neugarten, 1971; Baltzell, 1995). Membership almost always comes at birth, as suggested by the quip that the easiest way to become an upper-upper is to be born one. Most of these families possess enormous wealth, primarily inherited. For this reason, members of the upper-upper class are said to have *old money*.

Set apart by their wealth, upper-uppers live in old, exclusive neighborhoods, such as Beacon Hill in Boston, Rittenhouse Square or the Main Line in Philadelphia, the Gold Coast of Chicago, and Nob Hill in San Francisco. Their children typically attend private schools with others of similar background and high-prestige colleges and universities. In the tradition of European aristocrats, they study liberal arts rather than vocational skills.

Women of the upper-upper class often maintain a full schedule of volunteer work for charitable

People often distinguish between the "new rich" and those with "old money." Men and women who suddenly begin to earn high incomes tend to spend their money on "status symbols" because they enjoy the new thrill of high-roller living and they want others to know of their success. Those who grow up surrounded by wealth, on the other hand, are used to a privileged way of life and are more quiet about it. Thus, the "conspicuous consumption" of the lower-upper class (left) can differ dramatically from the more private pursuits and understatement of the upper-upper class (right).

organizations. While helping the larger community, such charitable activities also build networks that broaden this elite's power (Ostrander, 1980, 1984).

Lower-Uppers

Most upper-class people actually fall into the *lower-upper class*. To most of us, these people seem every bit as privileged as the upper-upper class. The major difference, however, is that lower-uppers (including Steve Jobs, profiled in the opening to this chapter) are the "working rich"; their primary source of income is earnings rather than inherited wealth. Although "new rich" families generally live in exclusive communities, most do not gain entry to the clubs and associations of "old money" families.

Historically, the American Dream has been to earn enough to join the ranks of the lower-upper class. The athlete who signs a million-dollar contract, the actor who lands a starring role in a Hollywood film, the computer whiz who becomes an Internet entrepreneur—these are the talented and lucky achievers who reach the lower-upper class. The box sharpens the distinction between "society" and the high achievers of the lower-upper class, people very much like the rest of us—except that they make a lot of money.

THE MIDDLE CLASS

Including 40 to 45 percent of the U.S. population, the large middle class has a tremendous influence on our culture. Television programs and movies usually depict middle-class people, and most commercial advertising is directed toward these "average" consumers. The middle class contains far more racial and ethnic diversity than the upper class.

Upper-Middles

The top half of this category is called the *upper-middle class*, based on above-average income in the range of $80,000 to $160,000 a year. Such income allows upper-middle-class families to accumulate valuable property: a comfortable house in a fairly expensive area, several automobiles, and investments. Two-thirds of upper-middle-class children receive college educations, and postgraduate degrees are common. Many go on to high-prestige careers as physicians, engineers, lawyers, accountants, and business executives. Lacking the power of the richest people to influence national or international events, upper-middles often play an important role in local political affairs.

Caste and Class: The *Social Register* and *Who's Who*

Small and exclusive, the upper-upper class comes closest to being a true social group. There is even a list of these privileged families: the *Social Register*, first published in 1887 as fortunes grew along with the industrial economy. Today, some 40,000 families are included in this inventory of our society's "blue bloods."

Because membership typically is based on birth, the upper-upper class operates much like a caste: You are either "in" or "out." Traditional upper-upper parents urge their children to seek partners of their own kind, sustaining the class into another generation. Family is thus crucial to the upper-upper class, as it is to all caste groups. This is why the *Social Register* lists *families*, not *individuals*.

The listing for David Rockefeller, a member of one of the most socially prominent U.S. families, indicates his family's address and home telephone number, Mrs. Rockefeller's maiden name, the names of the Rockefeller children and the boarding schools and colleges they are attending, and exclusive social clubs to which the family belongs. Because achievement is not the issue, the *Social Register* never mentions anyone's occupation or place of business.

The lower-upper class, by contrast, is an achievement elite. This larger category of "new rich" individuals has no clear boundaries, and its members do not engage in formal rituals (such as debutante parties) as many "old money" families do.

There is also a list—roughly speaking—of people at this class level: the national edition of *Who's Who in America*. Here, instead of established families, we find distinguished individuals: outstanding athletes, highly successful businesspeople, college presidents, Nobel prize winners, and famous entertainers.

Who's Who contains a few people, including David Rockefeller, who are also listed in the *Social Register*, but the information provided is quite different. David Rockefeller's entry in *Who's Who* includes a brief biography (date of birth, schooling, honorary degrees), a list of accomplishments (military decorations, government service, books authored), and—most important—his position as board chair of Chase Manhattan Bank. The address provided in *Who's Who* is his place of business.

These two publications show that there are two kinds of elites in the United States. The castelike *Social Register* lists high-prestige families according to *who they are*. The more classlike *Who's Who* lists individuals on the basis of *what they have done*. But as the dual listings for David Rockefeller suggest, social privilege and personal achievement sometimes go together.

What do you think?

1. *In what sense are the rich* not *all the same?*

2. *Why are "old money" families more a caste and "new money" families more a class?*

3. *With time, of course, "new money" becomes "old money." How did the ancestors of some of today's "old money" families (including the Rockefellers or the Kennedys) get their start?*

Average-Middles

The rest of the middle class falls near the center of the U.S. class structure. *Average-middles* typically work in less prestigious white-collar occupations (middle managers, high school teachers, and salesclerks) or in highly skilled blue-collar jobs (say, as building contractors). Household income is between $40,000 and $80,000 a year, which is roughly the national average.

Middle-class people accumulate a small amount of wealth over the course of their working lives (half of all U.S. households now own at least some stock and other investments). Yet most wealth for middle-class people is likely to be in the form of a house. Middle-class men and women are likely to be high school graduates, but the odds are just fifty-fifty that they will complete a college degree, generally at a less expensive, state-supported school.

THE WORKING CLASS

About one-third of the population is working class (sometimes called the *lower-middle class*). In Marxist terms, the working class forms the core of the industrial proletariat. Their blue-collar jobs usually yield a family income between $25,000 and $40,000 a year,

For decades, farm families who worked hard could expect to fall within the U.S. middle class. But the trend toward large-scale agribusiness has put the future of the small family farm in doubt. While many young people in rural areas are turning away from farming toward other careers, some carry on, incorporating high technology into their farm management in their determined efforts to succeed.

somewhat below the national average, and they have little or no wealth. Working-class families thus are vulnerable to financial problems caused by unemployment or illness.

Many working-class jobs provide little personal satisfaction—requiring discipline but rarely imagination—and subject workers to constant supervision. These jobs also offer fewer benefits, such as medical insurance and pension plans. About half of working-class families own their own homes, usually in lower-cost neighborhoods. College is a goal that only about one-third of working-class children realize.

THE LOWER CLASS

The remaining 20 percent of our population constitutes the lower class. Low income makes their lives unstable and insecure. In 2000, the federal government classified 31.1 million people (11.3 percent of the population) as poor. Millions more, called the "working poor," are just barely better off, holding low-prestige jobs that provide not only little satisfaction but close to minimum wage. Barely half manage to complete high school, and only one in four reaches college.

Society segregates the lower class, especially when the poor are racial or ethnic minorities. About 40 percent of lower-class families own their own homes, typically in the least desirable neighborhoods. Although poor neighborhoods usually are found in the inner cities, lower-class families also live in rural communities, especially across the South.

THE DIFFERENCE CLASS MAKES

September 2, Mount Vernon, Ohio. My bike leans right, leaving the trail for the rest station that offers a stretch and a drink of water. Here I encounter Linda, a thirty-something woman having trouble with her roller blades. Eye contact and a perplexed look are a call for help, so I walk over to see what I might do. Several of her boot buckles need adjustment. Close up, she doesn't look well. "Are you OK?" I ask gently. "Very tired," Linda responds, and goes on to explain why. Now divorced, she cannot pay off her debts with one low-income job. So she works an 11 A.M. to 7 P.M. shift as a computer clerk at a bank in town, catches four hours of sleep, and then drives an hour to Columbus, where she sits at another computer, processing catalog orders from 2 A.M. until 10 A.M. That leaves just enough time to drive back to Mount Vernon to start all over again at the bank.

Social stratification affects nearly every dimension of our lives. We will briefly examine some of the ways social standing is linked to our health, values, politics, and family life.

HEALTH

Health is closely related to social standing. Children born into poor families are three times more likely to die from disease, neglect, accidents, or violence during their first years of life than children born to rich families. Among adults, people with above-average incomes are twice as likely as low-income people to describe their health as excellent. Moreover, richer people live, on average, seven years longer because they eat more nutritious food, live in safer and less stressful environments, and receive better medical care (U.S. National Center for Health Statistics, 1999).

VALUES

Cultural values also vary from class to class. The "old rich" have an unusually strong sense of family history because their social position is based on wealth passed down from generation to generation (Baltzell, 1979b). With their birthright privileges, upper-uppers also favor understated manners and tastes, whereas many "new rich" practice *conspicuous consumption*, buying things they know others will notice. They use clothes, homes, cars, and even airplanes to make a statement about their social position.

Affluent people with more education and financial security also are more tolerant of controversial behavior such as homosexuality. Working-class people, who grow up in an atmosphere of greater supervision and discipline and are less likely to attend college, tend to be less tolerant (Kohn, 1977; NORC, 2001).

POLITICS

Political affiliations flow along class lines. By and large, more privileged people support the Republican party, and people with fewer advantages favor the Democrats.

But issue by issue, the pattern is more complex. A desire to protect their wealth prompts well-off people to be more conservative on *economic* issues, favoring, for example, lower taxes. But on *social* issues, such as abortion and other feminist concerns, highly educated, affluent people are more liberal. People of lower social standing, on the other hand, tend to be economic liberals, favoring expanded government social programs, but support a more conservative social agenda (Erikson, Luttbeg, & Tedin, 1980; NORC, 2001).

Another clear pattern emerges when it comes to political involvement. Higher-income people, who are better served by the system, are more likely to vote and to join political organizations than people in the lower class.

FAMILY AND GENDER

Social class also shapes family life. Most lower-class families are somewhat larger than middle-class families because of earlier marriage and less use of birth control. In addition, working-class parents encourage children to conform to conventional norms and respect authority figures. Parents of higher social standing

Compared to high-income people, low-income people are half as likely to report good health and, on average, live about seven fewer years. The toll of low income—played out in inadequate nutrition, little medical care, and high stress— is easy to see on the faces of the poor, who look old before their time.

transmit a different "cultural capital" to their children, teaching them to express their individuality and imagination. In both cases, parents are looking to the future: The odds are that less privileged children will take jobs that require them to closely follow rules, whereas more advantaged children will enter fields that require more creativity (Kohn, 1977; McLeod, 1995).

Of course, the more money a family has, the better parents can develop their children's talents and abilities. For example, an affluent family earning $95,800 a year will spend $241,770 raising a child born in 2000 to the age of eighteen. Middle-class people, with an income of $50,600 a year, will spend $165,630, and a lower-income family earning less than $38,000 will spend about $121,230 (Lino, 2001). Privilege, then, tends to beget privilege as family life reproduces the class structure in each generation.

Industrial class systems provide the opportunity for social mobility—both upward and downward. Typically, social mobility is modest and gradual. Sociologists track this change by comparing the social standing of people in different generations of the same family—for example, in the achievement of a son that makes his father proud.

Class also shapes our world of relationships. Elizabeth Bott (1971) found that most working-class couples divide their responsibilities according to gender; middle-class couples, by contrast, are more egalitarian, sharing more activities and expressing greater intimacy. More recently, Karen Walker (1995) discovered that working-class friendships typically provide material assistance; middle-class friendships, however, are likely to involve shared interests and leisure pursuits.

SOCIAL MOBILITY

Ours is a dynamic society marked by significant social movement. Earning a college degree, landing a higher-paying job, or marrying someone who earns a high income contributes to *upward social mobility;* dropping out of school, losing a job, or divorce (especially for women) may signal *downward social mobility.*

Over the long term, though, social mobility is not so much a matter of individual changes as changes in society itself. During the first half of the twentieth century, for example, industrialization expanded the U.S. economy, pushing up living standards. Even without being very good swimmers, so to speak, people rode a rising tide of prosperity. More recently, *structural social mobility* in a downward direction has dealt many people economic setbacks.

Sociologists distinguish between shorter- and longer-term changes in social position. **Intragenerational social mobility** is *a change in social position occurring*

during a person's lifetime. **Intergenerational social mobility,** *upward or downward social mobility of children in relation to their parents,* is important because it usually reveals long-term changes in society that affect almost everyone.

MYTH VERSUS REALITY

In few societies do people think about "getting ahead" as much as in the United States. After all, moving up is the American Dream. But is there as much social mobility as we like to think?

Studies of intergenerational mobility (almost all of which, unfortunately, have focused exclusively on men) show that almost 40 percent of the sons of blue-collar workers attain white-collar jobs and almost 30 percent of sons born into white-collar families end up doing blue-collar work. *Horizontal mobility*—a change of occupation at one class level—is even more common, so that about 80 percent of sons show at least some type of social mobility in relation to their fathers (Blau & Duncan, 1967; Featherman & Hauser, 1978; Hout, 1998).

Research points to four general conclusions about social mobility in the United States:

1. **Social mobility, at least among men, has been fairly high.** The widespread belief that social mobility in the United States is high is true. Mobility is what we would expect in an industrial class system.

2. **The long-term trend in social mobility has been upward.** Industrialization, which greatly expanded the U.S. economy, and the growth of white-collar work over the course of the twentieth century have boosted living standards.

3. **Within a single generation, social mobility usually is small.** Most young families increase their income over time (Duncan et al., 1998). Yet only a very few people move "from rags to riches." Although sharp rises or falls in individual fortunes may attract the media, social mobility usually involves limited movement *within* one class level rather than striking moves *between* classes.

4. **Social mobility since the 1970s has been uneven.** Real income (that is, adjusted for inflation) rose steadily during the twentieth century until the 1970s, when it hit a plateau. During the 1980s, real income changed little for many people, rising slowly by the end of the 1990s.

MOBILITY BY INCOME LEVEL

General trends often mask the experiences of different categories of people. Figure 11–4 shows how U.S. families at different income levels fared between 1980 and 2000. Well-to-do families (the highest 20 percent, but not all the same families over the entire period) saw their incomes jump 59 percent, from an average $97,991 in 1980 to $155,531 in 2000. People in the middle of the population saw more modest gains of about 20 percent during this time, while the lowest-income 20 percent saw a smaller gain of only 11.5 percent.

For families at the top of the income scale (the highest 1 percent), the last fifteen years have been a windfall. These families, with an average income of $132,451 in 1980, were earning $500,000 in 2000, almost four times as much (Edmondson, 1995; Nielsen & Alderson, 1997; U.S. Census Bureau, 2001).

MOBILITY: RACE, ETHNICITY, AND GENDER

White people, in a more privileged position to begin with, have been more upwardly mobile in recent decades than people of African or Hispanic ancestry. Through the economic expansion of the 1980s and 1990s, many more African Americans entered the ranks of the wealthy. But the real income of African Americans overall has changed little in two decades. African Americans earned only a slightly greater share of average white family income in 2000 (64 percent) as in 1970 (61 percent). Compared with non-Hispanic

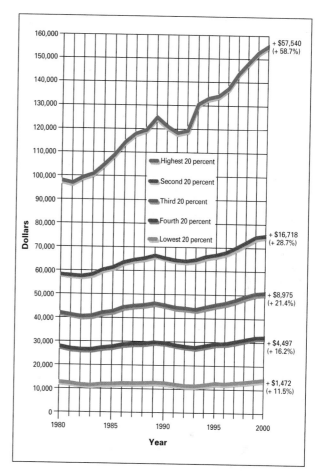

FIGURE 11–4 Mean Income, U.S. Families, 1980–2000 (in 2000 dollars, adjusted for inflation)

Source: U.S. Census Bureau (2001).

white families, Latinos lost ground between 1975 (when their average income was 67 percent of white family income) and 2000 (when it had fallen to 66 percent) (Featherman & Hauser, 1978; Pomer, 1986; U.S. Bureau of the Census, 2001).

Historically, women have had less opportunity for upward mobility than men because most working women hold clerical jobs (such as secretary) and service positions (say, serving food in a restaurant) that offer few promotions. In addition, when marriages end in divorce (as almost half do), women commonly experience downward social mobility; they lose not only income but a host of benefits, including health care and insurance coverage (Weitzman, 1996).

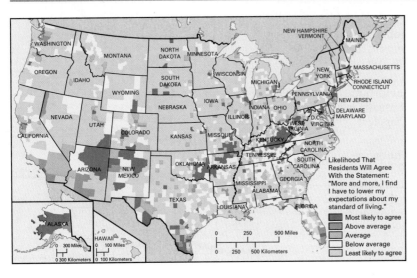

NATIONAL MAP 11–1
"Fear of Falling"
across the United States

This map shows, by county, how likely people are to agree with the statement "More and more, I find I have to lower my expectations about my standard of living." What characterizes regions (including Appalachia in Kentucky and West Virginia) where pessimism is high? But pessimism is pronounced not only in poor rural areas. In rich cities, including New York, Chicago, and Los Angeles, people are also afraid of losing their jobs.

Source: *American Demographics* magazine, February 1994, p. 60, Reprinted with permission. © 1994, *American Demographics* magazine, Ithaca, New York. Data from Yankelovich *Monitor* and Clarita's *Prizm* system.

Over time, however, the earnings gap between women and men has been narrowing. Women working full time in 1980 earned 60 percent as much as men working full time; by 2000, women earned 74 percent as much. Unfortunately, some of the change was due to a *drop* in men's earnings through the 1980s while women's income stayed about the same (U.S. Census Bureau, 2001).

THE AMERICAN DREAM: STILL A REALITY?

The expectation of upward social mobility is deeply rooted in our culture. Through most of our history, economic expansion fulfilled this promise by raising living standards. But about 1970 this upward trend leveled off, starting a period of income stagnation for many families that has shaken our national confidence. Note these recent trends:

1. **For many workers, earnings have stalled.** The annual income of a fifty-year-old man working full time climbed more than 50 percent between 1958 and 1974 (from $22,849 to $37,747 in constant 2000 dollars). Between 1974 and 2000, however, this worker's income rose only slightly, even as the number of hours worked increased and the cost of necessities such as housing,

education, and medical care went up (Russell, 1995a; U.S. Census Bureau, 2001).

2. **Multiple job-holding is up.** According to the Bureau of Labor Statistics, 4.7 percent of the U.S. labor force worked at two or more jobs in 1975; by 2000, the share had risen to 5.6 percent.

3. **More jobs offer little income.** In 1979, the Census Bureau classified 12 percent of full-time workers as "low-income earners" because they made less than $6,905; by 1998, this segment increased to 15.4 percent, earning less than the comparable figure of $15,208.

4. **Young people are remaining at home.** Fully 53 percent of young people aged eighteen to twenty-four are living with their parents. Since 1975, the average age at marriage has moved upward three years (to 25.0 years for women and 26.7 years for men).

In sum, over the last generation, the rich have become richer. Moreover, the number of rich people has also increased, to at least 5 million millionaires in the United States, four times the number a decade ago (D'Souza, 1999). So, for some at least, the American Dream is alive and well. But most are less optimistic about the future, and a significant share worry that the

FIGURE 11–5 Median Income, U.S. Families, 1950–2000

Source: U.S. Census Bureau (2001).

chance for a middle-class life is slipping away (Kerckhoff, Campbell, & Winfield-Laird, 1985; Newman, 1993). National Map 11–1 shows where in the United States pessimism about the future is most widespread.

Dubbed the *middle-class slide*, this downward structural mobility came along with a rising share of low-pay jobs. As Figure 11–5 shows, although median family income doubled between 1950 and 1973, it has grown by only 25 percent since then (U.S. Census Bureau, 2001).

THE GLOBAL ECONOMY AND U.S. CLASS STRUCTURE

Underlying the recent shifts in U.S. class structure is global economic change. Much of the industrial production that gave U.S. workers high-paying jobs a generation ago has moved overseas. With less industry at home, the United States now serves as a vast market for industrial goods such as cars and popular items such as stereos, cameras, and computers made in Japan, Korea, and elsewhere.

High-paying jobs in manufacturing, held by 26 percent of the U.S. labor force in 1960, support only 15 percent of workers today. In their place, the economy now offers service work, which often pays far less. A traditionally high-paying corporation such as USX (formerly United States Steel) now employs fewer people than McDonald's. Meanwhile, McDonald's continues to expand, and fast-food clerks make only a fraction of what steel workers earn.

The global reorganization of work is not bad news for everyone. On the contrary, the global economy creates upward social mobility for educated people who specialize in areas such as law, finance, marketing, and computer technology. Moreover, global economic expansion has helped push up the stock market (even with the recent declines) almost tenfold between 1980 and 2000, reaping profits for families with money to invest.

But the same trend has hurt many "average" workers who have seen their factory jobs disappear. Moreover, many companies have "downsized"—cut the ranks of their work force, blue-collar and white-collar alike—

FIGURE 11–6 The Poverty Rate in the United States, 1960–2000

Source: U.S. Census Bureau (2001).

to become competitive in world markets. As a result, although half of all households contain two or more workers—twice the share in 1950—many people are working harder simply to hold on to what they have (Reich, 1989, 1991; Nelson, 1998; Schlesinger, 1998; Sennett, 1998).

POVERTY IN THE UNITED STATES

Social stratification creates both "haves" and "have-nots." All systems of social inequality create poverty, or at least **relative poverty,** *the deprivation of some people in relation to those who have more.* A more serious but preventable problem is **absolute poverty,** *a deprivation of resources that is life threatening.*

As Chapter 12 ("Global Stratification") explains, upwards of 1 billion human beings—one in six—are at risk of absolute poverty. Even in the affluent United States, families go hungry, live in inadequate housing, and suffer poor health because of wrenching poverty.

THE EXTENT OF U.S. POVERTY

In 1964, the federal government established an official *poverty line* and began counting the poor and offering certain benefits. The idea was to identify people living close to absolute poverty. Mollie Orshansky, the architect of the poverty line, described it as the income needed "to purchase a nutritionally adequate diet on the assumption that no more than a third of the family income is used for food" (1969:38). In other words, the poverty threshold is three times what the government estimates people must spend to eat. The government sets the exact dollar amount according to family size, with annual adjustments to reflect the changing cost of living.

Figure 11–6 shows the official poverty rate as calculated annually since 1960. During the 1960s, poverty fell sharply, but there has been little overall change in the rate since. In 2000, the government tallied 31.1 million men, women, and children—11.3 percent of the U.S. population—as poor. Another 12.3 million people—the *near poor*—lived on income no greater than 125 percent of the poverty threshold.

For a family of four, the 2000 poverty line was set at $17,603. But the income of the average poor family was much lower—just $10,783. This means that the typical poor family must get by on about 60 percent of poverty-line income (U.S. Census Bureau, 2001).

Poor people know very well the consequences of living on the edge: not being able to afford the jackets or expensive sneakers their children want so badly and, worse, worrying about what will happen if one of the family becomes injured or ill. In short, poverty means a life of daily stress, insecurity, and—for several million adults and children in the United States—hunger.

WHO ARE THE POOR?

Although the poor fit no single stereotype, certain categories of our population are at high risk of poverty. Where these categories overlap, the problem is especially serious.

Age

A generation ago, it was the elderly who were at greatest risk for poverty, but no longer. From 30 percent in 1967, the poverty rate for seniors over the age of sixty-five fell to 10.2 percent in 2000, or 3.4 million elderly poor. The elderly now have a poverty rate below the national average because of better

In the 1952 painting Laundress, *U.S. artist George Tooker captures the humanity and humility of impoverished people. This message—that the poor are human beings, most doing the best they can to get by—is important to remember in a society that tends to define poor people as morally unworthy and deserving of their bitter plight.*

George Tooker (b. 1920), *Laundress*, 1952. Oil on gesso panel, 23 1/2 × 24 in. (59.7 × 61 cm). Christie's Images, N.Y. © George Tooker.

retirement programs from private employers and better government benefits. Even so, with the number of older people increasing, about 11 percent of the poor are elderly people.

Today, the burden of poverty falls most heavily on children. In 2000, 16.2 percent of people under age eighteen (11.6 million children) were poor. Tallied another way, nearly four in ten of the U.S. poor are children under the age of eighteen. The poverty problem contributes to the high *infant mortality rate*, a measure of how likely children are to survive their first year of life. Despite being the richest country in the world, the United States has one of the highest infant mortality rates among high-income nations. The box on page 288 takes a closer look at child poverty in the United States.

Race and Ethnicity

Two-thirds of all poor people are white; 25 percent are African Americans. But in relation to their overall numbers, African Americans are about three times as likely as non-Hispanic whites to be poor. In 2000, 22.1 percent of African Americans (7.7 million people) lived in poverty, compared to 21.2 percent of Hispanics (7.5 million), 10.8 percent of Asians and Pacific Islanders (1.1 million), and 7.5 percent of non-Hispanic white people (13.2 million). The poverty gap between whites and minorities has changed little since 1975 (U.S. Census Bureau, 2001).

Gender and Family Patterns

Of all poor people over age eighteen, 61 percent are women and 39 percent are men. This disparity reflects the fact that women who head households bear the brunt of poverty. Of all poor families, 50 percent are headed by women with no husband present, while just 8 percent of poor families are headed by single men.

The term **feminization of poverty** describes *the trend by which women represent an increasing proportion of the poor*. In 1960, 25 percent of all poor families were headed by women; the majority of poor families had

U.S. Children: Bearing the Burden of Poverty

We cringe at the sight of starving children in Somalia, the war-torn African nation where the average person struggles to live on less than $200 per year. But child poverty in the United States may be an even greater tragedy because ours is such a rich nation, with more than 100 times the per capita income of Somalia. Applying the sociological perspective, what can we learn about child poverty in the United States?

To begin, one in six (16.2 percent) U.S. children under age eighteen is poor—almost 12 million boys and girls. This is the same number as almost forty years ago, when the government began its "war on poverty." National Map 11–2 shows that the problem of child poverty is greatest across the South.

Like that of poverty in general, the risk of child poverty varies within our population. Whereas 9 percent of non-Hispanic white children are poor, 28 percent of Latino children and 31 percent of African American youngsters are poor.

From another angle, 63 percent of poor children are white, 30 percent are African American, and 4 percent are Asian; 29 percent of poor children are culturally Hispanic. But although poor children are a diverse lot, they share one trait: They all live in households with low income.

To explain the problem of child poverty, researchers point to the rising share of single-parent households. Today, about eight in ten poor children live in a household with a single mother. In the same share of cases, this household has no full-time worker.

The reasons for poverty are complex and controversial. But everyone agrees that children are not to blame. Tragically, however, this is precisely where the burden of poverty falls. Practically speaking, reducing child poverty is certainly cheaper than dealing with its later effects, including lower achievement in school and higher risk of drug use and crime. Whether we look at this issue from a moral or a practical standpoint, can we permit our society's most vulnerable members to suffer this way?

What do you think?

1. *National Map 11–2 shows that the problem of child poverty is greatest across the southern and southwestern United States. Why do you think this is the case?*

2. *More than twice as many poor children are white as are black. Does this surprise you? Why or why not?*

3. *Why, in your opinion, does the United States have such a high level of child poverty? What do you think U.S. society could do to address this problem?*

SEEING OURSELVES

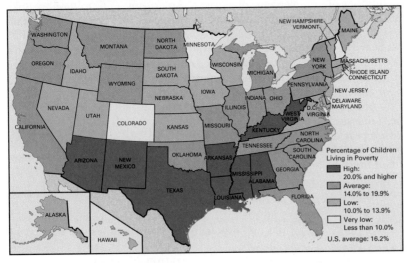

Percentage of Children Living in Poverty

- High: 20.0% and higher
- Average: 14.0% to 19.9%
- Low: 10.0% to 13.9%
- Very low: Less than 10.0%

U.S. average: 16.2%

NATIONAL MAP 11–2 Child Poverty across the United States

Source: U.S. Census Bureau (2001).

Sources: Children's Defense Fund (1995), Duncan et al. (1998), and U.S. Census Bureau (2001).

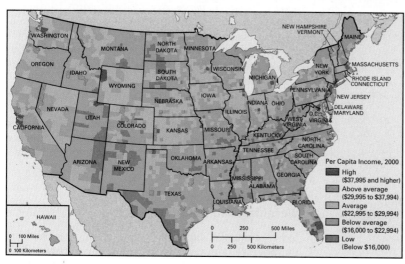

NATIONAL MAP 11–3
Per Capita Income across the United States, 2000

This map shows the median per-person income (that is, how much money, on average, a person has to spend) for the more than 3,000 counties that make up the United States for the year 2000. The richest counties, shown in dark green, are not spread randomly across the country. Nor are the poorest U.S. counties, which are shown in dark red. Looking at the map, what patterns do you see in the distribution of wealth and poverty across the United States? Do these patterns support our assertion linking affluence to urban living and poverty to rural places?

Per Capita Income, 2000

- High ($37,995 and higher)
- Above average ($29,995 to $37,994)
- Average ($22,995 to $29,994)
- Below average ($16,000 to $22,994)
- Low (Below $16,000)

both wives and husbands in the home. By 2000, however, the share of poor families headed by a single woman had doubled to 50 percent.

The feminization of poverty is thus part of a larger change: the rapidly increasing number of households at all class levels headed by single women. This trend, coupled with the fact that households headed by women are at high risk of poverty, is why women (and their children) make up an increasing share of the U.S. poor.

Urban and Rural Poverty

The greatest concentration of poverty is found in central cities, where the 2000 poverty rate stood at 16.1 percent. Suburbs also have destitute people, but their poverty rate is just 7.8 percent. Thus, the poverty rate for urban areas as a whole is 10.8 percent—a bit lower than the 13.4 percent found in rural areas. National Map 11–3 presents income levels across the United States and shows where poverty is most pronounced.

EXPLAINING POVERTY

For the richest nation on earth to have tens of millions of poor people raises serious questions. It is true, as

some analysts remind us, that many of the people counted among the officially poor in the United States are far better off than the poor in other countries:

 A report on food scarcity in the United States is found at this Internet address: http://www.econ.ag.gov/epubs/pdf/fanrr2/fanrr2.pdf

41 percent of U.S. poor families own their home (with an average of three bedrooms and a garage), 60 percent have a clothes washer, 70 percent own a car, and 97 percent have a color television. Moreover, only a few percent report often going without food (Rector, 1998; Gallagher, 1999). Nevertheless, millions of people in the United States have too little income to lead healthy lives.

Figure 11–7 on page 290 shows that the U.S. public is divided over what to do about poverty. One-fourth of respondents to this national survey look to the government to help poor people; slightly more than that think people must take responsibility for themselves. Almost 42 percent straddle the fence, thinking both government and individuals share this responsibility.

We now focus on two different explanations for poverty. Together, they lead to a lively and important political debate.

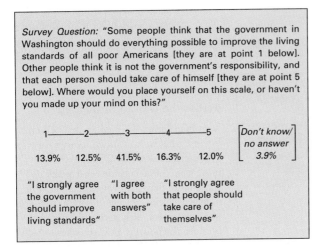

FIGURE 11–7 Government or Individuals: Who Is Responsible for Poverty?

Source: NORC (2001:311).

One View: Blame the Poor

One approach holds that *the poor are mostly responsible for their own poverty.* Throughout our history, people in the United States have valued self-reliance and believed that social standing is mostly a matter of individual talent and effort. This view sees society offering plenty of opportunity to anyone able and willing to take advantage of it. Thus, anyone who is poor either cannot or will not work. These are people with few skills, little schooling, and little motivation. This argument represents the right side of the continuum in Figure 11–7.

In a study of Latin American cities, the anthropologist Oscar Lewis (1961) concluded that the poor become trapped in a *culture of poverty,* a lower-class subculture that can destroy people's ambition. Socialized in poor families, children become resigned to their plight, producing a self-perpetuating cycle of poverty.

In 1996, hoping to break the cycle of poverty in the United States, Congress changed the welfare system that had provided federal funds to assist poor people since 1935. Now the federal government sends money to the states to give to needy people, but benefits carry strict time limits: in most cases, no more than two years at a stretch and a total of five years if a person moves in and out of the welfare system. The objective is to move people from depending on the government to supporting themselves.

Counterpoint: Blame Society

Another position, argued by William Julius Wilson (1996a, 1996b; Mouw, 2000), holds that *society is primarily responsible for poverty.* Wilson points to the loss of jobs in the inner cities as the primary cause of poverty, claiming that there is simply not enough work to support families. Thus, Wilson sees any lack of trying on the part of poor people as a *result of little opportunity* rather than a *cause of poverty.* From this point of view, Oscar Lewis's analysis amounts to blaming the victims for their own suffering (Ryan, 1976). The view that looks to government to overcome poverty is at the left side of the continuum in Figure 11–7. The box provides a closer look at Wilson's argument and how it would shape public policy.

Weighing the Evidence

What evidence supports one side or the other of the poverty controversy? Government statistics show that 48 percent of the heads of poor households did not work at all during 2000, and an additional 32 percent worked only part time (U.S. Census Bureau, 2001). Such facts seem to support the "blame the poor" side because one major cause of poverty is *not holding a job.*

But the *reasons* that people do not work seem more consistent with the "blame society" position. Middle-class women may be able to combine working and child rearing, but this is much harder for poor women who cannot afford child care, and few employers provide child-care programs for their employees. Moreover, as William Julius Wilson explains, many people are idle not because they are avoiding work but because there are not enough jobs. In short, most poor people in the United States find few options (Popkin, 1990; Schiller, 1994; Edin & Lein, 1996; Wilson, 1996a; Pease & Martin, 1997; Duncan, 1999).

The Working Poor

But not all poor people are jobless, and the *working poor* command the sympathy and support of people on both sides of the poverty debate (Schwartz & Volgy, 1992). In 2000, 20 percent of poor heads of households (1.3 million women and men) worked at least fifty weeks of the year and yet could not escape poverty. Another 32 percent of these heads of families (2.1 million people) remained poor despite part-time employment. Put differently, about 3 percent of

When Work Disappears: The Result Is Poverty

The U.S. economy has created tens of millions of new jobs in recent decades. Yet African Americans who live in inner cities have faced a catastrophic loss of work. William Julius Wilson points out that while people continue to talk about welfare reform, neither major political party (Democrats or Republicans) has said anything about the lack of work in central cities.

With the loss of inner-city jobs, Wilson continues, for the first time in U.S. history a large majority of the adults in our inner cities are not working. Studying the Washington Park area of Chicago, Wilson found a troubling trend. Back in 1950, most adults in the African American community had jobs, but by the mid-1990s, two-thirds did not. As one elderly woman who moved to the neighborhood in 1953 explains,

> When I moved in, the neighborhood was intact. It was intact with homes, beautiful homes, mini-mansions, with stores, laundromats, with Chinese cleaners. We had drugstores. We had hotels. We had doctors over on 39th Street. We had doctor's offices in the neighborhood. We had the middle class and the upper-middle class. It has gone from affluent to where it is today. (1996b:28)

But *why* has this neighborhood declined? Wilson's eight years of research point to one answer: There are barely any jobs. It is the loss of work that has pushed people into desperate poverty, weakened families, and made people turn to welfare. In nearby Woodlawn, Wilson identified more than 800 businesses that operated in 1950; today, just 100 remain. Moreover, a number of major employers a generation ago—including Western Electric and International Harvester—closed their plant doors in the late 1960s. The inner cities have fallen victim to economic change, including downsizing and jobs being moved overseas.

Wilson paints a grim picture. But he also believes there is an answer: Create jobs. Wilson proposes attacking the problem in stages. First, the government could hire people to do all kinds of work, including clearing slums and putting up new housing. Such a program, modeled on the Works Progress Administration (WPA) enacted in 1935 during the Great Depression, would move people from welfare to work and create much-needed hope. In addition, federal and state governments must improve schools by imposing performance standards and providing more funding. Of special importance is teaching

children language skills and computer skills to prepare them for the jobs being created by the Information Revolution. Improved regional public transportation would connect cities (where people need jobs) and suburbs (where most jobs are). In addition, more child-care programs would help single mothers and fathers balance the responsibilities of parenting and work.

Wilson claims that his proposals are well grounded in research. But he knows politics revolves around other considerations as well. For one thing, to the extent that the public *thinks* there are plenty of jobs, they will conclude that the poor are simply avoiding work, making any change unlikely. Moreover, he concedes that his proposals, at least in the short term, are more expensive than continuing to funnel welfare assistance to jobless communities.

But for the long term, he asks, what are the costs of allowing our cities to decay while suburbs prosper? Of allowing a new generation of preschoolers to join the ranks of the restless and often angry people for whom there is no work? What would be the benefits of affording everyone the hope and satisfaction that are supposed to define our way of life?

What do you think?

1. *According to Wilson, why are many of this country's inner-city neighborhoods so poor?*

2. *What does he think we can do to address this problem?*

3. *Do you agree with his analysis of poverty? Why or why not?*

Source: Based on Wilson (1996b).

About 2.4 million people in the United States work full time yet do not earn enough to escape poverty. These laundry workers in San Francisco's Chinatown earn $7 per hour, about $14,500 per year, in one of the most expensive cities in the country.

heads of families, people of color, people isolated from the larger society in inner-city areas—who face special barriers and limited opportunities.

HOMELESSNESS

There is no precise count of homeless people. Fanning out across the cities of the United States on the night of March 27, 2000, in a one-day tabulation of homeless people Census Bureau officials tallied 170,706 people at emergency and homeless shelters. But experts agree that a full count of the homeless might reach 500,000 *on any given night*, with as many as three times that number—1.5 million people—homeless *at some time during the course of a year* (Kozol, 1988; Wright, 1989; U.S. Census Bureau, 2000; Wickham, 2000).

The familiar stereotypes of homeless people—men sleeping in doorways and women carrying everything they own in a shopping bag—have been replaced by the "new homeless": people thrown out of work because of plant closings, those forced out of apartments by rent increases or condominium conversions, and others unable to meet mortgage or rent payments because of low wages or no work at all. Today, no stereotype paints a complete picture of the homeless.

Most homeless people report that they do not work, but 44 percent say they work at least part-time (HUD, 1999). But working or not, virtually all homeless people have one thing in common: *poverty*. For that reason, the explanations of poverty already offered also apply to homelessness. Some blame the *personal traits* of the homeless themselves. One-third of homeless people are substance abusers, and one-fourth are mentally ill. More broadly, it should not be surprising that a fraction of 1 percent of

 Find the HUD report on homelessness at http://www.huduser.org/publications/homeless/homelessness/contents.html

our population, for one reason or another, is unable to cope with our complex and highly competitive society (Bassuk, 1984; Whitman, 1989).

Others see homelessness resulting from *societal factors*, including low wages and a lack of low-income housing (Kozol, 1988; Schutt, 1989; Bohannan, 1991). Supporters of this position point out that one-third of all homeless people are entire families, and children are the fastest-growing category of the homeless. A minister in a Pennsylvania town that has lost hundreds of industrial jobs because of plant closings describes the real-life effects of economic recession:

full-time workers earn so little that they remain poor (U.S. Census Bureau, 2001). In short, the working poor suffer from low income because they work too few hours and earn low wages. Keep in mind that a full-time worker making $6 (above the minimum wage of $5.15 per hour) cannot lift an urban family of four above the poverty line.

To sum up, individual ability and personal initiative do play a part in shaping everyone's social position. However, the weight of sociological evidence points to society—not individual character traits—as the primary cause of poverty. Society must be at fault because the poor are *categories* of people—female

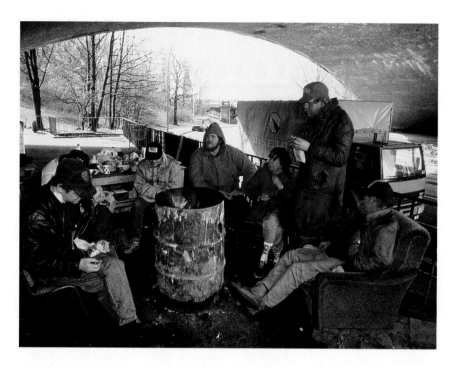

Homelessness is found throughout the United States as well as other high-income nations. Here, homeless people gather under a bridge in Hamburg, Germany. Why do you think that the public tends not to view homelessness (and, more generally, poverty) as a serious social problem?

Yes, there are new jobs. There's a new McDonald's and a Burger King. You can take home [enough to] barely pay the rent. What do you do if someone gets sick? What do you do for food and clothes? These may be good jobs for a teenager. Can you ask a thirty-year-old man who's worked for GM since he was eighteen to keep his wife and kids alive on jobs like that? There are jobs cleaning rooms in the hotel. . . . Can you expect a single mother with three kids to hold her life together with that kind of work? (Kozol, 1988:6)

No one disputes that a large proportion of homeless people are personally impaired to some degree, but how much is cause and how much is effect is difficult to untangle. Structural changes in the U.S. economy, coupled with reduced aid to low-income people and a real estate market that puts housing out of reach of low-income people, all contribute to homelessness (Ratnesar, 1999).

Most homeless people live in urban areas. A Housing and Urban Development (HUD) study of more than 4,000 poor people across the United States, most of them homeless at the time they were interviewed, reports that 92 percent are urban: 71 percent reside in central cities and 21 percent live in suburbs.

Just 8 percent live in rural areas (HUD, 1999). Rural homelessness is not only less common but also less visible. As one volunteer in a rural Ohio county explains, "Here, you don't see people sleeping in a park or under a bridge" (Splain, 2000:1a). Yet social services agencies in this small county (of 15,000 people) serve about 400 people a year. Some are transients, moving from place to place; some are living with friends or relatives; and some are sleeping in a car. This varied pattern explains why people who live in rural areas may not be aware that they, too, have homeless in their communities.

 A report by the U.S. Conference of Mayors on homelessness in this country is found at http://www.usmayors. org/uscm/news/press_releases/ documents/hunger_121101.asp

We close this chapter with a look at welfare, a topic that focuses our thinking about how to respond to issues such as poverty and homelessness.

Finally, social stratification extends far beyond the borders of the United States. In fact, the most striking social inequality is found not within any one nation but in the different living standards among nations of the world. In Chapter 12, we broaden our investigation of social stratification by looking at global inequality.

CONTROVERSY & DEBATE

The Welfare Dilemma

In 1996, Congress ended the federal public assistance that guaranteed some income to all poor people. Now state-run programs require that people receiving aid enroll in a job training program or find work—or have their benefits cut off.

Almost no one likes public assistance, or welfare. Liberals criticize welfare for doing too little to help the poor, conservatives charge that it hurts the people it is supposed to help, and the poor themselves find welfare a complex and often degrading program.

So what exactly *is* welfare? The term "welfare" refers to a host of policies and programs designed to improve the well-being of the U.S. population. Until the welfare reform of 1996, most people used the term to refer to one part of the overall system: Aid for Dependent Children (AFDC), a program of monthly financial support to parents (mostly single women) to care for themselves and their children. In 1996, some 5 million households received AFDC for some part of the year.

Did AFDC help or hurt the poor? There are two sides to the debate. Conservative critics argue that rather than reducing child poverty, AFDC actually made the problem worse for two reasons. First, this form of welfare weakened families by subsidizing living single as an alternative to marriage. For years, poor mothers received benefits *only if no husband lived in the home*. As conservatives saw it, therefore, AFDC was an economic incentive to women to have children outside marriage

and one reason for the increase in out-of-wedlock births among poor people. Conservatives see a clear connection between being poor and not being married: Fewer than one in ten married-couple families were poor; more than nine in ten families receiving AFDC were headed by an unmarried woman.

Second, conservatives also believe that welfare made poor people dependent on government handouts rather than working to support themselves. This, they say, is the main reason that eight of ten poor heads of households did not have steady, full-time jobs. Furthermore, more than half of nonpoor, single mothers worked full-time, compared to only 5 percent of single mothers receiving AFDC. Conservatives sum up by concluding that welfare strayed from its original purpose of giving temporary help to women with children (typically, after divorce or death of a husband) until they could find work. Instead, welfare became a way of life. Once trapped in dependency, poor

Do welfare programs such as food stamps do too much, or too little, to help the poor?

women are likely to raise children who will be poor as adults.

Liberals charge that their opponents use a double standard in evaluating government programs. Why, they ask, do people object to government money going to poor mothers and children when most "welfare" actually goes to relatively rich people? The AFDC budget was $25 billion annually—no small sum, to be sure, but just half of the $50 billion in home mortgage interest deductions that homeowners pocket each year. And it pales in comparison to the $300 billion in annual Social Security benefits Uncle Sam provides to senior citizens, most of whom are quite well-off. And what about "corporate welfare" to big companies? Their tax write-offs and other benefits amount to hundreds of billions of dollars a year. As liberals see it, "wealthfare" is far greater than "welfare."

Second, liberals claim that conservatives have a distorted picture of public assistance. The popular image of do-nothing "welfare queens" masks the fact that most poor families who turn to public assistance are truly needy. Moreover, the typical household receiving AFDC received barely $400 per month, hardly enough to attract people to a "life of welfare dependency." And, in constant dollars, AFDC payments actually declined over recent decades. In fact, liberals fault public assistance as a "Band-Aid approach" to the serious social problems of too few jobs and too much income inequality in the United States.

When natural disasters strike high-income countries, such as Hurricane Andrew that devasted much of southern Florida in 1992, property loss is great but the loss of life is low. In low-income countries, by contrast, the converse is true; the death toll from Hurricane Mitch's rampage through Honduras in 1998 reached 5,000.

recognize more than thirty official languages. But these societies share an industrial capacity that generates, on average, a rich material life for their people. Per capita income ranges from about $10,000 annually (in Slovakia and Saudi Arabia) to more than $25,000 annually (in the United States and Norway).[1] In fact, people in high-income countries enjoy more than half the world's total income.

Production in rich nations is capital-intensive; that is, it is based on factories, big machinery, and advanced technology. High-income countries also stand at the forefront of the Information Revolution; not only do these countries have the most computer users, but they are headquarters for most of the largest corporations that design and market computers. In addition, high-income countries control the world's financial markets, so that daily events on the financial exchanges of New York, London, and Tokyo affect people throughout the world.

[1]High-income countries have per capita annual income of at least $10,000. For middle- and low-income countries, the comparable figures are $2,500 to $10,000 and $2,500 and less. All data reflect the United Nations' concept of "purchasing power parities," which avoids distortion caused by exchange rates when converting currencies to U.S. dollars. Instead, the data represent the local purchasing power of each nation's currency.

MIDDLE-INCOME COUNTRIES

Middle-income countries have per capita income ranging between $2,500 and $10,000, roughly the median for the world's *nations* (but above that for the world's *people* because most people live in the poorest countries). Two-thirds of the people live in cities, and industrial jobs are common. The remaining one-third of the people live in rural areas, where most are poor and lack access to schools, medical care, adequate housing, and even safe drinking water.

Looking back at Global Map 1–2 (page 6), we see that about ninety of the world's nations fall in the middle-income category. At the high end are Chile (Latin America), South Africa (Africa), and Malaysia (Asia), where annual income is about $8,500. At the low end are Ecuador (Latin America), Albania (Europe), Egypt (Africa), and Indonesia (Asia) with roughly $3,000 annually in per capita income.

One cluster of middle-income countries includes the former Soviet Union and the nations of Eastern Europe (in the past, known as the Second World). These countries had mostly socialist economies until popular revolts between 1989 and 1991 swept aside their governments. Since then, these nations have begun to introduce market systems, but so far the results have been uneven. Some (including Estonia) have improving economies, whereas living standards in others (including Russia) have fallen.

Japan represents the world's high-income countries, in which industrial technology and economic expansion have produced material prosperity. The presence of market forces is evident in this view of downtown Tokyo (above, left). The Russian Federation represents the middle-income countries of the world. Industrial development and economic performance were sluggish under socialism; as a result, Moscow residents had to wait in long lines for their daily needs (above, right). The hope is that the introduction of a market system will raise living standards, although in the short run, Russian citizens must adjust to increasing economic disparity. Bangladesh (left) represents the world's low-income countries. As the photograph suggests, these nations have limited economic development and rapidly increasing populations. The result is widespread poverty.

A second, and larger, category of middle-income nations includes Chile and Brazil in South America, and Algeria and Botswana in Africa. Although South Africa's white minority lives as well as people in the United States, the country is considered less developed because its majority black population has far less income.

Taken together, middle-income countries span roughly 47 percent of the earth's land area and include about 3.3 billion people, or more than one-half of humanity. Some countries (such as Russia) are far less crowded than others (such as El Salvador), but compared with high-income countries, these societies are densely populated.

LOW-INCOME COUNTRIES

Low-income countries, where most people are very poor, are largely agrarian societies with some industry. Most of these sixty nations, identified in Global

Map 1–2, are found in Africa and in southern Asia. Low-income countries cover 28 percent of the planet's land area and are home to 28 percent of its people. Population density is generally high, although it is greater in Asian countries (such as Bangladesh and India) than in central African nations (such as Chad and the Democratic Republic of the Congo).

In poor countries, 31 percent of the people live in cities; most inhabit villages and farms, living much as their families have for centuries. In fact, half the world's people are peasants who, by and large, follow cultural traditions. With limited industrial technology, peasants are not very productive, one reason that many endure severe poverty. Hunger, disease, and unsafe housing frame the lives of the world's poorest people.

People living in affluent nations such as the United States find it hard to grasp the scope of human want in much of the world. From time to time, televised pictures of famine in very poor countries such as Ethiopia and Bangladesh give us a shocking glimpse of the poverty that makes every day a life-and-death struggle. Behind these images lie cultural, historical, and economic forces that we explore in the remainder of this chapter.

GLOBAL WEALTH AND POVERTY

<u>October 14, Manila, the Philippines.</u> What caught my eye was how clean she was—a girl no more than seven or eight years old. She was wearing a freshly laundered dress, and her hair was carefully combed. She followed us with her eyes: Camera-toting Americans stand out in this neighborhood, one of the poorest in the entire world.

Fed by methane from decomposing garbage, the fires never go out on Smokey Mountain, the vast garbage dump on the north side of Manila (referred to in the chapter opener). Smoke envelopes the hills of refuse like a thick fog. But Smokey Mountain is more than a dump; it is a neighborhood that is home to thousands of people. The residents of Smokey Mountain are the poorest of the poor. It is hard to imagine a setting more hostile to human life. Amid the smoke and the squalor, men and women do what they can to survive. They pick plastic bags from the garbage and wash them in the river and collect cardboard boxes or anything else they can sell. And all over Smokey Mountain are children who must already sense the enormous odds against them. What chance do they have, living in families that earn scarcely a few hundred dollars a year? With barely any opportunity for schooling? Year after year, breathing this air?

Against this backdrop of human tragedy, one lovely little girl has put on a fresh dress and gone out to play.

Now our taxi driver threads his way through heavy traffic as we head for the other side of Manila. The change is amazing: The smoke and smell of the dump give way to neighborhoods that could be in Miami or Los Angeles. On the bay in the distance floats a cluster of yachts. No more rutted streets; now we glide quietly along wide boulevards lined with trees and filled with expensive Japanese cars. We pass shopping plazas, upscale hotels, and high-rise office buildings. Every block or so we see the gated entrance to an exclusive residential enclave with security guards standing watch. Here, in large, air-conditioned homes, the rich of Manila live and many of the poor work.

A visit to the Philippines, which is a middle-income nation, or (even more so) India, which is a low-income country, reveals the striking extent of poverty. Indeed, in much of the world, most of the population gets by on incomes of barely several hundred dollars a year. Clearly, this means that the burden of poverty is far greater than among the poor of the United States. This is not to suggest that poverty at home is a minor problem. In so rich a country, too little food, substandard housing, and no medical care for tens of millions of people—almost half of them children—amount to a national tragedy. Yet poverty in poor countries is both *more severe* and *more extensive* than in the United States.

THE SEVERITY OF POVERTY

Poverty in poor countries is more severe than it is in rich countries. The data in Table 12–1 on page 304 show why. The first column of figures gives gross domestic product (GDP) for representative high-, middle-, and low-income countries.[2] The United States, a large

---

[2]Gross domestic product (GDP) includes all the goods and services on record as produced by a country's economy in a given year, excluding income earned outside the country by individuals or corporations. Gross national product (GNP) adds in the foreign earnings. For countries that invest heavily abroad (Kuwait, for example), GDP is much smaller than GNP; for countries in which other nations invest heavily (Hong Kong), GDP is much greater than GNP. For countries that both invest heavily abroad and have high foreign investment at home (including the United States), the two measures are about the same.

TABLE 12–1 Wealth and Well-Being in Global Perspective, 1999

Country	Gross Domestic Product ($ billion)	GDP per Capita (PPP$)*	Quality of Life Index
High Income			
Norway	153	28,433	.939
Australia	404	24,574	.936
Canada	635	26,251	.936
Sweden	239	22,636	.936
United States	9,152	31,872	.934
Japan	4,347	24,898	.928
France	1,432	22,897	.924
United Kingdom	1,442	22,093	.923
South Korea	407	15,712	.875
Middle Income			
Eastern Europe			
Poland	155	8,450	.828
Lithuania	11	6,656	.803
Russian Federation	401	7,473	.775
Ukraine	39	3,458	.742
Latin America			
Mexico	484	8,297	.790
Venezuela	102	5,495	.765
Brazil	752	7,037	.750
Asia			
Malaysia	79	8,209	.774
Thailand	124	6,132	.757
China, P.R.	990	3,617	.718
Middle East			
Iran	111	5,531	.714
Syria	19	4,454	.700
Africa			
Algeria	48	5,063	.693
Botswana	6	6,872	.577
Low Income			
Latin America			
Honduras	5	2,340	.634
Haiti	4	1,464	.467
Asia			
India	447	2,248	.571
Bangladesh	46	1,483	.470
Africa			
Democratic Republic of the Congo	6	801	.429
Guinea	4	1,934	.397
Ethiopia	6	628	.321
Sierra Leone	1	448	.258

*These data are the United Nations' purchasing power parity calculations, which avoid currency rate distortion by showing the local purchasing power of each domestic currency.

Source: United Nations Development Programme, *Human Development Report, 2001* (New York: Oxford University Press, 2001).

industrial nation, had a 1999 GDP of more than $9 trillion; Japan's GDP was more than $4 trillion. Comparing GDP figures shows that the world's richest nations are thousands of times more productive than the poorest countries.

The second column of figures in Table 12–1 indicates per capita GDP in terms of what the United Nations (1995) calls "purchasing power parities"—what people can buy using their income in the local economy. The per capita GDP for rich countries such as the United States, France, and Canada is very high— more than $20,000. For middle-income countries, such as Botswana and Lithuania, the figures are much lower—about $6,500. In the world's low-income countries, per capita annual income is just a few hundred dollars. In the Democratic Republic of the Congo or in Ethiopia, for example, a typical person labors all year to make what the average worker in the United States earns in several days.

The last column of Table 12–1 measures quality of life in these nations. This index, calculated by the United Nations, is based on income, education (extent of adult literacy and average years of schooling), and longevity (how long people typically live). Index values are decimals that fall between hypothetical extremes of 1 (highest) and zero (lowest). By this calculation, Norwegians enjoy the highest quality of life (.939), with residents of the United States close behind (.934). At the other extreme, people in the African nation of Sierra Leone have the lowest quality of life (.258).

One reason that quality of life differs so much around the world is that economic productivity is lowest in precisely the regions of the globe where population growth is highest. Figure 12–2 shows the division of global population and global income for countries at each level of economic development. High-income countries are by far the most advantaged, with 79 percent of global income supporting just 18 percent of humanity. In middle-income nations, 54 percent of the world's people earn 18 percent of global income. This leaves 28 percent of the planet's population with just 3 percent of global income. In short, for every dollar received by individuals in a low-income country, someone in a high-income nation takes home $41.

Relative versus Absolute Poverty

The distinction between relative and absolute poverty, made in Chapter 11, has an important application to global inequality. People living in rich countries generally focus on *relative poverty*, meaning that some people lack resources that others take for granted. Relative poverty, by definition, cuts across every society, rich or poor.

More important in global perspective, however, is *absolute poverty*, a lack of resources that is life threatening. Human beings in absolute poverty lack the nutrition necessary for health and long-term survival. To be sure, some absolute poverty exists in the United States. But such immediately life-threatening poverty strikes only a small proportion of the U.S. population; in low-income countries, by contrast, one-third or more of the people are in desperate need.

Because absolute poverty is deadly, one global indicator of this problem is median age at death. Global Map 12–1 on page 306 identifies the age by which half of all people born in a nation die. In rich societies, most people die after age seventy-five; in poor countries, half of all deaths occur among children under age ten.

THE EXTENT OF POVERTY

Poverty in poor countries is more extensive than it is in rich nations such as the United States. Chapter 11 ("Social Class in the United States") indicated that the U.S. government officially classifies about 11 percent of the population as poor. In low-income countries, however, most people live no better than the poor in the

 Read a report on world hunger by the Food and Agriculture Organization of the United Nations: http://www.fao.org/NEWS/1999/img/SOFI99-E.PDF

United States, and many are far worse off. As Global Map 12–1 shows, the high death rates among children in Africa indicate that absolute poverty is greatest there, where half the population is malnourished. In the world as a whole, at any given time, 15 percent of the people (about 1 billion) suffer from chronic hunger, which leaves them less able to work and puts them at high risk of disease (Kates, 1996; United Nations Development Programme, 2001).

The typical adult in a rich nation, such as the United States, consumes about 3,500 calories a day, an excess that contributes to obesity and related health problems. The typical adult in a low-income country not only does more physical labor but consumes just 2,000 calories a day. The result is undernourishment: too little food or not enough of the right kinds of food.

In the ten minutes it takes to read this section of the chapter, about 300 people in the world who are sick and weakened from hunger will die. This amounts to about 40,000 people a day, or 15 million people

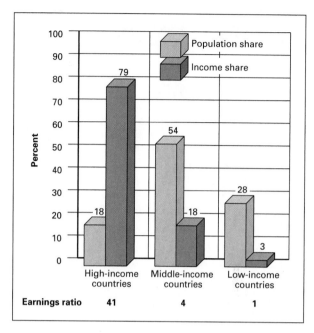

FIGURE 12–2 The Relative Share of Income and Population by Level of Economic Development

Sources: Calculated by the author based on United Nations Development Programme (2000) and The World Bank (2001).

each year. Clearly, easing world hunger is one of the most serious responsibilities facing humanity in the twenty-first century.

POVERTY AND CHILDREN

Death comes early in poor societies, where families lack adequate food, safe water, secure housing, and access to medical care. Organizations combating child poverty estimate that at least 100 million city children in poor countries beg, steal, sell sex, or work for drug gangs to provide income for their families. Such a life almost always means dropping out of school and puts children at high risk of disease and violence. Many girls, with little or no access to medical assistance, become pregnant: a case of children who cannot support themselves being forced to have still more children.

About 100 million of the world's children leave their families altogether, sleeping and living on the streets as best they can. Roughly half of all street children are found in Latin America (United Nations

GLOBAL MAP 12–1 Median Age at Death in Global Perspective

This map identifies the age below which half of all deaths occur in any year. In the high-income countries of the world, including the United States, it is mostly the elderly who face death—that is, people age seventy-five or older. In middle-income countries, including most of Latin America, most people die years or even decades earlier. In low-income countries, especially in Africa and parts of Asia, it is children who die, half of them never reaching their tenth birthday.

Sources: The World Bank (1993); map projection from *Peters Atlas of the World* (1990).

Development Programme, 2000). Some 10,000 homeless children roam throughout Mexico City alone (Ross, 1996). In Brazil, millions of street children live in makeshift huts, under bridges, or in alleyways. In Rio de Janeiro, known to many in the United States as Brazil's seaside resort, police try to keep the numbers of street children in check; at times, death squads may sweep

Tens of millions of children fend for themselves on the streets of Latin America, where many fall victim to disease, drug abuse, and outright violence. What do you think must be done to put an end to scenes like this one in San Salvador, the capital city of El Salvador?

through a neighborhood in a bloody ritual of "urban cleansing." Reports indicate that several hundred street children are murdered in that city each year (Larmer, 1992; U.S. House of Representatives, 1992).

POVERTY AND WOMEN

In rich societies, the work women do typically is unrecognized, undervalued, and underpaid. In poor societies, this is even more the case. Workers in sweatshops—factories that make much of the clothing and other products consumed in rich countries, including the United States—are mostly women.

At this site, read about a woman who spent six years working in a sweatshop in Saipan producing clothing for sale by the Gap in the United States: http://www.globalexchange.org/education/speakers/CarmencitaChieAbad.html

Families in poor societies depend on women's income. At the same time, tradition bars many women from attending school and gives them primary responsibility for raising children and maintaining the household. The United Nations estimates that in poor countries, men own 90 percent of the land, a far greater gender disparity in wealth than that in high-income nations. Thus, about 70 percent of the world's 1 billion people living near absolute poverty are women (Hymowitz, 1995).

Women in poor countries have limited access to birth control (which, in turn, raises the birth rate), and they typically give birth without the assistance of trained health personnel. Figure 12–3 on page 308 draws a stark contrast between low- and high-income countries in this regard.

SLAVERY

Poor societies are vulnerable to many problems: hunger, illiteracy, warfare, and slavery. The British Empire banned slavery in 1833; the United States followed suit in 1865. But according to Anti-Slavery International (ASI), as many as 400 million men, women, and children (almost 7 percent of humanity) live today in conditions that amount to slavery (Janus, 1996).

ASI distinguishes four types of slavery. In *chattel slavery*, one person owns another. The number of chattel slaves is difficult to estimate because this practice is against the law almost everywhere. Nevertheless, the buying and selling of slaves still takes place in many countries in Asia, the Middle East, and especially

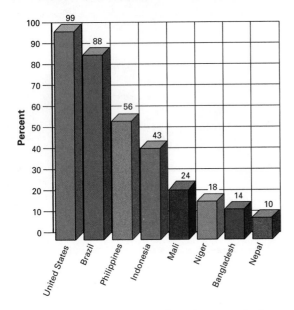

FIGURE 12–3 Percentage of Births Attended by Trained Health Personnel

Source: The World Bank (2001).

Africa. The box describes the reality of one slave's life in the African nation of Mauritania.

A second, more common form of bondage is *child slavery.* Desperately poor families make their children take to the streets to fend for themselves. Perhaps 100 million children—many in poor countries of Latin America—fall into this category.

Third, *debt bondage* is the practice by which employers hold workers by paying them too little to cover their debts. In this case, workers receive wages but not enough to cover the food and housing the employer provides. Thus, for practical purposes, they are enslaved. Many workers in sweatshops in poor countries fall into this category (McCarthy, 1998).

Fourth, *servile forms of marriage* may also amount to slavery. In India, Thailand, and some African nations, families marry off women against their will. Many end up as slaves working for their husband's family; some are forced into prostitution.

 Read the United Nations' Universal Declaration of Human Rights at http://www.un.org/rights/50/decla.htm

In 1948, the United Nations issued its Universal Declaration of Human Rights, which states; "No one shall be held in slavery or servitude; slavery and the slave trade shall be prohibited in all their forms." Unfortunately, more than fifty years later, this social evil persists.

CORRELATES OF GLOBAL POVERTY

What accounts for the severe and extensive poverty throughout much of the world? The rest of this chapter weaves together explanations from the following facts about poor societies:

1. **Technology.** About one-quarter of people in low-income countries farm the land using human muscle or beasts of burden. Because these energy sources fall far short of the force of steam, oil, or nuclear power, only limited use of complex machinery is possible.

2. **Population growth.** As Chapter 22 ("Population, Urbanization, and Environment") explains, the poorest countries have the world's highest birth rates. Despite the death toll from poverty, the populations of poor countries in Africa, for example, double every twenty-five years. In these countries, half the people are teenagers or younger. With such numbers entering their childbearing years, a wave of population growth will roll into the future. In recent years, for example, the population of Chad swelled by 3.3 percent annually, so that even with economic development living standards have fallen.

3. **Cultural patterns.** Poor societies usually are traditional. Adhering to long-established ways of life, people resist innovation, even if it promises a richer material life. The box on page 310 explains why traditional people in India respond to their poverty differently than poor people in the United States.

4. **Social stratification.** Low-income societies distribute their wealth very unequally. Chapter 10 ("Social Stratification") explained that social inequality is more pronounced in agrarian societies than in industrial societies. In Brazil, for example, half of all farmland is owned by just 1 percent of the people (Bergamo & Camarotti, 1996).

5. **Gender inequality.** Extreme gender inequality in poor societies deprives women of opportunities,

GLOBAL SOCIOLOGY

"God Made Me to Be a Slave"

Fatma Mint Mamadou is a young woman living in North Africa's Islamic Republic of Mauritania. Asked her age, she pauses and smiles. She has no idea when she was born. Nor can she read or write. What she knows is tending camels, herding sheep, hauling bags of water, washing clothes, sweeping, and serving tea to her owners. This young woman is one of perhaps 90,000 slaves in Mauritania.

In the central region of this nation, having dark brown skin almost always means being a slave to an Arab owner. Fatma accepts her situation; she has known nothing else. She explains in a matter-of-fact voice that she is a slave as was her mother before her. And her grandmother before that. "Just as God created a camel to be a camel," she shrugs, "he created me to be a slave."

Fatma, her mother, and her brothers and sisters live in a squatter settlement on the edge of Nauakchott, Mauritania's capital city. Their home is a nine- by twelve-foot hut that they built from wood scraps and other materials taken from construction sites. The roof is nothing more than a piece of cloth; there is no plumbing or furniture. The nearest water comes from a well a mile down the road.

Human slavery continues to exist in the twenty-first century.

In this region, slavery began 500 years ago, about the time Columbus sailed west toward the New World. Then, as Arab and Berber tribes moved across the region spreading Islam, they raided local villages and made slaves of the people. So it has been for dozens of generations ever since. In 1905, the French colonial rulers of Mauritania banned slavery. After the nation gained independence in 1961, the new government banned slavery once again. But such proclamations have done little to change strong traditions. Indeed, people like Fatma have no idea what freedom to choose means.

The next question is more personal: "Are you and other girls ever raped?" Again, Fatma hesitates. With no hint of emotion, she responds, "Of course, in the night the men come to breed us. Is that what you mean by rape?"

Source: Based on Burkett (1997).

which typically means they have many children. An expanding population, in turn, slows economic development. Thus, many analysts conclude, raising living standards in much of the world depends on improving the social standing of women.

6. **Global power relationships**. A final cause of global poverty lies in the relationships between the nations of the world. Historically, wealth flowed from poor societies to rich nations through **colonialism**, *the process by which some nations enrich themselves through political and economic control of other nations.* The countries of Western Europe colonized much of Latin America and Africa beginning roughly 500 years ago.

Such global exploitation allowed some nations to develop economically at the expense of other nations.

Although 130 former colonies gained their independence during the twentieth century, exploitation continues through **neocolonialism** (*neo* is the Greek word for "new"), *a new form of global power relationships that involves not direct political control but economic exploitation by multinational corporations.* **Multinational corporations**—*huge businesses that operate in many countries*—wield tremendous economic power. Corporate decision makers often impose their will on countries where they do business, just as colonizers did in the past.

A Different Kind of Poverty: A Report from India

Most North Americans know that India is one of the poorest nations on Earth. A vast country with per capita gross domestic product (GDP) of only $2,248 a year (see Table 12–1), India is home to one-third of all the world's hungry people.

But most North Americans do not readily understand the reality of poverty in India. Most of the country's 1 billion people live in conditions far worse than those our society labels "poor." A traveler's first experience of Indian life can be shocking. Madras, one of India's largest cities with 7 million inhabitants, seems chaotic to an outsider: streets choked with motorbikes, trucks, carts pulled by oxen, and waves of people. Along the roadway, vendors sit on burlap cloth and hawk fruit, vegetables, and cooked food while people nearby work, talk, bathe, and sleep.

Madras is dotted with thousands of shanty settlements, home to half a million people from rural villages who have come in search of a better life. Shantytowns are clusters of huts built with branches, leaves, and pieces of discarded cardboard and tin. These dwellings offer little privacy and lack refrigeration, running water, and bathrooms. A visitor from the United States may feel uneasy in such an area, knowing that the poorest sections of our own inner cities seethe with frustration and sometimes explode with violence.

But India's people understand poverty differently than we do. No restless young men hang out on corners, no drug dealers work the streets, and there is little danger of violence. In the United States, poverty often means anger and isolation; in India, even

shantytowns are organized around strong families—children, parents, and often grandparents—who offer a smile and a welcome to a stranger.

For traditional people in India, life is shaped by *dharma*, the Hindu concept of duty and destiny that teaches people to accept their fate, whatever it may be. Mother Teresa, who worked among the poorest of India's people, went to the heart of the cultural differences: "Americans have angry poverty," she explained. "In India, there is worse poverty, but it is a happy poverty."

Perhaps we should not describe anyone who clings to the edge of survival as happy. But poverty in India is eased by the strength and support of families and communities, a sense that existence has a purpose, and a worldview that encourages each person to accept whatever life offers. As a result, a visitor may well come away from a first encounter with Indian poverty in confusion: "How can people be so poor and yet apparently content, active, and *joyful*?"

Source: Based on the author's research in Madras, India, November 1988.

GLOBAL STRATIFICATION: THEORETICAL ANALYSIS

There are two major explanations for the unequal distribution of the world's wealth and power: *modernization theory* and *dependency theory*. Each theory suggests a different path toward relieving the suffering of hungry people in much of the world.

MODERNIZATION THEORY

Modernization theory is *a model of economic and social development that explains global inequality in terms of technological and cultural differences between societies.* Modernization theory emerged in the 1950s, a time when U.S. society was fascinated with new technology and many people in poor countries were hostile toward the United States. With the socialist Soviet

Mead studied three societies in New Guinea (1963; orig. 1935). In the mountainous home of the Arapesh, Mead observed men and women with remarkably similar attitudes and behavior. Both sexes were cooperative and sensitive to others—in short, what our culture would label "feminine."

Moving south, Mead then studied the Mundugumor, head-hunters and cannibals who stood in striking contrast to the gentle Arapesh. In this culture, both sexes typically were selfish and aggressive, traits we define as more "masculine."

Finally, traveling west to the Tchambuli, Mead discovered a culture that, like our own, defined females and males differently. But, Mead reported, the Tchambuli reversed many of our notions of gender: Females were dominant and rational, and males were submissive, emotional, and nurturing toward children. Based on her observations, Mead concluded that culture is the key to gender: What one culture defines as masculine, another may consider feminine.

Some critics view Mead's findings as "too neat," as if she saw in these three societies just the patterns she was looking for. Deborah Gewertz (1981) challenged Mead's "reversal hypothesis," claiming that Tchambuli males are really more aggressive and Tchambuli females more submissive. Gewertz explains that Mead visited the Tchambuli (who actually call themselves the Chambri) during the 1930s, after they had lost much of their property in tribal wars. Men working in the home, she claims, was a temporary role for Chambri men.

George Murdock's Research

In a broader study of more than 200 preindustrial societies, George Murdock (1937) found some global agreement on which tasks are feminine and which masculine. Hunting and warfare generally fall to men, and home-centered tasks such as cooking and child care tend to be women's work. With their simple technology, preindustrial societies apparently assign roles reflecting men's and women's physical attributes. With greater size and strength, men hunt game and protect the group; because women bear children, they assume domestic duties.

But beyond this general pattern, Murdock found significant variation. Consider agriculture: Women did the farming in about the same number of societies as men, but in most the two sexes divided this work. When it came to many other tasks—from building shelters to tattooing the body—Murdock found societies of the world were as likely to turn to one sex as the other.

DIVERSITY SNAPSHOT

FIGURE 13–1 Men's and Women's Athletic Performance

Do men naturally outperform women in athletic competition? The answer is not obvious. Early in the twentieth century, men outdistanced women by many miles in marathon races. But as opportunities for women in athletics increased, women have been closing the performance gap. Thirteen minutes separate the current world marathon records for women (set in 2001) and for men (set in 1999).

Sources: *The Christian Science Monitor* (1995) and www.marathonguide.com (2001). Adapted with permission of *The Christian Science Monitor.* © 1995 The Christian Science Publishing Society. All rights reserved.

In Sum: Gender and Culture

Global comparisons show us that societies do not consistently define most tasks as either feminine or masculine. With industrialization, moreover, the importance of muscle power declines, giving people even more options and further reducing gender differences (Nolan & Lenski, 1999). Thus, gender is simply too variable across cultures to be considered a simple expression of

In every society, people assume certain jobs, patterns of behavior, and ways of dressing are "naturally" feminine while others are just as obviously masculine. But in global perspective, we see remarkable variety in such social definitions. These men, Wodaabe pastoral nomads who live in the African nation of Niger, are proud to engage in a display of beauty most people in our society would consider feminine.

biology. Instead, as with many other elements of culture, what it means to be female and male is mostly a creation of society.

PATRIARCHY AND SEXISM

Although conceptions of gender vary, everywhere in the world we find some degree of **patriarchy** (literally, "the rule of fathers"), *a form of social organization in which males dominate females.* Despite mythical tales of societies dominated by female "Amazons," **matriarchy,** *a form of social organization in which females dominate males*, has never been documented in human history (Gough, 1971; Harris, 1977; Lengermann & Wallace, 1985).

Although some degree of patriarchy may be universal, Global Map 13–1 shows significant variation in the relative power and privilege of females and males around the world. According to the United Nations, three Nordic countries—Norway, Sweden, and Finland—afford women the highest social standing. By contrast, women in the central African nations of Niger and Chad, the East African nation of Djibouti, and the Asian nation of Afghanistan have the lowest social standing compared with men. Of the world's nations, the United States ranked eighth in terms of gender equality (United Nations, 1995).

Sexism, *the belief that one sex is innately superior to the other*, is the ideological basis of patriarchy. Sexism is not just a matter of individual attitudes; it is built into the institutions of our society. *Institutional*

sexism is part of the economy, for example, so that women are highly concentrated in low-paying jobs. Similarly, the legal system has long excused violence against women, especially on the part of boyfriends, husbands, and fathers (Landers, 1990).

The Costs of Sexism

Sexism stunts the talents and limits the ambitions of women, who make up half the population. Although men benefit in some respects from sexism, their privilege comes at a high price. Masculinity in our culture calls for men to engage in many high-risk behaviors, including greater use of tobacco and alcohol, participation in physically dangerous sports, and reckless driving, so that motor vehicle accidents are the leading cause of death among young males. Moreover, as Marilyn French (1985) argues, patriarchy compels men to seek control, not only of women but of themselves and their world. Thus, masculinity is closely linked not only to accidents but suicide, violence, and stress-related diseases. The Type A personality—characterized by chronic impatience, driving ambition, competitiveness, and free-floating hostility—is a recipe for heart disease and almost perfectly matches the behavior that our culture considers masculine (Ehrenreich, 1983).

Finally, insofar as men seek control over others, they lose opportunities for intimacy and trust. As one analyst put it, competition is supposed to separate "the men from the boys." In practice, however, it separates men from men and everyone else (Raphael, 1988).

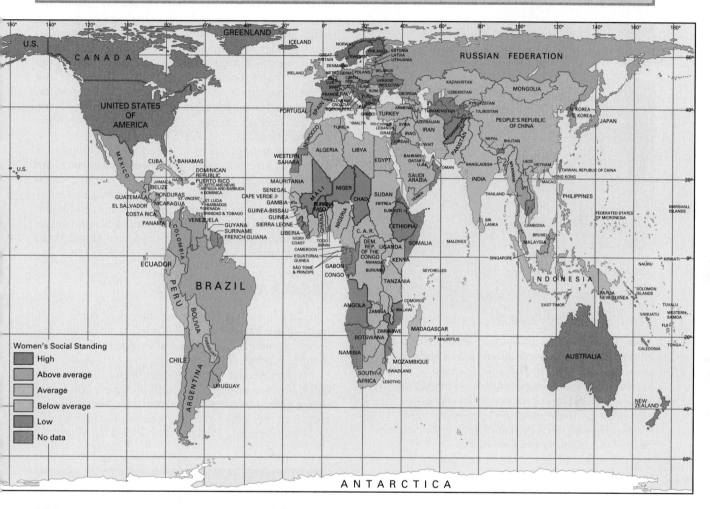

GLOBAL MAP 13–1 Women's Power in Global Perspective

Women's social standing, in relation to men's, varies around the world. In general, women fare better in rich countries than in poor countries. Even so, some nations stand out: In the Nordic nations of Norway, Sweden, and Finland, women come closest to social equality with men.

Source: Data from Seager (1997).

Is Patriarchy Inevitable?

In preindustrial societies, women have little say over pregnancy and childbirth, which limits the scope of their lives. At the same time, men's greater height and physical strength are highly valued resources. But industrialization—and especially the development of birth control technology—gives people choices about how to live. In today's postindustrial societies, such as our own, biological differences offer little justification for patriarchy.

But males are dominant in the United States and elsewhere. Does this mean that patriarchy is

Among the most striking consequences of patriarchy in China is the practice of foot-binding, by which the feet of young girls (especially those of high social position) are tightly wrapped as they grow, with predictable results. Conventional thinking suggests that this practice produces women of "dainty" proportions, but it also greatly limits women's physical mobility. Although rare today, cases of foot binding are still reported and documented with photographs.

inevitable? Some sociologists claim that biological factors set limits on the behavior of the two sexes so that, on average, females and males have different motivations and behaviors, with more aggressiveness in males. To the extent to which this is so, patriarchy may be difficult to eliminate (Goldberg, 1974, 1987; Rossi, 1985; Popenoe, 1993b; Udry, 2000). However, most sociologists believe that gender is a social construct that can be changed. Just because no society has yet eliminated patriarchy does not mean that we must be prisoners of the past.

To understand the persistence of patriarchy, we now examine how gender is rooted and reproduced in society, a process that begins in childhood and continues throughout our lives.

GENDER AND SOCIALIZATION

From birth until death, gender shapes human feelings, thoughts, and actions. Children quickly learn that their society considers females and males different kinds of people; by about age three, they begin to apply gender standards to themselves.

Table 13–1 presents the traits that people in the United States traditionally link to "feminine" and "masculine" behavior. Note the pattern of opposites, even though research suggests that most young people do not develop consistently feminine or masculine personalities (Bernard, 1980; Bem, 1993).

Just as gender affects how we think of ourselves, it teaches us how to act. **Gender roles** (or sex roles) are *attitudes and activities that a society links to each sex.* Insofar as our culture defines males as ambitious and competitive, we expect them to play team sports and aspire to positions of leadership. To the extent that we define females as deferential and emotional, we expect them to be supportive helpers and quick to cry.

GENDER AND THE FAMILY

The first question people usually ask about a newborn—"Is it a boy or a girl?"—looms large because the answer involves not just sex but the likely direction of the child's entire life.

In fact, gender is at work even before the birth of a child, because most parents hope to have a boy rather than a girl. Soon after birth, family members usher infants into the "pink world" of girls or the "blue world" of boys (Bernard, 1981). Parents even send gender

TABLE 13–1 Traditional Notions of Gender Identity	
Feminine Traits	**Masculine Traits**
Submissive	Dominant
Dependent	Independent
Unintelligent and incapable	Intelligent and competent
Emotional	Rational
Receptive	Assertive
Intuitive	Analytical
Weak	Strong
Timid	Brave
Content	Ambitious
Passive	Active
Cooperative	Competitive
Sensitive	Insensitive
Sex object	Sexually aggressive
Attractive because of physical appearance	Attractive because of achievement

Masculinity as Contest

By the time I was ten, the central fact in my life was the demand that I become a man. By then, the most important relationships by which I was taught to define myself were those I had with other boys. I already knew that I must see every encounter with another boy as a contest in which I must win or at least hold my own. . . . The same lesson continued [in school], after school, even in Sunday school. My parents, relatives, teachers, the books I read, movies I saw, all taught me that my self-worth depended on my manliness, my willingness to stand up to the other boys. This usually didn't mean a physical fight, though the willingness to stand up and "fight like a man" always remained a final test. But the relationships between us usually had the character of an armed truce. Girls weren't part of this social world at all yet, just because they weren't part of this contest. They didn't have to be bluffed, no credit was gained by cowing them, so they were more or less ignored. Sometimes when there were no grownups around we would let each other know that we liked each other, but most of the time we did as we were taught.

Source: Silverstein (1977).

messages in the way they handle daughters and sons. One researcher at an English university presented an infant dressed as either a boy or a girl to a number of women; her subjects handled the "female" child tenderly, with frequent hugs and caresses, and the "male" child more aggressively, often lifting him up high in the air or bouncing him on the knee (Bonner, 1984). The lesson is clear: The female world revolves around passivity and emotion, whereas the male world puts a premium on independence and action.

GENDER AND THE PEER GROUP

About the time they enter school, children move outside the family and make friends with others of the same age. Peer groups teach additional lessons about gender. The box explains how play groups shaped one young boy's sense of himself as masculine.

After spending a year watching children at play, Janet Lever (1978) concluded that boys favor team sports with complex rules and clear objectives such as scoring a run or making a touchdown. Such games nearly always have winners and losers, which reinforces masculine traits of aggression and control.

Girls, too, play team sports. But girls also play hopscotch, jump rope, or simply talk, sing, or dance. These activities have few rules, and rarely is "victory" the ultimate goal. Instead of teaching girls to be competitive, Lever explains, female peer groups promote interpersonal skills of communication and cooperation, presumably the basis for girls' future roles as wives and mothers.

Lever's observations recall Carol Gilligan's (1982) gender-based theory of moral reasoning, discussed in Chapter 5 ("Socialization"). Boys reason according to abstract principles, Gilligan contends. For them, "rightness" amounts to "playing by the rules." Girls, on the other hand, consider morality a matter of social responsibility to others. Thus, the games we play have serious implications for our later lives.

GENDER AND SCHOOLING

In high school, more girls than boys learn secretarial skills and take vocational classes such as cosmetology and food service. Classes in woodworking and auto maintenance, conversely, attract mostly young men.

In college, men are disproportionately represented in mathematics and the sciences, including physics, chemistry, and biology. Women cluster in the humanities (such as English), the fine arts (painting, music, dance, and drama), and the social sciences (including anthropology and sociology). New areas of study are also likely to be gender-typed. Computer science enrolls mostly men, for example, whereas courses in gender studies enroll more women.

Pretty Is As Pretty Does: The Beauty Myth

The Duchess of Windsor once quipped, "A woman cannot be too rich or too thin." The first half of her observation might apply to men as well, but certainly not the second. It is no surprise that most ads placed by the $20-billion-a-year cosmetics industry and the $40-billion diet industry target women.

According to Naomi Wolf (1990), our culture promotes a "beauty myth" that is damaging to women. The beauty myth arises, first, because society teaches women to measure themselves in terms of physical appearance (Backman & Adams, 1991). Yet the standards of beauty (such as the *Playboy* centerfold or the 100-pound New York fashion model) are unattainable for most women.

The beauty myth also teaches women to prize relationships with men and to use beauty to attract men. Striving for beauty drives women to be superficial and forces them to be highly attuned and responsive to men. Beauty-minded women try to please men and avoid challenging male power.

The beauty myth affects males as well: Men should want to possess beautiful women. Thus, our ideas about beauty

reduce women to objects and motivate men to possess women as if they were dolls rather than human beings.

In sum, there can be little doubt that the idea of beauty is important in everyday life. The question, according to Wolf, is whether beauty is about how we look or how we act.

What do you think?

1. *We might be tempted to say that physical attraction is simply a biological issue about "looks." How does Wolf's argument make beauty a social issue?*

2. *Do you think the beauty myth is still strong today? What messages about beauty and women does today's advertising send?*

3. *Are men harmed by the beauty myth? If so, how?*

Source: Based on Wolf (1990).

GENDER AND THE MASS MEDIA

Since television first captured the public imagination in the 1950s, white males have held center stage. Racial and ethnic minorities were all but absent from prominent television roles until the early 1970s. Even when both sexes appear on camera, men generally play the brilliant detectives, fearless explorers, and skilled surgeons. Women, by contrast, play the less capable characters, unnecessary except for the sexual interest they add to the story.

Historically, advertisements have presented women in the home, happily using cleaning products, serving food, trying out appliances, and modeling clothes. Men, on the other hand, predominate in ads for cars, travel, banking services, industrial companies, and alcoholic beverages. The authoritative voiceover—the faceless voice that describes a product on television and radio—is almost always male (Courtney & Whipple, 1983; Davis, 1993).

In studying magazine and newspaper ads, Erving Goffman (1979) documented the pattern by which men usually appear taller than women, implying male superiority. Women, he found, were more frequently presented lying down (on sofas and beds) or, like children, seated on the floor. Men's facial expressions exuded competence and authority, whereas women often appeared childlike. While men focused on the

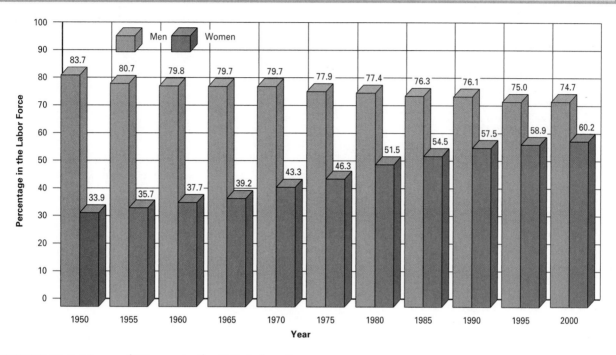

FIGURE 13–2 Men and Women in the U.S. Labor Force
Source: U.S. Department of Labor (2001).

products being advertised, women focused on the men, playing a supportive and submissive role.

In recent years, advertising has portrayed women and men in more equal terms. Still, advertising does not give women a fair shake, actively perpetuating what Naomi Wolf calls the "beauty myth." The box takes a closer look.

GENDER AND SOCIAL STRATIFICATION

Gender implies more than how people think and act. It is also about social hierarchy. The reality of gender stratification can be seen, first, in the world of work.

WORKING WOMEN AND MEN

Back in 1900, just one-fifth of U.S. women were in the labor force. In 2000, as shown in Figure 13–2, 60 percent

of women aged sixteen and over worked for income, and three-fourths of working women worked full time. The traditional view that earning an income is exclusively a man's role no longer holds true.

Factors that have changed the U.S. labor force include the decline of farming as an occupation, the growth of cities, a shrinking family size, and a rising divorce rate. Thus, the United States, along with most other nations of the world, considers women working for income the rule rather than the exception. In fact, 62 percent of U.S. married couples depend on two incomes. As Global Map 13–2 on page 334 shows, women represent almost half of the U.S. work force; however, this is not the case in many of the poorer nations of the world.

In the past, many women in the U.S. labor force were childless. But today, 62 percent of married women with children under age six work for income, as do 77 percent of married women with children between six and seventeen years of age. For divorced

GLOBAL MAP 13–2 Women's Paid Employment in Global Perspective

This map shows the percentage of the labor force made up of women. A country's level of technological development plays an important part here. In 2000, women were 47 percent of the labor force in the United States—up almost 10 percent over the last generation. In high-income nations, overall, nearly one-half of the labor force is made up of women. In poor societies, however, women work even harder than in this country, but they are less likely to be paid for their efforts. In Latin America, for example, women represent about one-third of the paid labor force; in Islamic societies of northern Africa and the Middle East, the figure is significantly lower. One exception to this rule is central and southern Africa, where, traditionally, women make up a large share of farmers.

Sources: *Peters Atlas of the World* (1990); updated by the author from The World Bank (2001).

women with children, the comparable figures are 77 percent of women with younger children and 82 percent of women with older children (U.S. Census Bureau, 2000).

Gender and Occupations

Although the shares of men and women in the labor force have been converging, the work they do remains different. The U.S. Department of Labor (2001) reports that nearly half of working women hold one of two types of jobs. Administrative support work draws 23 percent of working women. These office jobs sometimes are called "pink-collar" jobs because 79 percent are filled by women. Another 16 percent of employed women do service work. Most of these jobs are in food services, child care, and health care.

Table 13–2 shows the ten occupations with the highest concentrations of women. Overall, although more women now work for pay, they remain segregated in the labor force in jobs at the low end of the pay scale, with limited opportunities for advancement, and usually supervised by men (Charles, 1992; Bianchi & Spain, 1996; U.S. Department of Labor, 2001).

Men dominate most other job categories, including the building trades, where 99 percent of brick and stone masons, structural metalworkers, and heavy equipment

Read more about the small number of women in top corporate jobs at http://www.catalystwomen.org/press/factsheets/factscote00.html top

mechanics are men. Likewise, 90 percent of engineers, 83 percent of police officers, 72 percent of physicians, 70 percent of judges and lawyers, and 55 percent of corporate managers are men. According to a recent survey, the top earners in Fortune 500 corporations include 2,162 men and 93 women, or about 4 percent women. Just nine of the 1,000 largest corporations in the United States have a woman as their chief executive officer (Catalyst, 2001; U.S. Department of Labor, 2001).

Gender stratification in the workplace is easy to see: Female nurses assist male physicians, female administrative assistants serve male executives, and female flight attendants are under the command of male airplane pilots. Moreover, in any field, the greater the income and prestige associated with a job, the more likely it is to be held by a man. For example, 98 percent of kindergarten teachers, 83 percent of elementary school teachers, 58 percent of secondary school teachers, 42 percent of college and university professors, and 16 percent of college and university presidents are women (U.S. Department of Labor, 2001).

TABLE 13–2 Jobs with the Highest Concentrations of Women, 2000		
Occupation	Number of Women Employed	Percentage in Occupation Who Are Women
1. Secretary	2,594,000	98.9%
2. Dental hygienist	110,000	98.5
3. Prekindergarten and kindergarten teacher	617,000	98.5
4. Family child-care provider	446,000	97.7
5. Private household child-care worker	268,000	97.5
6. Receptionist	983,000	96.7
7. Dental assistant	210,000	96.4
8. Early childhood teacher's assistant	457,000	95.2
9. Private household cleaner or servant	474,000	94.8
10. Stenographer	146,000	94.7

Source: U.S. Department of Labor, Bureau of Labor Statistics, *Employment and Earnings*, vol. 48, no. 1, January 2001, pp. 178–83.

How are women kept out of certain jobs? By defining some kinds of work as "masculine," companies define women as unsuitable workers. In a study of coal mining in West Virginia, Suzanne E. Tallichet (2000) found that most men considered it "unnatural" for women to work in the mines. Women who did work in the mines were themselves defined as "unnatural" and subject to labeling as "sexually loose" or lesbian. Such labeling made these women outcasts, presented a challenge to holding the job, and made advancement all but impossible.

But one challenge to male domination in the workplace comes from women who are entrepreneurs. Women now own more than 9 million small businesses in the United States, twice the number just a decade ago and more than one-third of the total. Although the majority of women-owned businesses are one-person operations, these businesses employ one-fourth of the entire labor force. By starting their own businesses, women have shown that they can make opportunities for themselves outside larger, male-dominated companies (Ando, 1990; O'Hare & Larson, 1991; Mergenhagen, 1996c; NFWBO, 1996; Winters, 1999; U.S. Department of Labor, 2001).

HOUSEWORK

In the United States, housework has always been a cultural contradiction: We claim that it is essential for

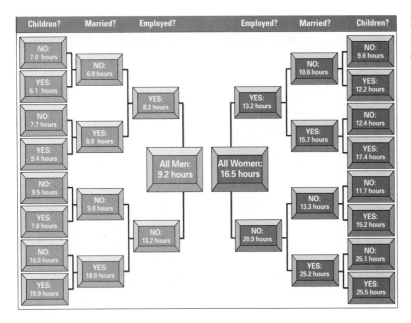

FIGURE 13–3 Housework: Who Does How Much?

Overall, women average 16.5 hours of housework per week, compared to 9.2 hours for men. This pattern holds whether people are employed or not, married or not, and parenting or not.

Source: Adapted from Stapinski (1998).

family life but give housework little prestige or other reward (Bernard, 1981). With women's entry into the labor force, the amount of housework performed by women has declined, but the *share* women do has stayed about the same. Figure 13–3 shows that, overall, women average 16.5 hours a week of housework, compared to 9.2 hours for men. Among all categories of people, the figure shows, women do significantly more housework than men (Stapinski, 1998).

In sum, men support the idea of women entering the labor force, and most count on the money women earn. But most men also resist taking on a more equal share of household duties. Holding primary responsibility for housework is likely to continue to reduce women's available time for paid work or schooling (Cowan, 1992; Robinson & Spitze, 1992; Lennon & Rosenfeld, 1994; Heath & Bourne, 1995; Harpster & Monk-Turner, 1998; Stratton, 2001).

GENDER, INCOME, AND WEALTH

In 2000, the median earnings for women working full time were $27,355, whereas men working full time earned $37,339. This means that, for every dollar earned by men, women earned about 73 cents.

Among full-time workers, 42 percent of women earned less than $25,000 in 2000, compared to 26 percent of comparable men. At the upper end of the income scale, men were three-and-one-half times more

likely than women (14.8 percent versus 4.1 percent) to earn more than $75,000 (U.S. Census Bureau, 2001).

The main reason women earn less is the *kind* of work they do: largely clerical and service jobs. In effect, jobs and gender interact. People still perceive jobs with less clout as "women's work," just as people devalue certain jobs simply because they are performed by women (Parcel, Mueller, & Cuvelier, 1986; Blum, 1991; England, 1992; Bellas, 1994; Huffman, Velasco, & Bielby, 1996; England, Hermsen, & Cotter, 2000).

During the 1980s, proponents of gender equality proposed a policy of comparable worth. That is, people should be paid not according to the historical double standard but according to the worth of what they actually do. Several nations, including Great Britain and Australia, have adopted comparable worth policies, but not the United States. As a result, women in this country lose as much as $1 billion annually.

A second cause of gender-based income disparity has to do with the family. Both men and women have children, of course, but our culture defines parenting as more a woman's duty than a man's. Pregnancy and raising small children keep many younger women out of the labor force at a time when their male peers are making significant career advancements. As a result, women workers have less job seniority than their male counterparts (Fuchs, 1986; Stier, 1996; Waldfogel, 1997).

Moreover, women who choose to have children may be reluctant or unable to maintain fast-paced jobs that tie up their evenings and weekends. To avoid role strain, they may take jobs that offer a shorter commuting distance, more flexible hours, or employer child-care services. Women pursuing both a career and a family are often torn between their dual responsibilities in ways that men are not. Consider what one researcher found: At age forty, 90 percent of men but only 35 percent of women in executive positions have at least one child (F. Schwartz, 1989).

These two factors—type of work and family responsibilities—account for about two-thirds of the earnings disparity between women and men. A third factor—discrimination against women—accounts for most of the remainder (Pear, 1987; Fuller & Schoenberger, 1991). Because discrimination is illegal, it is practiced in subtle ways. Corporate women often encounter a *glass ceiling*, a barrier that is invisible because it is denied by company officials even though it effectively prevents women from rising above middle management (Benokraitis & Feagin, 1995; Yamagata et al., 1997).

For all these reasons, then, women earn less than men in all major occupational categories. As shown in Table 13–3, this disparity varies from job to job, but in only five of the major job classifications do women earn more than 75 percent as much as men.

Finally, perhaps because women typically outlive men, many people think that women own most

 A report by the Department of Labor traces women's earnings over the second half of the twentieth century: http://www.dol.gov/dol/wb/public/wb_pubs/wagegap2000.htm

of this country's wealth. Government statistics tell a different story: Sixty-one percent of individuals with $1 million or more in assets are men, although widows are highly represented in this millionaires' club (U.S. Internal Revenue Service, 2000). Just 12 percent of the people identified in *Forbes* magazine as the richest people in the United States are women.

GENDER AND EDUCATION

In the past, women received little schooling because their lives revolved around the home. But times have changed. By 1980, women earned a majority of all associate and bachelor degrees; in 1998, that proportion stood at 56 percent (U.S. National Center for Education Statistics, 2001).

College doors have opened to women, and differences in men's and women's majors are becoming smaller. In 1970, for example, women earned just

TABLE 13–3 Earnings of Full-Time U.S. Workers,* by Sex, 2000

Selected Occupational Categories	Median Income		Women's Income as a Percentage of Men's
	Men	Women	
Executives, administrators, and managers	$57,162	$36,953	65%
Professional specialties	58,364	39,319	67
Technologists and technicians	46,717	35,818	77
Sales	41,266	25,619	62
Clerical and other administrative support workers	32,622	25,197	77
Precision production, craft, and repair workers	35,197	26,101	74
Machine operators and tenders	28,918	19,196	66
Material moving equipment operators	29,461	25,613	87
Handlers, equipment cleaners, helpers, and laborers	22,157	17,384	78
Service workers	25,052	16,873	67
Farming, forestry, and fishing workers	19,586	17,618	90
All occupations listed above	37,339	27,355	73

*Workers aged 15 and over.
Source: U.S. Census Bureau (2001).

17 percent of bachelor degrees in the natural sciences, computer science, and engineering; by 1998, that proportion had increased to 31 percent.

In 1993, for the first time, women also earned a majority of postgraduate degrees, often a springboard to high-prestige jobs. For all areas of study in 1998, women earned 57 percent of master's degrees and 42 percent of doctorates (including 56 percent of all Ph.D.s in sociology). Women have also broken into many graduate fields that used to be almost all male. For example, in 1970 only a few hundred women received a master's of business administration degree, compared to more than 39,000 in 1998 (39 percent of all such degrees) (U.S. National Center for Education Statistics, 2001).

Men continue to dominate some professional fields, however. In 1998, men received 56 percent of

TABLE 13–4 Significant "Firsts" for Women in U.S. Politics

1869	Law allows women to vote in Wyoming territory; Utah follows suit in 1870.
1872	First woman to run for the presidency (Victoria Woodhull) represents the Equal Rights party.
1917	First woman elected to the House of Representatives (Jeannette Rankin of Montana).
1924	First women elected state governors (Nellie Taylor Ross of Wyoming and Miriam ["Ma"] Ferguson of Texas); both followed their husbands into office. First woman to have her name placed in nomination for vice-presidency at the convention of a major political party (Lena Jones Springs).
1931	First woman to serve in the Senate (Hattie Caraway of Arkansas); completed the term of her husband upon his death and won reelection in 1932.
1932	First woman appointed to the presidential cabinet (Frances Perkins, secretary of labor in the cabinet of President Franklin D. Roosevelt).
1964	First woman to have her name placed in nomination for the presidency at the convention of a major political party (Margaret Chase Smith, a Republican).
1972	First African American woman to have her name placed in nomination for the presidency at the convention of a major political party (Shirley Chisholm, a Democrat).
1981	First woman appointed to the U.S. Supreme Court (Sandra Day O'Connor).
1984	First woman to be successfully nominated for the vice-presidency (Geraldine Ferraro, a Democrat).
1988	First woman chief executive to be elected to a consecutive third term (Madeleine Kunin, governor of Vermont).
1992	Political "Year of the Woman" yields record number of women in the Senate (six) and the House (forty-eight), as well as (1) first African American woman to win election to U.S. Senate (Carol Moseley-Braun of Illinois), (2) first state (California) to be served by two women senators (Barbara Boxer and Dianne Feinstein), and (3) first woman of Puerto Rican descent elected to the House (Nydia Valasquez of New York).
1996	First woman appointed secretary of state (Madeleine Albright).
2000	Record number of women in the Senate (thirteen) and the House (fifty-nine).
2000	First "First Lady" to win elected political office (Hillary Rodham Clinton, senator from New York).

Sources: Based on data compiled from Sandra Salmans, "Women Ran for Office before They Could Vote," *New York Times*, July 13, 1984, p. A11; and news reports.

law degrees, 58 percent of medical degrees, and 62 percent of dental degrees (U.S. National Center for Education Statistics, 2001). Our society still defines high-paying professions (and the drive and competitiveness needed to succeed in them) as masculine; this fact helps explain why an equal number of women and men begin most professional graduate programs, but women are less likely to complete their degrees (Fiorentine, 1987; Fiorentine & Cole, 1992). Nonetheless, the proportion of women in all these professions is rising steadily: For example, the American Bar Association reports that the law school class of 2004 across the United States is about evenly split between women and men (Gest, 2001).

 A report from the National Center for Educational Statistics on gender and education can be found at http://nces.ed.gov/pubs2000/2000030.pdf

GENDER AND POLITICS

A century ago, almost no women held elected office in the United States. In fact, women were legally barred from voting in national elections until passage of the Nineteenth Amendment to the Constitution in 1920. However, a few women were candidates for political office even before they could vote. The Equal Rights party supported Victoria Woodhull for the U.S. presidency in 1872; perhaps it was a sign of the times that she spent election day in a New York City jail. Table 13–4 identifies later milestones in women's gradual movement into political life.

Today, thousands of women serve as mayors of cities and towns across the United States, and tens of thousands hold responsible administrative posts in the federal government. At the state level, 22 percent of legislators in 2001 were women (up from just 6 percent in 1970). National Map 13–1 shows where in the United States women have made the greatest political gains.

Less change has occurred at the highest levels of politics, although a majority of U.S. adults claim they would support a qualified woman for any office, including the presidency. After the 2000 national elections, 5 of the 50 state governors were women (10 percent), and women held 59 of 435 seats in the House of Representatives (14 percent) and 13 of 100 seats (13 percent) in the Senate.

In global perspective, although women are half the Earth's population, they hold just 13.9 percent of seats in the world's 179 parliaments. Although this represents a rise from 3 percent fifty years ago, only in the Nordic nations of Norway, Sweden, Finland, and Denmark (38.7 percent) and Iceland (34.9 percent) and the Netherlands (32.9 percent) does the share of parliamentary seats held by women even approach

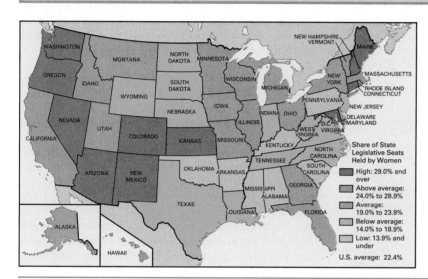

NATIONAL MAP 13–1
Women in State Government across the United States

Although women represent half of U.S. adults, just 22 percent of seats in state legislatures are held by women. Look at the state-by-state variation in the map. In which regions of the country have women gained the greatest political power? What factors do you think account for this pattern?

Source: Center for American Women and Politics, Eagleton Institute of Politics, Rutgers University, "Women in State Legislatures 2001." [Online] Available http://www.rci.rutgers.edu/~cawp/pdf/stleg.pdf, October 23, 2001.

Share of State Legislative Seats Held by Women

High: 29.0% and over
Above average: 24.0% to 28.9%
Average: 19.0% to 23.9%
Below average: 14.0% to 18.9%
Low: 13.9% and under

U.S. average: 22.4%

their share of the population (Inter-Parliamentary Union, 2001).

GENDER AND THE MILITARY

Since colonial times, women have served in the armed forces. Yet in 1940, at the outset of World War II, just 2 percent of armed forces personnel were women. By the 1991 Persian Gulf War, 35,000 women made up 6.5 percent of a total deployment of 540,000 U.S. troops. Five of the 148 Gulf War casualties were women.

In 2001, 15 percent of all armed forces personnel were women. Only the Coast Guard makes all assignments available to women; at the other extreme, the Marine Corps denies women access to two-thirds of its jobs. Those who defend limited roles for women in the military claim that, on average, women lack the physical strength of men. Critics counter that military women are better educated and score higher on intelligence tests than their male counterparts. But the heart of the issue is our society's deeply held view of women as *nurturers*—people who give life and help others—which clashes intolerably with the image of women trained to kill.

Although incorporating women into military culture has been difficult, women in all branches of the

U.S. armed forces are taking on more and more military assignments. One reason is that reliance on high technology blurs the distinction between combat and noncombat personnel. A combat pilot can fire missiles at a radar-screen target miles away, while nonfighting medical evacuation teams go to the battle site (McNeil, 1991; May, Segal, & Hansen, 1992; Wilcox, 1992; Kaminer, 1997).

ARE WOMEN A MINORITY?

Sociologists define a **minority**[2] as *any category of people, distinguished by physical or cultural difference, that a society sets apart and subordinates.* Given the clear economic disadvantage our society imposes on women, it seems reasonable to say that U.S. women are a minority even though they outnumber men.

Subjectively speaking, however, most white women do not think of themselves this way (Hacker, 1951; Lengermann & Wallace, 1985). This is partly because, unlike racial minorities (including African

---

[2]We use the term "minority" instead of "minority group" because, as explained in Chapter 7 ("Groups and Organizations"), a minority is a category, not a group.

Americans) and ethnic minorities (say, Hispanics), white women are well represented at all levels of the class structure, including the very top.

Bear in mind, however, that at every class level, women typically have less income, wealth, education, and power than men. In fact, patriarchy makes women dependent for much of their social standing on men—first their fathers and later their husbands (Bernard, 1981).

MINORITY WOMEN

If women are defined as a minority, what about minority women? Are they doubly handicapped? Generally speaking, they are, as we can show with some income comparisons. Looking first at race and ethnicity, the median income in 2000 for African American women working full time was $25,117, which is 85 percent as much as the $29,604 earned by non-Hispanic white women; Hispanic women earned $20,527—just 69 percent as much as their white, non-Hispanic counterparts. Looking at gender, African American women earned 83 percent as much as African American men, and Hispanic women earned 83 percent as much as Hispanic men.

Combining these disadvantages, African American women earned 61 percent as much as non-Hispanic white men, and Hispanic women earned 50 percent as much (U.S. Census Bureau, 2001). These disparities reflect minority women's lower positions in the occupational and educational hierarchies compared with white women (Bonilla-Santiago, 1990). These data confirm that, although gender has a powerful effect on our lives, it never operates alone. Class position, race and ethnicity, and gender intersect to form a multilayered system of disadvantage for some and privilege for others (Ginsburg & Tsing, 1990; St. Jean & Feagin, 1998).

VIOLENCE AGAINST WOMEN

As noted in the opening to this chapter, the phrase "rule of thumb" entered our language about 150 years ago when common decency prevented a man from beating his wife with a stick thicker than his thumb. Even today, a great deal of "manly" violence is directed at women. A U.S. government report estimates 383,000 sexual assaults against women annually, including 201,000 rapes or attempted rapes. To this number can be added perhaps 2 million physical assaults (Goetting, 1999; U.S. Bureau of Justice Statistics, 2001).

Gender violence is also an issue on college and university campuses. A new report from the Department of Justice (2001) states that in 2000, 1.7 percent of female college students were victims of rape, and another 1.1 percent were victims of attempted rape. In 90 percent of all cases, the victims knew the offenders, and most of the assaults took place in the woman's living quarters.

Off the campus as well, most gender-linked violence occurs where men and women interact most: in the home. Richard Gelles (cited in Roesch, 1984) argues that with the exception of the police and the military the family is the most violent organization in the United States. Both sexes suffer from family violence, although women sustain more serious injuries than men (Straus & Gelles, 1986; Schwartz, 1987; Shupe, Stacey, & Hazlewood, 1987; Gelles & Cornell, 1990; Smolowe, 1994).

Violence against women also occurs in casual relationships. As noted in Chapter 8 ("Deviance"), most rapes involve not strangers but men known and often trusted by the victim. Dianne Herman (2001) believes

 Here is a United Nations report on violence against women and girls around the world: http://www.unicef-icdc.org/publications/pdf/digest6e.pdf

that abuse of women is built into our way of life. All forms of violence against women—from the wolf whistles that intimidate women on city streets to a pinch in a crowded subway to physical assaults that occur at home—express what she calls a "rape culture" of men trying to dominate women. Sexual violence, she explains, is fundamentally about *power*, not sex, and therefore should be understood as a dimension of gender stratification.

In global perspective, violence against women is built into culture in other ways. One case in point is the practice of female genital mutilation, found in some

 This German site provides information on female genital mutilation. http://www.gtz.de/fgm/english/index.html

three dozen countries and known to occur in the United States, as shown in Global Map 13–3. The box on page 342 presents a case of genital mutilation that took place in California.

Sexual Harassment

Sexual harassment consists of *comments, gestures, or physical contact of a sexual nature that are deliberate, repeated, and unwelcome*. During the 1990s, sexual harassment became an issue of national importance that rewrote the rules for workplace interaction.

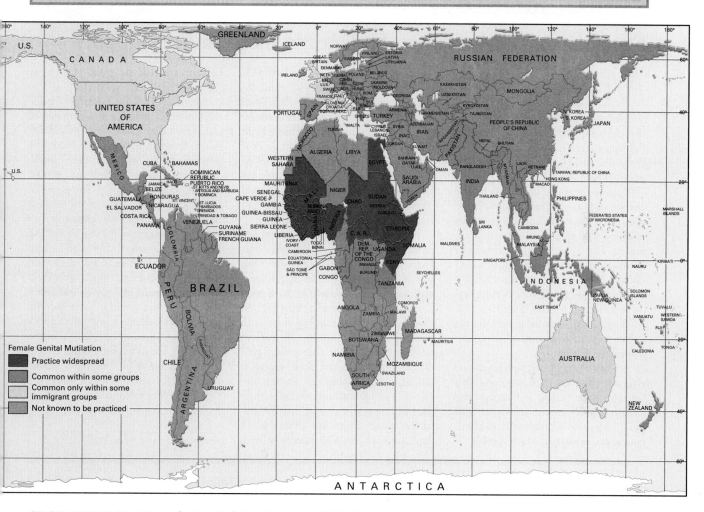

GLOBAL MAP 13–3 Female Genital Mutilation in Global Perspective

Female genital mutilation, also called female circumcision, is known to be performed in more than forty countries around the world. Across Africa, the practice is common and affects a majority of girls in the eastern African nations of Sudan, Ethiopia, and Somalia. In several Asian nations, including India, the practice is limited to a few ethnic minorities. In the United States, Canada, several European nations, and Australia, there are reports of the practice among some immigrants.

Source: Data from Seager (1997).

Most victims of sexual harassment are women. This is because, first, our culture encourages men to be sexually assertive and to perceive women in sexual terms. As a result, social interaction in the workplace, on campus, and elsewhere can readily take on sexual overtones. Second, most people in positions of power—including business executives, physicians, assembly line supervisors, professors, and military officers—are men

Female Genital Mutilation: Violence in the Name of Morality

Meserak Ramsey, a woman born in Ethiopia and now working as a nurse in California, paid a visit to a friend's home. Soon after arriving, she noticed her friend's eighteen-month-old daughter huddled in the corner of a room in obvious distress. "What's wrong?" she asked.

Ramsey was shocked when the woman said her daughter recently had a clitoridectomy, or female circumcision, whereby the clitoris is surgically removed. This procedure—performed by a midwife, a tribal practitioner, or a doctor and typically without anesthesia—is common in two dozen African nations, including Nigeria, Togo, Somalia, and Egypt, and is known to exist among certain cultural groups in other nations around the world.

Among members of highly patriarchal societies, husbands demand that their wives be virgins at marriage and remain sexually faithful thereafter. The point of genital mutilation is to eliminate sexual sensation, which, people as-sume, makes the girl less likely to violate sexual norms and thus be more desirable to men. In about one-fifth of all cases, an even more severe procedure, called infibulation, is performed, in which the entire external genital area is removed and the surfaces are stitched together, leaving only a small hole for urination. Before marriage, a husband retains the right to open the wound and assure himself of his bride's virginity.

How many women have undergone genital mutilation? Worldwide, estimates place the number at more than 100 million. In the United States, hundreds and probably thousands of such procedures are performed every year. In most cases, immigrant mothers and grandmothers who have themselves been mutilated insist that young girls in their family follow their example. Indeed, many immigrant women demand the procedure *because* their daughters now live in the United States, where sexual mores are more lax. "I don't have to worry about her now," one California parent explained to Meserak Ramsey; "She'll be a good girl."

Medically, the consequences of genital mutilation include more than loss of sexual pleasure. Pain is intense and can persist for years. There is also danger of infection, infertility, and even death. Meserak Ramsey underwent genital mutilation as a young girl. She is one of the lucky ones who has had few medical problems since. But the extent of her suffering is suggested by this story: She had invited a young U.S. couple to stay at her home. Late at night, she heard the woman's cries and burst into their room to investigate, only to learn that the couple was making love and the woman had just had an orgasm. "I didn't understand," Ramsey recalls; "I thought that there must be something wrong with American girls. But now I know that there is something wrong with me." Or with a system that inflicts such injury in the name of traditional morality.

Source: Based on Crossette (1995).

---

who oversee the work of women. In surveys carried out in widely different work settings, half of women respondents report receiving unwanted sexual attention (Paul, 1991; NORC, 2001).

Sexual harassment is sometimes blatant and direct: A supervisor solicits sexual favors from a subordinate by threatening reprisal if the advances are refused. Courts have declared such *quid pro quo* sexual harassment (the Latin phrase means "one thing in return for another") a violation of civil rights.

More often, however, sexual harassment involves subtle behavior—sexual teasing, off-color jokes, or pinups displayed in the workplace—that may not even be intended to harass anyone. But under the *effect* standard favored by many feminists, such actions create a hostile environment (Cohen, 1991; Paul, 1991). Incidents of this kind are far more complex because they involve different perceptions of the same behavior. For example, a man may think that complimenting a co-worker on her appearance is simply a friendly gesture; she, on the other hand, may feel his behavior hinders her job performance.

Pornography

Chapter 9 ("Sexuality") defined *pornography* as sexually explicit material that causes sexual arousal. However, people have different views of what is and what is not pornographic. Likewise, the law gives local municipalities the power to draw the lines that define what sexually

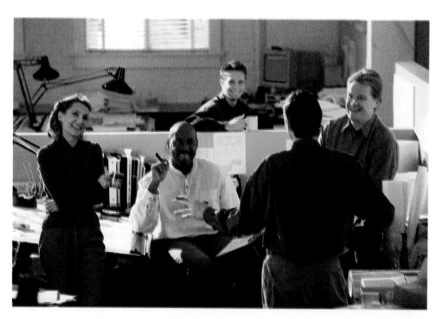

Many private companies and public organizations have adopted policies to discourage forms of behavior that might create a "hostile or intimidating environment." In practice, such policies seek to remove sexuality from the workplace so that employees can do their jobs while steering clear of traditional notions about female and male relationships. The hope is that sexual harassment policies will develop a comfortable informal atmosphere in which people can interact freely and easily.

explicit materials violate "community standards" of decency and lack redeeming social value.

People may disagree about what pornography is, but there is little doubt that in the United States pornography is big business. Taken together, sexually explicit videos, movies, magazines, telephone chat lines, and Internet sites represent more than $10 billion in sales each year.

Traditionally, U.S. society has viewed pornography as a *moral* issue. National survey data show that 57 percent of U.S. adults express concern that "sexual materials lead to a breakdown of morals" (NORC, 2001:244). But pornography also plays a part in gender stratification. From this point of view, pornography is a *power* issue because most pornography dehumanizes women as the playthings of men. It is worth noting that the term *pornography* comes from the Greek word *porne*, meaning a prostitute who acts as a man's sexual slave.

In addition, there is widespread concern that pornography promotes violence against women. Depicting women as merely the sexual playthings of men amounts to defining women as weak and undeserving of respect. Men may show contempt for women defined this way by striking out against them. Surveys show that about half of U.S. adults think that pornography encourages men to commit rape (NORC, 2001:245).

Like sexual harassment, pornography raises complex and conflicting issues. Most people object to offensive material, but many also think we must protect free speech and artistic expression. Nevertheless, public support to restrict pornography has increased, both from more conservative people who oppose pornography on moral grounds and from more liberal people who oppose it as demeaning and threatening to women.

THEORETICAL ANALYSIS OF GENDER

Each of sociology's major theoretical paradigms addresses the significance of gender in social organization.

STRUCTURAL-FUNCTIONAL ANALYSIS

The structural-functional paradigm views society as a complex system of many separate but integrated parts. From this point of view, gender functions to organize social life.

As Chapter 4 ("Society") explained, members of hunting and gathering societies had little power over the forces of biology. Lacking birth control, women often were pregnant, and the responsibilities of child care kept them close to home. At the same time, men's greater strength made them more suited for warfare and hunting. Over the centuries, this sexual division of labor became institutionalized and largely taken for granted (Lengermann & Wallace, 1985).

Industrial technology opens up vastly greater cultural possibilities. Because human muscles are no

In the 1950s, Talcott Parsons proposed that sociologists interpret gender as a matter of differences. As he saw it, masculine men and feminine women formed strong families and made for an orderly society. In recent decades, however, social-conflict theory has reinterpreted gender as a matter of inequality. From this point of view, U.S. society places men in a position of dominance over women.

longer the main energy source, the physical strength of men becomes less significant. In addition, the ability to control reproduction gives women greater choice in shaping their lives. Modern societies have come to see that traditional gender roles waste an enormous amount of human talent, yet change comes slowly because gender is deeply embedded in culture.

Talcott Parsons: Gender and Complementarity

As Talcott Parsons (1942, 1951, 1954) observed, gender helps to integrate society, at least in its traditional form. Gender forms a *complementary* set of roles that links men and women into family units for carrying out various important tasks. Women take primary responsibility for managing the household and raising children. Men connect the family to the larger world as they participate in the labor force.

Parsons further argued that socialization teaches the two sexes appropriate gender identity and skills needed for adult life. Thus, society teaches boys—presumably destined for the labor force—to be rational, competitive, and self-assured. This complex of traits Parsons called *instrumental*. To prepare girls for child rearing, their socialization stresses what Parsons called *expressive* qualities, such as emotional responsiveness and sensitivity to others.

Society promotes gender conformity, Parsons explained, by instilling in men and women a fear that straying too far from accepted standards courts rejection by the opposite sex. In simple terms, women learn to view nonmasculine men as sexually unattractive, and men learn to shun unfeminine women.

Critical evaluation. Structural functionalism puts forward a theory of complementarity by which gender integrates society both structurally (in terms of what people do) and morally (in terms of what they believe). Influential at midcentury, this approach has lost much of its standing today.

For one thing, functionalism assumes a singular vision of society that is not shared by everyone. For example, many women have always worked outside the home because of economic necessity, a fact not reflected in Parsons's conventional, middle-class view of family life. Second, Parsons's analysis ignores the personal strains and social costs of rigid, traditional gender roles (Giele, 1988). Third, for those who seek sexual equality, what Parsons describes as gender "complementarity" amounts to little more than women submitting to male domination.

SOCIAL-CONFLICT ANALYSIS

From a social-conflict point of view, gender involves differences not just in behavior but in power. Consider the striking parallel between the way ideas about gender have benefited men and the way oppression of racial and ethnic minorities has benefited whites (Hacker, 1951, 1974; Collins, 1971; Lengermann & Wallace, 1985). That is, conventional ideas about gender promote not cohesion but division and tension, with men seeking to protect their privileges as women challenge the status quo.

As earlier chapters explain, the social-conflict paradigm draws heavily on the ideas of Karl Marx. Yet Marx was a product of his time insofar as his writings focused almost exclusively on men. However, his friend and collaborator Friedrich Engels did develop a theory of gender stratification (1902; orig. 1884).

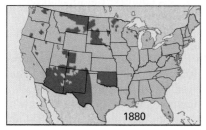

NATIONAL MAP 14–2
Land Controlled
by Native Americans, 1790–1998

Two hundred years ago, Native Americans controlled three-fourths of the land that would eventually become today's United States. Today, Native Americans control 314 reservations—scattered across the United States—that, together, account for just 2 percent of the country's land area. How would you characterize these locations?

Source: Copyright © 1998 by The New York Times Co. Reprinted by permission. All rights reserved.

Genocide also occurred in the twentieth century. Unimaginable horror befell European Jews during the Holocaust of the 1930s and 1940s, when Hitler's Nazis exterminated more than 6 million Jewish men, women, and children. Soviet dictator Josef Stalin murdered on an even greater scale, killing perhaps 30 million real and imagined enemies. Between 1975 and 1980, Pol Pot's communist regime in Cambodia butchered all "capitalists," including anyone able to speak a Western language and even people who wore eyeglasses, viewed as an elitist symbol. In all, some 2 million people (one-fourth of the population) perished in the Cambodian "killing fields" (Shawcross, 1979).

Tragically, genocide continues. Recent examples include Hutus killing Tutsis in Rwanda and Serbs killing Bosnians in the Balkans of Eastern Europe.

The four minority-majority patterns just described have all been played out in the United States. Although many people proudly point to patterns of pluralism and assimilation, it is also important to recognize the degree to which our society has been built on segregation (of African Americans) and genocide (of Native Americans). The remainder of this chapter examines how these four patterns have shaped the history and present social standing of major racial and ethnic categories in the United States.

RACE AND ETHNICITY IN THE UNITED STATES

> Give me your tired, your poor,
> Your huddled masses yearning to breathe free,
> The wretched refuse of your teeming shore,
> Send these, the homeless, tempest-tossed to me:
> I lift my lamp beside the golden door.

These words by Emma Lazarus, inscribed on the Statue of Liberty, express cultural ideals of human dignity, personal freedom, and opportunity. Indeed, the United States has provided more of the "good life" to more immigrants than any other nation. But as the history of this nation's racial and ethnic minorities reveals, our country's golden door has opened more widely for some than for others.

NATIVE AMERICANS

The term "Native Americans" refers to the societies—including Aleuts, Eskimos, Cherokee, Zuni, Sioux, Mohawk, Aztec, and Inca—who first settled the Western Hemisphere. Some 30,000 years before Christopher Columbus (1446–1506) stumbled on the Americas, migrating peoples crossed a land bridge from Asia to North America where the Bering Strait

TABLE 14–2 The Social Standing of Native Americans, 2000

	Native Americans	Entire United States
Median family income	$31,064	$50,891
Percentage in poverty	27.1%	11.3%
Completion of four or more years of college (age 25 and over)	9.3%*	25.6%

*Author estimate based on latest available data.

Source: U.S. Census Bureau (2001).

(off the coast of Alaska) lies today. Gradually, they made their way throughout North and South America.

When the first Europeans arrived late in the fifteenth century, Native Americans numbered in the millions. But by 1900, after relentless subjugation and acts of genocide, the "vanishing Americans" numbered a mere 250,000 (Dobyns, 1966; Tyler, 1973); the lands they controlled had also shrunk dramatically, as shown in National Map 14–2 on page 365.

It was Christopher Columbus who first called Native Americans "Indians" because he wrongly thought he had reached India. Actually, Columbus had landed in the Bahama Islands in the Caribbean. Columbus found the island people passive and peaceful, a stark contrast to materialistic and competitive Europeans (Matthiessen, 1984; Sale, 1990). Yet early Europeans justified seizing the land by calling their victims thieves and murderers (Unruh, 1979; Josephy, 1982).

After the Revolutionary War, the new U.S. government took a pluralist approach to Native American so-

For more information on Native Americans, visit this site, operated by Syracuse University: http://www.nativeweb.org

cieties and sought to gain more land through treaties. Payment for land was far from fair, however, and when Native Americans resisted surrendering their homeland, the U.S. government simply used superior military power to evict them. By the early 1800s, few Native Americans remained east of the Mississippi River.

In 1871, the United States declared Native Americans wards of the government and adopted a strategy of forced assimilation. Native Americans continued to lose their land and were well on their way to losing their culture. Reservation life fostered dependency, replacing ancestral languages with English and traditional religion with Christianity. Officials of the Bureau of Indian

Affairs took children from their parents and put them in boarding schools, where they were resocialized as "Americans." Authorities gave local control of reservation life to the few Native Americans who supported government policies, and they distributed reservation land—traditionally held collectively—as private property to individual families (Tyler, 1973).

Not until 1924 were Native Americans entitled to U.S. citizenship. After that, many migrated from reservations, adopting more mainstream cultural patterns and marrying non–Native Americans. Many large cities have sizable Native American populations. Overall, however, Native Americans control just a small share of land in this country; the median family income of Native Americans is far below the U.S. average, and relatively few Native Americans earn a college degree (see Table 14–2).[1]

From in-depth interviews with Native Americans in a western city, Joan Albon (1971) concluded that lower Native American social standing reflects a range of cultural factors, including a noncompetitive view of life and a reluctance to pursue higher education. In addition, she noted, many Native Americans have dark skin, which makes them victims of prejudice and discrimination.

Like other racial and ethnic minorities in the United States, Native Americans have recently reasserted pride in their cultural heritage. Native American organizations report a surge in membership, and many children can speak native languages better than their parents (Fost, 1991; Johnson, 1991; Nagel, 1996). Moreover, the legal autonomy of reservations has turned out to be an ace-up-the-sleeve for many tribes, who have built lucrative casinos and now control 20 percent of all U.S. gambling. But such financial windfalls affect relatively few Native peoples; most endure their disadvantages with a profound sense of the injustice they have suffered at the hands of white people.

WHITE ANGLO-SAXON PROTESTANTS

White Anglo-Saxon Protestants (WASPs) were not the first people to inhabit the United States, but they

---

[1]In making comparisons of education and, especially, income, keep in mind that various categories of the U.S. population have different median ages. The 2000 median age for all U.S. people was 35.3 years. Non-Hispanic white people have a median age of 38.6 years; for Native Americans, the figure is 28.0 years. Because people's schooling and income increase over time, such an age difference accounts for some of the disparities shown in Table 14–2.

TABLE 14–5 The Social Standing of Hispanic Americans, 2000

	All Hispanics	Mexican Americans	Puerto Ricans	Cuban Americans	Entire United States
Median family income	$35,050	$31,123*	$30,129*	$38,312*	$50,891
Percentage in poverty	21.2%	24.1%*	25.8%*	17.3%*	11.3%
Completion of four or more years of college (age 25 and over)	10.6%	6.9%	13.0%	23.0%	25.6%

*Data for 1999.

Source: U.S. Census Bureau (2001).

Median family income for all Hispanics—$35,050 in 2000—stands well below the national average.[4] As the following sections discuss, some categories of Hispanics have fared better than others.

Mexican Americans

Some Chicanos are descendants of people who lived in a part of Mexico annexed by the United States after the Mexican American War (1846–48). However, most Mexican Americans are more recent immigrants. In fact, in recent decades, more immigrants have come to the United States from Mexico than from any other country.

Like many other immigrants, many Mexican Americans have worked as low-wage laborers on farms or elsewhere. Table 14–5 shows that the 1999 median family income for Mexican Americans was $31,123, about two-thirds of the national standard. One-fourth of Chicano families are poor, more than twice the national average. And despite gains since 1980, Mexican Americans still acquire less schooling than U.S. adults as a whole and have a high dropout rate.

Puerto Ricans

Puerto Rico (like the Philippines) came under U.S. control with the end of the Spanish-American War in 1898. In 1917, Puerto Ricans (but not Filipinos) became U.S. citizens.

New York City is the center of Puerto Rican life in the continental United States and is home to about 1 million Puerto Ricans. However, about 40 percent of this community is counted among that city's poor, and only 13 percent aged twenty-five and older have

earned a college degree. Adjusting to cultural patterns on the mainland—including, for many, learning English—is one challenge. Also, Puerto Ricans with dark skin encounter especially strong prejudice and discrimination. As a result, more people return to Puerto Rico each year than arrive, so New York lost about 100,000 Puerto Ricans during the 1990s (Navarro, 2000).

This "revolving door" pattern hampers assimilation. Three-fourths of Puerto Rican families in the United States speak Spanish at home, compared to about half of Mexican American families (Sowell, 1981; Stevens & Swicegood, 1987). Speaking only Spanish maintains a strong ethnic identity, but it limits economic opportunity. Puerto Ricans also have a higher incidence of women-headed households than other Hispanics, a pattern that puts families at greater risk of poverty.

Table 14–5 shows that the 1999 median family income for Puerto Ricans was $30,129, 60 percent of the national average. Although long-term mainland residents have made economic gains, more recent immigrants from Puerto Rico struggle to find work. Averaging out the differences, Puerto Ricans remain the most socially disadvantaged Hispanic minority (Rivera-Batiz & Santiago, 1994; Holmes, 1996b).

Cuban Americans

Within a decade after the 1959 Marxist revolution led by Fidel Castro, 400,000 Cubans had immigrated to the United States. Those who fled were highly educated business and professional people who wasted little time becoming as successful in the United States as in their homeland (Fallows, 1983; Krafft, 1993).

Table 14–5 shows that the median household income for Cuban Americans in 1999 was $38,312, well above that of other Hispanics yet still below the national average. The 1 million Cuban Americans living in the United States have managed a delicate balancing act, achieving success in the larger society

[4]The 2000 median age of the U.S. Hispanic population was 25.8 years, well below the national median of 35.3 years. This differential accounts for some of the disparity in income and education.

The strength of family bonds and neighborhood ties is evident in this painting of street life in old San Juan, La Vida en Broma, *by Puerto Rican artist Nick Quijano.*

© Nick Quijano 1997. *La Vida en Broma, 1988: Streetlife in Old San Juan.*

while retaining much of their traditional culture. Of all Hispanics, Cubans are the most likely to speak Spanish in their homes: Eight out of ten families do. However, their cultural distinctiveness and highly visible communities, such as Miami's Little Havana, provoke hostility from some people.

WHITE ETHNIC AMERICANS

The term "white ethnics" recognizes the ethnic heritage and social disadvantages of many white people. White ethnics are non-WASPs whose ancestors lived in Ireland, Poland, Germany, Italy, or other European countries. More than half the U.S. population falls into a white ethnic category (U.S. Census Bureau, 2001).

Unprecedented emigration from Europe during the nineteenth century first brought Germans and Irish and then Italians and Jews to our shores. Despite cultural differences, all shared the hope that the United States would offer greater political freedom and economic opportunity than their homelands. Most did live better in this country, but the belief that "the streets of America were paved with gold" turned out to be a far cry from reality. Many immigrants found only hard labor for low wages.

White ethnics also endured their share of prejudice and discrimination. Nativist organizations opposed the entry of non-WASP Europeans to the United States, and many newspaper ads seeking workers warned new arrivals, "None need apply but Americans" (Handlin, 1941:67).

In 1921, the nativists declared victory when the federal government passed legislation that imposed a quota on immigration. Not until 1968 were restrictions lifted. The most severely targeted were southern and eastern Europeans—people likely to have darker skin and different cultural backgrounds from the dominant WASPs (Fallows, 1983).

In response to widespread bigotry, many white ethnics—like other immigrants—formed supportive residential enclaves. Some also established footholds in certain businesses and trades: Italian Americans entered the construction industry, the Irish worked in construction and civil service jobs, Jews predominated in the garment industry, and many Greeks (like the Chinese) worked in the retail food business (Newman, 1973).

Many working-class people still live in traditional neighborhoods, although those who prospered gradually assimilated. Most descendants of immigrants who labored in sweatshops and lived in overcrowded tenements now lead comfortable lives. As a result, their ethnic heritage is a source of pride.

RACE AND ETHNICITY: LOOKING AHEAD

The United States has been and will long remain a land of immigrants. Immigration has brought striking cultural diversity and tales of success, hope, and struggle told in hundreds of tongues.

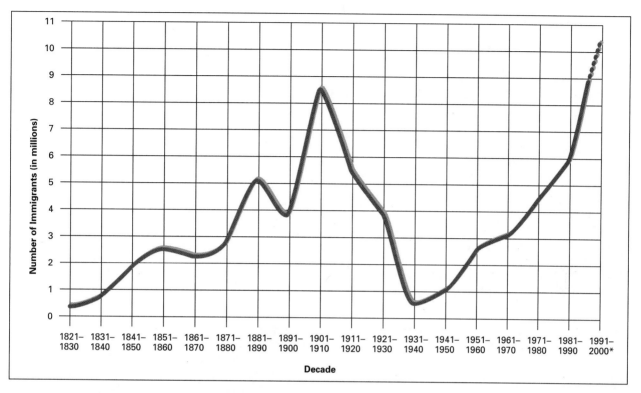

FIGURE 14–3 Immigration to the United States, by Decade

*Projection based on 1991–1998 data.

Source: U.S. Immigration and Naturalization Service (1999).

Most immigrants arrived in a great wave that peaked about 1910. The next two generations saw gradual economic gains and some assimilation. The government also extended citizenship to Native Americans (1924), foreign-born Filipinos (1942), Chinese Americans (1943), and Japanese Americans (1952).

As Figure 14–3 indicates, another wave of immigration began after World War II and swelled as the government relaxed immigration laws in the 1960s. During the 1990s, about 1 million people came to the United States each year, more than twice the number that arrived during the Great Immigration a century ago (although newcomers now enter a country that has five times as many people). However, today's immigrants come not from Europe but from Latin America and Asia, with Mexicans, Filipinos, and South Koreans arriving in the largest numbers.

New arrivals face the same kind of prejudice and discrimination experienced by those who came before them. Indeed, recent years have witnessed rising hostility toward foreigners (sometimes called *xenophobia*,

with Greek roots meaning "fear of what is strange"). In 1994, California voters passed Proposition 187, which cut off social services (including schooling) to illegal immigrants. More recently, voters there mandated that all children learn English in school. In 2000, some landowners along the southwest border of the United States took up arms to discourage the large number of immigrants crossing the border from Mexico, and some political candidates have called for drastic action to cut off further immigration. Furthermore, as the final box explains, the debate over affirmative action rages as hotly as ever.

Like their predecessors, many immigrants try to blend into U.S. society without completely giving up their traditional culture. Some have formed racial and ethnic enclaves, so that the Little Havanas and Korea-towns of today stand alongside the Little Italys and Germantowns of the past. Like those who came before them, new arrivals also share the hope that their racial and ethnic identity can be a source of strength and not a badge of inferiority.

CONTROVERSY & DEBATE

Affirmative Action: Solution or Problem?

Adarand Constructors, a white-owned Colorado highway construction company, submitted the low bid for a federal project erecting guard rails. But Adarand did not get the job. Despite having to pay a higher price, the government selected Gonzales Construction, a minority-owned firm. Adarand sued, and a bitter company manager, Randy Perch, explained, "What is prejudice? It's when government makes a decision based on something that doesn't matter, like race or gender."

Should race or ethnicity or gender matter in how we treat people? This question lies at the heart of the affirmative action debate. To begin, what exactly is this controversial policy, and how did it start?

After World War II, the U.S. government funded higher education for veterans of all races. The G.I. Bill held special promise for African Americans, most of whom needed financial assistance to enroll in college. The program was so successful that by 1960, some 350,000 black men and women were on college campuses with government funding.

But a problem remained: These people were not finding the kinds of jobs for which they were qualified. In short, *educational* opportunity was not producing *economic* opportunity.

Thus, in the early 1960s, the Kennedy administration introduced a program called "affirmative action" to provide a broader "net of opportunity" for qualified minorities in the job market.

Supporters argue that affirmative action in college admissions is needed to ensure a socially diverse campus.

Employers were instructed to monitor hiring, promotion, and admissions policies to eliminate discrimination—even if unintended—against minorities.

Defenders of affirmative action see it, first, as a sensible response to our nation's racial and ethnic history, especially for African Americans, who suffered through two centuries of slavery and a century of segregation under Jim Crow laws. Throughout our history, they claim, being white gave people a big advantage. Thus, minority preference today is a step toward just compensation for unfair majority preference in the past.

Second, given our racial history, the promise of a colorblind society strikes many analysts as hollow. Because prejudice and discrimination are deep in the fabric of U.S. society, simply endorsing the principle of colorblindness does not mean everyone will compete fairly.

Third, proponents maintain that affirmative action has worked. Where would minorities be if the government had not enacted this policy three decades ago? Major

SUMMARY

1. Races are socially constructed categories that set people apart according to various physical traits. Although a century ago scientists identified three broad categories—Caucasoids, Mongoloids, and Negroids—there are no pure races.

2. Ethnicity is based not on biology but on shared cultural heritage. Individuals may choose to emphasize or minimize their cultural distinctiveness. Likewise, societies may or may not set people apart because of cultural heritage.

3. Minorities—including people of various racial and ethnic categories—are people society sets apart as both socially distinct and socially disadvantaged.

4. Prejudice is a rigid and biased generalization about a category of people. Racism, a destructive type of prejudice, asserts that one race is innately superior or inferior to another.

5. Discrimination is a pattern of action by which a person treats various categories of people unequally.

APPLICATIONS AND EXERCISES

1. Does your college or university take account of race and ethnicity in its admissions policies? Ask to speak with an admissions officer to see what you can learn about your school's policies and the reasons for them. Ask whether there is a "legacy" policy that favors applicants with a parent who attended the school.

2. Give several of your friends or family members a quick quiz, asking them what share of the U.S. population is white, Hispanic, African American, and Asian (see Table 14–1). If they are like most people, they will exaggerate the share of all minorities and understate the white proportion (Labovitz, 1996). What do you make of the results?

3. There are probably immigrants on your campus or in your local community. Have you ever thought about asking them to tell you about their homeland and their experiences in the United States? Most immigrants are pleased to be asked, and you can learn a great deal.

4. Packaged in the back of this new textbook is an interactive CD-ROM that offers a variety of study and review materials intended to help you better understand the material covered in this chapter. For this chapter, the CD-ROM contains an author's tip video, Real Life Sociology videos, other relevant audio and video, interactive map animations, audio journal entries from the author, Web links, and much more.

 SITES TO SEE

http://www.prenhall.com/macionis

Visit the interactive *Companion Website*™ that accompanies this text. Begin by clicking on the cover of your book. You will find a chapter-by-chapter study guide, practice tests, and a significant portion of the text for online review, as well as many suggested Web links.

http://www.naacp.org
http://www.jdl.org

These two organizations—the National Association for the Advancement of Colored People and the Jewish Defense League—are concerned with combating prejudice and discrimination and advancing the social standing of

minorities in the United States. Determine each organization's strategies and goals.

http://w3.access.gpo.gov/eop/ca/index.html

This worthwhile data site, operated by the Council of Economic Advisors, provides an assessment of social and economic well-being of various racial and ethnic categories of this country's population.

http://www.collegeboard.org/research/html/991017r.html

Read the report of the College Board's National Task Force on Minority High Achievement, which analyzes racial and ethnic differences in higher education.

 INVESTIGATE WITH CONTENTSELECT

Follow the instructions found on page 23 of this textbook to enter this chapter of the book's *Companion Website*™. Once in the chapter, click on the ContentSelect icon at the bottom left of your screen and enter your personal

User ID and Password. Enter keywords such as "race," "ethnicity," and "discrimination," and the search engine will help you become an effective researcher.

CHAPTER

15

Boris Kustodiev (1878–1927)
Easter Morning, 1911

Regional Gallery of Art, Astrakhan, Russia.
Scala/Art Resource, N.Y.

AGING AND THE ELDERLY

Eldora Mitchell has just about seen it all: Born in 1903, she remembers when most homes had no electricity and there were more horses than cars on the streets. Looking back on her long life, what is most significant to her? "I have tried to live my life serving others and giving love," she explains. Growing up in a poor, African American family, she was scrubbing floors by the time she was twelve. She cleaned hospital rooms while she raised her own children, and later she spent years caring for her aging mother and her dying husband.

Now, at ninety-five, Mitchell smiles and says, "It's my turn." Four years ago, she moved across town to live with her son, Charles, who is fifty-five and divorced. Charles Mitchell works the night shift as a police dispatcher in Durham, North Carolina, so he can spend days caring for his mother. In his home, Eldora Mitchell has a bedroom of her own. Bright green curtains hang around the windows, and a Bible with large print lies on the nightstand.

Eldora Mitchell does not have much money. She receives $45 per month as a pension from the hospital where she worked; her monthly Social Security check adds $568. Her life's savings is little more than $8,000. But as long as she has the love and care of her son, in her mind she is rich indeed (based on Rimer, 1998).

Across the United States, there are millions of families like the Mitchells, caring for aging parents. The United States is witnessing a revolution in aging, with people living longer and many—especially those with low incomes—turning to family members for assistance. In this chapter, we explore the graying of U.S. society, the various meanings different societies attach to their oldest members, and the transitions people face as they grow old.

THE GRAYING OF THE UNITED STATES

A quiet but powerful revolution is reshaping the United States. In 1900, the United States was a young nation, with half the population under age twenty-three; just 4 percent had reached sixty-five. But the number of elderly people—that is, women and men aged sixty-five or older—has increased more than tenfold in the past century. By 2000, the number of seniors reached 35 million. Seniors already outnumber teenagers, and, as shown in Figure 15–1 on page 384, they accounted for 12.4 percent of the entire population in 2000.

By 2030, the number of seniors will double to 70 million, representing about 20 percent of the population. Then, almost half this country's people will be over age forty (U.S. Census Bureau, 2001).

Global Map 15–1 on page 385 shows that it is in the rich nations, such as the United States, that the share of elderly people is increasing most rapidly. Typically, two factors combine to drive up the elderly population: low birth rates (meaning that there are fewer children) and increasing longevity (meaning that people typically live longer).

In the United States, a third factor is also at work and will soon swell the ranks of the elderly: the aging of

Find information on aging and older people at the National Institute on Aging Web site: http://www.nia.nih.gov/

the baby boomers, the 75 million people born soon after the end of World War II. A generation later, after 1965, the birth rate took a sharp turn downward (the so-called baby bust

383

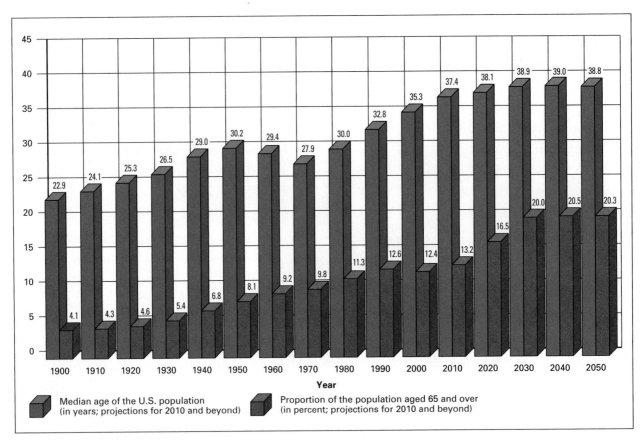

FIGURE 15–1 The Graying of U.S. Society

Source: U.S. Census Bureau (2000, 2001).

era), making the U.S. population more and more top-heavy in the twenty-first century.

THE BIRTH RATE: GOING DOWN

The first factor contributing to the graying of our society is a declining birth rate. The birth rate in the United States has been falling for more than a century. One reason is that as societies industrialize, children are more likely to survive to adulthood, so couples can have fewer. Another reason is that although children are an economic asset to farming families, they are an economic liability to families in industrial societies. Put otherwise, children no longer contribute to a family's financial well-being but are a major expense.

Also, as more and more women work outside the home for income, they want to have fewer children.

Advances in birth control technology during the twentieth century have provided the means to avoid unwanted births.

LIFE EXPECTANCY: GOING UP

The second factor contributing to the graying of U.S. society is an increase in life expectancy. It surprises many people to learn that in 1900, a typical female born in the United States lived just forty-eight years and a male lived just forty-six years. By contrast, females born in 2000 can look forward to living 79.5 years, and males can expect to live 74.1 years (U.S. National Center for Health Statistics, 2001).

A longer life span is one consequence of the Industrial Revolution. Greater material wealth and advances in medicine raise living standards; people benefit from better housing and nutrition and live

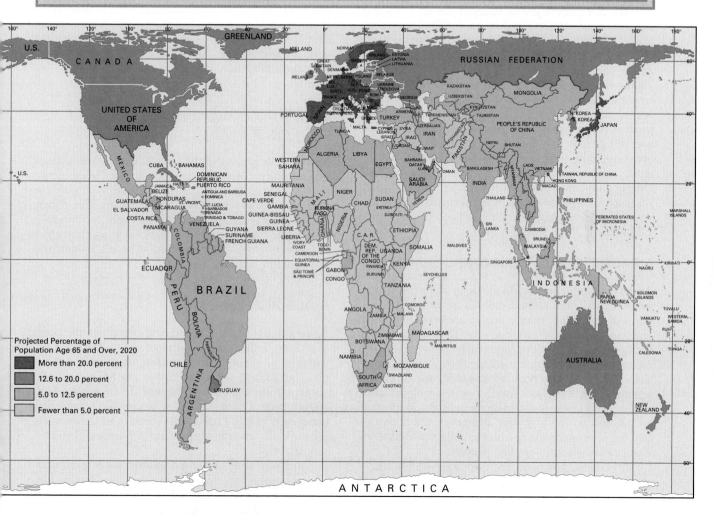

GLOBAL MAP 15–1 The Elderly in Global Perspective, 2020

Here we see projections for the share of population aged sixty-five and older in the year 2020, one generation from now. What relationship do you see between a country's income level and the size of its elderly population?

Source: U.S. Census Bureau (2000).

Projected Percentage of Population Age 65 and Over, 2020
- More than 20.0 percent
- 12.6 to 20.0 percent
- 5.0 to 12.5 percent
- Fewer than 5.0 percent

longer. At the same time, medical advances have almost eliminated infectious diseases such as smallpox, diphtheria, and measles that killed many infants and children a century ago. More recent medical strides help us fend off cancer and heart disease, which claim most of the U.S. population, but now later in life.

As life becomes longer, the fastest-growing segment of the U.S. population is people over eighty-five, who are already thirty-five times more numerous than they were in 1900. These men and women now number 4.2 million (about 1.5 percent of the total population). Projections put their number at 19 million (about 5 percent of the total) by the year 2050 (U.S. Census Office, 1902; Kaufman, 1990; Harbert & Ginsberg, 1991; U.S. Census Bureau, 2001).

We can only begin to imagine the changes that will accompany this major increase in the elderly population. As the number of older people retiring from the labor force goes up, the proportion of nonworking adults—already about ten times greater than in 1900—will demand more health care and other resources. Thus, the ratio of elderly people to working-age adults, called the *old-age dependency ratio*, will rise by 2050 from twenty to twenty-eight elderly people per 100 people aged eighteen to sixty-four. Government spending to support people over sixty-five is already increasing sharply. With tomorrow's swelling elderly population looking for support from a smaller share of younger workers, what security can today's young people expect in their old age? (Treas, 1995; Edmondson, 1996; Riche, 2000)

AN AGING SOCIETY: CULTURAL CHANGE

As the number of people and the share of the population over sixty-five push upward, cultural patterns are changing. For one thing, elderly people are becoming more and more visible in everyday life. Through much of the twentieth century, the young rarely mingled with the old, so that most people know little about old age. But as this country's elderly population steadily increases, age segregation will decline. Younger people will see more seniors at shopping malls, in movie theaters, at sporting events, and on the highways. Moreover, the design of buildings—from homes to stores to colleges—is likely to change to ease access for older people.

Of course, how frequently younger people interact with the elderly depends a great deal on where they live. This is because the elderly represent a far greater share of the population in some regions of the country than in others. National Map 15–1 looks at residential patterns of people aged sixty-five and older.

A larger share of old people certainly will change our way of life. Keep in mind, however, that seniors are socially diverse. Being "elderly" is a category open to everyone, if we are lucky to live long enough. Elders in the United States represent not just men and women but all cultures, classes, races, and ethnic backgrounds.

THE "YOUNG OLD" AND THE "OLD OLD"

Analysts sometimes distinguish two cohorts of the elderly. The younger elderly are between sixty-five and seventy-five and typically live independently, with good health and financial security; they are likely to be living as couples. The older elderly are past age seventy-five and more likely to have health and money problems and to be dependent on others. Because of their greater longevity, women outnumber men in the elderly population, an imbalance that grows greater with advancing age. Among the "oldest old," those over age eighty-five, about 60 percent are women.

GROWING OLD: BIOLOGY AND CULTURE

Studying the graying of the United States is the focus of **gerontology** (derived from the Greek word *geron*, meaning "an old person"), *the study of aging and the elderly*. Gerontologists—who work within many disciplines, including medicine, psychology, and sociology—investigate not only how people change as they grow old but also the different ways societies around the world define old age.

BIOLOGICAL CHANGES

Aging consists of gradual, ongoing changes in the body. But how individuals experience life's transitions—whether we welcome our maturity or complain about physical decline—depends largely on how a cultural system defines the various stages of life. In general, U.S. culture takes a positive view of biological changes that occur early in life. Through childhood and adolescence, people look forward to expanding opportunities and responsibilities.

But our youth-oriented culture takes a dimmer view of biological changes that develop later in life. Few people receive congratulations for getting old, at least not until they reach eighty-five or ninety. Rather, we commiserate with friends as they turn forty, fifty, and sixty and make jokes to avoid facing the fact that advancing age puts people, sooner or later, on a slippery slope of physical and mental decline. In short, we assume that by age fifty or sixty, people stop growing *up* and begin growing *down*.

Growing old brings on predictable changes: gray hair, wrinkles, loss of height and weight, and an overall decline in strength and vitality. After age fifty, bones become more brittle, so that injuries take longer to heal, and the odds of contracting chronic illnesses (such as arthritis and diabetes) and life-threatening conditions (such as heart disease and cancer) rise steadily. The sensory abilities—taste, sight, touch,

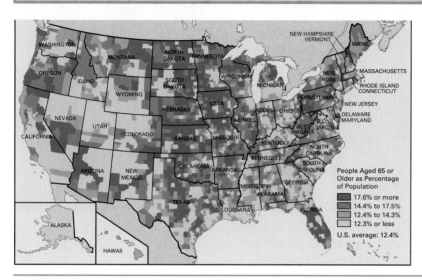

NATIONAL MAP 15–1
The Elderly Population of the United States

Common sense suggests that elderly people live in the Sunbelt, savoring the warmer climate of the South and Southwest. Although it is true that Florida has a disproportionate share of people over age sixty-five, it turns out that most counties with high percentages of older people are in the Midwest. What do you think accounts for this pattern? Hint: Which regions of the United States do *younger* people leave in search of jobs?

Source: U.S. Census Bureau (2001).

People Aged 65 or Older as Percentage of Population

- 17.6% or more
- 14.4% to 17.5%
- 12.4% to 14.3%
- 12.3% or less

U.S. average: 12.4%

smell, and especially hearing—become less keen with age (Colloway & Dollevoet, 1977; Treas, 1995).

Although health becomes more fragile with advancing age, most older people are not disabled by their physical condition. Only about one in ten seniors reports trouble walking, and fewer than one in twenty needs intensive care in a hospital or nursing home. No more than 1 percent of the elderly are bedridden. Overall, 27 percent of people over age sixty-five characterize their health as "fair" or "poor," and 73 percent consider their overall condition "good," "very good," or "excellent." In fact, the share of seniors reporting good or excellent health is going up (*Population Today*, 1997; U.S. National Center for Health Statistics, 1999).

However, patterns of well-being vary greatly within the elderly population. More health problems beset those over age seventy-five. Moreover, because women typically live longer than men, women spend more of their lives with chronic disabilities such as arthritis. In addition, well-to-do people live and work in healthful and safe environments and can afford better medical care. About 84 percent of elderly people with incomes exceeding $35,000 assess their own health as "excellent," "very good," or "good"; that figure drops below 60 percent among people with incomes under $10,000. Lower income and stress linked to prejudice and discrimination also explain

why 60 percent of older African Americans assess their health in positive terms, compared to three-fourths of elderly white people (Feagin, 1997; U.S. National Center for Health Statistics, 1999).

PSYCHOLOGICAL CHANGES

Just as we tend to overstate the physical problems of old age, it is easy to exaggerate the psychological changes that accompany growing old. The conventional belief about intelligence over the life course can be summed up as "What goes up, must come down" (Baltes & Schaie, 1974).

If we operationalize intelligence to refer to skills such as sensorimotor coordination—the ability to arrange objects to match a drawing—we do find a steady decline after midlife. The ability to learn new material and think quickly also declines, although not until around age seventy. But the ability to apply familiar ideas holds steady with advancing age, and some studies show improvement in verbal and mathematical skills (Baltes & Schaie, 1974; Schaie, 1980).

We all wonder whether we will think or feel differently as we get older. Gerontologists report that, for better or worse, the answer is usually no. The only common personality change with advancing age is greater introspection. That is, people become less materialistic

The reality of growing old is as much a matter of culture as it is of biology. In the United States, being elderly often means being inactive; yet, in rural regions of Iraq and other more traditional societies, old people commonly continue many familiar and productive routines.

and more engaged with their own thoughts and emotions. Generally, therefore, two elderly people who were childhood friends would recognize in each other the same personality traits that brought them together as youngsters (Neugarten, 1971, 1972, 1977; Wolfe, 1994).

AGING AND CULTURE

November 1, approaching Kandy, Sri Lanka. Our little van struggles up the steep mountain incline. Breaks in the lush vegetation offer spectacular views that interrupt our conversation about growing old. "Then there are no old age homes in your country?" I ask. "In Colombo and other cities, I am sure," our driver responds, "but not many. We are not like you Americans." "And how is that?" I counter, stiffening a bit. His eyes remain fixed on the road: "We would not leave our fathers and mothers to live alone."

When do people grow old? How do younger people regard society's oldest members? How do elderly people view themselves? The answers to these questions vary from place to place, showing that aging is not only a biological process but a matter of socially constructed meaning. In short, although aging is universal, the significance of growing old varies according to culture.

At one level, how well—and, more basically, how long—people live is closely linked to a society's technology and overall standard of living. Through most of human history, as English philosopher Thomas Hobbes (1588–1679) put it, people's lives have been "nasty, brutish, and short" (although Hobbes himself made it to the ripe old age of ninety-one). In his day, most people married and had children while in their teens, became middle-aged in their twenties, and succumbed to various illnesses in their thirties and forties. Thus, many greats of the past never reached what we would call old age at all: English poets Keats and Byron both died at age twenty-six; Mozart, the Austrian composer, died at thirty-five. Among famous writers, none of the three Brontë sisters lived to age forty, Edgar Allan Poe died at forty, Henry David Thoreau at forty-five, Oscar Wilde at forty-six, and Shakespeare at fifty-two.

About a century ago, rising living standards and advancing medical technology in the United States and Western Europe pushed longevity to about age fifty. As Global Map 15–2 shows, this life expectancy is still the case in many lower-income nations. During the twentieth century, increasing affluence in rich countries added almost thirty more years to the average life span.

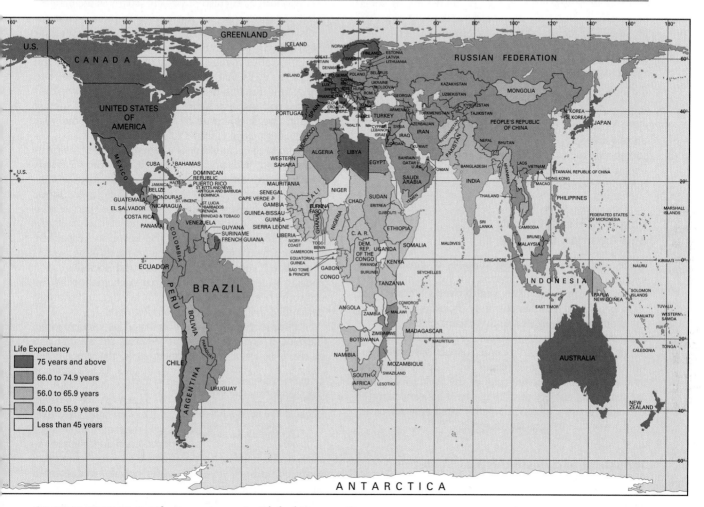

Life Expectancy
- 75 years and above
- 66.0 to 74.9 years
- 56.0 to 65.9 years
- 45.0 to 55.9 years
- Less than 45 years

GLOBAL MAP 15–2 Life Expectancy in Global Perspective

Life expectancy has shot upward over the course of the twentieth century in high-income countries, including Canada, the United States, Western Europe, Japan, and Australia. A newborn in the United States can expect to live about seventy-seven years, and our life expectancy would be greater still were it not for the high risk of death among infants born into poverty. Because poverty is the rule in much of the world, lives are correspondingly shorter, especially in parts of Africa, where life expectancy may be less than forty years.

Source: Population Reference Bureau (2001).

Just as important as life expectancy is the value societies attach to their senior members. As Chapter 10 ("Social Stratification") explains, all societies distribute basic resources unequally. We now turn to the importance of age in this process.

AGE STRATIFICATION: A GLOBAL ASSESSMENT

Like race, ethnicity, and gender, age is a basis for social ranking. **Age stratification** is *the unequal distribution of wealth, power, and privilege among people at*

For data and graphics on aging in global perspective, visit this UN site: http://www.un.org/ esa/population/publications/ aging99/fa99.htm *different stages of the life course.* As is true of other dimensions of social hierarchy, age stratification varies according to a society's level of technological development.

Hunting and Gathering Societies

As Chapter 4 ("Society") explains, without the technology to produce a surplus of food, hunters and gatherers must be nomadic. Therefore, survival depends on physical strength and stamina. As members of these societies grow old (in this case, about age thirty) they become less active and are considered an economic burden (Sheehan, 1976).

Pastoral, Horticultural, and Agrarian Societies

Once societies control food supplies by raising crops and animals, they can produce a surplus. Consequently, individuals can accumulate wealth over a lifetime. The most privileged members of these societies typically are the elderly, which gives rise to **gerontocracy,** *a form of social organization in which the elderly have the most wealth, power, and prestige.* Old people, particularly men, are honored (and sometimes feared) by their families, and, as the box reports in the case of the Abkhasians, they are leaders of society until they die. This veneration of the elderly also explains the widespread practice of ancestor worship in agrarian societies.

Industrial and Postindustrial Societies

We have noted that industrialization pushes living standards upward and advances medical technology, which increases human life expectancy. But although industrialization adds to the *quantity* of life, it does not necessarily improve the *quality* of life for old people. On the contrary, industrial societies give little power and prestige to the elderly. Why? Because the prime source of wealth shifts from land (typically controlled by the oldest members of society) to businesses and other goods (often owned and managed by younger people). Consider that in low-income countries the share of people over age sixty-five in the labor force is 76 percent of men and 44 percent of women. In high-income countries these percentages drop dramatically to 23 percent of men and 16 percent of women. These figures help explain why the peak earning years among

U.S. workers, on average, occur around age fifty; after that, earnings decline (UN Population Division, 1999; U.S. Census Bureau, 2000).

Modern living also physically separates the generations as younger people move away to pursue their careers, depending less on their parents and more on their own earning power. Furthermore, because industrial, urban societies change rapidly, the skills, traditions, and life experiences that served the old are not relevant to the young. Finally, the tremendous productivity of industrial nations means that not all members of a society need to work, so most of the very old and the very young play nonproductive roles (Cohn, 1982).

The long-term effect of all these factors transforms *elders* (a term with positive connotations) into *the elderly* (commanding far less prestige). In postindustrial societies such as the United States and Canada, economic and political leaders usually are middle-aged people who combine seasoned experience and up-to-date skills. In rapidly changing sectors of the economy, especially high-tech fields, many key executives are young, sometimes barely out of college. Industrial societies often consign older people to marginal participation in the economy because they lack the knowledge and training demanded in a fast-changing marketplace.

Some occupations are dominated by older people. Farming is one case in point: Whereas the average age of the U.S. labor force is thirty-eight, the average age of a U.S. farmer is A U.S. Department of Agriculture report on the effects of aging in rural communities is found at http://www.ers.usda.gov/ publications/rdrr90/rdrr90.pdf fifty-seven, with 35 percent of farmers over age sixty-five. Certainly some older men and women remain at the helm of corporations and other businesses; more commonly, however, older people predominate only in traditional occupations (working as farmers, barbers, tailors, and shop clerks) and in jobs that involve minimal activity (night security guards, for instance) (Kaufman & Spilerman, 1982; Yudelman & Kealy, 2000).

Japan: An Exceptional Case

Japan stands out as an exception to the rule. Japan has about the same share of seniors as the United States, but its traditional culture reveres older people. Most aged people in Japan live with an adult daughter or son, and they play a significant role in family life. Elderly men in Japan are also more likely than their U.S. counterparts to stay in the labor force, and in many Japanese corporations, the oldest employees enjoy the

If death was routine, it was also readily accepted. For example, medieval Christianity assured believers that death fit into the divine plan for human existence. Here is how the historian Philippe Ariès describes Sir Lancelot, one of King Arthur's Knights of the Round Table, preparing for death when he thinks he is mortally wounded:

> His gestures were fixed by old customs, ritual gestures which must be carried out when one is about to die. He removed his weapons and lay quietly upon the ground. . . . He spread his arms out, his body forming a cross . . . in such a way that his head faced east toward Jerusalem. (1974:7–8)

As societies gradually learned more about health and medicine, death became less of an everyday experience. Fewer children died at birth, and accidents and disease took a smaller toll among adults. People today view dying as extraordinary, except when it occurs among the very old or is associated with war or catastrophe. Consider that in 1900, about one-third of all deaths in the United States occurred before age five and fully two-thirds before age fifty-five. Today, by contrast, 85 percent of our population dies *after* age fifty-five. Death and old age are closely linked in our culture.

THE MODERN SEPARATION OF LIFE AND DEATH

Now removed from everyday experience, death somehow seems unnatural. If social conditions prepared our ancestors to accept their deaths, modern society, with its youth culture and aggressive medical technology, fosters a desire for eternal youth and immortality. Death has become separated from life.

Death is also *physically* removed from everyday activities. The clearest evidence of this is that many of us have never seen a person die. Our ancestors typically died at home in the presence of family and friends, but most deaths today occur in impersonal settings such as hospitals and nursing homes. Even in hospitals, dying patients occupy a special part of the building, and hospital morgues are located well out of sight of patients and visitors (Sudnow, 1967; Ariès, 1974).

ETHICAL ISSUES: CONFRONTING DEATH

Moral questions are more pressing than ever now that technological advances give humans the power to prolong life and thereby draw a line separating life from

In many traditional societies, people express great respect not only for elders but also for their ancestors. Dani villagers in New Guinea mummified the body of this elder in a sitting position so that they could continue to honor him and feel his presence in their daily lives.

death. We now grapple with how to use these new powers—or whether to use them at all.

When Does Death Occur?

Perhaps the most basic question is the most difficult: Exactly how do we define death? Common sense suggests that life ceases when breathing and heartbeat stop. But the ability of medical personnel to resuscitate someone after a heart attack and artificially sustain breathing makes such definitions of death obsolete. Medical and legal experts in the United States now define death as an *irreversible* state involving no response to stimulation, no movement or breathing, no reflexes, and no indication of brain activity (Ladd, 1979; Wall, 1980).

The Right-to-Die Debate

Today, many aging people are less afraid of death than the prospect of being kept alive at all costs. In other

Death on Demand: A Report from the Netherlands

Marcus Erich picked up the telephone and dialed his brother Arjen's number. In a quiet voice, thirty-two-year-old Marcus announced, "It's Friday at 5 o'clock." When the time came, Arjen was there, having driven to his brother's farmhouse an hour south of Amsterdam. They said their final goodbyes. Soon afterward, Marcus's physician arrived. Marcus and the doctor spoke for a few moments, and then the doctor prepared a "cocktail" of barbiturates and other drugs. As Marcus drank the mixture, he made a face, joking, "Can't you make this sweeter?"

As the minutes passed, Marcus lay back and his eyes closed. But after half an hour, he was still breathing. At that point, according to their earlier agreement, the doctor administered a lethal injection. In a few minutes, Marcus's life came to an end.

Events like this take us to the heart of the belief that people have a right to die. Marcus Erich was dying of AIDS. For five years, his body had been wasting away, and he suffered greatly with no hope of recovery. He wanted his doctor to end his life.

The Netherlands, a small nation in northwestern Europe, has gone further than any other in the world in allowing mercy killing or euthanasia. A 1981 Dutch law allows a physician to assist in a suicide if the following five conditions are met:

1. The patient must make a voluntary, well-considered, and repeated request to the doctor for help in dying.

2. The patient's suffering must be unbearable and without prospect of improvement.

3. The doctor and the patient must discuss alternatives.

4. The doctor must consult with at least one colleague who has access to the patient and the patient's medical records.

5. The assisted suicide must be performed in accordance with sound medical practice.

Official records indicate that doctors end 3,000 to 4,000 lives per year in the Netherlands. But because many cases are never reported, the actual number may well be twice that many.

Sources: Based on della Cava (1997) and Mauro (1997).

---

words, medical technology now threatens personal autonomy by letting doctors rather than the dying person decide when life is to end. In response, many people now seek control over their deaths just as they seek control over their lives.

After deliberation, patients, families, and doctors may decide to forgo heroic measures to keep a person alive. *Living wills*—documents stating which medical procedures a person wants and does not want under specific conditions—are now widespread.

A more difficult issue involves mercy killing, or **euthanasia,** *assisting in the death of a person suffering from an incurable disease.* Euthanasia (from the Greek term meaning "a good death") poses an ethical dilemma because it involves not just refusing life-extending treatment but actively taking steps to end life. In euthanasia, some see an act of kindness, and others see a form of killing.

Is there a right to die? People with incurable diseases can forgo treatment that might prolong their lives. But whether a doctor should be allowed to help bring about death is a matter of debate. In 1994, three states—Washington, California, and Oregon—voted on propositions that would allow physicians to help people who wanted to die. Only in Oregon did voters pass the initiative, and opposition tied up enactment of the law in Oregon's state courts until 1997, when voters again endorsed it. Since then, Oregon doctors have legally assisted in the death of terminally ill patients. In 1997, however, the U.S. Supreme Court declared that the U.S. Constitution recognizes no right to die. In 2001, the attorney general took action to prevent physician-assisted suicide in Oregon and any other states. However, no change has been made to the law pending resolution by Oregon courts.

In the Netherlands, we find the most permissive euthanasia law in the world. How does the Dutch system operate? The box takes a closer look.

Should the United States hold the line on euthanasia or follow the lead of the Dutch? Right to-die

Our society has long been concerned with the "good life"; more recently, attention has turned to the idea of a good death. The hospice movement is an important part of this trend. In some cases, terminally ill patients move to a hospice facility, where a professional staff provides medical support and emotional comfort. In other cases, hospice workers provide care in the familiar surroundings of a person's home.

advocates maintain that a person facing unbearable suffering should be able to choose whether to live or die. And if death is the choice, medical assistance can help people toward a "good death." Surveys show that a majority of U.S. adults support the option to die with a doctor's help (Rosenbaum, 1997; NORC, 2001).

On the other side of the debate, opponents fear that laws allowing physician-assisted suicide invite abuse. Pointing to the Netherlands, critics cite surveys indicating that in most cases the five conditions for physician-assisted suicide are not met. In particular, most physicians do not consult with another doctor or even report the euthanasia to authorities. Of greater concern, however, is the fact that in about one-fifth of all doctor-assisted suicides, the patient never explicitly asks to die. This is so even though half of these patients are conscious and capable of making decisions for themselves (Gillon, 1999). Therefore, opponents fear that legalizing doctor-assisted suicide puts a nation on a slippery slope toward more and more euthanasia. Can anyone deny, they ask, that ill people may be pushed into accepting death by doctors who consider suicide the right choice for the terminally ill or by family members who are weary of caring for them or want to avoid the expenses of medical care?

 For links to organizations worldwide advocating a right to die, see http://www.euthanasia.org/wfmap.html

However the right-to-die debate turns out in the future, our society has entered a new era when it comes to dying. Individuals, family members, and medical personnel must face death not as a medical fact but as a negotiated outcome (Flynn, 1991; Humphrey, 1991; Markson, 1992; Wolfson, 1998).

BEREAVEMENT

Elisabeth Kübler-Ross (1969) found that most people usually confront their own death in stages (see Chapter 5, "Socialization"). Initially, individuals react with *denial*, followed by *anger*; then they try to *negotiate* a divine intervention. Gradually, they fall into *resignation* and, finally, reach *acceptance*.

According to some researchers, bereavement follows the same pattern of stages. Those close to a dying person may initially deny the reality of impending death but with time gradually reach a point of acceptance. Other investigators question any linear "stage theory," arguing that bereavement is an unpredictable process (Lund, Caserta, & Dimond, 1986; Lund, 1989). However, experts do agree that how family and friends view an impending death affects the person who is dying. By accepting an approaching death, others help the dying person do the same; denying death isolates the dying person, who is unable to share feelings and experiences with others.

Many dying people find support in the *hospice movement*. Unlike a hospital, which is designed to cure disease, a hospice helps people have a good death. These care centers for dying people try to minimize

Looking ahead in the twenty-first century, the elderly will represent an increasing share of the U.S. population. How do you think this trend will affect the experiences and attitudes of the young?

pain and suffering—either there or at home—and encourage family members to stay close by.

Even under the most favorable circumstances, bereavement may involve profound grief and social disorientation that persist for some time. Research documents that bereavement is less intense for someone who accepts the death of a loved one and feels that the relationship with the dying person has reached a satisfactory resolution. Taking the opportunity to put appropriate closure on the relationship with a dying person allows family and friends to better comfort one another after death occurs (Atchley, 1983).

LOOKING AHEAD: AGING IN THE TWENTY-FIRST CENTURY

This chapter has explored the graying of the United States and other high-income nations. We can predict

 Government statistics and analysis of the well-being of the U.S. elderly population are available at http://www. agingstats.gov

with confidence that the ranks of the elderly will swell dramatically in the twenty-first century: By 2050, the elderly population will exceed the population of the entire country in 1900. Moreover, one in four of these seniors will be over eighty-five. Within the next fifty years, then, society's oldest

members will gain a far greater voice in everyday life. *Gerontology*—the study of the elderly—is also sure to gain in importance.

The reshaping of our society's age structure raises many serious concerns. With more people in their old age (and living longer once they enter old age), will we have the support services to sustain them? Remember that as the elderly make demands, proportionately fewer younger people will be there to respond. What about the spiraling medical care costs of an aging society? As the baby boomers enter old age, some analysts paint a doomsday picture of the United States as a "twenty-first century Calcutta," with desperate and dying elderly people everywhere (Longino, 1994:13).

But not all the signs are ominous. For one thing, the health of tomorrow's elderly people (that is, today's young and middle-aged adults) is better than ever: Smoking is way down, and people are eating more healthfully. Such trends probably mean that the elderly of the twenty-first century will be more vigorous and independent than their counterparts today. Moreover, tomorrow's seniors will enjoy the benefits of steadily advancing medical technology, although, as the final box explains, the claim of the old on our nation's resources is already hotly debated.

Another positive sign is the financial strength of the elderly. Although the cost of living is sure to rise, tomorrow's elderly will draw on greater affluence than ever before. Also the baby boomers will be the first generation of U.S. seniors with women who have been in the labor force most of their lives, a fact reflected in their substantial savings and pensions.

One concern, as we look ahead, is that younger adults will face a mounting responsibility to care for aging parents. Indeed, a falling birth rate coupled with a growing elderly population means that caregiving in our society increasingly will include both the very young and the very old.

More and more people in the United States are learning to care for aging parents. Caregiving includes more than meeting physical needs. Many of us have much to learn about communicating, expressing love, and facing eventual death. In caring for parents, of course, we will also teach important lessons to our children, including the skills they will need, one day, to care for us.

Finally, an aging population will almost certainly change the way we view death. In all likelihood, death will become less of a social taboo and reestablish itself as a natural part of the life course. As this comes to pass, both young and old will benefit.

Setting Limits: Must We "Pull the Plug" on Old Age?

Because death struck at any time, often without warning, our ancestors would have found the question, "Can people live too long?" absurd. In recent decades, however, as the elderly population soars in the United States, as new technology gives us more power to prolong life, and as life-extending care gets increasingly expensive, many now wonder just how much old age we can afford.

Currently, about half of the average person's lifetime spending for medical care occurs during the final years of life, and the share is rising. Against the spiraling costs of prolonging life, then, we well may ask whether what is technically possible is socially desirable. In this new century, warns gerontologist Daniel Callahan, an elderly population ready and eager to extend their lives will force us either to "pull the plug" on old age or shortchange everyone else.

To even raise this issue, Callahan concedes, seems cold and heartless. But consider that the bill for the elderly's health topped $200 billion in 2000—more than twice what it cost in 1980. This dramatic increase reflects our current policy of directing more and more

medical resources to studying and treating the diseases and disabilities of old age.

So Callahan makes the case for limits. He reasons, first, that to spend more on behalf of the elderly we must spend less on others. But with poverty a growing problem among children, how can we spend more and more on the oldest members of our society?

Second, Callahan reminds us, a *longer* life is not necessarily a *better* life. Cost aside, does heart surgery that prolongs the life of an eighty-four-year-old woman a year or two truly improve the quality of her life? Cost considered, would those resources yield more quality of life if used to give a ten-year-old child a kidney transplant?

Third, Callahan urges us to reconsider our view of death as an enemy to be conquered at all costs. Rather, he suggests, a more realistic stance for an aging society is to treat death as a natural end to the life course. If we cannot make peace with death for our own well-being, given limited financial resources, we must do it for the benefit of others.

But not everyone agrees. Shouldn't people who have worked all their lives

and made our society what it is enjoy our generosity in their final years? Moreover, given our cultural values of independence and responsibility, can we deny medical care to aging people able and willing to pay for it?

What is clear is that, in the twenty-first century, we will face questions that few would have imagined even fifty years ago: Is peak longevity good for everyone? Is it even *possible* for everyone?

Continue the debate . . .

1. *Should doctors and hospitals use a double standard, offering more complete care to the youngest people and more limited care to society's oldest members? Why or why not?*

2. *Do you think that a goal of the medical establishment should be to extend life at all costs?*

3. *Is the idea of rationing medical care really new? Hasn't our society always done this because some people have more wealth than others?*

Source: Callahan (1987).

SUMMARY

1. The proportion of elderly people in the U.S. population has risen from 4 percent in 1900 to 12 percent today; by 2030, 20 percent of our people will be elderly.

2. Gerontology, the study of aging and the elderly, focuses on how people change in old age and how various cultures define aging.

3. Most younger people exaggerate the extent of disability among the elderly. Growing old is accompanied by

a rising rate of disease and disability, but most seniors are healthy.

4. Psychological research confirms that growing old does not result in overall loss of intelligence or radical changes in personality.

5. The age at which people are defined as old varies historically: Until several centuries ago, old age began as early as thirty. In poor societies today,

where life expectancy is much lower than in North America, people become old at fifty or even forty.

6. In global perspective, industrialization fosters a decline in the social standing of elderly people.

7. As people age, they face social isolation brought on by retirement, physical disability, and the death of friends or spouse. Even so, most elderly people enjoy the support of family members.

8. Since 1960, poverty among the elderly has dropped sharply. The aged poor include categories of people—such as single women and people of color—who are at high risk of poverty at any age.

9. An increasing elderly population raises the demand for caregiving, most of which is performed by family members, typically women, who are likely to be caring for children as well.

10. Ageism—prejudice and discrimination against old people—is used to justify age stratification.

11. Although many seniors are socially disadvantaged, the elderly include men and women of all races, ethnicities, and social classes. Therefore, older people do not qualify as a minority.

12. Disengagement theory, based on structural-functional analysis, suggests that society helps the elderly disengage from positions of social responsibility before the onset of disability or death. This process allows the orderly transfer of statuses and roles from the older to the younger generation.

13. Activity theory, based on symbolic-interaction analysis, claims that a high level of activity affords people personal satisfaction in old age.

14. Age stratification is one focus of social-conflict analysis. Capitalist society's emphasis on economic efficiency leads us to devalue those who are less productive, including the elderly.

15. Modern society has set death apart from everyday life, prompting a cultural denial of human mortality. In part, this attitude is related to the fact that most people now die after reaching old age. Recent trends suggest that people are confronting death more directly and seeking control over the process of dying.

KEY CONCEPTS

gerontology (p. 386) the study of aging and the elderly

age stratification (p. 389) the unequal distribution of wealth, power, and privilege among people at different stages of the life course

gerontocracy (p. 390) a form of social organization in which the elderly have the most wealth, power, and prestige

caregiving (p. 395) informal and unpaid care provided to a dependent person by family members, other relatives, or friends

ageism (p. 396) prejudice and discrimination against the elderly

disengagement theory (p. 397) the idea that society enhances its orderly operation by disengaging people from positions of responsibility as they reach old age

activity theory (p. 397) the idea that a high level of activity enhances personal satisfaction in old age

euthanasia (mercy killing) (p. 400) assisting in the death of a person suffering from an incurable disease

CRITICAL-THINKING QUESTIONS

1. What factors are causing the populations of high-income nations to become, on average, older? What are some of the likely consequences of "the graying of the United States"?

2. In general, are the most popular faculty on the campus young instructors or old instructors? How does age play into the way students evaluate a professor?

3. In what ways does the United States have a "youth culture"? Provide specific examples.

4. Political analyst Irving Kristol (1996) praised the elderly as "our most exemplary citizens" because, compared with younger people, they do not kill, steal, use illegal drugs, or fall deeply into debt. Moreover, they are twice as likely as young people to vote. Overall, do you think the elderly in this country receive the respect and social support they deserve? Why or why not?

APPLICATIONS AND EXERCISES

1. What practices and policies does your college or university have for helping older faculty make the transition to retirement? Ask several faculty nearing retirement and several already retired for their views. In what ways does retiring from an academic career seem harder or easier than retiring from other kinds of work?

2. Look through an issue of any popular magazine—say, *Time*, *Newsweek*, or *People*—and notice the images of men and women featured in stories and pictured in advertising. Are elderly people fairly represented in such publications?

3. Obtain a copy of a living will and try to respond to all the questions it asks. Does filling out such a form help clarify your own thinking about confronting death?

4. The *Journal of Medical Ethics* (Vol. 25, No. 1, February 1999) has several research articles investigating alleged abuse of euthanasia laws in the Netherlands. Read the articles and decide whether you think, on balance, doctor-assisted suicide is a sound or unsound policy.

5. Packaged in the back of this new textbook is an interactive CD-ROM that offers a variety of study and review materials intended to help you better understand the material covered in this chapter. For this chapter, the CD-ROM contains an author's tip video, Real Life Sociology videos, other relevant audio and video, interactive map animations, audio journal entries from the author, Web links, and much more.

 ## SITES TO SEE

http://www.prenhall.com/macionis

Visit the interactive *Companion Website*™ that accompanies this text. Begin by clicking on the cover of your book. You will find a chapter-by-chapter study guide, practice tests, and a significant portion of the text for on-line review, as well as many suggested Web links.

http://www.nhpco.org

Learn about hospices by visiting the Web site for the National Hospice and Palliative Care Organization. Then check your local telephone book to contact people who operate a hospice in your community.

http://www.seniornet.org/php/

This is the site for SeniorNet, a nonprofit organization that is bringing seniors into the age of the Internet. Run by volunteers, SeniorNet offers low-cost computer and Internet instruction to the elderly at several hundred training sites across the United States.

http://www.aoa.gov

This site, operated by the Department of Health and Human Services, provides a look at likely trends involving the elderly over the course of the twenty-first century.

 ## INVESTIGATE WITH CONTENTSELECT

Follow the instructions found on page 23 of this textbook to enter this chapter of the book's *Companion Website*™. Once in the chapter, click on the ContentSelect icon at the bottom left of your screen and enter your personal User ID and Password. Enter keywords such as "aging," "retirement," and "euthanasia," and the search engine will help you become an effective researcher.

NEW INFORMATION TECHNOLOGY AND SOCIAL STRATIFICATION

Change in technology transforms the nature of work. Just as important, such shifts alter the reward structure, reshaping patterns of social inequality. This third cyber.scope considers several ways in which the spread of computer technology is linked to social stratification.

The Information Revolution and U.S. Stratification

Most analysts agree that recent decades have witnessed economic polarization in the United States, with economic growth primarily enriching families that already had high incomes (Persell, 1997; Keister, 2000). At the outset, at least, technological revolution typically concentrates income and wealth as a small number of people make key discoveries and, with the resulting products and services, establish and expand new markets. Just as John D. Rockefeller and Andrew Carnegie amassed great fortunes a century ago as captains of the Industrial Revolution, the Information Revolution has created a new elite today. For several years, the richest person in the country has been Bill Gates, a founder of Microsoft Corporation that produces not oil or steel but the operating systems found on most of today's personal computers. More broadly, it is those with money to invest (many of whom make up what Karl Marx called the capitalist class) who reap most of the profits from successful

new industries. During the 1990s, as the Information Revolution rolled ahead, key stock market indicators leaped fivefold, with new technology companies such as Microsoft (software), Intel (computer chips), Compaq (personal computers), and Cisco Systems (computer networking) making even more spectacular gains. A sharp downturn in the stock market during 2000 and 2001—especially affecting technology companies—trimmed these gains. Even so, high technology represents a larger and larger share of the U.S. economy.

But the wave of technological change does not benefit everyone. As companies adopt new technology in their efforts to become more efficient and profitable, some people lose out. In recent decades, for example, tens of millions of industrial jobs in the United States have simply disappeared. For each job lost, a worker—and usually an entire family—suffers.

Computers provide expanded opportunities for people with disabilities. This computer system, for example, is helping to teach lip reading to a young man who is deaf.

Another key link between new information technology and social inequality concerns the unequal spread of computing skills. In 2000, more than half the U.S. population over age fifteen were Internet users. Yet these users are not average people; they represent an information elite, privileged in more ways than one. About 95 percent are white (compared to 85 percent of the population), 60 percent are men (compared to half the population), and 40 percent are professionals or managers (compared to 18 percent of the population). In short, computer users are people with above-average incomes. College students stand out among computer users, but even among them, differences emerge. Figure Cyber III–1 shows that students attending private (and more expensive) colleges and universities are more likely to be frequent e-mail users than those attending public institutions. Similarly, students at two-year and at historically black colleges also make less use of computers.

The trend has been that, over time, computer users are coming to mirror more closely the population as a whole. But there can be little doubt that, at least for now, new information technology is contributing to higher levels of economic inequality as it creates a cyber-elite and generates a new underclass made up of those without crucial symbolic skills (Wynter, 1995; Edmondson, 1997b; Sax et al., 1999).

The Information Revolution: Gender, Race, and Age

The Industrial Revolution ushered in a trend by which women and men are becoming more socially equal. Machinery eroded the link between work and physical strength, and more women entered the labor force as birth control technology helped lower the birth rate by making motherhood a matter of individual choice. The Information Revolution promises to continue this trend. Work in the computer age involves not making or moving *things* but manipulating *ideas*—activity that favors neither men nor women.

Also, communication via computers obscures a person's sex—obvious in face-to-face interaction—placing men and women on a more equal footing. The same holds for race and ethnicity, so that the coming cyber-society may well be marked by greater contact between people of all races and cultural backgrounds.

But an important counterpoint involves access to computer technology. To date, cultural biases within the new cyber-society have favored males: Most games that introduce children to computers are designed for boys, just as computer science courses in colleges enroll mostly men. Similarly, to the extent that racial and ethnic minorities are economically disadvantaged and attend less well-funded schools, this segment of our population will have less opportunity to own and operate computers—the key to success in the labor force in this new century.

Finally, the effects of computing on age stratification are likely to be mixed. On one hand, the fact that computing demands mental more than physical vitality—and allows work to be performed almost anywhere—should expand opportunities for people to continue to work

well past the standard retirement age that emerged during the industrial era. On the other hand, new technology is almost always age biased in that it is readily adopted by the young but regarded more cautiously by the old, whose life experiences have been shaped by earlier ways. Unless our society expands programs of adult education, then, younger people are likely to predominate in, and benefit from, work and other activities that rely heavily on new information technology.

The Information Revolution and Global Stratification

Worldwide, the elite pattern we have described holds even more: The Information Revolution directly involves only a tiny share of the planet's people. A look back at Global Map 4–1, on page 104, and Global Map 7–1, on page 172, shows that it is the rich regions of the world where computers and Internet access

are readily available, at least to those who can afford them. In most of Africa, by contrast, people are far less likely to have a computer, and in some countries there are few computers and almost no Internet access. Moreover, the large number of African languages and alphabets will slow the spread of computing there.

Although Internet access is found in most of Asia, at present, a cultural and technical problem limits the spread of computing in this world region: Almost all computer keyboards use the Latin alphabet. In China and other Asian nations, although members of the technical elite are likely to speak and write English, most people use complex character sets that have yet to be incorporated into computer technology. Overall, then, the Information Revolution has come to the part of the world already benefiting from industrial technology—yet another case of the rich getting richer.

FIGURE Cyber III–1 Percentage of University and College Freshmen Reporting Frequent E-mail Use during the Past Year, 1999

Source: Sax et al. (1999).

CHAPTER

16

Christopher M. Chinn
Location and Dislocation
Courtesy of Latina/Latino Studies Program,
University of Illinois at Urbana–Champaign.

THE ECONOMY AND WORK

For more than thirty years, Alex Morris was a dockhand working the London waterfront. Today, at fifty-five, he considers himself retired. "I'm getting too old for the kind of work I used to do," he explains, "but the truth is there is no work for blokes like me anymore." These days, Morris spends most of his time in the company of other former dockworkers, sitting around the docks or in one of the local pubs.

It's not that the port of London is no longer operating; ships still come

and go much as they have for centuries. The difference is technology. "Back when I started," Morris explains, "it took a hundred guys five days to unload a ship. Then in the 1970s, they changed to container ships. Now it takes just eight people to unload a ship and they do it in just one day." Indeed, in ports around the world, enormous cranes lift the cargo containers, placing them directly on truck beds or railroad cars. Ships often are back to sea within twenty-four hours (based on Peters, 2000).

This chapter examines the economy, widely considered the most influential of all social institutions. The other major social institutions are examined in Chapter 17, "Politics and Government"; Chapter 18, "Family"; Chapter 19, "Religion"; Chapter 20, "Education"; and Chapter 21, "Health and Medicine.") As Alex Morris's story demonstrates, the economy has been changing, and the changes have not been to the benefit of everyone. Indeed, as we shall see, sociologists debate how the economy ought to work, whose interests it ought to serve, and what companies and workers owe each other.

THE ECONOMY: HISTORICAL OVERVIEW

The **economy** is *the social institution that organizes a society's production, distribution, and consumption of goods and services.* As an institution, the economy operates in a generally predictable manner. *Goods* are commodities ranging from necessities (food, clothing, shelter) to luxury items (cars, swimming pools, yachts). *Services* are activities that benefit others (for example, the work of priests, physicians, teachers, and software specialists).

We value goods and services because they ensure survival or because they make life easier or more interesting. Also, what people produce (as workers) and buy (as consumers) are important parts of social identity. How goods and services are distributed shapes the lives of everyone in a number of important ways.

The economies of modern high-income nations are the result of centuries of social change. We turn now to three technological revolutions that reorganized production and, in the process, transformed social life.

THE AGRICULTURAL REVOLUTION

Members of the earliest human societies were hunters and gatherers living off the land. In these technologically simple societies, there was no distinct economy. Rather, producing and consuming were all part of family life.

As Chapter 4 ("Society") explained, when people harnessed animals to plows some 5,000 years ago, the new agricultural economy was fifty times as productive as hunting and gathering. The resulting surplus meant that not everyone had to produce food, so many took on specialized work: making tools, raising animals, or building dwellings. Soon towns sprang up, linked by networks of traders dealing in food, animals, and other goods (Jacobs, 1970). These four factors—agricultural technology, job specialization, permanent

409

As societies industrialize, a smaller and smaller share of the labor force works in agriculture. In the United States, much of what agricultural work remains is performed by immigrants from lower-income nations. These people—new arrivals from Mexico—are harvesting aloe plants in south Texas.

settlements, and trade—made the economy a distinct social institution.

THE INDUSTRIAL REVOLUTION

By the mid-eighteenth century, a second technological revolution was underway, first in England and then in North America. The development of industry was to bring even greater changes than agriculture had. Industrialization changed the economy in five fundamental ways:

1. **New sources of energy.** Throughout history, "energy" meant the muscle power of people or animals. But in 1765, the English inventor James Watt introduced the steam engine. One hundred times more powerful than muscle power, early steam engines soon drove heavy machinery.

2. **Centralization of work in factories.** Steam-powered machines soon moved work out of homes and into factories, centralized and impersonal workplaces housing the machines.

3. **Manufacturing and mass production.** Before the Industrial Revolution, most people grew or gathered raw materials (such as grain, wood, or wool). In an industrial economy, the focus shifted so that most people's work day was spent turning raw materials into a wide range of finished products (such as furniture and clothing).

4. **Specialization.** Historically, artisans working at home made products from start to finish. In the factory, a laborer repeated a single task over and over, making only a small contribution to the finished product. Such specialization raised productivity but lowered the skill level of the average worker.

5. **Wage labor.** Instead of working for themselves in a household (called cottage industry), factory workers became wage laborers who sold their labor to strangers, who often cared less for them than for the machines they operated.

The Industrial Revolution gradually raised the standard of living as countless new products and services filled an expanding marketplace. Yet the benefits of industrial technology were not shared very equally, especially at the beginning. Some factory owners made vast fortunes, but the majority of industrial workers lived close to poverty. Children worked in factories or coal mines for pennies a day. Women factory workers, among the lowest paid, endured special problems, as the box explains.

THE INFORMATION REVOLUTION AND THE POSTINDUSTRIAL SOCIETY

By about 1950, the nature of production was changing once again. The United States was creating a

Women in the Mills of Lowell, Massachusetts

Few people paid much attention as Francis Cabot Lowell, ancestor of two prominent Boston families, the Cabots and the Lowells, stepped off a ship returning him from England in 1810. But Lowell carried with him documents that would change the course of the U.S. economy: plans, based on machinery operating in England, for this country's first power loom textile factory.

Lowell built his factory beside a waterfall on the Merrimack River in Massachusetts so he could use water power to turn large looms to weave cloth. Before long, Lowell's factory transformed a small farming village into a thriving industrial town that would be renamed at his death in his honor.

From the outset, 90 percent of the mill workers were women. Factory owners preferred women because they could be paid $2 to $3 a week, half the wages men received. Many immigrant men were willing to work for low wages, but prejudice disqualified "foreigners" from any job at all.

Recruiters, driving wagons through the small towns of New England, urged parents to send their daughters to the mills, where, they promised, the young women would be properly supervised as they learned skills and discipline. The offer appealed to many parents who could barely provide for their children, and the prospect of getting out on their own surely excited many young women. Back then, after all, there were few occupations open to women, and

those that were—including teaching and household service—paid even less than factory work.

At the Lowell factory, young women lived in dormitories, paying one-third of their wages for room and board. They were subject to a curfew and, as a condition of employment, regularly attended church. Any morally questionable conduct (such as bringing men to their rooms) brought firm disciplinary action.

Besides fulfilling their promise to parents, factory owners had another motive for their strict rules: They knew that closely supervised women could not organize among themselves. Working twelve or thirteen hours a day, six days a week, the Lowell employees had good reason to seek improvements in their working conditions. Yet any public criticism of the factory, or even possessing "radical" literature, could cost a worker her job.

Sources: Based on Eisler (1977) and Wertheimer (1982).

---

postindustrial economy, *a productive system based on service work and high technology.* Automated machinery (and, more recently, robotics) reduced the role of human labor in production so that fewer people work in industrial jobs and most now work in service positions, including sales, public relations, health care, advertising, and banking. Thus, the postindustrial era is distinguished by a shift from industrial work to service work.

Driving this change is a third technological breakthrough: the computer. Just as the Industrial Revolution introduced machines two centuries ago, the Information Revolution has introduced new kinds of products and new forms of communication that have

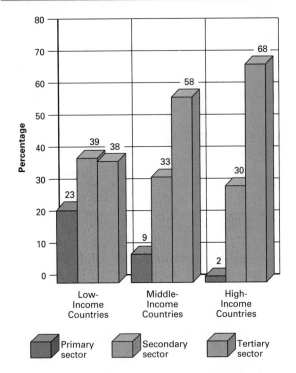

FIGURE 16–1 The Size of Economic Sectors by Income Level of Country

Source: Author estimates based on United Nations Development Programme (2000) and The World Bank (2000).

altered the fundamental character of work. In general, we see three changes:

1. **From tangible products to ideas.** As we discussed in earlier chapters, the industrial era was defined by the production of goods; in the postindustrial era, work involves manipulating symbols. Computer programmers, writers, financial analysts, advertising executives, architects, editors, and all sorts of consultants make up the labor force of the information age.

2. **From mechanical skills to literacy skills.** The Industrial Revolution required mechanical skills, but the Information Revolution requires literacy skills: speaking and writing well and, of course, using computers. People able to communicate

effectively enjoy new opportunities; people with limited literacy skills face declining prospects.

3. **From factories to almost anywhere.** Industrial technology drew workers into factories located near power sources, but computer technology allows workers to be almost anywhere. Laptop computers, cell phones, and portable fax machines now turn the home, car, or even an airplane into a "virtual office." New information technology blurs the line between work and home life.

SECTORS OF THE ECONOMY

The three revolutions we have just described reflect a shifting balance between the three sectors of a society's economy. The **primary sector** is *the part of the economy that draws raw materials from the natural environment.* The primary sector—agriculture, raising animals, fishing, forestry, and mining—is largest in low-income, preindustrial nations. Figure 16–1 shows that 23 percent of the economic output of low-income countries is in the primary sector, compared to 9 percent of economic activity in middle-income nations and just 2 percent in high-income countries such as the United States.

The **secondary sector** is *the part of the economy that transforms raw materials into manufactured goods.* This sector grows quickly as societies industrialize. It includes operations such as refining petroleum into gasoline and turning metals into tools and automobiles. The globalization of industry means that just about all the world's countries derive a significant share of their economic output from the secondary sector. Indeed, as Figure 16–1 shows, the secondary sector accounts for a greater share of economic output in low-income countries than it does in high-income nations.

The **tertiary sector** is *the part of the economy that involves services rather than goods.* Accounting for 38 percent of the economic output in low-income countries, the tertiary sector grows with industrialization and dominates the economies of middle-income countries (58 percent of economic output) and high-income, postindustrial nations (68 percent). Today, about 72 percent of the U.S. labor force is in service work, including clerical work and positions in food service, sales, law, health care, law enforcement, advertising, and teaching.

THE GLOBAL ECONOMY

New information technology is drawing people around the world closer together and creating a **global economy,** *expanding economic activity with little regard for national borders.*

GLOBAL MAP 16–1
Agricultural Employment in Global Perspective

The primary sector of the economy is largest in societies that are least developed. Thus, in the poor countries of Africa and Asia, up to half of all workers are farmers. This picture is altogether different in the world's most economically developed countries—including the United States, Canada, Great Britain, and Australia—which have 2 percent of their work force in agriculture.

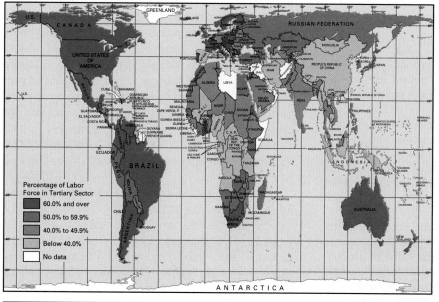

GLOBAL MAP 16–2
Service-Sector Employment in Global Perspective

The tertiary sector of the economy becomes ever larger as a nation's income level rises. In the United States, Canada, the countries of Western Europe, Australia, and Japan, about two-thirds of the labor force performs service work.

Sources: By the author, using data from United Nations Development Programme (2000) and The World Bank (2000, 2001); map projection from *Peters Atlas of the World* (1990).

The development of a global economy has four major consequences. First, we see a global division of labor so that different regions of the world specialize in one sector of economic activity. As Global Map 16–1 shows, agriculture represents more than half of the total economic output in the world's poorest countries. Global Map 16–2 indicates that most of the economic output in high-income countries is in the

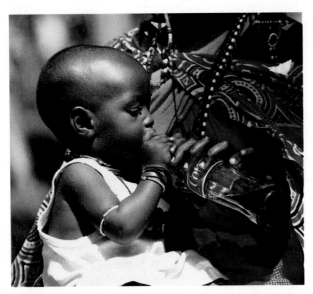

The rise of a global economy means that more and more products originally produced in one country are now made and consumed around the world. What do you see as some of the good consequences of globalization? What about harmful consequences?

service sector. Thus, the poorest nations specialize in producing raw materials, and the richest nations, including the United States, specialize in the production of various services.

Second, an increasing number of products pass through more than one nation. Look no farther than your morning coffee, which may well have been grown in Colombia and transported to New Orleans on a freighter registered in Liberia, made in Japan using steel from Korea, and fueled by oil from Venezuela.

A third consequence of the global economy is that national governments no longer control the economic activity that takes place within their borders. In fact, governments cannot even regulate the value of their national currencies as dollars, pounds sterling, yen, and other currencies are traded around the clock in the financial centers of Tokyo, London, and New York. Global markets are the result of satellite communications that link the world's cities.

A fourth consequence of the global economy is that a small number of businesses, operating internationally, now control a vast share of the world's economic

activity. According to one estimate, the 600 largest multinational companies account for half the world's entire economic output (Kidron & Segal, 1991).

The world is still divided into 192 politically distinct nations. But increasing international economic activity makes nationhood less significant than it was even a decade ago.

ECONOMIC SYSTEMS: PATHS TO JUSTICE

October 20, Saigon, Vietnam. Sailing up the narrow Saigon River is an unsettling experience for anyone who came of age during the 1960s. We need to remember that Vietnam is a country, not a war, and more than twenty years have passed since the last U.S. helicopter lifted off the rooftop of the U.S. embassy, ending our country's presence there.

Saigon is on the brink of becoming a boomtown. Neon signs bathe the city's waterfront in color; hotels, bankrolled by Western corporations, push skyward from a dozen construction sites; taxi meters record fares in U.S. dollars, not Vietnamese dong; Visa and American Express stickers decorate the doors of fashionable boutiques that cater to shoppers from Japan, France, and (since the U.S. embargo on visiting Vietnam was lifted in 1994) the United States.

There is a heavy irony here: After decades of fighting, the loss of millions of lives on both sides, and the victory of Communist forces, the Vietnamese are turning toward capitalism. What we see today is what might well have happened had the U.S. forces won the war.

Every society's economic system makes a statement about justice because the economy broadly determines who gets what. Two general economic models are capitalism and socialism. No society has an economy that is completely one or the other; capitalism and

Although the United States has a mostly capitalist economy, the role of government increased over the course of the twentieth century and is now a familiar part of everyday life. By contrast, back in the 1800s in small towns across the country, the only evidence of government was a single building—a post office. Shown here is the original post office for Duluth, Minnesota.

socialism are two ends of a spectrum along which all actual economies can be located. We will look at each type in turn.

CAPITALISM

Capitalism is *an economic system in which natural resources and the means of producing goods and services are privately owned.* Ideally, a capitalist economy has three distinctive features:

1. **Private ownership of property.** In a capitalist economy, individuals can own almost anything. The more capitalist an economy is, the more private ownership there is of wealth-producing property such as factories, real estate, and natural resources.

2. **Pursuit of personal profit.** A capitalist society encourages the accumulation of private property and considers the profit motive natural, simply a matter of "doing business." Furthermore, claimed Scottish philosopher Adam Smith (1723–1790), the individual pursuit of self-interest helps the entire society prosper (1937:508; orig. 1776).

3. **Competition and consumer sovereignty.** A purely capitalist economy is a free-market system with no government interference (sometimes called a *laissez-faire* economy, from the French words meaning "to leave alone"). Adam Smith

stated that a freely competitive economy regulates itself by the "invisible hand" of the laws of supply and demand.

Consumers regulate a free-market economy by selecting goods and services that offer the greatest value, Smith explained. Producers compete for customers' business by offering the highest-quality goods and services at the lowest price possible while still making a profit. As Smith put it, from narrow self-interest comes the "greatest good for the greatest number of people." Government control of the economy, on the other hand, distorts market forces by reducing producer motivation, diminishing quantity and quality of goods, and shortchanging consumers.

In a capitalist context, "justice" amounts to freedom of the marketplace, where one can produce, invest, and buy according to individual self-interest and the means to do so. The worth of products or workers is determined by the dynamic process of supply and demand. Replacing much of the work force with automatic machinery, as described in the opening to this chapter, is just if it is profitable to a company and its stockholders.

The United States is a capitalist nation in that the vast majority of businesses are privately owned. Even so, government plays an extensive role in economic affairs. The government itself owns and operates a number of businesses, including almost all of this country's

Capitalism still thrives in Hong Kong (left), evident in streets choked with advertising and shoppers. Socialism is more the rule in China's capital of Beijing (right), a city dominated by government buildings rather than a downtown business district.

schools, roads, parks and museums, the U.S. Postal Service, the Amtrak railroad system, and the entire U.S. military. The federal government also had a major part in building the Internet. In addition, governments use taxation and other forms of regulation to influence what companies produce, control the quality and cost of merchandise, influence what businesses import and export, and motivate consumers to conserve natural resources.

Furthermore, government sets minimum wage levels, enforces workplace safety standards, regulates corporate mergers, provides farm price supports, and supplements income in the form of Social Security, public assistance, student loans, and veterans' benefits for a majority of the people in the United States. In fact, local, state, and federal governments together are the country's biggest employer, with 14 percent of the labor force on their payrolls (U.S. Census Bureau, 2000).

SOCIALISM

Socialism is *an economic system in which natural resources and the means of producing goods and services are collectively owned.* In its ideal form, a socialist economy is the exact opposite of capitalism; its three distinctive features are:

1. **Collective ownership of property.** A socialist economy limits rights to private property, especially property used to generate income. Government controls such property and makes housing and other goods available to all, not just to people with the most money.

2. **Pursuit of collective goals.** The individualistic pursuit of profit is also at odds with the collective orientation of socialism. What capitalism celebrates as the entrepreneurial spirit, socialism condemns as greed. For this reason, socialist nations outlaw private transactions as "black market" activity.

3. **Government control of the economy.** Socialism rejects capitalism's laissez-faire approach in favor of a *centrally controlled* or *command economy* operated by the government. Socialism also rejects the idea that it is consumers who guide capitalist production, on the grounds that consumers lack the information necessary to evaluate products and are manipulated by advertising to buy what is profitable for factory owners rather than what

they genuinely need. Commercial advertising thus plays little role in socialist economies.

In a socialist context, "justice" is not freedom to compete and accumulate wealth but rather meeting everyone's basic needs in a roughly equal manner. From a socialist point of view, limiting workers' wages and benefits to boost company earnings is putting profits before people and is thus an injustice.

The People's Republic of China and some two dozen other societies in Asia, Africa, and Latin America model their economies on socialism, placing almost all wealth-generating property under state control (McColm et al., 1991; Freedom House, 2001). The extent of world socialism has declined in recent years as countries in Eastern Europe and the former Soviet Union have restructured their economies toward more of a market system.

Socialism and Communism

Many people think of *socialism* and *communism* as much the same. More precisely, **communism** is *a hypothetical economic and political system in which all members of a society are socially equal.* Karl Marx viewed socialism as a transitory stage on the path toward the ideal of a communist society that abolished all class divisions. In many socialist societies today, the dominant political party describes itself as communist, but nowhere has the communist goal been achieved.

Why? For one thing, social stratification involves differences of power as well as wealth. In general, socialist societies have reduced disparities in wealth by expanding government bureaucracies and extensively regulating daily life. In the process, government did not "wither away" as Karl Marx imagined. On the contrary, socialist political elites have enormous power and privilege.

Marx probably would have agreed that a communist society is a *utopia* (from the Greek words meaning "not a place"). Yet Marx considered communism a worthy goal and might well have disparaged reputedly Marxist societies such as the former Soviet Union, North Korea, the People's Republic of China, and Cuba for not fulfilling what he saw as the promise of communism.

WELFARE CAPITALISM AND STATE CAPITALISM

Some nations of Western Europe, including Sweden and Italy, have combined a market-based economy with broad social welfare programs. Analysts call this

Global comparisons indicate that socialist economies generate the greatest economic equality although living standards remain relatively low. Capitalist economies, by contrast, engender more income disparity although living standards are typically higher. As the former Soviet Union has moved towards a market system, however, the majority of people have suffered a decline in living standards, while some people have become quite rich.

"third way" **welfare capitalism,** *an economic and political system that combines a mostly market-based economy with extensive social welfare programs.*

Under welfare capitalism, the government owns some of the largest industries and services, such as transportation, the mass media, and health care. In Sweden and Italy, about 12 percent of economic production is "nationalized," or state controlled. That leaves most industry in private hands but subject to extensive government regulation. High taxation (aimed especially at the rich) funds a wide range of social welfare programs, including universal health care and child care (Olsen, 1996).

TABLE 16–1 Participation in the Labor Force by Sex, Race, and Ethnicity, 2000

Category of the Population	In the Labor Force	
	Number (in millions)	Percentage
Men (aged 16 and over)	**75.2**	**74.7%**
White	63.8	75.4
African American	7.8	69.0
Hispanic	8.9	80.6
Women (aged 16 and over)	**65.6**	**60.2**
White	53.7	59.8
African American	8.7	63.2
Hispanic	6.4	56.9

Source: U.S. Department of Labor, *Employment and Earnings*, vol. 48, no. 1 (January 2001), pp. 168–71.

Yet another blend of capitalism and socialism is **state capitalism,** *an economic and political system in which companies are privately owned but cooperate closely with the government.* State capitalism is the rule in rapidly developing Asian countries along the Pacific Rim. Japan, South Korea, and Singapore, for example, are all capitalist countries, but their governments work in partnership with large companies, supplying financial assistance and controlling foreign imports to help their businesses compete in world markets (Gerlach, 1992).

RELATIVE ADVANTAGES OF CAPITALISM AND SOCIALISM

In practice, which economic system works best? Comparing economic models is difficult because all countries mix capitalism and socialism to varying degrees. Moreover, nations differ in cultural attitudes toward work, available natural resources, levels of technological development, and patterns of trade (Gregory & Stuart, 1985). Despite these complicating factors, some crude comparisons are revealing.

Economic Productivity

One key dimension of economic performance is productivity. A commonly used measure of economic output is gross domestic product (GDP), the total value of all goods and services produced annually. "Per capita," or per person, GDP allows us to compare the economic performance of nations of different population sizes.

The output of mostly capitalist countries at the end of the 1980s varied somewhat, but averaging the

figures for the United States, Canada, and the nations of Western Europe yields a per capita GDP of about $13,500. The comparable figure for the former Soviet Union and nations of Eastern Europe is about $5,000. In other words, capitalist countries outproduced socialist nations by a ratio of 2.7 to 1 (United Nations Development Programme, 1990).

Economic Equality

How resources are distributed within a society is another important measure of how well an economic system works. A comparative study completed in the mid-1970s looked at income ratios based on the earnings of the richest and poorest 5 percent of the population (Wiles, 1977). The result was that societies with predominantly capitalist economies had an income ratio of about 10 to 1; the figure for socialist countries was 5 to 1. In other words, *capitalist economies support a higher overall standard of living but show greater income disparity.* Or, put another way, *socialist economies create more equality but with a lower overall living standard.*

Personal Freedom

One additional consideration in evaluating capitalism and socialism is the personal freedom of its people. Capitalism emphasizes *freedom to* pursue one's self-interest. After all, capitalism depends on the freedom of producers and consumers to interact, with little interference from the state. On the other hand, socialism emphasizes *freedom from* basic want. Equality is the goal, which requires state intervention in the economy, which in turn limits personal choices for citizens.

No system has yet been able to offer both political freedom and economic equality. In the capitalist United States, the political system guarantees many personal freedoms, but are these freedoms worth as much to a poor person as to a rich one? On the other side of the coin, China and Cuba have more economic equality but restrict the rights of their people to freely express themselves and move freely within and across their borders.

CHANGES IN SOCIALIST COUNTRIES

In 1989 and 1990, the nations of Eastern Europe that were seized by the Soviet Union at the end of World War II shook off their socialist regimes. These nations—including the German Democratic Republic, Czechoslovakia, Hungary, Romania, and Bulgaria—have introduced capitalist elements into

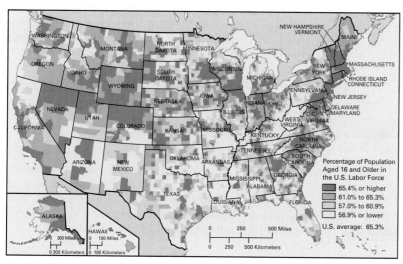

NATIONAL MAP 16–1
Labor Force Participation across the United States

Counties with high levels of labor force participation have steady sources of employment, including military bases, recreation areas, and large cities. By contrast, counties with low employment rates generally include a high proportion of elderly people (as well as students). Gender is another important consideration: What do you think is the typical level of employment in regions of the country (stretching from the South up into coal-mining districts of Kentucky and West Virginia) where traditional cultural norms encourage women to remain at home?

Percentage of Population Aged 16 and Older in the U.S. Labor Force
- 65.4% or higher
- 61.0% to 65.3%
- 57.0% to 60.9%
- 56.9% or lower

U.S. average: 65.3%

Sources: *American Demographics Desk Reference Series # 4*. Reprinted with permission. © 1992 *American Demographics* magazine, Ithaca, New York. Data from the 1990 decennial census.

what were centrally controlled economies. In 1992, the Soviet Union itself formally dissolved and has since introduced some free-market principles.

The reasons for these sweeping changes were complex. But two factors stand out: First, the mostly socialist economies grossly underproduced their capitalist counterparts. Although they achieved remarkable economic equality, living standards were low by Western European standards. Second, Soviet socialism was heavy-handed, rigidly controlling the media and restricting individual freedoms. In short, socialism did away with *economic* elites, as Karl Marx predicted. But as Max Weber foresaw, socialism increased the clout of *political* elites.

So far, the market reforms in Eastern Europe are proceeding unevenly. Some nations (Czech Republic, Slovakia, Poland, and the Baltic states of Latvia, Estonia, and Lithuania) are faring well, but others (Romania, Bulgaria, and the former Soviet republics) have been buffeted by price increases and falling living standards. Officials hope that expanding production eventually will bring a turnaround. However, there is already evidence that any improvement in living standards will be accompanied by increasing economic disparity (Pohl, 1996; Buraway, 1997; Specter, 1997a).

WORK IN THE POSTINDUSTRIAL ECONOMY

Economic change is not limited to the socialist world. In the United States in 2000, the government reported 141 million people in the U.S. labor force, representing two-thirds of the population age sixteen and over. As shown in Table 16–1, a larger proportion of men (74.7 percent) than women (60.2 percent) hold income-producing jobs, although this gap is closing. Among men, 69.0 percent of African Americans are in the labor force, compared to 75.4 percent of white people and 80.6 percent of Hispanics. Among women, 63.2 percent of African Americans are employed, compared to 59.8 percent of white people and 56.9 percent of Hispanics.

 Find a government report on youth in the U.S. labor force at this Web site: http://www.bls.gov/opub/rylf/rylfhome.htm

National Map 16–1 shows labor force participation across the United States. Because working is the major source of income for most people, regions of the country with greater labor force participation are more affluent.

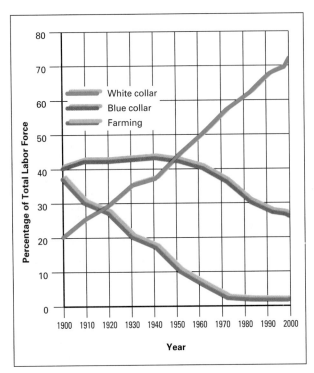

FIGURE 16–2 The Changing Pattern of Work in the United States, 1900–2000

Sources: Author estimates based on United Nations Development Programme (2000) and The World Bank (2000).

THE DECLINE OF AGRICULTURAL WORK

In 1900, almost 40 percent of the U.S. labor force engaged in farming. In 2000, just 2 percent were in agriculture. Figure 16–2 shows this rapid decline, which in turn reflects the shrinking role of the primary sector in the U.S. economy.

Although farming involves far fewer people today, it is more productive than ever. A century ago, a typical farmer grew food for five people; today, one farmer feeds seventy-five. This dramatic rise in productivity reflects new varieties of crops, pesticides that raise yields, and more efficient farm machinery and farming techniques. The average U.S. farm has also doubled in size since 1950, to about 500 acres.

The family farms of yesterday have been replaced by *corporate agribusinesses*. Agriculture may be more productive, but the transformation has required painful adjustments in farming communities across the country as a way of life is lost.

FROM FACTORY WORK TO SERVICE WORK

In the early 1900s, industrialization swelled the ranks of blue-collar workers. As shown in Figure 16–2, until about 1960, at least 40 percent of working people had industrial jobs—far more than were in agriculture. By 1950, however, a white-collar revolution had moved a majority of workers into service occupations. By 2000, 90 percent of new jobs were in the service sector, and 72 percent of the entire labor force performed service work.

As Chapter 11 ("Social Class in the United States") explained, the expansion of service work is one reason many people call the United States a middle-class society. But much service work—including sales and clerical positions and jobs in hospitals and restaurants—carries little of the income and prestige of white-collar professions and often fewer rewards than factory work. In sum, many jobs in this postindustrial era provide only a modest standard of living.

THE DUAL LABOR MARKET

Sociologists see the jobs in today's economy falling into two categories. The **primary labor market** includes *jobs that provide extensive benefits to workers.* This segment of the labor market includes the traditional white-collar professions such as medicine and law as well as upper-management positions. These are jobs that people think of as *careers,* interesting work that provides high income and job security. Such occupations require a broad education rather than specialized training and offer solid opportunity for advancement.

Few of these advantages apply to work in the **secondary labor market,** *jobs that provide minimal benefits to workers.* This segment of the labor force is employed in low-skilled, blue-collar assembly-line operations and low-level service-sector jobs, including clerical positions. Workers in the secondary labor market receive lower income, have less job security, and often feel dissatisfied with their jobs. One recent study found that about 15 percent of jobs in the United States lacked good pay, health benefits, or pension benefits. Women and other minorities are overrepresented in the secondary labor market work force (Hunnicutt, 1990; Greenwald, 1994; Nelson, 1994; Kalleberg, Reskin, & Hudson, 2000).

LABOR UNIONS

The changing U.S. economy has seen the role of labor unions diminish. **Labor unions** are *organizations of* *workers that seek to improve wages and working conditions through various strategies, including negotiations and strikes.* During the Great Depression of the 1930s, union membership increased rapidly until, by 1950, more than one-third of nonfarm workers belonged to a union. By 1970, the number of union members peaked at almost 25 million. Since then, union rolls have declined to about 14 percent of nonfarm workers, or 16.3 million men and women. Looking more closely, 37 percent of government workers are members of unions, compared to just 9 percent of private sector (nongovernment) workers (Clawson & Clawson, 1999; Goldfield, 2000).

The pattern of union decline holds in other high-income countries as well. Yet unions claim a far smaller share of workers in the United States than elsewhere. In Canada and Japan, about 33 percent of workers belong to unions; across Europe, the share is about 40 percent; in the Scandinavian countries, the share is 80 percent (Western, 1993, 1995).

The global decline in union membership follows the shrinking industrial sector of the economy. In addition, the newer service jobs are less likely to be unionized. But as some analysts see it, decreased job security may make unions popular again in years to come. Indeed, in 1999 unions gained more than 250,000 members. However, unions will have to adapt to the new global economy. Union members in the United States, used to seeing foreign workers as "the enemy," will have to build new international alliances (Mabry, 1992; Church, 1994).

PROFESSIONS

All kinds of jobs today are called *professional*; we hear of professional tennis players, professional babysitters, and even professional exterminators. As distinct from *amateur* (from the Latin for "lover," meaning someone who acts out of love for the activity itself), a professional pursues some task for a living.

A **profession** is *a prestigious, white-collar occupation that requires extensive formal education.* The term "profession" suggests a public declaration to abide by certain principles. Traditional professions include the ministry, medicine, law, academia, and, more recently, architecture, accounting, and social work. Occupations are professions to the extent that they demonstrate the following four characteristics (Goode, 1960; Ritzer & Walczak, 1990):

1. **Theoretical knowledge**. Professionals have a theoretical understanding of their field

An increasing share of jobs in the postindustrial economy of the United States involves working with computers. These jobs lack the hard manual labor and health hazards common to much factory work in the past; at the same time, they provide only modest pay and limited opportunities for advancement.

rather than mere technical training. Anyone can master first-aid skills, for example, but physicians have a theoretical understanding of human health and illness.

2. **Self-regulating practice**. The typical professional is self-employed, "in practice" rather than working for a company. Professionals oversee their own work and observe a code of ethics.

3. **Authority over clients**. Based on extensive training, professionals advise clients and expect them to follow their direction.

4. **Community orientation rather than self-interest**. The traditional professing of duty is a vow to serve the community rather than merely seek personal income.

Many new occupations in the postindustrial economy seek to *professionalize* their services. Claiming professional standing often begins by renaming the work to imply special, theoretical knowledge, which also distances the field from its previously less distinguished reputation. For example, stockroom workers call their work "inventory supply," and exterminators are reborn as "insect control specialists."

Interested parties may also form a professional association to formally attest to their specialized skills.

Jose Clemente Orozco's painting The Unemployed *is a powerful statement of the personal collapse and private despair that afflict men and women who are out of work. How does a sociological perspective help us to understand being out of work as more than a personal problem?*

Jose Clemente Orozco, *The Unemployed.* Oil. © Orozco Valladares Family. Reproduction authorized by the Instituto Nacional de Bellas Artes.

This organization then licenses people who perform the work and writes a code of ethics that emphasizes the occupation's role in the community. In its effort to win public acceptance, a professional association may also establish schools or other training facilities and perhaps start a professional journal (Abbott, 1988). Not all occupations try to claim professional status. Some *paraprofessionals*, including paralegals and medical technicians, possess specialized skills but lack the extensive theoretical education required of full professionals.

SELF-EMPLOYMENT

Self-employment—earning a living without working for an organization—was once common in the United States. About 80 percent of the labor force was self-employed in 1800, compared to 6.5 percent of workers today (8.2 percent of men and 5.7 percent of women) (U.S. Department of Labor, 2001).

Lawyers, physicians, and other professionals are well represented among the ranks of the self-employed. In addition, the number of people using the Internet to run small businesses is growing. But most self-employed workers are small business owners, plumbers, carpenters, freelance writers, editors, artists,

 Visit the Web site of the Small Business Administration: http://www.sba.gov

and long-distance truck drivers. Overall, the self-employed are more likely to have blue-collar than white-collar jobs.

Finally, a notable trend in the U.S. economy is that women now own nearly 40 percent of this country's small businesses, and the share is rising. Moreover, the 9.1 million firms owned by U.S. women now employ almost 30 million people and generate close to $4 trillion in annual sales (Small Business Administration, 2001).

UNEMPLOYMENT AND UNDEREMPLOYMENT

Every society has some unemployment. Few young people entering the labor force find a job right away, workers may temporarily leave their jobs to seek new work or have children, some may be on strike, others suffer from long-term illnesses, and still others are illiterate or lack the skills to perform useful work.

But unemployment is also caused by the economy itself. Jobs disappear as occupations become obsolete, businesses close in the face of foreign competition or economic recession, and companies downsize to become more profitable. Since 1980, the 500 largest U.S. businesses have eliminated some 5 million jobs, one-fourth of the total.

In 2000, 5.7 million people over the age of sixteen were unemployed, about 4.0 percent of the civilian labor force. As a glance back at National Map 16–1 on page 419 shows, some regions of the country, including parts of West Virginia and New Mexico, have high unemployment, in some cases twice the national average. Indeed, research shows that rural residents in the United States are especially likely to experience unemployment or underemployment (Stofferahn, 2000).

Figure 16–3 shows that unemployment among African Americans (7.6 percent) is more than twice the rate among white people (3.5 percent). Overall, men and women of each race have about the same rates of unemployment.

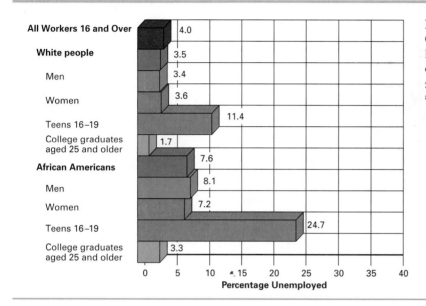

FIGURE 16–3
Official U.S. Unemployment Rates for Various Categories of Adults, 2000

Sources: U.S. Census Bureau (2000) and U.S. Department of Labor (2001).

Category	Percentage Unemployed
All Workers 16 and Over	4.0
White people	3.5
Men	3.4
Women	3.6
Teens 16–19	11.4
College graduates aged 25 and older	1.7
African Americans	7.6
Men	8.1
Women	7.2
Teens 16–19	24.7
College graduates aged 25 and older	3.3

Underemployment is a problem for millions of workers. The government reports that more than 30 million people work part time, meaning no more than thirty-four hours weekly. Of these, 80 percent are satisfied with the arrangement, but 20 percent (6 million workers) say they want more work but cannot find it (U.S. Department of Labor, 2001).

THE UNDERGROUND ECONOMY

The U.S. government requires individuals and businesses to report their economic activity, especially earnings. Unreported income makes a transaction part of the **underground economy,** *economic activity involving income unreported to the government as required by law.*

On a small scale, most people participate in the underground economy from time to time: A family makes extra money by holding a garage sale, or teenagers babysit for neighbors without reporting the income. Of course, far more of the underground economy is attributable to criminal activity, such as the sale of illegal drugs, prostitution, bribery, theft, illegal gambling, and loan-sharking.

But the single largest segment of contributors to the underground economy is people who fail to re-port some or all of their legally obtained income. Self-employed people such as carpenters, physicians, and owners of small businesses may understate their incomes on tax forms; food servers, taxicab drivers, and other service workers may not report their earnings from tips. Individually, the omissions and misrepresentations may be small, but millions of individuals hedging on income tax returns adds up to perhaps $170 billion annually in lost revenues (Speer, 1995).

DIVERSITY IN THE WORKPLACE: RACE AND GENDER

Traditionally, white men have been the mainstay of the U.S. labor force. As discussed in Chapter 14 ("Race and Ethnicity"), however, our nation's proportion of minorities is rising rapidly. Between 1990 and 2000, the African American population increased by 16 percent, more than five times the 3 percent rate for non-Hispanic white people. The jump in the Hispanic population was even greater, at 58 percent, and among Asian Americans, 41 percent. The box on page 424 takes a closer look at how the increasing social diversity of our society will affect the workplace.

Twenty-First Century Diversity: Changes in the Workplace

An upward trend in the U.S. minority population is changing the workplace. As the figure shows, the number of white men in the U.S. labor force will rise by a modest 7 percent between 1998 and 2008. The rate of increase among African American working men will be greater, at 18 percent, and that among Hispanic men will be greater still, at 29 percent. Among white women the projected increase is 13 percent, and among African American women it is 21 percent. Hispanic women will show the greatest gains, estimated at 49 percent.

The overall result is that within a decade, non-Hispanic white men will represent 38 percent of all workers, and that figure will continue to drop. Therefore, companies that welcome social diversity will tap the largest talent pool and enjoy a competitive advantage.

Welcoming social diversity means, first, recruiting talented workers of both sexes and all colors and cultural backgrounds. But developing the potential of all employees requires meeting the needs of women and other minorities, which may not be the same as those of white men. For example, corporations are being pressed to provide child care at the workplace.

Second, businesses must develop effective ways to defuse tensions that arise from social differences. They will have to work harder at treating workers equally and respectfully. Furthermore, no corporate culture can tolerate racial or sexual harassment.

Third, companies will have to rethink current promotion practices. At present, only 4 percent of Fortune 500 top executives are women, and just 1 percent are other minorities. In a broad survey of U.S. companies, the U.S. Equal Employment Opportunity Commission confirmed that white men (42 percent of adults aged twenty to sixty-four) hold 59 percent of management jobs; the comparable figures for white women are 42 and 28 percent; for African Americans, 12 and 6 percent; and for Hispanics, 13 and 4 percent.

In sum, "glass ceilings" that prevent skilled workers from advancing not only discourage effort but deprive companies of their largest source of talent: women and other minorities.

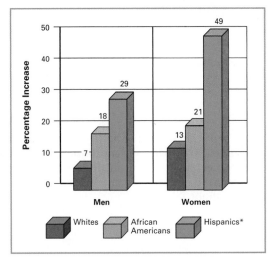

Projected Increase in the Numbers of People in the U.S. Labor Force, 1998–2008

*Hispanics can be of any race.

Source: U.S. Department of Labor (1999).

Sources: U.S. Department of Labor (1999), Catalyst (2001), and U.S. Equal Employment Opportunity Commission (2001).

NEW INFORMATION TECHNOLOGY AND WORK

July 2, Ticonderoga, New York. The manager of the local hardware store scans the barcodes on bags of lawn seed and fertilizer as I transfer them from my shopping cart to the counter. "The computer not only totals the costs," she explains, "it also keeps track of inventory, places orders from the warehouse, and decides which products to continue to sell and which to discontinue." "Sounds like what you used

Although the Information Revolution is centered in high-income countries such as the United States, the effects of high technology are becoming evident even in low-income nations. Do you think the expansion of information technology will change the lives of rural people such as these peasants in Vietnam? If so, how?

```
to do, Maureen," I respond with a
smile. "Yep," she nods, with no smile
at all.
```

Another workplace issue is the increasing role of computers and other new information technology. The Information Revolution is changing the kind of work people do and where they do it. Computers are also changing the character of work in more subtle ways (Zuboff, 1982; Rule & Brantley, 1992; Vallas & Beck, 1996):

1. **Computers are deskilling labor.** Just as industrial machinery replaced the master craftsworkers of an earlier era, computers now threaten the skills of managers. More and more business decisions are based not on executive training and experience but on computer modeling. In other words, as in the hardware store just described, a machine makes decisions that people used to make, determining when to resupply inventory or even whether or not to approve a loan application.

2. **Computers are making work more abstract.** Most industrial workers have a hands-on relationship with their product. Postindustrial workers manipulate symbols in pursuit of abstract goals such as making a Web site more attractive, a company more profitable, or software more user-friendly.

3. **Computers limit workplace interaction.** As workers spend more time at computer terminals, they become isolated from one another.

4. **Computers enhance employers' control of workers.** Computers allow supervisors to monitor employees' output precisely and continuously, whether they work at computer terminals or on assembly lines.

Such changes remind us that technology is not socially neutral. Rather, it shapes the way we work and alters the balance of power between employers and employees. Understandably, then, people welcome some aspects of the Information Revolution and oppose others.

CORPORATIONS

At the core of today's capitalist economy lies the **corporation,** *an organization with a legal existence, including rights and liabilities, apart from that of its members.* Incorporating makes an organization a legal entity unto itself, able to enter into contracts and own property. Of more than 24 million businesses in the United States, 5 million are incorporated (U.S. Census Bureau, 2000). Incorporating also protects the wealth of owners from lawsuits arising from business debts or as a result of harm to consumers; often, it also means a lower tax rate on profits.

Them That's Got, Gets: The Case of Corporate Welfare

What would you say if the government offered to slash your income taxes and abolish sales tax on your purchases? What if it offered you the money to buy a new house at a below-market interest rate? Would you like the government to hook up all your utilities for free and pay your water and electric bills?

For an ordinary individual, such deals sound too good to be true. But our tax money is doing exactly this—not for individuals but for big corporations. All a large company has to do is declare a willingness to relocate and then wait for the offers from state and local governments to come pouring in.

Supporters call government aid to corporations "public-private partnerships." They point to the jobs companies create, sometimes in areas hard hit by earlier business closings. For a city or county with a high unemployment rate, the promise of a new factory opening is simply too good to pass up. If some incentives in the form of tax relief or free utilities lure the company away

from another possible site, it is considered money well spent.

However, critics call these arrangements corporate welfare. They concede that companies do create new jobs, but they also point out that the corporations get much more than they give. In 1991, for example, the state of Indiana offered $451 million in incentives to lure United Airlines to build an aircraft maintenance facility there. United Airlines built the facility and hired 6,300 people. But some simple math shows that the cost to Indiana came out to be a whopping $72,000 *per job*. Much the same happened in 1993, when Alabama offered $253 million in incentives to Mercedes-Benz to build an automobile assembly plant in Tuscaloosa. The plant opened and 1,500 people were hired—at an average cost to Alabama of $169,000 per worker. In 1997, Pennsylvania gave $307 million in incentives to a Norwegian company to reopen part of Philadelphia's naval shipyard. Once the deal was signed, 950 people were hired, at a cost of $323,000 per job. Across the country, the

pattern is much the same. During the 1990s, in fact, government support to corporations exceeded $15 billion each year—more than the welfare given to poor people.

Corporations willing to relocate their facilities attract very generous offers from politicians eager to "create jobs." But nationwide, although new plants do create some jobs, more often jobs are simply moved from one place to another. Nor do all the jobs pay well. And there is no guarantee that, once settled, a corporation will stay because businesses are free to make a better deal to move again to another location. In 1993, state and local governments in Kentucky granted General Electric $19 million in tax breaks to build a washing machine factory near Louisville. In 1999, GE pulled up stakes, announcing the loss of 1,500 local jobs because the company was moving to new factories in Georgia and Mexico, where wages were lower.

Source: Adapted from Bartlett & Steele (1998).

ECONOMIC CONCENTRATION

About half of U.S. corporations are small, with assets under $100,000. However, the largest corporations dominate our country's economy. In 1997, 549 corporations had assets exceeding $1 billion, representing three-fourths of all corporate assets and profits (U.S. Census Bureau, 2000).

The largest U.S. corporation in terms of sales is automaker General Motors, with $303 billion in total assets. GM employs more people than the state governments of California, Oregon, Washington, Alaska, and Hawaii combined. Its sales ($185 billion in 2000) equal the total tax revenues of half the states.

CONGLOMERATES AND CORPORATE LINKAGES

The largest businesses are **conglomerates,** *giant corporations composed of many smaller corporations.* Conglomerates form as corporations enter new markets, spin off new companies, or merge with other companies. For example, RJR-Nabisco is a conglomerate that sells not only cigarettes but also dozens of familiar household products.

Even conglomerates are linked because they own each other's stock, resulting in worldwide corporate alliances of staggering size. For example, General Motors owns Opel (Germany), Vauxhall (Great Britain), and half of Saab (Sweden) and has partnerships with Suzuki, Isuzu, and Toyota (Japan). Similarly, Ford owns Jaguar and Aston Martin (Great Britain) and a share of Mazda (Japan), Kia (Korea), and Volvo (Sweden).

Corporations are also linked throughly *interlocking directorates*, networks of people who serve as directors of many corporations (Herman, 1981; Scott & Griff, 1985; Weidenbaum, 1995; Kono et al., 1998). These boardroom connections provide access to valuable information about each other's products and marketing strategies. Beth Mintz and Michael Schwartz (1981) found General Motors linked, through its board members, to 700 other companies. Such linkages do not in themselves run counter to the public interest, but they may encourage illegal activity, such as price-fixing, and they certainly concentrate wealth and power.

CORPORATIONS: ARE THEY COMPETITIVE?

According to the capitalist model, businesses operate independently in a competitive market. But large corporations have extensive linkages, which means they do not operate independently. Moreover, a small number of corporations dominate many large markets. Many large corporations therefore have little real competition.

Law forbids a large company from establishing a **monopoly,** *domination of a market by a single producer*, because a monopoly could simply dictate prices. But **oligopoly,** *domination of a market by a few producers*, is a legal and common practice. Oligopoly arises because the vast investment needed to enter a major market, such as the auto industry, is beyond the reach of all but the biggest companies. Moreover, true competition means risk, which big business tries to avoid.

Corporate power is now so great—and competition between corporations so limited—that government regulation may be the only way to protect the public interest. Yet the government is the corporate world's single biggest customer. The federal government also steps in to support struggling corporations, sometimes with billion-dollar bail-out programs. In addition, as the box explains, state government aid to corporations has drawn fire as "corporate welfare."

CORPORATIONS AND THE GLOBAL ECONOMY

Corporations have grown so big and powerful that they account for most of the world's economic output. The biggest corporations are based in the United

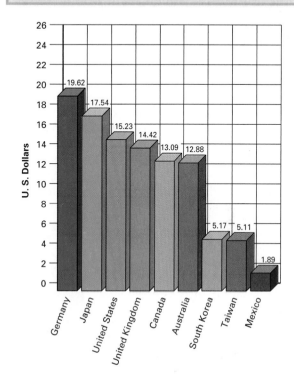

GLOBAL SNAPSHOT

U. S. Dollars

Germany 19.62
Japan 17.54
United States 15.23
United Kingdom 14.42
Canada 13.09
Australia 12.88
South Korea 5.17
Taiwan 5.11
Mexico 1.89

FIGURE 16–4 Average Hourly Wages for Workers in Manufacturing, 1999

Source: Calculations by the author based on U.S. Department of Labor (2000).

States, Japan, and Western Europe, but they consider the entire world one huge marketplace. In fact, many large U.S. companies such as McDonald's generate most of their sales outside the United States.

Poor nations attract the attention of global corporations because most of the world's people and resources are found there. In addition, as shown in Figure 16–4, labor costs are far lower: A factory worker in Mexico works for two weeks to earn what a German worker earns in a single day.

The impact of multinationals on poor societies is controversial, as Chapter 12 ("Global Stratification") explains. On one side of the argument, modernization theorists claim that multinationals unleash the great productive power of capitalism to raise living standards in poor nations. Specifically, corporations offer poor

The Market: Does the "Invisible Hand" Look Out for Us or Pick Our Pockets?

"The market" or "government planning"? Each is a means of economic decision making to determine what products and services companies will produce and what people will consume. So important is this process that the degree to which the market or government directs the economy largely determines how nations define themselves, choose their allies, and identify their enemies.

Historically, U.S. society has relied on the market's "invisible hand" for economic decisions. Market dynamics move prices up or down according to the supply of products and buyer demand. The market thus coordinates the efforts of countless people, each of whom—to return to Adam Smith's insight—is motivated only by self-interest.

Defenders of the market system praise it for discouraging social bad habits, such as racial prejudice. Industrialist J. P. Morgan, who once commented that he would sail only with a gentleman, would do business with *anyone*, making the point that market transactions focus on value, not the social traits of traders. Perhaps most important of all, as economists Milton Friedman and Rose Friedman remind us, a freely operating market system is

J. Pierpont Morgan, railroad tycoon and founder of U.S. Steel (the first billion-dollar corporation), symbolized the operation of the market system at a time of little government regulation.

the key to U.S. society's unprecedented economic standard of living.

But others point to the contributions government makes to the U.S. economy. First, government must step in to carry out tasks that no private company could do as well. For example, Adam Smith looked to government to defend the country against external enemies. Government (in partnership with private companies) also plays a key role in constructing and maintaining public projects such as roads, utilities, schools, libraries, and museums.

But the Friedmans, as well as other believers in the free-market system, counter that whatever task government undertakes usually ends up being performed inefficiently. The least satisfying goods and services available today—including public schools, postal service, and passenger railroad service—are government-operated. The products we most enjoy—computers and other new electronics, household appliances, and the myriad offerings of supermarkets and shopping centers—are products of the market. Thus, while some government presence in the economy

Statistics and analysis for any number of economic issues can be found at the Web site of the U.S. Department of Labor: http://www.dol.gov

societies capital investment, tax revenues, new jobs, and advanced technology that accelerate economic growth (Rostow, 1978; Madsen, 1980; Berger, 1986; Firebaugh & Beck, 1994; Firebaugh & Sandu, 1998).

On the other hand, dependency theorists respond that multinationals intensify global inequality. Multinationals, they contend, actually create few jobs because they block the development of local industries and push poor countries to make goods for export rather than food and other products for local consumption. From this standpoint, multinationals make poor societies poorer and increasingly dependent on rich nations is necessary, the Friedmans and other supporters of free markets believe that minimal state regulation best serves the public interest.

But supporters of government intervention in the economy have additional arguments in their arsenal. For one thing, they claim, the market has little incentive to produce anything that is not profitable. This is why few private companies set out to meet the needs of poor people because, by definition, poor people have little money to spend.

Second, the market has certain self-destructive tendencies that only the government can curb. In 1890, for example, the government passed the Sherman Antitrust Act to break up monopolies that controlled the nation's oil and steel production. Since then—and especially since President Franklin Roosevelt's New Deal of the 1930s—government has taken a strong regulatory role to control inflation (by setting interest rates), enhance the well-being of workers (by imposing workplace safety standards), and ensure consumer satisfaction (by setting standards for product quality). Despite such interventions, advocates for a stronger government role point out that corporations in U.S. society are so powerful that the government still cannot effectively challenge the capitalist elite.

Third, because the market magnifies social inequality, the government must step in on the side of social justice. Because capitalist economies concentrate income and wealth in the hands of a few, a government system of taxation that applies higher rates to the rich counters this tendency.

Does the market's "invisible hand" look out for us or pick our pockets?

Upon his election to the presidency, Franklin Delano Roosevelt announced a "New Deal" that greatly increased the role of government in the economic life of the United States. Here, Roosevelt signs historic Social Security legislation.

Although most people in the United States favor a free market, they also support government intervention that benefits the public. Indeed, government assists not only citizens but also business itself by providing investment capital, constructing roads and other infrastructures, and shielding companies from foreign competition. Yet in the United States and around the world, people continue to debate the optimal balance of market forces and government decision making.

Continue the debate . . .

1. *Why do free-market defenders assert that "a government is best that governs least"? What do you think?*

2. *What difference does it make in people's everyday lives if a society's economy is more a market system or more government-centered?*

3. *What is your impression of the successes and failures of socialist economic systems? What about welfare capitalism, as found in Sweden?*

Sources: Friedman & Friedman (1980) and Erber (1990).

(Vaughan, 1978; Wallerstein, 1979; Delacroix & Ragin, 1981; Bergesen, 1983; Walton & Ragin, 1990).

Whereas modernization theory hails the market as the key to progress and affluence for all the world's people, dependency theory calls for replacing market systems with government-based economic policies. The final box takes a closer look at the issue of market versus government economies.

LOOKING AHEAD: THE ECONOMY OF THE TWENTY-FIRST CENTURY

Social institutions are a society's way of meeting people's needs. But as we have seen, the U.S. economy only partly succeeds in this respect. Although highly

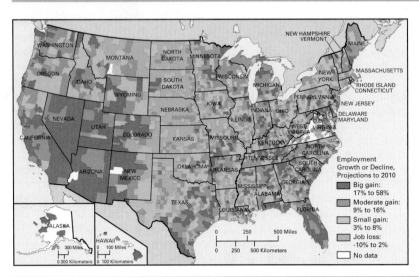

NATIONAL MAP 16–2
Where the Jobs Will Be: Projections to 2010

The economic prospects of counties across the United States are not the same. Much of the midsection of the country is projected to lose jobs. By contrast, the coastal regions and most of the West are rapidly gaining jobs. What factors might account for this pattern?

Source: Used with permission of Woods & Poole Economics, Washington, D.C.

Employment Growth or Decline, Projections to 2010

- ■ Big gain: 17% to 58%
- ■ Moderate gain: 9% to 16%
- □ Small gain: 3% to 8%
- ■ Job loss: -10% to 2%
- □ No data

productive, our economy provides for some much better than it does for others. Moreover, as we begin the twenty-first century, the Information Revolution continues to change our economy. In the postindustrial era, the share of the U.S. labor force engaged in manufacturing is half what it was in 1960; service work, especially computer-related jobs, makes up the difference. Therefore, our society must face the challenge of providing millions of men and women with the language and computer skills they need to succeed in the new information-based economy. We must also take into account that some regions of the country are experiencing an economic boom, as shown in National Map 16–2, whereas others—especially rural areas in the middle of the country—are projected to lose jobs. Can we afford to consign workers and their families to the margins of society because they happen to live in one region of the country rather than another?

In the new century the economy will also become increasingly global. Two centuries ago, the ups and downs of a local economy reflected events and trends in a single town. One century ago, communities were economically linked so that one town's prosperity depended on producing goods demanded by people elsewhere in the country. Today, it makes little sense to speak of a national economy because what people in a Kansas farm town produce and consume may be affected more by what happens in the wheat-growing region of Russia than by events in their own state capital. In short, U.S. workers and business owners are generating products and services in response to factors and forces that are distant and unseen.

Finally, analysts around the world are rethinking conventional economic models. The global economy shows that socialism is less productive than capitalism, one important reason for the collapse of socialist regimes in Eastern Europe and the former Soviet Union. But capitalism also is changing. It now operates with significant government regulation, partly to address the economic inequality generated by market systems.

What are the long-term effects of these changes? Two conclusions seem inescapable. First, the economic future of the United States and other nations will be played out in a global arena. After all, the emergence of the postindustrial economy in the United States is inseparable from the increasing industrial production of other nations. Second, we must address the related issues of global inequality and population increase (Firebaugh, 1999, 2000). Whether the world economy ultimately reduces or deepens the disparity between rich and poor societies may well be what steers our planet toward peace or war.

SUMMARY

1. The economy is the major social institution by which a society produces, distributes, and consumes goods and services.

2. In technologically simple societies, the economy is simply part of family life. Agrarian societies show some productive specialization. Industrialization rapidly expands the economy through greater specialization and new energy sources that power machines in large factories.

3. The postindustrial economy is characterized by a shift from producing goods to services. Just as the Industrial Revolution propelled the industrial economy of the past, the Information Revolution is now advancing the postindustrial economy.

4. The primary sector of the economy, which generates raw materials, dominates in preindustrial societies. The secondary, manufacturing sector prevails in industrial societies. The tertiary, service sector dominates in postindustrial societies.

5. The expanding global economy now produces and consumes products and services with little regard for national boundaries. Today, the 600 largest corporations, operating internationally, account for half of the world's economic output.

6. Capitalism is based on private ownership of productive property and the pursuit of profit in a competitive marketplace. Socialism is grounded in collective ownership of productive property through government control of the economy.

7. Although the economy of the United States is predominantly capitalist, government is broadly involved in economic life. Government plays a greater role in the welfare capitalist economies of some Western European nations, such as Sweden, and the state capitalism of many Asian nations, including Japan.

8. Capitalism is very productive, providing a high average standard of living. A capitalist system allows freedom to act according to one's self-interest. Socialism is less productive but generates greater economic equality. A socialist system offers freedom from basic want.

9. In the United States, agricultural work has declined to just 2 percent of the labor force. Blue-collar jobs have also dwindled, accounting for one-fourth of the labor force. The share of white-collar service occupations has risen to more than 70 percent of the labor force.

10. Although work in the primary labor market may provide greater rewards, many new jobs in the United States are service positions in the secondary labor market.

11. A profession is a special category of white-collar work based on theoretical knowledge, occupational autonomy, authority over clients, and a claim to serving the community.

12. Today, 6.5 percent of U.S. workers are self-employed. Although many professionals fall into this category, most self-employed workers have blue-collar occupations.

13. Unemployment has many causes, including the operation of the economy itself; in 2000, 4.0 percent of the U.S. labor force was without work.

14. The underground economy, which includes criminal as well as legal activity, generates income unreported to the government.

15. Corporations form the core of the U.S. economy. The largest corporations, which are conglomerates, account for most corporate assets and profits. Many large corporations operate as multinationals, producing and distributing products in nations around the world.

KEY CONCEPTS

economy (p. 409) the social institution that organizes a society's production, distribution, and consumption of goods and services

postindustrial economy (p. 411) a productive system based on service work and high technology

primary sector (p. 412) the part of the economy that draws raw materials from the natural environment

secondary sector (p. 412) the part of the economy that transforms raw materials into manufactured goods

tertiary sector (p. 412) the part of the economy that involves services rather than goods

global economy (p. 412) expanding economic activity with little regard for national borders

capitalism (p. 415) an economic system in which natural resources and the means of producing goods and services are privately owned

socialism (p. 416) an economic system in which natural resources and the means of producing goods and services are collectively owned

communism (p. 417) a hypothetical economic and political system in which all members of a society are socially equal

welfare capitalism (p. 417) an economic and political system that combines a mostly market-based economy with extensive social welfare programs

state capitalism (p. 418) an economic and political system in which companies are privately owned but cooperate closely with the government

primary labor market (p. 420) jobs that provide extensive benefits to workers

secondary labor market (p. 420) jobs that provide minimal benefits to workers

labor unions (p. 420) organizations of workers that seek to improve wages and working conditions through various strategies, including negotiations and strikes

profession (p. 421) a prestigious, white-collar occupation that requires extensive formal education

underground economy (p. 423) economic activity involving income unreported to the government as required by law

corporation (p. 425) an organization with a legal existence, including rights and liabilities, apart from that of its members

conglomerate (p. 426) a giant corporation composed of many smaller corporations

monopoly (p. 427) domination of a market by a single producer

oligopoly (p. 427) domination of a market by a few producers

CRITICAL-THINKING QUESTIONS

1. As a social institution, what is the economy supposed to do? How well do you think our economy does its job?

2. How did the Industrial Revolution alter the economy of the United States? How is the Information Revolution changing the economy once again?

3. What key characteristics distinguish capitalism from socialism? Compare these two systems in terms of productivity, economic inequality, and personal freedoms.

4. What does it mean to say that we now have a global economy? How does the operation of the global economy affect your life?

APPLICATIONS AND EXERCISES

1. Overall, a profile of the U.S. economy looks like this: 72 percent of output is in the service sector, 26 percent in the industrial sector, and 2 percent in the primary sector. But in any specific area, the percentages vary widely. Visit the library and locate data that profile your own city, county, or state.

2. Visit a discount store such as Wal-Mart or K-Mart and select a product area that interests you. Do a little fieldwork, inspecting the merchandise to see where it is made. Does your research support the existence of a global economy?

3. What share of the faculty on your campus has temporary teaching contracts? Talk with several tenured faculty, as well as several visiting professors: What differences can you discover in their working conditions and their attitude toward their jobs?

4. Packaged in the back of this new textbook is an interactive CD-ROM that offers a variety of study and review materials intended to help you better understand the material covered in this chapter. For this chapter, the CD-ROM contains an author's tip video, Real Life Sociology videos, other relevant audio and video, interactive map animations, audio journal entries from the author, Web links, and much more.

SITES TO SEE

http://www.prenhall.com/macionis

Visit the interactive *Companion Website*™ that accompanies this text. Begin by clicking on the cover of your book. You will find a chapter-by-chapter study guide, practice tests, and a significant portion of the text for on-line review, as well as many suggested Web links.

http://www.bls.gov

Visit this Web site, operated by the Bureau of Labor Statistics, where you will find a wide range of interesting data and reports.

http://www.nber.org

Another worthwhile site, run by the National Bureau of Economic Research, explains the operation of the economy.

http://www2.kenyon.edu/projects/famfarm/

Students at Kenyon College, in central Ohio, prepared this Web site to study family farms in the local, rural county.

http://www.fao.org

The Food and Agriculture Organization is a part of the United Nations concerned with how well the global economy meets the needs of the world's people. From their main page, look for their annual report, titled "State of Food Insecurity in the World."

INVESTIGATE WITH CONTENTSELECT

Follow the instructions found on page 23 of this textbook to enter this chapter of the book's *Companion Website*™. Once in the chapter, click on the ContentSelect icon at the bottom left of your screen and enter your personal User ID and Password. Enter keywords such as "professions," "monopoly," and "underground economy," and the search engine will help you become an effective researcher.

CHAPTER
17

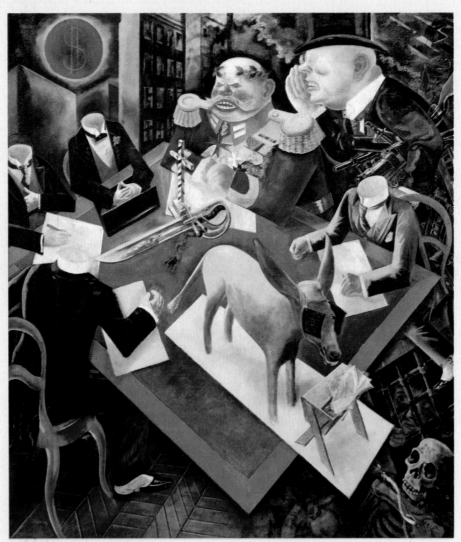

George Grosz (1893–1959)
Sonnenfinsternis (Eclipse of the Sun)

Oil on canvas, 207.3 × 182.6 cm. Huntington (N.Y.), Heckscher Museum.
Photo: AKG London. © Estate of George Grosz/Licensed by VAGA, New York, N.Y.

POLITICS
AND GOVERNMENT

Charlotte Williams sat straight up in the metal folding chair behind the ballot box, her eyes fixed on the open door in front of her. It was election day, and she was four hours into her day-long shift overseeing the voting in Washington, D.C., Precinct Number 15. To her left, a man of about sixty leaned over a table, completing his ballot. But except for the man and Williams herself, the large room was empty.

As the man walked over to deposit his ballot, he smiled and shrugged his shoulders. "Today we are picking a president," he began, "yet nobody bothers to come out to vote." "Tell me about it," Charlotte Williams responded, glad for the opportunity for conversation. "People ought to care, but—you know what—they don't. The welfare system is changing. You know what's happening in our schools. There's way too much crime. I'm sorry, but I can't see it. I just can't see people not caring."

In the 2000 presidential election—a contest that turned on a few hundred votes—only about half the voting-age population of the United States bothered to go to the polls. And no category of the population is less likely to vote than the poor. In fact, more than three-fourths of high-income people vote in presidential elections compared to about 40 percent of low-income people.

What does this apathy mean? Is our political system failing to meet the needs of the people, especially the poor? Indeed, is it realistic to describe our nation as a democracy when most people don't participate in politics, even as once-a-year voters?

This chapter investigates *politics*, the dynamics of power within societies and between nations. Formally, **politics,** or "the polity," is *the social institution that distributes power, sets a society's agenda, and makes decisions.* But as the low turnout in many voting precincts suggests, politics may address the concerns of some far better than others.

POWER AND AUTHORITY

Every society rests on **power,** which sociologist Max Weber (1978; orig. 1921) defined as *the ability to achieve desired ends despite resistance from others.* To a

large degree, the exercise of power is the business of **government,** *a formal organization that directs the political life of a society.* Yet as Weber explained, few governments obtain compliance by openly threatening their people. Most of the time, people respect (or at least accept) their political system.

Practically speaking, it would be difficult for any large, complex society to persist if power derived *only* from sheer force, and life in such a society would be a nightmare of terror. Social organization depends on some degree of consensus among members of a society about proper goals (often in the form of cultural values) and suitable means of pursuing them (cultural norms).

435

Every society, then, seeks to establish its power as legitimate. Weber therefore focused on the concept of **authority,** *power that people perceive as legitimate rather than coercive.* How is sheer power transformed into stable authority? Weber pointed to three ways, which vary according to a society's level of economic development.

TRADITIONAL AUTHORITY

Preindustrial societies, Weber explained, rely on **traditional authority,** *power legitimized through respect for long-established cultural patterns.* In ideal terms, traditional authority is power woven into a society's collective memory, so that people consider social arrangements almost sacred. Chinese emperors in antiquity were legitimized by tradition, as were nobles in medieval Europe. In both cases, the power of tradition was strong enough that—for better or worse—people typically viewed members of a hereditary ruling family as almost godlike.

But traditional authority declines as societies industrialize. Hannah Arendt (1963) pointed out that traditional authority is compelling only as long as everyone shares the same heritage and worldview. This form of authority is undermined by the specialization demanded by industrial production, by modern scientific thinking, and by the social change and cultural diversity that accompany immigration. Thus, it is quite unlikely that today's President George W. Bush would ever make the claim of ruling by grace of God. Even so, some well-established upper-class families with names such as Bush, Kennedy, Roosevelt, and Rockefeller have occupied a privileged position for several generations, so that when one of their number enters the political arena, it is with some measure of traditional authority (Baltzell, 1964).

If traditional authority plays only a small part in U.S. national politics, it persists in other aspects of everyday life. *Patriarchy,* the domination of women by men, is a traditional form of power that remains widespread, even though it is increasingly challenged. Less controversial is the traditional authority parents exert over their children. The fact that traditional authority is linked to a person's status as parent is obvious every time a parent answers a doubting child's "Why?" with "Because I said so!" There is no debating the parent's decision because that would defeat the parent's traditional authority over the child by putting the two on equal footing.

RATIONAL-LEGAL AUTHORITY

Weber defined **rational-legal authority** (sometimes called *bureaucratic authority*) as *power legitimized by legally enacted rules and regulations.* Rational-legal authority is power legitimized in the operation of lawful government.

As Chapter 7 ("Groups and Organizations") explained, Weber viewed bureaucracy as the organizational backbone of rational-thinking, modern societies. Moreover, just as a rational worldview promotes bureaucracy, it erodes traditional customs and practices. Instead of venerating the past, members of today's high-income societies look to formally enacted rules—especially law—for principles of justice.

Rationally enacted rules also underlie many power relationships in everyday life. For example, the authority of deans and classroom teachers rests on the offices they hold in bureaucratic colleges and universities. The police also are officers within the bureaucracy of local government. In contrast to traditional authority, rational-legal authority flows not from family background but from one's position in the formal organization of government. Thus, whereas a traditional monarch rules for life, a modern president accepts and gives up power according to law because presidential authority lies in the office, not the person.

CHARISMATIC AUTHORITY

Finally, Weber claimed power could be transformed into authority through charisma. **Charismatic authority** is *power legitimized through extraordinary personal abilities that inspire devotion and obedience.* Unlike tradition and rational law, then, charisma has less to do with social organization and is more a mark of an exceptionally forceful and magnetic personality.

Throughout history, some members of societies have been regarded as charismatic. Charisma enhances the stature of an established leader or strengthens the appeal of a challenger. Charismatics have the

 Learn more about Dr. King and the civil rights movement at this Web site: http://www.stanford.edu/group/King

personal skills to turn an audience into followers and, in the process, they may make their own rules and challenge the status quo. In 1917, for example, Vladimir Lenin guided the overthrow of Russia's feudal monarchy; after World War II, Mahatma Gandhi inspired the struggle to free India from British colonialism; soon after, Martin Luther King, Jr., galvanized the civil rights movement in the United States; and, over a lifetime of work ministering to the poor in Calcutta, India, Mother Teresa asked the world to confront its stunning poverty.

Because charismatic authority emanates from a single individual, any charismatic movement faces a

In 2000, just 28 of the world's 192 nations were political monarchies where single families pass power from generation to generation. The African nation of Swaziland recently celebrated the coronation of a young king.

crisis of survival upon the death of its leader. Thus, Weber explained, the persistence of a charismatic organization depends on the **routinization of charisma,** *the transformation of charismatic authority into some combination of traditional and bureaucratic authority.* For example, Christianity began as a cult driven by the personal charisma of Jesus of Nazareth. After the death of Jesus, followers institutionalized his teachings in a church eventually centered in Rome and built on both tradition and bureaucracy. Routinized in this way, the Roman Catholic church has flourished for 2,000 years.

POLITICS IN GLOBAL PERSPECTIVE

Political systems have taken many forms throughout history. The technologically simple hunting and gathering societies that once were found all over the planet operated like one large family. Leadership generally fell to a man with unusual strength, hunting skill, or personal charisma. But these leaders exercised little power because they lacked the resources to control their own people, much less extend their rule. In the simplest societies, then, leaders were barely discernible from everyone else, and government did not exist as a distinct sphere of life (Nolan & Lenski, 1999).

Larger and more complex agrarian societies are characterized by specialized activity and a material surplus. These societies become hierarchical, with a small elite gaining control of most wealth and power; politics moves outside the family to become a social institution

in its own right. Leaders who manage to pass along their power over several generations may acquire traditional authority, perhaps even claiming divine right to govern. Such leaders also may benefit from Weber's rational-legal authority because they are served by a bureaucratic political administration and system of law.

As societies expand, politics eventually takes the form of a national government or *political state*. But the emergence of a political state depends on technology. Just a few centuries ago, armies moved slowly, and communication over even short distances was uncertain. For this reason, the early political empires—such as Mesopotamia in the Middle East about 5,000 years ago—took the form of many small *city-states*.

More complex technology helped the modern world develop the larger-scale system of *nation-states*. Currently, the world has 192 independent nation-states, each with a distinctive political system. Generally speaking, however, the world's political systems can be analyzed in terms of four categories: monarchy, democracy, authoritarianism, and totalitarianism.

MONARCHY

Monarchy (with Latin and Greek roots meaning "one ruler") is *a type of political system in which a single family rules from generation to generation.* Monarchy is typical in ancient agrarian societies; for example, the Bible tells of great kings such as David and Solomon. Today's British monarchy, the Windsor family, traces its lineage back roughly 1,000 years. In Weber's terms, then, monarchy is legitimized by tradition.

During the medieval era, *absolute monarchy*, in which hereditary rulers claimed a monopoly of power based on divine right, flourished from England to China and in parts of the Americas. Monarchs in some nations, including Saudi Arabia, still exercise nearly absolute control over their people.

During the twentieth century, however, a more egalitarian climate gradually weakened monarchs in favor of elected officials. Monarchs remain in several European nations—Great Britain, Spain, Norway, Sweden, Belgium, Denmark, and the Netherlands—but they now preside over *constitutional monarchies*. In other words, they are merely symbolic heads of state, and elected politicians, led by a prime minister, govern according to political principles embodied in a constitution. In these nations, then, the nobility may formally reign, but elected officials actually rule.

DEMOCRACY

The historical trend in the modern world is toward **democracy,** *a type of political system which gives power to the people as a whole.* But members of democratic societies rarely participate directly in decision making; numbers alone make this an impossibility. Instead, a system of *representative democracy* places authority in the hands of elected leaders, who are accountable to the people.

Most rich countries of the world claim to be democratic. Economic development and democratic government go together because both depend on a literate populace. Moreover, the traditional legitimization of power in an agrarian monarchy gives way, with industrialization, to rational-legal authority. A rational election process puts leaders in offices regulated by law. Thus democracy and rational-legal authority are linked just as monarchy and traditional authority are.

But countries such as the United States are not truly democratic for two reasons: First, there is the problem of bureaucracy. All democratic political systems rely on large numbers of bureaucratic officials. The federal government of the United States, for example, has more than 2 million regular, full-time employees, 6 million contract workers, 1.5 million uniformed military personnel, and 2.4 million workers paid for by various grants and special funding—about 12 million workers in all. In addition, another 15 million people work in 80,000 local governments across the country. Most people who operate the government are never elected by anyone and are not directly accountable to the people (Scaff, 1981; Edwards, 1985; Etzioni-Halevy, 1985; Light, 1999).

The second problem involves economic inequality. In a highly stratified society, the rich have far more political clout than the poor. One reason George W. Bush got off to such a fast start in the 2000 presidential race was that, as a rich man with many rich friends, he was able to raise more than $50 million in a short time. Magazine magnate Steve Forbes financed his own run for the White House, spending more than $50 million of his own fortune in 1996 and 2000 (although he did not get very far in the primaries). In short, in the game of politics, few doubt that "money talks." Given the even greater resources of billion-dollar corporations and labor unions, how can we think our "democratic" system responds to—or even hears—the voices of "average people"? (Burns, Francia, & Herrnson, 2000)

Democracy and Freedom: Capitalist and Socialist Approaches

Despite the problems we have just described, rich capitalist nations such as the United States claim to operate as democracies. Of course, socialist countries such as Cuba and the People's Republic of China make the same claim. This curious fact suggests that we need to look more closely at *political economy:* the interplay of politics and economics.

The political life of the United States, Canada, and the nations of Europe is shaped largely by the economic principles of capitalism. The pursuit of profit within a market system requires that "freedom" be defined in terms of people's right to act in their own self-interest. Thus, the capitalist approach to political freedom translates into personal liberty, the freedom to act in whatever ways maximize personal profit or other advantage. From this point of view, moreover, "democracy" means that individuals have the right to select their leaders from among those running for office.

However, as we noted earlier, capitalist societies are marked by a striking inequality of income and wealth. In other words, if everyone acts according to self-interest, the inevitable result is that some people have much more power to get their way than others. It is this elite that dominates the economic and political life of the society.

By contrast, socialist systems claim they are democratic because their economies meet everyone's basic needs for housing, schooling, work, and medical care. Despite being a much poorer country than the United States, for example, Cuba provides basic medical care to all without regard for people's ability to pay.

But critics of socialism counter that the extensive government regulation of social life in these countries

Mixed Positions

Pegging the political views of individuals is difficult because most people do not hold the same positions on economic and social issues. Well-to-do men and women tend to be conservative on economic issues (because they have wealth to protect) but liberal on social issues (largely because of higher levels of education). Working-class people display the opposite pattern, combining economic liberalism with social conservatism (Nunn, Crockett, & Williams, 1978; Erikson, Luttbeg, & Tedin, 1980; McBroom & Reed, 1990). African Americans, both rich and poor, tend to be liberal (especially on economic issues) and, for half a century, have voted Democratic (more than 90 percent supported Democrat Al Gore in 2000). Historically, Latinos, Asian Americans, and Jews have also supported the Democratic party.

Party Identification

Because so many people hold mixed political attitudes—espousing liberal views on some issues and taking conservative stands on others—party identification in the United States is weak. In this way, our nation differs from European countries, where most people adhere strongly to one political party. Table 17–2 shows the results of a recent national survey of party identification among U.S. adults (NORC, 2001). Some 44 percent identified themselves to some degree as Democrats and about 34 percent as Republicans. Twenty percent claimed to be independents, voicing no preference for either party. Even though a large majority declare a party preference, their allegiance is weak. Republicans scored a landslide victory in the 1994 congressional elections, for example, while the Democrats held the White House in 1996 and gained ground in Congress in 1996, 1998, and 2000.

There is also an urban-rural divide in U.S. politics, by which people in urban areas typically vote Democratic and those in rural areas vote Republican.

 To learn more about how researchers conduct political polls, go to http://faculty.vassar.edu/lowry/polls.html

The box on page 446 takes a closer look at the national political scene, and National Map 17–1 on page 447 shows the county-by-county results for the 2000 election.

SPECIAL-INTEREST GROUPS

Just about everyone is aware of the recent shootings in a number of public schools across the United States; in

TABLE 17–2 Political Party Identification in the United States, 2000

Party Identification	Percentage of Respondents
Democrat	**44.2%**
Strong Democrat	14.7
Not very strong Democrat	18.0
Independent, close to Democrat	11.5
Republican	**33.6**
Strong Republican	9.3
Not very strong Republican	14.2
Independent, close to Republican	10.1
Independent	**20.1**
Other party, no response	**2.1**

Source: *General Social Surveys, 1972–2000: Cumulative Codebook* (Chicago: National Opinion Research Center, 2001), p. 88.

the wake of these events, public support for gun control has been rising. The National Rifle Association, representing several million people who are active hunters and millions of social conservatives, has steadily worked in opposition to this goal.

The "gun lobby," which has been successful so far in fending off change, is an example of a **special-interest group**: *a political alliance of people interested in some economic or social issue.* Special-interest groups, which include associations of elderly people, tour bus operators, women's organizations, farmers, fireworks producers, environmentalists, and countless others, flourish in nations such as the United States where political parties tend to be weak. Special-interest groups employ *lobbyists* (Washington, D.C., is home to more than 75,000 of them) as their professional advocates in political circles.

One example of a special-interest group concerned with economic issues is the American Federation of Labor–Congress of Industrial Organizations (AFL-CIO), this nation's largest labor union. Special-interest groups lobbying on social issues include not only the conservative National Rifle Association but also the liberal American Civil Liberties Union.

Political action committees (PACs) are *organizations formed by special-interest groups, independent of political parties, to pursue political aims by raising and spending money.* Political action committees channel most of their funds directly to candidates likely to support their interests. Although legal reforms have limited direct contributions to candidates, since the 1970s the number of PACs has grown rapidly to 4,400 (U.S. Federal Election Commission, 2000).

The Rural-Urban Divide: Election 2000

An important and often overlooked dimension of diversity in the United States involves where people live: in rural versus urban places. Sociologists have long debated how the two settings differ (see Chapter 22, "Population, Urbanization, and Environment"). But one thing is certain: Rural and urban politics are quite different.

Take a look at National Map 17–1, which shows the county-by-county results from the 2000 presidential election. The first thing that is striking about the map is that Republican George W. Bush won in almost 80 percent of U.S. counties: 2,477 out of a total of 3,153 (which appear in various shades of red). By contrast, Democrat Al Gore won in just 676 counties (which appear in a shade of blue). At the same time, Gore actually won the popular vote across the country (Bush was victorious in the election by winning the majority of votes in the electoral college).

The reason for this apparent contradiction is that the many counties won by Bush were mostly rural, with low populations. By contrast, Gore won the fewer counties containing large cities. In Nevada, for example, the map shows just the Las Vegas area in "Gore blue," but the remainder of the state is painted "Bush red." In Oregon, Gore won enough votes in Portland to carry the entire state, even though almost all the remaining counties went for Bush.

As political analyst Stuart Rothenberg (cited in Simon, 2000) concluded, "There is a cultural gap between liberal, urban, Democratic America and rural, small-town Republican America." In Washington, D.C., a politically divided Congress is trying to work together for the good of the country. Yet as the results of the 2000 election show, the country itself is divided in a way that is not likely to be overcome anytime soon.

Source: Based on Bai (2001).

Because of the rising costs of campaigns, most candidates eagerly accept support from political action committees. In the 1998 congressional elections, 40 percent of all funding came from PACs, and two-thirds of all senators seeking reelection received more than $1 million each in PAC contributions. Supporters maintain that PACs represent interests of a vast array of businesses, unions, and church groups, thereby increasing political participation. Critics counter that organizations supplying cash to politicians expect to be treated favorably in return so that, in effect, PACs try to buy political influence (Allen & Broyles, 1991; Cook, 1993; Center for Responsive Politics, 1998).

In 2000, the campaigns of presidential candidates cost a total of $3 billion, and another $3 billion was spent by congressional candidates and people running in state and local elections. Does having the most money matter? The evidence suggests that it is crucial because 90 percent of the candidates with the most money won their race. Concern about the power of money has prompted much discussion of campaign finance reform, but to date there has been little real change.

VOTER APATHY

As noted at the beginning of this chapter, a disturbing fact of U.S. political life is that many people seem indifferent to their right to vote. The long-term trend has been for greater *eligibility* to vote: The Fifteenth Amendment, ratified in 1870, enfranchised African American men; the Nineteenth Amendment extended voting rights to women in 1920; and in 1971 the Twenty-Sixth

 For more information on voter apathy, visit this Harvard University site: http://www.vanishingvoter.org

Amendment lowered the voting age to eighteen years. However, a countertrend shows that over the last century, a smaller and smaller share of eligible citizens *actually do vote*. In the 2000 presidential election, less than half the registered voters took the time to cast a ballot, below the comparable share in almost all other high-income nations. This was so despite the fact that

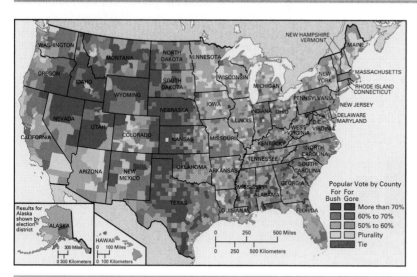

NATIONAL MAP 17–1
The Presidential Election, 2000:
Popular Vote by County

The 2000 presidential election was the closest in more than a century. Almost 80 percent of the nation's counties went for George W. Bush, but densely populated areas—especially along both coasts— provided strong support for Al Gore. What social differences do you think distinguish the areas that voted Republican and Democratic? Why are rural areas mostly Republican whereas cities tend to be Democratic?

Source: "Red Zone vs. Blue Zone," *Newsweek*, January 22, 2001. Copyright © 2001 Newsweek, Inc. All rights reserved. Reprinted by permission.

the 2000 presidential race was decided in Florida (which gave George W. Bush enough electoral votes to win) by 537 votes (plus or minus a hanging chad or two) out of 2.5 million cast.

Who is and is not likely to vote? Women and men are equally likely to cast a ballot. White people are more likely to vote (64 percent voted in 2000) than African Americans (58 percent), with Hispanics (30 percent) the least likely of all to vote. Generally speaking, people with a bigger stake in society—homeowners, parents with children at home, people with good jobs and extensive schooling—are most likely to vote. Income matters, too: People earning more than $75,000 are twice as likely to vote (76 percent voted) as people earning between $5,000 and $10,000 (38 percent voted) (Lewis, McCracken, & Hunt, 1994; DeLuca, 1998; Fetto, 1999; U.S. Census Bureau, 2000).

Age is perhaps the most significant factor of all: People over sixty-five are three times as likely to vote as young adults aged eighteen to twenty-four. In fact, barely half of these young people even even bothered to register in 2000.

Of course, we should expect some nonvoting, because at any given time millions of people are sick, disabled, or away from home. Many more people move to a new neighborhood and forget to reregister. Registering and voting also depend on the ability to read

and write, which discourages the tens of millions of U.S. adults who have limited literacy skills. Finally, people with physical disabilities that limit mobility have a lower turnout than the general population (Schur & Kruse, 2000).

Even so, the problem of political apathy is widespread in the population as a whole. Conservatives suggest that this apathy is not a serious problem because it reflects *indifference* to politics. That is, most people who do not vote are reasonably content with their lives. But liberals (and especially political radicals) counter that apathy is a symptom of a serious problem: Most nonvoters are *alienated* from politics. Although dissatisfied with the way society operates, they doubt that elections will make any real difference. Figure 17–2 on page 448 provides data that confirm the link between income and voting: In simple terms, most high-income people *do* and most low-income people *don't*. The fact that it is disadvantaged people who are least likely to vote suggests that the liberal explanation for low voter turnout probably is closer to the truth.

Are there small reforms that might make a difference in voting rates? Currently, many states require people to complete their voting registration well before election day. Research suggests that allowing people to register as late as election day would raise the turnout by about 7 percent (Brians & Grofman, 2001).

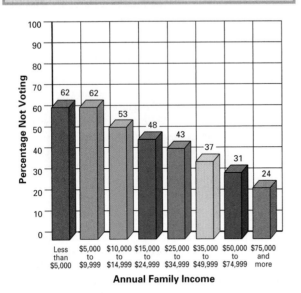

FIGURE 17–2 Political Apathy by Income Level

Percentage of adults who reported not voting in the 1996 presidential election, presented according to their annual family income.

Source: U.S. Census Bureau (1998).

THEORETICAL ANALYSIS OF POWER IN SOCIETY

Sociologists have long debated how power is distributed in the United States. Power is one of the most difficult topics to study scientifically because decision making is complex and takes place behind closed doors. Moreover, it is difficult to separate a theory of power from the theorist's political attitudes and personal values. Nevertheless, three competing models of power in the United States have emerged.

THE PLURALIST MODEL: THE PEOPLE RULE

The **pluralist model** is *an analysis of politics that sees power as dispersed among many competing interest groups.* This approach is closely tied to structural-functional theory.

Pluralists claim, first, that politics is an arena of negotiation. With limited resources, no organization can expect to realize all its goals. Organizations therefore operate as *veto groups*, realizing some success but mostly keeping opponents from achieving all their goals. The political process relies heavily on negotiating alliances and compromises between numerous interest groups so that policies gain wide support. In short, pluralists see power as widely dispersed throughout society, with all people having at least some voice in the political system (Dahl, 1961, 1982; Rothman & Black, 1998).

THE POWER-ELITE MODEL: A FEW PEOPLE RULE

The **power-elite model** is *an analysis of politics that sees power as concentrated among the rich.* This second approach is closely allied with the social-conflict paradigm.

The term *power elite* was coined by sociologist and social critic C. Wright Mills (1956), who argued that a small number of people in the United States control this nation's political system. Mills claimed that the power elite stands atop each of three major sectors of U.S. society: the economy, the government, and the military. Thus, the power elite is made up of the "super rich" (namely, the executives and large stockholders of major corporations), top officials in government (the most powerful figures in Washington, D.C., and state capitals around the country), and the highest-ranking officers in the U.S. military (senior Pentagon officials).

Furthermore, Mills explained, these elites move from one sector to another, consolidating their power as they go. For example, Alexander Haig has served as a top corporate executive, a member of Ronald Reagan's cabinet (and 1988 presidential candidate), and a general of the army. Haig is far from the exception: A majority of national political leaders enter government from powerful and highly paid positions—when President George W. Bush took office and assembled his cabinet in 2001, all but one person were already millionaires—and most return to the corporate world later on.

Power-elite theorists challenge the claim that the United States is a political democracy. They maintain that the concentration of wealth and power is simply too great for the average person's voice to be heard. They reject the pluralist idea that various centers of power serve as checks and balances on one another.

TABLE 17–3 Three Models of U.S. Politics: A Summary

	Pluralist Model	Power-Elite Model	Marxist Model
How is power distributed in U.S. society?	Highly dispersed	Concentrated	Concentrated
Is the United States basically democratic?	Yes, because voting offers everyone a voice, and no one group or organization dominates society	No, because a small share of the people dominates the economy, government, and military	No, because the bias of the capitalist system is to concentrate wealth and power
How should we understand voter apathy?	Apathy is indifference; after all, even poor people can organize for a greater voice if they want	Apathy is understandable, given how difficult it is for ordinary people to oppose the rich and powerful	Apathy is alienation generated by a system that will always leave most people powerless

Instead, the power-elite model holds that people at the top encounter no real opposition (Bartlett & Steele, 2000).

THE MARXIST MODEL: BIAS IN THE SYSTEM ITSELF

A third approach to understanding U.S. politics is the **Marxist political-economy model,** *an analysis that explains politics in terms of the operation of a society's economic system.* Like the power-elite model, the Marxist model rejects the idea that the United States operates as a political democracy. But whereas the power-elite model focuses on the disproportionate wealth of certain individuals and the control they have over our political system, the Marxist model highlights bias rooted in this nation's institutions, especially its economy. As noted in Chapter 4 ("Society"), Karl Marx claimed that a society's economic system (capitalist or socialist) goes a long way toward shaping how the political system operates. Therefore, the power elites do not simply appear on the scene; they are creations of capitalism itself.

From this point of view, any attempts to reform the political system—say, by limiting the amount of money rich people can contribute to political candidates—are unlikely to bring about true democracy. The problem does not lie in the *people* who exercise great power or the *people* who don't vote; the problem is rooted in the *system* itself, what Marxists call the political economy of capitalism. In other words, as long as the United States remains a predominantly capitalist economy, just as the majority of people are exploited in the workplace, they will be shut out of politics.

Critical evaluation. Table 17–3 summarizes the three models of the U.S. political system. Which of the models is correct? Over the years, research shows that a case can be made for all three. In the end, how one views this country's political system and how one thinks it ought to operate turn out to be a matter of political values as much as scientific fact.

Research by Nelson Polsby (1959) supports the pluralist model. Polsby studied the political scene in New Haven, Connecticut, and concluded that key decisions on various issues—including renewing urban areas, nominating political candidates, and operating the schools—were made by different groups. He found, too, that few of the upper-class families listed in New Haven's *Social Register* were also economic leaders. Thus, Polsby concluded, no one segment of society rules all the others.

Robert Dahl also investigated New Haven's history, finding that over time power had become more and more dispersed. Thus, Dahl's research also supports the pluralist model. As he put it, "No one, and certainly no group of more than a few individuals, is entirely lacking in [power]" (1961:228).

Supporting the power-elite position is research by Robert Lynd and Helen Lynd (1937) in Muncie, Indiana (which they called "Middletown," to suggest that it was a typical city). They documented the fortune amassed by a single family, the Balls, from their business manufacturing glass canning jars, and showed how the Ball family dominated the city's life. If anyone doubted the Balls' prominence, the Lynds explained, there was no need to look further than the local bank, a university, a hospital, and a department store, which all bear the family name. In Muncie, according to the Lynds, the power elite more or less boiled down to a single family.

In a study of Atlanta, Georgia, Floyd Hunter (1963; orig. 1953) found further support for the power-elite model. No one family dominated Atlanta, as was the case in Muncie. Yet Hunter found that about forty people held all the top positions in the city's businesses and controlled the city's politics.

From the Marxist perspective, the point is not to look at which individuals make political decisions at the local or even the national level. Rather, as Alexander Liazos (1982:13) explains, "The basic tenets of capitalist society shape everyone's life: the inequalities of social classes and the importance of profits over people." As long as the basic institutions of society are organized to meet the needs of the few rather than the many, Liazos concludes, a democratic society will elude us.

In the end, what are we to make of the U.S. political system? At one level, it affords almost everyone the right to participate in the political process through elections. This is an important opportunity, one that is not enjoyed by a majority of the world's people. At the same time, however, the power-elite and Marxist models point out that, at the very least, the U.S. political system is far less democratic than most people think. Most citizens may have the right to vote, but the major political parties and their candidates typically support only the positions acceptable to the most powerful segments of society and consistent with the operation of our capitalist economy (Bachrach & Baratz, 1970).

Whatever the reasons, many people in the United States do not report having very much confidence in their leaders. More than 80 percent of U.S. adults report having, at best, only "some confidence" that members of Congress and other government officials will do what is best for the country (NORC, 2001:904, 1037).

POWER BEYOND THE RULES

Politics always involves disagreement over a society's goals and the means to achieve them. Therefore, political systems try to resolve controversy within a system of rules. But political activity sometimes exceeds—or tries to do away with—established practices.

REVOLUTION

Political revolution is *the overthrow of one political system in order to establish another*. In contrast to reform, which involves change *within* a system, revolution involves change *of the system itself*. Thus, even one leader deposing another—called a *coup d'état* (in French, literally, "stroke concerning the state")—falls short of revolution because it involves only a change at the top. Whereas reform rarely escalates into violence, revolution often does. The revolutions in Eastern Europe beginning in 1989 were surprisingly peaceful, with the exception of Romania, where violence claimed thousands of lives.

No type of political system is immune to revolution, nor does revolution invariably produce any one kind of government. Our country's Revolutionary War transformed colonial rule by the British monarchy into democratic government. French revolutionaries in 1789 also overthrew a monarch, only to set the stage for the return of monarchy in the person of Napoleon. In 1917, the Russian Revolution replaced monarchy with a socialist government built on the ideas of Karl Marx. Then in 1992, the Soviet Union was reborn as the Russian Federation, moving toward a market system and a greater political voice for its people.

Despite their striking variety, revolutions share a number of traits (Tocqueville, 1955, orig. 1856; also Davies, 1962; Brinton, 1965; Skocpol, 1979; Lewis, 1984; Tilly, 1986):

1. **Rising expectations**. Although common sense suggests that revolution would be more likely when people are grossly deprived, history shows that most revolutions occur when people's lives are improving. Rising expectations, rather than bitter resignation, fuel revolutionary fervor.

2. **Unresponsive government**. Revolutionary zeal gains strength when a government is unwilling or unable to reform, especially when such demands are made by powerful segments of society.

3. **Radical leadership by intellectuals**. The English philosopher Thomas Hobbes (1588–1679) observed that intellectuals often provide the justification for revolution, and universities often are the center of sweeping political change. During the 1960s in the United States, students were at the forefront of much of the political unrest. Students also played a critical role in China's prodemocracy movement and the uprisings in Eastern Europe.

4. **Establishing a new legitimacy**. Overthrowing a political system is not easy, but more difficult still is ensuring a revolution's long-term success. Some revolutionary movements are unified

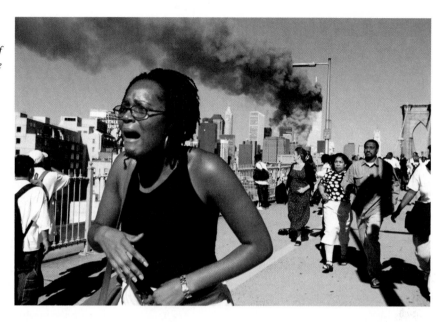

According to many analysts, our way of life changed with the events of September 11, 2001. Why? The power of terror lies in creating fear—fear that the unimaginable can actually happen. Unless we can take basic safety for granted, in short, it is difficult to get on with our lives. How has your life been different since that fateful day?

mostly by hatred of the past regime and fall apart once new leaders are installed. Revolutionaries must also guard against counterrevolutionary drives led by the deposed leaders. This explains the speed and ruthlessness with which victorious revolutionaries dispose of previous rulers.

Scientific analysis cannot declare that a revolution is good or bad. The full consequences of such an upheaval depend on one's values and become evident only after many years. In the wake of recent revolution, for example, the future of the former Soviet Union remains unsettled.

TERRORISM

On September 11, 2001, terrorists hijacked four commercial airliners, and although one airliner crashed in a wooded area, the other three were flown into public buildings full of people. The attack, which killed some 3,500 innocent people and injured many thousands more, completely destroyed the World Trade Center in New York City and seriously damaged the Pentagon in Washington, D.C. Not since the attack on Pearl Harbor at the outbreak of World War II had the United States suffered such a blow. Indeed, this event was the most serious terrorist act ever recorded, resulting in greater loss of life than all previous acts of terrorism combined.

Terrorism consists of *acts of violence or the threat of such violence used by an individual or group as a political strategy.* Like revolution, terrorism is a political act beyond the rules of established political systems. According to Paul Johnson (1981), terrorism has four distinguishing characteristics.

First, terrorists try to paint violence as a legitimate political tactic, despite the fact that such acts are condemned by nearly every nation. Terrorists also bypass (or are excluded from) established channels of political negotiation. Therefore, terror is a weak organization's strategy to harm a stronger foe. Indeed, terrorism has become almost common in international politics. In 2000, according to the U.S. State Department, there were 423 acts of terrorism worldwide, which claimed 405 lives and injured 791 people. Of these 423 terrorist acts, 200 (47 percent) were directed against the United States (U.S. State Department, 2001). Of course, in light of the September 11th attack on the United States, the 2001 casualties will be much higher.

Second, terrorism is used not just by groups but also by governments against their own people. *State terrorism* is the use of violence, generally without support of law, by government officials. State terrorism is lawful in some authoritarian and totalitarian states, which survive by inciting fear and intimidation. For example, Saddam Hussein shores up his power in Iraq through state terrorism.

Not all terrorism is the work of individuals or groups. Since 1950, China has sought to maintain control of Tibet by force. This Tibetan refugee displays instruments of torture used against him by officials of the Chinese government.

Third, democratic societies reject terrorism in principle, but they are especially vulnerable to terrorists because they afford extensive civil liberties to their people and have less extensive police networks. In contrast, totalitarian regimes make widespread use of state terrorism although, at the same time, their extensive police power minimizes opportunities for individual acts of terror.

Hostage-taking and outright killing provoke popular anger, but responding to such acts is difficult. Before taking action, a government must identify those responsible. However, because most terrorist groups are shadowy organizations with no formal connection to any established state, a reprisal may be all but impossible. Yet as terrorism expert Brian Jenkins warns, the failure to respond "encourages other terrorist groups, who begin to realize that this can be a pretty cheap way to wage war" (quoted in Whitaker, 1985:29). At the same time, a forcible military reaction to terrorism may risk confrontation with other governments.

Fourth, terrorism is always a matter of definition. Governments claim the right to maintain order, even

Read the U.S. State Department's latest annual report on global terrorism at http://www.usis.usemb.se/terror/rpt2000/index.html

by force, but brand opposition groups who use violence as "terrorists." Similarly, political differences may explain why one person's "terrorist" is another's "freedom fighter." Ironically, in Afghanistan, some of the "terrorists" that the United States and other nations targeted in the wake of the September 11th attacks were the same people who were widely praised as "freedom fighters" in the 1980s when they fought the invading Soviet army.

WAR AND PEACE

Perhaps the most critical political issue is **war,** *organized, armed conflict between the people of various societies, directed by their governments.* War is as old as humanity, of course, but understanding it now takes on greater urgency. Because we have the technological capacity to destroy ourselves, war poses unprecedented danger to the entire planet. Most scholarly investigation of war aims to promote peace, meaning the absence of war (but not necessarily the end of all political conflict).

Many people think of war as an extraordinary occurrence, yet for almost all of the twentieth century, nations somewhere on Earth were in violent conflict. In our nation's short history, we have participated in eleven large-scale wars, resulting in the deaths of more than 1.3 million U.S. men and women and injury to many times that number, as shown in Figure 17–3. Thousands more died in "undeclared wars" and "limited military actions" in the Dominican Republic, Lebanon, Grenada, Panama, and elsewhere.

THE CAUSES OF WAR

The frequency of war in human affairs might imply that there is something natural about armed confrontation. But whereas many animals are naturally aggressive, research provides no basis for concluding that human beings inevitably wage war under any particular circumstances. Indeed, as Ashley Montagu (1976) observes, governments around the world have to use considerable coercion to mobilize their people for war.

Like all other forms of social behavior, warfare is a product of society that varies in purpose and intensity from place to place. The Semai of Malaysia, among the most peace-loving of the world's people, rarely resort to violence. In contrast, the Yanomamö, described in Chapter 3 ("Culture"), are far more likely to wage war.

If society holds the key to war or peace, under what circumstances do humans go to battle? Quincy Wright (1987) identifies five factors that promote war:

1. **Perceived threats**. Societies mobilize in response to a perceived threat to their people, territory, or culture. For example, the prospect of armed conflict between the United Sates and the former Soviet Union diminished as the two nations have become less fearful of each other; Russia even voiced support for the 2001 anti-terrorist attacks by the United States.

2. **Social problems**. When internal problems generate widespread frustration at home, a society's leaders may divert public attention by attacking an external "enemy" as a form of scapegoating. Some analysts see the lack of economic development in the People's Republic of China as underlying that nation's hostility toward Vietnam, Tibet, and the former Soviet Union.

3. **Political objectives**. Leaders sometimes use war as a political strategy. Poor societies, such as Algeria and Vietnam, have fought wars to end foreign domination. For powerful societies such as the United States, a periodic show of force (recall the recent deployments of troops in Somalia, Haiti, and Bosnia) enhances their global political stature.

4. **Moral objectives**. Rarely do nations claim to fight merely to increase their wealth and power. Leaders infuse military campaigns with moral urgency, rallying their people around visions of "freedom" or the "fatherland." U.S. leaders characterized the recent attack on the Taliban and the al Qaeda network in Afghanistan as a clear case of good against evil.

5. **The absence of alternatives**. A fifth factor promoting war is the absence of alternatives. Although it is the United Nations' job to maintain international peace, the UN has had limited success in resolving tensions between self-interested societies.

In short, war is rooted in social dynamics on both national and international levels. Moreover, even combat has rules, and breaking them can lead to charges of *war crimes*. The box on page 454 takes a closer look.

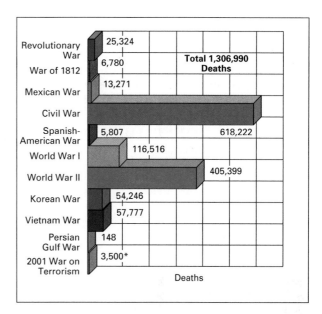

FIGURE 17–3 Deaths of Americans in Eleven U.S. Wars

*Preliminary, as of December 1, 2001.

Sources: Compiled from various sources by Maris A. Vinovskis (1989) and the author.

TERRORISM: A NEW KIND OF WAR?

In the wake of the terrorist attacks on September 11, 2001, U.S. government officials spoke of terrorism as a new kind of war. As we have explained, war is usually played out according to at least some rules, the warring parties are known to each other, and they clearly state their objectives, which generally involve control of territory.

Terrorism, however, breaks from these patterns. In cases of terrorism, the identity of terrorist individuals and organizations may not be known, those involved may deny their responsibility, and their goals may be unclear. Indeed, the recent terrorist attacks against the United States were not attempts to defeat the nation militarily, nor to secure territory. They were carried out by people representing not a country but a cause—one not well understood in the United States. In short, they were expressions of anger and hate, an effort to destabilize the country and shatter public morale by inciting widespread anger and fear.

Conventional warfare is "symmetrical," with two nations sending their armies into battle. By contrast,

GLOBAL SOCIOLOGY

Violence beyond the Rules: A Report from the Former Yugoslavia

War is violent, but it also has rules. Many of our current rules of warfare were written at the end of World War II, when the victorious Allies, including the United States, charged German and Japanese military officials with war crimes. The United Nations spells out the rules of war in a document called the Geneva Conventions.

One of the most important principles is that whatever violence soldiers inflict on each other, they should not imprison, torture, rape, or murder civilians. Nor should they deliberately destroy civilian property or wantonly bomb or shell cities. Even so, for years—and especially during the Balkan conflict in the 1990s—Serbs, Croats, and Muslims committed all these war crimes in the former Yugoslavia. Tens of thousands of civilians were killed, raped, and seriously injured; the loss of property was enormous. As early as 1993, a UN tribunal convened in the Netherlands to consider possible responses.

After World War II, the Allies successfully prosecuted (and, in several cases, executed) German officers for their crimes against humanity based on evidence obtained from extensive Nazi records. This time around, however,

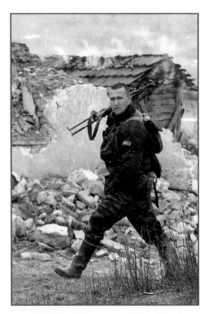

the task of punishing offenders has turned out to be far more difficult. For one thing, there are few written records of the Balkan conflict; for another, UN officials fear that arrests may upset delicate diplomatic efforts to bring peace to the region.

Even so, since beginning its investigations, the United Nations has indicted dozens of military officers on all sides of the conflict and begun to hand down prison sentences. In 2001, Serbian president Slobodan Milosevic was taken to the Netherlands to stand trial for war crimes. Overall, however, only a handful of the many charged with such crimes have been taken into custody, so that it is doubtful that more than a few people responsible for a staggering number of civilian deaths will ever pay for their crimes.

Sources: Adapted from Nelan (1993), Sebastian (1996), Watson (1999), Hundley (2001), and various news reports.

---

terrorism is a new form of war, an "asymmetrical conflict" in which the small number of attackers use terror and their own willingness to die as a means to "level the playing field" against a much more powerful enemy. Furthermore, while the terrorists may be ruthless, the nation under attack must exercise restraint in its response to terror because little may be known about the identity and location of those responsible. It is for this reason that U.S. officials maintain that the reaction to the 2001 attacks is likely to unfold over a period of years.

THE COSTS AND CAUSES OF MILITARISM

The cost of armed conflict extends far beyond battlefield casualties. Together, the world's nations spend more than $1 trillion annually (roughly $160 for every person on the planet) for military purposes. Such expenditures divert resources from alleviating the desperate struggle for survival of millions of people. If the world's nations could muster the will and the political wisdom to redirect their military spending, they could greatly reduce global poverty.

Early to Wed: A Report from Rural India

Sumitra Jogi cries as her wedding is about to begin. Are they tears of joy? Not exactly. This "bride" is an eleven-month-old squirming in the arms of her mother. The groom? A boy of six.

In a remote, rural village in India's western state of Rajasthan, two families gather at midnight to celebrate a traditional wedding ritual. It is May 2, an especially good day to marry in Hindu tradition. Sumitra's father smiles as the ceremony begins; her mother cradles the infant, who has fallen asleep. The groom, dressed in a special costume with a red and gold turban on his head, gently reaches up and grasps the baby's hand. Then, as the ceremony reaches its conclusion, the young boy leads the child and mother around the wedding fire three-and-one-half times, as the audience beams at the couple's first steps together as husband and wife.

Child weddings are illegal in India, but in the rural regions traditions are strong and marriage laws are hard to enforce. Thus, experts estimate, thousands of children marry each year. "In rural Rajasthan," explains one social welfare worker, "all the girls are married by age fourteen. These are poor, illiterate families, and they don't want to keep girls past their first menstrual cycle."

For the immediate future, Sumitra Jogi will remain with her parents. But in eight or ten years, a second ceremony will send her to live with her husband's family, and her married life will begin.

If the responsibilities of marriage lie years in the future, why do families push their children to marry at such an early age? Parents of girls know that the younger the bride, the smaller the dowry offered to the groom's family. Also, when girls marry this young, there is no question about their virginity, which raises their value on the marriage market. Arranged marriages are an alliance between families. No one thinks about love or the fact that the children are too young to understand what is taking place.

Source: Based on Anderson (1995).

STAGES OF FAMILY LIFE

The family is a dynamic institution, with marked changes across the life course. New families begin with courtship and evolve as partners settle into the realities of married life. Next, for most couples at least, are the years spent raising children and, finally, the later years after children have left home to form families of their own. We will look briefly at each of these four stages.

COURTSHIP

November 2, Kandy, Sri Lanka. Winding through the rain forest of this beautiful island, our van driver, Harry, recounts how he met his wife. Actually, it was more of an arrangement: The two families were both Buddhist and of the same caste. "We got along well, right from the start," recalls Harry. "We had the same background. I suppose she or I could have said 'no.' But love marriages happen in the city, not in the village where I grew up."

In rural Sri Lanka and in rural areas of low-and middle-income societies throughout the world, most people consider courtship too important to be left to the young (Stone, 1977). Arranged marriages represent an alliance between two extended families of similar social standing and usually involve not just an exchange of children but also wealth and favors. Romantic love has little to do with it, and parents may make such arrangements when their children are very young. A century ago in Sri Lanka and India, for example, half of all girls married before reaching age fifteen (Mayo, 1927; Mace & Mace, 1960). As the box explains, in some parts of the world, child marriage persists today.

Because traditional societies are culturally homogeneous, almost any member of the opposite sex has been suitably socialized to be a good spouse. Therefore,

People in every society recognize the reality of physical attraction. But the power of romantic love, captured in Christian Pierre's painting, I Do, *holds surprisingly little importance in traditional societies. In much of the world, it would be less correct to say that individuals marry individuals and more true to say that families marry families. In other words, parents arrange marriages for their children with an eye to the social position of the kin-groups involved.*

parents can arrange marriages with little thought to whether the two individuals involved are *personally* compatible; they can be confident that the partners will be *culturally* compatible.

Industrialization erodes the importance of extended families as it weakens tradition. Young people choose their own mates and delay marriage until they have financial security and the experience needed to select a suitable partner. Dating sharpens courtship skills and allows sexual experimentation.

Romantic Love

Our culture celebrates *romantic love*—affection and sexual passion for another person—as the basis for marriage. We find it hard to imagine marriage without love, and popular culture—from fairy tales such as "Cinderella" to today's romance novels—portrays love as the key to a successful marriage. However, as Figure 18–1 shows, in Pakistan, India, and many other countries where traditions remain strong, romantic love plays a much smaller role in marriage.

 Take a look at "virtual courtship" using the Internet to find a partner: http://www.loveme.com

Our society's emphasis on romance motivates young people to "leave the nest" to form new families of their own, and physical passion can help a new couple through difficult adjustments of living together (Goode, 1959). On the other hand, because feelings wax and wane, romantic love is a less stable foundation for marriage than social and economic considerations—one reason that the divorce rate is much higher in the United States than in nations where culture limits choices in partners.

But even here, sociologists point out, society aims Cupid's arrow more than we like to think. Most people fall in love with others of the same race, comparable age, and similar social class. Our society "arranges" marriages by encouraging **homogamy** (literally, "like marrying like"), *marriage between people with the same social characteristics.*

SETTLING IN: IDEAL AND REAL MARRIAGE

Our culture gives the young an idealized, "happily ever after" picture of marriage. Such optimism can lead to disappointment, especially for women, who are taught that marriage is the key to happiness. Then, too, romantic love involves a good deal of fantasy. We fall in love with others not necessarily as they are but as we want them to be (Berscheid & Hatfield, 1983). Only after marriage do many spouses face up to day-to-day responsibilities and routines.

Sexuality, too, can be a source of disappointment. In the romantic haze of falling in love, people may unrealistically expect marriage to be an endless sexual

First, divorce rates are likely to remain high, even in the face of evidence that marital breakups harm children. At the same time, bear in mind that today's marriages are no less durable than they were a century ago, when many were cut short by death (Kain, 1990). The difference is that more couples now *choose* to end marriages that fail to live up to their expectations. Thus, although the divorce rate has recently stabilized, it is unlikely to return to the low rates that marked the early decades of the twentieth century.

Second, family life in the twenty-first century will be highly variable. Cohabiting couples, one-parent families, gay and lesbian families, and blended families are all on the increase. Most families are still based on marriage, and most married couples still have children. But, taken together, the variety of family forms reveals a trend toward more personal choice.

Third, men will continue to play a limited role in child rearing. In the 1950s, a decade many people see as the "golden age" of families, men began to withdraw from active parenting (Snell, 1990; Stacey, 1990). In recent years, a small countertrend, the "stay-at-home dad," is evi-

Here is a resource Web site for stay-at-home fathers: http://www.slowlane.com

dent, with some older, highly educated fathers of young children staying at home yet remaining active in their careers by using computer technology. But

they represent no more than 15 percent of fathers with preschool children (Gardner, 1996). The bigger picture is that with the high U.S. divorce rate and the surge in single motherhood, more children are growing up with weak ties to fathers. At the same time, the evidence is building that the absence of fathers is harmful to children, at the very least because such families are at high risk of being poor.

Fourth, we will continue to feel the effects of economic changes in our families (Hochschild & Machung, 1989). In most homes, both household partners work, rendering marriage the interaction of weary men and women who try to squeeze in a little "quality time" for themselves and their children (Dizard & Gadlin, 1990). Two-career couples may advance the goal of gender equality, but the long-term effects on families as we have known them are likely to be mixed.

Fifth and finally, the importance of new reproductive technology will increase. Ethical concerns about whether what *can* be done *should* be done will surely slow these developments, but new forms of reproduction will continue to alter the traditional experience of parenthood.

Despite the changes and controversies that have buffeted the family in the United States, most people still report being happy as partners and parents. Marriage and family life will remain a foundation of our society for some time to come.

SUMMARY

1. All societies are built on kinship, although family forms vary across cultures and over time.

2. In industrial societies such as the United States, marriage is monogamous. Many preindustrial societies permit polygamy, of which there are two types: polygyny and polyandry.

3. In global perspective, patrilocality is most common, whereas industrial societies favor neolocality and a few societies have matrilocal residence. Industrial societies use bilateral descent, whereas preindustrial societies are either patrilineal or matrilineal.

4. Structural-functional analysis identifies major family functions: socialization of the young, regulation of sexual activity, social placement, and material and emotional support.

5. Social-conflict theories explore how the family perpetuates social inequality by transmitting divisions

based on class, ethnicity, race, and gender from one generation to the next.

6. Micro-level analysis highlights the variety of family life as experienced by various family members.

7. Courtship leads to the formation of families. Romantic love is central to mate selection in the United States but not in much of the world. Even in this country, moreover, romantic love usually joins people with similar social backgrounds.

8. The vast majority of married couples have children, although family size has decreased over time. The main reason for this decline is industrialization, which transforms children into economic liabilities, encourages women to acquire an education and join the labor force, and reduces infant mortality.

9. Married life changes as children leave home to form families of their own. However, many middle-aged

Should We Save the Traditional Family?

What are "traditional families"? Are they vital to our way of life or a barrier to progress? To begin, people use the term "traditional family" to mean a married couple who, at some point in their lives, raise children. Statistically speaking, traditional families are less common than they used to be. In 1950, as the figure shows, 90 percent of U.S. households were families: two or more people related by blood, marriage, or adoption. By 2000, just 68 percent of households were families because of rising levels of divorce, cohabitation, and singlehood.

Of course, "traditional family" is more than just a term; it is also a moral statement. That is, belief in the traditional family implies putting a high value on becoming and remaining married, placing children ahead of careers, and favoring two-parent families over various "alternative lifestyles."

On one side of the debate, David Popenoe warns that there has been a serious erosion of the traditional family since 1960. Then, married couples with young children accounted for almost half of all households; today, the figure is 24 percent. Singlehood is up, from 10 to 26 percent of present households.

The divorce rate has doubled since 1960, so that almost half of today's marriages will end in permanent separation. Moreover, because of both divorce and out-of-wedlock births, the share of youngsters who will live with a single parent before age eighteen has quadrupled since 1960, to 50 percent. In other words, just one in four of

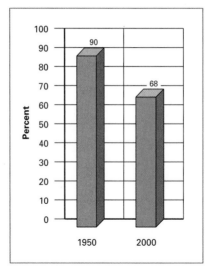

Share of U.S. Households That the Census Bureau Classifies as Families, 1950 and 2000

today's children will grow up with two parents and go on to maintain a stable marriage as an adult.

In light of such data, Popenoe concludes, it may not be an exaggeration to say that the family is falling apart. He sees a fundamental shift from a "culture of marriage" to a "culture of divorce." Traditional vows of marital commitment—"'til death us do part"—now amount to little more than "as long as I am happy." Daniel Yankelovich (1994:20) sums it up this way:

> The quest for greater individual choice clashed directly with the obligations and social norms that held families and communities together in earlier years. People came to feel that questions of how to live and with whom to live were a matter of individual choice not to be governed by restrictive norms. As a nation, we came to experience the bonds of marriage, family, children, job, community, and country as constraints that were no longer necessary. Commitments have loosened.

The negative consequences of the cultural trend toward weaker families, Popenoe continues, are obvious and

---

couples care for aging parents, and many older couples are active grandparents. The final transition in marriage begins with the death of one's spouse, usually the husband.

10. Families differ according to class position, race, and ethnicity. For example, Hispanic families are more likely than others to maintain extended kinship ties. African American families are more likely than others to be headed by single women. Among all

categories of people, well-to-do families enjoy the most options and greatest financial security.

11. Gender affects family dynamics because husbands dominate in most marriages. Research suggests that marriage has more benefits for men than for women.

12. The divorce rate today is ten times what it was a century ago; at least four in ten current marriages will end in divorce. Most people who divorce—especially

can be found everywhere: As we pay less and less attention to children, the juvenile crime rate goes up along with a host of other troublesome behaviors such as underage smoking and drinking and premarital sex.

As Popenoe sees it, then, we must act quickly and work hard to reverse current trends. Government cannot be the solution and may even be part of the problem: Since 1960, as government spending on social programs has soared fivefold, families have become weaker and weaker. Instead, says Popenoe, we need a cultural turnaround. We must replace our "me-first" attitudes in favor of commitment to our spouse and children. Such a switch is entirely possible, he continues; just look at how attitudes toward smoking have changed in recent decades. We can save the traditional family in two steps: first, by publicly affirming the value of staying married and, second, by endorsing the two-parent family as best for the well-being of children.

But Judith Stacey is unconvinced. She says "good riddance" to the traditional family and provides a counterpoint. To her, the traditional family is more problem than solution. Striking to the heart of the matter, Stacey writes (1990:269),

The family is not here to stay. Nor should we wish it were. On the contrary, I believe that all democratic people, whatever their kinship preferences, should work to hasten its demise.

The main reason for rejecting the traditional family is that it perpetuates social inequality, Stacey explains. Families play a key role in maintaining the class hierarchy, transferring wealth and "cultural capital" from one generation to another. Moreover, feminists criticize the traditional family's patriarchal form, which subjects women to their husbands' authority and saddles them with most of the responsibility for housework and child care. From a gay rights perspective, she adds, a society that values traditional families inevitably denies homosexual men and women equal participation in social life.

Stacey thus applauds the breakdown of the family as social progress. She does not consider the family a necessary social institution but rather a political construct that elevates one category of people—affluent white males—at the expense of others, including women, homosexuals, and poor people.

Stacey also claims that the concept of "traditional family" is increasingly irrelevant in a diverse society where both men and women work for income. What our society needs, Stacey concludes, is not a return to some "golden age" of the family but political and economic change, including income parity for women, universal health care and child care, programs to reduce unemployment, and expanded sex education in the schools. Only with such programs can we support our children and ensure that people in diverse family forms receive the respect everyone deserves.

Continue the debate . . .

1. *To strengthen families, David Popenoe suggests that parents put children ahead of their own careers by limiting their joint work week to sixty hours. Do you agree? Why or why not?*

2. *Judith Stacey thinks that marriage is weaker today because women are rejecting patriarchal relationships. What do you think about this argument?*

3. *Do we need to change family patterns for the well-being of our children? As you see it, what specific changes are called for?*

Sources: Popenoe (1993a), Stacey (1990, 1993), and Council on Families in America (1995).

men—remarry, often forming blended families that include children from previous marriages.

13. Most family violence victimizes women and children and is far more common than official records indicate. Most adults who abuse family members were themselves abused as children.

14. Our society's family life is becoming more varied. One-parent families, cohabitation, gay and lesbian couples, and singlehood have proliferated in recent years. Although the law does not recognize homosexual marriages, many gay men and lesbians form long-lasting relationships and increasingly are becoming parents.

15. Although ethically controversial, new reproductive technology is changing conventional ideas of parenthood.

KEY CONCEPTS

family (p. 463) a social institution found in all societies that unites people in cooperative groups to oversee the bearing and raising of children

kinship (p. 463) a social bond based on blood, marriage, or adoption

family unit (p. 464) a social group of two or more people, related by blood, marriage, or adoption, who usually live together

marriage (p. 464) a legally sanctioned relationship, usually involving economic cooperation as well as sexual activity and childbearing, that people expect to be enduring

extended family (consanguine family) (p. 464) a family unit that includes parents and children as well as other kin

nuclear family (conjugal family) (p. 464) a family unit composed of one or two parents and their children

endogamy (p. 465) marriage between people of the same social category

exogamy (p. 465) marriage between people of different social categories

monogamy (p. 465) marriage that unites two partners

polygamy (p. 465) marriage that unites three or more people

polygyny (p. 465) marriage that unites one male and two or more females

polyandry (p. 465) marriage that unites one female and two or more males

patrilocality (p. 465) a residential pattern in which a married couple lives with or near the husband's family

matrilocality (p. 465) a residential pattern in which a married couple lives with or near the wife's family

neolocality (p. 465) a residential pattern in which a married couple lives apart from both sets of parents

descent (p. 465) the system by which members of a society trace kinship over generations

patrilineal descent (p. 465) a system tracing kinship through men

matrilineal descent (p. 466) a system tracing kinship through women

bilateral descent (p. 466) a system tracing kinship through both men and women

incest taboo (p. 467) a norm forbidding sexual relations or marriage between certain relatives

homogamy (p. 472) marriage between people with the same social characteristics

infidelity (p. 473) sexual activity outside marriage

family violence (p. 481) emotional, physical, or sexual abuse of one family member by another

cohabitation (p. 482) the sharing of a household by an unmarried couple

CRITICAL-THINKING QUESTIONS

1. Identify several changes in the family since 1960. What factors are responsible for these changes?

2. A rising number of companies are extending marital benefits (such as health insurance) to unmarried gay partners. Do you approve of this trend? Why or why not? Should companies also extend benefits to cohabiting heterosexual partners?

3. Do you think that single-parent households do as good a job as two-parent households in raising children? Why or why not?

4. On balance, are families in the United States becoming weaker or simply different? What evidence can you cite?

APPLICATIONS AND EXERCISES

1. Parents and grandparents can be a wonderful source of information about changes in marriage and the family. Spend an hour or two with married people of two different generations and ask about when they married, what their married lives have been like, and what changes in family life today stand out for them.

2. Relationships with various family members differ. With which family member—mother, father, brother, sister—do you most readily and least readily share secrets? Why? Which family member would you turn to first in a crisis? Why?

3. Organize a debate for one class period with one team arguing each side of the "family values controversy." Present arguments for and against the statement: "Resolved: The traditional family is necessary for the survival of our country's way of life."

4. Packaged in the back of this new textbook is an interactive CD-ROM that offers a variety of study and review materials intended to help you better understand the material covered in this chapter. For this chapter, the CD-ROM contains an author's tip video, Real Life Sociology videos, other relevant audio and video, interactive map animations, audio journal entries from the author, Web links, and much more.

 SITES TO SEE

http://www.prenhall.com/macionis

Visit the interactive *Companian Website*™ that accompanies this text. Begin by clicking on the cover of your book. You will find a chapter-by-chapter study guide, practice tests, and a significant portion of the text for on-line review as well as many suggested Web links.

http://www.frc.org

This is the Web address for the Family Research Council, a conservative organization supporting what it calls "traditional family values." What does the council consider a "traditional family"? What values does it defend? Why? Are there family problems that it ignores?

http://www.redthreadmag.com

This site provides information about cross-cultural adoptions—specifically, the experiences of people in the United States adopting young girls from China.

http://childstats.gov

This is the site for the Federal Interagency Forum on Child and Family Statistics, which compiles information from eighteen government agencies.

http://www.polyamorysociety.org

Survey the increasing diversity of family life at the Web site for the Polyamory Society. What do you make of the society's views of family life?

 INVESTIGATE WITH CONTENTSELECT

Follow the instructions found on page 23 of this textbook to enter this chapter of the book's *Companion Website*™. Once in the chapter, click on the ContentSelect icon at the bottom left of your screen and enter your personal User ID and Password. Enter keywords such as "family values," "cohabitation," and "new reproductive technology," and the search engine will help you become an effective researcher.

William Penhallow Henderson (1877–1943)
Feast Day: San Juan Pueblo (New Mexico), ca. 1924

Smithsonian American Art Museum,
Washington, D.C./Art Resource, N.Y.

RELIGION

A warm July wind blows through the open windows of the white-steepled New England church as it has this time of year for three centuries, since the Puritans settled the town of Chelmsford, Massachusetts. Many in the congregation slowly fan themselves with the worship program as they wait for the service to begin. Like Puritans of times past, these are conservative people, men and women who believe in prayer and follow a strict code of conduct, even abstaining from alcohol. Then their voices rise together, declaring, "God is great!" But these New Englanders are speaking Arabic: "Allah-u

Akhbar!" Muslims make up an increasing share of this Yankee town, as they do in communities all across the United States.

According to the most recent count, there are now between 7 and 10 million Muslims in the United States—more, in fact, than there are Episcopalians, Presbyterians, or Jews. In fact, Muslims in this nation now outnumber Mormons, Quakers, Unitarians, Seventh-Day Adventists, Christian Scientists, and Jehovah's Witnesses combined. As some see it, after Christianity, Islam is this country's second religion (adapted from Blank, 1998).

The names, languages, and rituals may change, but religion has always held a central part in U.S. society. This chapter explains what religion is, explores the changing face of religious belief throughout history and around the world, and examines the vital yet sometimes controversial place of religion in today's modern, scientific culture.

Here is a new report on Muslims in the United States from the Council on American-Islamic Relations: http://www.cair-net.org/mosquereport/

RELIGION: BASIC CONCEPTS

The French sociologist Emile Durkheim stated that religion involves "things that surpass the limits of our knowledge" (1965:62; orig. 1915). As human beings, we define most objects, events, and experiences as **profane** (from Latin, meaning "outside the temple"), *that which people define as an ordinary element of everyday life*. But we define some things as **sacred,** *that which people set apart as extraordinary, inspiring a sense of awe and reverence*. Distinguishing the sacred from the profane is the essence of all religious belief. **Religion,** then, is *a social institution involving beliefs and practices based on a conception of the sacred.*

A global perspective reveals great variety in matters of faith, with nothing sacred to everyone on Earth. Although people regard most books as profane, Jews believe the Torah (the first five books of the Hebrew Bible or Old Testament) is sacred, in the same way that Christians revere the Old and New Testaments of the Bible and Muslims exalt the Qur'an (Koran).

But no matter how a community of believers draws religious lines, Durkheim (1965:62) explained, people understand profane things in terms of their everyday usefulness: We log onto the Web with our computer or turn a key to start our car. What is sacred we reverently set apart from everyday life and denote as "forbidden." Marking the boundary between the sacred and the profane, for example, Muslims remove their shoes before entering a mosque to avoid defiling a sacred place with soles that touch the profane ground outside.

The sacred is embodied in **ritual,** *formal, ceremonial behavior*. Holy communion is the central ritual of Christianity; to the Christian faithful, the wafer and wine consumed during communion are not treated in a profane way as food but as the sacred symbols of the body and blood of Jesus Christ.

Religion is founded on the concept of the sacred: that which is set apart as extraordinary and which demands our submission. Bowing, kneeling, or prostrating oneself are all ways of symbolically surrendering to a higher power. This monk is performing an act of prostration circumambulation, a complicated way of saying that he falls flat on the ground every few steps as he moves around a holy shrine. In this way, he expresses his complete surrender to his faith.

RELIGION AND SOCIOLOGY

Because religion deals with ideas and truth that transcend everyday experience, neither sociology nor any other scientific discipline can verify or disprove religious doctrine. Religion is a matter of **faith,** *belief anchored in conviction rather than scientific evidence.* The New Testament of the Bible, for instance, describes faith as "the assurance of things hoped for, the conviction of things not seen" (Heb. 11:1) and exhorts Christians to "walk by faith, not by sight" (2 Cor. 5:7).

Some people with strong faith may be disturbed by the thought of sociologists turning a scientific eye to what they hold sacred. However, a sociological study of religion poses no threat to anyone's faith. Sociologists study religion just as they study the family: to understand religious experiences around the world and how religion is tied to other social institutions. They make no judgments that a specific religion is right or wrong. Rather, scientific sociology takes a more worldly approach by delving into why religions take particular forms in one society or another and how religious activity affects society as a whole.

THEORETICAL ANALYSIS OF RELIGION

Sociologists have applied various theoretical paradigms to the study of religion. Each provides distinctive insights into the way religion shapes social life.

FUNCTIONS OF RELIGION: STRUCTURAL-FUNCTIONAL ANALYSIS

According to Durkheim (1965; orig. 1915), society has an existence and power of its own beyond the life of any individual. In other words, society itself is "god-like," surviving the death of its members, whose lives it shapes. Thus, people engage in religious life to celebrate the awesome power of their society.

No wonder, then, that people around the world transform certain everyday objects into sacred symbols of their collective life. Members of technologically simple societies do this with the **totem,** *an object in the natural world collectively defined as sacred.* The totem—perhaps an animal or an elaborate work of art—becomes the centerpiece of ritual, symbolizing the power of collective life over any individual. In our society, the flag is a quasi-sacred totem. It is not to be used in a profane manner (say, as clothing) or allowed to touch the ground.

Similarly, putting the inscription "In God We Trust" on all currency (a practice begun in the 1860s, at the time of the Civil War) implies that our society is bound by common beliefs. Local communities across the United States also create a sense of unity through totemic symbolism attached to sports teams, from the New England Patriots, to the Ohio State University Buckeyes, to the San Francisco 49ers.

Why is the religious dimension of social life so important? Durkheim pointed out three major functions of religion for the operation of society:

1. **Social cohesion**. Religion unites people through shared symbolism, values, and norms. Religious thought and ritual establish rules of fair play that make organized social life possible.

2. **Social control**. Every society uses religious ideas to promote conformity. Societies give many cultural norms—especially mores that deal with marriage and reproduction—religious justification. Religion even legitimizes the political system. Although few of today's politicians claim to rule by divine right (as they did centuries ago), many publicly ask for God's blessing, implying to audiences that their efforts are right and just.

3. **Providing meaning and purpose**. Religious belief offers the comforting sense that our brief lives serve some greater purpose. Strengthened by their faith, people are less likely to despair when one of life's calamities strikes. For this reason, we mark major life course transitions—including birth, marriage, and death—with religious observances.

Critical evaluation. In Durkheim's structural-functional analysis, religion represents the collective life of society. The major weakness of this approach, however, is that it downplays religion's dysfunctions, especially the fact that strongly held beliefs can generate social conflict. During the early Middle Ages, for example, religious faith was the driving force behind the Crusades—the battles between European Christians and Muslims over the Holy Land, which both religions considered sacred. Conflict between Muslims, Jews, and Christians is still a source of political instability in the Middle East today. Similarly, tensions continue to divide Protestants and Catholics in Northern Ireland, and religious conflict persists in Algeria, India, Sri Lanka, and elsewhere. In short, many nations have marched to war under the banner of their God; in fact, few doubt that religious beliefs have provoked more violence in human history than differences in social class.

CONSTRUCTING THE SACRED: SYMBOLIC-INTERACTION ANALYSIS

From a symbolic-interaction point of view, religion (like all of society) is socially constructed (although perhaps with divine inspiration). Through various rituals—from daily prayers to annual religious observances such as Easter and Passover—individuals sharpen the distinction between the sacred and profane. Furthermore, as Peter Berger (1967:35–36)

explains, placing our fallible, brief lives within some "cosmic frame of reference" gives us "the semblance of ultimate security and permanence."

Marriage is a good example. If two people look on marriage as merely a contract, they can walk away whenever they want. But defined as holy matrimony, their bond makes far stronger claims on each of them. Indeed, the more religious people are, the less likely they are to divorce. More generally, whenever humans confront uncertainty or life-threatening situations—such as illness, war, and natural disaster—we turn to our sacred symbols.

Critical evaluation. Following the symbolic-interaction approach, religion puts everyday life under a "sacred canopy" of meaning (Berger, 1967). Of course, Berger adds, the sacred's ability to give meaning and stabilize society requires that people ignore its constructed character. After all, how much strength could we derive from beliefs we saw as mere strategies for coping with tragedy? Also, this micro-level analysis ignores religion's link to social inequality, to which we now turn.

INEQUALITY AND RELIGION: SOCIAL-CONFLICT ANALYSIS

The social-conflict paradigm highlights religion's support of social hierarchy. Religion serves ruling elites by legitimizing the status quo and diverting people's attention from social inequities, Karl Marx proclaimed.

Even today, for example, the British monarch is the formal head of the Church of England, showing the close alliance between religious and political elites. In practical terms, working for political change may mean opposing the church and, by implication, God. Religion also encourages people to look hopefully to a "better world to come," minimizing the social problems of this world. In a well-known statement, Marx dismissed religion as "the sigh of the oppressed creature, the sentiment of a heartless world, and the soul of soulless conditions. It is the opium of the people" (1964b:27; orig. 1848).

Religion and social inequality are also linked through gender. Virtually all the world's major religions are patriarchal, as the box on pages 494–95 explains.

For centuries, the powerful Christian nations of Western Europe justified the conquest of Africa, the Americas, and Asia by claiming that they were "converting heathens." In the United States, churches in

Religion and Patriarchy: Does God Favor Males?

Why do two-thirds of U.S. adults envision God as father rather than mother (NORC, 2001:144)? Probably because we link "godly" attributes such as wisdom and power to men. Thus, it is hardly surprising that organized religions tend to favor males, a fact evident in passages from the sacred writings of major world religions.

The Qur'an (Koran), the sacred text of Islam, stipulates that men dominate women:

> Men are in charge of women. . . . Hence good women are obedient.
> . . . As for those whose rebelliousness you fear, admonish them, banish them from your bed, and scourge them. (quoted in Kaufman, 1976:163)

Christianity, the major religion of the Western world, also supports patriarchy. Although many Christians revere Mary, the mother of Jesus, the New Testament also includes the following passages:

> A man . . . is the image and glory of God; but woman is the glory of man. For man was not made from woman, but woman from man.

Neither was man created for woman, but woman for man. (1 Cor. 11:7–9)

> As in all the churches of the saints, the women should keep silence in the churches. For they are not permitted to speak, but should be subordinate, as even the law says. If there is anything they desire to know, let them ask their husbands at home. For it is shameful for a woman to speak in church. (1 Cor. 14:33–35)

> Wives, be subject to your husbands, as to the Lord. For the husband is the head of the wife as Christ is the head of the church. . . . As the church is subject to Christ, so let wives also be subject in everything to their husbands. (Eph. 5:22–24)

the South believed enslaving African Americans was consistent with God's will. To this day, churches across the country remain segregated. In the words of African American author Maya Angelou, "Sunday at 11:30 A.M., America is more segregated than at any other time of the week."

Critical evaluation. Social-conflict analysis reveals the power of religion to legitimize social inequality. Yet religion also promotes change toward equality. For example, nineteenth-century religious groups in the United States were at the forefront of the movement to abolish slavery. During the 1950s and 1960s, religious organizations led by the Reverend Martin Luther King, Jr. and others formed the core of the civil rights movement. During the 1960s and 1970s, many clergy actively opposed the Vietnam War, and, as will be explained, some support revolutionary change in Latin America and elsewhere.

RELIGION AND SOCIAL CHANGE

Religion is not just the conservative force portrayed by Karl Marx. At some points in history, as Max Weber (1958; orig. 1904–5) noted, religion has promoted dramatic social transformation.

MAX WEBER: PROTESTANTISM AND CAPITALISM

Max Weber contended that new ideas often are engines of change. It was the religious doctrine of Calvinism, for example, that sparked the Industrial Revolution in Western Europe.

As Chapter 4 ("Society") explains in detail, John Calvin (1509–1564), a leader in the Protestant Reformation, preached the doctrine of predestination. According to Calvin, an all-powerful and all-knowing God predestined some people for salvation but condemned most

Let a woman learn in silence with all submissiveness. I permit no woman to teach or to have authority over men; she is to keep silent. For Adam was formed first, then Eve; and Adam was not deceived, but the woman was deceived and became a transgressor. Yet woman will be saved through bearing children, if she continues in faith and love and holiness, with modesty. (1 Tm. 2:11–15)

Judaism also traditionally supports patriarchy. Male Orthodox Jews say the following as part of their daily prayers:

Blessed art thou, O Lord our
    God, King of the Universe, that
    I was not born a gentile.
Blessed art thou, O Lord our
    God, King of the Universe, that
    I was not born a slave.
Blessed art thou, O Lord our
    God, King of the Universe, that
    I was not born a woman.

Major religions have also excluded women from the clergy. Even today, Islam and the Roman Catholic church ban women from the priesthood, as do about half of Protestant denominations. But a growing number of Protestant religious organizations, including the Church of England, ordain women, who now represent 15 percent of U.S. clergy. Orthodox Judaism upholds the traditional prohibition against women serving as rabbis, but Reform and Conservative Judaism look to both men and women as spiritual leaders. Across the United States, the proportion of women in seminaries has never been higher (now roughly one-third), further evidence that change is ongoing (Chaves, 1996, 1997; Nesbitt, 1997).

Challenges to the patriarchal structure of organized religion—from ordaining women to gender-neutral language in hymnals and prayers—have sparked heated controversy between progressives and traditionalists. Propelling these developments is a lively feminism in many religious communities. According to feminist Christians, for example, patriarchy in the church stands in stark contrast to the largely feminine image of Jesus Christ in the Scriptures as "nonaggressive, noncompetitive, meek and humble of heart, a nurturer of the weak and a friend of the outcast" (Sandra Schneiders, quoted in Woodward, 1989:61).

Feminists argue that unless traditional notions of gender are removed from our understanding of God, women will never be equal to men in the church. The theologian Mary Daly puts the matter bluntly: "If God is male, then male is God" (quoted in Woodward, 1989:58).

to eternal damnation. Each person's fate, sealed before birth and known only to God, is either eternal glory or endless hellfire.

Driven by anxiety over their fate, Calvinists understandably sought evidence of God's favor and gradually came to regard prosperity as a sign of divine blessing. Religious conviction and a rigid sense of duty led Calvinists to work all the time, and many amassed great wealth. But money was not for self-indulgent spending or for sharing with the poor, whose plight they saw as a mark of God's rejection. As agents of God's work on Earth, Calvinists believed that they best fulfilled their calling by reinvesting profits and reaping ever-greater success in the process.

All the while, Calvinists lived thrifty lives and embraced technological advances, thereby laying the groundwork for the rise of industrial capitalism. In time, the religious fervor that motivated early Calvinists weakened, leaving a profane "Protestant work ethic." To Max Weber, industrial capitalism was a "disenchanted" religion. Weber's analysis clearly shows the power of religious thinking to alter the basic shape of society.

LIBERATION THEOLOGY

Christianity has a long-standing concern for poor and oppressed people, urging all to strengthen their faith in a better life to come. In recent decades, however, some church leaders and theologians have endorsed **liberation theology,** *a fusion of Christian principles with political activism, often Marxist in character.*

This social movement started in the late 1960s in Latin America's Roman Catholic church and continues today with Christian activists working to liberate people in poor nations from abysmal poverty. The message of liberation theology is simple: Social oppression runs counter to Christian morality, so as a matter of faith and justice, Christians must promote greater social equality.

Despite its Roman Catholic beginnings, Pope John Paul II condemns liberation theology for distorting traditional church doctrine with left-wing politics. But over the pontiff's objections, the liberation theology movement remains powerful in Latin America, where many people find that their Christian faith drives them to improve conditions for the world's poor (Boff & Boff, 1984; Neuhouser, 1989; Rowland, 1999).

TYPES OF RELIGIOUS ORGANIZATION

Sociologists categorize the hundreds of different religious organizations found in the United States along a continuum, with *churches* at one end and *sects* at the other. We can describe any existing religious organization in relation to these two ideal types by locating it on the church-sect continuum.

CHURCH

Drawing on the ideas of his teacher Max Weber, Ernst Troeltsch (1931) defined a **church** as *a type of religious organization that is well integrated into the larger society.* Churchlike organizations usually persist for centuries and include generations of the same families. Churches have well-established rules and regulations and expect their leaders to be formally trained and ordained.

Though concerned with the sacred, a church tries to fit in with the profane world, which gives it broad appeal. The religious doctrine of a church conceives of God in highly intellectualized terms (say, as a force for good), and favors abstract moral standards ("Do unto others as you would have them do unto you") over specific rules for day-to-day living. By teaching morality in safely abstract terms, church leaders avoid social controversy. For example, many congregations may celebrate the unity of all peoples but nevertheless have all-white memberships. Such duality minimizes conflict between a church and political life (Troeltsch, 1931).

December 11, Casablanca, Morocco. The waves of the Atlantic crash along the walls of Casablanca's magnificent coastline mosque, reputedly the largest in the world. From the top of the towering structure, a green laser cuts through the night sky, pointing eastward to Mecca, the holy city of Islam toward which the faithful bow in prayer. To pay for this monumental house of worship, King Hassam II, Morocco's head of state and religious leader, levied a tax on every citizen in his realm, all of whom are officially Muslim. This example of government religion contrasts sharply with our ideas about the separation of church and state.

A church may operate with or apart from the state. A **state church** is *a church formally allied with the state,* as illustrated by Islam in Morocco. State churches have existed throughout human history; for centuries Roman Catholicism was the official religion of the Roman Empire, as was Confucianism in China until early in the twentieth century. Today, the Anglican church is the official Church of England, as Islam is the official religion of Pakistan and Iran. State churches count everyone in the society as members, a practice that severely limits tolerance of religious difference.

A **denomination,** by contrast, is *a church, independent of the state, that accepts religious pluralism.* Denominations exist in nations that formally separate church and state, such as the United States, which has dozens of Christian denominations—including Catholics, Baptists, Methodists, and Lutherans—as well as various categories of Judaism, Islam, and other traditions. Members of a denomination hold to their own beliefs, but they accept the right of others to disagree.

SECT

The second general religious form is the **sect,** *a type of religious organization that stands apart from the larger society.* Sect members have rigid religious convictions and deny the beliefs of others. Generally, to members of a sect, religion is not just one aspect of life but a firm plan for how to live. In some cases, then, members of a sect may withdraw completely from society in order to practice their religion without interference. The Amish are one example of a North American sect that isolates itself (Kraybill, 1994). Because our culture holds up religious tolerance as a virtue, members of sects are sometimes accused of being narrow-minded in insisting that they alone follow the true religion.

through Muhammad, God's messenger. In Arabic, the word "Islam" means both "submission" and "peace," and the Qur'an urges submission to Allah as the path to inner peace. Muslims express this personal devotion in ritual prayers five times a day.

Islam spread rapidly after the death of Muhammad, although divisions arose, as they did within Christianity. However, all Muslims accept the Five Pillars of Islam: (1) recognizing Allah as the one, true God and Muhammad as God's messenger; (2) ritual prayer; (3) giving alms to the poor; (4) fasting during the month of Ramadan; and (5) making a pilgrimage at least once to the Sacred House of Allah in Mecca (Weeks, 1988; El-Attar, 1991). Like Christianity, Islam holds people accountable to God for their deeds on Earth. Those who live obediently will be rewarded in heaven, and evildoers will suffer unending punishment.

Muslims are also obligated to defend their faith, which has led to holy wars against unbelievers (in roughly the same way that medieval Christians fought in the Crusades). Recently, in Afghanistan, Algeria, Egypt, Iran, and elsewhere, some fundamentalist Muslims have sought to rid their society of Western influences that they consider morally wrong (Martin, 1982; Arjomand, 1988).

To many Westerners, Muslim women are among the most socially oppressed people on Earth. Of course, Muslim nations differ in this regard: For example, Tunisia allows women far more opportunities than, say, Saudi Arabia (Ganley, 1998). In general, however, Muslim women lack many of the personal freedoms enjoyed by Muslim men, yet many—and perhaps most—accept the mandates of their religion and find security in a system that guides the behavior of both women and men (S. Peterson, 1996). Muslims also point out that patriarchy was well established in the Middle East long before the birth of Muhammad, and some defenders argue that Islam actually improved the social position of women by requiring that husbands deal justly with their wives. Furthermore, although Islam permits a man to have up to four wives, it admonishes men to have only one wife if having more would cause him to treat any woman unjustly (Qur'an, "The Women," v. 3).

JUDAISM

Simply in terms of numbers, Judaism's total of 15 million followers worldwide makes it something less than a world religion. Moreover, only in Israel do Jews represent a national majority. But Judaism has special significance to the United States because the largest concentration of Jews (6 million people) is found in North America.

Jews look to the past as a source of guidance in the present and for the future. Judaism has deep historical roots that extend some 4,000 years before the birth of Christ to the ancient cultures of Mesopotamia. At this time, Jews were animistic, but this belief changed after Jacob—grandson of Abraham, the earliest great ancestor—led his people to Egypt.

Jews endured centuries of slavery in Egypt. In the thirteenth century B.C.E., Moses, the adopted son of an Egyptian princess, was called by God to lead the Jews from bondage. This exodus (this word's Latin and Greek roots mean "a marching out") from Egypt is commemorated by Jews today in the annual ritual of Passover. Once liberated, Jews became monotheistic, recognizing a single, all-powerful God.

A distinctive concept of Judaism is the *covenant*, a special relationship with God by which Jews became the "chosen people." The covenant also implies a duty to observe God's law, especially the Ten Commandments as revealed to Moses on Mount Sinai. Jews regard the Old Testament of the Bible as both a record of their history and a statement of the obligations of Jewish life. Of special importance are the Bible's first five books (Genesis, Exodus, Leviticus, Numbers, and Deuteronomy), designated the *Torah* (a word roughly meaning "teaching" and "law"). In contrast to Christianity's central concern with personal salvation, therefore, Judaism emphasizes moral behavior in this world.

Judaism has three main denominations. Orthodox Jews (including more than 1 million people in the United States) strictly observe traditional beliefs and practices, wear traditional dress, segregate men and women at religious services, and eat only kosher foods. Such traditional practices set off Orthodox Jews in the United States as the most sectlike. In the mid-nineteenth century, many Jews sought greater acceptance by the larger society, leading to the formation of more churchlike Reform Judaism (now including more than 1.3 million people in this country). A third segment, Conservative Judaism (with about 2 million adherents), has since established a middle ground between the other two denominations.

Whatever their denomination, Jews share a history of prejudice and discrimination. A collective memory of centuries of slavery in Egypt, conquest by Rome, and persecution in Europe has shaped Jewish identity. It was Jews in Italy who first lived in an urban ghetto (derived from the Italian word *borghetto*, meaning "settlement outside of the city walls"), and this residential segregation soon spread to other parts of Europe.

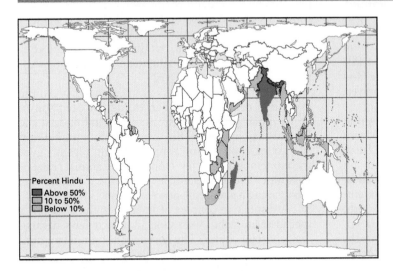

GLOBAL MAP 19–3
Hinduism in Global Perspective

Source: *Peters Atlas of the World* (1990).

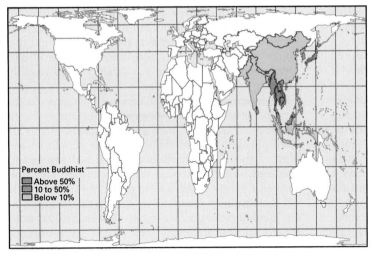

GLOBAL MAP 19–4
Buddhism in Global Perspective

Source: *Peters Atlas of the World* (1990).

Jewish immigration to the United States began in the mid-1600s. Many early immigrants prospered, and many were also assimilated into largely Christian communities. But as larger numbers entered the country toward the end of the nineteenth century, prejudice and discrimination against them—commonly called *anti-Semitism*—increased. During World War II, anti-Semitism reached a vicious peak as the Nazi regime in Germany systematically annihilated 6 million Jews.

On average, Jews have prospered, with social standing well above average. Still, many Jews are concerned about the future of their religion because in recent years more than half the Jews in the United States have married non-Jews. In only a few cases are non-Jewish spouses converting to Judaism. Just as significantly, about half the children raised in Jewish households are not learning Jewish culture and ritual. For the present, such patterns symbolize Jewish success in gaining acceptance into society. At the same time, however, they cast some doubt on the future of Judaism in North America (Bedell, Sandon, & Wellborn, 1975; Holm, 1977; Schmidt, 1980; Seltzer, 1980; B. Wilson, 1982; Eisen, 1983; Dershowitz, 1997; Van Biema, 1997a).

HINDUISM

Hinduism is the oldest of all the world religions, originating in the Indus River valley about 4,500 years ago. Hindus number some 800 million (14 percent of humanity). Global Map 19–3 shows that Hinduism remains an Eastern religion, practiced mostly in India and Pakistan but with a significant presence in southern Africa and Indonesia.

Over the centuries, Hinduism and the culture of India have become intertwined, so that now one is not easily described apart from the other (although India also has a sizable Muslim population). This connection also explains why Hinduism, unlike Christianity, Islam, and Judaism, has not diffused widely to other nations. Nevertheless, with 1.4 million followers in the United States, Hinduism is a significant part of this country's cultural diversity.

Hinduism differs from most other religions by not being linked to the life of any single person. Hinduism also has no sacred writings comparable to the Bible or the Qur'an. Nor does Hinduism envision God as a specific entity. For this reason, Hinduism—like other Eastern religions, as we shall see—is sometimes described as an ethical religion. Hindu beliefs and practices vary widely, but all Hindus recognize a moral force in the universe that presents everyone with responsibilities, called *dharma*. For example, dharma calls people to observe the traditional caste system, described in Chapter 10 ("Social Stratification").

Another Hindu principle, *karma*, is a belief in the spiritual progress of the human soul. To a Hindu, all actions have spiritual consequences, and proper living contributes to moral development. Karma works through *reincarnation*, a cycle of death and rebirth by which the individual is reborn into a spiritual state corresponding to the moral quality of a previous life. Unlike Christianity and Islam, Hinduism proclaims no ultimate judgment at the hands of a supreme god, although in the cycle of rebirth, people reap what they have sown. *Moksha* is the state of spiritual perfection: When a soul reaches this level, it is no longer reborn.

Hinduism stands as evidence that not all religions can be neatly labeled monotheistic or polytheistic. Hinduism is monotheistic insofar as it envisions the universe as a single moral system, yet Hindus see this

The spiritual leader of Tibetan Buddhism is the Dalai Lama, shown here teaching a large assembly of followers. For more information on the Dalai Lama, go to http://www.dalailama.com

moral order at work in every element of nature. Moreover, many Hindus participate in public rituals, such as the *Kumbh Mela*, which every twelve years brings some 20 million pilgrims to the sacred Ganges River to bathe in its purifying waters. At the same time, Hindus practice private devotions, which vary from village to village across the vast nation of India.

Elements of Hindu thought have characterized some cults in the United States over the years, but Hinduism is still unfamiliar to most Westerners. Nonetheless, like religions better known to us, Hinduism is a powerful force offering both explanation and guidance in life (Pitt, 1955; Sen, 1961; Embree, 1972; Kaufman, 1976; Schmidt, 1980).

BUDDHISM

Twenty-five hundred years ago, the rich culture of India also gave rise to Buddhism. Today some 350 million people (6 percent of humanity) are Buddhists,

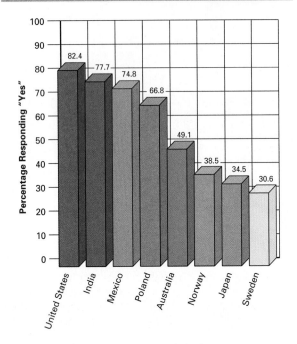

GLOBAL SNAPSHOT

FIGURE 19–1 Religiosity in Global Perspective

Survey Question: "Do you gain comfort and strength from religion?"

Source: Inglehart et al. (2000).

almost all of whom are Asians. As shown in Global Map 19–4, Buddhists make up more than half the populations of Myanmar (Burma), Thailand, Cambodia, and Japan; Buddhism is also widespread in India and the People's Republic of China. Of the world religions considered so far, Buddhism most resembles Hinduism in doctrine, but, like Christianity, its inspiration stems from the life of one person.

Siddhartha Gautama was born to a high-caste family in Nepal about 563 B.C.E. As a young man, he was preoccupied with spiritual matters. At age twenty-nine, he underwent a radical personal transformation and set off for years of travel and meditation. His journey ended when he achieved what Buddhists describe as *bodhi*, or enlightenment. Understanding the essence of life, Gautama became a Buddha.

Energized by his personal charisma, followers spread Buddha's teachings—the *dhamma*—across India.

In the third century B.C.E., the ruler of India became a Buddhist and sent missionaries throughout Asia, making Buddhism a world religion.

Buddhists believe that much of life involves suffering. This idea is rooted in the Buddha's own travels in a society rife with poverty. But the solution to suffering is not wealth, Buddha claimed. On the contrary, materialism limits spiritual development. Instead, Buddha taught that we must transcend our selfish concerns and desires through meditation, with the goal of obtaining *nirvana*, a state of enlightenment and peace.

Buddhism closely parallels Hinduism in recognizing no god of judgment, yet each daily action has spiritual consequences. Another similarity is a belief in reincarnation. Here, again, only enlightenment ends the cycle of death and rebirth and finally liberates a person from the suffering of the world (Schumann, 1974; Thomas, 1975; Van Biema, 1997b).

CONFUCIANISM

From about 200 B.C.E. until the beginning of the twentieth century, Confucianism was a state church, the official religion of China. A dramatic change took place after the 1949 Revolution when the communist government of the new People's Republic of China vigorously repressed religion. Today, although officials provide no precise count, hundreds of millions of Chinese are still influenced by Confucianism. Almost all Confucianists live in China, although Chinese immigration has spread this religion to other nations in Southeast Asia. Perhaps 100,000 followers of Confucius live in North America.

Confucius or, more properly, K'ung Fu-tzu, lived between 551 and 479 B.C.E. Like Buddha, Confucius was deeply concerned about people's suffering. The Buddha's response was a sectlike spiritual withdrawal from the world; By contrast, Confucius instructed his followers to engage the world according to a code of moral conduct. Thus it was that Confucianism became fused with the traditional culture of China. Here we see a second example of what might be called a national religion: As Hinduism has remained largely synonymous with Indian culture, Confucianism is enshrined in the Chinese way of life.

A central concept of Confucianism is *jen*, meaning "humaneness." In practice, this means that we must always subordinate our self-interest to moral principle. In the family, the individual must be loyal and considerate. Families also must remain mindful of their duties toward the larger community. In this way, layer upon layer of moral obligation integrates society as a whole.

Most of all, Confucianism stands out as lacking a clear sense of the sacred. Recalling Durkheim's analysis, we might view Confucianism as the celebration of the sacred character of society itself. Or we might argue that Confucianism is less a religion than a model of disciplined living. Certainly the historical dominance of Confucianism helps explain why Chinese culture is skeptical of the supernatural. But even as a disciplined way of life, Confucianism shares with religion a body of beliefs and practices that have as their goal goodness, concern for others, and social harmony (Kaufman, 1976; Schmidt, 1980; McGuire, 1987).

RELIGION: EAST AND WEST

This overview of world religions points up two general differences between the belief systems of Eastern and Western societies. First, Western religions (Christianity, Islam, Judaism) typically are deity-based, with a clear focus on God. However, Eastern religions (Hinduism, Buddhism, Confucianism) tend to be ethical codes; therefore, they make a less clear-cut distinction between what is sacred and what is secular.

Second, believers in Western religions form congregations. That is, people join an organization and worship formally in groups at a specific time and place. By contrast, Eastern religions are informally fused with culture itself. For this reason, for example, a visitor finds a Japanese temple filled with both tourists and worshipers, who come and go as they please and pay little attention to those around them.

But these two distinctions do not overshadow the common element of all religions: a conception of a higher moral force or purpose that transcends individualism and the concerns of everyday life. Although they take different paths, all religions give people a spiritual sense that their lives can serve some larger purpose.

 For information on various religions, visit http://www.adherents.com

RELIGION IN THE UNITED STATES

In global perspective, the United States is a relatively religious nation. As Figure 19–1 shows, eight in ten members of our society say they gain "comfort and strength from religion," a substantially higher share than in most other high-income countries.

That said, scholars debate exactly how religious this nation is. Whereas some claim that religion is central to our way of life, others conclude that a decline

TABLE 19–1 Religious Identification in the United States, 2000	
Religion	**Percentage Indicating Preference**
Protestant denominations	**56.2%**
Baptist	20.6
Methodist	9.3
Lutheran	5.4
Presbyterian	3.4
Episcopalian	1.9
All others or no denomination	15.6
Catholic	**25.1**
Jewish	**2.3**
Other or no answer	**1.7**
No religious preference	**14.7**

Source: *General Social Surveys, 1972–2000: Cumulative Codebook* (Chicago: National Opinion Research Center, 2001), pp. 129–30.

of the traditional family and the advancing role of science and technology are undermining religious commitment and faith (Collins, 1982; Greeley, 1989; Woodward, 1992a; Hadaway, Marler, & Chaves, 1993).

RELIGIOUS AFFILIATION

Most people in the United States identify with a religion. On national surveys, 85 percent of U.S. adults claim a religious preference (NORC, 2001:129). Table 19–1 shows that more than half of U.S. adults consider themselves Protestants, one-fourth are Catholics, and 2 percent Jews. Significant numbers of people also adhere to dozens of other religions, from animism to Zen Buddhism, making our society as religiously diverse as any on Earth.

About 60 percent consider themselves a member of some religious organization, and 90 percent say they had at least some formal religious instruction growing up (NORC, 2001:373–74). National Map 19–1 on page 506 shows the share of people who claim to belong to any church across the United States.

National Map 19–2 takes us one more step, showing that the religion most people identify with varies by region. New England and the Southwest are predominantly Catholic, the South is overwhelmingly Baptist, and in the northern Plains states, Lutherans predominate. In and around Utah, there is a heavy concentration of members of the Church of Jesus Christ of Latter Day Saints (Mormons).

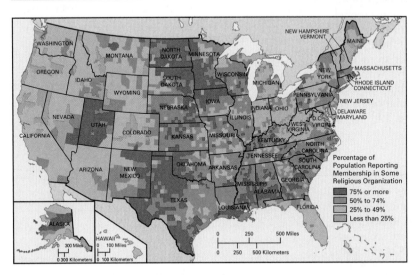

NATIONAL MAP 19–1
Religious Membership across the United States

In general, people in the United States are more religious than people in other high-income nations. Yet membership in a religious organization is more common in some parts of the country than in others. What pattern do you see in the map? Can you explain the pattern?

Source: From Rodger Doyle, *Atlas of Contemporary America*. Map copyright © 1994 by Facts on File, Inc. Reprinted with the permission of Facts on File, Inc.

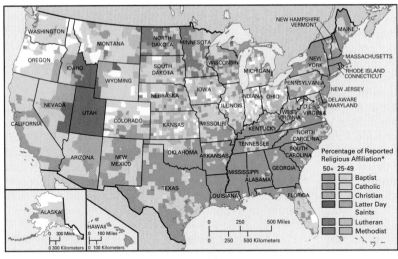

NATIONAL MAP 19–2
Religious Diversity across the United States

In the vast majority of counties, at least 25 percent of people who report having an affiliation are members of the same religious organization. Thus, although the United States is religiously diverse at the national level, most people live in communities where one denomination predominates. What historical facts might account for this pattern?

*When two or more churches have 25 to 49 percent of the membership in a county, the largest is shown. When no church has 25 percent of the membership that county is left blank. A few exceptions include Palm Beach County in southern Florida, which is primarily Jewish, and Holmes County in central Ohio, which is largely Amish.

Source: The Glenmary Research Center, Atlanta, Georgia (1990).

RELIGIOSITY

Religiosity is *the importance of religion in a person's life.* Identifying with a religion is only one measure of religiosity, of course, and a superficial one at that. How religious people turn out to be depends on how we operationalize the concept.

Years ago, Charles Glock (1959, 1962) suggested that we could measure five distinct dimensions of religiosity. *Experiential* religiosity refers to how emotionally tied to a religion someone is. *Ritualistic* religiosity means how often someone prays or goes to church. *Ideological* religiosity describes how much a person believes in religious doctrine. *Consequential* religiosity has to do with how strongly religious beliefs figure in one's daily behavior. Finally, *intellectual* religiosity refers to how much someone knows about the history and doctrines of a religion. Anyone is likely to be more religious on some dimensions and less on others, so assessing religiosity is a difficult task.

When asked directly, 86 percent of U.S. adults claim to believe in a divine power of some kind, although just 61 percent claim that they "know that God exists and have no doubts about it" (NORC, 2001:375). These measures of experiential religiosity are relatively high.

Measures of ideological religiosity yield lower numbers. Seventy-two percent of U.S. adults report a belief in life after death. And the numbers for ritualistic religiosity drop further: Fifty-five percent of adults say they pray at least once a day, and just 29 percent claim to attend religious services on a weekly or almost-weekly basis (NORC, 2001:133, 138, 131).

Clearly, the question "How religious are we?" offers no easy answers. Keep in mind, too, that many people probably claim to be more religious than they really are. For example, a team of researchers posted observers at every place of worship in Ashtabula County, Ohio, and estimated the number of people attending Sunday services; in a subsequent survey of county residents, twice as many people claimed that they attended church that Sunday than really did. The researchers concluded that no more than 20 percent of people attend church regularly (Hadaway, Marler, & Chaves, 1993). Critics charge that this study may have underestimated the actual number of people attending religious services. Based on all available evidence, it is likely that 25 to 35 percent of the population attends church regularly (Caplow, 1998; Hout & Greeley, 1998; Woodberry, 1998).

Overall, although most people in the United States claim to be at least somewhat religious, probably no more than about one-third actually are. Moreover,

 Access Gallup polls on religion at http://www.gallup.com/poll/topics

religiosity varies among denominations. Members of sects are the most religious of all, followed by Catholics and then "mainstream" Protestants. In general, older people are more religious than younger people, and women are more religious than men (Stark & Glock, 1968; Hadaway, Marler, & Chaves, 1993; Sherkat & Ellison, 1999).

RELIGION AND SOCIAL STRATIFICATION

Sociologists who study religion have found that religious affiliation is related to other familiar social patterns. We shall consider three: social class, race, and ethnicity.

Social Class

A recent study of *Who's Who in America*, which profiles high achievers, showed that 33 percent of the people who gave a religious affiliation were Episcopalians, Presbyterians, and United Church of Christ members, denominations that together account for less than 10 percent of the population. Jews also enjoy high social position, with their 2 percent of the U.S. population accounting for 12 percent of the listings in *Who's Who*.

Research also shows that other denominations—including Congregationalists, Methodists, and Catholics—have a moderate social position. Lower social standing is typical of Baptists, Lutherans, and members of sects. Within all denominations, of course, there is wide variation (Roof, 1979; Davidson, Pyle, & Reyes, 1995; Waters, Heath, & Watson, 1995).

By and large, Protestants with high social standing are people of northern European background whose families came to the United States at least a century ago. They encountered little prejudice and discrimination and have had the longest time to establish themselves socially. Roman Catholics, more recent immigrants to the United States, have faced greater social barriers because of their religion.

Jews command unexpectedly high social standing considering that they often contend with anti-Semitism from the Christian majority. The reason for this achievement is mostly cultural, because Jewish tradition places great value on education and hard work. Although a large proportion of Jews began life in the United States in poverty, many improved their social position in subsequent generations.

Ethnicity and Race

Throughout the world, religion is tied to ethnicity. Many religions predominate in a single nation or geographic region. Islam predominates in the Arab societies of the Middle East, Hinduism is fused with the culture of India, and Confucianism runs deep in Chinese society. Christianity and Judaism do not follow this pattern; although these religions are mostly Western, Christians and Jews are found all over the world.

Religion and national identity come together in the United States as well. For example, we have *Anglo-Saxon* Protestants, *Irish* Catholics, *Russian* Jews, and people who are *Greek* Orthodox. This linking of nation and creed results from the influx of immigrants from nations with a single major religion. Still, nearly every ethnic category displays some religious diversity. For instance, people of English ancestry may be

Protestants, Roman Catholics, Jews, Hindus, Muslims, or followers of other religions.

Historically, the church has been central to the spiritual—and political—lives of African Americans. Transported to the Western Hemisphere in slave ships, most Africans became Christians—the dominant religion in the Americas—but they blended Christian belief with elements of African religions. Guided by this religious mix, Christian people of color therefore have developed rituals that, by European standards, are quite spontaneous and emotional (Frazier, 1965; Roberts, 1980).

When African Americans migrated from the rural South to the industrial cities of the North around 1940, the church played a major role in addressing problems of dislocation, poverty, and prejudice (cf. Pattillo-McCoy, 1998). Furthermore, black churches have provided an important avenue of achievement for talented men and women. The Reverends Ralph Abernathy, Martin Luther King, Jr., and Jesse Jackson have all won recognition as national, even world leaders.

RELIGION IN A CHANGING SOCIETY

`June 4, Ticonderoga, New York.` Our summer church is small—maybe forty people attend on a Sunday in summer. These days, says long-time member Ed Keller, it's tough for churches to survive, with kids' sports teams scheduling Sunday games, Wal-Mart and the other stores opening early, and many people looking forward to a chance to sleep a little later after a hectic week. The people here seem very committed to the church, but there are not very many of them.

All social institutions evolve over time. Just as the economy, politics, and family have changed over the past century, so has our society's religious life.

SECULARIZATION

Secularization is *the historical decline in the importance of the supernatural and the sacred.* For society as a whole, secularization involves a declining influence of religion in everyday life. For religious organizations, becoming more secular means less focus on otherworldly issues (such as life after death) and more on worldly affairs (such as sheltering the homeless and feeding the

hungry). Secularization also means that functions once performed by the church (such as charity) are now primarily the responsibility of nonreligious organizations, such as the United Way and government.

With Latin roots meaning "the present age," secularization is associated with modern, technologically advanced societies in which science is the dominant mode of understanding. Today, for example, people are more likely to experience the transitions of birth, illness, and death in the presence of physicians (with scientific knowledge) than religious leaders (whose knowledge is based on faith). This shift alone suggests that religion's relevance for our everyday lives has declined. Harvey Cox elaborates,

> The world looks less and less to religious rules and rituals for its morality or its meanings. For some, religion provides a hobby, for others a mark of national or ethnic identification, for still others an aesthetic delight. For fewer and fewer does it provide an inclusive and commanding system of personal and cosmic values and explanations. (1971:3; orig. 1965)

If Cox is right, should we expect religion to disappear someday? The consensus among sociologists is "no." The vast majority of people in the United States still profess a belief in God, and as many people claim to pray each day as vote in national elections. In fact, religious affiliation today is higher than it was in 1850. Secularization, then, does not signal the death of religion. For one thing, although some dimensions of religiosity (such as belief in life after death) have declined, others (such as religious affiliation) have increased. Furthermore, while affiliation with some religious organizations is declining, the numbers joining others are increasing. In short, the secularization thesis remains highly controversial among scholars (Hammond, 1985; Hout & Greeley, 1987; McGuire, 1987; Gorski, 2000).

Our society is of two minds as to whether secularization is good or bad. Conservatives take any weakening of religion as a mark of moral decline. Progressives think secularization liberates people from the all-encompassing beliefs of the past, so people can choose what to believe. Secularization has also helped bring some practices (such as ordaining only men) into line with widespread social attitudes (by opening clerical positions to both women and men).

Back in 1963, the U.S. Supreme Court banned prayer in school as violating the Constitutional separation of church and state. In recent years, however, religion has returned to many public schools; the box takes a closer look.

CRITICAL THINKING

Should Students Pray in School?

It is late afternoon on a cloudy spring day in Minneapolis, and two dozen teenagers have come together to pray. They share warm smiles as they enter the room. As soon as everyone is seated, the prayers begin, with one voice following another. One girl prays for her brother, a boy prays for the success of an upcoming food drive, another asks God to comfort a favorite teacher who is having a hard time. Then they join their voices to pray for all the teachers at their school who are not Christians. Following the prayers, the young people sing Christian songs, discuss a Scripture lesson, and bring their meeting to a close with a group hug.

What is so unusual about this prayer meeting is that it is taking place in room 133 of Patrick Henry High School, a *public* institution. Indeed, in public schools from coast to coast, something of a religious revival is taking place as more and more students hold meetings like this one.

You would have to be at least in your mid-forties to remember when it was routine for public school students to begin the day with Bible reading and prayer. In 1963, the Supreme Court ruled that this practice violated the separation of church and state mandated by the U.S. Constitution.

Most school officials took this decision to mean that any religious activity anywhere in public schools was illegal. But from the outset critics charged that by supporting a wide range of other activities and clubs while banning any religious activity, schools were really being *anti*religious. In 1990, the Supreme Court handed down a new ruling, stating that religious groups can meet on school property if group membership is voluntary, meetings are held outside regular class hours, and students rather than adults run them.

Today, student religious groups have formed in perhaps one-fourth of all public schools. Evangelical Christian organizations such as First Priority and National Network of Youth are using the Internet and word of mouth to expand

the place of religion in every public school across the country. However, opponents of school prayer worry that religious zeal may lead some students to pressure others to join their groups, which ensures that the controversy over prayer in public schools will continue.

What do you think?

1. *Do you think that religious clubs should have the same freedom to operate on school grounds as other organizations? Why or why not?*

2. *The writers of our Constitution stated in the First Amendment that Congress should not establish any official religion and also pass no law that would interfere with the free practice of religion. How do you think this amendment applies to prayer in school?*

3. *In 1995, President Bill Clinton said, "Nothing in the First Amendment converts our public schools into religion-free zones." Do you think schools should support spiritual education and development, be neutral to religious activity, or oppose such activity? Why?*

Source: Based on Van Biema (1998, 1999).

CIVIL RELIGION

One dimension of secularization is the rise of what Robert Bellah (1975) calls **civil religion,** *a quasi-religious loyalty binding individuals in a basically secular society.* In other words, although some dimensions of religiosity are weakening, citizenship has taken on religious qualities.

Certainly, most people in the United States consider our way of life a force for moral good in the world. Many people also find religious qualities in political movements, whether liberal or conservative (Williams & Demerath, 1991). Civil religion also involves a range of rituals, from singing the national anthem at sporting events to waving the flag at public parades. At all such events, the U.S. flag serves as a sacred symbol of our national identity, and we expect people to treat it with respect.

Civil religion is not a specific doctrine. However, it does incorporate many elements of traditional religion into the political system of a secular society.

A POST-DENOMINATION SOCIETY

In a society with no formal ties between church and state, religious organizations take the form of denominations. Yet in recent decades, an increasing number of people are pursuing spiritual growth outside established religious organizations. This trend toward spirituality but away from established religious organizations suggests that the United States is becoming a *post-denomination society*. In simple terms, more people seem to be saying that they are interested in spirituality but are "none of the above" in terms of conventional denominations.

Exactly what is the difference between a focus on spirituality and a concern with religion? Spirituality is a form of religious expression that is

> the search for . . . a religion of the heart, not the head. It's a religious expression that downplays doctrine and dogma, and revels in direct experience of the divine—whether it's called the 'holy spirit' or 'divine consciousness' or 'true self.' It's practical and personal, more about stress reduction than salvation, more therapeutic than theological. It's about feeling good rather than being good. It's as much about the body as the soul. (Cimino & Lattin, 1999:62)

From a traditional point of view, this concept of spirituality may seem more like psychology than religion. Yet as seen in the case of civil religion, religious interest in the modern world can take new forms.

Finally, keep in mind the effect of high immigration on religious life in the United States. As people come from Latin America, Asia, and other regions and join the U.S. cultural mix, they are likely to fuse traditional religious ideas with ideas they encounter in their new land. The result is religious innovation (Yang & Ebaugh, 2001).

RELIGIOUS REVIVAL

At the same time that "new age" spirituality is flourishing, a great deal of change has been going on in the world of organized religion. Membership in established, mainstream churches such as the Episcopalian and Presbyterian denominations has plummeted by almost 50 percent since 1960. During the same period, however, affiliation with conservative religious organizations (including the Mormons, Seventh-Day Adventists, and especially Christian sects) has risen just as dramatically. As many churchlike organizations have become more worldly, many people apparently abandon them in favor of more sectlike communities that offer a more intense religious experience (Stark & Bainbridge, 1981; Roof & McKinney, 1987; Jacquet & Jones, 1991; Warner, 1993; Iannaccone, 1994).

Religious Fundamentalism

One of the striking religious trends today is the growth of **fundamentalism,** *a conservative religious doctrine that opposes intellectualism and worldly accommodation in favor of restoring traditional, otherworldly religion.* In the United States, fundamentalism has made the greatest gains among Protestants. Southern Baptists, for example, are the largest religious community in the United States. But fundamentalism has also made gains among Roman Catholics, Jews, and Muslims.

In response to what they see as the growing influence of science and the erosion of the conventional family, religious fundamentalists defend what they call "traditional values." As they see it, liberal churches are simply too open to change. Religious fundamentalism is distinctive in five ways (Hunter, 1983, 1985, 1987):

1. **Fundamentalists interpret sacred texts literally.** Fundamentalists insist on a literal interpretation of the Bible and other sacred texts in order to counter what they consider excessive intellectualism among more liberal religious organizations. For example, fundamentalist Christians believe that God created the world precisely as described in Genesis.

2. **Fundamentalists reject religious pluralism.** Fundamentalists believe that tolerance and relativism water down personal faith. Therefore they maintain that their religious beliefs are true and other beliefs are not.

3. **Fundamentalists pursue the personal experience of God's presence.** In contrast to the worldliness and intellectualism of other religious organizations, fundamentalism seeks a return to "good ol' time religion" and spiritual revival. To fundamentalist Christians, being "born again" and having a personal relationship with Jesus Christ should be evident in a person's everyday life.

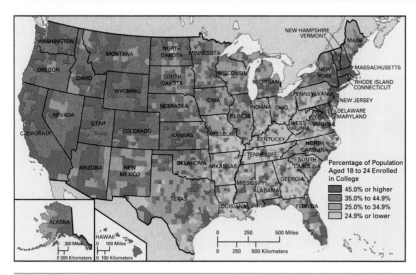

NATIONAL MAP 20–1
College Attendance across the United States

Generally speaking, college attendance is highest among adults along the Northeast and West coasts. By contrast, adults in the Midwest and the South (especially the Appalachian region) are the least likely members of our society to attend college. How would you explain this pattern? (Income is one obvious consideration. Would people's ideas about gender equality be another?)

Source: *American Demographics* magazine, April 1993, p. 60. Reprinted with permission. ©1993 *American Demographics* magazine.

Beyond the city limits, affluent suburban school districts offer better schooling than less well-funded systems in central cities. This disparity—which benefits whites—led to *busing*, or transporting students to achieve racial balance and equal opportunity in schools. Although only 5 percent of U.S. schoolchildren are bused to schools outside their neighborhoods, this policy has generated heated controversy. Busing advocates claim that the only way government will adequately fund schools in poor, minority neighborhoods is if white children from richer neighborhoods attend them. Critics respond that busing is expensive and undermines the concept of neighborhood schools. But both sides acknowledge that given the racial imbalance of our nation's urban areas, an effective busing scheme would have to join inner cities and suburbs, a plan that is almost never politically feasible.

A classic report by a research team headed by James Coleman (1966) confirmed that predominantly minority schools suffer more problems, ranging from larger class size to insufficient libraries and fewer science labs. But the Coleman report cautioned that money will not magically improve academic quality. Even more important are the cooperative efforts and enthusiasm of teachers, parents, and the students themselves. In other words, even if school funding were exactly the same everywhere, students who benefit from more *social capital*—that is, those whose parents value schooling, read to their children, and encourage the development of imagination—would still perform better. Reacting to differences in Ohio schools, state governor Bob Taft (cited in Troy, 2000:A1) put it, "Some children may have been read to 1,000 hours before they come to school. Some children have parents who cannot read themselves." Thus, we should not expect schools alone to overcome marked social inequality in the United States (Schneider et al., 1998; Israel, Beaulieu, & Hartless, 2001).

ACCESS TO HIGHER EDUCATION

In industrial societies, higher education is the main path to occupational achievement. In the United States, 63 percent of high school graduates enroll in college the following fall (U.S. National Center for Education Statistics, 2001). Moreover, among young people eighteen to twenty-four years old, about 33 percent are enrolled in college: National Map 20–1 shows where in the United States college attendance is most and least likely.

The most crucial factor affecting access to U.S. higher education is money. College is expensive, and the cost is rising rapidly. Even at state-supported institutions, annual tuition averages about $3,000, and

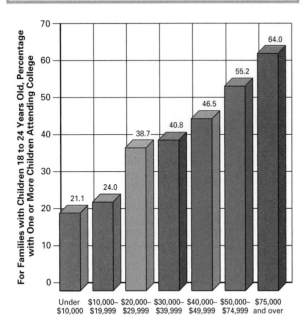

FIGURE 20–2 College Attendance and Family Income, 2000

Source: U.S. Census Bureau (2001).

admission to the most exclusive private colleges and universities exceeds $30,000 a year. As shown in Figure 20–2, families with incomes above $75,000 annually (roughly the richest 20 percent, who fall within the upper and upper-middle classes) send two-thirds of their children to college because they can afford to, but fewer than one-fourth of young people from families earning less than $20,000 each year reach college.

The cost of higher education prevents many minorities, typically with below-average incomes, from attending college. As Figure 20–3 shows, whites are more likely than African Americans and Hispanics to complete high school, and this disparity remains with each step up in the educational system. For some, schooling is a path to social mobility, but it has not overcome persistent racial inequality in the United States (Epps, 1995).

Completing college carries numerous rewards, including intellectual and personal growth as well as higher income. Over a person's working lifetime, a college degree adds almost $500,000 to income (Speer, 1994). Table 20–2 shows why. In 1999, women with an eighth-grade education typically earned $14,375, high school graduates averaged $21,970, and college graduates averaged $36,340. The ratios in parentheses show that a woman with a bachelor's degree earns two-and-one-half times as much as a woman with eight or fewer years of schooling. Across the board, men earn considerably more than women; moreover, more schooling boosts income faster for men than for women. Finally, for both men and women, some of the greater earnings that come with more schooling have to do with social background, because the people with the most schooling are likely to come from upper-class families to begin with.

CREDENTIALISM

Sociologist Randall Collins (1979) calls the United States a *credential society* because people regard diplomas and degrees highly. In modern, technologically advanced societies, credentials say "who you are" as much as family background.

Credentialism, then, is *evaluating a person on the basis of educational degrees.* On one hand, credentialism is simply the way our modern society goes about filling jobs with well-trained people. On the other hand, Collins explains that credentials often bear little relation to the responsibilities of a specific job. In reality, advanced degrees often are an easy way to sort out the people with the manners, attitudes, and even skin color many employers are looking for. Credentialism thus is a gatekeeping strategy that restricts important occupations to a small segment of the population.

PRIVILEGE AND PERSONAL MERIT

If attending college is a rite of passage for affluent men and women, as social-conflict analysis suggests, then *schooling transforms social privilege into personal merit.* But given our cultural emphasis on individualism, we tend to see credentials as "badges of ability" rather than as symbols of family affluence (Sennett & Cobb, 1973). When we congratulate the new graduate, we rarely recognize the resources—both financial and cultural—that made this achievement possible. Yet the fact is that young people from families with incomes exceeding $100,000 a year average 1,130 on college board exams—more than 200 points higher than young people from families with $15,000 income.

erode our nation's commitment to public education, especially in the central cities, where the need is greatest (Martinez et al., 1995; Godwin et al., 1998; Cohen, 1999; Forstmann, 1999). Despite pressure from the Bush administration, Congress has so far resisted enacting any voucher system.

A more modest form of school choice involves *magnet schools*, 1,000 of which now exist across the country. Magnet schools offer special facilities and programs to promote educational excellence in a particular area, such as computer science, foreign languages, science, mathematics, or the arts. In school districts with magnet schools, parents can choose the one best suited to their child's particular talents and interests.

Another successful choice program involves *charter schools*, public schools that are given more freedom to operate in order to try out new policies and programs. There are about 1,500 such schools in the United States. In many of these schools, students demonstrate high academic achievement—a necessary condition for the charter to be renewed.

A final development in the school choice movement is *schooling for profit*. Advocates of this plan say school systems operated by private profit-making companies would be more efficient than schools run by local governments. Private schooling is nothing new; across the United States, more than 25,000 schools are run by private organizations and religious groups. What is new, however, is the small number of public schools—about 250 in 2000 enrolling some 120,000 students—that are run by private businesses for profit (Greenwald, 2000).

Research confirms that many public school systems suffer from bureaucratic bloat, spending too much and teaching too little. And our society has long looked to competition and private initiative to improve quality and cut costs. Evidence suggests that for-profit schools have reduced administrative costs far below those of regular public schools. But the educational results of schooling for profit appear mixed. Several companies claim to have improved student learning, yet some cities have cut back on business-run schools. In 1995, for example, Baltimore canceled the contract of the corporation that had taken over nine of its schools in 1992; school boards in Miami and Hartford, Connecticut, have also canceled contracts. In short, public school systems perform poorly in many cities; but whether private business can improve on their record remains unclear (Putka & Stecklow, 1994; Kanamine, 1995; Ravitch & Viteritti, 1996; Bennett, 1997; Toch, 1998).

Educators have long debated the proper manner in which to school children with disabilities. On one hand, such children may benefit from distinctive facilities and specially trained teachers. On the other hand, they are less likely to be stigmatized as "different" if included in regular classroom settings. What do you consider to be the ramifications of the "special education" versus "inclusive education" debate for the classroom experience of all *children, not only those who have disabilities?*

SCHOOLING PEOPLE WITH DISABILITIES

Bureaucratic schools do not readily meet the special needs of some people, including many of the 5 million U.S. children with physical impairments. Many children with disabilities have difficulty getting to and from school, and many with crutches or wheelchairs cannot negotiate stairs and other obstacles inside school buildings. Children with developmental disabilities such as mental retardation require extensive personal attention from specially trained teachers. As a result, many children with mental and physical disabilities have received a public education only because of persistent efforts by parents and other concerned citizens.

About one-fourth of children with disabilities are schooled in special facilities; the rest attend public schools, many participating in regular classes. Thus, most schools avoid expensive "special education" in favor of **mainstreaming,** *integrating special students into the overall educational program.* Mainstreaming is a form of *inclusive education* that works best for physically impaired students who have no difficulty keeping up with the rest of the class. Moreover, putting children with and without disabilities in the same classroom allows everyone to learn more about interacting with people who differ from themselves.

ADULT EDUCATION

Most schooling involves young people. However, the share of U.S. students aged twenty-five and older has risen sharply in recent years and now accounts for 36 percent of people in the classroom.

In 1999, more than 76 million U.S. adults enrolled in some type of schooling. These older students range in age from the mid-twenties to the seventies and beyond. Adults in school are twice as likely to be women as men and generally have above-average incomes. Some are people who dropped out of high school in the past; others are part-time students completing college degrees. Still others already have a college diploma and other advanced degrees and are trying to advance their careers or are simply returning to the classroom to experience the joy of learning (Speer, 1996; Miller, 1997a).

THE TEACHER SHORTAGE

A final challenge for U.S. schools is hiring enough teachers to fill the classrooms. A number of factors—including low salaries, frustration, and retirement, as well as rising enrollment and reductions in class size—have combined to create more than 200,000 teaching vacancies in the United States each year.

How will these slots be filled? About the same number of people graduate with education degrees annually, but most lack a degree in a specific field (such as mathematics, biology, or English). In fact, many have trouble passing state certification tests in the area they wish to teach.

As a result, schools have adopted new recruitment strategies. One is to encourage more people who have already established successful careers to switch to teaching. To attract people, schools are making it easier to obtain teaching certification, offering higher salaries and signing bonuses, and pointing out that there is probably no work more important than training our children. In addition, many school districts are going

 For a National Center for Education Statistics (NCES) report titled "Trends in Educational Equity of Girls & Women," go to http://nces.ed. gov/pubs2000/2000030.pdf

global, actively recruiting in countries such as Spain, India, and the Philippines to bring talented women and men to U.S. classrooms (Dervarics, 1999; Lord, 2001; Philadelphia, 2001).

Of course, the debates about education in the United States spread beyond the issues noted here. The final box takes a look at the recent trend by which men represent a declining share of students on college campuses.

LOOKING AHEAD: SCHOOLING IN THE TWENTY-FIRST CENTURY

Despite the fact that the United States leads the world in providing a college education to its people, our public school system continues to struggle with serious problems, many of which have their roots in the larger society. Thus, during this new century, we cannot expect schools *by themselves* to improve the quality of education. Schools will improve only to the extent to which students, teachers, parents, and local communities commit to educational excellence. In short, educational dilemmas are *social* problems, and there is no quick fix.

For much of the twentieth century, there were just two models for education in the United States: public schools run by the government and private schools operated by nongovernment organizations. In the last decade, however, many new ideas about schooling have come on the scene, including schooling for profit and a wide range of "choice" programs (Finn & Gau, 1998). In the decades ahead, we will probably see some significant changes in mass education, guided in part by social science research on the consequences of different strategies.

Whatever decisions are made about who controls education, one factor that will continue to reshape schools is new information technology. Today, 97 percent of conventional primary and secondary schools have instructional computers. The promise of this new technology goes beyond helping students learn basic skills; computers can improve the overall quality of learning. Computers help students be more active learners and allow them to progress at their own pace. For students with disabilities who cannot write using a pencil, computers permit easier self-expression. For all students, using computers in schools—in some cases as early as kindergarten—appears to increase significantly how fast students learn and helps prepare them for the workplace of the twenty-first century.

3. From a structural-functional perspective, why is schooling important to the operation of society? From a social-conflict point of view, how does formal education reproduce social inequality in each generation?

4. Do you agree with research chapter that college studen class? If so, what do you make everyone more active

APPLICATIONS AND EXERCISES

1. Arrange to visit a secondary school near your college or home. Does it have a tracking policy? If so, find out how it works. How much importance does a student's social background have in making a track assignment?

2. Most people agree that teaching our children is a vital task. Yet most teachers earn relatively low salaries. Check the prestige ranking for teachers back in Table 11–2. See what you can learn about the average salaries of teachers compared to those of other workers. Can you explain this pattern?

3. After the passage of the Americans with Disabilities Act in 1990, schools have sought to "accommodate"

students with a broader ran disabilities. Do some resear your campus to learn hov changing education.

4. Packaged in the back of thi teractive CD-ROM that off review materials intended t stand the material covered chapter, the CD-ROM co video, Real Life Sociology audio and video, interactive journal entries from the a much more.

SITES TO SEE

http://www.prenhall.com/macionis

Visit the interactive *Companion Website*™ that accompanies this text. Begin by clicking on the cover of your book. You will find a chapter-by-chapter study guide, practice tests, and a significant portion of the text for on-line review, as well as many suggested Web links.

http://nces.ed.gov/

The National Center for Education Statistics provides data about U.S. education, including a profile of those who have earned various degrees by gender and race.

http://www.acpe.asu.edu/VirtualU/

To explore how new information technology is reshaping education, read about the founding of Western Virtual University, this country's first "cyber-college." Think

about the advantages and disadv schooling.

http://www2.kenyon.edu/proje

Visit the Family Farm Web site at site was created by students to learned about farming and rural l central Ohio.

http://www.nces.ed.gov/pubs98,

The issue of school violence is th ment Web site.

http://www.chronicle.com

This site provides general news a higher education.

INVESTIGATE WITH CONTENTSELECT

Follow the instructions found on page 23 of this textbook to enter this chapter of the book's *Companion Website*™. Once in the chapter, click on the ContentSelect icon at the bottom left of your screen and enter your personal

User ID and Password. Enter key ing," "functional illiteracy," and " the search engine will help you researcher.

CONTROVERSY & DEBATE

The Twenty-First Century Campus: Where Are the Men?

A century ago, the campuses of colleges and universities across the United States might as well have hung out a sign that read "Men Only!" Almost all of the students and faculty were male. Although there were a number of women's colleges, many more schools, including some of the best-known U.S. universities (such as Yale, Harvard, and Princeton), barred women outright.

As the twentieth century proceeded, however, women won greater social equality. Therefore, few people were surprised when, in 1980, the number of women enrolled at U.S. colleges finally matched the number of men.

What is surprising is what has happened since then: The share of women on the campus has continued to increase. As a result, in 2000 men accounted for only 44 percent of all U.S. undergraduates. Student Meg DeLong noticed the gender imbalance right away when she moved into her dorm at the University of Georgia at Athens. In fact, 39 percent of the first-year students were men. In classes, DeLong found there were few men, and women dominated discussions. Out of class, she and many other women complained that having so few men on campus was

hurting their social life (not surprisingly, the men felt otherwise about their own social life).

Why the shifting gender balance on U.S. campuses? No one knows for sure, but several theories have been put forward. Some suggest that young men are drawn away from college by the lure of jobs, especially in high technology. This pattern is sometimes called the "Bill Gates syndrome," after the Microsoft founder who dropped out of college to become the world's richest person. In addition, analysts point to an anti-intellectual male culture. That is, whereas young women are drawn to learning and seek to do well in school, young men are more likely to consider studying and schoolwork as "something for girls." In short, rightly or wrongly, more men seem to think they can get a good job without investing years of their lives and a lot of money to get a college degree.

The gender gap is evident among all racial and ethnic categories. In fact, only 37 percent of African American college students are men. It is also found at all class levels. Indeed, the lower the income level, the greater the gender gap in college attendance.

Many college officials are concerned about this trend. In an effort to attract

more balanced enrollments, some colleges adopted what amounts to affirmative action programs that favor males. In several states, however, courts have ruled that such policies are illegal. Therefore, many colleges are turning to more vigorous recruitment, having admission officers pay special attention to male applicants and stressing a college's strength in mathematics and science—areas that traditionally have attracted men. Although colleges across the country are striving to increase their number of minority students, the hope is that they can also succeed in attracting more men.

Continue the debate . . .

1. *Do you think that among high school students, men are less concerned than women with academic achievement? Why?*

2. *Is there a lack of males on your campus? Does it create problems? What problems? For whom?*

3. *What programs or policies do you think might increase the number of men going to college?*

Source: Based on Fonda (2000).

The numerous benefits of computers should not blind us to their limitations, however. Computers will never bring to the educational process the personal insight or imagination of a motivated teacher. Nor can computers tap what one teacher calls the "springs of human identity and creativity" that we discover by exploring literature and language rather than simply manipulating mathematical codes. Indeed, despite their proliferation in the classroom, computers have yet to

change teaching and learning in any fundamental sense or even replace the traditional blackboard (Berger, 1991; Elmer-DeWitt, 1991; Skinner, 1997). Therefore, we should not look to technology to solve the problems—including violence and rigid bureaucracy—that plague our schools. What we need is a broad plan for social change that refires this country's early ambition to provide high-quality universal schooling—a goal that has so far eluded us.

SUMMARY

1. Education is the major social institution for transmitting knowledge and skills and teaching cultural norms and values. In preindustrial societies, education occurs informally within the family; industrial societies develop formal systems of schooling.

2. The United States was among the first countries to institute compulsory mass education, reflecting both democratic political ideals and the needs of the industrial-capitalist economy.

3. Structural-functional analysis highlights major functions of schooling, including socialization, cultural innovation, social integration, and perpetuation of the social hierarchy. Latent functions of schooling include providing child care and building social networks.

4. Social-conflict analysis links schooling to hierarchy involving class, race, and gender. Formal education also promotes conformity to produce compliant adult workers.

5. Standardized achievement tests are controversial. Some see them as a reasonable measure of academic aptitude and learning; others say they are culturally biased tools used to label less privileged students as personally deficient.

6. Tracking also is controversial. Some see tracking as the way schools provide appropriate instruction for students with different interests and aptitudes; others say tracking gives privileged youngsters a richer education.

7. Most young people in the United States attend state-funded public schools. Most private schools offer a reli-

gious education. A sma[...] well-to-do, attend elite[...]

8. One-fourth of U.S. a[...] college graduates, ma[...] dential society." Peop[...] much higher lifetime [...]

9. Most adults in the Un[...] schools. Violence pe[...] cially those in poor [...] cratic character of sch[...] rates and student pass[...]

10. Declining academic st[...] lower average scores [...] functional illiteracy [...] high school graduates [...]

11. The school choice mo[...] more responsive to t[...] include magnet scho[...] charter schools, all of [...] policy debate.

12. Children with mental[...] cally have been schoole[...] Mainstreaming affords[...]

13. Adults are a growing [...] United States. Most [...] are engaged in job-rel[...]

14. The Information Rev[...] through increasing u[...] computers permit int[...] they are not suitable fo[...]

KEY CONCEPTS

education (p. 517) the social institution through which society provides its members with important knowledge, including basic facts, job skills, and cultural norms and values

schooling (p. 517) formal instruction under the direction of specially trained teachers

hidden curriculum (p. 524) subtle presentations of political or cultural ideas in the classroom

tracking (p. 524) assigning[...] educational programs

credentialism (p. 528) ev[...] of educational degrees

functional illiteracy (p. 53[...] ing skills needed for everyd[...]

mainstreaming (p. 535) [...] into the overall educational[...]

CRITICAL-THINKING QUESTIONS

1. Why does industrialization lead societies to expand their systems of schooling?

2. In what ways is schooli[...] by our economic, politi[...]

CHAPTER
21

Jacob Lawrence (b. 1917)
Harlem Hospital Surgery, 1953

Tempera on masonite, 20 × 24 in., signed and dated.
Courtesy of Michael Rosenfeld Gallery, New York. © Jacob Lawrence.

HEALTH AND MEDICINE

In 1995, television came to Fiji, a small island in the South Seas of the Pacific Ocean. A single cable channel carried programming from the United States, Great Britain, and Australia. When Anne Becker, a Harvard researcher specializing in eating disorders, read the news, her sociological imagination led her to wonder what effect watching television would have on young women there.

Becker knew that Fijian culture emphasized good nutrition and

looking strong and healthy. Dieting to look very thin had never been common in Fiji. Indeed, in 1995, Becker found, just 3 percent of teenage girls reported ever vomiting to control their weight. By 1998, however, a striking change was evident: Fifteen percent of teenage girls—a fivefold increase—reported this practice. Moreover, Becker found that 62 percent of girls said they had dieted during the previous month, and 74 percent reported feeling "too big" or "fat" (Becker, 1999).

The rapid rise in eating disorders in Fiji after television was introduced shows the power of society to shape patterns of health. Eating disorders, including anorexia nervosa (medically, a practice of severe caloric restriction, commonly understood as compulsive dieting) and bulimia (binge eating followed by vomiting), are even more common in the United States. In fact, about half of college women report engaging in such behavior, even though most, medically speaking, are not overweight.

Consider, too, that 95 percent of people with an eating disorder are female. Why? Because weight control is part of our cultural definition of femininity: As the Duchess of Windsor once put it, "A woman cannot be too rich or too thin." In the United States—and now Fiji as well—society teaches young women that they are "never too thin to feel fat" (Wooley, Wooley, & Dyrenforth, 1979; Levine, 1987; Parrott, 1987; Robinson, 1987).

WHAT IS HEALTH?

The World Health Organization defines **health** as *a state of complete physical, mental, and social well-being*

For the Web site of the World Health Organization, go to http://www.who.int

(1946:3). This definition underscores the major theme of this chapter: *health is as much a social as a biological issue because well-being and illness have their roots in the organization of society.*

HEALTH AND SOCIETY

Society shapes people's health in five major ways:

1. **Cultural patterns define health.** Standards of health vary from society to society. Early in the twentieth century, yaws, a contagious skin disease, was so common in sub-Saharan Africa that people there considered it normal. Similarly, according to the U.S. Centers for Disease Control and Prevention (2000), the rich foods that people in the United States consume are responsible for almost two-thirds of adults being overweight. "Health" is sometimes a matter of having the same disease as one's neighbors (Dubos, 1980; Pinhey, Rubinstein, & Colfax, 1997).

2. **What is considered healthy often is the same as what people define as morally good.** Members of our society (especially men) think a competitive way of life is healthy because it fits our cultural mores. This is so even though stress contributes to heart disease and many other illnesses. On the other hand, some people who object to homosexuality on moral grounds call this sexual orientation "sick," even though it is natural from a biological point of view. Thus, ideas about good health amount to a form of social control that encourages conformity to cultural norms.

541

The profession of surgery has existed only for several centuries. Before that, barbers offered their services to the very sick, often cutting the skin to "bleed" a patient. Of course, this "treatment" was rarely effective, but it did produce plenty of bloody bandages, which practitioners hung out to dry. This practice identifies the origin of the red and white barber poles we see today.

Lucas van Leyden, *The Surgeon and the Peasant*, Rijksmuseum, Amsterdam.

3. **Cultural standards of health change over time.** In the early twentieth century, some physicians warned women not to go to college because higher education strained the female brain. Others denounced masturbation as a danger to health. Today, on both counts, we know differently. Similarly, in 1950, about 30 percent of U.S. adults reported bathing every day, compared to about 75 percent in 2000 (Gallup, 2000).

4. **A society's technology affects people's health.** In poor societies, infectious diseases are rampant because of malnutrition and poor sanitation. As industrialization raises living standards, people become more healthy. But industrial technology also creates new threats to health. As Chapter 22 ("Population, Urbanization, and Environment") explains, high-income countries threaten human health by overtaxing the world's resources and creating pollution.

5. **Social inequality affects people's health.** All societies distribute resources unequally. Therefore, some people are healthier than others. This pattern starts at birth, with infant mortality highest among the poor. Poor people also live fewer years than rich people.

HEALTH: A GLOBAL SURVEY

Because health is closely linked to social life, we find that humans have fared better and better over the long course of history. For the same reason, we see striking differences in health around the world today.

HEALTH IN HISTORY

Many hunting and gathering people had fairly healthful diets, eating a range of vegetation and, when available, lean meat. With only simple technology, however, our ancestors were vulnerable to drought and other natural events that could cause widespread hunger. In addition, they faced injuries and illnesses for which there was little or no treatment. Thus, in these societies, few people lived to age forty, and about half never made it to twenty (Nolan & Lenski, 1999; Scupin, 2000).

With the discovery of agriculture, food became more plentiful. At the same time, many societies began to rely on single crops, which led to a less nutritious diet. Moreover, social inequality increased, so that elites enjoyed better health and peasants and slaves lived in crowded, unsanitary shelters and often went hungry. In the growing cities of medieval Europe, human waste and other refuse piled up in the streets, spreading infectious diseases and plagues that periodically wiped out entire towns (Mumford, 1961).

HEALTH IN LOW-INCOME COUNTRIES

November 1, central India. Poverty is not just a matter of what you have; it shapes what you are. Probably most of the people we see in the villages here

Our national view of medicine has changed during the last several decades. Television viewers in the 1970s watched doctors like Marcus Welby, M.D., confidently take charge of situations in a fatherly— and almost godlike—manner. By the 1990s, programs like E.R. gave a more realistic view of the limitations of medicine to address illness, as well as the violence that wracks our society.

for people who are ill. According to Parsons, the sick role has three characteristics:

1. **Illness exempts people from routine responsibilities**. Serious illness relaxes or suspends normal obligations such as going to work or attending school. To prevent abuse of this privilege, however, people do not simply declare themselves ill; they must enlist the support of others—especially a recognized medical expert— before assuming the sick role.

2. **A sick person must want to be well**. We assume that no one wants to be sick, and we withdraw the benefits of the sick role when someone feigns illness in order to avoid responsibility or get attention.

3. **A sick person must seek competent help**. People who are ill must seek out and cooperate with medical care practitioners. By failing to get medical help or to follow doctor's orders, a person risks losing the benefits of the sick role.

The Physician's Role

Physicians evaluate people's claims of sickness and try to restore the sick to normal routines. To do this,

Parsons explained, physicians use their specialized knowledge. Physicians expect patients to provide whatever personal information may assist their efforts and to follow doctor's orders in completing treatment.

Parsons saw the doctor-patient relationship as hierarchical. Yet this pattern varies from society to society. For example, Japanese tradition gives physicians great authority over their patients. Japanese physicians even take it upon themselves to decide how much information about the seriousness of an illness they will share with the patient (Darnton & Hoshia, 1989). Until about thirty years ago, physicians in the United States made similar decisions. But the patient's rights movement embodies the public demand that physicians readily share medical information, and a more equal relationship between doctor and patient, now commonplace in the United States, is developing also in Europe and even in Japan.

Critical evaluation. Parsons's analysis links illness and medicine to the broader organization of society. Others have usefully extended the concept of the sick role to some nonillness situations such as pregnancy (Myers & Grasmick, 1989).

One limitation of the sick role concept is that it applies to acute conditions (such as the flu or a broken leg) better than chronic illnesses (like heart disease), which may not be reversible. Moreover, a sick person's ability to regain health depends on available resources. Many poor people simply cannot afford either medical care or time off from work.

Finally, critics point out that Parsons's analysis implies that doctors—rather than people themselves—bear the primary responsibility for health. A more prevention-oriented approach makes physicians and patients equal partners in the pursuit of health.

SYMBOLIC-INTERACTION ANALYSIS

According to the symbolic-interaction paradigm, society is less a grand system than a series of complex and changing realities. Health and medical care, therefore, are socially constructed by people in everyday interaction.

The Social Construction of Illness

If we socially construct our ideas of health and illness, it follows that members of a very poor society may view hunger and malnutrition as normal. Similarly, people in rich nations, such as our own, may give little thought to the harmful effects of a rich diet.

How we respond to illness, too, is based on social definitions that may or may not square with medical facts. For instance, people with AIDS contend with fear and sometimes outright bigotry that have no medical basis. Likewise, students may pay no attention to signs of illness on the eve of a vacation, but they dutifully report to the infirmary hours before a midterm examination. In short, health is less an objective commodity than a negotiated outcome.

Indeed, how people define a medical situation may actually affect how they feel. Medical experts marvel at *psychosomatic* disorders (a fusion of Greek words for "mind" and "body"), when state of mind guides physical sensations (Hamrick, Anspaugh, & Ezell, 1986). Applying sociologist W. I. Thomas's theorem (1931), we can say that when health or illness is defined as real, it becomes real in its consequences.

The Social Construction of Treatment

In Chapter 6 ("Social Interaction in Everyday Life"), we used Erving Goffman's dramaturgical approach to explain how physicians tailor their physical surroundings ("the office") and their behavior ("the presentation of self") so that others see them as competent and in charge.

Sociologist Joan Emerson (1970) further illustrates this process of constructing reality in her analysis of the gynecological examination carried out by a male doctor. This situation is vulnerable to serious misinterpretation because a man touching a woman's genitals is conventionally viewed as a sexual act or possibly even an assault.

To ensure that people define the situation as impersonal and professional, the medical staff wear uniforms and furnish the examination room with nothing but medical equipment. The doctor's manner and overall performance are designed to make the patient feel that, to him, examining the genital area is no different from treating any other part of the body. A female nurse usually is present during the examination not only to assist the physician but also to dispel any impression that a man and woman are "alone in a room."

Managing situational definitions in this way is rarely taught in medical schools. The oversight is unfortunate because, as Emerson's analysis shows, understanding how people construct reality in the examination room is as important as mastering the medical skills required for treatment.

Critical evaluation. A strength of the symbolic-interaction paradigm lies in revealing that what people view as healthful or harmful depends on numerous factors, many of which are not, strictly speaking, medical. This approach also shows that in any medical procedure, both patient and medical staff engage in a subtle process of reality construction.

Critics fault this approach, however, for implying that there are no objective standards of well-being. Certain physical conditions do indeed cause definite changes in people, regardless of how we view those conditions. For example, people who lack sufficient nutrition and safe water suffer from their unhealthy environment, whether they define their surroundings as normal or not.

SOCIAL-CONFLICT ANALYSIS

Social-conflict analysis draws a connection between health and social inequality and, taking a cue from Karl Marx, ties medicine to the operation of capitalism. Researchers have focused on three main issues: access to medical care, the effects of the profit motive, and the politics of medicine.

free of government control, how can a totalitarian political order persist?

On the other hand, if governments gain control of computer-based communication, they will have a powerful new tool for spreading propaganda and manipulating their populations. Governments bent on tyranny may not be able to control the global Internet, but they may try to control access to computer technology within their borders. Such regulation of information would be a blow to democracy, of course. At the same time, however, any nation would pay a high price for isolating itself from the expanding world of computer-based information and trade.

New information technology is spreading ideas and images around the world as never before. These young women live in Malaysia, a relatively traditional society. How do you think the spread of culture via the Internet from the United States and other rich countries will affect the labor force, family patterns, and the desire for education in societies like this one? Will changes be for the better or worse? Why?

more effective treatments. In recent years, for example, computer links have been vital in helping physicians in central Africa share news, skills, and equipment while fighting the outbreak of the deadly Ebola virus.

New information technology is also making an important contribution to the lives of people with mental and physical disabilities. On one level, new computer programs allow officials to determine whether plans for new public buildings and private homes will include sufficient access for people with disabilities. On another level, specialists at numerous universities and hospitals use computer simulations to train children to operate wheelchairs and to teach mentally retarded adults to ride the train or bus. More broadly, computers now allow people with various physical and mental limitations to enjoy and learn from virtual experiences, including travel, skiing, and even hang-gliding, that seemed impossible a generation ago (Biggs, 1996).

Families of the Future

Over the centuries, new technology has shaped and reshaped the family. The Industrial Revolution moved work from farm and home to factories, making the job and the family separate spheres of life.

More recently, the Information Revolution is creating the opposite effect as new communication technology allows people to work at home (or, with portable computers and telephones, to work almost anywhere). The trend toward *decentralizing* work means that, for more and more people, the line between the office and the home is disappearing.

In some respects, this trend should strengthen families, allowing parents to create more flexible work schedules and placing both fathers and mothers closer to children. Yet in the cyber-age, televisions and computers are playing a larger role in socializing the young. In short, families may be able to spend more time together in this

new century, but whether they will actually do so is less certain.

Medicine and the Pursuit of Health

Just as computer technology is decentralizing work, it is making medical care more readily available. In the years to come, many routine health checks (pulse rate, blood pressure, and heart function) will be performed at home by people with computer access who transmit data via modem to personnel at medical centers.

Around the world, new information technology is making better health care available to more and more people. In the United States, hospitals rely on Internet sites to match patients and available organs, saving lives. In villages throughout poor nations, practitioners in clinics can log on to computers to consult with specialists in medical centers in the world's largest cities, gaining the information they need to provide

Institutions and Technology: Each Shaping the Other

New technology is bringing changes to all aspects of our lives. But although technology is a powerful agent of change, it does not determine the shape of society. On the contrary, technology alters the boundaries of what is possible. Therefore, *how* and even *if* we employ new information technology is an important decision that societies must make. How we decide these questions comes back to our social institutions, which, after all, define *for whom* society should operate in the first place.

CHAPTER

22

W. Louis Sonntag, Jr.
The Bowery at Night, 1895
Copyright Museum of the City of New York.
32.275.2

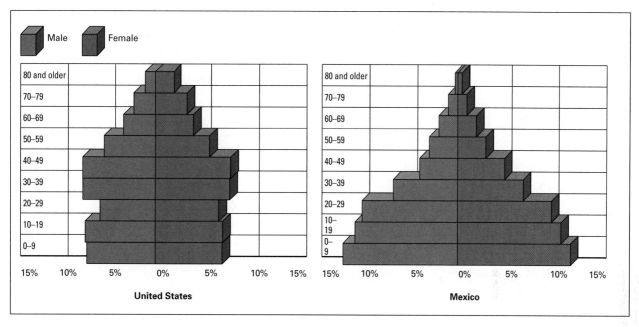

FIGURE 22–2 Age-Sex Population Pyramids for the United States and Mexico, 2000

Source: U.S. Census Bureau (2000).

birth rate of 14.6 minus the crude death rate of 8.5), or about 0.61 percent annual growth.

Global Map 22–1 shows that population growth in the United States and other high-income nations is well below the world average of 1.3 percent. The earth's low-growth continents are Europe (currently posting a slight decline, expressed as −0.1 percent annual growth), North America (0.5 percent), and Oceania (1.1 percent). Close to the global average are Asia (1.4 percent) and Latin America (1.7 percent). The highest-growth region in the world is Africa (2.4 percent).

A handy rule of thumb for estimating population growth is to divide a society's population growth rate into the number 70 to calculate the *doubling time* in years. Thus, an annual growth rate of 2 percent (common in parts of Latin America) doubles a population in thirty-five years, and a 3 percent growth rate (found in some of Africa) drops the doubling time to just twenty-four years. The rapid population growth of the poorest countries is deeply troubling because they can barely support the populations they have now.

POPULATION COMPOSITION

Demographers also study the makeup of a society's population at a given point in time. One variable is the **sex ratio,** *the number of males for every hundred females in a nation's population.* In 2000, the sex ratio in the United States was 96, or 96 males for every 100 females. Sex ratios usually are below 100 because, on average, women outlive men. In India, however, the sex ratio is 107 because parents value sons more than daughters and may either abort a female fetus or, after birth, give more care to a male infant, raising the odds that a female child will die.

A more complex measure is the **age-sex pyramid,** *a graphic representation of the age and sex of a population.* Figure 22–2 presents the age-sex pyramids for the populations of the United States and Mexico. Higher mortality with advancing age gives these figures a roughly pyramidal shape. In the U.S. pyramid, the bulge corresponding to ages thirty through the mid-fifties reflects high birth rates during the *baby boom* from the mid-1940s to 1970. The contraction just below—that is, people under thirty—reflects the subsequent *baby bust* as the birth rate dipped from 25.3 in 1957 to 14.6 in 2000.

Comparing the U.S. and Mexican age-sex pyramids shows different demographic trends. The age-sex pyramid for Mexico, like that of other low-income nations, is wide at the bottom (reflecting higher birth rates) and narrows quickly by what we would call

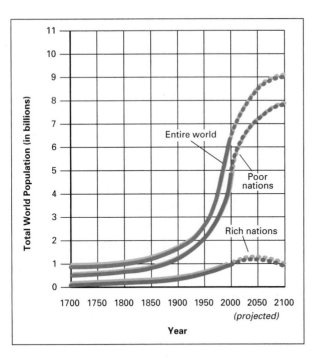

FIGURE 22–3 The Increase in World Population, 1700–2100

middle age (because of higher mortality). In short, Mexico is a much younger society, with a median age of twenty compared to thirty-five in the United States.

 To find out more about U.S. demography, go to http://www.census.gov

With a larger share of females still in their childbearing years, therefore, Mexico's crude birth rate (24) is nearly twice our own (14.6), and its annual rate of population growth (1.9 percent) is four times the U.S. rate (0.61 percent).

HISTORY AND THEORY OF POPULATION GROWTH

In the past, people favored large families because human labor was the key to productivity. Moreover, until rubber condoms appeared 150 years ago, preventing pregnancy was an uncertain proposition at best. But high death rates from widespread infectious diseases put a constant brake on population growth.

However, as shown in Figure 22–3, a major demographic shift began about 1750 as the world's population turned upward, reaching the 1 billion mark by 1800. This milestone (which took all of human history

up to this point) was repeated by 1930—barely a century later—when a second billion people were added to the planet. In other words, not only was population increasing but the *rate* of growth was accelerating. Global population reached 3 billion by 1962 (just thirty-two years later) and 4 billion by 1974 (a scant twelve years later). The rate of world population increase has slowed recently, but our planet passed the 5 billion mark in 1987 and the 6 billion mark late in 1999. In no previous century did the world's population even double. In the twentieth century, it quadrupled.

Currently, the world is gaining 77 million people each year, with 96 percent of this increase in poor countries. Experts predict that the Earth's population will reach between 8 billion and 9 billion by 2050 (Wattenberg, 1997; Thirunarayanapuram, 1998). Given the world's troubles in feeding the present population, such an increase is a matter of urgent concern.

MALTHUSIAN THEORY

It was the sudden population growth 250 years ago that sparked the development of demography. Thomas Robert Malthus (1766–1834), an English economist and clergyman, warned that population increase would soon lead to social chaos. Malthus (1926; orig. 1798) calculated that population would increase by what mathematicians call a *geometric progression*, illustrated by the series of numbers 2, 4, 8, 16, 32, and so on. At such a rate, Malthus concluded, world population would soon soar out of control.

Food production would also increase, Malthus explained, but only in *arithmetic progression* (as in the series 2, 3, 4, 5, 6) because even with new agricultural technology, farmland is limited. Thus, Malthus presented a distressing vision of the future: people reproducing beyond what the planet could feed, leading ultimately to widespread starvation.

Malthus recognized that artificial birth control or abstinence might change the equation. But he found one morally wrong and the other quite unlikely. Thus, famine and war stalked humanity in Malthus's scheme, and he was justly known as "the dismal parson."

Critical evaluation. Fortunately, Malthus's prediction was flawed. First, by 1850, the European birth rate began to drop, partly because children were becoming an economic liability rather than an asset and partly because people began using artificial birth control. Second, Malthus underestimated human ingenuity: Irrigation, fertilizers, and pesticides have increased farm production far more than he imagined.

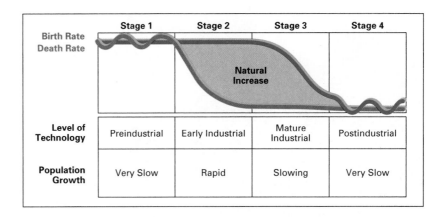

FIGURE 22–4
Demographic Transition Theory

	Stage 1	Stage 2	Stage 3	Stage 4
Birth Rate Death Rate		Natural Increase		
Level of Technology	Preindustrial	Early Industrial	Mature Industrial	Postindustrial
Population Growth	Very Slow	Rapid	Slowing	Very Slow

Some criticized Malthus for ignoring the role of social inequality in world abundance and famine. Karl Marx (1967; orig. 1867), for one, objected to viewing suffering as a "law of nature" rather than the curse of capitalism. More recently, "critical demographers" claim that saying the high birth rate in low-income countries is responsible for poverty amounts to blaming the victims. On the contrary, they continue, global inequality is the real problem that is yet to be addressed (Horton, 1999; Kuumba, 1999).

Still, Malthus offers an important lesson. Habitable land, clean water, and fresh air are limited resources, and as we explain presently, greater economic productivity has taken a heavy toll on the natural environment. In addition, medical advances have lowered death rates, pushing up world population. Common sense tells us that no level of population growth can go on forever. Therefore, people everywhere must become aware of the dangers of population increase.

DEMOGRAPHIC TRANSITION THEORY

Malthusian theory has been superseded by **demographic transition theory**, *the thesis that population patterns reflect a society's level of technological development.* Figure 22–4 shows the demographic consequences at four levels of technological development. Preindustrial, agrarian societies—those at Stage 1—have high birth rates because of the economic value of children and the absence of birth control. Death rates are also high because of low living standards and little medical technology. Outbreaks of disease neutralize births, so population rises and falls with only a modest overall increase. This was the case for thousands of years in Europe before the Industrial Revolution.

Stage 2—the onset of industrialization—brings a demographic transition as death rates fall because of greater food supplies and scientific medicine. But birth rates remain high, resulting in rapid population growth. It was during Europe's Stage 2 that Malthus formulated his ideas, which explains his pessimistic view of the future. The world's poorest countries today are in this high-growth stage.

In Stage 3—a mature industrial economy—the birth rate drops, curbing population growth once again. Fertility falls because most children survive to adulthood and because high living standards make raising children expensive. In short, affluence transforms children from economic assets into economic liabilities. Smaller families, made possible by effective birth control, are also favored by women working outside the home. As birth rates follow death rates downward, population growth slows further.

In Stage 4—a postindustrial economy—the demographic transition is complete. The birth rate keeps falling, partly because dual-income couples gradually become the norm and partly because the cost of raising children continues to rise. This trend, coupled with steady death rates, means that at best, population grows only very slowly or even decreases. This is the case now in Japan, Europe, and the United States.

Critical evaluation. Demographic transition theory suggests that the key to population control lies in technology. Instead of the runaway population increase feared by Malthus, this theory sees technology reining in growth and spreading material plenty.

Demographic transition theory dovetails with modernization theory, one approach to global development discussed in Chapter 12 ("Global Stratification").

The Getu family, on the left, lives in the low-income African nation of Ethiopia. The de Frutos family, to the right, lives in the high-income European nation of Spain. Comparing the two photographs, what can you learn about the relationship between a society's level of material affluence and family size? In fact, the fertility rate in Ethiopia is about five times higher than in Spain. Thus, while population levels are stable or declining in most of the world's richest countries, they are increasing in the world's poorest nations. This is why poor countries now account for 96 percent of global population increase.

Modernization theorists are optimistic that poor countries will solve their population problems as they industrialize. But critics—notably dependency theorists—strongly disagree. Unless there is a significant redistribution of global resources, they maintain, our planet will become increasingly divided into industrialized "haves," enjoying low population growth, and nonindustrialized "have-nots," struggling in vain to feed more and more people.

GLOBAL POPULATION TODAY: A BRIEF SURVEY

What can we say about population in today's world? Drawing on the discussion so far, we can reach several conclusions.

The Low-Growth North

When the Industrial Revolution began, population growth in Western Europe and North America peaked at 3 percent annually. But in the centuries since, the growth rate steadily declined and, in 1970, fell below 1 percent. As our postindustrial society enters Stage 4, the U.S. birth rate is less than the replacement level of 2.1 children per woman, a point demographers term **zero population growth**: *the level of reproduction that maintains population at a steady state.* Some fifty nations, almost all of them rich, have passed the point of zero population growth (Wattenberg, 1997).

To find out more about zero population growth, go to http://www.zpg.org

Factors holding down population in these postindustrial societies include a high proportion of men and women in the labor force, rising costs of raising children, trends toward later marriage and singlehood, and widespread use of contraceptives and abortion.

In postindustrial nations, therefore, population increase is not the pressing problem that it is in poor countries. Indeed, some analysts point to a future problem of *underpopulation* in countries such as Japan, Italy, and the United States, where the swelling ranks of the elderly have fewer and fewer young people to support them in old age (Chesnais, 1997).

The High-Growth South

Population is a critical problem in poor nations of the Southern Hemisphere. No nation in the world lacks industrial technology entirely; demographic transition

The rural rebound has been most pronounced in towns that offer spectacular natural beauty. There are times when people living in the scenic town of Park City, Utah, cannot even find a parking space.

eighteen. Heading the list is New York and adjacent urban areas in Long Island, western Connecticut, and northern New Jersey, with a total population of more than 21 million. Next in size is the CMSA in southern California that includes Los Angeles, Riverside, and Anaheim, with a population of more than 16 million.

As regional cities grow, they begin to overlap each other. For example, along the East Coast a 400-mile supercity stretches all the way from New England to Virginia. In the early 1960s, French geographer Jean Gottmann (1961) coined the term **megalopolis** to designate *a vast urban region containing a number of cities and their surrounding suburbs.* Other supercities cover the eastern coast of Florida and stretch from Cleveland west to Chicago. More megalopolises undoubtedly will emerge, especially in the fast-growing Sunbelt.

EDGE CITIES

Urban decentralization has also created *edge cities,* business centers some distance from the old downtowns. Edge cities—a mix of corporate office buildings, shopping malls, hotels, and entertainment complexes—differ from suburbs, which contain mostly homes. Thus, whereas the population of suburbs peaks at night, the population of edge cities peaks during the work day.

As part of expanding urban regions, most edge cities have no clear physical boundaries. Some have

names, including Los Colinas (near the Dallas–Fort Worth airport), Tyson's Corner (in Virginia, near Washington, D.C.), and King of Prussia (northwest of Philadelphia). Other edge cities are known only by the major highways that flow through them, including Route 1 in Princeton, New Jersey, and Route 128 near Boston (Garreau, 1991; Macionis & Parrillo, 2001).

THE RURAL REBOUND

Over the course of U.S. history, as the data in Table 22–1 show, the urban population has steadily increased. Immigration has played a part in the increase because most newcomers settle in cities. Urban growth can also be traced to migration from rural areas, typically by people seeking more economic opportunity.

Even so, since 1990 rural areas have been gaining population, a trend analysts call the "rural rebound." During the 1990s, three-fourths of the rural counties across the United States added population. Most of this increase resulted from migration of people from urban areas, as illustrated by the family in the chapter opening. This trend has not affected all rural places, however; for example, the Great Plains and the Mississippi Delta still show losses, as you can see by looking back at National Map 22–1. But even those losses are smaller than those during previous decades (Johnson, 1999).

Peasant Dance *(above, c. 1565), by Pieter Breughel the Elder, conveys the essential unity of rural life forged by generations of kinship and neighborhood. By contrast, Ernest Fiene's* Nocturne *(left) communicates the impersonality common to urban areas. Taken together, these paintings capture Tönnies's distinction between* Gemeinschaft *and* Gesellschaft.

Pieter Breughel the Elder (c. 1525/30–1569), *Peasant Dance*, c. 1565, Kunsthistorisches Museum, Vienna/Superstock. Ernest Fiene (1894–1965), *Nocturne*. Photograph © Christie's Images.

The rural rebound has been especially marked in rural communities that offer scenic and recreational attractions such as lakes, mountains, and ski areas. But the trend to live in rural communities has become widespread and reflects both decisions by urban people to relocate and decisions by rural people to stay where they are. In most cases, lifestyle is the impetus, with people preferring the slower pace, less traffic, less crime, and cleaner air found in the country and small towns. An increasing number of companies have also relocated to rural counties, which has increased economic opportunity for the rural population (Baldauf, 1996; Johnson, 1999; Johnson & Fuguitt, 2000).

URBANISM AS A WAY OF LIFE

How does rural life differ from urban life? This question has long attracted the attention of sociologists both in Europe and the United States. Here, we survey the ideas of a number of people who sought to answer this question.

FERDINAND TÖNNIES:
GEMEINSCHAFT AND *GESELLSCHAFT*

In the late nineteenth century, the German sociologist Ferdinand Tönnies (1855–1937) studied how life in the new industrial metropolis differed from life in rural villages. From this contrast, he developed two concepts that have become a lasting part of sociology's terminology.

Tönnies (1963; orig. 1887) used the German word ***Gemeinschaft*** (meaning roughly "community") to refer to *a type of social organization by which people are closely tied by kinship and tradition.* The *Gemeinschaft* of the rural village joins people in what amounts to a single primary group.

By and large, argued Tönnies, *Gemeinschaft* is absent in the modern city. On the contrary, urbanization fosters ***Gesellschaft*** (a German word meaning roughly "association"), *a type of social organization by which people come together only on the basis of individual self-interest.* In the *Gesellschaft* way of life, individuals are motivated by their own needs rather than a drive to

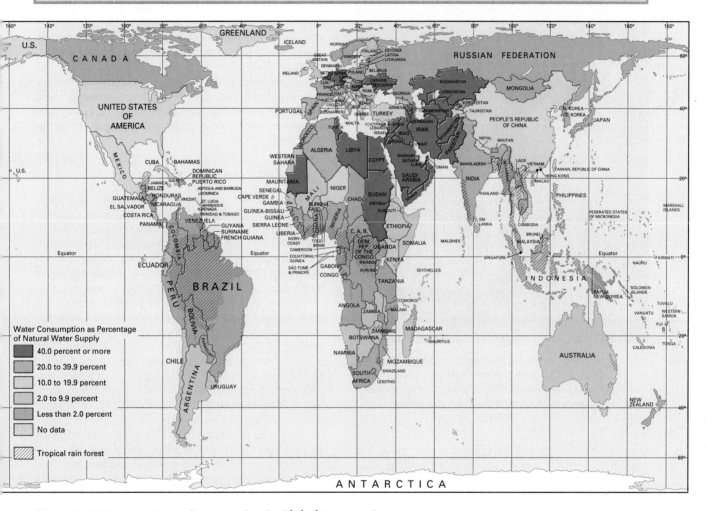

GLOBAL MAP 22–2 Water Consumption in Global Perspective

This map shows water consumption as a percentage of each country's renewable water resources. Nations near the equator consume only a tiny share of their available resources; indeed, much of this region is covered with rain forest. Northern Africa and the Middle East are a different story, however, with dense populations drawing on very limited water resources. As a result, in countries like Libya, Egypt, and Saudi Arabia, people (especially the poor) do not have as much water as they would like or, often, as they need.

Source: United Nations Development Programme (2000).

are becoming frequent. Egyptians today must make do with one-sixth the amount of water per person from the Nile compared to 1900. Furthermore, experts predict that within thirty years, as many as 1 billion people in northern Africa and the Middle East may lack the water they need for irrigation and drinking (Myers, 1984c; Postel, 1993).

Throughout the world, soaring population and complex technology have greatly increased societies' appetite for water. The global consumption of water

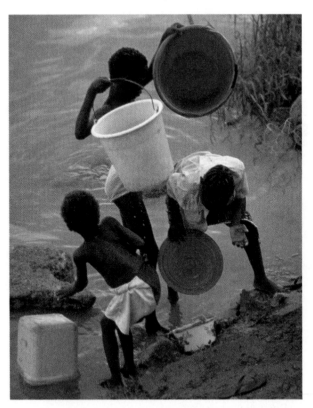

In the United States, most of us take safe water for granted. But people, and especially children, in poor countries around the world are at high risk from infectious diseases that are spread by unclean water used for bathing, cooking, and drinking.

(now more than 6 billion cubic feet per year) has tripled since 1950 and is expanding even faster than the world's population. As a result, even in the parts of the world that receive plenty of rainfall, people are using groundwater faster than it can be naturally replenished. In the Tamil Nadu region of southern India, for example, so much groundwater is being used that the water table has fallen 100 feet over the last several decades. Mexico City—which has sprawled to some 1,400 square miles—has pumped so much water from its underground aquifer that the city has sunk thirty feet during the last century and is dropping about two inches per year. Farther north in the United States, pumping from the Ogallala aquifer, which lies below seven states from South Dakota to Texas, is now so rapid that some experts fear it could run dry within several decades.

In light of such developments, we must face the reality that water is a valuable, finite resource. Greater conservation of water by individuals (the average person consumes 10 million gallons in a lifetime) is part of the answer. However, households around the world account for just 10 percent of water use. We need to curb water consumption by industry, which uses 25 percent of the global total, and farming, which consumes two-thirds of the total for irrigation.

New irrigation technology may reduce the demand for water in the future. But, here again, we see how population increase, as well as economic growth, strains our ecosystem (Goldfarb, 1991; Falkenmark & Widstrand, 1992; Postel, 1993; Population Action International, 2000).

Water Pollution

In large cities—from Mexico City to Cairo to Shanghai—many people have no choice but to drink contaminated water. Infectious diseases such as typhoid, cholera, and dysentery—all caused by waterborne microorganisms—spread rapidly (Clarke, 1984b; Falkenmark & Widstrand, 1992). Besides ensuring ample *supplies* of water, then, we must protect the *quality* of water.

Water quality in the United States is generally good by global standards. However, even here the problem of water pollution is growing steadily. According to the Sierra Club, an environmental activist organization, rivers and streams across the United States absorb some 500 million pounds of toxic waste each year. This pollution results not just from intentional dumping but also from the runoff of agricultural fertilizers and lawn chemicals.

A special problem is *acid rain*, rain made acidic by air pollution that destroys plant and animal life. Acid rain (or snow) begins with power plants burning fossil fuels (oil and coal) to generate electricity; this burning releases sulfuric and nitrous oxides into the air. As the wind sweeps these gases into the atmosphere, they react with the air to form sulfuric and nitric acids, which turns atmospheric moisture acidic.

This is a clear case of one type of pollution causing another: Air pollution (from smokestacks) ends up contaminating water (in lakes and streams that collect acid rain). Moreover, acid rain is truly a global phenomenon because the regions that suffer the harmful effects may be thousands of miles from the original pollution. For instance, British power plants have caused acid rain that has devastated forests and fish in Norway and Sweden, up to a thousand miles to the northeast. In the United States, we see a similar pattern as midwestern smokestacks have harmed the natural environment of New England.

Air Pollution

Because we are surrounded by air, most people in the United States are more aware of air pollution than contaminated water. One of the unexpected consequences of industrial technology, especially the factory and the motor vehicle, has been a decline in air quality. In 1950, exhaust fumes from automobiles shrouded cities such as Los Angeles. In London, factory smokestacks, automobiles, and coal fires used to heat households all added to what was probably the worst urban air quality of the last century. What some British jokingly called "pea soup" was, in reality, a deadly mix of pollution. For five days in 1952, an especially thick haze that hung over London killed 4,000 people (Clarke, 1984a).

In the final decades of the twentieth century air quality improved. Rich nations passed laws that banned high-pollution heating, including the coal fires that choked London fifty years ago. In addition, scientists devised ways to reduce the noxious output of factories and the growing numbers of automobiles and trucks.

If high-income countries can breathe a bit more easily than they once did, the problem of air pollution in poor societies is becoming more serious. One reason is that people in low-income countries still rely on wood, coal, peat, and other "dirty" fuels to cook and to heat their homes. Moreover, nations eager to encourage short-term industrial development often pay little heed to the longer-term dangers of air pollution. As a result, many cities in Latin America, Eastern Europe, and Asia are plagued by air pollution as bad as London's fifty years ago.

THE RAIN FORESTS

Rain forests are *regions of dense forestation, most of which circle the globe close to the equator.* A glance back at Global Map 22–2, on page 591, shows that the largest tropical rain forests are in South America (notably Brazil), west central Africa, and Southeast Asia. In all, the world's rain forests cover some 2 billion acres, or 7 percent of the Earth's total land surface.

Like other global resources, rain forests are falling victim to the needs and appetites of the surging world population. As noted earlier, to meet the demand for beef, ranchers in Latin America burn forested areas to increase their supply of grazing land. We are also losing rain forests to the hardwood trade. People in rich nations pay high prices for mahogany and other woods because, as environmentalist Norman Myers (1984b:88) puts it, they have "a penchant for parquet floors, fine furniture, fancy paneling, weekend yachts,

and high-grade coffins." Under such economic pressure, the world's rain forests are now just half their original size, and they continue to shrink by about 1 percent (65,000 square miles) annually. Unless we stop this loss, the rain forests will vanish before the end of the twenty-first century, and with them will go protection for the earth's biodiversity and climate.

Global Warming

Why are rain forests so important? One reason is that they cleanse the atmosphere of carbon dioxide (CO_2). Since the beginning of the Industrial Revolution, the amount of carbon dioxide produced by humans (mostly from factories and automobiles) has risen tenfold. Much of this carbon dioxide is absorbed by the oceans. But plants take in carbon dioxide and expel oxygen. This is why rain forests are vital to maintaining the chemical balance of the atmosphere.

The problem, then, is that carbon dioxide production is rising while the amount of plant life on the Earth is shrinking. To make matters worse, rain forests are being destroyed mostly by burning, which releases even more carbon dioxide into the atmosphere. Experts estimate that the atmospheric concentration of carbon dioxide is now 20 to 30 percent higher than it was 150 years ago.

High above the Earth, carbon dioxide acts like the glass roof of a greenhouse, letting heat from the sun pass through to the Earth while preventing much of it from escaping back into outer space. The result of this *greenhouse effect*, say ecologists, is **global warming,** *a rise in the Earth's average temperature caused by an increasing concentration of carbon dioxide and other gases in the atmosphere.* Over the last century, the global temperature has risen about 1.0° Fahrenheit (to an average of 58°F). And scientists warn that it could rise by 5° to 10° during this century, which would melt vast areas of the polar ice caps and raise the sea level to cover low-lying land around the world. Were this to happen, water would cover all of Bangladesh, for example, and much of the coastal United States, including Washington, D.C., right up to the steps of the White House. On the other hand, the U.S. Midwest, currently one of the most productive agricultural regions in the world, probably would become arid.

 A FEMA study (2000) claims that one in four houses within 500 feet of a shoreline is in danger over the next 60 years: http://www.heinzcenter.org

Mounting evidence suggests that the danger of global warming is real. Even so, some scientists point out that global temperature changes have been taking

Members of small, simple societies, such as the Tan't Batu, who thrive in the Philippines, live in harmony with nature; such people do not have the technological means to greatly affect the natural world. Although we in complex societies like to think of ourselves as superior to such people, the truth is that there is much we can—and must—learn from them.

place throughout history, apparently with little or nothing to do with rain forests. Moreover, higher concentrations of carbon dioxide in the atmosphere might speed up plant growth (because plants thrive on this gas), which would correct the imbalance and nudge the Earth's temperature downward once again. Still other scientists think global warming might even have benefits, including longer growing seasons and lower food prices (Silverberg, 1991; Moore, 1995; Begley, 1997; McDonald, 1999).

Declining Biodiversity

Destroying rain forests also reduces the Earth's *biodiversity*. This is because rain forests are home to almost half of this planet's living species.

On Earth, there are as many as 30 million species of animals, plants, and microorganisms. Several dozen unique species of plants and animals cease to exist each day, but given the vast number of living species, why should we be concerned? Environmentalists give three reasons. First, our planet's biodiversity provides a varied source of human food. Using agricultural technology, scientists can interbreed or genetically combine familiar crops with more exotic plant life, making food more bountiful and more resistant to insects and disease. Thus, biodiversity is needed to feed our planet's rapidly increasing population.

Second, the Earth's biodiversity is a vital genetic resource. Medical and pharmaceutical researchers look to animal and plant biodiversity for new compounds that cure disease and improve our lives. For example, children in the United States now have a good chance of surviving leukemia, a disease that was almost a sure killer two generations ago, because of a compound derived from a pretty tropical flower called the rosy periwinkle. The oral birth control pill, used by tens of millions of women in this country, is another product of plant research, this time involving the Mexican forest yam.

Third, with the loss of any species of life—whether it is the magnificent California condor, the famed Chinese panda, the spotted owl, or even one variety of ant—the beauty and complexity of our natural environment are diminished. And there are clear warning signs of such loss: Three-fourths of the world's 9,000 species of birds are declining in number.

Finally, note that, unlike pollution, the extinction of any species is irreversible and final. An important ethical question, then, is whether we who live today have the right to impoverish the world for those who live tomorrow (Myers, 1984b, 1991; E. Wilson, 1991; Brown et al., 1993).

ENVIRONMENTAL RACISM

Conflict theory has given rise to the concept of **environmental racism,** *the pattern by which environmental hazards are greatest for poor people, especially minorities.* Historically, factories that spew pollution stand near neighborhoods of the poor and people of color. Why? In part because the poor themselves were drawn to factories in search of work, and their low incomes often meant they could afford housing only in undesirable neighborhoods. Sometimes the only housing that fit their budgets stood in the very shadow of the plants and mills where they worked.

Nobody wants a "locally undesirable land use" (LULU) such as a factory or dump nearby, but communities face proposals for such development all the time. When businesses or other large organizations seek to establish a LULU, poor communities often have little power to resist. Through the years, then, the most serious environmental hazards have been located near Newark, New Jersey (not in upscale Bergen County), in southside Chicago (not wealthy Lake Forest), or on Native American reservations in the West (not in affluent suburbs of Denver or Phoenix) (Perrolle, 1993; Commission for Racial Justice, United Church of Christ, 1994; Szasz, 1994; Pollock & Vittas, 1995; Bohon & Humphrey, 2000).

LOOKING AHEAD: TOWARD A SUSTAINABLE WORLD

The demographic analysis presented in this chapter points to some disturbing trends. We see, first, that Earth's population has reached record levels because birth rates remain high in poor nations and death rates have fallen just about everywhere. Lowering fertility will remain a pressing problem throughout this century. Even with some recent decline in population increase, the nightmare Thomas Malthus described is still a real possibility, as the box on page 596 explains.

Furthermore, population growth remains greatest in the poorest countries of the world, those without the means to support their present populations, much less their future ones. Supporting 77 million additional people on our planet each year—almost 74 million of whom are in low-income societies—will require a global commitment to provide not only food but housing, schools, and employment. The well-being of the entire world may ultimately depend on resolving the economic and social problems of poor, overly populated countries and bridging the widening gulf between "have" and "have-not" societies.

Urbanization, too, is continuing, especially in poor countries. Throughout human history, people have sought out cities with the hope of finding a better life. But the sheer numbers of people who live in the emerging global supercities—Mexico City, São Paulo (Brazil), Kinshasa (Democratic Republic of the Congo), Bombay (India), and Manila (the Philippines)—have created urban problems on a massive scale.

Throughout the entire world, humanity is facing a serious environmental challenge. Part of this problem is population increase, which is greatest in poor societies. But another part of the problem is the high levels of consumption typical of rich nations such as our own. By increasing the planet's environmental deficit, our present way of life is borrowing against the well-being of our children and their children. Globally, members of rich societies, who currently consume so much of the Earth's resources, are mortgaging the future security of the poor countries of the world.

The answer, in principle, is to form an **ecologically sustainable culture,** *a way of life that meets the needs of the present generation without threatening the environmental legacy of future generations.* Sustainable living depends on three strategies.

First, the world needs to bring population growth under control. The current population of more than 6 billion is already straining the natural environment. Clearly, the higher the world's population climbs, the more difficult environmental problems will become. Even if the recent slowing of population growth continues, the world will have 8 billion people by 2050. Few analysts think that the Earth can support this many people; most argue that we must hold the line at about 7 billion, and some argue that we must *decrease* population in the coming decades (Smail, 1997).

A second strategy is *conservation of finite resources.* This means meeting our needs with a responsible eye toward the future by using resources efficiently, seeking alternative sources of energy, and, in some cases, learning to live with less.

A third strategy is *reducing waste.* Whenever possible, simply using less is the best solution. But recycling programs also are part of the answer.

In the end, making all these strategies work depends on a more basic change in the way we think about ourselves and our world. Our *egocentric* outlook sets our own interests as standards for how to live, but a sustainable environment demands an *ecocentric* outlook that helps us see how the present is tied to the future and why everyone must work together. Most nations in the southern half of the world are *underdeveloped,* unable to meet the basic needs of their people. At the same time, most countries in the northern half of the world are *overdeveloped,* using more resources than the Earth can sustain over time. Changes needed to create a sustainable ecosystem will not come easily. But the cost of not responding to the growing environmental deficit will certainly be greater (Humphrey & Buttel, 1982; Burke, 1984; Kellert & Bormann, 1991; Brown et al., 1993; Population Action International, 2000).

In closing, consider that the great dinosaurs dominated this planet for some 160 million years and then perished forever. Humanity is far younger, having existed for a mere 250,000 years. Compared to the dimwitted dinosaurs, our species has the gift of great intelligence. But how will we use this ability? What are the chances that our species will continue to flourish 160 million years—or even 1,000 years—from now? The shape of tomorrow's world depends on the choices we make today.

Apocalypse: Will People Overwhelm the Earth?

Are you worried about the world's increasing population? Think about this: By the time you finish reading this box, more than 1,000 people will be added to our planet. By this time tomorrow, global population will rise by 210,000. Currently, as the following table shows, there are about four births for every two deaths on the planet, pushing the world's population upward by 77 million annually. Put another way, global population growth amounts to adding another Philippines to the world every year.

It is no wonder that demographers and environmentalists are deeply concerned about the future. The Earth has an unprecedented population: The 2 billion people we have *added* since 1974 alone exceeds the planet's total in 1900.

neo-Malthusians by predicting an apocalypse if we do not change our ways. Brown concedes that Malthus failed to imagine how much technology (especially fertilizers and genetically modified plants) could boost agricultural output. But he maintains that the Earth's rising population is nevertheless rapidly outstripping its finite resources. Families in many poor countries can find little firewood, members of rich societies are depleting the oil reserves, and everyone is draining our supply of clean water.

Moreover, according to the neo-Malthusians, we are steadily poisoning the planet with waste. There is a limit to the Earth's capacity to absorb pollution, they warn, and as the number of people continues to increase, the quality of life will decline. Some analysts, in

as many people who, on average, live longer, healthier lives than ever before. As Simon sees it, the current state of the planet is cause for celebration.

The mistake of the neo-Malthusians, Simon argues, is assuming the world has finite resources that are spread thinner and thinner as population increases. Rather, people have the ability to control population growth and to improve their lives in many ways. Furthermore, we do not know what number of people the Earth can support because humans keep rewriting the rules, in effect, by developing new fertilizers, new crops, and new forms of energy. Simon notes that today's global economy makes available more resources than ever (including energy and consumer goods) at increasingly low prices. He looks optimistically to the future because technology, economic investment, and, above all, human ingenuity have consistently proven the doomsayers wrong. And he is betting they will continue to do so.

Global Population Increase			
	Births	**Deaths**	**Net Increase**
Per Year	131,571,719	55,001,289	76,570,430
Per Month	10,964,310	4,583,441	6,380,869
Per Day	360,470	150,688	209,782
Per Hour	15,020	6,279	8,741
Per Minute	250	105	146
Per Second	4.2	1.7	2.4

Might Thomas Robert Malthus—who predicted that population would outstrip the Earth's resources and plunge humanity into war and suffering—be right after all?

Lester Brown, a population and environmental activist, speaks for the

 Explore connections between population increase, global inequality, and the natural environment at http://www.peopleandtheplanet.net

fact, argue that we have already passed the Earth's "carrying capacity" for population. Holding the line will not be enough; as they see it, we need to *reduce* global population to perhaps half of what it is today (Smail, 1997).

But other analysts, the *anti-Malthusians*, sharply disagree. Asks Julian Simon, "Why the doom and gloom?" More than two centuries ago, he points out, Malthus predicted catastrophe. But today the Earth supports almost six times

Continue the debate . . .

1. *Where do you place your bet? Do you think the Earth can support 4, 6, 8, or 10 billion people? Why?*

2. *Ninety-six percent of current population growth is in poor countries. What does this mean for the future of rich nations? For the future of poor ones?*

3. *What should people in rich countries do to ensure the future of children everywhere?*

Sources: Based, in part, on Brown et al. (1993), Brown (1995), Simon (1995), and Smail (1997).

SUMMARY

Population

1. Fertility and mortality, measured as crude birth and death rates, are major factors affecting population size. In global terms, U.S. population growth is low.

2. Migration, another key demographic concept, has special importance to the historical growth of the United States and to cities everywhere.

3. Age-sex pyramids show graphically the composition of a population and project population trends. Sex ratio is a society's balance of females and males.

4. Historically, world population grew slowly because high birth rates were offset by high death rates. About 1750, a demographic transition began as world population rose sharply, mainly due to falling death rates.

5. Malthus warned that population growth would outpace food production, threatening society. Demographic transition theory counters that technological advances gradually slow population increase.

6. World population is expected to reach between 8 billion and 9 billion by 2050, with most of the increase in poor societies.

Urbanization

1. The first urban revolution began with the appearance of cities about 8000 B.C.E.. By the start of the common era, cities had emerged in most regions of the world except for North America.

2. Preindustrial cities have low-rise buildings, narrow, winding streets, and personal social ties.

3. A second urban revolution began about 1750 with the Industrial Revolution in Europe. An emphasis on commerce, as well as the increasing size of cities, made urban life more anonymous.

4. Urbanism came to North America with Europeans, who settled in a string of colonial towns along the Atlantic coastline. By 1850, hundreds of new cities were founded from coast to coast.

5. By 1920, a majority of the U.S. population lived in urban areas, and the largest metropolises were home to millions of people.

6. About 1950, cities began to decentralize with the growth of suburbs and edge cities. Nationally, Sunbelt cities—but not the older Snowbelt cities—are increasing in size and population.

7. Rapid urbanization in Europe during the nineteenth century led early sociologists to contrast rural and urban life. Ferdinand Tönnies built his analysis on the concepts of *Gemeinshaft* and *Gesellschaft*, and Emile Durkheim proposed parallel concepts of mechanical solidarity and organic solidarity. Georg Simmel claimed that the overstimulation of city life produced a blasé attitude in urbanites.

8. Robert Park believed cities permit greater social freedom. Louis Wirth saw large, dense, heterogeneous populations creating an impersonal and self-interested, though tolerant, way of life. Other researchers have explored urban ecology and urban political economy.

9. A third urban revolution is occurring in poor countries, where most of the world's largest cities will soon be found.

Environment

1. How human beings organize social life has the greatest effect on the natural environment.

2. Societies increase the environmental deficit by focusing on short-term benefits and ignoring the long-term consequences of their way of life.

3. Our ability to alter the natural world lies in our capacity for culture. Humanity's effect on the environment has increased along with the development of complex technology.

4. The "logic of growth" thesis supports economic development, stating that people can solve environmental problems as they arise. The opposing "limits to growth" thesis states that societies must curb development to prevent eventual environmental collapse.

5. Environmental issues include disposing of solid waste and protecting the quality of air and water. The supply of clean water is already low in some parts of the world.

6. Rain forests help remove carbon dioxide from the atmosphere and are home to a large share of this planet's living species. Under pressure from commercial interests, the world's rain forests are now half their original size and are shrinking by about 1 percent annually.

7. Environmental racism is the pattern by which the poor, especially minorities, suffer most from environmental hazards.

8. To achieve a sustainable environment that does not threaten the well-being of future generations, we must control world population, conserve finite resources, and reduce waste and pollution.

KEY CONCEPTS

Population

demography (p. 569) the study of human population

fertility (p. 570) the incidence of childbearing in a country's population

crude birth rate (p. 570) the number of live births in a given year for every thousand people in a population

mortality (p. 570) the incidence of death in a country's population

crude death rate (p. 570) the number of deaths in a given year for every thousand people in a population

infant mortality rate (p. 571) the number of deaths among infants under one year of age for each thousand live births in a given year

life expectancy (p. 571) the average life span of a country's population

migration (p. 571) the movement of people into and out of a specified territory

sex ratio (p. 573) the number of males for every hundred females in a nation's population

age-sex pyramid (p. 573) a graphic representation of the age and sex of a population

demographic transition theory (p. 575) the thesis that population patterns reflect a society's level of technological development

zero population growth (p. 576) the level of reproduction that maintains population at a steady state

Urbanization

urbanization (p. 578) the concentration of humanity into cities

metropolis (p. 580) a large city that socially and economically dominates an urban area

suburbs (p. 580) urban areas beyond the political boundaries of a city

megalopolis (p. 581) a vast urban region containing a number of cities and their surrounding suburbs

Gemeinschaft (p. 582) a type of social organization by which people are closely tied by kinship and tradition

Gesellschaft (p. 582) a type of social organization by which people come together only on the basis of self-interest

urban ecology (p. 584) the study of the link between the physical and social dimensions of cities

Environment

ecology (p. 586) the study of the interaction of living organisms and the natural environment

natural environment (p. 586) the Earth's surface and atmosphere, including living organisms, air, water, soil, and other resources necessary to sustain life

ecosystem (p. 586) a system composed of the interaction of all living organisms and their natural environment

environmental deficit (p. 587) profound and long-term harm to the natural environment caused by humanity's focus on short-term material affluence

rain forests (p. 593) regions of dense forestation, most of which circle the globe close to the equator

global warming (p. 593) a rise in the Earth's average temperature caused by an increasing concentration of carbon dioxide and other gases in the atmosphere

environmental racism (p. 594) the pattern by which environmental hazards are greatest for poor people, especially minorities

ecologically sustainable culture (p. 595) a way of life that meets the needs of the present generation without threatening the environmental legacy of future generations

CRITICAL-THINKING QUESTIONS

1. What are fertility and mortality rates? Which one has been more important in increasing global population?

2. Evaluate the environmental prediction of Thomas Robert Malthus. On balance, do you think he was more wrong or more right? Why?

3. How does demographic transition theory explain population patterns in terms of technological development?

4. According to Ferdinand Tönnies, Emile Durkheim, Georg Simmel, and Louis Wirth, what characterizes urbanism as a way of life? Note several differences in the ideas of these thinkers.

APPLICATIONS AND EXERCISES

1. Here is an illustration of the problem of runaway growth (Milbrath, 1989:10): *A pond has a single water lily growing on it. The lily doubles in size each day. In thirty days, it covers the entire pond. On which day does it cover half the pond?* When you realize the answer, discuss the implications of this example for population increase.

part, McCartney is barefoot, which is how Tibetan ritual prepares a corpse for burial. Behind Paul, a Volkswagen nearby displays the license plate "28 IF," apparently stating that McCartney would be 28 *if* he were alive.

The rumor explained that McCartney had died of head injuries suffered in an automobile accident in November 1966. After the accident, record company executives had secretly replaced Paul with a double.

Of course, Paul McCartney is very much alive and still jokes about the episode. Few doubt that Paul himself dreamed up some of the details of his "death" with a little help from his friends to encourage the interest of their fans. But the incident has a serious side,

showing how quickly rumors can arise and persist in a climate of distrust. In the late 1960s, many disaffected young people were quite ready to believe that the media and other powerful interests were concealing McCartney's death.

In 1969, McCartney himself denied the rumor in a *Life* magazine story. But thousands of suspicious readers noticed that on the other side of the page with McCartney's picture was an ad for an automobile: If one held this page up to the light, the car lay across McCartney's chest and blocked his head. Another clue!

What do you think?

1. *What can we say about the kind of issues that give rise to rumors?*

2. *Have there been rumors this year on your campus? About what?*

3. *On balance, do you think rumors are helpful or harmful? Why?*

Sources: Based on Rosnow & Fine (1976) and Kapferer (1992).

---

collective behavior among people dispersed over a wide geographical area.

RUMOR AND GOSSIP

A common type of mass behavior is **rumor**, *unsubstantiated information spread informally, often by word of mouth*. People pass along rumors through face-to-face communication, of course, but today's modern technology—including telephones, the mass media, and now the Internet—spreads rumors faster and farther than ever before.

Rumor has three essential characteristics.

1. **Rumor thrives in a climate of ambiguity.** Rumors arise when people lack definitive information about an important issue. A lack of knowledge about terrorism and the threat of catching anthrax from the mail led to widespread fear in the wake of the September 11, 2001, attacks (Kaplan, 2001).

2. **Rumor is unstable.** People change a rumor as they pass it along, usually giving it a "spin" that serves their own interests. Before long, many competing versions exist.

3. **Rumor is difficult to stop.** The number of people aware of a rumor increases exponentially as each person spreads information to several others. Rumors dissipate with time, but the only way to control rumors is for a believable source to issue a clear and convincing statement of the facts.

 To check the truth about recent rumors making the rounds on the Internet, visit http://www.nonprofit.net/hoax/

Rumor can trigger the formation of crowds or other collective behavior. For this reason, officials establish rumor control centers during a crisis in order to manage information. Yet some rumors persist for years, perhaps just because people enjoy them; the box gives one notable example.

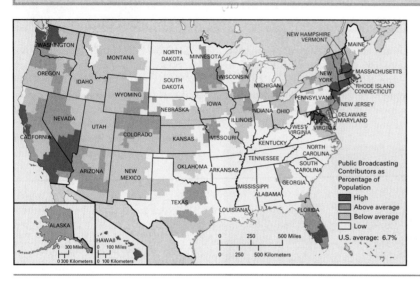

NATIONAL MAP 23–1
Support for Public Broadcasting across the United States

About 7 percent of people in the United States pledge money to support the Public Broadcasting System (PBS). As the map shows, PBS supporters are concentrated in particular regions of the country. What do you think accounts for this pattern?

Source: *Time* (January 16, 1995). Copyright © 1995 Time, Inc. Reprinted by permission.

Gossip is *rumor about people's personal affairs.* According to Charles Horton Cooley (1962; orig. 1909), rumor involves an issue of concern to a large audience, but gossip interests only a small circle of people who know a particular person. Rumors therefore spread widely, whereas gossip tends to be more localized.

Communities use gossip as a means of social control, praising or scorning someone to encourage conformity to local norms. Moreover, people gossip about others to raise their own standing as social "insiders," just as more powerful people use gossip to keep those who are socially marginal "in their place" (Baumgartner, 1998; Nicholson, 2001). Yet no community wants gossip to get out of control, which may be the reason people who gossip *too* much are criticized as "busybodies."

PUBLIC OPINION AND PROPAGANDA

Another form of dispersed collective behavior is **public opinion,** *widespread attitudes about controversial issues.* Exactly who is or is not included in any "public" depends on the issue involved. Over the years in the United States, "publics" have formed over numerous controversial issues, from water fluoridation, air pollution, and the social standing of women to handguns and health care (Lang & Lang, 1961; Turner, Killian, & Sow, 2001). More recently, the public has debated affirmative action, welfare reform, and government funding of public radio and television. National Map 23–1 shows where supporters of public broadcasting reside.

On any given issue, anywhere from 2 to 10 percent of people offer no opinion at all because of ignorance or indifference. Moreover, over time, public interest in issues rises and falls. For example, interest in the social position of women in the United States ran high a century ago during the women's suffrage movement but declined after 1920 when women gained the right to vote. Since the 1960s, a second wave of feminism has again created a public with strong opinions on gender-related issues.

Also, keep in mind that on any issue, not everyone's opinion carries the same weight. Some categories of people have more clout because they are better educated, wealthier, or better connected. As Chapter 17 ("Politics and Government") explained, many special interest groups shape public policy in the United States even though they represent just a small fraction of the population. For example, physicians are a well-organized and well-funded interest group that greatly influences U.S. health care policy, just as members of the National Education Association have a great deal to say about public education in the United States.

Special interest groups and political leaders all try to shape public tastes and attitudes by using

propaganda, *information presented with the intention of shaping public opinion.* Although the term has negative connotations, propaganda is not necessarily false. A thin line separates information from propaganda; the difference depends mostly on the presenter's intention. We offer *information* to enlighten others; we use *propaganda* to sway an audience toward some viewpoint. Political speeches, commercial advertising, and even some college lectures may disseminate propaganda in an effort to steer people toward thinking or acting in some specific way.

PANIC AND MASS HYSTERIA

A **panic** is *a form of localized collective behavior by which people react to a threat or other stimulus with irrational, frantic, and often self-destructive behavior.* The classic illustration of a panic is people streaming toward exits of a crowded theater after someone yells "Fire!" As they flee, they trample one another, blocking exits so that few actually escape.

Closely related to panic is **mass hysteria** or **moral panic,** *a form of dispersed collective behavior by which people react to a real or imagined event with irrational and even frantic fear.* Whether the cause of the hysteria is real or not, a large number of people certainly take it very seriously.

Some causes of mass hysteria or moral panic emerge within popular culture. In recent years, moral panics have centered on fear of AIDS (or people with AIDS), concern about missing children (whose numbers were greatly exaggerated during the 1980s), cybersmut (that is, pornography widely available to young people via the Internet), and political correctness (a liberal viewpoint that allegedly dominates academia and the media).

As these examples suggest, the real danger involved in such cases is debatable. Why, then, are these concerns widespread? As Erich Goode (2000:549) puts it, "the mass media *thrives* on scares; contributing to moral panics is the media's stock in trade." Therefore, many people become fearful about issues that are not really so dangerous because of what they learn about them from the mass media (Glassner, 1999).

Mass hysteria can be triggered by an event, which, at the extreme, sends people into chaotic flight. Of course, people who see others overcome by fear may become more afraid themselves, so that hysteria feeds on itself. So it was on the morning or September 11, 2001, in the wake of terrorist attacks. Although there were countless acts of heroism, panic was also widespread, especially in Washington, D.C., after a plane crashed into the Pentagon. Within an hour and a half, evacuation orders had been given and the streets of the city were choked with cars trying to get out. Yet the city's main bridges had been closed, which soon led to a citywide gridlock. People thought they were in danger, they found that they were unable to escape, and fear built on itself. Because no one knew what might happen next, rumors were everywhere: More attacks were coming, and even the city's water had been poisoned (Gibbs, 2001).

FASHIONS AND FADS

Two more kinds of collective behavior—fashions and fads—involve people spread over a large area. A **fashion** is *a social pattern favored by a large number of people.* Some fashions last for years, whereas others change after just a few months. The arts (including painting, music, drama, and literature), the shape of buildings, automobiles, clothes, our use of language, and public opinion all change as ideas go in and out of fashion.

Lyn Lofland (1973) explains that in preindustrial societies, clothing and personal appearance reflect traditional *style*, which changes very little. Women and men, the rich and the poor, lawyers and carpenters wear distinctive clothes and hairstyles that indicate their occupations and social standing.

In industrial societies, however, established style gives way to changing fashion. For one thing, modern people care less about tradition and often eagerly embrace new ways of living. Also, high social mobility means that people use their looks to make statements about themselves. German sociologist Georg Simmel (1971; orig. 1904) explained that affluent people usually are the trendsetters because people look to them and because they have the money to spend on luxuries. Or as U.S. sociologist Thorstein Veblen (1953; orig. 1899) put it, fashion involves *conspicuous consumption*, as people buy expensive products (from bottled water to Range Rovers) simply to show off their wealth.

Ordinary people who want to appear wealthy often snap up less expensive copies of what the rich make fashionable. In this way, a fashion trickles downward through the class structure. But before long, the fashion loses its prestige when too many average people share "the look," so the rich move on to something new. In short, fashions are born along the Fifth Avenues and Rodeo Drives of the rich but reach mass popularity in discount stores across the country.

Because change in high-income societies is so rapid, we see differences in personal appearance—one important element of fashion—over relatively short periods of time. These six photographs (beginning at the top, left) show hair styles commonly worn by women in the 1950s, 1960s, 1970s, 1980s, 1990s, and since 2000.

A reversal of this pattern has been occurring since the 1960s, as better-off people mimic fashions found among people of lower social position. This pattern began when affluent college students began buying blue jeans, or dungarees (from a Hindi word for a coarse fabric). For decades, manual laborers had worn blue jeans. But in the era of civil rights and antiwar movements, jeans became the uniform of liberal political activists and soon were popular on college campuses across the country. Cargo pants and other emblems of the hip-hop culture do much the same today, allowing even the most affluent entertainers and celebrities to mimic the styles of those with much less.

A **fad** is *an unconventional social pattern that people embrace briefly but enthusiastically.* Fads, sometimes called *crazes*, are common in high-income societies, where many people have the money to spend on amusing, if often frivolous, products. During the 1950s, two young entrepreneurs in California produced a brightly colored plastic version of a popular Australian toy, a three-foot-diameter hoop that one could swing around the waist by gyrating the hips. In no time, the "hula hoop" was a national craze. But in less than a year, hula hoops vanished from the scene.

In recent years, collecting Pokémon cards has been a fad among young people. But Pokémon's popularity already has begun to fade, showing that fads enter and depart from our culture all the time (Aguirre, Quarantelli, & Mendoza, 1988).

How do fads differ from fashions? Fads are passing fancies that capture the mass imagination but quickly burn out. Fashions, by contrast, reflect basic cultural values such as individuality and sexual attractiveness and tend to evolve over time. Therefore, a fashion—but rarely a fad—is incorporated into a society's culture. For instance, the fad of streaking came out of nowhere and soon vanished; the fashion of wearing blue jeans, on the other hand, originated in the rough mining camps of Gold Rush California more than a century ago and still influences clothing designs today. This "staying power" explains why we are happy to be called "fashionable" but put off by being called "faddish" (Blumer, 1968; Turner & Killian, 1993).

SOCIAL MOVEMENTS

A **social movement** is *an organized activity that encourages or discourages social change.* Social movements may be the most important type of collective behavior because they are deliberately organized and often have lasting effects on the shape of our society.

Social movements occur more frequently in today's world than in the past. Preindustrial societies are tightly bound by tradition, making social movements extremely rare. However, industrial and post-industrial societies foster diverse subcultures and countercultures so that social movements develop around a wide range of public issues. In recent decades, for example, the gay rights movement has won legal changes in numerous cities and several states, forbidding discrimination based on sexual orientation and allowing formal domestic partnership. Like any social movement that seeks change, the gay rights movement has prompted a countermovement made up of traditionalists who want to limit social acceptance of homosexuality. In today's society, almost every important public issue gives rise to a social movement favoring change and an opposing countermovement resisting it (Lo, 1982; Meyer & Staggenborg, 1996).

TYPES OF SOCIAL MOVEMENTS

Sociologists classify social movements according to two variables (Aberle, 1966; Cameron, 1966; Blumer, 1969). One variable asks *who is changed?* Some movements target selected people, and others try to change everyone. A second variable asks *how much change?* Some movements seek only limited change in our lives, and others are radical. Combining these variables results in four types of social movements, shown in Figure 23–1.

Alternative social movements are least threatening to the status quo because they seek limited change

 Visit the Promise Keepers Web site at http://www. promisekeepers.org

in only a part of the population. Promise Keepers, one example of an alternative social movement, encourages men to be more spiritual and supportive of their families.

Redemptive social movements also have a selective focus, but they seek radical change in those they engage. For example, Alcoholics Anonymous is an organization that helps alcoholics achieve a sober life.

Reformative social movements aim for only limited social change but target everyone. Multiculturalism, described in Chapter 3 ("Culture"), is an educational and political movement that advocates working toward social equality for people of all races and ethnicities. Reformative social movements generally work inside the existing political system. Some are *progressive*

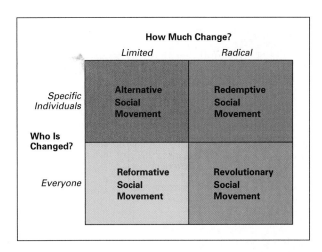

FIGURE 23–1 Four Types of Social Movements
Source: Based on Aberle (1966).

(promoting a new social pattern), whereas others are *reactionary* (countermovements trying to preserve the status quo or to revive past social patterns). Thus, just as multiculturalists push for greater racial equality, white supremacist organizations try to maintain the historical dominance of white people.

Revolutionary social movements are the most extreme of all, striving for basic transformation of an entire society. Sometimes pursuing specific goals, sometimes spinning utopian dreams, these social movements reject existing social institutions as flawed while promoting radically new alternatives. Both the left-wing Communist Party (pushing for government control of the economy) and right-wing militia groups (advocating the destruction of "big government") seek to radically change our way of life.

EXPLAINING SOCIAL MOVEMENTS

Because social movements are intentional and long-lasting, sociologists find this type of collective behavior easier to explain than fleeting incidents of mob behavior or mass hysteria. Several theories have come to the fore.

Deprivation Theory

Deprivation theory holds that social movements arise among people who feel deprived. People who feel they lack enough income, safe working conditions, basic political rights, or plain human dignity may organize a

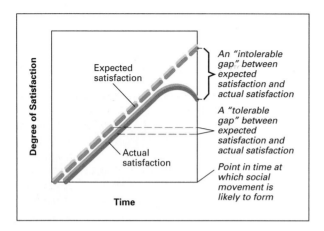

FIGURE 23–2 Relative Deprivation and Social Movements

In this diagram, the solid line represents a rising standard of living over time. The dotted line indicates the expected standard of living, which is typically somewhat higher. James C. Davies describes the difference between the two as "a tolerable gap between what people want and what they get." If the standard of living suddenly drops in the midst of rising expectations, however, the gap becomes intolerable. At this point, we can expect social movements to form.

Source: Davies (1962).

social movement to bring about a more just state of affairs (Morrison, 1978; Rose, 1982).

The rise of the Ku Klux Klan and passage of Jim Crow laws by whites intent on enforcing segregation in the South after the Civil War illustrate deprivation theory. With the end of slavery, white people lost a source of free labor and the claim that they were socially superior to African Americans. Many whites reacted to their sense of deprivation by trying to keep all people of color "in their place" (Dollard et al., 1939). African Americans had experienced much greater deprivation, of course, but as slaves they had little opportunity to organize. During the twentieth century, however, African Americans organized successfully in pursuit of racial equality.

For information on the Ku Klux Klan and other hate groups, visit http://www.splcenter. org/intelligenceproject/ip-index.html

As Chapter 7 ("Groups and Organizations") explained, deprivation is a relative concept. Regardless of anyone's absolute amount of money and power, people feel either better or worse off than some category of others. **Relative deprivation,** then, is *a perceived disadvantage arising from some specific comparison* (Stouffer et al., 1949; Merton, 1968).

More than a century ago, Alexis de Tocqueville (1955; orig. 1856) studied the French Revolution. Why, he asked, did rebellion occur in progressive France rather than in more traditional Germany, where peasants were, by any objective measure, worse off? Tocqueville's answer was that as bad as their condition was, German peasants had known nothing but feudal servitude and thus had no basis for feeling deprived. French peasants, on the other hand, had seen improvements in their lives that whetted their appetites for more. Thus the French—not the Germans—felt a keen sense of relative deprivation. The irony, as Tocqueville saw it, was that increasing freedom and prosperity did not satisfy people as much as stimulate their desire for an even better life (1955:175; orig. 1856).

Closer to home, Tocqueville's insight helps explain patterns of rioting during the 1960s. Protest riots involving African Americans began not in the South, where many black people lived in miserable poverty and most were not even registered to vote, but in Detroit, where the auto industry was booming, black unemployment was low, and black home ownership was the highest in the country (Thernstrom & Thernstrom, 1998).

James C. Davies (1962) agrees that as life gets better, people take their rising fortunes for granted and expect even more. But what happens if the standard of living suddenly stops improving or begins to drop? As Figure 23–2 illustrates, relative deprivation is the result, generating unrest and social movements aimed at change.

Critical evaluation. Deprivation theory challenges our common-sense assumption that the worst-off people are the most likely to organize for change. People do not organize simply because they suffer in an absolute sense; rather, they form social movements because of *relative* deprivation. Indeed, both Tocqueville and Marx—as different as they were in many ways—agreed on the importance of relative deprivation in the formation of social movements.

But most people experience some discontent all the time, so deprivation theory leaves us wondering why social movements arise among some categories of people and not others. A second problem is that deprivation theory suffers from circular reasoning: We assume that deprivation causes social movements, but often the only evidence of deprivation is the social movement itself (Jenkins & Perrow, 1977). A third limitation of this approach is that it focuses exclusively on the cause of a social movement and tells us little about movements themselves (McAdam, McCarthy, & Zald, 1988).

Mass-Society Theory

William Kornhauser's mass-society theory (1959) argues that social movements attract socially isolated people who feel personally insignificant. From this point of view, social movements occur in large *mass* societies. Social movements are *personal* as well as *political* in that they offer a sense of purpose and belonging to people otherwise adrift in society (Melucci, 1989).

It follows, says Kornhauser, that categories of people with weak social ties are those who most readily join a social movement. People who are well integrated socially, by contrast, are unlikely to seek membership in a social movement.

Like Gustave Le Bon, discussed earlier, Kornhauser offers a conservative view of social movements. Activists tend to be psychologically vulnerable people who eagerly join groups and often are manipulated by group leaders. In Kornhauser's view, social movements are unlikely to be very democratic.

Critical evaluation. To Kornhauser's credit, his theory focuses on both the kind of society that produces social movements and the kinds of people who join them. But one criticism is that if we try to test the idea that mass societies foster social movements, we run up against the problem of having no clear standard for measuring the extent to which we live in a "mass society."

A second criticism is that explaining social movements in terms of people hungry to belong belittles the social justice issues that movements address. Put otherwise, mass society theory suggests that flawed people—rather than a flawed society—are responsible for social movements.

What does research show about mass society theory? The record is mixed. On the down side, some studies conclude that the Nazi movement in Germany did not draw heavily from socially isolated people (Lipset, 1963; Oberschall, 1973). Similarly, many of the people who took part in urban riots during the 1960s had strong ties to their communities (Sears & McConahay, 1973). Evidence also suggests that most young people who join religious movements have fairly normal family ties (Wright & Piper, 1986).

Finally, researchers who have examined the biographies of 1960s political activists find evidence of deep and continuing commitment to political goals rather than isolation from society (McAdam, 1988, 1989; Whalen & Flacks, 1989).

On the up side, research by Frances Piven and Richard Cloward (1977) supports mass-society theory. Piven and Cloward found that a breakdown of routine social patterns encourages poor people to form social movements. Also, in a study of the New Mexico State Penitentiary, Bert Useem (1985) found that when prison programs promoting social ties between inmates were suspended, inmates were more likely to protest their conditions.

Structural-Strain Theory

One of the most influential theories about social movements was developed by Neil Smelser (1962). *Structural-strain theory* identifies six factors that encourage the development of social movements. Smelser's theory also suggests which kinds of situations lead to unorganized mobs or riots and which to highly organized social movements. We will use the prodemocracy movement that transformed Eastern Europe during the late 1980s to illustrate Smelser's theory.

1. **Structural conduciveness.** Social movements arise as people come to think their society has some serious problems. In Eastern Europe, these problems included low living standards and political repression by national governments.

2. **Structural strain.** People begin to experience relative deprivation when their society fails to meet their expectations. Eastern Europeans joined the prodemocracy movement because they knew their living standards were far lower than living standards in Western Europe and much below what years of propaganda about prosperous socialism had led them to expect.

3. **Growth and spread of an explanation.** Forming a well-organized social movement requires a clear statement of a problem, its causes, and its solutions. If people are confused about their suffering, they are likely to express their dissatisfaction in an unorganized way such as rioting. In the case of Eastern Europe, intellectuals played a key role in the prodemocracy movement by pointing out economic and political flaws in the system and proposing strategies to increase democracy.

4. **Precipitating factors.** Discontent often festers for a long time, only to be transformed into collective action by a specific event. In Eastern Europe, such an event occurred in 1985 when Mikhail Gorbachev came to power in the Soviet Union and began his program of *perestroika* (restructuring). As Moscow relaxed its rigid control over Eastern Europe, people there saw a historic opportunity to reorganize political and economic life and claim greater freedom.

5. **Mobilization for action.** Once people share a concern about some public issue, they are ready to take action—to distribute leaflets, stage protest rallies, and build alliances with sympathetic organizations. The initial success of the Solidarity movement in Poland—covertly aided by the Reagan administration in the United States and by Pope John Paul II in the Vatican—mobilized people throughout Eastern Europe to press for change. The rate of change accelerated as reform movements gained strength: What had taken a decade in Poland took only months in Hungary and only weeks in other Eastern European nations.

6. **Lack of social control.** The success of any social movement depends, in large part, on how political officials, police, and the military respond. Sometimes the state moves swiftly to crush a social movement, as happened to the prodemocracy forces in the People's Republic of China. But Gorbachev adopted a policy of nonintervention in Eastern Europe, thereby opening the door for change. Ironically, the movements that began in Eastern Europe soon spread to the Soviet Union itself, ending the historic domination of the Communist party and producing a new political confederation in 1992.

Critical evaluation. Smelser's analysis recognizes the complexity of social movements and suggests how various factors encourage or inhibit their development. Structural-strain theory also explains why people may respond to their problems either by forming organized social movements or participating in spontaneous mob action or rioting.

Yet Smelser's theory contains some of the same circularity of argument found in Kornhauser's analysis. A social movement is caused by strain, says Smelser, but the only evidence of underlying strain appears to be the social movement itself. Finally, structural-strain theory is incomplete, overlooking the important role that resources such as the mass media or international alliances play in the success or failure of a social movement (Oberschall, 1973; Jenkins & Perrow, 1977; McCarthy & Zald, 1977; Olzak & West, 1991).

Resource-Mobilization Theory

Resource-mobilization theory points out that no social movement is likely to succeed—or even get off the ground—without substantial resources, including money, human labor, office and communication facilities, access to the mass media, and a positive public image. In short, any social movement rises or falls on its ability to attract resources, mobilize people, and forge alliances. The 1989 prodemocracy movement in China was fueled by students whose location on campuses clustered together in Beijing allowed them to build networks and recruit new members (Zhao, 1998). Similarly, to challenge socialism in Eastern Europe, Poles and others needed fax machines, copiers, telecommunication gear, money, and moral support provided by other nations. In recent years, the Internet has been a vital resource enabling organizations to link tens of thousands of people across the United States and to draw large numbers of demonstrators to Washington, D.C., or cities such as Seattle in order to stage protests.

According to resource mobilization theory, outsiders can be just as important as insiders in affecting the outcome of a social movement. Because socially disadvantaged people, by definition, lack the money, contacts, leadership skills, and organizational know-how that a successful movement requires, sympathetic outsiders fill the resource gap. In U.S. history, well-to-do white people, including college students, performed a vital service to the black civil rights movement in the 1960s, and affluent men have joined women as leaders of the current women's movement (Snow, Zurcher, & Ekland-Olson, 1980; Killian, 1984; Snow et al., 1986; Baron, Mittman, & Newman, 1991; Burstein, 1991; Meyer & Whittier, 1994; Valocchi, 1996).

On the other side of the coin, a lack of resources limits efforts to bring about change. The history of the AIDS epidemic is a case in point. Initially, in the early 1980s, the government paid little attention to the rising incidence of AIDS, leaving gay communities in San Francisco, New York, and other cities to shoulder the responsibility for treatment and educational programs. Gradually, as more people began to grasp the scope of the problem, public pressure prompted local, state, and federal governments to allocate more

The mass media often play an important part in guiding public opinion toward or away from change. Media performances do this by providing symbols that mobilize support for some point of view. Soviet-backed governments throughout Eastern Europe were collapsing, one after another, during the early 1990s; Roger Waters (former member of Pink Floyd) performed "The Wall" at the site of the Berlin Wall, celebrating the fact that this barrier was finally coming down.

resources for research, education, and treatment. Members of the Hollywood-based entertainment industry in particular lent their money, visibility, and prestige to the movement. These resources were crucial in transforming a fledgling social movement into a well-organized, global coalition of political leaders, educators, and medical specialists.

Critical evaluation. Resource-mobilization theory recognizes that both resources and discontent are necessary to the success of a social movement. Research confirms that forging alliances to gain resources is especially important and notes that movements with few resources may, in desperation, turn to violence to call attention to their cause (Grant & Wallace, 1991).

Critics of this theory counter that even relatively powerless segments of a population can promote change if they are able to organize effectively and have strongly committed members (Donnelly & Majka, 1998). Research by Aldon Morris (1981) shows that people of color drew largely on their own skills and resources to fuel the civil rights movement of the 1950s and 1960s. A second problem with this theory is that it overstates the extent to which powerful people are willing to challenge the status quo. Some rich white people did provide valuable resources to the black civil rights movement, but probably more often, elites were indifferent or opposed to significant change (McAdam, 1982, 1983; Pichardo, 1995).

Overall, the success or failure of a social movement is determined by political struggle. A strong and united establishment (perhaps aided by a counter-movement) reduces the odds that a social movement will succeed. However, if the established powers are divided, the movement's chances of success improve.

Culture Theory

In recent years, sociologists have recognized that social movements depend not only on material resources and the structure of political power but also on cultural symbols. That is, people in any particular situation are likely to mobilize to form a social movement only to the extent that they develop "shared understandings of the world that legitimate and motivate collective action" (McAdam, McCarthy, & Zald, 1996:6).

In part, mobilization depends on a sense of injustice, as suggested by deprivation theory. In addition, people must come to believe that they are not able to respond to their situation effectively acting as individuals. Finally, social movements gain strength as they develop symbols and a sense of community that both generate strong feelings and direct this emotional energy into organized action. News photographs of children harmed by bombing during the Vietnam War, for example, bolstered the antiwar movement. Likewise, the media presentation of the attack on the World Trade Center in 2001 (a site later referred to simply as "ground zero") helped mobilize public support for a military response against terrorists in Afghanistan (Morris & Mueller, 1992; Giugni, 1998; Staggenborg, 1998; Gibbs, 2001).

One example of a new social movement is the worldwide effort to eliminate land mines. Years after hostilities cease, these mines remain in place and take a staggering toll in civilian lives. At a protest in Berlin, Germany, a mountain of shoes stands as a memorial to the tens of thousands of people who have been crippled or died as a result of stepping on underground mines.

Critical evaluation. This approach reminds us that not just material resources but also cultural symbols form the foundation of social movements. At the same time, powerful symbols (such as the flag and ideas about patriotism and respecting our leaders) help support the status quo. How and when symbols turn people from supporting the system toward protest are questions that warrant further research.

New Social Movements Theory

A final, more recent theoretical approach addresses the changing character of social movements. *New social movements theory* emphasizes the distinctive features of recent social movements in postindustrial societies of North America and Western Europe (Melucci, 1980; McAdam, McCarthy, & Zald, 1988; Kriesi, 1989; Pakulski, 1993).

First, most of today's social movements are international, focusing on global ecology, the social standing of women and gay people, animal rights, and the risks of terrorism. As the process of globalization connects the world's nations in more and more ways, in other words, social movements are becoming global.

For information on laws involving animal rights, see http://www.animal-law.org

Second, whereas traditional social movements such as labor organizations are concerned mostly with economic issues, new social movements tend to focus on cultural change and improving our social and physical surroundings. The international environmental movement, for example, opposes practices that aggravate global warming and other environmental dangers.

Third, whereas most social movements of the past drew strong support from working-class people, new social movements, with their noneconomic agendas, usually draw support from the middle and upper-middle classes. This is because, as discussed in Chapter 17 ("Politics and Government"), more affluent people tend to be more conservative on economic issues (because they have wealth to protect) but more liberal on social issues (partly as a result of extended education). Furthermore, in the United States and other rich nations, the number of highly educated professionals—the people who most support new social movements—is increasing, which suggests that these movements will grow (Jenkins & Wallace, 1996; Rose, 1997).

Critical evaluation. One clear strength of this theory is its recognition that social movements have increased in scale in response to the development of a global economy and international political connections. This theory also highlights the power of the mass media and new information technology to unite people around the world in pursuit of political goals.

However, critics claim that this approach exaggerates the differences between past and present social movements. The women's movement, for example, focuses on many of the same issues—workplace conditions and pay—that have concerned labor organizations for decades. Similarly, many of those protesting the rising power of the World Trade Organization (described in the opening to this chapter) consider economic equality around the world their primary goal.

Each of the five theories we have presented offers some explanation for the emergence of social movements; no single theory can stand alone (Kowalewski & Porter, 1992). Table 23–1 summarizes the theories.

GENDER AND SOCIAL MOVEMENTS

Gender figures prominently in the operation of social movements. In keeping with traditional ideas about gender in the United States, men more than women tend to take part in public life, including spearheading social movements.

Investigating "Freedom Summer," a 1964 voter registration project in Mississippi, Doug McAdam (1992) found that most people believed registering African-American voters in the midst of considerable hostility from whites was dangerous and therefore "men's work" unsuitable for women. He also discovered that project leaders were likely to assign women volunteers to clerical and teaching assignments, leaving the field activities to men. This was so even though women who participated in Freedom Summer were more qualified than their male counterparts in terms of years of activism and organizational affiliations. McAdam concluded that only the most committed women were able to overcome the movement's gender barriers. In short, although women have played leading roles in many social movements (including the abolitionist and feminist movements in the United States), male dominance has been the norm even in social movements that otherwise oppose the status quo (Herda-Rapp, 1998).

STAGES IN SOCIAL MOVEMENTS

Despite the many differences that set one social movement off from another, all unfold in roughly the same way, as shown in Figure 23–3 on page 618. Researchers have identified four stages in the life of the typical social movement (Blumer, 1969; Mauss, 1975; Tilly, 1978).

Stage 1: Emergence. Social movements are driven by the perception that all is not well. Some, such as the civil rights and women's movements, are born of widespread dissatisfaction. Others emerge only as a small vanguard group increases public awareness of some issue. Gay activists, for example, initially raised public concern about the threat posed by AIDS.

Stage 2: Coalescence. After emerging, a social movement must define itself and develop a strategy for "going public." Leaders must determine policies, decide on tactics, build morale, and recruit new members. At this stage, the movement may engage in collective action such as rallies or demonstrations to attract media attention and thereby public notice. The movement may also form alliances with other organizations to acquire necessary resources.

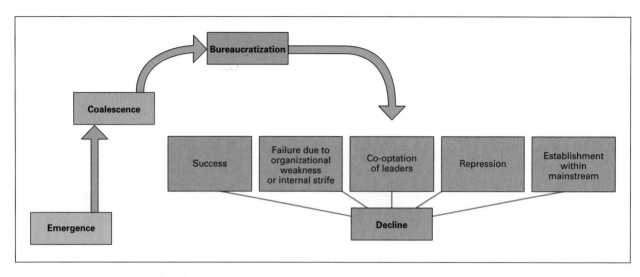

FIGURE 23–3 Stages in the Lives of Social Movements

Stage 3: Bureaucratization. To become a political force, a social movement must take on bureaucratic traits, described in Chapter 7 ("Groups and Organizations"). Thus, as it becomes established, the social movement depends less on the charisma and talents of a few leaders and more on a capable staff. When social movements do not become established in this way, they risk dissolving. For example, many activist organizations on college campuses during the late 1960s were energized by a single charismatic leader and consequently did not last long. On the other hand, the National Organization for Women (NOW), despite its changing leadership, is well established and can be counted on to speak for feminists.

Even so, bureaucratization can sometimes hinder a social movement. In reviewing social movements in U.S. history, Frances Piven and Richard Cloward (1977) found that leaders can become so engrossed in building an organization that they neglect the need to keep people fired up for change. In such cases, the radical edge of protest is lost.

Stage 4: Decline. Eventually, most social movements begin to decline. Frederick Miller (1983) suggests four reasons that this can occur.

First, if members have met their goals, decline may simply signal success. For example, the women's suffrage movement disbanded after it won women in the United States the right to vote. Such clear-cut successes are rare, however, because few social movements

have a single goal. More commonly, winning one victory leads to new campaigns. Because issues related to gender extend far beyond voting, the women's movement has recast itself time and again.

Second, a social movement may fold because of organizational factors, such as poor leadership, loss of interest among members, insufficient funds, or repression by authorities. Some people lose interest when the excitement of early efforts is replaced by day-to-day routine. Fragmentation by internal conflicts over goals and strategies is another common problem. Students for a Democratic Society (SDS), a student movement promoting participatory democracy and opposing the war in Vietnam, splintered into several small factions by the end of the 1960s as members disagreed over strategies for social change.

Third, a social movement can fall apart if the established power structure, through offers of money, prestige, and other rewards, diverts leaders from their goals. "Selling out" is one facet of the iron law of oligarchy, discussed in Chapter 7 ("Groups and Organizations"). That is, organizational leaders use their positions to enrich themselves. For example, Vernon Jordan, once head of the National Urban League became a close advisor to President Clinton and a rich and powerful Washington "insider" as a result. But this process can also work the other way: Some people leave lucrative, high-prestige occupations to become activists. Cat Stevens, a rock star of the 1970s, became a Muslim, changed his name to Yusuf

Islam, and has devoted himself in recent decades to spreading his religion.

Fourth and finally, a social movement can collapse because of repression. Officials may crush a social movement by frightening away participants, discouraging new recruits, and even imprisoning leaders. In general, the more revolutionary the social movement, the more officials try to repress it. Until 1990, the government of South Africa banned the African National Congress (ANC), a political organization seeking to overthrow the state-supported system of apartheid. Even suspected members of the ANC were subject to arrest. In 1990, the government lifted the decades-old ban and released ANC leader Nelson Mandela from prison; in 1994, the South African people elected Mandela president and began the journey away from apartheid.

Beyond the reasons noted by Miller, a fifth cause of decline is that a social movement may "go mainstream." Some movements become an accepted part of the system—typically after realizing some of their goals—so that although they continue to flourish, they no longer challenge the status quo. For example, the U.S. labor movement is now well established; its leaders control vast sums of money and, according to some critics, now have more in common with the business tycoons they opposed in the past than with rank-and-file workers.

SOCIAL MOVEMENTS AND SOCIAL CHANGE

Social movements exist to encourage—or to resist—social change. Whatever the intention, their success varies from case to case. The civil rights movement has certainly pushed this country toward racial equality, despite opposition from a handful of white supremacist countermovements such as the Aryan Nation and what's left of the Ku Klux Klan.

Sometimes we overlook the success of past social movements and take for granted the changes other people struggled so hard to win. Beginning a century ago, workers' movements in the United States fought to end child labor in factories, limit working hours, make the workplace safer, and establish the right to bargain collectively with employers. Laws protecting the environment are another product of successful social movements during this century. In addition, women today have greater legal rights and economic opportunities because of the efforts of earlier generations of women.

Seen one way, major social transformations such as the Industrial Revolution and capitalism give rise to social movements, including those involving workers and women. On the other hand, the efforts of workers, women, racial and ethnic minorities, and gay people have sent ripples of change throughout our society. In short, social change is both the cause and the consequence of social movements.

LOOKING AHEAD: SOCIAL MOVEMENTS IN THE TWENTY-FIRST CENTURY

Especially since the turbulent 1960s, a decade marked by widespread social protests, U.S. society has been pushed and pulled by many social movements and countermovements. Sometimes tension explodes into violence, as when demonstrators faced off against police at meetings of world leaders in Seattle in 1999, Washington, DC, in 2000, and Stockholm, Sweden, in 2001. In other cases, the struggles are more restrained, as with political debate between congressional Democrats supporting greater social "safety nets" and Republicans opposed to "big government." Yet people on all sides agree that this nation faces a number of pressing issues, including poor public schools, racial tension, the soaring costs of political campaigns, and tens of millions of people without health care insurance. Of course, different people define the problems in different ways, just as they are likely to settle on different policies as solutions. In short, social movements and the problems they address are always *political* (Macionis, 2002).

Just as social movements have always been part of U.S. society, there is little doubt that they will continue to shape our way of life throughout the twenty-first century. Indeed, for three reasons, the scope of social movements is likely to increase. First, protest should increase as women, African Americans, and other historically marginalized categories of people gain a greater political voice. Second, at a global level, the technology of the Information Revolution means that anyone with a cable or satellite television or a personal computer can stay abreast of political events, often as they happen. Third, new technology and the emerging global economy mean that social movements are now uniting people throughout the entire world. Moreover, because many problems are global in scope, only international cooperation can solve them.

Are You Willing to Take a Stand?

Are you satisfied with our society as it is? Surely, everyone would change some things about our way of life. And surveys show just that: If they could, a lot of people would change plenty! There is considerable pessimism about the state of U.S. society. Two-thirds of U.S. adults think that the average person's situation "is getting worse, not better," and three-fourths of respondents state that most government officials are "not interested" in the average person's problems (NORC, 2001:210–11).

But in light of such concerns, few people are willing to stand up and try to bring about change. Only 10 percent of

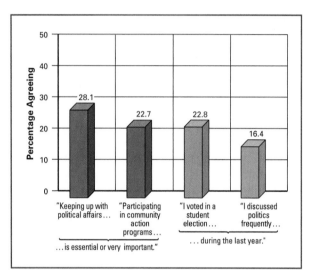

Political Involvement of Students Entering College in 2000: A Survey

Source: Sax et al. (2000).

U.S. adults have ever picketed during a labor strike; just 5 percent say they have ever taken part in any other kind of demonstration (NORC, 2001:249–50).

Many college students probably suspect age has something to do with such apathy. That is, young people have the interest and idealism to challenge the status quo, whereas older adults worry only about their families and their jobs. Indeed, one of the popular sayings of the activist 1960s was "You can't trust people over thirty!" But the facts are otherwise: Students entering college in 2000 expressed less interest in political issues than their parents.

SUMMARY

1. Collective behavior differs from group behavior because it involves limited social interaction within vague social boundaries and also weak and often unconventional norms.

2. Crowds, an important type of collective behavior, take various forms: casual crowds, conventional crowds, expressive crowds, acting crowds, and protest crowds.

3. Crowds that become emotionally intense spawn violence in the form of mobs and riots. Mobs pursue a specific goal; rioting involves undirected destructiveness.

4. Crowds have figured heavily in social change throughout history, although the value of their action depends on one's political outlook.

5. Contagion theory views crowds as anonymous, suggestible, and subject to rising emotions. Convergence theory links crowd behavior to the traits of participants. Emergent-norm theory suggests that crowds develop their own behavioral norms.

6. One form of mass behavior is rumor, which thrives in a climate of ambiguity. Whereas rumor involves public issues, gossip deals with personal issues.

7. Public opinion consists of people's positions on important, controversial issues. Public attitudes change over time; at any time on any given issue, a small share of people hold no opinion at all.

8. Panic (in a local area) and mass hysteria (across an entire society) are types of collective behavior by which people respond to a significant event, real or

Asked to select important goals in life from a list, 28 percent of first-year students included "keeping up with political affairs," and just 22 percent checked off "participating in community action programs." As the figure shows, only a handful of students (22 percent) say they voted in a student election during the past year. An even smaller share (16 percent) claimed to discuss politics frequently in the past year.

Certainly, people cite some good reasons to avoid political controversy. Anytime we challenge the system—whether on campus or in the national political arena—we risk making enemies, losing a job, or perhaps even sustaining physical injury.

But the most important reason that people in the United States avoid joining in social movements may have to do with cultural norms about how change should occur. In our individualistic culture, people favor taking personal responsibility over collective action as a means of addressing social problems. For example, when asked about the best way for women or African Americans to improve their social position, most U.S. adults say that individuals should rely on their own efforts. Only a few point to women's groups or civil rights activism as the best way to bring about change (NORC, 2001:228, 362, 364). This individualistic orientation explains why U.S. adults are half as likely as their European counterparts to join in lawful demonstrations (Inglehart et al., 2000).

Of course, sociology poses a counterpoint to our cultural individualism. As C. Wright Mills (1959) explained decades ago, many of the problems we encounter as individuals are caused by the structure of society. Thus, said Mills, solutions to many of life's problems depend on collective effort—that is, people willing to take a stand for what they believe.

Continue the debate . . .

1. Do you think the reluctance of people in the United States to address problems through collective action shows that they are basically satisfied with their lives? Or that they think individuals acting together can't make a difference?

2. Have you ever participated in a political demonstration? What were its goals? What did it accomplish?

3. Identify ways in which life today has been affected by people who took a stand in the past (think about race relations, animal welfare, the state of the environment, the standing of women and other issues).

imagined, with irrational, frantic, and often self-destructive behavior.

9. In industrial societies, people use fashion as a source of social prestige. A fad is more unconventional than a fashion and also of shorter duration, although people embrace fads with greater enthusiasm.

10. Social movements exist to promote or discourage change. Sociologists classify social movements according to the range of people they seek to involve and the extent of the change they seek.

11. According to deprivation theory, social movements arise as people feel deprived in relation to some standard of well-being.

12. Mass-society theory holds that people join social movements to gain a sense of belonging and moral direction.

13. Structural-strain theory explains the development of a social movement as a cumulative effect of six factors. Well-formulated grievances and goals encourage the formation of social movements; undirected anger, by contrast, promotes rioting.

14. Resource-mobilization theory ties the success or failure of a social movement to the availability of resources such as money, human labor, and alliances with other organizations.

15. Culture theory notes the importance of symbols and material resources to the success of a social movement.

16. New social movements theory focuses on quality-of-life issues that are usually international in scope.

17. A typical social movement proceeds through consecutive stages: emergence (defining the public issue),

coalescence (entering the public arena), bureaucratization (becoming formally organized), and decline (caused by failure or, sometimes, success).

18. Past social movements have shaped society in ways that people now take for granted. Just as movements produce change, change itself causes social movements.

KEY CONCEPTS

collective behavior (p. 601) activity involving a large number of people, often spontaneous and sometimes controversial

collectivity (p. 602) a large number of people whose minimal interaction occurs in the absence of well-defined and conventional norms

crowd (p. 603) a temporary gathering of people who share a common focus of attention and who influence one another

mob (p. 603) a highly emotional crowd that pursues a violent or destructive goal

riot (p. 604) a social eruption that is highly emotional, violent, and undirected

mass behavior (p. 606) collective behavior among people dispersed over a wide geographical area

rumor (p. 607) unsubstantiated information spread informally, often by word of mouth

gossip (p. 608) rumor about people's personal affairs

public opinion (p. 608) widespread attitudes about controversial issues

propaganda (p. 609) information presented with the intention of shaping public opinion

panic (p. 609) a form of localized collective behavior by which people react to a threat or other stimulus with irrational, frantic, and often self-destructive behavior

mass hysteria or **moral panic** (p. 609) a form of dispersed collective behavior by which people react to a real or imagined event with irrational and even frantic fear

fashion (p. 609) a social pattern favored by a large number of people

fad (p. 610) an unconventional social pattern that people embrace briefly but enthusiastically

social movement (p. 610) organized activity that encourages or discourages social change

relative deprivation (p. 612) a perceived disadvantage arising from a specific comparison

CRITICAL-THINKING QUESTIONS

1. The concept of collective behavior encompasses a broad range of social patterns. List some of these patterns. What traits do they all have in common?

2. Imagine the aftermath of a football game when the revelry turns into a destructive rampage. How might contagion theory, convergence theory, and emergent-norm theory explain such behavior?

3. The 1960s were a decade of both great affluence and widespread social protest. What sociological insights help explain this apparent paradox?

4. In what respects do some recent social movements (those concerned with the environment, animal rights, and gun control) differ from much earlier crusades (focusing on, say, the right of workers to form unions or the right of women to vote)?

George Tooker's 1950 painting The Subway *depicts a common problem of modern life: Weakening social ties and eroding traditions create a generic humanity in which everyone is alike yet each person is an anxious stranger in the midst of others.*

George Tooker, *The Subway*, 1950, egg tempera on gesso panel, 18¼ × 36¼", Whitney Museum of American Art, New York. Purchased with funds from the Julianna Force Purchase Award, 50.23. Photograph © 2000 Whitney Museum of American Art.

Inevitable tensions and conflicts—sometimes based on race, ethnicity, or religion—divided these small communities. But according to Tönnies, because of the traditional spirit of *Gemeinschaft*, people were "essentially united in spite of all separating factors" (1963:65; orig. 1887).

Modernity turns societies inside out so that, as Tönnies put it, people are "essentially separated in spite of uniting factors" (1963:65; orig. 1887). This is the world of *Gesellschaft*, where, especially in large cities, most people live among strangers and ignore others they pass on the street. Trust is hard to come by in a mobile and anonymous society; people tend to put their personal needs ahead of group loyalty, and a majority of adults believe "you can't be too careful" in dealing with people (NORC, 2001:178). No wonder that millions of men and women attend weekly support groups (also made up of strangers) to establish even temporary emotional ties and find someone who is willing simply to listen (Leerhsen, 1990).

Critical evaluation. Tönnies's theory of *Gemeinschaft* and *Gesellschaft* is the most widely cited model of modernization. The theory's strength lies in its synthesis of various dimensions of change: growing population, the rise of cities, increasing impersonality in social interaction.

One problem with Tönnies's theory is that modern life, though often impersonal, is not completely devoid of *Gemeinschaft*. Even in a world of strangers, friendships can be strong and lasting. Traditions are especially pronounced in many ethnic neighborhoods, where residents maintain close community ties.

Another criticism is that Tönnies said little about which factors (industrialization, urbanization, weakening

of families) are cause and which are effect. Some analysts also think that Tönnies favored—perhaps even romanticized—traditional societies while overlooking bonds of family, neighborhood, and friendship in modern societies.

EMILE DURKHEIM: THE DIVISION OF LABOR

The French sociologist Emile Durkheim, whose work is discussed in Chapter 4 ("Society"), shared Tönnies's interest in the profound social changes wrought by the Industrial Revolution. For Durkheim, modernization is defined by an increasing *division of labor*, or specialized economic activity (1964a; orig. 1893). Whereas all members of a traditional society usually perform the same daily round of activities, modern societies function by having people perform highly specific roles.

Durkheim explained that preindustrial societies are held together by *mechanical solidarity*, or shared moral sentiments. In other words, members of preindustrial societies view everyone as basically alike, doing the same kind of work and belonging together. Durkheim's concept of mechanical solidarity is virtually the same as Tönnies's *Gemeinschaft*.

With modernization, the division of labor becomes more and more pronounced. To Durkheim, this change means less mechanical solidarity but more of another kind of tie: *organic solidarity*, or the mutual dependency of people engaged in specialized work. Put simply, modern societies are held together not by likeness but by difference: All of us must depend on others to meet most of our needs. Organic solidarity corresponds to Tönnies's concept of *Gesellschaft*.

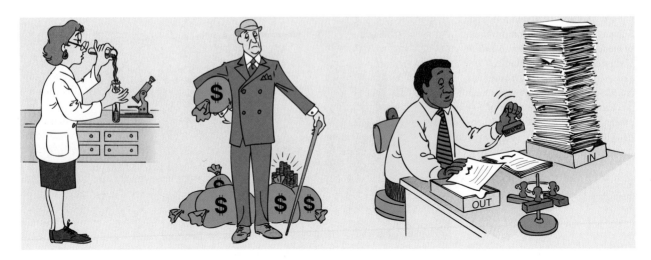

Max Weber maintained that the distinctive character of modern society was its rational worldview. Virtually all of Weber's work on modernity centered on types of people he considered typical of their age: the scientist, the capitalist, and the bureaucrat. Each is rational to the core: The scientist is committed to the orderly discovery of truth, the capitalist to the orderly pursuit of profit, and the bureaucrat to orderly conformity to a system of rules.

Despite obvious similarities in their thinking, Durkheim and Tönnies viewed modernity somewhat differently. To Tönnies, the change from *Gemeinschaft* to *Gesellschaft* amounts to the loss of social solidarity because modern people lose the "natural" and "organic" bonds of the rural village, leaving only the "artificial" and "mechanical" ties of the big city. Durkheim had a different take on modernity, even reversing Tönnies's language to bring home the point. Durkheim labeled modern society "organic," arguing that modern society is no less natural than any other, and he described traditional societies as "mechanical" because they are so regimented. Thus Durkheim viewed modernization not as the loss of community but as a change from community based on bonds of likeness (kinship and neighborhood) to community based on economic interdependence (the division of labor). Durkheim's view of modernity is both more complex and more positive than Tönnies's.

Critical evaluation. Durkheim's ideas stand alongside those of Tönnies as a highly influential analysis of modernity. Of the two thinkers, Durkheim is the more optimistic; still, he feared that modern societies might become so diverse that they would collapse into a state of *anomie*, a condition in which norms and values are so weak and inconsistent that society provides little moral guidance to individuals. Without strong moral ties to society, modern people become egocentric and find little purpose in life.

The suicide rate—which Durkheim considered a good index of anomie—has increased in the United States over the twentieth century. Moreover, in a recent survey, the vast majority of U.S. adults reported that they see moral questions not in clear terms of right and wrong but in confusing "shades of gray" (NORC, 2001:377).

Even so, in modern societies, shared norms and values are still strong enough to give most people some sense of meaning and purpose. Moreover, whatever the hazards of anomie, most people seem to value the personal freedom modern society affords.

MAX WEBER: RATIONALIZATION

For Max Weber, whose work is also discussed in Chapter 4 ("Society"), modernity means replacing a traditional worldview with a rational way of thinking. In preindustrial societies, tradition acts as a constant brake on change. To traditional people, "truth" is roughly the same as "what has always been" (1978:36; orig. 1921). To modern people, however, "truth" is the result of rational calculation. Because they value efficiency and have little reverence for the past, modern people adopt whatever social patterns allow them to achieve their goals.

short, they conclude, despite our pretensions of democracy, most people are all but powerless in the face of wealthy elites.

Critical evaluation. Table 24–3 summarizes the interpretations of modernity offered by mass-society theory and class-society theory. Whereas the former focuses on the increasing scale of life and the growth of government, the latter stresses the expansion of capitalism and the persistence of inequality.

Class-society theory also dismisses Durkheim's argument that people in modern societies suffer from anomie, claiming instead that they suffer from alienation and powerlessness. Not surprisingly, then, the class-society interpretation of modernity enjoys widespread support among liberals (and radicals) who favor greater equality and call for extensive regulation (or abolition) of the capitalist marketplace.

A basic criticism of class-society theory is that it overlooks the many ways in which equality in modern societies has increased. For example, discrimination based on race, ethnicity, and gender is now illegal and widely regarded as a social problem. Tolerance for people with same-sex orientation has increased dramatically, and people with disabilities have more rights and opportunities than ever before. It is true that differences in income remain large; however, most people in the United States favor unequal rewards, at least insofar as they reflect differences in personal talent and effort.

Moreover, few observers think a centralized economy would cure the ills of modernity in light of socialism's failure to generate a high overall standard of living. Many other problems in the United States—from unemployment, homelessness, and industrial pollution to unresponsive government—are also found in socialist nations such as the former Soviet Union.

MODERNITY AND THE INDIVIDUAL

Both mass- and class-society theories look at the broad societal changes that have taken place since the Industrial Revolution. But from these macro-level approaches we can also draw micro-level insights into how modernity shapes individual lives.

Mass Society: Problems of Identity

Modernity liberated individuals from small, tightly knit communities of the past. Most people in modern societies, therefore, have the privacy and freedom to express their individuality. However, mass-society theory suggests that so much social diversity, widespread

TABLE 24–3 Two Interpretations of Modernity: A Summary		
	Mass Society	**Class Society**
Process of Modernization	Industrialization; growth of bureaucracy	Rise of capitalism
Effects of Modernization	Increasing scale of life; rise of the state and other formal organizations	Expansion of the capitalist economy; persistence of social inequality

isolation, and rapid social change make it difficult to establish a coherent identity (Wheelis, 1958; Riesman, 1970; Berger, Berger, & Kellner, 1974).

Chapter 5 ("Socialization") explained that a person's personality is largely a product of social experience. The small, homogeneous, and slowly changing societies of the past provided a firm, if narrow, foundation for building a meaningful identity. Even today, the Amish communities that flourish in the United States and Canada teach young men and women "correct" ways to think and behave. Not everyone born into an Amish community can tolerate strict demands for conformity, but most members establish a well-integrated and satisfying personal identity (cf. Hostetler, 1980; Kraybill & Olshan, 1994).

Mass societies are quite another story. Socially diverse and rapidly changing, they offer only shifting sands on which to build a personal identity. Left to make many life decisions on our own, many people—especially those with greater affluence and thus more freedom—face a bewildering range of options. Choice has little value without standards to guide our selections, and in a tolerant mass society, people may find one path no more compelling than the next. Not surprisingly, many people shuttle from one identity to another, changing their lifestyles, relationships, and even religions in search of an elusive "true self." Beset by the widespread "relativism" of modern societies, people without a moral compass lack the security and certainty once provided by tradition.

To David Riesman (1970; orig. 1950), modernization brings changes in **social character,** *personality patterns common to members of a particular society.* Preindustrial societies foster what Riesman calls **tradition-directedness,** *rigid conformity to time-honored ways of living.* Members of traditional societies model their lives on those of their ancestors, so that "living a good

Mass-society theory attributes feelings of anxiety, isolation, and lack of meaning in the modern world to rapid social change that washes away tradition. Edvard Munch captured this vision of modern emptiness in his painting The Scream *(left). Class-society theory, by contrast, ties such feelings to social inequality, by which some categories of people are made into second-class citizens (or not made citizens at all). Paul Marcus portrays modern injustice in the painting* Crossing the Rio Grande *(right).*

Edvard Munch, *The Scream,* Oslo, National Gallery, Scala/Art Resource, NY. © 1998 Artists Rights Society (ARS), NY/ADAGP, Paris. © Paul Marcus, *Crossing the Rio Grande,* 1999, oil painting on canvas, 63 × 72 in. Studio SPM Inc.

life" amounts to "doing what our people have always done."

Tradition-directedness corresponds to Tönnies's *Gemeinschaft* and Durkheim's mechanical solidarity. Culturally conservative, tradition-directed people think and act alike. Unlike the conformity sometimes found in modern societies, the uniformity of tradition-directedness is not an effort to mimic one another. Instead, people are alike because they all draw on the same solid cultural foundation. Amish women and men exemplify tradition-directedness; in Amish culture, tradition ties everyone to ancestors and descendants in an unbroken chain of righteous living.

Members of diverse and rapidly changing societies consider a tradition-directed personality deviant because it seems so rigid. Modern people prize personal flexibility and sensitivity to others, what Riesman describes as **other-directedness,** *a receptiveness to the latest trends and fashions, often expressed by imitating others.* Because their socialization occurs in societies that are constantly in flux, other-directed people develop fluid identities marked by superficiality, inconsistency, and

change. They try on different "selves," almost like new pieces of clothing. They seek out role models, try to maintain self-esteem, and engage in varied performances as they move from setting to setting (Goffman, 1959). In a traditional society, such "shiftiness" makes a person untrustworthy, but in a changing, modern society, the chameleon-like ability to fit in virtually anywhere is very useful.

In societies that value the up-to-date rather than the traditional, people anxiously solicit the approval of others, looking to members of their own generation rather than to elders as significant role models. Peer pressure can be irresistible to people with no enduring standards to guide them. Our society urges individuals to be true to themselves. But when social surroundings change so rapidly, how can people develop the self to which they should be true? This problem lies at the root of the identity crisis so widespread in industrial societies today. "Who am I?" is a nagging question that many of us struggle to answer. In truth, this problem is not so much us as the society in which we live, that is, the inherent instability of modern mass society.

CRITICAL-THINKING QUESTIONS

1. How well do you think Tönnies, Durkheim, Weber, and Marx predicted the character of modern society? How are their visions of modernity the same? How do they differ?

2. What traits lead some to call the United States a "mass society"? Why do other analysts describe the United States as a "class society"?

3. What is the difference between *anomie* (a trait of mass society) and *alienation* (a characteristic of class society)? In which categories of the U.S. population would you expect each to be pronounced?

4. Why do some analysts see the United States as a postmodern society? Do you agree? Why or why not?

APPLICATIONS AND EXERCISES

1. Do you have an elderly relative or friend? Most older people will be happy to tell you about the social changes they have seen in their lifetimes.

2. Ask people in your class or your friends to make five predictions about U.S. society in the year 2050, when today's twenty-year-olds will be senior citizens. Compare notes: On what issues is there agreement?

3. Has the rate of social change been increasing? Do some research about inventions over time and see for yourself. For example, consider modes of travel, including walking, riding animals, trains, cars, airplanes, and rockets in space. The first two characterized society for tens of thousands of years; the last four emerged in barely two centuries.

4. Packaged in the back of this new textbook is an interactive CD-ROM that offers a variety of study and review materials intended to help you better understand the material covered in this chapter. For this chapter, the CD-ROM contains an author's tip video, Real Life Sociology videos, other relevant audio and video, interactive map animations, audio journal entries from the author, Web links, and much more.

 ## SITES TO SEE

http://www.prenhall.com/macionis

Visit the interactive *Companion Website*™ that accompanies this text. Begin by clicking on the cover of your book. You will find a chapter-by-chapter study guide, practice tests, and a significant portion of the text for on-line review, as well as many suggested Web links.

http://www.gwu.edu/~ccps/

This Web site describes the Communitarian Network, including its goals and how it proposes to achieve them.

http://www.utoronto.ca/utopia/

Deliberate change sometimes is inspired by visions of utopia, ideal societies that exist nowhere. Read about the Society for Utopian Studies at this Web site.

http://www.TheSociologyPage.com or
http://www.macionis.com

Finally, on a personal note, I hope this book has helped you and will be a useful resource for courses later on. Please visit my Web page, and send an e-mail message (macionis@kenyon.edu) with your thoughts and suggestions. And, yes, I *will* write back!

John J. Macionis

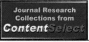 ## INVESTIGATE WITH CONTENTSELECT

Follow the instructions found on page 23 of this textbook to enter this chapter of the book's *Companion Website*™. Once in the chapter, click on the ContentSelect icon at the bottom left of your screen and enter your personal User ID and Password. Enter keywords such as "social change," "mass society," and "postmodernity," and the search engine will help you become an effective researcher.

NEW INFORMATION TECHNOLOGY AND SOCIAL CHANGE

Chapter 3 ("Culture") presented William Ogburn's (1964) concept of *cultural lag*, the pattern by which some elements of culture change faster than others. Usually, Ogburn explained, technology changes quickly; getting used to new technology, on the other hand, takes people much longer. This cultural pattern of lagging behind probably explains why we use old terminology to describe new developments, such as measuring the "horsepower" of gasoline engines or, more recently, exploring the "superhighway" of cyberspace.

The fact that developments in science and technology outpace our ability to comprehend them makes many people uneasy about social change. In a national survey, about 40 percent of U.S. adults agreed with the statement, "One trouble with science is that it makes our way of life change too fast" (NORC, 2001:365). But the majority of people are more optimistic, expecting that new technology will improve our lives. This final cyber.scope highlights how the age of computers is altering the shape of cities, forming new kinds of human communities, and bringing people together in new ways to form social movements.

The New Shape of Cities
As Chapter 22 ("Population, Urbanization, and Environment") explains, the metropolis stands as the greatest monument to the industrial era. A century ago, factories full of huge machines offered jobs that drew people from across the countryside to form cities of unprecedented size. Industrial

metropolises such as New York, Chicago, Philadelphia, and Detroit churned with activity, and new buildings of mortar, steel, and glass stretched skyward.

These cities became busier and denser as industrial technology centralized people. Businesses fused together into a central business district, where executives and managers could easily establish face-to-face communication. Factories were situated together near rivers and railroads, which brought them fuel and raw materials and took away their finished products.

The industrial cities of the United States reached their peak populations about 1950, just as scientists were building their first computers. Computer technology helped push the economy from industry to service and information work, and this shift spurred the decentralization of cities. Population began radiating farther away from the central city so that, by 1970, most city dwellers were actually living in suburbs miles from the central city. Businesses followed suit, deserting the downtowns for industrial parks and outlying shopping malls. Today's urban sprawl is the result.

Why have the old central cities lost much of their attraction? One reason is that in the business world, having a central city address is no longer so important. That is, with new information technology, people can communicate efficiently without working in the same area. Thus, today's cities are growing "out" more than they are growing "up." The urban scene early in the twenty-first century shows steady central city populations surrounded

by swelling suburbs and rapidly growing "edge cities"—clusters of office buildings, shopping malls, hotels, and entertainment complexes miles from the old "downtowns."

Change in the shape of cities highlights, once again, one of the most important consequences of new information technology: Physical distance no longer separates people the way it used to. Thus, people who work together do not need to share an office building or even live in the same city. The other side of the same coin is that in the cyber-age, we may not pay very much attention to the people who are—physically speaking—all around us. In short, new information technology is forming new kinds of human communities while eroding older ones.

The Rise of Virtual Communities
Consider some dramatic changes taking place at Dartmouth College, in Hanover, New Hampshire, one of the country's most academically competitive schools and a college at the forefront of the Information Revolution. Since the college wired all dormitories—sometimes called the "one plug per pillow" model—life on campus has not been the same. In the cyber-age, students such as Arthur Desrosiers have discovered that they have fewer and fewer reasons to leave their rooms. Desrosiers, a Dartmouth sophomore, relies on his computer to browse the college library, write papers, ask questions of his professors, send notes to his girlfriend, keep up with old high school friends, and even order pizza while joining in 2:00 A.M.

online chat sessions. Perhaps strangest of all, Desrosiers often fires messages back and forth to his two roommates, even though they are silently staring at screens of their own just a few feet away in the same room.

It may be a sign of the times that a once-popular restaurant just down the street from dorms that house 3,000 students has closed its doors. Similarly, the student union is far less busy that it was just a few years ago. There, some of the space once used for socializing now accommodates—you guessed it—computer terminals for students who want to check their e-mail between classes.

At Dartmouth, computers have never been more popular. All together, the 8,000 students, faculty, and staff send and receive some 250,000 messages each day. No one doubts that new information technology has opened up more possibilities for accessing more information than ever before and contacting people almost anywhere in the world. But some people are beginning to see that an older form of local community is being lost in the process. Some faculty worry that they see less and less of their students. Some students, too, are beginning to think that they ought to see more of each other. As senior Abigail Butler puts it, "I know people who sit home Friday and Saturday night and e-mail back and forth to people they only know by nicknames, while the rest of the world is going by. After a while it starts to be really unfulfilling. It's easier to just meet someone in

With access to the Internet, these Thai students have joined an international social movement to advance the opportunities of people with disabilities.

person and actually talk" (Gabriel, 1996).

Social Movements: New Ways to Connect

New ways to connect with people means a rising potential for starting and expanding social movements. Today, anyone with an interest in some issue and a computer can make contact, ask questions, and spread ideas—in short, play a role in intentional social change. In addition, computers offer access to almost unlimited information by accessing the Web pages of countless organizations and individuals with programs for change.

Perhaps most important, computer technology has made it easy to make connections on a global scale. Take the students at the Redemptorist Vocational School in Pattaya, Thailand. These young men and women have physical disabilities, which, before the information age, might have kept them

from learning at all. But using their school's computers, the students have established contact with hundreds of other people with disabilities in dozens of countries, including the United States. From these contacts and from visiting the Web sites of national and international organizations representing people with disabilities, the students have received a rich education indeed. They have been surprised to learn that many countries have laws that protect people with disabilities from discrimination and that mandate access ramps for sidewalks and buildings; they have discovered that cities abroad feature buses that "kneel" to permit entry by people in wheelchairs, as well as public restrooms designed to accommodate everyone. Armed with their new knowledge, the students at the Redemptorist Vocational School are now taking the lead in their own country, using the Internet to educate people about disabilities and lobbying government officials to make changes in Thailand's laws.

The Internet is a powerful communication resource for anyone. But it is especially important for people whose ability to make contact with others is otherwise limited, including people with disabilities. As one Thai student reports, "On the 'Net, I don't feel like a handicapped person" (Smolan & Erwitt, 1996:150). Even though computer access is far from equal around the world, the Internet is providing more and more people in poor countries with the power of a global reach.

GLOSSARY

abortion the deliberate termination of a pregnancy

absolute poverty a deprivation of resources that is life-threatening

achieved status a social position a person assumes voluntarily that reflects personal ability and effort

activity theory the idea that a high level of activity enhances personal satisfaction in old age

Afrocentrism the dominance of African cultural patterns

ageism prejudice and discrimination against the elderly

age-sex pyramid a graphic representation of the age and sex of a population

age stratification the unequal distribution of wealth, power, and privilege among people at different stages of the life course

agriculture large-scale cultivation using plows harnessed to animals or more powerful energy sources

alienation the experience of isolation and misery resulting from powerlessness

animism the belief that elements of the natural world are conscious life forms that affect humans

anomie Durkheim's term for a condition in which society provides little moral guidance to individuals

anticipatory socialization learning that helps a person achieve a desired position

ascribed status a social position a person receives at birth or assumes involuntarily later in life

asexuality a sexual orientation in which a person is not attracted to people of either sex

assimilation the process by which minorities gradually adopt patterns of the dominant culture

authoritarianism a political system that denies popular participation in government

authority power that people perceive as legitimate rather than coercive

beliefs specific statements that people hold to be true

bilateral descent a system tracing kinship through both men and women

bisexuality a sexual orientation in which a person is attracted to people of both sexes

blue-collar occupations lower-prestige work that involves mostly manual labor

bureaucracy an organizational model rationally designed to perform tasks efficiently

bureaucratic inertia the tendency of bureaucratic organizations to perpetuate themselves

bureaucratic ritualism a preoccupation with rules and regulations to the point of thwarting an organization's goals

capitalism an economic system in which natural resources and the means of producing goods and services are privately owned

capitalists people who own and operate factories and other businesses in pursuit of profits

caregiving informal and unpaid care provided to a dependent person by family members, other relatives, or friends

caste system social stratification based on ascription

cause and effect a relationship in which change in one variable (the independent variable) causes change in another (the dependent variable)

charisma extraordinary personal qualities that can turn an audience into followers

charismatic authority power legitimized through extraordinary personal abilities that inspire devotion and obedience

church a type of religious organization well integrated into the larger society

civil religion a quasi-religious loyalty binding citizens in a basically secular society

class conflict conflict between entire classes over the distribution of a society's wealth and power

class consciousness Marx's term for workers' recognition of themselves as a class united in opposition to capitalists and, ultimately, to capitalism itself

class society a capitalist society with pronounced social stratification

class system social stratification based on both birth and individual achievement

cohabitation the sharing of a household by an unmarried couple

cohort a category of people who share some trait, usually their age

collective behavior activity involving a large number of people, often spontaneous and sometimes controversial

collectivity a large number of people whose minimal interaction occurs in the absence of well-defined and conventional norms

colonialism the process by which some nations enrich themselves through political and economic control of other nations

communism a hypothetical economic and political system in which all members of a society are socially equal

concept a mental construct that represents some part of the world, inevitably in a simplified form

concrete operational stage Piaget's term for the level of human development at which individuals first perceive causal connections in their surroundings

conglomerate a giant corporation composed of many smaller corporations

control holding constant all variables except one to see clearly the effect of that variable

corporate crime the illegal actions of a corporation or people acting on its behalf

corporation an organization with a legal existence, including rights and liabilities, apart from those of its members

correlation a relationship by which two (or more) variables change together

counterculture cultural patterns that strongly oppose those widely accepted within a society

credentialism evaluating a person on the basis of educational degrees

crime the violation of society's formally enacted criminal law

crimes against the person (violent crimes) crimes that direct violence or the threat of violence against others

crimes against property (property crimes) crimes that involve theft of property belonging to others

criminal justice system a formal response by police, courts, and prison officials to alleged violations of the law

criminal recidivism subsequent offenses by people convicted of crimes

critical sociology the study of society that focuses on the need for social change

crowd a temporary gathering of people who share a common focus of attention and who influence one another

crude birth rate the number of live births in a given year for every thousand people in a population

crude death rate the number of deaths in a given year for every thousand people in a population

cult a religious organization that is largely outside a society's cultural traditions

cultural integration the close relationship between various elements of a cultural system

cultural lag the fact that some cultural elements change more quickly than others, which may disrupt a cultural system

cultural relativism the practice of evaluating a culture by its own standards

cultural transmission the process by which one generation passes culture to the next

cultural universals traits that are part of every known culture

culture the values, beliefs, behavior, and material objects that, together, form a people's way of life

culture shock personal disorientation when experiencing an unfamiliar way of life

Davis-Moore thesis the assertion that social stratification has beneficial consequences for the operation of a society

deductive logical thought reasoning that transforms general theory into specific hypotheses suitable for testing

democracy a type of political system in which power is exercised by the people as a whole

demographic transition theory the thesis that population patterns reflect a society's level of technological development

demography the study of human population

denomination a church, independent of the state, that accepts religious pluralism

dependency theory a model of economic development that explains global inequality in terms of the historical exploitation of poor societies by rich ones

dependent variable a variable that is changed by another (independent) variable

descent the system by which members of a society trace kinship over generations

deterrence the attempt to discourage criminality through punishment

deviance the recognized violation of cultural norms

direct-fee system a medical care system in which patients pay directly for the services of physicians and hospitals

discrimination any action that involves treating various categories of people unequally

disengagement theory the idea that society enhances its orderly operation by disengaging people from positions of responsibility as they reach old age

division of labor specialization of economic activity

dramaturgical analysis Erving Goffman's term for the study of social interaction in terms of theatrical performance

dyad a social group with two members

dysfunction (*see* social dysfunction)

eating disorder an intense form of dieting or other unhealthy method of weight control driven by the desire to be very thin

ecologically sustainable culture a way of life that meets the needs of the present generation without threatening the environmental legacy of future generations

ecology the study of the interaction of living organisms and the natural environment

economy the social institution that organizes a society's production, distribution, and consumption of goods and services

ecosystem a system composed of the interaction of all living organisms and their natural environment

education the social institution through which society provides its members with important knowledge, including basic facts, job skills, and cultural norms and values

ego Freud's designation for a person's conscious efforts to balance innate pleasure-seeking drives with the demands of society

empirical evidence information we can verify with our senses

endogamy marriage between people of the same social category

environmental deficit profound and long-term harm to the natural environment caused by humanity's focus on short-term material affluence

environmental racism the pattern by which environmental hazards are greatest for poor people, especially minorities

ethnicity a shared cultural heritage

ethnocentrism the practice of judging another culture by the standards of one's own culture

ethnomethodology Harold Garfinkel's term for the study of the way people make sense of their everyday surroundings

Eurocentrism the dominance of European (especially English) cultural patterns

euthanasia (mercy killing) assisting in the death of a person suffering from an incurable disease

exogamy marriage between people of different social categories

experiment a research method for investigating cause and effect under highly controlled conditions

expressive leadership group direction that focuses on collective well-being

extended family (consanguine family) a family unit that includes parents and children as well as other kin

fad an unconventional social pattern that people embrace briefly but enthusiastically

faith belief anchored in conviction rather than scientific evidence

false consciousness Marx's term for explanations of social problems as the shortcomings of individuals rather than the flaws of society

family a social institution found in all societies that unites people into cooperative groups to oversee the bearing and raising of children

family unit a social group of two or more people, related by blood, marriage, or adoption, who usually live together

family violence emotional, physical, or sexual abuse of one family member by another

fashion a social pattern favored by a large number of people

feminism the advocacy of social equality for men and women, in opposition to patriarchy and sexism

feminization of poverty the trend by which women represent an increasing proportion of the poor

fertility the incidence of childbearing in a country's population

folkways norms for routine, casual interaction

formal operational stage Piaget's term for the level of human development at which individuals think abstractly and critically

formal organization a large secondary group organized to achieve its goals efficiently

functional illiteracy a lack of reading and writing skills needed for everyday living

fundamentalism a conservative religious doctrine that opposes intellectualism and worldly accommodation in favor of restoring traditional, otherworldly religion

Gemeinschaft a type of social organization by which people are closely tied by kinship and tradition

gender the personal traits and social positions that members of a society attach to being female and male

gender roles (sex roles) attitudes and activities that a society links to each sex

gender stratification the unequal distribution of wealth, power, and privilege between men and women

generalized other George Herbert Mead's term for the widespread cultural norms and values we use as a reference in evaluating ourselves

genocide the systematic annihilation of one category of people by another

gerontocracy a form of social organization in which the elderly have the most wealth, power, and prestige

gerontology the study of aging and the elderly

Gesellschaft a type of social organization by which people come together only on the basis of individual self-interest

global economy expanding economic activity with little regard for national borders

global perspective the study of the larger world and our society's place in it

global warming a rise in the Earth's average temperature caused by an increasing concentration of carbon dioxide and other gases in the atmosphere

gossip rumor about people's personal affairs

government a formal organization that directs the political life of a society

groupthink the tendency of group members to conform, resulting in a narrow view of some issue

hate crime a criminal act against a person or person's property by an offender motivated by racial or other bias

Hawthorne effect a change in a subject's behavior caused simply by the awareness of being studied

health a state of complete physical, mental, and social well-being

health maintenance organization (HMO) an organization that provides comprehensive medical care to subscribers for a fixed fee

hermaphrodite a human being with some combination of female and male genitalia

heterosexism a view stigmatizing anyone who is not heterosexual as "queer"

heterosexuality a sexual orientation in which a person is attracted to someone of the other sex

hidden curriculum subtle presentations of political or cultural ideas in the classroom

high culture cultural patterns that distinguish a society's elite

high-income countries nations with very productive economic systems in which most people have high incomes

holistic medicine an approach to health care that emphasizes prevention of illness and takes into account the person's entire physical and social environment

homogamy marriage between people with the same social characteristics

homophobia the dread of close personal interaction with people thought to be gay, lesbian, or bisexual

homosexuality a sexual orientation in which a person is attracted to someone of the same sex

horticulture the use of hand tools to raise crops

hunting and gathering the use of simple tools to hunt animals and gather vegetation

hypothesis an unverified statement of a relationship between variables

id Freud's designation for the human being's basic drives

ideal type an abstract statement of the essential characteristics of any social phenomenon

ideology cultural beliefs that justify social stratification

incest taboo a cultural norm forbidding sexual relations or marriage between certain relatives

income wages or salary from work and earnings from investments

independent variable a variable that causes change in another (dependent) variable

inductive logical thought reasoning that transforms specific observations into general theory

industrialism the production of goods using advanced sources of energy to drive large machinery

infant mortality rate the number of deaths among infants under one year of age for each thousand live births in a given year

infidelity sexual activity outside marriage

ingroup a social group commanding a member's esteem and loyalty

institutional prejudice and discrimination bias inherent in the operation of society's institutions

instrumental leadership group direction that emphasizes the completion of tasks

intergenerational social mobility upward or downward social mobility of children in relation to their parents

interpretive sociology the study of society that focuses on the meanings people attach to their social world

interview a series of questions a researcher administers in person to respondents

intragenerational social mobility a change in social position occurring during a person's lifetime

kinship a social bond based on blood, marriage, or adoption

labeling theory the assertion that deviance and conformity result not so much from what people do as from how others respond to those actions

labor unions organizations of workers that seek to improve wages and working conditions through various strategies, including negotiations and strikes

language a system of symbols that allows people to communicate with one another

latent functions the unrecognized and unintended consequences of any social pattern

liberation theology a fusion of Christian principles with political activism, often Marxist in character

life expectancy the average life span of a country's population

looking-glass self Cooley's term for a self-image based on how we think others see us

low-income countries nations with less productive economic systems in which most people are poor

macro-level orientation a broad focus on social structures that shape society as a whole

mainstreaming integrating special students into the overall educational program

manifest functions the recognized and intended consequences of any social pattern

marriage a legally sanctioned relationship, usually involving economic cooperation as well as sexual activity and childbearing, that people expect to be enduring

Marxist political-economy model an analysis that explains politics in terms of the operation of a society's economic system

mass behavior collective behavior among people dispersed over a wide geographic area

mass hysteria a form of dispersed collective behavior by which people react to a real or imagined event with irrational and even frantic fear

mass media impersonal communications aimed at a vast audience

mass society a society in which industry and bureaucracy have eroded traditional social ties

master status a status that has special importance for social identity, often shaping a person's entire life

material culture the tangible things created by members of a society

matriarchy a form of social organization in which females dominate males

matrilineal descent a system tracing kinship through women

matrilocality a residential pattern in which a married couple lives with or near the wife's family

measurement the process of determining the value of a variable in a specific case

mechanical solidarity Durkheim's term for social bonds, based on common sentiments and shared moral values, that are strong among members of preindustrial societies

medicalization of deviance the transformation of moral and legal deviance into a medical condition

medicine the social institution that focuses on combating disease and improving health

megalopolis a vast urban region containing a number of cities and their surrounding suburbs

meritocracy social stratification based on personal merit

metropolis a large city that socially and economically dominates an urban area

micro-level orientation a close-up focus on social interaction in specific situations

middle-income countries nations with moderately productive economic systems in which personal income is about the global average

migration the movement of people into and out of a specified territory

military-industrial complex the close association of the federal government, the military, and defense industries

minority any category of people, distinguished by physical or cultural difference, that a society sets apart and subordinates

miscegenation biological reproduction by partners of different racial categories

mob a highly emotional crowd that pursues a violent or destructive goal

modernity social patterns resulting from industrialization

modernization the process of social change begun by industrialization

modernization theory a model of economic and social development that explains global inequality in terms of technological and cultural differences between societies

monarchy a type of political system in which a single family rules from generation to generation

monogamy marriage uniting two partners

monopoly domination of a market by a single producer

monotheism belief in a single divine power

mores norms that are widely observed and have great moral significance

mortality the incidence of death in a country's population

multiculturalism an educational program recognizing the cultural diversity of the United States and promoting the equality of all cultural traditions

multinational corporation a large business that operates in many countries

natural environment the Earth's surface and atmosphere, including living organisms as well as the air, water, soil, and other resources necessary to sustain life

neocolonialism a new form of global power relationships that involves not direct political control but economic exploitation by multinational corporations

neolocality a residential pattern in which a married couple lives apart from both sets of parents

network a web of weak social ties

nonmaterial culture the intangible world of ideas created by members of a society

nonverbal communication communication using body movements, gestures, and facial expressions rather than speech

norms rules and expectations by which a society guides the behavior of its members

nuclear family (conjugal family) a family unit composed of one or two parents and their children

nuclear proliferation the acquisition of nuclear-weapons technology by more and more nations

objectivity a state of personal neutrality in conducting research

oligarchy the rule of the many by the few

oligopoly domination of a market by a few producers

operationalizing a variable specifying exactly what one is to measure before assigning a value to a variable

organic solidarity Durkheim's term for social bonds based on specialization and interdependence that are strong among members of industrial societies

organizational environment a range of factors outside an organization that affect its operation

organized crime a business supplying illegal goods or services

other-directedness a receptiveness to the latest trends and fashions, often expressed by imitating others

outgroup a social group toward which one feels competition or opposition

panic a form of localized collective behavior by which people react to a threat or other stimulus with irrational, frantic, and often self-destructive behavior

paradigm (*see* theoretical paradigm)

participant observation a method in which investigators systematically observe people while joining in their routine activities

pastoralism the domestication of animals

patriarchy a form of social organization in which males dominate females

patrilineal descent a system tracing kinship through men

patrilocality a residential pattern in which a married couple lives with or near the husband's family

peer group a social group whose members have interests, social position, and age in common

personality a person's fairly consistent patterns of acting, thinking, and feeling

personal space the surrounding area over which a person makes some claim to privacy

plea bargaining a legal negotiation in which a prosecutor reduces a charge in exchange for a defendant's guilty plea

pluralism a state in which racial and ethnic minorities are distinct but have social parity

pluralist model an analysis of politics that sees power as dispersed among many competing interest groups

political action committee (PAC) an organization formed by a special-interest group, independent of political parties, to pursue political aims by raising and spending money

political revolution the overthrow of one political system in order to establish another

politics the social institution that distributes power, sets a society's agenda, and makes decisions

polyandry marriage uniting one female and two or more males

polygamy marriage uniting three or more people

polygyny marriage uniting one male and two or more females

polytheism belief in many gods

popular culture cultural patterns that are widespread among a society's population

population the people who are the focus of research

pornography sexually explicit material that causes sexual arousal

positivism a way of understanding based on science

postindustrial economy a productive system based on service work and high technology

postindustrialism technology that supports an information-based economy

postmodernity social patterns characteristic of postindustrial societies

power the ability to achieve desired ends despite resistance from others

power-elite model an analysis of politics that sees power as concentrated among the rich

prejudice a rigid and irrational generalization about an entire category of people

preoperational stage Piaget's term for the level of human development at which individuals first use language and other symbols

presentation of self an individual's effort to create specific impressions in the minds of others

primary group a small social group whose members share personal and enduring relationships

primary labor market jobs that provide extensive benefits to workers

primary sector the part of the economy that draws raw materials from the natural environment

primary sex characteristics the genitals, organs used for reproduction

profane that which people define as an ordinary element of everyday life

profession a prestigious, white-collar occupation that requires extensive formal education

proletarians people who sell their productive labor for wages

propaganda information presented with the intention of shaping public opinion

prostitution the selling of sexual services

public opinion widespread attitudes about controversial issues

queer theory a growing body of knowledge that challenges a perceived heterosexual bias in sociology

questionnaire a series of written questions a researcher presents to subjects

race a socially constructed category composed of people who share biologically transmitted traits that members of a society consider important

racism the belief that one racial category is innately superior or inferior to another

rain forests regions of dense forestation, most of which circle the globe close to the equator

rationality deliberate, matter-of-fact calculation of the most efficient means to accomplish a particular task

rationalization of society Weber's term for the historical change from tradition to rationality as the dominant mode of human thought

rational-legal authority (also **bureaucratic authority**) power legitimized by legally enacted rules and regulations

reference group a social group that serves as a point of reference in making evaluations and decisions

rehabilitation a program for reforming the offender to prevent subsequent offenses

relative deprivation a perceived disadvantage arising from a specific comparison

FLAHERTY, MICHAEL G. "A Formal Approach to the Study of Amusement in Social Interaction." *Studies in Symbolic Interaction.* Vol. 5. New York: JAI Press, 1984:71–82.

———. "Two Conceptions of the Social Situation: Some Implications of Humor." *The Sociological Quarterly.* Vol. 31, No. 1 (Spring 1990).

FLORIDA, RICHARD, and MARTIN KENNEY. "Transplanted Organizations: The Transfer of Japanese Industrial Organization to the U.S." *American Sociological Review.* Vol. 56, No. 3 (June 1991):381–98.

FLYNN, PATRICIA. "The Disciplinary Emergence of Bioethics and Bioethics Committees: Moral Ordering and its Legitimation." *Sociological Focus.* Vol. 24, No. 2 (May 1991):145–56.

FOBES, RICHARD. "Creative Problem Solving." *The Futurist.* Vol. 30, No. 1 (January–February 1996):19–22.

FONDA, DAREN. "The Male Minority." *Time.* Vol. 156, No. 24 (December 11, 2000):58–60.

FORBES. "The Forbes Four Hundred." [Online] Available October 6, 2001, at http://www.forbes.com/2001/09/27/400.html

FORD, CLELLAN S., and FRANK A. BEACH. *Patterns of Sexual Behavior.* New York: Harper & Row, 1951.

FORREST, HUGH. "They Are Completely Inactive . . ." *The Gambier Journal.* Vol. 3, No. 4 (February 1984):10–11.

FORSTMANN, THEODORE J. "A Competitive Vision for American Education." *Imprimis.* Vol. 28, No. 9 (September 1999):1–4.

FOST, DAN. "American Indians in the 1990s." *American Demographics.* Vol. 13, No. 12 (December 1991):26–34.

FOUCAULT, MICHEL. *The History of Sexuality: An Introduction.* Vol. 1, trans. Robert Hurley. New York: Vintage, 1990; orig. 1978.

FRANK, ANDRÉ GUNDER. *On Capitalist Underdevelopment.* Bombay: Oxford University Press, 1975.

———. *Crisis: In the World Economy.* New York: Holmes & Meier, 1980.

———. *Reflections on the World Economic Crisis.* New York: Monthly Review Press, 1981.

FRANK, JOHN DAVID, JOHN W. MEYER, and DAVID MIYAHARA. "The Individualist Polity and the Prevalence of a Professionalized Psychology: A Cross-National Study." *American Sociological Review.* Vol. 60, No. 3 (June 1995):360–77.

FRANKLIN, JOHN HOPE. *From Slavery to Freedom: A History of Negro Americans.* 3d ed. New York: Vintage Books, 1967.

FRANKLIN ASSOCIATES. *Characterization of Municipal Solid Waste in the United States, 1960–2000.* Prairie Village, Kans.: Franklin Associates, 1986.

FRAZIER, E. FRANKLIN. *Black Bourgeoisie: The Rise of a New Middle Class.* New York: Free Press, 1965.

FREDRICKSON, GEORGE M. *White Supremacy: A Comparative Study in American and South African History.* New York: Oxford University Press, 1981.

FREE, MARVIN D. "Religious Affiliation, Religiosity, and Impulsive and Intentional Deviance." *Sociological Focus.* Vol. 25, No. 1 (February 1992):77–91.

FREEDOM HOUSE. *Freedom in the World 2000–2001.* New York: Freedom House, 2001.

FRENCH, MARILYN. *Beyond Power: On Women, Men, and Morals.* New York: Summit Books, 1985.

FRIEDAN, BETTY. *The Fountain of Age.* New York: Simon & Schuster, 1993.

FRIEDMAN, MEYER, and RAY H. ROSENMAN. *Type A Behavior and Your Heart.* New York: Fawcett Crest, 1974.

FRIEDMAN, MILTON, and ROSE FRIEDMAN. *Free to Choose: A Personal Statement.* New York: Harcourt Brace Jovanovich, 1980.

FRIEDRICH, CARL J., and ZBIGNIEW BRZEZINSKI. *Totalitarian Dictatorship and Autocracy.* 2d ed. Cambridge, Mass.: Harvard University Press, 1965.

FRUM, DAVID, and FRANK WOLFE. "If You Gotta Get Sued, Get Sued in Utah." *Forbes.* Vol. 153, No. 2 (January 1994):70–73.

FRUMKIN, PETER. "Are Nonprofit CEOs Overpaid?" *The Public Interest.* Vol. 142 (Winter 2001):83–94.

FUCHS, VICTOR R. "Sex Differences in Economic Well-Being." *Science.* Vol. 232 (April 25, 1986):459–64.

FUGITA, STEPHEN S., and DAVID J. O'BRIEN. "Structural Assimilation, Ethnic Group Membership, and Political Participation among Japanese Americans: A Research Note." *Social Forces.* Vol. 63, No. 4 (June 1985):986–95.

FUJIMOTO, ISAO. "The Failure of Democracy in a Time of Crisis." In Amy Tachiki et al., eds., *Roots: An Asian American Reader.* Los Angeles: UCLA Asian American Studies Center, 1971:207–14.

FULLER, REX, and RICHARD SCHOENBERGER. "The Gender Salary Gap: Do Academic Achievement, Intern Experience, and College Major Make a Difference?" *Social Science Quarterly.* Vol. 72, No. 4 (December 1991):715–26.

FUREDI, FRANK. "New Britain: A Nation of Victims." *Society.* Vol. 35, No. 3 (April 1998):80–84.

FURSTENBERG, FRANK F., JR., and ANDREW CHERLIN. *Divided Families: What Happens to Children When Parents Part.* Cambridge, Mass.: Harvard University Press, 1991.

GABRIEL, TRIP. "Computers Help Unite Campuses but Also Drive Some Students Apart." *New York Times* (November 11, 1996).

GAGLIANI, GIORGIO. "How Many Working Classes?" *American Journal of Sociology.* Vol. 87, No. 2 (September 1981):259–85.

GAGNÉ, PATRICIA, and RICHARD TEWKSBURY. "Conformity Pressures and Gender Resistance among Transgendered Individuals." *Social Problems.* Vol. 45, No. 1 (February 1998):81–101.

GAGNÉ, PATRICIA, RICHARD TEWKSBURY, and DEANNA MCGAUGHEY. "Coming Out and Crossing Over: Identity Formation and Proclamation in a Transgender Community." *Gender and Society.* Vol. 11, No. 4 (August 1997):478–508.

GALLAGHER, MAGGIE. "Does Bradley Know What Poverty Is?" *The New York Post* (October 28, 1999):37.

GALLUP. Poll results reported in "Numbers," *Time,* Vol. 155, No. 9 (February 28, 2000):25.

GALSTER, GEORGE. "Black Suburbanization: Has It Changed the Relative Location of Races?" *Urban Affairs Quarterly.* Vol. 26, No. 4 (June 1991):621–28.

GAMBLE, ANDREW, STEVE LUDLAM, and DAVID BAKER. "Britain's Ruling Class." *The Economist.* Vol. 326, No. 7795 (January 23, 1993):10.

GAMORAN, ADAM. "The Variable Effects of High-School Tracking." *American Sociological Review.* Vol. 57, No. 6 (December 1992):812–28.

GAMSON, WILLIAM A. "Beyond the Science-versus-Advocacy Distinction." *Contemporary Sociology.* Vol. 28, No. 1 (January 1999):23–26.

GANLEY, ELAINE. "Among Islamic Countries, Women's Roles Vary Greatly." *The Washington Times* (April 15, 1998):A13.

GANS, HERBERT J. *People and Plans: Essays on Urban Problems and Solutions.* New York: Basic Books, 1968.

———. *Deciding What's News: A Study of CBS Evening News, NBC Nightly News, Newsweek and Time.* New York: Vintage Books, 1980.

GARDNER, MARILYN. "At-Home Dads Give Their New Career High Marks." *Christian Science Monitor* (May 30, 1996):1, 12.

GARDYN, REBECCA. "Retirement Redefined." *American Demographics.* Vol. 22, No. 11 (November 2000):52–57.

GARFINKEL, HAROLD. "Conditions of Successful Degradation Ceremonies." *American Journal of Sociology.* Vol. 61, No. 2 (March 1956):420–24.

———. *Studies in Ethnomethodology.* Cambridge, Mass.: Polity Press, 1967.

GARREAU, JOEL. *Edge City.* New York: Doubleday, 1991.

GEERTZ, CLIFFORD. "Common Sense as a Cultural System." *The Antioch Review.* Vol. 33, No. 1 (Spring 1975):5–26.

GEIST, WILLIAM. *Toward a Safe and Sane Halloween and Other Tales of Suburbia.* New York: Times Books, 1985.

GELLES, RICHARD J., and CLAIRE PEDRICK CORNELL. *Intimate Violence in Families.* 2d ed. Newbury Park, Calif.: Sage, 1990.

GEORGE, SUSAN. *How the Other Half Dies: The Real Reasons for World Hunger.* Totowa, N.J.: Rowman & Allanheld, 1977.

GERBER, THEODORE P., and MICHAEL HOUT. "More Shock Than Therapy: Market Transition, Employment, and Income in Russia, 1991–1995." *American Journal of Sociology.* Vol. 104, No. 1 (July 1998):1–50.

GERLACH, MICHAEL L. *The Social Organization of Japanese Business.* Berkeley: University of California Press, 1992.

GERSTEL, NAOMI. "Divorce and Stigma." *Social Problems.* Vol. 43, No. 2 (April 1987):172–86.

GERTH, H. H., and C. WRIGHT MILLS, eds. *From Max Weber: Essays in Sociology.* New York: Oxford University Press, 1946.

GESCHWENDER, JAMES A. *Racial Stratification in America.* Dubuque, Iowa: Wm. C. Brown, 1978.

GEST, TED. "Law Schools' New Female Face." *U.S. News & World Report.* Vol. 130, No. 14 (April 9, 2001):76–77.

GEWERTZ, DEBORAH. "A Historical Reconsideration of Female Dominance among the Chambri of Papua New Guinea." *American Ethnologist.* Vol. 8, No. 1 (1981):94–106.

GIBBONS, DON C., and MARVIN D. KROHN. *Delinquent Behavior.* 4th ed. Englewood Cliffs, N.J.: Prentice Hall, 1986.

GIBBS, NANCY. "When Is It Rape?" *Time.* Vol. 137, No. 22 (June 3, 1991a):48–54.

———. "The Clamor on Campus." *Time.* Vol. 137, No. 22 (June 3, 1991b):54–55.

———. "How Much Should We Teach Our Children about Sex?" *Time.* Vol. 141, No. 21 (May 24, 1993):60–66.

———. "Cause Celeb." *Time.* Vol. 147, No. 25 (June 17, 1996):28–30.

———. "The Pulse of America Along the River." *Time.* Vol. 156, No. 2 (July 10, 2000):42–46.

———. "What Kids (Really) Need." *Time.* Vol. 157, No. 17 (April 30, 2001):48–49.

———. "If You Want to Humble an Empire." *Time.* September 11, 2001. Special issue.

GIDDENS, ANTHONY. *Sociology: A Brief but Critical Introduction.* New York: Harcourt Brace Jovanovich, 1982.

———. *The Transformation of Intimacy.* Cambridge, UK: Polity Press, 1992.

GIELE, JANET Z. "Gender and Sex Roles." In Neil J. Smelser, ed., *Handbook of Sociology.* Newbury Park, Calif.: Sage, 1988:291–323.

GIGLIOTTI, RICHARD J., and HEATHER K. HUFF. "Role Related Conflicts, Strains, and Stresses of Older-Adult College Students." *Sociological Focus.* Vol. 28, No. 3 (August 1995):329–42.

GILBERT, NEIL. "Realities and Mythologies of Rape." *Society.* Vol. 29, No. 4 (May–June 1992):4–10.

GILBERTSON, GRETA A., and DOUGLAS T. GURAK. "Broadening the Enclave Debate: The Dual Labor Market Experiences of Dominican and Colombian Men in New York City." *Sociological Forum.* Vol. 8, No. 2 (June 1993):205–20.

GILL, RICHARD T. "What Happened to the American Way of Death?" *The Public Interest.* Vol. 127 (Spring 1996):105–17.

GILLIARD, DARRELL K., and ALLEN J. BECK. *Prisoners in 1997.* Washington, D.C.: U.S. Bureau of Justice Statistics, 1998.

GILLIGAN, CAROL. *In a Different Voice: Psychological Theory and Women's Development.* Cambridge, Mass.: Harvard University Press, 1982.

———. *Making Connections: The Relational Worlds of Adolescent Girls at Emma Willard School.* Cambridge, Mass.: Harvard University Press, 1990.

GILLON, RAANAN. "Euthanasia in the Netherlands: Down the Slippery Slope?" *Journal of Medical Ethics.* Vol. 25, No. 1 (February 1999):3–4.

GIMENEZ, MARTHA E. "Silence in the Classroom: Some Thoughts about Teaching in the 1980s." *Teaching Sociology.* Vol. 17, No. 2 (April 1989):184–91.

GINSBURG, FAYE, and ANNA LOWENHAUPT TSING, eds. *Uncertain Terms: Negotiating Gender in American Culture.* Boston: Beacon Press, 1990.

GIOVANNINI, MAUREEN. "Female Anthropologist and Male Informant: Gender Conflict in a Sicilian Town." In John J. Macionis and Nijole V. Benokraitis, eds., *Seeing Ourselves: Classic, Contemporary, and Cross-Cultural Readings in Sociology*. 2d ed. Englewood Cliffs, N.J.: Prentice Hall, 1992:27–32.

GIROUX, GREGORY L. "GOP Maintains Thin Edge." *CQ Weekly*. Vol. 58, No. 44 (November 11, 2000):2652.

GIUGNI, MARCO G. "Structure and Culture in Social Movements Theory." *Sociological Forum*. Vol. 13, No. 2 (June 1998):365–75.

GLADUE, BRIAN A., RICHARD GREEN, and RONALD E. HELLMAN. "Neuroendocrine Response to Estrogen and Sexual Orientation." *Science*. Vol. 225, No. 4669 (September 28, 1984):1496–99.

GLASSNER, BARRY. *The Culture of Fear: Why Americans Are Afraid of the Wrong Things*. New York: Basic Books, 1999.

GLEICK, ELIZABETH. "The Marker We've Been Waiting For." *Time*. Vol. 149, No. 14 (April 7, 1997):28–42.

GLENN, NORVAL D., and BETH ANN SHELTON. "Regional Differences in Divorce in the United States." *Journal of Marriage and the Family*. Vol. 47, No. 3 (August 1985):641–52.

GLOCK, CHARLES Y. "The Religious Revival in America." In Jane Zahn, ed., *Religion and the Face of America*. Berkeley: University of California Press, 1959:25–42.

——. "On the Study of Religious Commitment." *Religious Education*. Vol. 62, No. 4 (1962):98–110.

GLUECK, SHELDON, and ELEANOR GLUECK. *Unraveling Juvenile Delinquency*. New York: Commonwealth Fund, 1950.

GNIDA, JOHN J. "Teaching 'Nature versus Nurture': The Case of African American Athletic Success." *Teaching Sociology*. Vol. 23, No. 4 (October 1995):389–95.

GODWIN, KENNETH, FRANK KEMERER, VALERIE MARTINEZ, and RICHARD RUDERMAN. "Liberal Equity in Education: A Comparison of Choice Options." *Social Science Quarterly*. Vol. 79, No. 3 (September 1998):502–22.

GOETTING, ANN. *Getting Out: Life Stories of Women Who Left Abusive Men*. New York: Columbia University Press, 1999.

GOFFMAN, ERVING. *The Presentation of Self in Everyday Life*. Garden City, N.Y.: Anchor Books, 1959.

——. *Asylums: Essays on the Social Situation of Mental Patients and Other Inmates*. Garden City, N.Y.: Anchor Books, 1961.

——. *Stigma: Notes on the Management of Spoiled Identity*. Englewood Cliffs, N.J.: Prentice Hall, 1963.

——. *Interactional Ritual: Essays on Face to Face Behavior*. Garden City, N.Y.: Anchor Books, 1967.

——. *Gender Advertisements*. New York: Harper Colophon, 1979.

GOLASH, TANYA. From "Proposed American Sociological Association Statement on Race." [Online] Available 2001 at http://www.unc.edu/~tatiana

GOLDBERG, STEVEN. *The Inevitability of Patriarchy*. New York: William Morrow, 1974.

——. Personal communication, 1987.

GOLDEN, FREDERIC. "Good Eggs, Bad Eggs." *Time*. Vol. 153, No. 1 (January 11, 1999a):56–59.

——. "Lying Faces Unmasked." *Time*. Vol. 153, No. 13 (April 5, 1999b):52.

GOLDEN, FREDERIC, and MICHAEL D. LEMONICK. "The Race Is Over." *Time*. Vol. 156, No. 1 (July 3, 2000):18–23.

GOLDFARB, WILLIAM. "Groundwater: The Buried Life." In F. Herbert Bormann and Stephen R. Kellert, eds., *Ecology, Economics, and Ethics: The Broken Circle*. New Haven, Conn.: Yale University Press, 1991:123–35.

GOLDFIELD, MICHAEL. "Rebounding Unions Target Service Sector." *Population Today*. Vol. 28, No. 7 (October 2000):3, 10.

GOLDSMITH, H. H. "Genetic Influences on Personality from Infancy." *Child Development*. Vol. 54, No. 2 (April 1983):331–35.

GOODE, ERICH. "No Need to Panic? A Bumper Crop of Books on Moral Panics." *Sociological Forum*. Vol. 15, No. 3 (September 2000):543–52.

GOODE, WILLIAM J. "The Theoretical Importance of Love." *American Sociological Review*. Vol. 24, No. 1 (February 1959):38–47.

——. "Encroachment, Charlatanism, and the Emerging Profession: Psychology, Sociology and Medicine." *American Sociological Review*. Vol. 25, No. 6 (December 1960):902–14.

GORDON, JAMES S. "The Paradigm of Holistic Medicine." In Arthur C. Hastings et al., eds., *Health for the Whole Person: The Complete Guide to Holistic Medicine*. Boulder, Colo.: Westview Press, 1980:3–27.

GORDON, SOL, and CRAIG W. SNYDER. *Personal Issues in Human Sexuality: A Guidebook for Better Sexual Health*. 2d ed. Boston: Allyn & Bacon, 1989.

GORING, CHARLES BUCKMAN. *The English Convict: A Statistical Study*. Montclair, N.J.: Patterson Smith, 1972; orig. 1913.

GORMAN, CHRISTINE. "Stressed Out Kids." *Time*. Vol. 156, No. 26 (December 25, 2000/January 1, 2001):168.

GORSKI, PHILIP S. "Historicizing the Secularization Debate: Church, State, and Society in Late Medieval and Early Modern Europe, ca. 1300 to 1700." *American Sociological Review*. Vol. 65, No. 1 (February 2000):138–67.

GOTHAM, KEVIN FOX. "Race, Mortgage Lending, and Loan Rejections in a U.S. City." *Sociological Focus*. Vol. 31, No. 4 (October 1998):391–405.

GOTTFREDSON, MICHAEL R., and TRAVIS HIRSCHI. "National Crime Control Policies." *Society*. Vol. 32, No. 2 (January–February 1995):30–36.

GOTTMANN, JEAN. *Megalopolis*. New York: Twentieth Century Fund, 1961.

GOUGH, KATHLEEN. "The Origin of the Family." *Journal of Marriage and the Family*. Vol. 33, No. 4 (November 1971):760–71.

——. "The Origin of the Family." In John J. Macionis and Nijole V. Benokraitis, eds., *Seeing Ourselves: Classic, Contemporary, and Cross-Cultural Readings in Sociology*. Englewood Cliffs, N.J.: Prentice Hall, 1989.

GOULD, STEPHEN J. "Evolution as Fact and Theory." *Discover* (May 1981):35–37.

GOULDNER, ALVIN. *The Coming Crisis of Western Sociology*. New York: Avon Books, 1970.

GRAHAM, JOHN W., and ANDREA H. BELLER. "Child Support in Black and White: Racial Differentials in the Award and Receipt of Child Support during the 1980s." *Social Science Quarterly*. Vol. 77, No. 3 (September 1996):528–42.

GRANT, DON SHERMAN, II, and MICHAEL WALLACE. "Why Do Strikes Turn Violent?" *American Journal of Sociology*. Vol. 96, No. 5 (March 1991):1117–50.

GRANT, DONALD L. *The Anti-Lynching Movement*. San Francisco: R & E Research Associates, 1975.

GRANT, KAREN R. "The Inverse Care Law in the Context of Universal Free Health Insurance in Canada: Toward Meeting Health Needs through Public Policy." *Sociological Focus*. Vol. 17, No. 2 (April 1984):137–55.

GRATETT, RYKEN. "Hate Crimes: Better Data or Increasing Frequency?" *Population Today*. Vol. 28, No. 5 (July 2000):1, 4.

GREELEY, ANDREW M. *Religious Change in America*. Cambridge, Mass.: Harvard University Press, 1989.

GREEN, GARY PAUL, LEANN M. TIGGES, and DANIEL DIAZ. "Racial and Ethnic Differences in Job-Search Strategies in Atlanta, Boston, and Los Angeles." *Social Science Quarterly*. Vol. 80, No. 2 (June 1999):263–90.

GREEN, JOHN C. "Pat Robertson and the Latest Crusade: Resources and the 1988 Presidential Campaign." *Social Sciences Quarterly*. Vol. 74, No. 1 (March 1993):156–68.

GREENBERG, DAVID F. *The Construction of Homosexuality*. Chicago: University of Chicago Press, 1988.

GREENFIELD, LAWRENCE A. *Child Victimizers: Violent Offenders and Their Victims*. Washington, D.C.: U.S. Bureau of Justice Statistics, 1996.

GREENHOUSE, LINDA. "Justices Uphold Stiffer Sentences for Hate Crimes." *New York Times* (June 12, 1993):1, 8.

GREENWALD, JOHN. "The New Service Class." *Time*. Vol. 144, No. 20 (November 14, 1994):72–74.

——. "School for Profit." *Time*. Vol. 155, No. 11 (March 20, 2000):56–57.

GREGORY, PAUL R., and ROBERT C. STUART. *Comparative Economic Systems*. 2d ed. Boston: Houghton Mifflin, 1985.

GROSS, JANE. "New Challenge of Youth: Growing Up in a Gay Home." *New York Times* (February 11, 1991):A1, B7.

GROTH, NICHOLAS A., and H. JEAN BIRNBAUM. *Men Who Rape: The Psychology of the Offender*. New York: Plenum, 1979.

GUP, TED. "What Makes This School Work?" *Time*. Vol. 140, No. 25 (December 21, 1992):63–65.

GURAK, DOUGLAS T., and JOSEPH P. FITZPATRICK. "Intermarriage among Hispanic Ethnic Groups in New York City." *American Journal of Sociology*. Vol. 87, No. 4 (January 1982):921–34.

GURNETT, KATE. "On the Forefront of Feminism." *Albany Times Union* (July 5, 1998):G-1, G-6.

GUSTAFASSON, BJORN, and MATS JOHANSSON. "In Search of Smoking Guns: What Makes Income Inequality Vary over Time in Different Countries?" *American Sociological Review*. Vol. 64, No. 4 (August 1999):585–605.

GWARTNEY-GIBBS, PATRICIA A. "The Institutionalization of Premarital Cohabitation: Estimates from Marriage License Applications, 1970 and 1980." *Journal of Marriage and the Family*. Vol. 48, No. 2 (May 1986):423–34.

GWYNNE, S. C., and JOHN F. DICKERSON. "Lost in the E-Mail." *Time*. Vol. 149, No. 15 (April 21, 1997):88–90.

HABERMAS, JÜRGEN. *Toward a Rational Society: Student Protest, Science, and Politics*. Jeremy J. Shapiro, trans. Boston: Beacon Press, 1970.

HACKER, HELEN MAYER. "Women as a Minority Group." *Social Forces*. Vol. 30 (October 1951):60–69.

——. "Women as a Minority Group: 20 Years Later." In Florence Denmark, ed., *Who Discriminates against Women?* Beverly Hills, Calif.: Sage, 1974:124–34.

HADAWAY, C. KIRK, PENNY LONG MARLER, and MARK CHAVES. "What the Polls Don't Show: A Closer Look at U.S. Church Attendance." *American Sociological Review*. Vol. 58, No. 6 (December 1993):741–52.

HADDEN, JEFFREY K., and CHARLES E. SWAIN. *Prime Time Preachers: The Rising Power of Televangelism*. Reading, Mass.: Addison-Wesley, 1981.

HAFNER, KATIE. "Making Sense of the Internet." *Newsweek* (October 24, 1994):46–48.

HAGAN, JACQUELINE MARIA. "Social Networks, Gender, and Immigrant Incorporation: Resources and Restraints." *American Sociological Review*. Vol. 63, No. 1 (February 1998):55–67.

HAGAN, JOHN, and PATRICIA PARKER. "White-Collar Crime and Punishment: The Class Structure and Legal Sanctioning of Securities Violations." *American Sociological Review*. Vol. 50, No. 3 (June 1985):302–16.

HAIG, ROBIN ANDREW. *The Anatomy of Humor: Biopsychosocial and Therapeutic Perspectives*. Springfield, Ill.: Charles C. Thomas, 1988.

HALBERSTAM, DAVID. *The Reckoning*. New York: Avon Books, 1986.

HALEDJIAN, DEAN. "How to Tell a Businessman from a Businesswoman." Annandale, Va.: Northern Virginia Community College, 1997.

HALL, JOHN R., and MARY JO NEITZ. *Culture: Sociological Perspectives*. Englewood Cliffs, N.J.: Prentice Hall, 1993.

HALL, KELLEY J., and BETSY LUCAL. "Tapping in Parallel Universes: Using Superhero Comic Books in Sociology Courses." *Teaching Sociology*. Vol. 27, No. 1 (January 1999):60–66.

HALLINAN, MAUREEN T. "The Sociological Study of Social Change." *American Sociological Review*. Vol. 62, No. 1 (February 1997):1–11.

HALLINAN, MAUREEN T., and RICHARD A. WILLIAMS. "Interracial Friendship Choices in Secondary Schools." *American Sociological Review*. Vol. 54, No. 1 (February 1989):67–78.

LORD, MARY. "Good Teachers, the Newest Imports." *U.S. News & World Report.* Vol. 130, No. 13 (April 9, 2001):54.

LORD, WALTER. *A Night to Remember.* Rev. ed. New York: Holt, Rinehart & Winston, 1976.

LORENZ, FREDERICK O., and BRENT T. BRUTON. "Experiments in Surveys: Linking Mass Class Questionnaires to Introductory Research Methods." *Teaching Sociology.* Vol. 24, No. 3 (July 1996):264–71.

LOVEMAN, MARA. "Is 'Race' Essential?" *American Sociological Review.* Vol. 64, No. 6 (December 1999):890–98.

LOVGREN, STEFEN. "Will All the Blue Men End Up in Timbuktu?" *U.S. News & World Report* (December 7, 1998):40.

LUBLIN, JOANN S. "Pay for No Performance." *Wall Street Journal* (April 22, 1998):R1.

LUKER, KRISTEN. *Abortion and the Politics of Motherhood.* Berkeley: University of California Press, 1984.

LUND, DALE A. "Conclusions about Bereavement in Later Life and Implications for Interventions and Future Research." In Dale A. Lund, ed., *Older Bereaved Spouses: Research with Practical Applications.* London: Taylor-Francis-Hemisphere, 1989:217–31.

———. "Caregiving." *Encyclopedia of Adult Development.* Phoenix, Ariz.: Oryx Press, 1993:57–63.

LUND, DALE A., MICHAEL S. CASERTA, and MARGARET F. DIMOND. "Gender Differences through Two Years of Bereavement among the Elderly." *The Gerontologist.* Vol. 26, No. 3 (1986):314–20.

LUNDMAN, RICHARD L. Correspondence to author, 1999.

LUNSFORD, JACK. Remarks at a meeting of the Arizona Task Force on the Western Virtual University. [Online] Available May 6, 1996, at http://www.acpe.asu.edu/VirtualU/

LUO, JAR-DER. "The Significance of Networks in the Initiation of Small Businesses in Taiwan." *Sociological Focus.* Vol. 12, No. 2 (June 1997):297–317.

LUTZ, CATHERINE A. *Unnatural Emotions: Everyday Sentiments on a Micronesia Atoll and Their Challenge to Western Theory.* Chicago: University of Chicago Press, 1988.

LUTZ, CATHERINE A., and GEOFFREY M. WHITE. "The Anthropology of Emotions." In Bernard J. Siegel, Alan R. Beals, and Stephen A. Tyler, eds., *Annual Review of Anthropology.* Palo Alto, Calif.: Annual Reviews, Vol. 15 (1986):405–36.

LYNCH, MICHAEL, and DAVID BOGEN. "Sociology's Asociological 'Core': An Examination of Textbook Sociology in Light of the Sociology of Scientific Knowledge." *American Sociological Review.* Vol. 62, No. 3 (June 1997):481–93.

LYND, ROBERT S. *Knowledge for What? The Place of Social Science in American Culture.* Princeton, N.J.: Princeton University Press, 1967.

LYND, ROBERT S., and HELEN MERRELL LYND. *Middletown in Transition.* New York: Harcourt, Brace & World, 1937.

LYNOTT, PATRICIA PASSUTH, and BARBARA J. LOGUE. "The 'Hurried Child': The Myth of Lost Childhood on Contemporary American Society." *Sociological Forum.* Vol. 8, No. 3 (September 1993):471–91.

MA, LI-CHEN. Personal communication, 1987.

MABRY, MARCUS. "New Hope for Old Unions?" *Newsweek* (February 24, 1992):39.

MABRY, MARCUS, and TOM MASLAND. "The Man after Mandela." *Newsweek* (June 7, 1999):54–55.

McADAM, DOUG. *Political Process and the Development of Black Insurgency, 1930–1970.* Chicago: University of Chicago Press, 1982.

———. "Tactical Innovation and the Pace of Insurgency." *American Sociological Review.* Vol. 48, No. 6 (December 1983):735–54.

———. *Freedom Summer.* New York: Oxford University Press, 1988.

———. "The Biographical Consequences of Activism." *American Sociological Review.* Vol. 54, No. 5 (October 1989):744–60.

———. "Gender as a Mediator of the Activist Experience: The Case of Freedom Summer." *American Journal of Sociology.* Vol. 97, No. 5 (March 1992):1211–40.

McADAM, DOUG, JOHN D. McCARTHY, and MAYER N. ZALD. "Social Movements." In Neil J. Smelser, ed., *Handbook of Sociology.* Newbury Park, Calif.: Sage, 1988:695–737.

———, eds. *Comparative Perspectives on Social Movements: Political Opportunities, Mobilizing Structures, and Cultural Framings.* Cambridge: Cambridge University Press, 1996.

McALLISTER, J. F. O. "Cinderella, Career Gal." *Time.* Vol. 157, No. 16 (April 23, 2001):8.

McBROOM, WILLIAM H., and FRED W. REED. "Recent Trends in Conservatism: Evidence of Non-Unitary Patterns." *Sociological Focus.* Vol. 23, No. 4 (October 1990):355–65.

McCARTHY, JOHN D., and MAYER N. ZALD. "Resource Mobilization and Social Movements: A Partial Theory." *American Journal of Sociology.* Vol. 82, No. 6 (May 1977):1212–41.

McCARTHY, TERRY. "Give Me Your Tired, Your Poor . . ." *Time.* Vol. 151, No. 4 (February 2, 1998):4.

MACCOBY, ELEANOR EMMONS, and CAROL NAGY JACKLIN. *The Psychology of Sex Differences.* Palo Alto, Calif.: Stanford University Press, 1974.

McCOLM, R. BRUCE, JAMES FINN, DOUGLAS W. PAYNE, JOSEPH E. RYAN, LEONARD R. SUSSMAN, and GEORGE ZARYCKY. *Freedom in the World: Political Rights & Civil Liberties, 1990–1991.* New York: Freedom House, 1991.

McCONNELL, SCOTT. "New Liberal Fear: Hyperdemocracy." *The New York Post* (January 18, 1995):19.

McCORMICK, NAOMI B. *Sexual Salvation.* Westport, Conn.: Praeger, 1994.

MacDONALD, J. FRED. *Blacks and White TV: African Americans in Television since 1948.* Chicago: Nelson-Hall, 1992.

McDONALD, KIM A. "Debate over How to Gauge Global Warming Heats Up Meeting of Climatologists." *Chronicle of Higher Education.* Vol. 45, No. 22 (February 5, 1999):A17.

MACE, DAVID, and VERA MACE. *Marriage East and West.* Garden City, N.Y.: Doubleday (Dolphin), 1960.

McGEARY, JOHANNA. "Nukes . . . They're Back." *Time.* Vol. 151, No. 20 (May 25, 1998):34–42.

McGUIRE, MEREDITH B. *Religion: The Social Context.* 2d ed. Belmont, Calif.: Wadsworth, 1987.

MACIONIS, JOHN J. "Intimacy: Structure and Process in Interpersonal Relationships." *Alternative Lifestyles.* Vol. 1, No. 1 (February 1978):113–30.

———. "A Sociological Analysis of Humor." Presentation to the Texas Junior College Teachers Association, Houston, 1987.

———. "Making Society (and, Increasingly, the World) Visible." In Earl Babbie, ed., *The Spirit of Sociology.* Belmont, Calif.: Wadsworth, 1993:221–24.

———. *Social Problems.* Upper Saddle River, N.J.: Prentice Hall, 2002.

MACIONIS, JOHN J., and LINDA GERBER. *Sociology: Third Canadian Edition.* Scarborough, Ontario: Prentice Hall Allyn & Bacon Canada, 2001.

———. *Sociology: Fourth Canadian Edition.* Scarborough, Ontario: Prentice Hall Allyn & Bacon Canada, 2002.

MACIONIS, JOHN J., and VINCENT R. PARRILLO. *Cities and Urban Life.* 2d ed. Upper Saddle River, N.J.: Prentice Hall, 2001.

MacKAY, JUDITH. *The Penguin Atlas of Human Sexual Behavior.* New York: Penguin Group, 2000.

McKEE, VICTORIA. "Blue Blood and the Color of Money." *New York Times* (June 9, 1996):49–50.

MACKLIN, ELEANOR D. "Nonmarital Heterosexual Cohabitation: An Overview." In Eleanor D. Macklin and Roger H. Rubin, eds., *Contemporary Families and Alternative Lifestyles: Handbook on Research and Theory.* Beverly Hills, Calif.: Sage, 1983:49–74.

McLEOD, JANE D., and MICHAEL J. SHANAHAN. "Poverty, Parenting, and Children's Mental Health." *American Sociological Review.* Vol. 58, No. 3 (June 1993):351–66.

McLEOD, JAY. *Ain't No Makin' It: Aspirations and Attainment in a Low-Income Neighborhood.* Boulder, Colo.: Westview Press, 1995.

McLUHAN, MARSHALL. *The Gutenberg Galaxy.* New York: New American Library, 1969.

McNEIL, DONALD G., JR. "Should Women Be Sent into Combat?" *New York Times* (July 21, 1991):E3.

McNULTY, PAUL J. "Who's in Jail and Why They Belong There." *Wall Street Journal* (November 9, 1994):A23.

McPHAIL, CLARK. *The Myth of the Maddening Crowd.* New York: Aldine, 1991.

McPHAIL, CLARK, and RONALD T. WOHLSTEIN. "Individual and Collective Behaviors within Gatherings, Demonstrations, and Riots." *Annual Review of Sociology.* Vol. 9. Palo Alto, Calif.: Annual Reviews, 1983:579–600.

MacPHERSON, KAREN. "Children Have a Full-Time Media Habit, Study Says." *Toledo Blade* (November 18, 1999):3.

McRAE, SUSAN. *Cross-Class Families: A Study of Wives' Occupational Superiority.* New York: Oxford University Press, 1986.

MADDOX, SETMA. "Organizational Culture and Leadership Style: Factors Affecting Self-Managed Work Team Performance." Paper presented at the annual meeting of the Southwest Social Science Association, Dallas, February 1994.

MADSEN, AXEL. *Private Power: Multinational Corporations for the Survival of Our Planet.* New York: William Morrow, 1980.

MAINES, DAVID R. "Charting Futures for Sociology: Culture and Meaning." *Contemporary Sociology.* Vol. 29, No. 4 (July 2000):577–84.

MALTHUS, THOMAS ROBERT. *First Essay on Population 1798.* London: Macmillan, 1926; orig. 1798.

MANZA, JEFF, and CLEM BROOKS. "The Religious Factor in U.S. Presidential Elections, 1960–1992." *American Journal of Sociology.* Vol. 103, No. 1 (July 1997):38–81.

———. "The Gender Gap in U.S. Presidential Elections: When? Why? Implications?" *American Journal of Sociology.* Vol. 103, No. 5 (March 1998):1235–66.

MARCUSE, HERBERT. *One-Dimensional Man.* Boston: Beacon Press, 1964.

MARE, ROBERT D. "Five Decades of Educational Assortative Mating." *American Sociological Review.* Vol. 56, No. 1 (February 1991):15–32.

MARÍN, GERARDO, and BARBARA VANOSS MARÍN. *Research with Hispanic Populations.* Newbury Park, Calif.: Sage, 1991.

MARINI, MARGARET MOONEY, and PI-LING FAN. "The Gender Gap in Earnings at Career Entry." *American Sociological Review.* Vol. 62, No. 4 (August 1997):588–604.

MARKLEIN, MARY BETH. "Optimism Rises as SAT Math Scores Hit 30-Year High." *USA Today* (August 30, 2000):1A.

MARKOFF, JOHN. "Remember Big Brother? Now He's a Company Man." *New York Times* (March 31, 1991):7.

MARKOVSKY, BARRY, JOHN SKVORETZ, DAVID WILLER, MICHAEL J. LOVAGLIA, and JEFFREY ERGER. "The Seeds of Weak Power: An Extension of Network Exchange Theory." *American Sociological Review.* Vol. 58, No. 2 (April 1993):197–209.

MARKSON, ELIZABETH W. "Moral Dilemmas." *Society.* Vol. 29, No. 5 (July–August 1992):4–6.

MARQUAND, ROBERT. "Worship Shift: Americans Seek Feeling of 'Awe'." *Christian Science Monitor* (May 28, 1997):1, 8.

MARQUAND, ROBERT, and DANIEL B. WOOD. "Rise in Cults as Millennium Approaches." *Christian Science Monitor* (March 28, 1997):1, 18.

MARSHALL, SUSAN E. "Ladies against Women: Mobilization Dilemmas of Antifeminist Movements." *Social Problems.* Vol. 32, No. 4 (April 1985):348–62.

MARTIN, JOHN M., and ANNE T. ROMANO. *Multinational Crime: Terrorism, Espionage, Drug and Arms Trafficking.* Newbury Park, Calif.: Sage, 1992.

MARTIN, RICHARD C. *Islam: A Cultural Perspective.* Englewood Cliffs, N.J.: Prentice Hall, 1982.

MARTINEZ, RAMIRO, JR. "Latinos and Lethal Violence: The Impact of Poverty and Inequality." *Social Problems.* Vol. 43, No. 2 (May 1996):131–46.

MARTINEZ, VALERIE J., R. KENNETH GODWIN, FRANK R. KEMERER, and LAURA PERNA. "The Consequences of School Choice: Who Leaves and Who Stays in the Inner City." *Social Science Quarterly.* Vol. 76, No. 1 (September 1995):485–501.

MARULLO, SAM. "The Functions and Dysfunctions of Preparations for Fighting Nuclear War." *Sociological Focus.* Vol. 20, No. 2 (April 1987):135–53.

MARX, GARY T., and JAMES L. WOOD. "Strands of Theory and Research in Collective Behavior." In Alex Inkeles et al., eds., *Annual Review of Sociology.* Vol. 1. Palo Alto, Calif.: Annual Reviews, 1975:363–428.

MARX, KARL. Excerpt from "A Contribution to the Critique of Political Economy." In Karl Marx and Friedrich Engels, *Marx and Engels: Basic Writings on Politics and Philosophy,* Lewis S. Feurer, ed. Garden City, N.Y.: Anchor Books, 1959:42–46.

———. *Karl Marx: Early Writings.* T. B. Bottomore, ed. New York: McGraw-Hill, 1964a.

———. *Karl Marx: Selected Writings in Sociology and Social Philosophy.* T. B. Bottomore, trans. New York: McGraw-Hill, 1964b.

———. *Capital.* Friedrich Engels, ed. New York: International Publishers, 1967; orig. 1867.

———. "Theses on Feuer." In Robert C. Tucker, ed., *The Marx-Engels Reader.* New York: Norton, 1972:107–9; orig. 1845.

MARX, KARL, and FRIEDRICH ENGELS. "Manifesto of the Communist Party." In Robert C. Tucker, ed., *The Marx-Engels Reader.* New York: Norton, 1972:331–62; orig. 1848.

———. *The Marx-Engels Reader.* 2d ed. Robert C. Tucker, ed. New York: Norton, 1978.

MARX, LEO. "The Environment and the 'Two Cultures' Divide." In James Rodger Fleming and Henry A. Gemery, eds., *Science, Technology, and the Environment: Multidisciplinary Perspectives.* Akron, Ohio: University of Akron Press, 1994:3–21.

MASSEY, DOUGLAS. "Housing Discrimination 101." *Population Today.* Vol. 28, No. 6 (August/September 2000):1, 4.

MASSEY, DOUGLAS S., and NANCY A. DENTON. "Hypersegregation in U.S. Metropolitan Areas: Black and Hispanic Segregation along Five Dimensions." *Demography.* Vol. 26, No. 3 (August 1989):373–91.

MASTERS, WILLIAM H., VIRGINIA E. JOHNSON, and ROBERT C. KOLODNY. *Human Sexuality.* 3d ed. Glenview, Ill.: Scott, Foresman/Little, Brown, 1988.

MATLOFF, JUDITH. "Nomadic 'Blue Men' of the Desert Try to Go Roam Again." *Christian Science Monitor* (September 9, 1997):7.

MATTHIESSEN, PETER. *Indian Country.* New York: Viking Press, 1984.

MAUER, MARC. "Americans behind Bars: U.S. and International Use of Incarceration 1995." [Online] Available April 1, 2000, at http://www.sentencingproject.org/pubs/tsppubs/9030data.html

MAURO, TONY. "Ruling Likely Will Add Fuel to Already Divisive Debate." *USA Today* (January 7, 1997):1A, 2A.

MAUSS, ARMAND L. *Social Problems of Social Movements.* Philadelphia: Lippincott, 1975.

MAYO, KATHERINE. *Mother India.* New York: Harcourt, Brace, 1927.

MEAD, GEORGE HERBERT. *Mind, Self, and Society.* Charles W. Morris, ed. Chicago: University of Chicago Press, 1962; orig. 1934.

MEAD, MARGARET. *Sex and Temperament in Three Primitive Societies.* New York: William Morrow, 1963; orig. 1935.

MEADOWS, DONELLA H., DENNIS L. MEADOWS, JORGAN RANDERS, and WILLIAM W. BEHRENS, III. *The Limits to Growth: A Report on the Club of Rome's Project on the Predicament of Mankind.* New York: Universe, 1972.

MELTZER, BERNARD N. "Mead's Social Psychology." In Jerome G. Manis and Bernard N. Meltzer, eds., *Symbolic Interaction: A Reader in Social Psychology.* 3d ed. Needham Heights, Mass.: Allyn & Bacon, 1978.

MELUCCI, ALBERTO. "The New Social Movements: A Theoretical Approach." *Social Science Information.* Vol. 19, No. 2 (May 1980):199–226.

———. *Nomads of the Present: Social Movements and Individual Needs in Contemporary Society.* Philadelphia: Temple University Press, 1989.

MENCKEN, F. CARSON, and IDEE WINFIELD. "Employer Recruiting and the Gender Composition of Jobs." *Sociological Focus.* Vol. 32, No. 2 (May 1999):210–20.

MENJIVAR, CECILIA. "Immigrant Kinship Networks and the Impact of the Receiving Context: Salvadorans in San Francisco in the Early 1990s." *Social Problems.* Vol. 44, No. 1 (February 1997):104–23.

MERGENHAGEN, PAULA. "Rethinking Retirement." *American Demographics.* Vol. 16, No. 6 (June 1994):28–34.

———. "Black-Owned Businesses." *American Demographics.* Vol. 18, No. 6 (June 1996a):24–27, 30–33.

———. "Sun City Gets Boomerized." *American Demographics.* Vol. 18, No. 8 (August 1996b):16–20.

———. "Her Own Boss." *American Demographics.* Vol. 18, No. 12 (December 1996c):37–41.

MERTON, ROBERT K. "Social Structure and Anomie." *American Sociological Review.* Vol. 3, No. 6 (October 1938):672–82.

———. *Social Theory and Social Structure.* New York: Free Press, 1968.

———. "Discrimination and the American Creed." In *Sociological Ambivalence and Other Essays.* New York: Free Press, 1976:189–216.

MEYER, DAVID S., and SUZANNE STAGGENBORG. "Movements, Countermovements, and the Structure of Political Opportunity." *American Journal of Sociology.* Vol. 101, No. 6 (May 1996):1628–60.

MEYER, DAVIS S., and NANCY WHITTIER. "Social Movement Spillover." *Social Problems.* Vol. 41, No. 2 (May 1994):277–98.

MICHELS, ROBERT. *Political Parties.* Glencoe, Ill.: Free Press, 1949; orig. 1911.

MILBRATH, LESTER W. *Envisioning A Sustainable Society: Learning Our Way Out.* Albany: State University of New York Press, 1989.

MILGRAM, STANLEY. "Behavioral Study of Obedience." *Journal of Abnormal and Social Psychology.* Vol. 67, No. 4 (1963):371–78.

———. "Group Pressure and Action against a Person." *Journal of Abnormal and Social Psychology.* Vol. 69, No. 2 (August 1964):137–43.

———. "Some Conditions of Obedience and Disobedience to Authority." *Human Relations.* Vol. 18 (February 1965):57–76.

———. "The Small World Problem." *Psychology Today.* Vol. 2 (1967):60–67.

MILIBAND, RALPH. *The State in Capitalist Society.* London: Weidenfeld & Nicolson, 1969.

MILLER, ARTHUR G. *The Obedience Experiments: A Case of Controversy in Social Science.* New York: Praeger, 1986.

MILLER, BERNA. "The Quest for Lifelong Learning." *American Demographics.* Vol. 19, No. 3 (March 1997a):20, 22.

———. "Population Update for April." *American Demographics.* Vol. 19, No. 4 (April 1997b):18.

MILLER, DAVID L. *Introduction to Collective Behavior.* Belmont, Calif.: Wadsworth, 1985.

MILLER, FREDERICK D. "The End of SDS and the Emergence of Weatherman: Demise through Success." In Jo Freeman, ed., *Social Movements of the Sixties and Seventies.* New York: Longman, 1983:279–97.

MILLER, G. TYLER, JR. *Living in the Environment: An Introduction to Environmental Science.* Belmont, Calif.: Wadsworth, 1992.

MILLER, WALTER B. "Lower Class Culture as a Generating Milieu of Gang Delinquency." In Marvin E. Wolfgang, Leonard Savitz, and Norman Johnston, eds., *The Sociology of Crime and Delinquency.* 2d ed. New York: Wiley, 1970:351–63; orig. 1958.

MILLET, KATE. *Sexual Politics.* Garden City, N.Y.: Doubleday, 1970.

MILLS, C. WRIGHT. *The Power Elite.* New York: Oxford University Press, 1956.

———. *The Sociological Imagination.* New York: Oxford University Press, 1959.

MINK, BARBARA. "How Modernization Affects Women." *Cornell Alumni News.* Vol. 3, No. 3 (April 1989):10–11.

MINTZ, BETH, and MICHAEL SCHWARTZ. "Interlocking Directorates and Interest Group Formation." *American Sociological Review.* Vol. 46, No. 6 (December 1981):851–69.

MIRINGOFF, MARC, and MARQUE-LUISA MIRINGOFF. "The Social Health of the Nation." *The Economist.* Vol. 352, No. 8128 (July 17, 1999):suppl. 6–7.

MIROWSKY, JOHN. "The Psycho-Economics of Feeling Underpaid: Distributive Justice and the Earnings of Husbands and Wives." *American Journal of Sociology.* Vol. 92, No. 6 (May 1987):1404–34.

MIROWSKY, JOHN, and CATHERINE ROSS. "Working Wives and Mental Health." Presentation to the American Association for the Advancement of Science, New York, 1984.

MOEN, PHYLLIS, DONNA DEMPSTER-McCLAIN, and ROBIN M. WILLIAMS. "Successful Aging: A Life-Course Perspective on Women's Multiple Roles and Health." *American Journal of Sociology.* Vol. 97 (May 1992):1612–38.

MOGELONSKY, MARCIA. "Reconfiguring the American Dream (House)." *American Demographics.* Vol. 19, No. 1 (January 1997):31–35.

MOLM, LINDA D. "Risk and Power Use: Constraints on the Use of Coercion in Exchange." *American Sociological Review.* Vol. 62, No. 1 (February 1997):113–33.

MOLOTCH, HARVEY. "The City as a Growth Machine." *American Journal of Sociology.* Vol. 82, No. 2 (September 1976):309–33.

MONTAGU, ASHLEY. *The Nature of Human Aggression.* New York: Oxford University Press, 1976.

MOORE, GWEN. "Structural Determinants of Men's and Women's Personal Networks." *American Sociological Review.* Vol. 55, No. 5 (October 1991):726–35.

———. "Gender and Informal Networks in State Government." *Social Science Quarterly.* Vol. 73, No. 1 (March 1992):46–61.

MOORE, JOAN, and HARRY PACHON. *Hispanics in the United States.* Englewood Cliffs, N.J.: Prentice Hall, 1985.

MOORE, WILBERT E. "Modernization as Rationalization: Processes and Restraints." In Manning Nash, ed., *Essays on Economic Development and Cultural Change in Honor of Bert F. Hoselitz.* Chicago: University of Chicago Press, 1977:29–42.

———. *World Modernization: The Limits of Convergence.* New York: Elsevier, 1979.

MORAN, JOHN S., S. O. ARAL, W. C. JENKINS, T. A. PETERMAN, and E. R. ALEXANDER. "The Impact of Sexually Transmitted Diseases on Minority Populations." *Public Health Reports.* Vol. 104, No. 6 (November–December 1989):560–65.

MORGAN, LAURIE A. "Glass Ceiling or Cohort Effect? A Longitudinal Study of the Gender Earnings Gap for Engineers, 1982 to 1989." *American Sociological Review.* Vol. 63, No. 4 (August 1998):479–93.

MORRIS, ALDON. "Black Southern Sit-In Movement: An Analysis of Internal Organization." *American Sociological Review.* Vol. 46, No. 6 (December 1981):744–67.

MORRIS, JIM, and MARIANNE LAVELLE. "Secret Data Reveal Why Tires Went Bad." *U.S. News & World Report.* Vol. 129, No. 12 (September 25, 2000):42–43.

MORRISON, DENTON E. "Some Notes toward Theory on Relative Deprivation, Social Movements, and Social Change." In Louis E. Genevie, ed., *Collective Behavior and Social Movements.* Itasca, Ill.: Peacock, 1978:202–9.

MOSLEY, W. HENRY, and PETER COWLEY. "The Challenge of World Health." *Population Bulletin.* Vol. 46, No. 4 (December 1991). Washington, D.C.: Population Reference Bureau.

MOUW, TED. "Job Relocation and the Racial Gap in Unemployment in Detroit and Chicago, 1980 to 1990." *American Sociological Review.* Vol. 65, No. 5 (October 2000):730–53.

MOYNIHAN, DANIEL PATRICK. "Toward a New Intolerance." *The Public Interest.* No. 112 (Summer 1993):119–22.

MUFSON, STEVEN. "China's Growing Inequality." *Washington Post* (January 1, 1997):A1, A26–A27.

MULFORD, MATTHEW, JOHN ORBELL, CATHERINE SHATTO, and JEAN STOCKARD. "Physical Attractiveness, Opportunity, and Success in Everyday Exchange." *American Journal of Sociology.* Vol. 106, No. 6 (May 1998):1565–92.

MUMFORD, LEWIS. *The City in History: Its Origins, Its Transformations, and Its Prospects.* New York: Harcourt, Brace & World, 1961.

MURDOCK, GEORGE PETER. "Comparative Data on the Division of Labor by Sex." *Social Forces.* Vol. 15, No. 4 (May 1937):551–53.

———. "The Common Denominator of Cultures." In Ralph Linton, ed., *The Science of Man in World Crisis.* New York: Columbia University Press, 1945:123–42.

———. *Social Structure.* New York: Free Press, 1965; orig. 1949.

MURRAY, CHARLES. *Losing Ground: American Social Policy 1950–1980.* New York: Basic Books, 1984.

———. "Keeping Priorities Straight on Welfare Reform." *Society.* Vol. 33, No. 5 (July/August 1996):10–12.

MURRAY, STEPHEN O., and WILL ROSCOE, eds. *Studies of African Homosexualities.* New York: St. Martin's Press, 1998.

MUTCHLER, JAN E. "Living Arrangements and Household Transitions among the Unmarried in Later Life." *Social Science Quarterly.* Vol. 73 (Spring 1992):565–80.

MYERS, NORMAN. "Humanity's Growth." In Sir Edmund Hillary, ed., *Ecology 2000: The Changing Face of the Earth.* New York: Beaufort Books, 1984a:16–35.

———. "The Mega-Extinction of Animals and Plants." In Sir Edmund Hillary, ed., *Ecology 2000: The Changing Face of the Earth.* New York: Beaufort Books, 1984b:82–107.

———. "Disappearing Cultures." In Sir Edmund Hillary, ed., *Ecology 2000: The Changing Face of the Earth.* New York: Beaufort Books, 1984c:162–69.

———. "Biological Diversity and Global Security." In F. Herbert Bormann and Stephen R. Kellert, eds., *Ecology, Economics, and Ethics: The Broken Circle.* New Haven, Conn.: Yale University Press, 1991:11–25.

MYERS, SHEILA, and HAROLD G. GRASMICK. "The Social Rights and Responsibilities of Pregnant Women: An Application of Parsons' Sick Role Model." Paper presented to the Southwestern Sociological Association, Little Rock, Arkansas, March 1989.

MYERSON, ALLEN R. "This Man Wants to Bury You." *New York Times* (August 1, 1993):section 3, pp. 1, 6.

MYRDAL, GUNNAR. *An American Dilemma: The Negro Problem and Modern Democracy.* New York: Harper & Brothers, 1944.

NAGEL, JOANE. "Constructing Ethnicity: Creating and Recreating Ethnic Identity and Culture." *Social Problems.* Vol. 41, No. 1 (February 1994):152–76.

———. *American Indian Ethnic Renewal: Red Power and the Resurgence of Identity and Culture.* New York: Oxford University Press, 1996.

NAJAFIZADEH, MEHRANGIZ, and LEWIS A. MENNERICK. "Sociology of Education or Sociology of Ethnocentrism: The Portrayal of Education in Introductory Sociology Textbooks." *Teaching Sociology.* Vol. 20, No. 3 (July 1992):215–21.

NASH, J. MADELEINE. "To Know Your Own Fate." *Time.* Vol. 145, No. 14 (April 3, 1995):62.

NATIONAL COMMISSION ON EXCELLENCE IN EDUCATION. *A Nation at Risk.* Washington, D.C.: U.S. Government Printing Office, 1983.

NAVARRO, MIREYA. "Puerto Rican Presence Wanes in New York." *The New York Times* (February 28, 2000):A1, A20.

NEERGAARD, LAUREN. "Cigarette Smoking Jumps 28% on Campus." *Bowling Green Sentinel Tribune* (November 18, 1998):9.

NELAN, BRUCE W. "Crimes without Punishment." *Time.* Vol. 141, No. 2 (January 11, 1993):21.

NELSON, AMY L. "The Effect of Economic Restructuring on Family Poverty in the Industrial Heartland, 1970–1990." *Sociological Focus.* Vol. 31 No. 2 (May 1998):201–16.

NELSON, JOEL I. "Work and Benefits: The Multiple Problems of Service Sector Employment." *Social Problems.* Vol. 42, No. 2 (May 1994):240–55.

NESBITT, PAULA D. *Feminization of the Clergy in America: Occupational and Organizational Perspectives.* New York: Oxford University Press, 1997.

NESSMAN, RAVI. "Stampede at Soccer Match Kills 47." Associated Press news report, April 11, 2001. [Online]. Accessed at http://www.dailynews.yahoo.com

NEUGARTEN, BERNICE L. "Grow Old with Me. The Best Is Yet to Be." *Psychology Today.* Vol. 5 (December 1971):45–48, 79, 81.

———. "Personality and the Aging Process." *The Gerontologist.* Vol. 12, No. 1 (Spring 1972):9–15.

———. "Personality and Aging." In James E. Birren and K. Warner Schaie, eds., *Handbook of the Psychology of Aging.* New York: Van Nostrand Reinhold, 1977:626–49.

NEUHOUSER, KEVIN. "The Radicalization of the Brazilian Catholic Church in Comparative Perspective." *American Sociological Review.* Vol. 54, No. 2 (April 1989):233–44.

NEUMAN, W. LAURENCE. *Social Research Methods: Qualitative and Quantitative Approaches.* 3d ed. Boston: Allyn & Bacon, 1997.

NEWMAN, KATHERINE S. *Declining Fortunes: The Withering of the American Dream.* New York: Basic Books, 1993.

NEWMAN, WILLIAM M. *American Pluralism: A Study of Minority Groups and Social Theory.* New York: Harper & Row, 1973.

NFWBO. NATIONAL FOUNDATION FOR WOMEN BUSINESS OWNERS. "Women Business Owners Economic Impact Re-Affirmed." [Online] Accessed in 1996 at http:www.nfwbo.org/nfwbo

NIELSEN, A. C. Survey data cited in *Information Please Almanac 1997.* Boston: Houghton Mifflin, 1997.

NIELSEN, FRANCOIS, and ARTHUR S. ALDERSON. "The Kuznets Curve: The Great U-Turn: Income Inequality in U.S. Counties, 1970 to 1990." *American Sociological Review.* Vol. 62, No. 1 (February 1997):12–33.

NIELSEN, JOYCE MCCARL, ed. *Feminist Research Methods: Exemplary Readings in the Social Sciences.* Boulder, Colo.: Westview Press, 1990.

1991 Green Book. U.S. House of Representatives. Washington, D.C.: U.S. Government Printing Office, 1991.

NISBET, ROBERT A. *The Sociological Tradition.* New York: Basic Books, 1966.

———. *The Quest for Community.* New York: Oxford University Press, 1969.

NOCK, STEVEN L., JAMES D. WRIGHT, and LAURA SANCHEZ. "America's Divorce Problem." *Society.* Vol. 36, No. 4 (May/June 1999):43–52.

NOLAN, PATRICK and GERHARD LENSKI. *Human Societies: An Introduction to Macrosociology.* 8th ed. New York: McGraw-Hill, 1999.

NORBECK, EDWARD. "Class Structure." In *Kodansha Encyclopedia of Japan.* Tokyo: Kodansha, 1983:322–25.

NORC. *General Social Surveys, 1972–2000: Cumulative Codebook.* Chicago: National Opinion Research Center, 2001.

NORD, MARK. "Does It Cost Less to Live in Rural Areas? Evidence from New Data on Food Scarcity and Hunger." *Rural Sociology.* Vol. 65, No. 1 (March 2000):104–25.

NOVAK, VIVECA. "The Cost of Poor Advice." *Time.* Vol. 154, No. 1 (July 5, 1999):38.

NUNN, CLYDE Z., HARRY J. CROCKETT, JR., and J. ALLEN WILLIAMS, JR. *Tolerance for Nonconformity.* San Francisco: Jossey-Bass, 1978.

OAKES, JEANNIE. "Classroom Social Relationships: Exploring the Bowles and Gintis Hypothesis." *Sociology of Education.* Vol. 55, No. 4 (October 1982):197–212.

———. *Keeping Track: How High Schools Structure Inequality.* New Haven, Conn.: Yale University Press, 1985.

OBERSCHALL, ANTHONY. *Social Conflict and Social Movements.* Englewood Cliffs, N.J.: Prentice Hall, 1973.

O'BRIEN, DAVID J., EDWARD W. HASSINGER, and LARRY DERSHEM. "Size of Place, Residential Stability, and Personal Social Networks." *Sociological Focus.* Vol. 29, No. 1 (February 1996):61–72.

O'CONNOR, RORY J. "Internet Declared Protected Speech." *Post-Star* (Glens Fall, N.Y.: June 27, 1997):A1–A2.

OGBURN, WILLIAM F. *On Culture and Social Change.* Chicago: University of Chicago Press, 1964.

O'HARE, WILLIAM P. "In the Black." *American Demographics.* Vol. 11, No. 11 (November 1989):25–29.

———. "The Rise of Hispanic Affluence." *American Demographics.* Vol. 12, No. 8 (August 1990):40–43.

———. "Managing Multiple-Race Data." *American Demographics.* Vol. 20, No. 4 (April 1998):42–44.

O'HARE, WILLIAM P., WILLIAM H. FREY, and DAN FOST. "Asians in the Suburbs." *American Demographics.* Vol. 16, No. 9 (May 1994):32–38.

O'HARE, WILLIAM P., and JAN LARSON. "Women in Business: Where, What, and Why." *American Demographics.* Vol. 13, No. 7 (July 1991):34–38.

OKRENT, DANIEL. "Raising Kids Online: What Can Parents Do?" *Time.* Vol. 154, No. 18 (May 10, 1999):38–43.

OLSEN, GREGG M. "Re-Modeling Sweden: The Rise and Demise of the Compromise in a Global Economy." *Social Problems.* Vol. 43, No. 1 (February 1996):1–20.

OLZAK, SUSAN. "Labor Unrest, Immigration, and Ethnic Conflict in Urban America, 1880–1914." *American Journal of Sociology.* Vol. 94, No. 6 (May 1989):1303–33.

OLZAK, SUSAN, and ELIZABETH WEST. "Ethnic Conflict and the Rise and Fall of Ethnic Newspapers." *American Sociological Review.* Vol. 56, No. 4 (August 1991):458–74.

ORLANSKY, MICHAEL D., and WILLIAM L. HEWARD. *Voices: Interviews with Handicapped People.* Columbus, Ohio: Merrill, 1981:85, 92, 133–34, 172.

ORSHANSKY, MOLLIE. "How Poverty Is Measured." *Monthly Labor Review.* Vol. 92, No. 2 (February 1969):37–41.

ORWIN, CLIFFORD. "All Quiet on the Western Front?" *The Public Interest.* Vol. 123 (Spring 1996): 3–9.

OSGOOD, D. WAYNE, JANET K. WILSON, PATRICK M. O'MALLEY, JERALD G. BACHMAN, and LLOYD D. JOHNSTON. "Routine Activities and Individual Deviant Behavior." *American Sociological Review.* Vol. 61, No. 4 (August 1996):635–55.

OSTRANDER, SUSAN A. "Upper Class Women: The Feminine Side of Privilege." *Qualitative Sociology.* Vol. 3, No. 1 (Spring 1980):23–44.

———. *Women of the Upper Class.* Philadelphia: Temple University Press, 1984.

OUCHI, WILLIAM. *Theory Z: How American Business Can Meet the Japanese Challenge.* Reading, Mass.: Addison-Wesley, 1981.

OWEN, DAVID. *None of the Above: Behind the Myth of Scholastic Aptitude.* Boston: Houghton Mifflin, 1985.

PAGE, SUSAN. "New Tactics Pushed in Terror War." *USA Today* (January 7, 2000):1A.

PAKULSKI, JAN. "Mass Social Movements and Social Class." *International Sociology.* Vol. 8, No. 2 (June 1993):131–58.

PALLONE, NATHANIEL J., and JAMES J. HENNESSY. "Brain Dysfunction and Criminal Violence." *Society.* Vol. 35, No. 6 (September–October 1998):20–27.

PALMORE, ERDMAN. "Predictors of Successful Aging." *The Gerontologist.* Vol. 19, No. 5 (October 1979):427–31.

————. "What Can the USA Learn from Japan about Aging?" In Steven H. Zarit, ed., *Readings in Aging and Death: Contemporary Perspectives.* New York: Harper & Row, 1982:166–69.

PARCEL, TOBY L., CHARLES W. MUELLER, and STEVEN CUVELIER. "Comparable Worth and Occupational Labor Market: Explanations of Occupational Earnings Differentials." Paper presented to the American Sociological Association, New York, 1986.

PARENTI, MICHAEL. *Inventing Reality: The Politics of the Mass Media.* New York: St. Martin's Press, 1986.

PARINI, JAY. "The Meaning of Emeritus." *Dartmouth Alumni Magazine* (July/August 2001):40–43.

PARK, ALICE. "Suffer the Children." *Time.* Vol. 156, No. 2 (July 10, 2000):99.

PARK, ROBERT E. *Race and Culture.* Glencoe, Ill.: Free Press, 1950.

PARRILLO, VINCENT N. "Diversity in America: A Sociohistorical Analysis." *Sociological Forum.* Vol. 9, No. 4 (December 1994):42–45.

PARROTT, JULIE. "The Effects of Culture on Eating Disorders." Paper presented to Southwestern Social Science Association, Dallas, Texas, March 1987.

PARSONS, TALCOTT. "Age and Sex in the Social Structure of the United States." *American Sociological Review.* Vol. 7, No. 4 (August 1942):604–16.

————. *Essays in Sociological Theory.* New York: Free Press, 1954.

————. *The Social System.* New York: Free Press, 1964; orig. 1951.

————. *Societies: Evolutionary and Comparative Perspectives.* Englewood Cliffs, N.J.: Prentice Hall, 1966.

PARSONS, TALCOTT, and ROBERT F. BALES, eds. *Family, Socialization and Interaction Process.* New York: Free Press, 1955.

PATTILLO-MCCOY, MARY. "Church Culture as a Strategy of Action in the Black Community." *American Sociological Review.* Vol. 63, No. 6 (December 1998):767–84.

PAUL, ELLEN FRANKEL. "Bared Buttocks and Federal Cases." *Society.* Vol. 28, No. 4 (May–June, 1991):4–7.

PEAR, ROBERT. "Women Reduce Lag in Earnings, but Disparities with Men Remain." *New York Times* (September 4, 1987):1, 7.

PEAR, ROBERT, and ERIK ECKHOLM. "When Healers Are Entrepreneurs: A Debate over Costs and Ethics." *New York Times* (June 2, 1991):1, 17.

PEARSON, DAVID E. "Post-Mass Culture." *Society.* Vol. 30, No. 5 (July–August 1993):17–22.

————. "Community and Sociology." *Society.* Vol. 32, No. 5 (July–August 1995):44–50.

PEASE, JOHN, and LEE MARTIN. "Want Ads and Jobs for the Poor: A Glaring Mismatch." *Sociological Forum.* Vol. 12. No. 4 (December 1997):545–64.

PERROLLE, JUDITH A. "Comments from the Special Issue Editor: The Emerging Dialogue on Environmental Justice." *Social Problems.* Vol. 40, No. 1 (February 1993):1–4.

PERSELL, CAROLINE HODGES. "The Interdependence of Social Justice and Civil Society." *Sociological Forum.* Vol. 12, No. 2 (June 1997):149–72.

PESSEN, EDWARD. *Riches, Class, and Power: America before the Civil War.* New Brunswick, N.J.: Transaction Books, 1990.

PETERS, TOM. "What Will We Do for Work?" *Time.* Vol. 155, No. 21 (May 22, 2000):68–71.

Peters Atlas of the World. New York: Harper & Row, 1990.

PETERSEN, TROND, ISHAK SAPORTA, and MARC-DAVID L. SEIDEL. "Offering a Job: Meritocracy and Social Networks." *American Journal of Sociology.* Vol. 106, No. 3 (November 2000):763–816.

PETERSILIA, JOAN. "Probation in the United States: Practices and Challenges." *National Institute of Justice Journal.* No. 233 (September 1997):4.

PETERSON, SCOTT. "Women Live on Own Terms behind the Veil." *Christian Science Monitor* (July 31, 1996):1, 10.

PHELAN, JO, BRUCE G. LINK, ANN STUEVE, and ROBERT E. MOORE. "Education, Social Liberalism, and Economic Conservatism: Attitudes toward Homeless People." *American Sociological Review.* Vol. 60, No. 1 (February 1995):126–40.

PHILADELPHIA, DESA. "Rookie Teacher, Age 50." *Time.* Vol. 157, No. 14 (April 9, 2001):66–68.

PHILIPSON, ILENE J., and KAREN V. HANSEN. "Women, Class, and the Feminist Imagination." In Karen V. Hansen and Ilene J. Philipson, eds., *Women, Class, and the Feminist Imagination: A Socialist-Feminist Reader.* Philadelphia: Temple University Press, 1992:3–40.

PHILLIPSON, CHRIS. *Capitalism and the Construction of Old Age.* London: Macmillan, 1982.

PICHARDO, NELSON A. "The Power Elite and Elite-Driven Countermovements: The Associated Farmers of California during the 1930s." *Sociological Forum.* Vol. 10, No. 1 (March 1995):21–49.

PIERCE, EMILY. "Momentum Swing." *C Q Weekly.* Vol. 58, No. 44 (Nov. 11, 2000):2646.

PILLEMER, KARL. "Maltreatment of the Elderly at Home and in Institutions: Extent, Risk Factors, and Policy Recommendations." In U.S. Congress. House, Select Committee on Aging and Senate, Special Committee on Aging. *Legislative Agenda for an Aging Society: 1988 and Beyond.* Washington, D.C.: U.S. Government Printing Office, 1988.

PINCHOT, GIFFORD, and ELIZABETH PINCHOT. *The End of Bureaucracy and the Rise of the Intelligent Organization.* San Francisco: Berrett-Koehler, 1993.

PINES, MAYA. "The Civilization of Genie." *Psychology Today.* Vol. 15 (September 1981):28–34.

PINHEY, THOMAS K., DONALD H. RUBINSTEIN, and RICHARD S. COLFAX. "Overweight and Happiness: The Reflected Self-Appraisal Hypothesis Reconsidered." *Social Science Quarterly.* Vol. 78, No. 3 (September 1997):747–55.

PIRANDELLO, LUIGI. "The Pleasure of Honesty." In *To Clothe the Naked and Two Other Plays.* New York: Dutton, 1962:143–98.

PIROG, MAUREEN A., and CHRIS MAGEE. "High School Completion: The Influence of Schools, Families, and Adolescent Parenting." *Social Science Quarterly.* Vol. 78, No. 3 (September 1997):710–24.

PITNEY, JOHN J., JR. "What Scholars Don't Know about Term Limits." *The Chronicle of Higher Education.* Vol. 41, No. 33 (April 28, 1995):A76.

PITT, MALCOLM. *Introducing Hinduism.* New York: Friendship Press, 1955.

PITTS, LEONARD, JR. "When a Win Sparks a Riot." *The Philadelphia Inquirer* (June 26, 2000):A11.

PIVEN, FRANCES FOX, and RICHARD A. CLOWARD. *Poor People's Movements: Why They Succeed, How They Fail.* New York: Pantheon Books, 1977.

PLOMIN, ROBERT, and TERRYL T. FOCH. "A Twin Study of Objectively Assessed Personality in Childhood." *Journal of Personality and Social Psychology.* Vol. 39, No. 4 (October 1980):680–88.

PODOLNY, JOEL M., and JAMES N. BARON. "Resources and Relationships: Social Networks and Mobility in the Workplace." *American Sociological Review.* Vol. 62, No. 5 (October 1997):673–93.

POHL, RUDIGER. "The Transition from Communism to Capitalism in East Germany." *Society.* Vol. 33, No. 4 (June 1996):62–65.

POLENBERG, RICHARD. *One Nation Divisible: Class, Race, and Ethnicity in the United States since 1938.* New York: Pelican Books, 1980.

POLLACK, ANDREW. "Happy in the East (^-^) or Smiling :-) in the West." *New York Times* (August 12, 1996).

————. "Overseas, Smoking Is One of Life's Small Pleasures." *New York Times* (August 17, 1997):E5.

POLLARD, KELVIN. "Play Ball! Demographics and Major League Baseball." *Population Today.* Vol. 24, No. 4 (April 1996a):3.

————. "Speaking Graphically: Per Capita Fresh Water Availability . . ." *Population Today.* Vol. 24, No. 12 (December 1996b):6.

POLLOCK, PHILIP H., III, and M. ELLIOT VITTAS. "Who Bears the Burdens of Environmental Pollution: Race, Ethnicity, and Environmental Equity in Florida." *Social Science Quarterly.* Vol. 76, No. 2 (June 1995):294–310.

POLSBY, NELSON W. "Three Problems in the Analysis of Community Power." *American Sociological Review.* Vol. 24, No. 6 (December 1959):796–803.

POMER, MARSHALL I. "Labor Market Structure, Intragenerational Mobility, and Discrimination: Black Male Advancement out of Low-Paying Occupations, 1962–1973." *American Sociological Review.* Vol. 51, No. 5 (October 1986):650–59.

PONIEWOZIK, JAMES. "Postnuclear Explosion." *Time.* Vol. 156, No. 19 (November 6, 2000):110–11.

POOLEY, ERIC. "The Great Escape." *Time.* Vol. 150, No. 24 (December 8, 1997):52–64.

POPENOE, DAVID. *Disturbing the Nest: Family Change and Decline in Modern Societies.* New York: Aldine, 1988.

————. "Family Decline in the Swedish Welfare State." *The Public Interest.* No. 102 (Winter 1991):65–77.

————. "The Controversial Truth: Two-Parent Families Are Better." *New York Times* (December 26, 1992):21.

————. "American Family Decline, 1960–1990: A Review and Appraisal." *Journal of Marriage and the Family.* Vol. 55, No. 3 (August 1993a):527–55.

————. "Parental Androgyny." *Society.* Vol. 30, No. 6 (September–October 1993b):5–11.

————. "Scandinavian Welfare." *Society.* Vol. 31, No. 6 (September–October, 1994):78–81.

————. "Can the Nuclear Family Be Revived?" *Society.* Vol. 36, No. 5 (July/August 1999):28–30.

POPENOE, DAVID, and BARBARA DAFOE WHITEHEAD. *Should We Live Together? What Young Adults Need to Know about Cohabitation before Marriage.* New Brunswick, N.J.: The National Marriage Project, 1999.

POPKIN, SUSAN J. "Welfare: Views from the Bottom." *Social Problems.* Vol. 17, No. 1 (February 1990):64–79.

POPULATION ACTION INTERNATIONAL. *People in the Balance: Population and Resources at the Turn of the Millennium.* Washington, D.C.: PAI, 2000.

POPULATION REFERENCE BUREAU. *2000 World Population Data Sheet.* Washington, D.C.: Population Reference Bureau, 2000.

————. *2001 World Population Data Sheet.* Washington, D.C.: Population Reference Bureau, 2001.

Population Today. "Majority of Children in Poverty Live with Parents Who Work." Vol. 23, No. 4 (April 1995):6.

PORTER, EDUARDO. "Even 126 Sizes Do Not Fit All." *The Wall Street Journal* (March 2, 2001):B1.

PORTES, ALEJANDRO, and LEIF JENSEN. "The Enclave and the Entrants: Patterns of Ethnic Enterprise in Miami before and after Mariel." *American Sociological Review.* Vol. 54, No. 6 (December 1989):929–49.

POSTEL, SANDRA. "Facing Water Scarcity." In Lester R. Brown et al., eds., *State of the World 1993: A Worldwatch Institute Report on Progress toward a Sustainable Society.* New York: Norton, 1993:22–41.

POWELL, CHRIS, and GEORGE E. C. PATON, eds. *Humour in Society: Resistance and Control.* New York: St. Martin's Press, 1988.

PRESS, ANDREA L. Review of *Enlightened Racism: "The Cosby Show," Audiences, and the Myth of the American Dream,* by Sut Jhally and Justin Lewis. *American Journal of Sociology.* Vol. 99, No. 1 (July 1993):219–21.

PRESSER, HARRIET B. "The Housework Gender Gap." *Population Today.* Vol. 21, No. 7/8 (July–August 1993):5.

PRESSLEY, SUE ANNE, and NANCY ANDREWS. "For Gay Couples, the Nursery Becomes the New Frontier." *Washington Post* (December 20, 1992):A1, A22–23.

PRESTON, LEE E. "Corporate Boards and Corporate Governance." *Society.* Vol. 32, No. 3 (March–April 1995):17–20.

PRIMEGGIA, SALVATORE, and JOSEPH A. VARACALLI. "Southern Italian Comedy: Old to New World." In Joseph V. Scelsa, Salvatore J. LaGumina, and Lydio Tomasi, eds., *Italian Americans in Transition*. New York: The American Italian Historical Association, 1990:241–52.

PRINDLE, DAVID F. *Risky Business: The Political Economy of Hollywood*. Boulder, Colo.: Westview Press, 1993.

PRINDLE, DAVID F., and JAMES W. ENDERSBY. "Hollywood Liberalism." *Social Science Quarterly*. Vol. 74, No. 1 (March 1993):136–49.

PUTERBAUGH, GEOFF, ed. *Twins and Homosexuality: A Casebook*. New York: Garland, 1990.

PUTKA, GARY. "SAT to Become a Better Gauge." *Wall Street Journal* (November 1, 1990):B1.

PUTKA, GARY, and STEVE STECKLOW. "Do For-Profit Schools Work? These Seem to for One Entrepreneur." *Wall Street Journal* (June 8, 1994):A1, A4.

QUEENAN, JOE. "The Many Paths to Riches." *Forbes*. Vol. 144, No. 9 (October 23, 1989):149.

QUINNEY, RICHARD. *Class, State and Crime: On the Theory and Practice of Criminal Justice*. New York: David McKay, 1977.

RABKIN, JEREMY. "The Supreme Court in the Culture Wars." *The Public Interest*. Vol. 125 (Fall 1996):3–26.

RALEY, R. KELLY. "A Shortage of Marriageable Men? A Note on the Role of Cohabitation in Black-White Differences in Marriage Rates." *American Journal of Sociology*. Vol. 61, No. 6 (December 1996):973–83.

RAMO, JOSHUA COOPER. "Finding God on the Web." *Time* (December 16, 1996):60–67.

RAPHAEL, RAY. *The Men from the Boys: Rites of Passage in Male America*. Lincoln: University of Nebraska Press, 1988.

RATAN, SUNEEL. "A New Divide between Haves and Have-Nots?" *Time*. Special Issue. Vol. 145, No. 12 (Spring 1995):25–26.

RATNESAR, ROMESH. "Lost in the Middle." *Time*. Vol. 152, No. 17 (September 14, 1998):60–62.

———. "Not Gone, but Forgotten?" *Time*. Vol. 153, No. 15 (February 8, 1999):30–31.

RAVITCH, DIANE, and JOSEPH VITERITTI. "A New Vision for City Schools." *The Public Interest*. Vol. 122 (Winter 1996):3–16.

RAY, PAUL H. "The Emerging Culture." *American Demographics*. Vol. 19, No. 2 (February 1997):29–34, 56.

RECKLESS, WALTER C., and SIMON DINITZ. "Pioneering with Self-Concept as a Vulnerability Factor in Delinquency." *Journal of Criminal Law, Criminology, and Police Science*. Vol. 58, No. 4 (December 1967):515–23.

RECTOR, ROBERT. "America Has the World's Richest Poor People." *Wall Street Journal* (September 24, 1998):A18.

REED, HOLLY E. "Kosovo and the Demography of Forced Migration." *Population Today*. Vol. 27, No. 6 (June 1999):4.

REICH, ROBERT B. "As the World Turns." *The New Republic* (May 1, 1989):23, 26–28.

———. *The Work of Nations: Preparing Ourselves for 21st-Century Capitalism*. New York: Alfred A. Knopf, 1991.

REIMAN, JEFFREY. *The Rich Get Richer and the Poor Get Prison: Ideology, Class, and Criminal Justice*. Boston: Allyn & Bacon, 1998.

REINGOLD, BETH, and RICHARD S. WIKE. "Confederate Symbols, Southern Identity, and Racial Attitudes: The Case of the Georgia State Flag." *Social Science Quarterly*. Vol. 79, No. 3 (September 1998):568–80.

REINHARZ, SHULAMIT. *Feminist Methods in Social Research*. New York: Oxford University Press, 1992.

REITZES, DONALD C., ELIZABETH J. MUTRAN, and MARIA E. FERNANDEZ. "The Decision to Retire: A Career Perspective." *Social Science Quarterly*. Vol. 79, No. 3 (September 1998):607–19.

REMOFF, HEATHER TREXLER. *Sexual Choice: A Woman's Decision*. New York: Dutton/Lewis, 1984.

REMY, JACQUELINE. "Interview with Agnes Fournier de Saint-Maur, Interpol Police Lieutenant." For *L'Express*. Reprinted in *World Press Review* (November 1996):7.

RESKIN, BARBARA F., and DEBRA BRANCH MCBRIER. "Why Not Ascription? Organizations' Employment of Male and Female Managers." *American Sociological Review*. Vol. 65, No. 2 (April 2000):210–33.

REYNOLDS, JOHN R., and CATHERINE E. ROSS. "Social Stratification and Health: Education's Benefit beyond Economic Status and Social Origins." *Social Problems*. Vol. 45, No. 2 (May 1998):221–45.

RHODES, STEVE. "The Luck of the Draw." *Newsweek* (April 26, 1999):41.

RICHARDSON, JAMES T. "Definitions of Cult: From Sociological-Technical to Popular Negative." Paper presented at the American Psychological Association, Boston, August 1990.

RICHE, MARTHA FARNSWORTH. "America's Diversity and Growth: Signposts for the 21st Century." *Population Bulletin*. Vol. 55, No. 2 (June 2000).

RIDDLE, JOHN M., J. WORTH ESTES, and JOSIAH C. RUSSELL. "Ever since Eve: Birth Control in the Ancient World." *Archaeology*. Vol. 47, No. 2 (March/April 1994):29–35.

RIDGEWAY, CECILIA L. *The Dynamics of Small Groups*. New York: St. Martin's Press, 1983.

RIDGEWAY, CECILIA L. and KRISTAN GLASGOW ERICKSON. "Creating and Spreading Status Beliefs." *American Journal of Sociology*. Vol. 106, No. 3 (November 2000):579–615.

RIESMAN, DAVID. *The Lonely Crowd: A Study of the Changing American Character*. New Haven, Conn.: Yale University Press, 1970; orig. 1950.

RILEY, MATILDA WHITE, ANNE FONER, and JOAN WARING. "Sociology of Age." In Neil J. Smelser, ed., *Handbook of Sociology*. Newbury Park, Calif.: Sage, 1988:243–90.

RILEY, NANCY E. "Gender, Power, and Population Change." *Population Bulletin*. Vol. 52, No. 1 (May 1997).

RIMER, SARA. "Blacks Carry Load of Care for Their Elderly." *The New York Times* (March 15, 1998):1, 22.

RITZER, GEORGE. *The McDonaldization of Society: An Investigation into the Changing Character of Contemporary Social Life*. Thousand Oaks, Calif.: Pine Forge Press, 1993.

———. *The McDonaldization of Society*. Revised ed. Thousand Oaks, Calif.: Sage, 1996.

———. *The McDonaldization Thesis: Explorations and Extensions*. Thousand Oaks, Calif.: Sage, 1998.

———. "The Globalization of McDonaldization." *The Spark* (February 2000):8–9.

RITZER, GEORGE, and DAVID WALCZAK. *Working: Conflict and Change*. 4th ed. Englewood Cliffs, N.J.: Prentice Hall, 1990.

RIVERA-BATIZ, FRANCISCO L., and CARLOS SANTIAGO, cited in Sam Roberts, "Puerto Ricans on Mainland Making Gains, Study Finds." *New York Times* (October 19, 1994):A20.

ROBERT, STEPHANIE A. "Socioeconomic Position and Health: The Independent Contribution of Community Socioeconomic Context." *Annual Review of Sociology*. Vol. 25 (1999):489–516.

ROBERTS, J. DEOTIS. *Roots of a Black Future: Family and Church*. Philadelphia: Westminster Press, 1980.

ROBERTS, STEVEN V. "Open Arms for Online Democracy." *U.S. News & World Report*. Vol. 118, No. 2 (January 16, 1995):10.

ROBINSON, DAWN. "Toward a Synthesis of Sociological and Psychological Theories of Eating Disorders." Paper presented to Southwestern Social Science Association, Dallas, Texas, March 1987.

ROBINSON, JOHN P., PERLA WERNER, and GEOFFREY GODBEY. "Freeing Up the Golden Years." *American Demographics*. Vol. 19, No. 10 (October 1997):20–24.

ROBINSON, JOYCE, and GLENNA SPITZE. "Whistle While You Work? The Effect of Household Task Performance on Women's and Men's Well-Being." *Social Science Quarterly*. Vol. 73, No. 4 (December 1992):844–61.

ROBINSON, THOMAS N., MARTA L. WILDE, LISA C. NAVRACRUZ, K. FARISH HAYDEL, and ANN VARADY. "Effects of Reducing Children's Television and Video Game Use on Aggressive Behavior." *Archives of Pediatrics and Adolescent Medicine*. Vol. 155 (January 2001):17–23.

ROBINSON, VERA M. "Humor and Health." In Paul E. McGhee and Jeffrey H. Goldstein, eds., *Handbook of Humor Research, Vol. II, Applied Studies*. New York: Springer-Verlag, 1983:109–28.

ROCHE, TIMOTHY. "A Psychotic Killer Sues His Psychiatrist." *Time*. Vol. 153, No. 15 (April 19, 1999):8.

ROCKETT, IAN R. H. "Population and Health: An Introduction to Epidemiology." *Population Bulletin*. Vol. 49, No. 3 (November 1994). Washington, D.C.: Population Reference Bureau.

RODGERS, JOAN R. "An Empirical Study of Intergenerational Transmission of Poverty in the United States." *Social Science Quarterly*. Vol. 76, No. 1 (March 1995):178–94.

ROESCH, ROBERTA. "Violent Families." *Parents*. Vol. 59, No. 9 (September 1984):74–76, 150–52.

ROETHLISBERGER, F. J., and WILLIAM J. DICKSON. *Management and the Worker*. Cambridge, Mass.: Harvard University Press, 1939.

ROGERS-DILLON, ROBIN H. "What Do We Really Know about Welfare Reform?" *Society*. Vol. 38, No. 2 (January/February 2001):7–15.

ROHLEN, THOMAS P. *Japan's High Schools*. Berkeley: University of California Press, 1983.

ROMAINE, SUZANNE. *Communicating Gender*. Mahwah, NJ: Erlbaum, 1999.

RÓNA-TAS, AKOS. "The First Shall Be Last? Entrepreneurship and Communist Cadres in the Transition from Socialism." *American Journal of Sociology*. Vol. 100, No. 1 (July 1994):40–69.

ROOF, WADE CLARK. "Socioeconomic Differentials among White Socioreligious Groups in the United States." *Social Forces*. Vol. 58, No. 1 (September 1979):280–89.

ROOF, WADE CLARK, and WILLIAM MCKINNEY. *American Mainline Religion: Its Changing Shape and Future*. New Brunswick, N.J.: Rutgers University Press, 1987.

ROSE, FRED. "Toward a Class-Cultural Theory of Social Movements: Reinterpreting New Social Movements." *Sociological Forum*. Vol. 12, No. 3 (September 1997):461–94.

ROSE, JERRY D. *Outbreaks*. New York: Free Press, 1982.

ROSEN, ELLEN ISRAEL. *Bitter Choices: Blue-Collar Women In and Out of Work*. Chicago: University of Chicago Press, 1987.

ROSEN, JEFFREY. *The Unwanted Gaze*. New York: Random House, 2000.

ROSENBAUM, DAVID E. "Americans Want a Right to Die. Or So They Think." *New York Times* (June 8, 1997):E3.

ROSENDAHL, MONA. *Inside the Revolution: Everyday Life in Socialist Cuba*. Ithaca, N.Y.: Cornell University Press, 1997.

ROSENFELD, MEGAN. "Little Boys Blue: Reexamining the Plight of Young Males." *Washington Post* (March 26, 1998):A1, A17–A18.

ROSENFELD, MICHAEL J. "Celebration, Politics, and Selective Looting and Riots: A Micro-Level Study of the Bulls Riot of 1992 in Chicago." *Social Problems*. Vol. 44, No. 4 (November 1997):483–502.

ROSENFELD, SARAH. "Labeling Mental Illness: The Effects of Received Services and Perceived Stigma on Life Satisfaction." *American Sociological Review*. Vol. 62, No. 4 (August 1997):660–72.

ROSENTHAL, ELIZABETH. "Canada's National Health Plan Gives Care to All, with Limits." *New York Times* (April 30, 1991):A1, A16.

ROSENTHAL, JACK. "The Rapid Growth of Suburban Employment." In Lois H. Masotti and Jeffrey K. Hadden, eds., *Suburbia in Transition*. New York: New York Times Books, 1974:95–100.

ROSNOW, RALPH L., and GARY ALAN FINE. *Rumor and Gossip: The Social Psychology of Hearsay.* New York: Elsevier, 1976.

ROSS, CATHERINE E., JOHN MIROWSKY, and JOAN HUBER. "Dividing Work, Sharing Work, and In-Between: Marriage Patterns and Depression." *American Sociological Review.* Vol. 48, No. 6 (December 1983):809–23.

ROSS, JOHN. "To Die in the Street: Mexico City's Homeless Population Boom as Economic Crisis Shakes Social Protections." *SSSP Newsletter.* Vol. 27, No. 2 (Summer 1996):14–15.

ROSSI, ALICE S. "Gender and Parenthood." In Alice S. Rossi, ed., *Gender and the Life Course.* New York: Aldine, 1985:161–91.

ROSSI, PETER H. Review of Christopher Jencks, *The Homeless* (Cambridge, Mass.: Harvard University Press). *Society.* Vol. 32, No. 4 (May–June 1995):80–81.

ROSTOW, WALT W. *The Stages of Economic Growth: A Non-Communist Manifesto.* Cambridge, U.K.: Cambridge University Press, 1960.

———. *The World Economy: History and Prospect.* Austin: University of Texas Press, 1978.

ROSZAK, THEODORE. *The Cult of Information: The Folklore of Computers and the True Art of Thinking.* New York: Pantheon Books, 1986.

ROTHMAN, BARBARA KATZ. "Of Maps and Imaginations: Sociology Confronts the Genome." *Social Problems.* Vol. 42, No. 1 (February 1995):1–10.

ROTHMAN, STANLEY, and AMY E. BLACK. "Who Rules Now? American Elites in the 1990s." *Society.* Vol. 35, No. 6 (September–October 1998):17–20.

ROTHMAN, STANLEY, and S. ROBERT LICHTER. "Social Science and Ideology: A Reply to Prindle, Endersby, and Gans." *Social Science Quarterly.* Vol. 75 (June 1994):455–57.

ROTHMAN, STANLEY, STEPHEN POWERS, and DAVID ROTHMAN. "Feminism in Films." *Society.* Vol. 30, No. 3 (March–April 1993):66–72.

ROWE, DAVID C. "Biometrical Genetic Models of Self-Reported Delinquent Behavior: A Twin Study." *Behavior Genetics.* Vol. 13, No. 5 (1983):473–89.

ROWE, DAVID C., and D. WAYNE OSGOOD. "Heredity and Sociological Theories of Delinquency: A Reconsideration." *American Sociological Review.* Vol. 49, No. 4 (August 1984):526–40.

ROWLAND, CHRISTOPHER, ed. *The Cambridge Companion to Liberation Theology.* Cambridge, U.K.: Cambridge University Press, 1999.

ROZELL, MARK J., CLYDE WILCOX, and JOHN C. GREEN. "Religious Constituencies and Support for the Christian Right in the 1990s." *Social Science Quarterly.* Vol. 79, No. 4 (December 1998):815–27.

RUBENSTEIN, ELI A. "The Not So Golden Years." *Newsweek* (October 7, 1991):13.

RUBIN, LILLIAN BRESLOW. *Worlds of Pain: Life in the Working-Class Family.* New York: Basic Books, 1976.

RUDÉ, GEORGE. *The Crowd in History: A Study of Popular Disturbances in France and England, 1730–1848.* New York: Wiley, 1964.

RUDEL, THOMAS K., and JUDITH M. GERSON. "Postmodernism, Institutional Change, and Academic Workers: A Sociology of Knowledge." *Social Science Quarterly.* Vol. 80, No. 2 (June 1999):213–28.

RUDOLPH, ELLEN. "Women's Talk: Japanese Women." *New York Times Magazine* (September 1, 1991).

RULE, JAMES, and PETER BRANTLEY. "Computerized Surveillance in the Workplace: Forms and Delusions." *Sociological Forum.* Vol. 7, No. 3 (September 1992):405–23.

RUSSELL, CHERYL. "Are We in the Dumps?" *American Demographics.* Vol. 17, No. 1 (January 1995a):6.

———. "True Crime." *American Demographics.* Vol. 17, No. 8 (August 1995b):22–31.

RUSSELL, CHERYL, and MARCIA MOGELONSKY. "Riding High on the Market." *American Demographics.* Vol. 22, No. 4 (April 2000):44–54.

RUTHERFORD, MEGAN. "Women Run the World." *Time.* Vol. 153, No. 25 (June 28, 1999):72.

———. "Simply Grand." *Time.* Vol. 154, No. 15 (October 11, 1999). Special section.

RYAN, WILLIAM. *Blaming the Victim.* Rev. ed. New York: Vintage Books, 1976.

RYMER, RUSS. *Genie.* New York: HarperPerennial, 1994.

SACHS, JEFFREY. "The Real Causes of Famine." *Time.* Vol. 152, No. 17 (October 26, 1998):69.

SADIK, NAFIS, ed. *Population Policies and Programmes: Lessons Learned from Two Decades of Experience.* New York: New York University Press, 1991.

ST. JEAN, YANICK, and JOE R. FEAGIN. *Double Burden: Black Women and Everyday Racism.* Armonk, N.Y.: M. E. Sharpe, 1998.

SALE, KIRKPATRICK. *The Conquest of Paradise: Christopher Columbus and the Columbian Legacy.* New York: Alfred A. Knopf, 1990.

SAMPSON, ANTHONY. *The Changing Anatomy of Britain.* New York: Random House, 1982.

SAMPSON, ROBERT J. "Urban Black Violence: The Effects of Male Joblessness and Family Disruption." *American Journal of Sociology.* Vol. 93, No. 2 (September 1987):348–82.

SAMPSON, ROBERT J., and JOHN H. LAUB. "Crime and Deviance over the Life Course: The Salience of Adult Social Bonds." *American Sociological Review.* Vol. 55, No. 5 (October 1990):609–27.

SANCHEZ, RENE. "Urban Students Not Making the Mark." *Washington Post* (January 8, 1998):A18.

SANTOLI, AL. "Fighting Child Prostitution." *Freedom Review.* Vol. 25, No. 5 (September–October 1994):5–8.

SAPIR, EDWARD. "The Status of Linguistics as a Science." *Language.* Vol. 5 (1929):207–14.

———. *Selected Writings of Edward Sapir in Language, Culture, and Personality.* David G. Mandelbaum, ed. Berkeley: University of California Press, 1949.

SAX, LINDA J., ALEXANDER W. ASTIN, WILLIAM S. KORN, and KATHRYN M. MAHONEY. *The American Freshman: National Norms for Fall 1999.* Los Angeles: UCLA Higher Education Research Institute, 1999.

SCAFF, LAWRENCE A. "Max Weber and Robert Michels." *American Journal of Sociology.* Vol. 86, No. 6 (May 1981):1269–86.

SCANLON, JAMES P. "The Curious Case of Affirmative Action for Women." *Society.* Vol. 29, No. 2 (January–February 1992):36–42.

SCHAIE, K. WARNER. "Intelligence and Problem Solving." In James E. Birren and R. Bruce Sloane, eds., *Handbook of Mental Health and Aging.* Englewood Cliffs, N.J.: Prentice Hall, 1980:262–84.

SCHAUB, DIANA. "From Boys to Men." *The Public Interest.* No. 127 (Spring 1997):108–14.

SCHEFF, THOMAS J. *Being Mentally Ill: A Sociological Theory.* 2d ed. New York: Aldine, 1984.

SCHERER, RON. "Worldwide Trend: Tobacco Use Grows." *Christian Science Monitor* (July 17, 1996):4, 8.

SCHILLER, BRADLEY. "Who Are the Working Poor?" *The Public Interest.* Vol. 155 (Spring 1994):61–71.

SCHLESINGER, ARTHUR. "The City in American Civilization." In A. B. Callow, Jr., ed., *American Urban History.* New York: Oxford University Press, 1969:25–41.

SCHLESINGER, ARTHUR, JR. "The Cult of Ethnicity: Good and Bad." *Time.* Vol. 137, No. 27 (July 8, 1991):21.

SCHLESINGER, JACOB M. "Finally, U.S. Median Income Approaches Old Heights." *Wall Street Journal* (September 25, 1998):B1.

SCHMIDT, ROGER. *Exploring Religion.* Belmont, Calif.: Wadsworth, 1980.

SCHMITT, ERIC. "Whites in Minority in Largest Cities, the Census Shows." *New York Times* (April 30, 2001):A1, A12.

SCHNAIBERG, ALLAN, and KENNETH ALAN GOULD. *Environment and Society: The Enduring Conflict.* New York: St. Martin's Press, 1994.

SCHNEIDER, MARK, MELISSA MARSCHALL, PAUL TESKE, and CHRISTINE ROCH. "School Choice and Culture Wars in the Classroom: What Different Parents Seek from Education." *Social Science Quarterly.* Vol. 79, No. 3 (September 1998):489–501.

SCHOR, JUDITH B. Cited in Cheryl Russell, "Overworked? Overwhelmed?" *American Demographics.* Vol. 17, No. 3 (March 1995):8.

SCHULTZ, T. PAUL. "Inequality in the Distribution of Personal Income in the World: How It Is Changing and Why." *Journal of Population Economics.* Vol. 11, No. 2 (1998):307–44.

SCHULTZ & HECKHAUSEN, 1996.

SCHUMAN, HOWARD, and MARIA KRYSAN. "A Historical Note on Whites' Beliefs about Racial Inequality." *American Sociological Review.* Vol. 64, No. 6 (December 1999):847–55.

SCHUMANN, HANS WOLFGANG. *Buddhism: An Outline of Its Teachings and Schools.* Wheaton, Ill.: The Theosophical Publishing House/Quest Books, 1974.

SCHUR, LISA A., and DOUGLAS L. KRUSE. "What Determines Voter Turnout? Lessons from Citizens with Disabilities." *Social Science Quarterly.* Vol. 81, No. 2 (June 2000): 571–87.

SCHUTT, RUSSELL K. "Objectivity versus Outrage." *Society.* Vol. 26, No. 4 (May–June 1989):14–16.

SCHWARTZ, BARRY. "Memory as a Cultural System: Abraham Lincoln in World War II." *American Sociological Review.* Vol. 61, No. 5 (October 1996):908–27.

SCHWARTZ, FELICE N. "Management, Women, and the New Facts of Life." *Harvard Business Review.* Vol. 89, No. 1 (January–February 1989):65–76.

SCHWARTZ, MARTIN D. "Gender and Injury in Spousal Assault." *Sociological Focus.* Vol. 20, No. 1 (January 1987):61–75.

SCHWARZ, JOHN E., and THOMAS J. VOLGY. *The Forgotten Americans: Thirty Million Working Poor in the Land of Opportunity.* New York: Norton, 1992.

SCOTT, JOHN, and CATHERINE GRIFF. *Directors of Industry: The British Corporate Network, 1904–1976.* New York: Blackwell, 1985.

SCOTT, JOSEPH E., and J. CUVELIER. "Violence in *Playboy* Magazine: A Longitudinal Analysis." *Archives of Sexual Behavior.* Vol. 16 (1987):279–88.

SCOTT, W. RICHARD. *Organizations: Rational, Natural, and Open Systems.* Englewood Cliffs, N.J.: Prentice Hall, 1981.

SCUPIN, RAY. Personal communication, 2000.

SEAGER, JONI. *The State of Women in the World Atlas.* New revised 2d ed. New York: Penguin Group, 2000.

SEARS, DAVID O., and JOHN B. McCONAHAY. *The Politics of Violence: The New Urban Blacks and the Watts Riot.* Boston: Houghton Mifflin, 1973.

SEBASTIAN, TIM. "Massacred: 1,000; Tried, 0." *World Press Review* (June 1996):6–10.

SEIDMAN, STEVEN. *Queer Theory/Sociology.* Oxford, U.K.: Blackwell, 1996.

SEKULIC, DUSKO, GARTH MASSEY, and RANDY HODSON. "Who Were the Yugoslavs? Failed Sources of Common Identity in the Former Yugoslavia." *American Sociological Review.* Vol. 59, No. 1 (February 1994):83–97.

SELLIN, THORSTEN. *The Penalty of Death.* Beverly Hills, Calif.: Sage, 1980.

SELTZER, ROBERT M. *Jewish People, Jewish Thought: The Jewish Experience in History.* New York: Macmillan, 1980.

SEN, K. M. *Hinduism.* Baltimore: Penguin Books, 1961.

SENNETT, RICHARD. *The Corrosion of Character: The Personal Consequences of Work in the New Capitalism.* New York: Norton, 1998.

SENNETT, RICHARD, and JONATHAN COBB. *The Hidden Injuries of Class.* New York: Vintage Books, 1973.

THE SENTENCING PROJECT. [Online] Available October 18, 2000, at http://www.sentencingproject.org/brief/facts-pp.pdf

SEPLOW, STEPHEN, and JONATHAN STORM. "How TV Defined Our Lives." *Philadelphia Inquirer* (November 30, 1997):A1, A16–17.

SHAPIRO, JOSEPH P., and JOANNIE M. SCHROF. "Honor Thy Children." *U.S. News & World Report.* Vol. 118, No. 8 (February 27, 1995):39–49.

SHARPE, ANITA. "The Rich Aren't So Different After All." *Wall Street Journal* (November 12, 1996):B1, B10.

SHAWCROSS, WILLIAM. *Sideshow: Kissinger, Nixon and the Destruction of Cambodia.* New York: Pocket Books, 1979.

SHEEHAN, TOM. "Senior Esteem as a Factor in Socioeconomic Complexity." *The Gerontologist*. Vol. 16, No. 5 (October 1976):433–40.

SHELDON, WILLIAM H., EMIL M. HARTL, and EUGENE McDERMOTT. *Varieties of Delinquent Youth*. New York: Harper, 1949.

SHELEY, JAMES F., JOSHUA ZHANG, CHARLES J. BRODY, and JAMES D. WRIGHT. "Gang Organization, Gang Criminal Activity, and Individual Gang Members' Criminal Behavior." *Social Science Quarterly*. Vol. 76, No. 1 (March 1995):53–68.

SHERKAT, DARREN E., and CHRISTOPHER G. ELLISON. "Recent Developments and Current Controversies in the Sociology of Religion." *Annual Review of Sociology*. Vol. 25 (1999):363–94.

SHERMAN, LAWRENCE W., and DOUGLAS A. SMITH. "Crime, Punishment, and Stake in Conformity: Legal and Informal Control of Domestic Violence." *American Sociological Review*. Vol. 57, No. 5 (October 1992):680–90.

SHEVKY, ESHREF, and WENDELL BELL. *Social Area Analysis*. Stanford, Calif.: Stanford University Press, 1955.

SHIPLER, DAVID K. *Russia: Broken Idols, Solemn Dreams*. New York: Penguin Books, 1984.

SHIPLEY, JOSEPH T. *Dictionary of Word Origins*. Totowa, N.J.: Roman & Allanheld, 1985.

SHIVELY, JoELLEN. "Cowboys and Indians: Perceptions of Western Films among American Indians and Anglos." *American Sociological Review*. Vol. 57, No. 6 (December 1992):725–34.

SHUPE, ANSON. *In the Name of All That's Holy: A Theory of Clergy Malfeasance*. Westport, Conn.: Praeger, 1995.

SHUPE, ANSON, WILLIAM A. STACEY, and LONNIE R. HAZLEWOOD. *Violent Men, Violent Couples: The Dynamics of Domestic Violence*. Lexington, Mass.: Lexington Books, 1987.

SIDEL, RUTH, and VICTOR W. SIDEL. *A Healthy State: An International Perspective on the Crisis in United States Medical Care*. Rev. ed. New York: Pantheon Books, 1982a.

———. *The Health Care of China*. Boston: Beacon Press, 1982b.

SILVERBERG, ROBERT. "The Greenhouse Effect: Apocalypse Now or Chicken Little?" *Omni* (July 1991):50–54.

SILVERSTEIN, MICHAEL. In Jon Snodgrass, ed., *A Book of Readings for Men against Sexism*. Albion, Calif.: Times Change Press, 1977:178–79.

SIMMEL, GEORG. *The Sociology of Georg Simmel*. Kurt Wolff, ed. New York: Free Press, 1950:118–69; orig. 1902.

———. "Fashion." In Donald N. Levine, ed., *Georg Simmel: On Individuality and Social Forms*. Chicago: University of Chicago Press, 1971; orig. 1904.

SIMON, JULIAN. *The Ultimate Resource*. Princeton, N.J.: Princeton University Press, 1981.

———. "More People, Greater Wealth, More Resources, Healthier Environment." In Theodore D. Goldfarb, ed., *Taking Sides: Clashing Views on Controversial Environmental Issues*. 6th ed. Guilford, Conn.: The Dushkin Publishing Group, 1995.

SIMON, ROGER. "The Dems' New Tune: Tryin' to Go Country." *U.S. News & World Report*. Vol. 130, No. 23 (June 11, 2001):22–23.

SIMON, ROGER, and ANGIE CANNON. "An Amazing Journey." *U.S. News & World Report*. Vol. 131, No. 5 (August 6, 2001):10–19.

SIMONS, CAROL. "Japan's *Kyoiku* Mamas." In John J. Macionis and Nijole V. Benokraitis, eds., *Seeing Ourselves: Classic, Contemporary, and Cross-Cultural Readings in Sociology*. Englewood Cliffs, N.J.: Prentice Hall, 1989:281–86.

SIMONS, MARLISE. "The Price of Modernization: The Case of Brazil's Kaiapo Indians." In John J. Macionis and Nijole V. Benokraitis, eds., *Seeing Ourselves: Classic, Contemporary, and Cross-Cultural Readings in Sociology*. 5th ed. Upper Saddle River, N.J.: Prentice Hall, 2001:496–502.

SIMPSON, GEORGE EATON, and J. MILTON YINGER. *Racial and Cultural Minorities: An Analysis of Prejudice and Discrimination*. 4th ed. New York: Harper & Row, 1972.

SINGER, JEROME L., and DOROTHY G. SINGER. "Psychologists Look at Television: Cognitive, Developmental, Personality, and Social Policy Implications." *American Psychologist*. Vol. 38, No. 7 (July 1983):826–34.

SIPES, RICHARD G. "War, Sports and Aggression: An Empirical Test of Two Rival Theories." *American Anthropologist*. Vol. 75, No. 1 (January 1973):64–86.

SIVARD, RUTH LEGER. *World Military and Social Expenditures, 1987–88*. 12th ed. Washington, D.C.: World Priorities, 1988.

———. *World Military and Social Expenditures, 1992–93*. 17th ed. Washington, D.C.: World Priorities, 1993.

SIZER, THEODORE R. *Horace's Compromise: The Dilemma of the American High School*. Boston: Houghton Mifflin, 1984.

SKINNER, DAVID. "Computers: Good for Education?" *The Public Interest*. No. 128 (Summer 1997):98–109.

SKOCPOL, THEDA. *States and Social Revolutions: A Comparative Analysis of France, Russia, and China*. Cambridge, U.K.: Cambridge University Press, 1979.

SMAIL, J. KENNETH. "Beyond Population Stabilization: The Case for Dramatically Reducing Global Human Numbers." Roundtable: World Population Policy commentary and responses. *Politics and the Life Sciences*. Vol. 16, No. 2 (September 1997):183–236.

SMALL BUSINESS ADMINISTRATION. *The Facts about Small Business 1999*. U.S. Small Business Administration, Office of Advocacy. [Online] Available February 13, 2001, at http://www.sba.gov/ADVO/stats/facts99.pdf

SMART, NINIAN. *The Religious Experience of Mankind*. New York: Charles Scribner's Sons, 1969.

SMELSER, NEIL J. *Theory of Collective Behavior*. New York: Free Press, 1962.

SMITH, ADAM. *An Inquiry into the Nature and Causes of the Wealth of Nations*. New York: The Modern Library, 1937; orig. 1776.

SMITH, CRAIG S. "Authorities Took Victim's Organs, His Brother Says." *Columbus Dispatch* (March 11, 2001):A3.

SMITH, DOUGLAS A. "Police Response to Interpersonal Violence: Defining the Parameters of Legal Control." *Social Forces*. Vol. 65, No. 3 (March 1987):767–82.

SMITH, DOUGLAS A., and PATRICK R. GARTIN. "Specifying Specific Deterrence: The Influence of Arrest on Future Criminal Activity." *American Sociological Review*. Vol. 54, No. 1 (February 1989):94–105.

SMITH, DOUGLAS A., and CHRISTY A. VISHER. "Street-Level Justice: Situational Determinants of Police Arrest Decisions." *Social Problems*. Vol. 29, No. 2 (December 1981):167–77.

SMITH, EARL, and WILBERT M. LEONARD II. "Twenty-Five Years of Stacking Research in Major League Baseball: An Attempt at Explaining This Re-Occurring Phenomenon." *Sociological Focus*. Vol. 30, No. 4 (October 1997):321–31.

SMITH, ROBERT B. "Health Care Reform Now." *Society*. Vol. 30, No. 3 (March–April 1993):56–65.

SMITH, TOM W. Research results reported in "Anti-Semitism Decreases but Persists." *Society*. Vol. 33, No. 3 (March/April 1996):2.

SMITH-LOVIN, LYNN, and CHARLES BRODY. "Interruptions in Group Discussions: The Effects of Gender and Group Composition." *American Journal of Sociology*. Vol. 54, No. 3 (June 1989):424–35.

SMOCK, PAMELA J. "Cohabitation in the United States: An Appraisal of Research Themes, Findings, and Implications." *Annual Review of Sociology*. Vol. 26 (2000):1–20.

SMOLAN, RICK, and JENNIFER ERWITT. *24 Hours in Cyberspace*. New York: Macmillan, 1996.

SMOLOWE, JILL. "When Violence Hits Home." *Time*. Vol. 144, No. 1 (July 4, 1994):18–25.

SNELL, MARILYN BERLIN. "The Purge of Nurture." *New Perspectives Quarterly*. Vol. 7, No. 1 (Winter 1990):1–2.

SNOW, DAVID A., E. BURKE ROCHFORD, JR., STEVEN K. WORDEN, and ROBERT D. BENFORD. "Frame Alignment Processes, Micromobilization, and Movement Participation." *American Sociological Review*. Vol. 51, No. 4 (August 1986):464–81.

SNOW, DAVID A., LOUIS A. ZURCHER, JR., and SHELDON EKLAND-OLSON. "Social Networks and Social Movements: A Macrostructural Approach to Differential Recruitment." *American Sociological Review*. Vol. 45, No. 5 (October 1980):787–801.

SOUTH, SCOTT J., and KIM L. LLOYD. "Spousal Alternatives and Marital Dissolution." *American Sociological Review*. Vol. 60, No. 1 (February 1995):21–35.

SOUTH, SCOTT J., and STEVEN F. MESSNER. "Structural Determinants of Intergroup Association: Interracial Marriage and Crime." *American Journal of Sociology*. Vol. 91, No. 6 (May 1986):1409–30.

SOUTH, SCOTT J., and GLENNA SPITZE. "Housework in Marital and Nonmarital Households." *American Sociological Review*. Vol. 59, No. 3 (June 1994):327–47.

SOWELL, THOMAS. *Ethnic America*. New York: Basic Books, 1981.

———. *Race and Culture*. New York: Basic Books, 1994.

———. "Ethnicity and IQ." In Steven Fraser, ed., *The Bell Curve Wars: Race, Intelligence and the Future of America*. New York: Basic Books, 1995:70–79.

SOYINKA, WOLE. "Africa's Culture Producers." *Society*. Vol. 28, No. 2 (January–February 1991):32–40.

SPALTER-ROTH, ROBERTA, FELICE J. LEVINE, and ANDREW SUTTER. "The Pipeline of Faculty of Color in Sociology." *Footnotes*. Vol. 27, No. 4 (April 1999):4–5.

SPATES, JAMES L. "Counterculture and Dominant Culture Values: A Cross-National Analysis of the Underground Press and Dominant Culture Magazines." *American Sociological Review*. Vol. 41, No. 5 (October 1976):868–83.

———. "The Sociology of Values." In Ralph Turner, ed., *Annual Review of Sociology*. Vol. 9. Palo Alto, Calif.: Annual Reviews, 1983:27–49.

SPATES, JAMES L., and H. WESLEY PERKINS. "American and English Student Values." *Comparative Social Research*. Vol. 5. Greenwich, Conn.: JAI Press, 1982:245–68.

SPECTER, MICHAEL. "Plunging Life Expectancy Puzzles Russia." *New York Times* (August 2, 1995):A1, A2.

———. "Deep in the Russian Soul, a Lethal Darkness." *New York Times* (June 8, 1997a): section 4, pp. 1, 5.

———. "Moscow on the Make." *New York Times Magazine* (June 1, 1997b):48–55, 72, 75, 80, 84.

———. "Yogurt? Caucasus Centenarians 'Never Eat It.'" *New York Times* (March 14, 1998):A1, A4.

SPEER, JAMES A. "The New Christian Right and Its Parent Company: A Study in Political Contrasts." In David G. Bromley and Anson Shupe, eds., *New Christian Politics*. Macon, Ga.: Mercer University Press, 1984:19–40.

SPEER, TIBBETT L. "Are College Costs Cutting Enrollment?" *American Demographics*. Vol. 16, No. 11 (November 1994):9–10.

———. "Digging Into the Underground Economy." *American Demographics*. Vol. 17, No. 2 (February 1995):15–16.

———. "A Nation of Students." *American Demographics*. Vol. 48, No. 8 (August 1996):32–39.

SPEIER, HANS. "Wit and Politics: An Essay on Laughter and Power." Ed. and trans. by Robert Jackall. *American Journal of Sociology*. Vol. 103, No. 5 (March 1998):1352–1401.

SPENCER, MARTIN E. "Multiculturalism, 'Political Correctness,' and the Politics of Identity." *Sociological Forum*. Vol. 9, No. 4 (December 1994):547–67.

SPITZER, STEVEN. "Toward a Marxian Theory of Deviance." In Delos H. Kelly, ed., *Criminal Behavior: Readings in Criminology*. New York: St. Martin's Press, 1980:175–91.

SPLAIN, CHERYL S. "Homeless Problem Not Just in Big Cities." *Mount Vernon News* (March 6, 2000):1A, 3A.

STACEY, JUDITH. *Patriarchy and Socialist Revolution in China*. Berkeley: University of California Press, 1983.

———. *Brave New Families: Stories of Domestic Upheaval in Late Twentieth-Century America*. New York: Basic Books, 1990.

———. "Good Riddance to 'The Family': A Response to David Popenoe." *Journal of Marriage and the Family*. Vol. 55, No. 3 (August 1993):545–47.

STACK, CAROL B. *All Our Kin: Strategies for Survival in a Black Community*. New York: Harper & Row, 1975.

STAGGENBORG, SUZANNE. "Social Movement Communities and Cycles of Protest: The Emergence and Maintenance of a Local Women's Movement." *Social Problems*. Vol. 45, No. 2 (May 1998):180–204.

STAHURA, JOHN M. "Suburban Development, Black Suburbanization and the Black Civil Rights Movement since World War II." *American Sociological Review*. Vol. 51, No. 1 (February 1986):131–44.

STANLEY, LIZ, ed. *Feminist Praxis: Research, Theory, and Epistemology in Feminist Sociology*. London: Routledge & Kegan Paul, 1990.

STAPINSKI, HELENE. "Let's Talk Dirty." *American Demographics*. Vol. 20, No. 11 (November 1998):50–56.

STARK, RODNEY. *Sociology*. Belmont, Calif.: Wadsworth, 1985.

STARK, RODNEY, and WILLIAM SIMS BAINBRIDGE. "Of Churches, Sects, and Cults: Preliminary Concepts for a Theory of Religious Movements." *Journal for the Scientific Study of Religion*. Vol. 18, No. 2 (June 1979):117–31.

———. "Secularization and Cult Formation in the Jazz Age." *Journal for the Scientific Study of Religion*. Vol. 20, No. 4 (December 1981):360–73.

STARK, RODNEY, and CHARLES Y. GLOCK. *American Piety: The Nature of Religious Commitment*. Berkeley: University of California Press, 1968.

STARR, PAUL. *The Social Transformation of American Medicine*. New York: Basic Books, 1982.

STAVRIANOS, L. S. *A Global History: The Human Heritage*. 3d ed. Englewood Cliffs, N.J.: Prentice Hall, 1983.

STEELE, RANDY. "Awful but Lawful." *Boating* (June 2000):36.

STEELE, SHELBY. *The Content of Our Character: A New Vision of Race in America*. New York: St. Martin's Press, 1990.

STEIN, MAURICE R. *The Eclipse of Community: An Interpretation of American Studies*. Princeton, N.J.: Princeton University Press, 1972.

STEINBERG, LAURENCE. "Failure outside the Classroom." *Wall Street Journal* (July 11, 1996):A14.

STEPHENS, JOHN D. *The Transition from Capitalism to Socialism*. Urbana: University of Illinois Press, 1986.

STERN, LARRY. Personal communication, 1998.

STERNLIEB, GEORGE, and JAMES W. HUGHES. "The Uncertain Future of the Central City." *Urban Affairs Quarterly*. Vol. 18, No. 4 (June 1983):455–72.

STEVENS, GILLIAN, and GRAY SWICEGOOD. "The Linguistic Context of Ethnic Endogamy." *American Sociological Review*. Vol. 52, No. 1 (February 1987):73–82.

STIER, HAYA. "Continuity and Change in Women's Occupations following First Childbirth." *Social Science Quarterly*. Vol. 77, No. 1 (March 1996):60–75.

STODGHILL, RON, II. "Where'd You Learn That?" *Time*. Vol. 151, No. 23 (1998).

STOFFERAHN, CURTIS W. "Underemployment: Social Fact or Socially Constructed Reality?" *Rural Sociology*. Vol. 65, No. 2 (June 2000):311–30.

STOHL, MICHAEL, and GEORGE A. LOPEZ. *The State as Terrorist: The Dynamics of Government Violence and Repression*. Westport, Conn.: Greenwood Press, 1984.

STONE, LAWRENCE. *The Family, Sex and Marriage in England 1500–1800*. New York: Harper & Row, 1977.

STONE, ROBYN, GAIL LEE CAFFERATA, and JUDITH SANGL. *Caregivers of the Frail Elderly: A National Profile*. Washington, D.C.: U.S. Department of Health and Human Services, 1987.

STOUFFER, SAMUEL A., et al. *The American Soldier: Adjustment during Army Life*. Princeton, N.J.: Princeton University Press, 1949.

STRATTON, LESLIE S. "Why Does More Housework Lower Women's Wages? Testing Hypotheses Involving Job Effort and Hours Flexibility." *Social Sciences Quarterly*. Vol. 82, No. 1 (March 2001):67–76.

STRAUS, MURRAY A., and RICHARD J. GELLES. "Societal Change and Change in Family Violence from 1975 to 1985 as Revealed by Two National Surveys." *Journal of Marriage and the Family*. Vol. 48, No. 4 (August 1986):465–79.

STREIB, GORDON F. "Are the Aged a Minority Group?" In Bernice L. Neugarten, ed., *Middle Age and Aging: A Reader in Social Psychology*. Chicago: University of Chicago Press, 1968:35–46.

SUDNOW, DAVID N. *Passing On: The Social Organization of Dying*. Englewood Cliffs, N.J.: Prentice Hall, 1967.

SULLIVAN, BARBARA. "McDonald's Sees India as Golden Opportunity." *Chicago Tribune*. Business section (April 5, 1995):1.

SUMNER, WILLIAM GRAHAM. *Folkways*. New York: Dover, 1959; orig. 1906.

SUN, LENA H. "WWII's Forgotten Internees Await Apology." *The Washington Post* (March 9, 1998):A1, A5, A6.

SUNG, BETTY LEE. *Mountains of Gold: The Story of the Chinese in America*. New York: Macmillan, 1967.

SUPLEE, CURT. "1 in 8 Plants in Global Study Threatened." *Washington Post* (April 8, 1998):A1, A8.

SUTHERLAND, EDWIN H. "White Collar Criminality." *American Sociological Review*. Vol. 5, No. 1 (February 1940):1–12.

SUTHERLAND, EDWIN H., and DONALD R. CRESSEY. *Criminology*. 10th ed. Philadelphia: J.B. Lippincott, 1978.

SUTTON, JOHN R. "Imprisonment and Social Classification in Five Common-Law Democracies: 1955–1985." *American Journal of Sociology*. Vol. 106, No. 2 (September 2000):350–86.

SWARTZ, STEVE. "Why Michael Milken Stands to Qualify for Guinness Book." *Wall Street Journal*. Vol. 70, No. 117 (March 31, 1989):1, 4.

SZASZ, THOMAS S. *The Manufacture of Madness: A Comparative Study of the Inquisition and the Mental Health Movement*. New York: Dell, 1961.

———. *The Myth of Mental Illness: Foundations of a Theory of Personal Conduct*. New York: Harper & Row, 1970; orig. 1961.

———. "Mental Illness Is Still a Myth." *Society*. Vol. 31, No. 4 (May–June 1994):34–39.

———. "Idleness and Lawlessness in the Therapeutic State." *Society*. Vol. 32, No. 4 (May–June 1995):30–35.

TAJFEL, HENRI. "Social Psychology of Intergroup Relations." *Annual Review of Psychology*. Palo Alto, Calif.: Annual Reviews, 1982:1–39.

TALLICHET, SUZANNE E. "Barriers to Women's Advancement in Underground Coal Mining." *Rural Sociology*. Vol. 65, No. 2 (June 2000):234–52.

TANBER, GEORGE J. "Freed from Death Row." *Toledo Blade* (November 22, 1998):B1, B2.

TANNAHILL, REAY. *Sex in History*. Scarborough House Publishers, 1992.

TANNEN, DEBORAH. *You Just Don't Understand: Women and Men in Conversation*. New York: Wm. Morrow, 1990.

———. *Talking from 9 to 5: How Women's and Men's Conversational Styles Affect Who Gets Heard, Who Gets Credit, and What Gets Done at Work*. New York: Wm. Morrow, 1994.

TANNENBAUM, FRANK. *Slave and Citizen: The Negro in the Americas*. New York: Vintage Books, 1946.

TANNER, MICHAEL, and STEPHEN MOORE. "Why Welfare Pays." *Wall Street Journal* (September 28, 1995):A20.

TARROW, SIDNEY. *Social Movements, Collective Action and Politics*. New York: Cambridge University Press, 1994.

TAVRIS, CAROL, and SUSAN SADD. *The Redbook Report on Female Sexuality*. New York: Delacorte Press, 1977.

TAX FOUNDATION. [Online] Available March 30, 2000, at http://www.taxfoundation.org

TAYLOR, JOHN. "Don't Blame Me: The New Culture of Victimization." *New York Magazine* (June 3, 1991):26–34.

TERKEL, STUDS. *Working*. New York: Pantheon Books, 1974:1–2, 57–59, 65, 66, 69, 221–22.

TERRY, DON. "In Crackdown on Bias, A New Tool." *New York Times* (June 12, 1993):8.

TEWKSBURY, RICHARD, and PATRICIA GAGNÉ. "Transgenderists: Products of Non-normative Intersections of Sex, Gender, and Sexuality." *The Journal of Men's Studies*. Vol. 5, No. 2 (November 1996):105–29.

THERNSTROM, ABIGAIL, and STEPHAN THERNSTROM. "American Apartheid? Don't Believe It." *Wall Street Journal* (March 2, 1998):A18.

THIRUNARAYANAPURAM, DESIKAN. "Population Explosion Is Far from Over." *Popline*. Vol. 20 (January–February, 1998):1, 4.

THOMAS, EDWARD J. *The Life of Buddha as Legend and History*. London: Routledge & Kegan Paul, 1975.

THOMAS, EVAN, JOHN BARRY, and MELINDA LIU. "Ground Zero." *Newsweek* (May 25, 1998):28–32A.

THOMAS, PAULETTE. "Success at a Huge Personal Cost." *Wall Street Journal* (July 26, 1995):B1, B6.

THOMAS, PIRI. *Down These Mean Streets*. New York: Signet, 1967.

THOMAS, W. I. "The Relation of Research to the Social Process." In Morris Janowitz, ed., *W. I. Thomas on Social Organization and Social Personality*. Chicago: University of Chicago Press, 1966:289–305; orig. 1931.

———. *The Unadjusted Girl*. New York: Harper & Row, 1967:42; orig. 1923.

THOMMA, STEVEN. "Christian Coalition Demands Action from GOP." *Philadelphia Inquirer* (September 14, 1997):A2.

THOMPSON, DICK. "Gene Maverick." *Time*. Vol. 153, No. 1 (January 11, 1999):54–55.

THOMPSON, LARRY. "Fertility with Less Fuss." *Time*. Vol. 144, No. 20 (November 14, 1994):79.

THOMPSON, MARK. "Fatal Neglect." *Time*. Vol. 150, No. 17 (October 27, 1997):34–38.

———. "Shining a Light on Abuse." *Time*. Vol. 152, No. 5 (August 3, 1998):42–43.

THOMPSON, MARK, and DOUGLAS WALLER. "Shield of Dreams." *Time*. Vol. 155, No. 19 (May 8, 2001):45–47.

THORLINDSSON, THOROLFUR, and THORODDUR BJARNASON. "Modeling Durkheim on the Micro Level: A Study of Youth Suicidality." *American Sociological Review*. Vol. 63, No. 1 (February 1998):94–110.

THORNBERRY, TERRANCE, and MARGARET FARNSWORTH. "Social Correlates of Criminal Involvement: Further Evidence on the Relationship between Social Status and Criminal Behavior." *American Sociological Review*. Vol. 47, No. 4 (August 1982):505–18.

THORNE, BARRIE, CHERIS KRAMARAE, and NANCY HENLEY, eds. *Language, Gender and Society*. Rowley, Mass.: Newbury House, 1983.

THORNTON, ARLAND. "Changing Attitudes toward Separation and Divorce: Causes and Consequences." *American Journal of Sociology*. Vol. 90, No. 4 (January 1985):856–72.

THORNTON, ARLAND, WILLIAM G. AXINN, and DANIEL H. HILL. "Reciprocal Effects of Religiosity, Cohabitation, and Marriage." *American Journal of Sociology*. Vol. 98, No. 3 (November 1992):628–51.

THUROW, LESTER C. "A Surge in Inequality." *Scientific American*. Vol. 256, No. 5 (May 1987):30–37.

TILLY, CHARLES. *From Mobilization to Revolution*. Reading, Mass.: Addison-Wesley, 1978.

———. "Does Modernization Breed Revolution?" In Jack A. Goldstone, ed., *Revolutions: Theoretical, Comparative, and Historical Studies*. New York: Harcourt Brace Jovanovich, 1986:47–57.

Time Almanac 2001. Boston: Information Please, 2000.

TIRYAKIAN, EDWARD A. "Revisiting Sociology's First Classic: The Division of Labor in Society and Its Actuality." *Sociological Forum*. Vol. 9, No. 1 (March 1994):3–16.

TITTLE, CHARLES R., and WAYNE J. VILLEMEZ. "Social Class and Criminality." *Social Forces.* Vol. 56, No. 22 (December 1977):474–502.

TITTLE, CHARLES R., WAYNE J. VILLEMEZ, and DOUGLAS A. SMITH. "The Myth of Social Class and Criminality: An Empirical Assessment of the Empirical Evidence." *American Sociological Review.* Vol. 43, No. 5 (October 1978):643–56.

TOBIN, GARY. "Suburbanization and the Development of Motor Transportation: Transportation Technology and the Suburbanization Process." In Barry Schwartz, ed., *The Changing Face of the Suburbs.* Chicago: University of Chicago Press, 1976.

TOBY, JACKSON. "Getting Serious about School Discipline." *The Public Interest.* Vol. 133 (Fall 1998):68–83.

TOCH, THOMAS. "The New Educational Bazaar." *U.S. News & World Report* (April 27, 1998):35–45.

TOCQUEVILLE, ALEXIS DE. *The Old Regime and the French Revolution.* Stuart Gilbert, trans. Garden City, N.Y.: Anchor/Doubleday Books, 1955; orig. 1856.

TOFFLER, ALVIN, and HEIDI TOFFLER. *War and Anti-War: Survival at the Dawn of the 21st Century.* Boston: Little, Brown, 1993.

TOLSON, JAY. "The Trouble with Elites." *The Wilson Quarterly.* Vol. 19, No. 1 (Winter 1995):6–8.

TÖNNIES, FERDINAND. *Community and Society (Gemeinschaft und Gesellschaft).* New York: Harper & Row, 1963; orig. 1887.

TREAS, JUDITH. "Socialist Organization and Economic Development in China: Latent Consequences for the Aged." *The Gerontologist.* Vol. 19, No. 1 (February 1979):34–43.

———. "Older Americans in the 1990s and Beyond." *Population Bulletin.* Vol. 50, No. 2 (May 1995). Washington, D.C.: Population Reference Bureau.

TREIMAN, DONALD J. "Industrialization and Social Stratification." In Edward O. Laumann, ed., *Social Stratification: Research and Theory for the 1970s.* Indianapolis: Bobbs-Merrill, 1970.

TRENT, KATHERINE. "Family Context and Adolescents' Expectations about Marriage, Fertility, and Nonmarital Childbearing." *Social Science Quarterly.* Vol. 75, No. 2 (June 1994):319–39.

TROELTSCH, ERNST. *The Social Teaching of the Christian Churches.* New York: Macmillan, 1931.

TROIDEN, RICHARD R. *Gay and Lesbian Identity: A Sociological Analysis.* Dix Hills, N.Y.: General Hall, 1988.

TROY, TOM. "Money Does Matter." *Toledo Blade* (October 23, 2000):A1, 5, 7.

TUMIN, MELVIN M. "Some Principles of Stratification: A Critical Analysis." *American Sociological Review.* Vol. 18, No. 4 (August 1953):387–94.

———. *Social Stratification: The Forms and Functions of Inequality.* 2d ed. Englewood Cliffs, N.J.: Prentice Hall, 1985.

TURNER, RALPH H., and LEWIS M. KILLIAN. *Collective Behavior.* 2d ed. Englewood Cliffs, N.J.: Prentice Hall, 1972; 3d ed., 1987; 4th ed., 1993.

TYLER, S. LYMAN. *A History of Indian Policy.* Washington, D.C.: United States Department of the Interior, Bureau of Indian Affairs, 1973.

TYREE, ANDREA, MOSHE SEMYONOV, and ROBERT W. HODGE. "Gaps and Glissandos: Inequality, Economic Development, and Social Mobility in 24 Countries." *American Sociological Review.* Vol. 44, No. 3 (June 1979):410–24.

UDRY, J. RICHARD. "Biological Limitations of Gender Construction." *American Sociological Review.* Vol. 65, No. 3 (June 2000):443–57.

UGGEN, CHRISTOPHER. "Ex-Offenders and the Conformist Alternative: A Job-Quality Model of Work and Crime." *Social Problems.* Vol. 46, No. 1 (February 1999):127–51.

UNITED NATIONS. "AIDS Epidemic Update: December 2000." [Online] Available October 22, 2001, at http://www.unaids.org/wac/2000/wad00/files/WAD–epidemic–report.PDF

UNITED NATIONS DEVELOPMENT PROGRAMME. *Human Development Report 1990.* New York: Oxford University Press, 1990.

———. *Human Development Report 1994.* New York: Oxford University Press, 1994.

———. *Human Development Report 1995.* New York: Oxford University Press, 1995.

———. *Human Development Report 1996.* New York: Oxford University Press, 1996.

———. *Human Development Report 1997.* New York: Oxford University Press, 1997.

———. *Human Development Report 1998.* New York: Oxford University Press, 1998.

———. *Human Development Report 1999.* New York: Oxford University Press, 1999.

———. *Human Development Report 2000.* New York: Oxford University Press, 2000.

———. *Human Development Report 2001.* New York: Oxford University Press, 2001.

UNITED NATIONS POPULATION DIVISION. *Population Aging, 1999.* New York: United Nations, 1999.

UNIVERSITY OF AKRON RESEARCH CENTER. *National Survey of Religion and Politics 1992.* Akron, Ohio: University of Akron Research Center, 1993.

UNNEVER, JAMES D., CHARLES E. FRAZIER, and JOHN C. HENRETTA. "Race Differences in Criminal Sentencing." *The Sociological Quarterly.* Vol. 21, No. 2 (Spring 1980):197–205.

UNRUH, JOHN D., JR. *The Plains Across.* Urbana: University of Illinois Press, 1979.

UPTHEGROVE, TAYNA R., VINCENT J. ROSCIGNO, and CAMILLE ZUBRINSKY CHARLES. "Big Money Collegiate Sports: Racial Concentration, Contradictory Pressures, and Academic Performance." *Social Science Quarterly.* Vol. 80, No. 4 (December 1999):718–37.

U.S. BUREAU OF ECONOMIC ANALYSIS. *Foreign Direct Investment in the United States. Country Detail for Selected Items.* Washington, D.C.: The Bureau, 1999.

U.S. BUREAU OF JUSTICE STATISTICS. *Violence against Women.* Washington, D.C.: U.S. Government Printing Office, 1994.

———. *Criminal Victimization 1994.* Washington, D.C.: U.S. Government Printing Office, 1996.

———. *Violence by Intimates.* Washington, D.C.: The Bureau, 1998.

———. *Criminal Victimization 1998: Changes 1997–98 with Trends 1993–98.* Washington, D.C.: The Bureau, 1999.

———. *Sourcebook of Criminal Justice Statistics 1998.* Washington, D.C.: The Bureau, 1999.

———. *Capital Punishment 1999.* Washington, D.C.: The Bureau, 2000.

———. *Criminal Victimization 1999: Changes 1998–99 with Trends 1993–99.* Washington, D.C.: The Bureau, 2000.

———. *Sourcebook of Criminal Justice Statistics 1999.* Washington, D.C.: The Bureau, 2000.

———. *Intimate Partner Violence and Age of Victim, 1993–99.* Washington, D.C.: The Bureau, 2001. [Online] Available December 4, 2001, at http://www.ojp.usdoj.gov/bjs/pub/pdf/ipva99.pdf

———. *Sourcebook of Criminal Justice Statistics Online.* [Online] Available November 11, 2001, at http://www.albany.edu/sourcebook/1995/pdf/

U.S. CENSUS BUREAU. *Asset Ownership of Households: 1993.* Current Population Reports, Series P-70, No. 47. Washington, D.C.: U.S. Government Printing Office, 1995.

———. *Household and Family Characteristics: March 1994.* Current Population Reports, Series P-20, No. 483, Washington, D.C.: U.S. Government Printing Office, 1995.

———. *Income, Poverty, and Valuation of Noncash Benefits: 1993.* Current Population Reports, Series P-60, No. 188. Washington, D.C.: U.S. Government Printing Office, 1995.

———. *Marital Status and Living Arrangements:* March 1995. PPL-52. Washington, D.C.: U.C. Government Printing Office, 1996.

———. *School Enrollment: Social and Economic Characteristics of Students: October 1995 (Update).* PPL-55: The Bureau, 1997.

———. "Who's Minding Our Preschoolers?" Fall 1994 (Update). P70–62. Washington, D.C.: U.S. Government Printing Office, 1997.

———. *Educational Achievement in the United States: March 1998 (Update).* Current Population Reports, P20-515. Washington, D.C.: U.S. Government Printing Office, 1998.

———. *Educational Attainment in the United States: March 1998 (Update).* Current Population Reports, P20-513. Washington, D.C.: U.S. Government Printing Office, 1998.

———. *Household and Family Characteristics: March 1998 (Update).* Current Population Reports, P20-515. Washington, D.C.: U.S. Government Printing Office, 1998.

———. *Poverty in the United States 1997.* Current Population Reports, P60-201. Washington, D.C.: U.S. Government Printing Office, 1998.

———. *Statistical Abstract of the United States 1998.* Washington, D.C.: U.S. Government Printing Office, 1998.

———. *Educational Attainment in the United States: March 1998 (Update).* Washington, D.C.: U.S. Government Printing Office, 1999.

———. *Grandchildren Living in the Home of Their Grandparents: 1970 to Present* (CH-7). Washington, D.C.: The Bureau, 1999.

———. *Health Insurance Coverage* (P60-208). Washington, D.C.: The Bureau, 1999.

———. *Household and Family Characteristics: March 1998 (Update).* Washington, D.C.: The Bureau, 1999.

———. *Metropolitan Area Population Estimates for July 1, 1998, and Population Change for April 1, 1990, to July 1, 1998.* Washington, D.C.: The Bureau, 1999.

———. *Money Income in the United States 1998* (P60-206). Washington, D.C.: U.S. Government Printing Office, 1999.

———. *Population Estimates for Cities with Populations of 100,000 and Greater (Sorted by 1998 Population Size Rank in U.S.).* Washington, D.C.: The Bureau, 1999.

———. *Poverty in the United States 1998* (P60-207). Washington, D.C.: U.S. Government Printing Office, 1999.

———. *School Enrollment—Social and Economic Characteristics of Students: October 1998 (Update).* Current Population Report, P20-521. Washington, D.C.: The Bureau, 1999.

———. *Statistical Abstract of the United States 1999.* Washington, D.C.: U.S. Government Printing Office, 1999.

———. *Educational Attainment in the United States: March 1998 (Update).* [Online] Available March 21, 2000, at http://www.census.gov/prod/3/98pubs/p20-513u.pdf

———. *Educational Attainment in the United States: March 2000* (Update). Current Population Reports, P20-536. Washington, D.C.: U.S. Government Printing Office, 2000.

———. *Health Insurance Coverage 1999* (P60–211). Washington, D.C.: The Bureau, 2000.

———. *Historical Income Tables: Families,* Tables F-1, F-2, and F-3. [Online] Available March 21, 2000, at http://www.census.gov/hhes/income/histinc/f02.html

———. Vols. Table F-3, "Mean Income Received by Each Fifth and Top 5 Percent of Families (All Races): 1966 to 1999." [Online] Available December 6, 2000, at http://www.census.gov/hhes/income/histinc/f03.html

———. *Housing Vacancies and Home Ownership: Annual Statistics: 1998.* Table 20. [Online] Available March 21, 2000, at http://www.census.gov/hhes/www/housing/hvs/annual98/ann98t20.html

———. *International Data Base.* [Online] Available February 24, 2000, at http://www.census.gov/ipc/www/idbprint.html

———. *Metropolitan Area Population Estimates for July 1, 1999, and Population Change for April 1, 1990, to July 1, 1999.* Washington, D.C.: The Bureau, 2000.

———. *Money Income in the United States 1999.* Current Population Reports (P60–209). Washington, D.C.: U.S. Government Printing Office, 2000.

———. *Poverty in the United States 1999.* Current Population Reports (P60–210). Washington, D.C.: U.S. Government Printing Office, 2000.

———. *Projections of the Total Resident Population by 5-Year Age Groups and Sex with Special Age Categories: Middle Series.* [Online] Available February 24, 2000, at http://www.census.gov/population/projections/nation/summary/np-t3-?.pdf

———. *Projections of the Total Resident Population by 5-Year Age Groups and Sex with Special Age Categories: Middle Series 2050 to 2070.* [Online] Available February 24, 2000, at http://www.census.gov/population/projections/nation/summary/np-t-g.pdf

———. *Resident Estimates of the United States by Age and Sex: April 1, 1990 to November 1, 1999.* [Online] Available February 24, 2000, at http://www.census.gov/population/estimates/nation/intfile2-1.txt

———. *Resident Population Estimates of the United States by Sex, Race, and Hispanic Origin: April 1, 1990 to November 1, 1999.* [Online] Available April 22, 2000, at http://www.census.gov/population/estimates/nation/intfile3-1.txt

———. *Statistical Abstract of the United States 2000.* Washington, D.C.: U.S. Government Printing Office, 2000.

———. Table F-1, "Income Limits for Each Fifth and Top 5 Percent of Families (All Races): 1947 to 1999." [Online] Available December 6, 2000, at http://www.census.gov/hhes/income/histinc/f01.html

———. Table F-2, "Share of Aggregate Income Received by Each Fifth and Top 5 Percent of Families (All Races): 1947 to 1999." [Online] Available December 6, 2000, at http://www.census.gov/hhes/income/histinc/f02.html

———. Table F-7, "Type of Family (All Races) by Median and Mean Income: 1947 to 1998." [Online] Available March 21, 2000, at http://www.census.gov/hhes/income/histinc/f07.html

———. Table P-10, "Age—People (Both Sexes Combined—All Races) by Median and Mean Income: 1974 to 1998." [Online] Available January 28, 2000, at http://www.census.gov/hhes/income/histinc/p10.html

———. Table P-28, "Years of School Completed: Workers 18 Years Old and Over by Mean Earnings, Age, and Sex: 1991 to 1998." [Online] Available December 6, 2000, at http://www.census.gov/hhes/income/histinc/p28.html

———. Table P-31, "Years of School Completed: Workers 18 Years Old and Over by Mean Earnings, Age, and Sex: 1974 to 1979." [Online] Available December 6, 2000, at http://www.census.gov/hhes/income/histinc/p31.html

———. *Age: 2000. Census 2000 Brief, C2KBR/01-12.* [Online] Available September 2001 at http://www.census.gov/population/www/cen2000/briefs.html

———. *America's Families and Living Arrangements: March 2000. Current Population Reports, P20-537.* [Online] Available December 6, 2001, at http://www.census.gov/population/www/socdemo/hh-fam/p20-537–00.html

———. *The Black Population: 2000. Census 2000 Brief, C2KBR/01-5.* [Online] Available August 2001 at http://www.census.gov/population/www/cen2000/briefs.html

———. *Census 2000 PHC-T-5. Ranking Tables for Incorporated Places of 100,000 or More: 1990 and 2000.* [Online] Available October 24, 2001, at http://www.census.gov/population/cen2000/phc-t5/tab02.pdf

———. *Census 2000 PHC-T-15. General Demographic Characteristics by Race for the United States: 2000.* [Online] Available October 10, 2001, at http://www.census.gov/population/www/cen2000/phc-t15.html

———. *Census 2000 Supplementary Survey Summary Tables.* Tables QT-01, QT-02, and QT-03. [Online] Available September 12, 2001, at http://factfinder.census.gov/

———. *CPS Annual Demographic Survey, March Supplement.* [Online] Available March 2001 at http://ferret.bls.census.gov/macro/032001/perinc/new06–000.htm

———. *Child Support 1997.* [Online] Revised version, October 13, 2000. Available December 4, 2001, at http://www.census.gov/hhes/www/childsupport/97tables/tab4.html

———. *Gender: 2000. Census 2000 Brief, C2KBR/01-9.* [Online] Available September 2001 at http://www.census.gov/population/www/cen2000/briefs.html

———. *The Hispanic Population: 2000. Census 2000 Brief, C2KBR/01-3.* [Online] Available May 2001 at http://www.census.gov/population/www/cen2000/briefs.html

———. *Hispanic Population of the United States. Current Population Survey, March 2000.* Washington, D.C.: U.S. Government Printing Office, 2001. [Online] Available November 28, 2001, at http://www.census.gov/population/www/socdemo/hispanic/ho00-04.html

———. *Historical Income Tables: Families.* [Online] Available October 6, 2001, at http://www.census.gov/hhes/income/histinc/

———. *Historical Income Tables: People,* Table P-10. [Online] Available March 1, 2001, at http://www.census.gov/hhes/income/histinc/p10.html

———. *Households and Families: 2000. Census 2000 Brief, C2KBR/01-8.* [Online] Available September 2001 at http://www.census.gov/population/www/cen2000/briefs.html

———. *Interracial Tables.* Table 2, "Race of Couples: 1990." [Online] Available December 4, 2001, at http://www.census.gov/population/socdemo/race/interractab2.txt

———. *Mapping Census 2000: The Geography of U.S. Diversity.* Census Special Reports, Series CENSR/01-1. Washington, D.C.: U.S. Government Printing Office, 2001.

———. *Money Income in the United States: 2000.* Current Population Reports, P60-213. Washington, D.C.: U.S. Government Printing Office, 2001.

———. *Overview of Race and Hispanic Origin: 2000.* Census 2000 Brief, C2KBR/01-1. [Online] Available March 2001 at http://www.census.gov/population/www/cen2000/briefs.html

———. *Population Change and Distribution: 1990 to 2000.* Census 2000 Brief, C2KBR/01-2. [Online] Available April 2001 at http://www.census.gov/population/www/cen2000/briefs.html

———. *Poverty in the United States: 2000.* Current Population Reports, P60-214. Washington, D.C.: U.S. Government Printing Office, 2001.

———. *Resident Population Estimates of the United States by Sex, Race, and Hispanic Origin: April 1, 1990 to July 1, 1999, with Short-Term Projection to November 1, 2000.* [Online] Available September 19, 2001, at http://www.census.gov/population/estimates/nation/intfile3-1.txt

———. *School Enrollment: Social and Economic Characteristics of Students: October 2000.* PPL-148. Washington, D.C.: The Bureau, 2001. [Online] Available October 17, 2001, athttp://www.census.gov/population/socdemo/school/ppl-148/

———. *The 65 Years and Over Population: 2000.* Census 2000 Brief, C2KBR/01-10. [Online] Available October 2001 at http://www.census.gov/population/www/cen2000/briefs.html

———. Table DP-1, "Profile of General Demographic Characteristics: 2000." [Online] Available November 21, 2001, at http://www.census.gov/prod/cen2000/dp1/2khus.pdf

———. *The White Population: 2000.* Census 2000 Brief, C2KBR/01-4. [Online] Available August 2001 at http://www.census.gov/population/www/cen2000/briefs.html

U.S. CENSUS OFFICE. *Census of the United States (1900).* Vol. II: Population. Washington, D.C.: The Office, 1902.

U.S. CENTERS FOR DISEASE CONTROL AND PREVENTION. *Morbidity and Mortality Weekly Report.* Vol. 46, No. 51 (December 26, 1997).

———. *HIV/AIDS Surveillance Report.* Vol. 11, No. 1 (Midyear 1999).

———. *Sexually Transmitted Disease Surveillance 1998.* Atlanta, Ga.: The Centers, 1999.

———. *HIV/AIDS Surveillance Report.* Vol. 12, No. 1 (Midyear 2000).

———. *Morbidity and Mortality Weekly Report.* Vol. 49, No. 43 (November 3, 2000):978–82. [Online] Available http://www.cdc.gov/mmwr/preview/mmwrhtml/mm4943a2.htm

———. *Sexually Transmitted Disease Surveillance 1999.* Atlanta, Ga.: The Centers, 2000.

———. *HIV/AIDS Surveillance Report.* Vol. 12, No. 2 (December 2000 Year-end edition, 2001).

———. *Morbidity and Mortality Weekly Report.* Vol. 50, No. 40 (October 12, 2001).

U.S. DEPARTMENT OF HEALTH AND HUMAN SERVICES. *Administration for Children and Families. Temporary Assistance for Needy Families (TANF) Program;* Third Annual Report to Congress, August 2000. Washington, D.C.: The Administration, 2000.

U.S. DEPARTMENT OF JUSTICE. "Nearly Three Percent of College Women Experienced a Completed Rape or Attempted Rape During the College Year, According to a New Justice Department Report." [Online]. Accessed February 15, 2001, at http://www.ojp.usdoj/bjs/pub/press/svcw.pr

U.S. DEPARTMENT OF LABOR. Bureau of Labor Statistics. *Employment and Earnings.* Vol. 46, No. 1 (January 1999).

———. Bureau of Labor Statistics. *Employment Projections.* Table 5, "Civilian Labor Force by Sex, Age, Race, and Hispanic Origin, 1978, 1988, 1998, and Projected 2008." Washington, D.C.: The Bureau, 1999.

———. Bureau of Labor Statistics. *Employment and Earnings.* Vol. 47, No. 1 (January 2000).

———. *International Comparisons of Hourly Compensation Costs for Production Workers in Manufacturing, 1975–1998.* Supplementary tables for BLS News Release USDL 00–07, January 11, 2000. Washington, D.C.: The Bureau, 2000.

———. *International Comparisons of Hourly Compensation Costs for Production Workers in Manufacturing, 1975–1999.* Supplementary tables for BLS News Release USDL 00-254, September 7, 2000. Washington, D.C.: The Bureau, 2000.

———. Women's Bureau. *Women Business Owners: 1999.* [Online] Available February 12, 2000, at http://www.dol.gov/dol/wb/public/wb–pubs/wbo.htm

———. *Employment and Earnings.* Vol. 48, No. 1 (January 2001).

U.S. DEPARTMENT OF STATE. Bureau of Arms Control. *World Military Expenditures and Arms Transfers 1998.* Washington, D.C.: The Bureau, 1999.

———. *Patterns of Global Terrorism 1998.* Washington, D.C.: The Department, 1999.

———. *Patterns of Global Terrorism 1999.* Washington, D.C.: The Department, 2000.

———. *Patterns of Global Terrorism 2000.* [Online] Available July 8, 2001, at http://www.usis.usemb.se/terror/rpt2000/index.html

USEEM, BERT. "Disorganization and the New Mexico Prison Riot of 1980." *American Sociological Review.* Vol. 50, No. 5 (October 1985):677–88.

U.S. EQUAL EMPLOYMENT OPPORTUNITY COMMISSION. *Job Patterns for Minorities and Women in Private Industry, 1996.* Washington, D.C.: The Commission, 1997.

———. *Job Patterns for Minorities and Women in Private Industry 1997.* Washington, D.C.: The Commission, 1998.

———. *Job Patterns for Minorities and Women in Private Industry, 1998.* Washington, D.C.: The Commission, 2000.

———. Table 1, "Occupational Employment in Private Industry by Race/Ethnic Group/Sex, United States, 1998." [Online] Available October 18, 2000, at http://www.eeoc.gov/stats/jobpat/tables-1.html

———. *Job Patterns for Minorities and Women in Private Industry 1999.* [Online] Available September 19, 2001, at http://www.eeoc.gov/stats/jobpat/1999/national.html

U.S. FEDERAL BUREAU OF INVESTIGATION. *Crime in the United States 1998.* Washington, D.C.: The Bureau, 1999.

———. *Crime in the United States 1999.* Washington, D.C.: The Bureau, 2000.

———. *Crime in the United States 2000.* Washington, D.C.: The Bureau, 2001. [Online] Available November 11, 2001, at http://www.fbi.gov/ucr/cius-00/

U.S. FEDERAL ELECTION COMMISSION. "18-Month Summary on Political Action Committees." News release, September 27, 2000. [Online] Available http://www.fec.gov

U.S. HOUSE OF REPRESENTATIVES. "Street Children: A Global Disgrace." Hearing on November 7, 1991. Washington, D.C.: U.S. Government Printing Office, 1992.

U.S. IMMIGRATION AND NATURALIZATION SERVICE. Table 3, "Immigrants Admitted by Region and Selected Country of Birth, Fiscal Years 1984–94." Fax received from INS January 1996.

———. Table 5, "Immigrants Admitted by Region and Selected Country of Birth, Fiscal Years 1994–96." [Online] Available December 5, 1997, at http://www.ins.doj.gov/stats/annual/fy96/1005.htm

———. *Legal Immigration, Fiscal Year 1998.* Washington, D.C.: The Service, 1999.

U.S. INTERNAL REVENUE SERVICE. *Statistics of Income Bulletin* (Spring 1993).

———. *Statistics of Income Bulletin.* Winter 1999/2000. Publication 1136, Rev. 2/00.

U.S. NATIONAL CENTER FOR EDUCATION STATISTICS. *Digest of Education Statistics 1998.* Washington, D.C.: U.S. Government Printing Office, 1999.

———. *Dropout Rates in the United States: 1997.* Washington, D.C.: The Center, 1999.

———. *Digest of Education Statistics 2000.* Washington, D.C.: U.S. Government Printing Office, 2001.

U.S. NATIONAL CENTER FOR HEALTH STATISTICS. *National Vital Statistics Report.* Vol. 47, No. 4 (October 7, 1998).

———. *Current Estimates from the National Health Interview Survey 1996.* Series 10, No. 200. Hyattsville, Md.: The Center, 1999.

———. *National Vital Statistics Report.* Vol. 47, No. 18 (April 29, 1999).

———. *National Vital Statistics Report.* Vol. 47, No. 19 (June 30, 1999).

———. *National Vital Statistics Report.* Vol. 47, No. 21 (July 6, 1999).

———. *National Vital Statistics Report.* Vol. 47, No. 25 (October 5, 1999).

———. "Births, Marriages, Divorces, and Deaths: Provisional Data for November 1999." *National Vital Statistics Report.* Vol. 48, No. 17 (October 31, 2000).

———. *National Vital Statistics Report.* Vol. 48, No. 11 (July 24, 2000). [Online] Available http://www.cdc.gov/nchs/data/nvs48-11.pdf

———. "Nonmarital Childbearing in the United States, 1940–99." *National Vital Statistics Report.* Vol. 48, No. 16 (revised) (October 18, 2000). [Online] Available http://www.cdc.gov/nchs/data/nvs48-16.pdf

———. *National Vital Statistics Report.* Vol. 48, No. 18 (February 7, 2001). [Online] Available February 6, 2001, at http://www.cdc.gov/nchs/data/nvsr/nvsr48/nvs48-18.pdf

———. *National Vital Statistics Report.* Vol. 49, No. 1 (April 17, 2001).

———. *National Vital Statistics Report.* Vol. 49, No. 6 (August 22, 2001).

———. *National Vital Statistics Report.* Vol. 49, No. 12 (October 9, 2001).

———. News release. October 10, 2001.

U.S. NATIONAL CLEARINGHOUSE ON CHILD ABUSE AND NEGLECT. *Child Maltreatment 1996.* Washington, D.C.: The Clearinghouse, 1998.

———. *Child Abuse and Neglect National Statistics* (April 2000). Washington, D.C.: The Clearinghouse, 2000.

VALDEZ, A. "In the Hood: Street Gangs Discover White-Collar Crime." *Police.* Vol. 21, No. 5 (May 1997):49–50, 56.

VALLAS, STEPHEN P., and JOHN P. BECK. "The Transformation of Work Revisited: The Limits of Flexibility in American Manufacturing." *Social Problems.* Vol. 43, No. 3 (August 1996):339–61.

VALOCCHI, STEVE. "The Emergence of the Integrationist Ideology in the Civil Rights Movement." *Social Problems.* Vol. 43, No. 1 (February 1996):116–30.

VAN BIEMA, DAVID. "Parents Who Kill." *Time.* Vol. 144, No. 20 (November 14, 1994):50–51.

———. "Sparse at Seder?" *Time.* Vol. 149, No. 17 (April 28, 1997a):67.

———. "Buddhism in America." *Time.* Vol. 150, No. 15 (October 13, 1997b):71–81.

———. "Spiriting Prayer into School." *Time.* Vol. 152, No. 20 (April 27, 1998):38–41.

———. "A Surge of Teen Spirit." *Time.* Vol. 153, No. 20 (May 31, 1999):58–59.

———. "Strangers in a Land of Strange Mountains." *Time.* Vol. 156, No. 11 (September 11, 2000):7.

VAN DEN HAAG, ERNEST, and JOHN P. CONRAD. *The Death Penalty: A Debate.* New York: Plenum Press, 1983.

VAUGHAN, MARY KAY. "Multinational Corporations: The World as a Company Town." In Ahamed Idris-Soven et al., eds., *The World as a Company Town: Multinational Corporations and Social Change.* The Hague: Mouton Publishers, 1978:15–35.

VAYDA, EUGENE, and RAISA B. DEBER. "The Canadian Health Care System: An Overview." *Social Science and Medicine.* Vol. 18, No. 3 (1984):191–97.

VEBLEN, THORSTEIN. *The Theory of the Leisure Class.* New York: The New American Library, 1953; orig. 1899.

VEDDER, RICHARD, and LOWELL GALLAWAY. "Declining Black Employment." *Society.* Vol. 30, No. 5 (July–August 1993):56–63.

VINOVSKIS, MARIS A. "Have Social Historians Lost the Civil War? Some Preliminary Demographic Speculations." *Journal of American History.* Vol. 76, No. 1 (June 1989):34–58.

VOGEL, EZRA F. *The Four Little Dragons: The Spread of Industrialization in East Asia.* Cambridge, Mass.: Harvard University Press, 1991.

VOGEL, LISE. *Marxism and the Oppression of Women: Toward a Unitary Theory.* New Brunswick, N.J.: Rutgers University Press, 1983.

VOLD, GEORGE B., and THOMAS J. BERNARD. *Theoretical Criminology.* 3d ed. New York: Oxford University Press, 1986.

VON HIRSH, ANDREW. *Past or Future Crimes: Deservedness and Dangerousness in the Sentencing of Criminals.* New Brunswick, N.J.: Rutgers University Press, 1986.

VOSS, JACQUELINE, and LORI KOGAN. Research reported in Keith Mulvihill, "Sex Education Does Not Up Sexual Activity: Study." Accessed at http://dailynews.yahoo.com (May 1, 2001).

VOYDANOFF, PATRICIA., and BRENDA W. DONNELLY. *Adolescent Sexuality and Pregnancy.* Newbury Park, Calif.: Sage, 1990.

WAITE, LINDA J., GUS W. HAGGSTROM, and DAVID I. KANOUSE. "The Consequences of Parenthood for the Marital Stability of Young Adults." *American Sociological Review.* Vol. 50, No. 6 (December 1985):850–57.

WALDER, ANDREW G. "Career Mobility and the Communist Political Order." *American Sociological Review.* Vol. 60, No. 3 (June 1995):309–28.

WALDFOGEL, JANE. "The Effect of Children on Women's Wages." *American Sociological Review.* Vol. 62, No. 2 (April 1997):209–17.

WALDMAN, STEVEN. "Deadbeat Dads." *Newsweek* (May 4, 1992):46–52.

WALDROP, JUDITH. "Live Long and Prosper." *American Demographics.* Vol. 14 (October 1992):40–45.

WALKER, BOB. "Bob Walker's Official New Orleans Area Wedding Guide: Louisiana's Covenant Marriage Law." [Online] Available August 13, 1998, at http://www.acadiacom.net/walker/covenant–marriage.htm

WALKER, KAREN. "'Always There For Me': Friendship Patterns and Expectations among Middle- and Working-Class Men and Women." *Sociological Forum.* Vol. 10, No. 2 (June 1995):273–96.

WALL, THOMAS F. *Medical Ethics: Basic Moral Issues.* Washington, D.C.: University Press of America, 1980.

WALLER, DOUGLAS. "Onward Cyber Soldiers." *Time.* Vol. 146, No. 8 (August 21, 1995):38–44.

WALLERSTEIN, IMMANUEL. *The Modern World-System: Capitalist Agriculture and the Origins of the European World-Economy in the Sixteenth Century.* New York: Academic Press, 1974.

———. *The Capitalist World-Economy.* New York: Cambridge University Press, 1979.

———. "Crises: The World Economy, the Movements, and the Ideologies." In Albert Bergesen, ed., *Crises in the World-System.* Beverly Hills, Calif.: Sage, 1983:21–36.

———. *The Politics of the World Economy: The States, the Movements, and the Civilizations.* Cambridge, U.K.: Cambridge University Press, 1984.

WALLERSTEIN, JUDITH S., and SANDRA BLAKESLEE. *Second Chances: Men, Women, and Children a Decade after Divorce.* New York: Ticknor & Fields, 1989.

WALLIS, DAVID. "After Cyberoverkill Comes Cyberburnout." *New York Times* (August 4, 1996):43, 46.

WALMSLEY, ROY. *World Prison Population.* 2d ed. United Kingdom Home Office Research, Development, and Statistics Directorate, July 2000.

WALSH, MARY WILLIAMS. "No Time to Put Your Feet Up as Retirement Comes in Stages." *The New York Times* (April 15, 2001):1, 18.

WALTON, JOHN, and CHARLES RAGIN. "Global and National Sources of Political Protest: Third World Responses to the Debt Crisis." *American Sociological Review.* Vol. 55, No. 6 (December 1990):876–90.

WARNER, R. STEPHEN. "Work in Progress toward a New Paradigm for the Sociological Study of Religion in the United States." *American Journal of Sociology.* Vol. 98, No. 5 (March 1993):1044–93.

WARNER, W. LLOYD, and PAUL S. LUNT. *The Social Life of a Modern Community.* New Haven, Conn.: Yale University Press, 1941.

WARR, MARK, and CHRISTOPHER G. ELLISON. "Rethinking Social Reactions to Crime: Personal and Altruistic Fear in Family Households." *American Journal of Sociology.* Vol. 106, No. 3 (November 2000):551–78.

WARREN, JOHN ROBERT, and ROBERT M. HAUSER. "Social Stratification across Three Generations: New Evidence from the Wisconsin Longitudinal Study." *American Sociological Review.* Vol. 62 (August 1997):561–72.

WASKUL, DENNIS. "Selfhood in the Age of Computer Mediated Symbolic Interaction." Paper presented to the annual meeting of the Southwest Social Science Association, New Orleans, La., March 1997.

WATERS, MELISSA S., WILL CARRINGTON HEATH, and JOHN KEITH WATSON. "A Positive Model of the Determination of Religious Affiliation." *Social Science Quarterly.* Vol. 76, No. 1 (March 1995):105–23.

WATSON, RUSSELL. "Milosevic in His Bunker." *Newsweek* (June 7, 1999):49–51.

WATTENBERG, BEN J. "The Attitudes behind American Exceptionalism." *U.S. News & World Report.* Vol. 107, No. 6 (August 7, 1989):25.

———. "The Population Explosion Is Over." *New York Times Magazine* (November 23, 1997):60–63.

WATTS, DUNCAN J. "Networks, Dynamics, and the Small-World Phenomenon." *American Journal of Sociology.* Vol. 105, No. 2 (September 1999):493–527.

WEBER, ADNA FERRIN. *The Growth of Cities.* New York: Columbia University Press, 1963; orig. 1899.

WEBER, MAX. *The Protestant Ethic and the Spirit of Capitalism.* New York: Charles Scribner's Sons, 1958; orig. 1904–5.

———. *Economy and Society*. G. Roth and C. Wittich, eds. Berkeley: University of California Press, 1978; orig. 1921.

WEBSTER, ANDREW. *Introduction to the Sociology of Development*. London: Macmillan, 1984.

WEBSTER, MURRAY, JR., and STUART J. HYSOM. "Creating Status Characteristics." *American Sociological Review*. Vol. 63, No. 3 (June 1998):351–78.

WEBSTER, PAMELA S., TERRI ORBUCH, and JAMES S. HOUSE. "Effects of Childhood Family Background on Adult Marital Quality and Perceived Stability." *American Journal of Sociology*. Vol. 101, No. 2 (September 1995):404–32.

WEEKS, JOHN R. "The Demography of Islamic Nations." *Population Bulletin*. Vol. 43, No. 4 (December 1988). Washington, D.C.: Population Reference Bureau.

WEICHER, JOHN C. "Getting Richer (at Different Rates)." *Wall Street Journal* (June 14, 1995):A18.

WEIDENBAUM, MURRAY. "The Evolving Corporate Board." *Society*. Vol. 32, No. 3 (March/April 1995):9–20.

WEINBERG, GEORGE. *Society and the Healthy Homosexual*. Garden City, N.Y.: Anchor Books, 1973.

WEINER, TIM. "Head of C.I.A. Plans Center to Protect U.S. Cyberspace." *New York Times* (June 26, 1996):B7.

WEINRICH, JAMES D. *Sexual Landscapes: Why We Are What We Are, Why We Love Whom We Love*. New York: Charles Scribner's Sons, 1987.

WEISBERG, D. KELLY. *Children of the Night: A Study of Adolescent Prostitution*. Lexington, Mass.: D.C. Heath, 1985.

WEISBURD, DAVID, STANTON WHEELER, ELIN WARING, and NANCY BODE. *Crimes of the Middle Class: White Collar Defenders in the Courts*. New Haven, Conn.: Yale University Press, 1991.

WEITZMAN, LENORE J. *The Divorce Revolution: The Unexpected Social and Economic Consequences for Women and Children in America*. New York: Free Press, 1985.

———. "The Economic Consequences of Divorce Are Still Unequal: Comment on Peterson." *American Sociological Review*. Vol. 61, No. 3 (June 1996):537–38.

WELLER, JACK M., and E. L. QUARANTELLI. "Neglected Characteristics of Collective Behavior." *American Journal of Sociology*. Vol. 79, No. 3 (November 1973):665–85.

WELLFORD, CHARLES. "Labeling Theory and Criminology: An Assessment." In Delos H. Kelly, ed., *Criminal Behavior: Readings in Criminology*. New York: St. Martin's Press, 1980:234–47.

WELLINGTON, SHEILA. "Cracking the Ceiling." *Time*. Vol. 152, No. 23 (December 7, 1998):187.

WERTHEIMER, BARBARA MAYER. "The Factory Bell." In Linda K. Kerber and Jane De Hart Mathews, eds., *Women's America: Refocusing the Past*. New York: Oxford University Press, 1982:130–40.

WESOLOWSKI, WLODZIMIERZ. "Transition from Authoritarianism to Democracy." *Social Research*. Vol. 57, No. 2 (Summer 1990):435–61.

WESTERN, BRUCE. "Postwar Unionization in Eighteen Advanced Capitalist Countries." *American Sociological Review*. Vol. 58, No. 2 (April 1993):266–82.

———. "A Comparative Study of Working-Class Disorganization: Union Decline in Eighteen Advanced Capitalist Countries." *American Sociological Review*. Vol. 60, No. 2 (April 1995):179–201.

WESTERN, MARK, and ERIK OLIN WRIGHT. "The Permeability of Class Boundaries to Intergenerational Mobility among Men in the United States, Canada, Norway and Sweden." *American Sociological Review*. Vol. 59, No. 4 (August 1994):606–29.

WHALEN, JACK, and RICHARD FLACKS. *Beyond the Barricades: The Sixties Generation Grows Up*. Philadelphia: Temple University Press, 1989.

WHEELIS, ALLEN. *The Quest for Identity*. New York: Norton, 1958.

WHELAN, CHRISTINE B. "No Honeymoon for Covenant Marriage." *Wall Street Journal* (August 17, 1998):A14.

WHITAKER, MARK. "Ten Ways to Fight Terrorism." *Newsweek* (July 1, 1985):26–29.

WHITE, JACK E. "I'm Just Who I Am." *Time*. Vol. 149, No. 18 (May 5, 1997):32–36.

WHITE, RALPH, and RONALD LIPPITT. "Leader Behavior and Member Reaction in Three 'Social Climates." In Dorwin Cartwright and Alvin Zander, eds., *Group Dynamics*. Evanston, Ill.: Row, Peterson, 1953:586–611.

WHITE, WALTER. *Rope and Faggot*. New York: Arno Press and *New York Times*, 1969; orig. 1929.

WHITMAN, DAVID. "Shattering Myths about the Homeless." *U.S. News & World Report* (March 20, 1989):26, 28.

WHORF, BENJAMIN LEE. "The Relation of Habitual Thought and Behavior to Language." In *Language, Thought, and Reality*. Cambridge, Mass.: The Technology Press of MIT/New York: Wiley, 1956:134–59; orig. 1941.

WHYTE, WILLIAM FOOTE. *Street Corner Society*. 3d ed. Chicago: University of Chicago Press, 1981; orig. 1943.

WHYTE, WILLIAM H., JR. *The Organization Man*. Garden City, N.Y.: Anchor Books, 1957.

WIARDA, HOWARD J. "Ethnocentrism and Third World Development." *Society*. Vol. 24, No. 6 (September–October 1987):55–64.

WIATROWSKI, MICHAEL A., DAVID B. GRISWOLD, and MARY K. ROBERTS. "Social Control Theory and Delinquency." *American Sociological Review*. Vol. 46, No. 5 (October 1981):525–41.

WICKHAM, DEWAYNE. "Homeless Receive Little Attention from Candidates." Accessed October 24, 2000, at http://www.usatoday.com/usatonline

WIDOM, CATHY SPATZ. "Childhood Sexual Abuse and Its Criminal Consequences." *Society*. Vol. 33, No. 4 (May/June 1996):47–53.

WILCOX, CLYDE. "Race, Gender, and Support for Women in the Military." *Social Science Quarterly*. Vol. 73, No. 2 (June 1992):310–23.

WILES, P. J. D. *Economic Institutions Compared*. New York: Halsted Press, 1977.

WILKINSON, DORIS. "Transforming the Social Order: The Role of the University in Social Change." *Sociological Forum*. Vol. 9, No. 3 (September 1994):325–41.

WILLIAMS, RHYS H., and N. J. DEMERATH, III. "Religion and Political Process in an American City." *American Sociological Review*. Vol. 56, No. 4 (August 1991):417–31.

WILLIAMS, ROBIN M., JR. *American Society: A Sociological Interpretation*. 3d ed. New York: Alfred A. Knopf, 1970.

WILLIAMSON, JEFFREY G., and PETER H. LINDERT. *American Inequality: A Macroeconomic History*. New York: Academic Press, 1980.

WILSON, BARBARA. "National Television Violence Study." Reported by Julia Duin, "Study Finds Cartoon Heroes Initiate Too Much Violence." *Washington Times* (April 17, 1998):A4.

WILSON, BRYAN. *Religion in Sociological Perspective*. New York: Oxford University Press, 1982.

WILSON, EDWARD O. "Biodiversity, Prosperity, and Value." In F. Herbert Bormann and Stephen R. Kellert, eds., *Ecology, Economics, and Ethics: The Broken Circle*. New Haven, Conn.: Yale University Press, 1991:3–10.

WILSON, JAMES Q. *Bureaucracy: What Government Agencies Do and Why They Do It*. New York: Basic Books, 1991.

———. "Crime, Race, and Values." *Society*. Vol. 30, No. 1 (November–December 1992):90–93.

WILSON, JAMES Q., and RICHARD J. HERRNSTEIN. *Crime and Human Nature*. New York: Simon & Schuster, 1985.

WILSON, LOGAN. *American Academics Then and Now*. New York: Oxford University Press, 1979.

WILSON, THOMAS C. "Urbanism and Tolerance: A Test of Some Hypotheses Drawn from Wirth and Stouffer." *American Sociological Review*. Vol. 50, No. 1 (February 1985):117–23.

———. "Urbanism and Unconventionality: The Case of Sexual Behavior." *Social Science Quarterly*. Vol. 76, No. 2 (June 1995):346–63.

WILSON, WILLIAM JULIUS. *The Declining Significance of Race*. Chicago: University of Chicago Press, 1978.

———. *When Work Disappears: The World of the New Urban Poor*. New York: Alfred A. Knopf, 1996a.

———. "Work." *New York Times Magazine* (August 18, 1996b):26–31, 40, 48, 52, 54.

WINKLER, KAREN J. "Scholar Whose Ideas of Female Psychology Stir Debate Modifies Theories, Extends Studies to Young Girls." *Chronicle of Higher Education*. Vol. 36, No. 36 (May 23, 1990):A6–A8.

WINNICK, LOUIS. "America's 'Model Minority.'" *Commentary*. Vol. 90, No. 2 (August 1990):22–29.

WINSHIP, CHRISTOPHER, and JENNY BERRIEN. "Boston Cops and Black Churches." *The Public Interest*. Vol. 136 (Summer 1999):52–68.

WINTERS, REBECCA. "Who Needs an M.B.A.?" *Time Select: Business*. Vol. 153, No. 19 (May 17, 1999).

WIRTH, LOUIS. "Urbanism as a Way of Life." *American Journal of Sociology*. Vol. 44, No. 1 (July 1938):1–24.

WITKIN, GORDON. "The Crime Bust." *U.S. News & World Report*. Vol. 124, No. 20 (May 25, 1998):28–40.

WITKIN-LANOIL, GEORGIA. *The Female Stress Syndrome: How to Recognize and Live with It*. New York: Newmarket Press, 1984.

WITT, G. EVANS. "Say What You Mean." *American Demographics*. Vol. 21, No. 2 (February 1999):23.

WOLF, DIANE L., ed. *Feminist Dilemma of Fieldwork*. Boulder, Colo.: Westview Press, 1996.

WOLF, NAOMI. *The Beauty Myth: How Images of Beauty Are Used against Women*. New York: William Morrow, 1990.

WOLFE, DAVID B. "Targeting the Mature Mind." *American Demographics*. Vol. 16, No. 3 (March 1994):32–36.

WOLFGANG, MARVIN E., ROBERT M. FIGLIO, and THORSTEN SELLIN. *Delinquency in a Birth Cohort*. Chicago: University of Chicago Press, 1972.

WOLFGANG, MARVIN E., TERRENCE P. THORNBERRY, and ROBERT M. FIGLIO. *From Boy to Man, From Delinquency to Crime*. Chicago: University of Chicago Press, 1987.

WOLFSON, ADAM. "Killing Off the Dying?" *The Public Interest*. No. 131 (Spring 1998):50–70.

WOLKOMIR, MICHELLE, MICHAEL FUTREAL, ERIC WOODRUM, and THOMAS HOBAN. "Substantive Religious Belief and Environmentalism." *Social Science Quarterly*. Vol. 78, No. 1 (March 1997):96–108.

WONG, BUCK. "Need for Awareness: An Essay on Chinatown, San Francisco." In Amy Tachiki et al., eds., *Roots: An Asian American Reader*. Los Angeles: UCLA Asian American Studies Center, 1971:265–73.

WOOD, PETER B., and MICHELE CHESSER. "Black Stereotyping in a University Population." *Sociological Focus*. Vol. 27, No. 1 (February 1994):17–34.

WOODBERRY, ROBERT D. "When Surveys Lie and People Tell the Truth: Church Attenders." *American Sociological Review*. Vol. 63, No. 1 (February 1998):119–22.

WOODWARD, KENNETH L. "Feminism and the Churches." *Newsweek*. Vol. 13, No. 7 (February 13, 1989):58–61.

———. "Talking to God." *Newsweek*. Vol. 119, No. 1 (January 6, 1992a):38–44.

———. "The Elite, and How to Avoid It." *Newsweek* (July 20, 1992b):55.

WOOLEY, ORLAND W., SUSAN C. WOOLEY, and SUE R. DYRENFORTH. "Obesity and Women—II: A Neglected Feminist Topic." *Women's Studies International Quarterly*. Vol. 2 (1979):81–92.

THE WORLD BANK. *World Development Report 1993*. New York: Oxford University Press, 1993.

———. *World Development Report 1995: Workers in an Integrating World*. New York: Oxford University Press, 1995.

680   References

———. *World Development Report 1997: The State in a Changing World*. New York: Oxford University Press, 1997.

———. *World Development Report: Knowledge for Development*. New York: Oxford University Press, 1999.

———. *Entering the 21st Century: World Development Report 1999/2000*. New York: Oxford University Press, 2000.

———. *World Bank Atlas 2001*. Washington, D.C.: The World Bank, 2001.

———. *World Development Indicators 2001*. Washington, D.C.: The World Bank, 2001.

———. *World Development Report 2000/2001*. Washington, D.C.: The World Bank, 2001.

WORLD HEALTH ORGANIZATION. *Constitution of the World Health Organization*. New York: World Health Organization Interim Commission, 1946.

World Values Survey, 1990–1993. Ann Arbor, Mich.: Interuniversity Consortium for Political and Social Research, 1994.

WORSLEY, PETER. "Models of the World System." In Mike Featherstone, ed., *Global Culture: Nationalism, Globalization, and Modernity*. Newbury Park, Calif.: Sage, 1990:83–95.

WREN, CHRISTOPHER S. "In Soweto-by-the-Sea, Misery Lives on as Apartheid Fades." *New York Times* (June 9, 1991):1, 7.

WRIGHT, ERIK OLIN. "Typologies, Scales, and Class Analysis: A Comment on Halaby and Weakliem." *American Sociological Review*. Vol. 58, No. 1 (February 1993):31–34.

WRIGHT, ERIK OLIN, and BILL MARTIN. "The Transformation of the American Class Structure, 1960–1980." *American Journal of Sociology*. Vol. 93, No. 1 (July 1987):1–29.

WRIGHT, ERIC R. "Personal Networks and Anomie: Exploring the Sources and Significance of Gender Composition." *Sociological Focus*. Vol. 28, No. 3 (August 1995):261–82.

WRIGHT, JAMES D. "Address Unknown: Homelessness in Contemporary America." *Society*. Vol. 26, No. 6 (September–October 1989):45–53.

———. "Ten Essential Observations on Guns in America." *Society*. Vol. 32, No. 3 (March–April 1995):63–68.

WRIGHT, QUINCY. "Causes of War in the Atomic Age." In William M. Evan and Stephen Hilgartner, eds., *The Arms Race and Nuclear War*. Englewood Cliffs, N.J.: Prentice Hall, 1987:7–10.

WRIGHT, RICHARD A. "Curing Doonesbury's Disease: A Prescription for Dialogue in the Classroom." *Quarterly Journal of Ideology*. Vol. 9, No. 4 (1985):3–8.

———. *In Defense of Prisons*. Westport, Conn.: Greenwood Press, 1994.

WRIGHT, ROBERT. "Hyperdemocracy." *Time*. Vol. 145, No. 3 (January 23, 1995):15–21.

———. "Sin in the Global Village." *Time*. Vol. 152, No. 16 (October 19, 1998):130.

WRIGHT, STUART A., and ELIZABETH S. PIPER. "Families and Cults: Familial Factors Related to Youth Leaving or Remaining in Deviant Religious Groups." *Journal of Marriage and the Family*. Vol. 48, No. 1 (February 1986):15–25.

WU, LAWRENCE L. "Effects of Family Instability, Income, and Income Instability on the Risk of a Premarital Birth." *American Sociological Review*. Vol. 61, No. 3 (June 1996):386–406.

WYNTER, LEON E. "Business and Race." *Wall Street Journal* (May 10, 1995):B1.

YAMAGATA, HISASHI, KUANG S. YEH, SHELBY STEWMAN, and HIROKO DODGE. "Sex Segregation and Glass Ceilings: A Comparative Static Model of Women's Career Opportunities in the Federal Government over a Quarter Century." *American Journal of Sociology*. Vol. 103, No. 3 (November 1997):566–632.

YANG, FENGGANG, and HELEN ROSE EBAUGH. "Transformations in New Immigrant Religions and Their Global Implications." *American Sociological Review*. Vol. 66, No. 2 (April 2001):269–88.

YANKELOVICH, DANIEL. "How Changes in the Economy Are Reshaping American Values." In Henry J. Aaron, Thomas E. Mann, and Timothy Taylor, eds., *Values and Public Policy*. Washington, D.C.: The Brookings Institution, 1994:20.

YATES, RONALD E. "Growing Old in Japan; They Ask Gods for a Way Out." *Philadelphia Inquirer* (August 14, 1986):3A.

YEATTS, DALE E. "Self-Managed Work Teams: Innovation in Progress." *Business and Economic Quarterly* (Fall–Winter 1991):2–6.

———. "Creating the High Performance Self-Managed Work Team: A Review of Theoretical Perspectives." Paper presented at the annual meeting of the Southwest Social Science Association, Dallas, February 1994.

YODER, JAN D., and ROBERT C. NICHOLS. "A Life Perspective: Comparison of Married and Divorced Persons." *Journal of Marriage and the Family*. Vol. 42, No. 2 (May 1980):413–19.

YOELS, WILLIAM C., and JEFFREY MICHAEL CLAIR. "Laughter in the Clinic: Humor in Social Organization." *Symbolic Interaction*. Vol. 18, No. 1 (1995):39–58.

YUDELMAN, MONTAGUE, and LAURA J. M. KEALY. "The Graying of Farmers." *Population Today*. Vol. 28, No. 4 (May/June, 2000):6.

ZACHARY, G. PASCAL. "Not So Fast: Neo-Luddites Say an Unexamined Cyberlife Is a Dangerous One." *Wall Street Journal* (June 16, 1997):R18.

ZALMAN, MARVIN, and STEVEN STACK. "The Relationship between Euthanasia and Suicide in the Netherlands: A Time Series Analysis, 1950–1990." *Social Science Quarterly*. Vol. 77, No. 3 (September 1996):576–93.

ZANGWILL, ISRAEL. *The Melting Pot*. Macmillan, 1921; orig. 1909.

ZBOROWSKI, MARK. *People in Pain*. San Francisco: Jossey-Bass, 1969.

ZEITLIN, IRVING M. *The Social Condition of Humanity*. New York: Oxford University Press, 1981.

ZHAO, DINGXIN. "Ecologies of Social Movements: Student Mobilization during the 1989 Prodemocracy Movement in Beijing." *American Journal of Sociology*. Vol. 103, No. 6 (May 1998):1493–1529.

ZHOU, MIN, and JOHN R. LOGAN. "Returns of Human Capital in Ethnic Enclaves: New York City's Chinatown." *American Sociological Review*. Vol. 54, No. 5 (October 1989):809–20.

ZHOU, XUEGUANG, and LIREN HOU. "Children of the Cultural Revolution: The State and the Life Course in the People's Republic of China." *American Sociological Review*. Vol. 64, No. 1 (February 1999):12–36.

ZICKLIN, G. "Re-Biologizing Sexual Orientation: A Critique." Paper presented at the Annual Meeting of the Society for the Study of Social Problems, Pittsburgh, Penn., 1992.

ZIMBARDO, PHILIP G. "Pathology of Imprisonment." *Society*. Vol. 9 (April 1972):4–8.

ZUBOFF, SHOSHANA. "New Worlds of Computer-Mediated Work." *Harvard Business Review*. Vol. 60, No. 5 (September–October 1982):142–52.

ZURCHER, LOUIS A., and DAVID A. SNOW. "Collective Behavior and Social Movements." In Morris Rosenberg and Ralph Turner, eds., *Social Psychology: Sociological Perspectives*. New York: Basic Books, 1981:447–82.

PHOTO CREDITS

Paul W. Liebhardt, *ii*; George Breithaupt, *xxxiii*

CHAPTER 1: Smithsonian American Art Museum/Art Resource, N.Y., *xxxiv*; Ed Bock/Corbis/Stock Market, *1*; Caroline Penn/Corbis, *2 (top, left)*; Paul W. Liebhardt, *2 (top, center; bottom, left; bottom, center; bottom, right)*; Minh-Thu Pham, *2 (top, right)*; Lineair/Peter Arnold, Inc., *7*; Getty Images, Inc., *11 (left)*; Simon Bening, *April: Farmyard with Woman Milking Cow*, from *Da Costa Book of Hours*. Bruges, c. 1515. © The Pierpont Morgan Library, New York. M.399,F.5V/Art Resource, N.Y., *11 (right)*; Private Collection/The Stapleton Collection/The Bridgeman Art Library International Ltd., *12*; Corbis, *13 (left)*; Brown Brothers, *13 (right)*; Janet Marqusee Fine Arts Ltd., *15*; Brown Brothers, *16*; Paul Marcus/Studio SPM Inc., *17*; Christie's Images/The Bridgeman Art Library International Ltd., *18*.

CHAPTER 2: Scala/Art Resource, N.Y., *24*; Photo by Ruben Burrell/Courtesy of Hampton University, *25*; Index/The Bridgeman Art Library. ©2003 Banco de Mexico Diego Rivera & Frida Kahlo Museums Trust. Av. Cinco de Mayo No., 2, Col. Centro, Del. Cuauhtemoc 06059, Mexico, D.F., *27*; John Eastcott/Yva Momatiuk/The Image Works, *28*; Bob Daemmrich/Stock Boston, *30*; Doranne Jacobson/International Images, *32*; Argas/Getty Images, *33 (right)*; Steve McCurry/Magnum Photos, Inc., *33 (left)*; Tony Freeman/PhotoEdit, *37*; Philip G. Zimbardo, Inc., Department of Psychology, Stanford University, *38*; Congressional Black Caucus of the U.S. Congress, *41*; Carol Beckwith and Angela Fisher/Robert Estall Photo Agency, *44 (right)*; David Bradnum/Robert Estall Photo Agency, *44 (left)*.

CYBER.SCOPE PART I: Eugene Fisher Photography Worldwide, *54*; General Electric Company, *55*.

CHAPTER 3: Schalkwijk/Art Resource, N.Y., *58*; Sion Touhig/Corbis/Sygma, *59*; Paul W. Liebhardt, *60 (top, left; middle, left)*; Carlos Humberto/TDC/Contact/Corbis/Stock Market, *60 (top, center)*; Doranne Jacobson/International Images, *60 (top, right)*; David Austen/Stock Boston, *60 (middle, center)*; Getty Images, Inc., *60 (middle, right)*; Doranne Jacobson/International Images, *60 (bottom, left)*; Jack Fields/Photo Researchers, Inc., *60 (bottom, right)*; J. Humer/Getty Images, Inc., *62*; Dimitri Lovetsky/AP/Wide World Photos, *61*; Jeff Greenberg/Index Stock Imagery, Inc., *64 (left)*; Pedrick/The Image Works, *64 (center)*; CLEO Photo/Jeroboam, Inc., *64 (right)*; *Mrs. Picasso Dusts the Mantlepiece*, from *Great Housewives of Art* by Sally Swain. Copyright ©1988, 1989 by Sally Swain. Used by permission of Viking Penguin, a division of Penguin Putnam, Inc., *67*; Jeff Greenberg/PhotoEdit, *68*; Margaret Courtney-Clarke/Tom Keller and Associates LLC, *70*; Canapress/E.J. Flynn, *75*; Catherine Karnow/Corbis, *76*; J. P. Laffont/Corbis/Sygma, *79*; Jessie Levine, Laguna Sales, Palo Alto, *80*; Photographer Bill Coleman, www.amishphoto.com, (814) 238-8495 #174 *One Day's Work*, *82*; Copyright 1952, 1980 Ruth Orkin/Getty Images, Inc., *83*.

CHAPTER 4: Arnaudet/Art Resource, N.Y., *88*; ©1996, *The Washington Post*, photo by Carol Guzy, reprinted with permission, *89*; Patrick Bordes/Photo Researchers, Inc., *90*; Victor Englebert/Photo Researchers, Inc., *91*; Robert Frerck/Woodfin Camp & Associates, *92*; Getty Images, Inc., *95 (left)*; Corbis/Sygma, *95 (right)*; Corbis, *100*; Norbert Goeneutte *The Paupers' Meal on a Winter Day in Paris*. Waterhouse and Dodd, London. Fine Art Photographic Library, London/Art Resource, N.Y., *98*; Charles Steiner/The Image Works, *102*; The Granger Collection, *103*; D.C. Moore Gallery, *106*; Elliot Landy/Magnum Photos, Inc., *107 (left; center; left; center right)*; Robert Sorbo/AP/Wide World Photos, *107 (right)*; Paul W. Liebhardt, *108*.

CHAPTER 5: The Bridgeman Art Library International Ltd., *114*; Blair Seitz/Photo Researchers, Inc., *115*; Ted Horowitz/

Corbis/Stock Market, *116 (left)*; Henley & Savage/Corbis/Stock Market, *116 (center)*; Tom Pollack, *116 (right)*; Bettmann/Corbis, *117*; William Kurelek, *Prairie Childhood*, by permission of the Estate of William Kurelek, courtesy of the Isaacs Gallery of Toronto, *118*; Elizabeth Crews/Elizabeth Crews Photography, *120*; Rimma Gerlovina and Valeriy Gerlovin. *122*; Hampton University Museum, *124*; Mary Ellen Mark, *129*; Eastcott/Momatiuk/Woodfin Camp & Associates, *133*.

CHAPTER 6: Manu Sassoonian /Art Resource, N.Y., *138*; John Macionis, *139*; Jim Anderson/Woodfin Camp & Associates, *140*; AP/Wide World Photos, *141*; Richard Lord Enterprises, Inc., *142*; DiMaggio/Kalish/Corbis/Stock Market, *144*; David Cooper/Getty Images, Inc., *149 (top, left)*; Alan Weiner/Getty Images, Inc., *149 (top, center)*; Lynn McLaren/Index Stock Imagery, Inc., *149 (top, right)*; Guido Rossi/Getty Images, Inc., *149 (left)*; Richard Pan, *149 (bottom, center)*; Costa Manos/Magnum Photos, Inc., *149 (bottom, right)*; Paul Ekman, Ph.D. Professor of Psychology, University of California, San Francisco, *151 (left and right)*; Paul W. Liebhardt, *150 (left; center; right)*; Michael Newman/PhotoEdit, *154*; Jason Plotkin/*The York Dispatch*/AP/Wide World Photos, *157*; Angela Maynard/Getty Images, Inc./PhotoDisc, Inc., *153*; Myrleen Ferguson/PhotoEdit, *158*.

CHAPTER 7: The Bridgeman Art Library International Ltd, *162*; Nik Wheeler/Corbis, *163*; Galen Rowell/Peter Arnold, Inc., *164*; Jonathan Green Studios, Inc., *169*; Dan Habib/Impact Visuals Photo & Graphics, Inc., *170*; Cliché Bibliotheque nationale de France, Paris. From *The Horizon History of China* by the editors of Horizon Magazine, The Horizon Publishing Co., Inc., 551 5th Avenue, New York, N.Y. 10017. ©1969, *174*; Paul W. Liebhardt, *177*; The Metropolitan Museum of Art, *176*; Jose Luis Pelaez, Inc./Corbis/Stock Market, *179*; Michael S. Yamashita/Corbis, *180*; Gabe Palmer/Corbis/Stock Market, *182*; Saleh Rifai/AP/Wide World Photos, *184*.

CHAPTER 8: Noah's Ark Fine Art, *190*; Pat Sullivan/AP/Wide World Photos, *191*; SIPA Press, *193*; Cliff Owen/UPI/Corbis, *194*; Paul W. Liebhardt, *196*; Edward Gargan/New York Times Pictures, *199*; Stan Honda/Agence France-Presse, *200*; Andrew Lichtenstein/The Image Works, *201*; Danny Hellman, *203*; S. Liss/Corbis/Sygma, *205*; Rich Pedroncelli/AP/Wide World Photos, *207*; Paul Marcus/Studio SPM Inc., *209*; Washoe County, Nevada Police Department, *213*.

CHAPTER 9: Tate Gallery/Art Resource, N.Y., *220*; Kim D. Johnson/*The Sacramento Bee*, *221*; Andre Gallant/Getty Images, Inc., *222 (top, left)*; Pete Turner/Getty Images, Inc., *222 (top, center)*; Brun/Photo Researchers, Inc., *222 (top, right)*; Bruno Hadijh/Getty Images, Inc., *222 (bottom, left)*; Elliot Erwitt/Magnum Photos, Inc., *222 (bottom, center)*; George Holton/Photo Researchers, Inc., *222 (bottom, right)*; Thomas Friedmann/Photo Researchers, Inc., *223*; David McCoy/Rainbow, *225*; John Marshall Mantel/Corbis, *231*; Mark Peterson/Corbis/SABA Press Photos, Inc., *237*; AKG London Ltd, *239*.

CYBER.SCOPE PART II: T. Crosby/Getty Images, Inc., *244*; The Cartoon Bank, *245*.

CHAPTER 10: Paul Marcus/Studio SPM Inc., *246*; Illustration by Ken Marshall ©1992 from *Titanic: An Illustrated History*, a Viking Studio/Madison Press Book, *247*; Sebastiao Salgado/Contact Press Images Inc., *248*; Doranne Jacobson/International Images, *249*; Per-Anders Pettersson/Black Star, *251*; John Launois/Black Star, *253*; Francisco Conde/Impact Visuals Photo & Graphics, Inc., *254*; Bridgeman Art Library/London/SuperStock, Inc., *256*; Kevork Djansezian/AP/Wide World Photos, *258*; The Granger Collection, *260*; Doranne Jacobson/International Images, *262*; Ford Madox Brown (1821-93) *Work*. SuperStock, Inc., *265*.

CHAPTER 11: Smithsonian American Art Museum/Art Resource, N.Y., *270*; Stan Godlewski/Getty Images, Inc., *271*; Bill Bachmann/The Image Works, *277*; Grapes/Michaud/Photo Researchers, Inc., *278 (left)*; Burt Glinn/Magnum Photos, Inc., *278 (right)*; Ed Bock/Corbis/Stock Market, *280*; Russell Lee/Corbis, *281*; Bob Krist/Corbis, *282*; Christie's Images, Inc., *287*; William Julius Wilson, *291*; Phil Schermeister/Corbis, *292*; Argus Fotoarchiv/Peter Arnold, Inc., *293*; Brooks Kraft/Corbis/Sygma, *294*.

CHAPTER 12: The Bridgeman Art Library International Ltd, *298*; Romeo Ranoco/Reuters NewMedia Inc./Corbis, *299*; Tony Arruza/Corbis, *301 (left)*; Reuters/Juan Carlos Ulate/Getty Images Inc., *301 (right)*; Martin Benjamin/The Image Works, *302 (top, left)*; Peter Turnley/Corbis, *302 (top, right)*; Pablo Bartholomew/Getty Images, Inc., *302 (bottom)*; Yuri Cortez/AFP Photo/Corbis, *307*; Malcolm Linton/Getty Images, Inc., *309*; Steve Maines/Stock Boston, *310*; Joe McDonald/Corbis, *311 (left)*; Robert van der Hilst/Corbis, *311(center)*; Wolfgang Kaehler/Corbis, *311 (right)*; Sean Sprague, *313*; The Granger Collection, *317*.

CHAPTER 13: Getty Images, Inc., *324*, *325*; Jon Feingersh/Corbis/Stock Market, *326*; Angela Fisher/Carol Beckwith/Robert Estall Photo Agency, *328*; Underwood & Underwood/Corbis, *330*; Ed Malitsky/Index Stock Imagery, Inc., *332*; R.W. Jones/Corbis, *343*; Willinger/Getty Images, Inc., *344*; Bettmann/Corbis, *346 (left)*; APA/Getty Images, Inc., *346 (center)*; Hulton-Deutsch Collection/Corbis, *346 (right)*; UNICEF/HQ96-1041/Tapas Barua, *348*.

CHAPTER 14: Paul Marcus/Studio SPM Inc., *352*; AP/Wide World Photos, *353*; Joel Gordon/Joel Gordon Photography, *354 (top, left)*; Leong Ka Tai/Material World, *354 (top, center)*; Owen Franken/Corbis, *354 (top, right)*; Charles O'Rear/Corbis, *354 (bottom, left)*; Paul W. Liebhardt, *354 (bottom, center)*; Lisi Dennis/Getty Images, Inc., *354 (bottom, right)*; Bob Daemmrich Photography, Inc., *358*; Peter Turnley/Corbis, *359*; Corbis, *368 (left)*; Culver Pictures, Inc., *368 (center, left)*; Photographs and Prints Division, Schomburg Center for Research in Black Culture/The New York Public Library/Astor, Lenox and Tilden Foundations, *368 (center, right)*; UPI/Corbis, *368 (center, right)*; National Baseball Hall of Fame Library, Cooperstown, N.Y., *364*; UPI/Corbis, *372*; Jim West, *371*; Nick Quijano, *376*; Bob Daemmrich Photography, Inc., *378*.

CHAPTER 15: Scala/Art Resource, N.Y., *382*; Jim Erickson/Corbis/Stock Market, *383*; Elliot Erwitt/Magnum Photos, Inc., *388 (left)*; AP/Wide World Photos, *388 (right)*; Eve Arnold/Magnum Photos, *391*; Alese and Mort Pechter/Corbis/Stock Market, *393*; Bob Daemmrich Photography, Inc., *395*; Chris Rainier/Corbis, *399*; Robin Sachs/PhotoEdit, *397*; Ira Wyman/Corbis/Sygma, *401*; Alan Oddie/PhotoEdit, *402*.

CYBER.SCOPE PART III: Richard T. Nowitz/Science Source/Photo Researchers, Inc., *406*.

CHAPTER 16: Latina/Latino Studies Program, University of Illinois at Urbana-Champaign, *408*; Mike Feeney/Eye Ubiquitous/Corbis, *409*; Underwood & Underwood/Library of Congress, *411*; Bob Daemmrich Photography, Inc., *410*; Courtesy of the Library of Congress, *415*; Bellavia/REA/Corbis/SABA Press Photos, Inc., *416 (left)*; John Bryson/Corbis/Sygma, *416 (right)*; Patrick Ward/Stock Boston, *417*; Bob Daemmrich Photography, Inc., *421*; Sven-Olof Lindblad/Photo Researchers, Inc., *414*; Fundacion Jose Clemente Orozco, *422*; Getty Images, Inc., *428*; UPI/Corbis, *429*; Chris Brown/Corbis/SABA Press Photos, Inc., *425*.

CHAPTER 17: AKG London Ltd, *434*; Tomas Muscionico/Contact Press Images, Inc., *435*; Durand/SIPA Press, *437*; David Ball/Index Stock Imagery, Inc., *441*; A. Ramey/Woodfin Camp & Associates, *444 (left)*; Joel Gordon/Joel Gordon Photography, *444 (right)*; David Hoffman Photo Library, *452*; Srdjan Ilic/AP/Wide World Photos, *454*; Joe McNally, Life Magazine ©TimePix, *455*; Andrade Patrick/Gamma Press, *451*.

CHAPTER 18: Smithsonian American Art Museum/Art Resource, N.Y., *462*; AP/Wide World Photos, *463*; M. Lee Fatherree/Carmen Lomas Garza, *464*; Bo Zaunders/Corbis/Stock Market, *466*; The Bridgeman Art Library International Ltd, *469*; Judy Reed/Carmen Lomas Garza, *470*; Christian Pierre, B. 1962, *I Do*. American Private Collection, Superstock, Inc., *472*; Paul Marcus/Studio SPM Inc., *478*; Sheldon Memorial Art Gallery, *482*; Stern (Ullah)/Black Star, *484*.

CHAPTER 19: Smithsonian American Art Museum/Art Resource, N.Y., *490*; David H. Wells/Corbis, *491*; Micael Freeman/Corbis, *492*; Mathieu Polak/Corbis/Sygma, *494*; Doranne Jacobson/International Images, *497*; Topham/The Image Works, *498*; Annie Griffiths Belt/NGS Image Collection, *500*; Thomas Caplain/Corbis/Sygma, *503*; James L. Amos/Corbis, *509*; Nick Kelsh/Kelsh Wilson Design Inc., *511*.

CHAPTER 20: Philadelphia Museum of Art/Corbis, *516*; *The Toledo Blade*, *517 (left and right)*; Doranne Jacobson/International Images, *518*; Tom McCarthy/Corbis/Stock Market, *525 (left)*; Michael Newman/PhotoEdit, *525 (right)*; Bob Daemmrich Photography, Inc., *532*; Tom & Dee Ann McCarthy/Corbis/Stock Market, *530*; Mugshots/Corbis/Stock Market, *535*.

CHAPTER 21: Michael Rosenfield Gallery, *540*; Reuters/Fred Prouser/Getty Images, Inc., *541*, Rijksmuseum, *542*; W. Campbell/Corbis/Sygma, *543 (left)*; Steve Lehman/Corbis/SABA Press Photos, Inc., *543 (right)*; Steve Prezant/Corbis/Stock Market, *547*; Tom Prettyman/PhotoEdit, *552*; Adalbert Franz Selgmann *Allgemeines Krankenhaus* (General Hospital) 19ᵗʰ Century Painting, canvas. *Professor Theodor Billroth lectures at the General Hospital, Vienna. 1880.* Erich Lessing/Art Resource, N.Y., *554*; Galen Rowell/Mountain Light Photography, Inc., *555*; ABC Television/Globe Photos, Inc., *559 (left)*; NBC/Everett Collection, Inc., *559 (right)*; Steve Murez/Black Star, *562*; Al Diaz, *561*.

CYBER.SCOPE PART IV: Ed Bock/Corbis/Stock Market, *566*; ©Tara Sosrowardovo/Indo-pix, *567*.

CHAPTER 22: Museum of the City of New York, *568*; AP/Wide World Photos, *569*; Shawn G. Henry/Material World, *576 (left)*; Jose Manuel Navia/Material World, *576 (right)*; Lauren Goodsmith/The Image Works, *577*; Steve C. Wilson/Online USA, Inc./Getty Images, Inc., *581*; Christie's Images, *582 (left)*; SuperStock,, *582 (right)*; Chip Simons/Getty Images, Inc., *587*; Culver Pictures, Inc., *590*; Paul W. Liebhardt, *592*; Eric Pasquier/Corbis/Sygma, *594*.

CHAPTER 23: ©Franklin McMahon/Corbis, *600*; ©Reuters NewMedia Inc./Corbis, *601*; Rose Palmisano, *602*; Christopher Morris/Black Star, *605*; Sabina Dowell, *607*; Tom Kelley/Getty Images, Inc., *610 (top, left)*; Inge Morath/Magnum Photos, Inc., *610 (top, center, left)*; Kimberly Maier, *610 (top, center, right)*; Willie L. Hill, Jr./Stock Boston, *610 (top, right)*; Michael Grecco/Stock Boston, *610 (bottom, left)*; ©Mike Blake/Reuters NewMedia Inc./Corbis, *610 (bottom, right)*; Steve Weinberg/Corbis/Sygma, *615*; Hans Edinger/AP/Wide World Photos, *616*.

CHAPTER 24: ©Forrest J. Ackerman Collection/Corbis, *624*; Culver Pictures, Inc., *625 (left)*; Robert Brenner/PhotoEdit, *625 (right)*; Mark Peters, *627*; Chrisie's Images, Inc., *629*; Whitney Museum of American Art, *631*; Pearson Education/PH College, *632*; Christie's Images, Inc., *636*; Scala/Art Resource, N.Y., *638 (left)*; Paul Marcus/Studio SPM Inc., *638 (right)*; John Launois/Black Star, *639*; Mauri Rautkari/WWF UK (World Wide Fund For Nature), *640*.

CYBER.SCOPE PART V: Corbis/SABA Press Photos, Inc., *649*.

NAME INDEX

SUBJECT INDEX

Egypt, 92, 93, 301, 321, 342, 347, 501, 585, 590–91
population control and women, 577
Egypt, ancient, 224
El Salvador, 2, 302, 358
Elderly (*see also* Aging)
in global population (2020), global map, 385
as outsiders, 8
population statistics for U.S., 385–86
as share of population, national map, 387
Electronic church, 511, 513
Electronic mail, 56, 176, 442
survey research, 40
Electronic town meetings, 458
Embarrassment, 152–53
Emergent-norm theory of crowd behavior, 606
Emigration, 571
Emotions, expression and culture, 148–49
Empirical evidence, 26
Empty nest, 474
Enclosure movement, 10
Endogamous marriage, 249, 465, 468
Energy consumption, 587
Energy sources, steam engine, 410
English language, 66, 76, 81, 153–55, 355, 367
Enlightenment, 214
Environment, organizational, 175
Environment (*see* Natural environment)
Environmental deficit, 587, 595
Environmental movement, strategies of, 595
Environmental racism, 594–95
Equal opportunity, 67, 521
Equal Rights Amendment (ERA), 345–46
Equality, value of, 271
Eros, 118–19
Eskimo, 229
Espionage, 211
Estate system, 252
Estonia, 301, 419
Ethics
and death, 399–401, 403, 552–53
and health, 399–401, 552–53
and reproductive technology, 484
and research, 36
Ethiopia, 2, 302, 317, 321, 440, 543
gross domestic product (GDP), 304
Ethnicity (*see also* specific categories of people)
categories, 356
defined, 355
and Information Revolution, 407
minority-majority population, national map, 357
and poverty, 287
and religion, 507–8
and social mobility, 283
and social stratification, 275–76
Ethnic jokes, 158–59
Ethnic villages, 363, 376, 377
Ethnocentrism, 79
Ethnographies, 43
Ethnomethodology, 145–46
Eurocentrism, 76

Euthanasia, 400–401, 553
Evolution, 83, 257
creationism issue, 512
sociocultural, 90–96, 262
Exogamy, 465
Experiment, 36–39
goal of, 36
Experimental group, 37
Expressions, facial, 148–49
Expressive crowds, 603
Expressive leadership, 165–66
Expressive traits, 344
Extended family, 464
Extinction, plants and animals, 594
Extramarital sex, 228, 473
Eye contact, in communication, 150

Facial expressions, 148–49
Facsimile (fax) machines, 54, 412
Factory system, 10, 54, 410, 420
Fads, 610
Faith, religious, 492
False consciousness, 98
Family
African American, 209, 275, 476–77, 482
and aging, 474
alternative forms, 481–84
Asian American, 210, 482
and authority, 463
basic concepts, 463–64
blended, 480
and caregiving, 394
and child rearing, 336–37, 473–74
defined, 463
and divorce, 463, 478–80, 485, 486
female-headed, 287, 289, 375, 476–77, 482
and gender, 477–78
and gender socialization, 330–31
in global perspective, 464–66
homeless families, 292
incest taboo, 224
and industrialization, 94
and Information Revolution, 567
in later life, 474
in modern society, 11
and new reproductive technology, 484
patterns of descent, 465–66
and race and ethnicity, 476–77
recent trends in, 463
residential patterns, 465
single-parent, 209, 275, 287, 289, 482
size, 473, 474
and social class, 474–75
social class and experiences, 281–82
social-conflict analysis of, 469–70
social-exchange analysis of, 470
and socialization, 467
stages of life, 471–74
structural-functional analysis of, 467–69
in Sweden, 466–67, 483
symbolic-interaction analysis of, 470
traditional, 486–87
in twenty-first century, 484–85
violence in, 340, 481
Family of affinity, 464
Family and Medical Leave Act, 474
Family of orientation, 464

Family of procreation, 464
Family unit, 464
"Family values" agenda, 226, 444, 474
Fascism, 440
Fashions, 609–10
Fecundity, 570
Federal Bureau of Investigation (FBI), crime statistics, 206, 207
"Female advantage," 179–80
Female circumcision, 238
Female genital mutilation, 340, 341–42
Female-headed families, 287, 289, 375, 476–77, 482
Female infanticide, 465
Feminine traits, 327, 330 (*see also* Gender)
Feminism, 345–348, 641 (*see also* Women's movement)
basic concepts, 345–46
defined, 345
forms of, 346–47
opposition to, 347–48
and religion, 495
Feminist research, 34
Feminization of poverty, 287, 289
Fertility, 570, 576–78
Feudalism, 98, 253
Fieldwork, 43–45
Fifteenth Amendment, 369, 446
Fiji, 541
Filipino Americans, 370, 373, 377
Financial exchanges, 301
Finland, 126, 328
First estate, 252
First World, 299–300
Flexibility, organizational, 182–83, 185
Flirting, 144
Folkways, as norm, 70
Food production, 312–13, 316
Foot-binding, 330
Force, versus authority, 435
Foreign aid, 314
Formal communications, and bureaucracy, 175
Formal operational stage (Piaget), 120
Formal organizations (*see also* Bureaucracy)
future view, 185
and gender, 179–80
Japanese, 180–81
and personal privacy, 186–87
and race, 178, 179
compared to small groups, 175
types of, 173–75
France, 71, 232, 295, 442, 455, 557
gross domestic product (GDP), 304
Freedom
and capitalism, 418
culture as, 85
economic (capitalism versus socialism), 418
political, global map, 439
and socialization, 135
value of, 68
versus social responsibility, 644–45
Freedom fighters, 452, 453
Freedom Summer, 617
Free enterprise, as value, 68
Free will, 1
French Revolution, 11, 450, 612
Function, social, 107 (*see also* Structural-functional paradigm)

Functional illiteracy, 533–34
Fundamentalism, religious, 318, 501, 510–11, 513
Funerals, 82

Gambling, 193, 198
Games
and gender, 331
and learning, 123
"Gay gene," 229
Gay people (*see also* Homosexuality; Lesbians)
and AIDS, 550–52, 614–15
couples, 483, 485
gay rights movement, 231, 628
and hate crimes, 204, 205
homophobia, 231
in military, 69, 329
as outsiders, 8
prostitution by, 235
sexual orientation theories, 229–30
in U.S. population, 230
Gay rights movement, 231, 628
GDP (*see* Gross domestic product [GDP])
Gemeinschaft, 582, 630–31, 634, 638
Gender (*see also* Feminism; Men; Women)
and aging, 386, 392–93, 394
and athletic performance, 326, 327
and caregiving, 394
and child rearing, 336–37
and college degrees, 337–38, 528
and complementarity, 344
and crime, 208, 349
and cultural variables, 325–30
defined, 325
and deviance, 204–5
and discrimination, 337–38
and divorce, 479–80
and double standard, 35, 225, 226
and education, 331, 337–38, 521, 524, 527
equality, global view, 328
extramarital sex, 228
and eye contact, 152
and family, 331, 477–78
feminine traits, 327, 330
and formal organization, 179–80
global comparisons, 326–27
and health, 546
and income, 283–84, 336–37, 528
and inequality, 325–30
and infanticide, 465
and Information Revolution, 407
and intelligence, 326
Japan, stratification, 253
and language, 153–55
and leadership, 165
and life expectancy, 326, 349, 384
and marriage, 477–78
masculine traits, 327, 328, 330, 547
in mass media, 332–33
Mead's study, 326–27
and military, 339
and moral development, 121–22, 331
and networks, 171
and occupations, 274, 283, 335
in organizations, 274
and patriarchy, 328–30, 469